MITSUBISHI | ECLIPSE
1990-98 REPAIR MANUAL

Covers all U.S. and Canadian models of
Mitsubishi Eclipse, Eagle Talon and
Plymouth Laser

by Christine Sheeky, S.A.E.

CHILTON *Automotive Books*

PUBLISHED BY **HAYNES NORTH AMERICA. Inc.**

Manufactured in USA
© 1998 Haynes North America, Inc.
ISBN 0-8019-8957-4
Library of Congress Catalog Card No. 97-78115
7890123456 9876543210

Haynes Publishing Group
Sparkford Nr Yeovil
Somerset BA22 7JJ England

Haynes North America, Inc
861 Lawrence Drive
Newbury Park
California 91320 USA

ABCDE
FGHIJ
KLM

Contents

Contents

DRIVE TRAIN   7

STEERING   8

BRAKES   9

BODY AND TRIM   10

GLOSSARY

MASTER INDEX

SAFETY NOTICE

Proper service and repair procedures are vital to the safe, reliable operation of all motor vehicles, as well as the personal safety of those performing repairs. This manual outlines procedures for servicing and repairing vehicles using safe, effective methods. The procedures contain many NOTES, CAUTIONS and WARNINGS which should be followed, along with standard procedures to eliminate the possibility of personal injury or improper service which could damage the vehicle or compromise its safety.

It is important to note that repair procedures and techniques, tools and parts for servicing motor vehicles, as well as the skill and experience of the individual performing the work vary widely. It is not possible to anticipate all of the conceivable ways or conditions under which vehicles may be serviced, or to provide cautions as to all possible hazards that may result. Standard and accepted safety precautions and equipment should be used when handling toxic or flammable fluids, and safety goggles or other protection should be used during cutting, grinding, chiseling, prying, or any other process that can cause material removal or projectiles.

Some procedures require the use of tools specially designed for a specific purpose. Before substituting another tool or procedure, you must be completely satisfied that neither your personal safety, nor the performance of the vehicle will be endangered.

Although information in this manual is based on industry sources and is complete as possible at the time of publication, the possibility exists that some car manufacturers made later changes which could not be included here. While striving for total accuracy, the authors or publishers cannot assume responsibility for any errors, changes or omissions that may occur in the compilation of this data.

PART NUMBERS

Part numbers listed in this reference are not recommendations by Haynes North America, Inc. for any product brand name. They are references that can be used with interchange manuals and aftermarket supplier catalogs to locate each brand supplier's discrete part number.

SPECIAL TOOLS

Special tools are recommended by the vehicle manufacturer to perform their specific job. Use has been kept to a minimum, but where absolutely necessary, they are referred to in the text by the part number of the tool manufacturer. These tools can be purchased, under the appropriate part number, from your local dealer or regional distributor, or an equivalent tool can be purchased locally from a tool supplier or parts outlet. Before substituting any tool for the one recommended, read the SAFETY NOTICE at the top of this page.

ACKNOWLEDGMENTS

The publisher expresses appreciation to Mitsubishi Motors Corporation and Chrysler Corporation for their generous assistance.

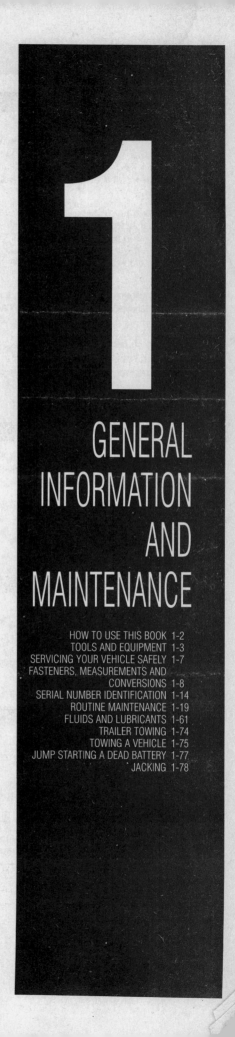

1

GENERAL INFORMATION AND MAINTENANCE

HOW TO USE THIS BOOK

Chilton's Total Car Care Manual for the 1990–98 Mitsubishi Eclipse, Plymouth Laser and Eagle Talon is intended to help you learn more about the inner workings of your vehicle and save you money on its maintenance and repairs.

The beginning of the book will likely be referred to the most, since that is where you will find information for maintenance and tune-up. The other sections deal with the more complex systems of your vehicle. Operating systems from engine through brakes are covered to the extent that the average do-it-yourselfer becomes mechanically involved. This book will not explain such things as rebuilding a differential for the simple reason that the expertise required and the investment in special tools make this task uneconomical. It will, however, give you detailed instructions to help you change your own brake pads and shoes, replace spark plugs, and perform many more jobs that can save you money, give you personal satisfaction and help you avoid expensive problems.

A secondary purpose of this book is a reference for owners who want to understand their vehicle and/or their mechanics better. In this case, no tools at all are required.

Where to Begin

Before removing any bolts, read through the entire procedure. This will give you the overall view of what tools and supplies will be required. There is nothing more frustrating than having to walk to the bus stop on Monday morning because you were short one bolt on Sunday afternoon. So read ahead and plan ahead. Each operation should be approached logically and all procedures thoroughly understood before attempting any work.

All sections contain adjustments, maintenance, removal and installation procedures, and in some cases, repair or overhaul procedures. When repair is not considered practical, we tell you how to remove the part and then how to install the new or rebuilt replacement. In this way, you at least save the labor costs. Backyard repair of some components is just not practical.

Avoiding Trouble

Many procedures in this book require you to "label and disconnect . . ." a group of lines, hoses or wires. Don't be lulled into thinking you can remember where everything goes—you won't. If you hook up vacuum or fuel lines incorrectly, the vehicle will run poorly, if at all. If you hook up electrical wiring incorrectly, you may instantly learn a very expensive lesson.

You don't need to know the official or engineering name for each hose or line. A piece of masking tape on the hose and a piece on its fitting will allow you to assign your own label such as the letter A or a short name. As long as you remember your own code, the lines can be reconnected by matching similar letters or names. Do remember that tape will dissolve in gasoline or other fluids; if a component is to be washed or cleaned, use another method of identification. A permanent felt-tipped marker can be very handy for marking metal parts. Remove any tape or paper labels after assembly.

Maintenance or Repair?

It's necessary to mention the difference between maintenance and repair. Maintenance includes routine inspections, adjustments, and replacement of parts which show signs of normal wear. Maintenance compensates for wear or deterioration. Repair implies that something has broken or is not working. A need for repair is often caused by lack of maintenance. Example: draining and refilling the automatic transmission fluid is maintenance recommended by the manufacturer at specific mileage intervals. Failure to do this can ruin the transmission/transaxle, requiring very expensive repairs. While no maintenance program can prevent items from breaking or wearing out, a general rule can be stated: MAINTENANCE IS CHEAPER THAN REPAIR.

Two basic mechanic's rules should be mentioned here. First, whenever the left side of the vehicle or engine is referred to, it is meant to specify the driver's side. Conversely, the right side of the vehicle means the passenger's side. Second, most screws and bolts are removed by turning counterclockwise, and tightened by turning clockwise.

Safety is always the most important rule. Constantly be aware of the dangers involved in working on an automobile and take the proper precautions. See the information in this section regarding SERVICING YOUR VEHICLE SAFELY and the SAFETY NOTICE on the acknowledgment page.

Avoiding the Most Common Mistakes

Pay attention to the instructions provided. There are 3 common mistakes in mechanical work:

1. Incorrect order of assembly, disassembly or adjustment. When taking something apart or putting it together, performing steps in the wrong order usually just costs you extra time; however, it CAN break something. Read the entire procedure before beginning disassembly. Perform everything in the order in which the instructions say you should, even if you can't immediately see a reason for it. When you're taking apart something that is very intricate, you might want to draw a picture of how it looks when assembled at one point in order to make sure you get everything back in its proper position. We will supply exploded views whenever possible. When making adjustments, perform them in the proper order; often, one adjustment affects another, and you cannot expect even satisfactory results unless each adjustment is made only when it cannot be changed by any other.

2. Overtorquing (or undertorquing). While it is more common for overtorquing to cause damage, undertorquing may allow a fastener to vibrate loose causing serious damage. Especially when dealing with aluminum parts, pay attention to torque specifications and utilize a torque wrench in assembly. If a torque figure is not available, remember that if you are using the right tool to perform the job, you will probably not have to strain yourself to get a fastener tight enough. The pitch of most threads is so slight that the tension you put on the wrench will be multiplied many times in actual force on what you are tightening. A good example of how critical torque is can be seen in the case of spark plug installation, especially where you are putting the plug into an aluminum cylinder head. Too little torque can fail to crush the gasket, causing leakage of combustion gases and consequent overheating of the plug and engine parts. Too much torque can damage the threads or distort the plug, changing the spark gap.

There are many commercial products available for ensuring that fasteners won't come loose, even if they are not torqued just right (a very common brand is Loctite®). If you're worried about getting something together tight enough to hold, but loose enough to avoid mechanical damage during assembly, one of these products might offer substantial insurance. Before choosing a threadlocking compound, read the label on the package and make sure the product is compatible with the materials, fluids, etc. involved.

3. Crossthreading. This occurs when a part such as a bolt is screwed into a nut or casting at the wrong angle and forced. Crossthreading is more likely to occur if access is difficult. It helps to clean and lubricate fasteners, then to start threading with the part to be installed positioned straight in. Then, start the bolt, spark plug, etc. with your fingers. If you encounter resistance, unscrew the part and start over again at a different angle until it can be inserted and turned several times without much effort. Keep in mind that many parts, especially spark plugs, have tapered threads, so that gentle turning will automatically bring the part you're threading to the proper angle, but only if you don't force it or resist a change in angle. Don't put a wrench on the part until it's been tightened a couple of turns by hand. If you suddenly encounter resistance, and the part has not seated fully, don't force it. Pull it back out to make sure it's clean and threading properly.

Always take your time and be patient; once you have some experience, working on your vehicle may well become an enjoyable hobby.

TOOLS AND EQUIPMENT

▶ **See Figures 1 thru 15**

Naturally, without the proper tools and equipment it is impossible to properly service your vehicle. It would also be virtually impossible to catalog every tool that you would need to perform all of the operations in this book. Of course, It would be unwise for the amateur to rush out and buy an expensive set of tools on the theory that he/she may need one or more of them at some time.

The best approach is to proceed slowly, gathering a good quality set of those tools that are used most frequently. Don't be misled by the low cost of bargain tools. It is far better to spend a little more for better quality. Forged wrenches, 6 or 12-point sockets and fine tooth ratchets are by far preferable to their less expensive counterparts. As any good mechanic can tell you, there are few worse experiences than trying to work on a vehicle with bad tools. Your monetary savings will be far outweighed by frustration and mangled knuckles.

Begin accumulating those tools that are used most frequently: those associated with routine maintenance and tune-up. In addition to the normal assortment of screwdrivers and pliers, you should have the following tools:

• Wrenches/sockets and combination open end/box end wrenches in sizes from ⅛–¾ in. or 3mm–19mm (depending on whether your vehicle uses standard or metric fasteners) and a $^{13}/_{16}$ in. or ⅝ in. spark plug socket (depending on plug type).

➡**If possible, buy various length socket drive extensions. Universal-joint and wobble extensions can be extremely useful, but be careful when using them, as they can change the amount of torque applied to the socket.**

• Jackstands for support.
• Oil filter wrench.
• Spout or funnel for pouring fluids.
• Grease gun for chassis lubrication (unless your vehicle is not equipped with any grease fittings—for details, please refer to information on Fluids and Lubricants found later in this section).
• Hydrometer for checking the battery (unless equipped with a sealed, maintenance-free battery).
• A container for draining oil and other fluids.
• Rags for wiping up the inevitable mess.

In addition to the above items there are several others that are not absolutely necessary, but handy to have around. These include Oil Dry® (or an equivalent oil absorbent gravel—such as cat litter) and the usual supply of lubricants, antifreeze and fluids, although these can be purchased as needed. This is a basic list for routine maintenance, but only your personal needs and desire can accurately determine your list of tools.

After performing a few projects on the vehicle, you'll be amazed at the other tools and non-tools on your workbench. Some useful household items

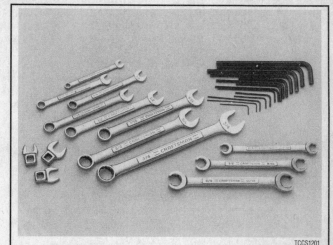

TCCS1201

Fig. 2 In addition to ratchets, a good set of wrenches and hex keys will be necessary

TCCS1202

Fig. 3 A hydraulic floor jack and a set of jackstands are essential for lifting and supporting the vehicle

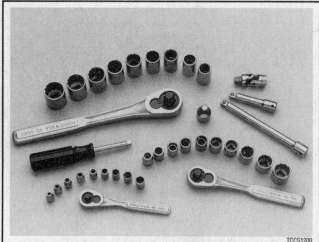

TCCS1200

Fig. 1 All but the most basic procedures will require an assortment of ratchets and sockets

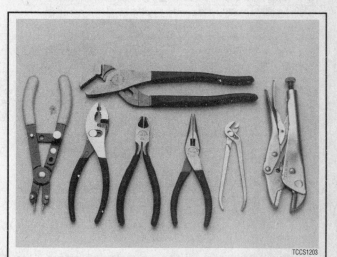

TCCS1203

Fig. 4 An assortment of pliers, grippers and cutters will be handy for old rusted parts and stripped bolt heads

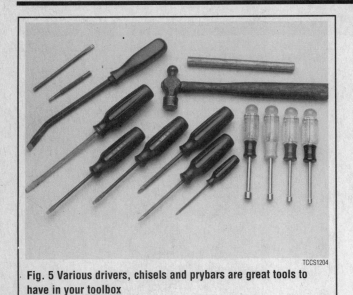

Fig. 5 Various drivers, chisels and prybars are great tools to have in your toolbox

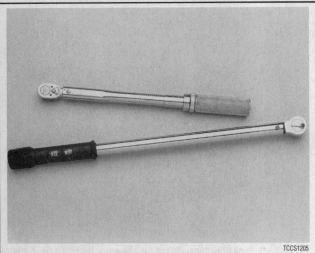

Fig. 6 Many repairs will require the use of a torque wrench to assure the components are properly fastened

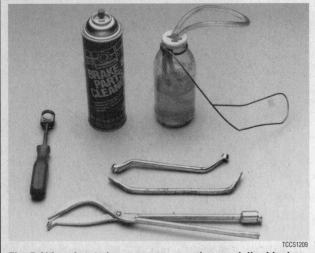

Fig. 7 Although not always necessary, using specialized brake tools will save time

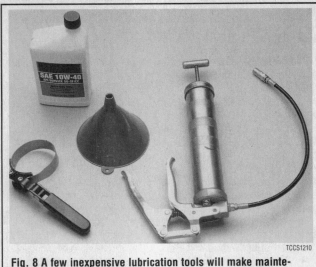

Fig. 8 A few inexpensive lubrication tools will make maintenance easier

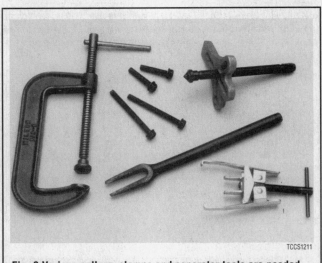

Fig. 9 Various pullers, clamps and separator tools are needed for many larger, more complicated repairs

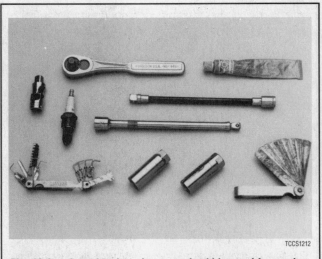

Fig. 10 A variety of tools and gauges should be used for spark plug gapping and installation

are: a large turkey baster or siphon, empty coffee cans and ice trays (to store parts), ball of twine, electrical tape for wiring, small rolls of colored tape for tagging lines or hoses, markers and pens, a note pad, golf tees (for plugging vacuum lines), metal coat hangers or a roll of mechanics's wire (to hold things out of the way), dental pick or similar long, pointed probe, a strong magnet, and a small mirror (to see into recesses and under manifolds).

A more advanced set of tools, suitable for tune-up work, can be drawn up easily. While the tools are slightly more sophisticated, they need not be outrageously expensive. There are several inexpensive tach/dwell meters on the market that are every bit as good for the average mechanic as a professional model. Just be sure that it goes to a least 1200–1500 rpm on the tach scale and that it

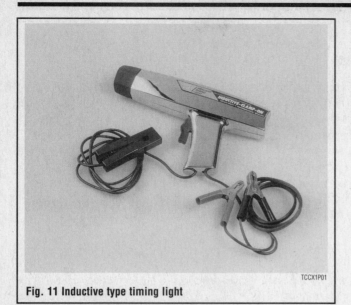

Fig. 11 Inductive type timing light

Fig. 12 A screw-in type compression gauge is recommended for compression testing

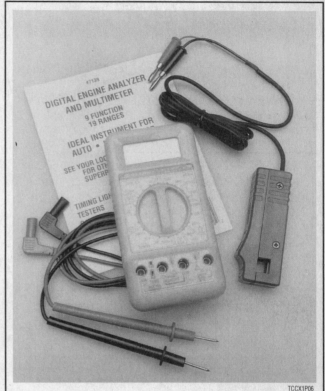

Fig. 14 Most modern automotive multimeters incorporate many helpful features

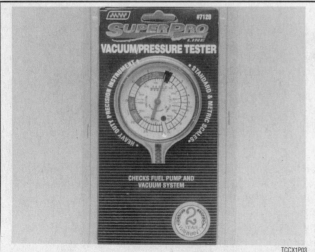

Fig. 13 A vacuum/pressure tester is necessary for many testing procedures

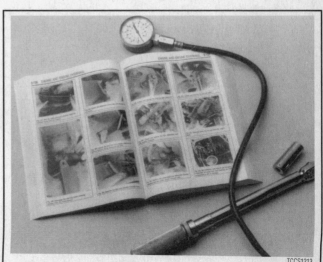

Fig. 15 Proper information is vital, so always have a Chilton Total Car Care manual handy

Modern vehicles equipped with computer-controlled fuel, emission and ignition systems require modern electronic tools to diagnose problems. Many of these tools are designed solely for the professional mechanic and are too costly and difficult to use for the average do-it-yourselfer. However, various automotive aftermarket companies have introduced products that address the needs of the average home mechanic, providing sophisticated information at affordable cost. Consult your local auto parts store to determine what is available for your vehicle.

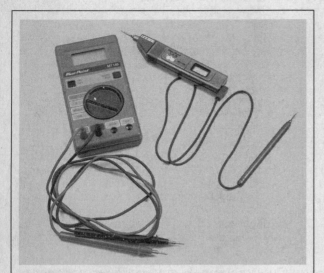

Digital multimeters come in a variety of styles and are a "must-have" for any serious home mechanic. Digital multimeters measure voltage (volts), resistance (ohms) and sometimes current (amperes). These versatile tools are used for checking all types of electrical or electronic components

Trouble code tools allow the home mechanic to extract the "fault code" number from an on-board computer that has sensed a problem (usually indicated by a Check Engine light). Armed with this code, the home mechanic can focus attention on a suspect system or component

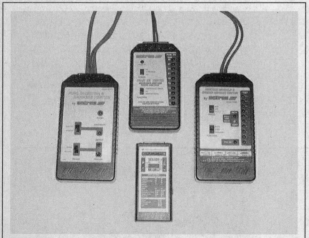

Sensor testers perform specific checks on many of the sensors and actuators used on today's computer-controlled vehicles. These testers can check sensors both on or off the vehicle, as well as test the accompanying electrical circuits

Hand-held scanners represent the most sophisticated of all do-it-yourself diagnostic tools. These tools do more than just access computer codes like the code readers above; they provide the user with an actual interface into the vehicle's computer. Comprehensive data on specific makes and models will come with the tool, either built-in or as a separate cartridge

works on 4, 6 and 8-cylinder engines. (If you have one or more vehicles with a diesel engine, a special tachometer is required since diesels don't use spark plug ignition systems). The key to these purchases is to make them with an eye towards adaptability and wide range. A basic list of tune-up tools could include:

• Tach/dwell meter.
• Spark plug wrench and gapping tool.
• Feeler gauges for valve or point adjustment. (Even if your vehicle does not use points or require valve adjustments, a feeler gauge is helpful for many repair/overhaul procedures).

A tachometer/dwell meter will ensure accurate tune-up work on vehicles without electronic ignition. The choice of a timing light should be made carefully. A light which works on the DC current supplied by the vehicle's battery is the best choice; it should have a xenon tube for brightness. On any vehicle with an electronic ignition system, a timing light with an inductive pickup that clamps around the No. 1 spark plug cable is preferred.

In addition to these basic tools, there are several other tools and gauges you may find useful. These include:

• Compression gauge. The screw-in type is slower to use, but eliminates the possibility of a faulty reading due to escaping pressure.
• Manifold vacuum gauge.
• 12V test light.
• A combination volt/ohmmeter

• Induction Ammeter. This is used for determining whether or not there is current in a wire. These are handy for use if a wire is broken somewhere in a wiring harness.

As a final note, you will probably find a torque wrench necessary for all but the most basic work. The beam type models are perfectly adequate, although the newer click types (breakaway) are easier to use. The click type torque wrenches tend to be more expensive. Also keep in mind that all types of torque wrenches should be periodically checked and/or recalibrated. You will have to decide for yourself which better fits your purpose.

Special Tools

Normally, the use of special factory tools is avoided for repair procedures, since these are not readily available for the do-it-yourself mechanic. When it is possible to perform the job with more commonly available tools, it will be pointed out, but occasionally, a special tool was designed to perform a specific function and should be used. Before substituting another tool, you should be convinced that neither your safety nor the performance of the vehicle will be compromised.

Special tools can usually be purchased from an automotive parts store or from your dealer. In some cases special tools may be available directly from the tool manufacturer.

SERVICING YOUR VEHICLE SAFELY

▶ **See Figures 16, 17, 18 and 19**

It is virtually impossible to anticipate all of the hazards involved with automotive maintenance and service, but care and common sense will prevent most accidents.

The rules of safety for mechanics range from "don't smoke around gasoline," to "use the proper tool(s) for the job." The trick to avoiding injuries is to develop safe work habits and to take every possible precaution.

Do's

• Do keep a fire extinguisher and first aid kit handy.
• Do wear safety glasses or goggles when cutting, drilling, grinding or prying, even if you have 20–20 vision. If you wear glasses for the sake of vision, wear safety goggles over your regular glasses.
• Do shield your eyes whenever you work around the battery. Batteries contain sulfuric acid. In case of contact with the eyes or skin, flush the area with water or a mixture of water and baking soda, then seek immediate medical attention.
• Do use safety stands (jackstands) for any undervehicle service. Jacks are for raising vehicles; jackstands are for making sure the vehicle stays

raised until you want it to come down. Whenever the vehicle is raised, block the wheels remaining on the ground and set the parking brake.
• Do use adequate ventilation when working with any chemicals or hazardous materials. Like carbon monoxide, the asbestos dust resulting from some brake lining wear can be hazardous in sufficient quantities.
• Do disconnect the negative battery cable when working on the electrical system. The secondary ignition system contains EXTREMELY HIGH VOLTAGE. In some cases it can even exceed 50,000 volts.
• Do follow manufacturer's directions whenever working with potentially hazardous materials. Most chemicals and fluids are poisonous if taken internally.
• Do properly maintain your tools. Loose hammerheads, mushroomed punches and chisels, frayed or poorly grounded electrical cords, excessively worn screwdrivers, spread wrenches (open end), cracked sockets, slipping ratchets, or faulty droplight sockets can cause accidents.
• Likewise, keep your tools clean; a greasy wrench can slip off a bolt head, ruining the bolt and often harming your knuckles in the process.
• Do use the proper size and type of tool for the job at hand. Do select a wrench or socket that fits the nut or bolt. The wrench or socket should sit straight, not cocked.

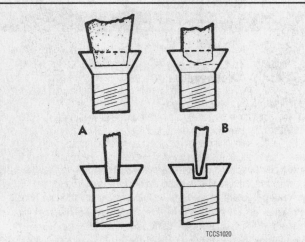

TCCS1020

Fig. 16 Screwdrivers should be kept in good condition to prevent injury or damage which could result if the blade slips from the screw

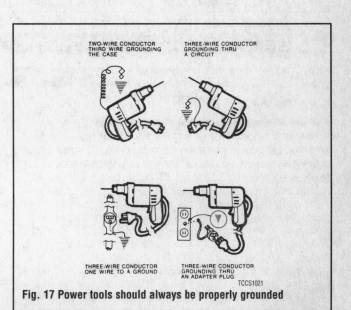

TWO-WIRE CONDUCTOR THIRD WIRE GROUNDING THE CASE   THREE-WIRE CONDUCTOR GROUNDING THRU A CIRCUIT

THREE-WIRE CONDUCTOR ONE WIRE TO A GROUND   THREE-WIRE CONDUCTOR GROUNDING THRU AN ADAPTER PLUG

TCCS1021

Fig. 17 Power tools should always be properly grounded

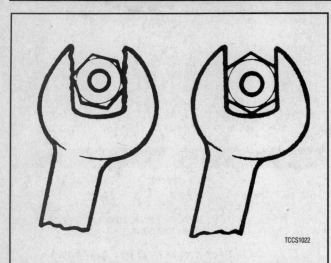

Fig. 18 Using the correct size wrench will help prevent the possibility of rounding off a nut

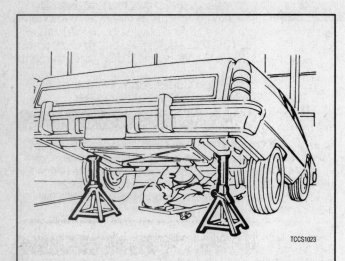

Fig. 19 NEVER work under a vehicle unless it is supported using safety stands (jackstands)

• Do, when possible, pull on a wrench handle rather than push on it, and adjust your stance to prevent a fall.

• Do be sure that adjustable wrenches are tightly closed on the nut or bolt and pulled so that the force is on the side of the fixed jaw.

• Do strike squarely with a hammer; avoid glancing blows.

• Do set the parking brake and block the drive wheels if the work requires a running engine.

Don'ts

• Don't run the engine in a garage or anywhere else without proper ventilation—EVER! Carbon monoxide is poisonous; it takes a long time to leave the human body and you can build up a deadly supply of it in your system by simply breathing in a little every day. You may not realize you are slowly poisoning yourself. Always use power vents, windows, fans and/or open the garage door.

• Don't work around moving parts while wearing loose clothing. Short sleeves are much safer than long, loose sleeves. Hard-toed shoes with neoprene soles protect your toes and give a better grip on slippery surfaces. Jewelry such as watches, fancy belt buckles, beads or body adornment of any kind is not safe working around a vehicle. Long hair should be tied back under a hat or cap.

• Don't use pockets for toolboxes. A fall or bump can drive a screwdriver deep into your body. Even a rag hanging from your back pocket can wrap around a spinning shaft or fan.

• Don't smoke when working around gasoline, cleaning solvent or other flammable material.

• Don't smoke when working around the battery. When the battery is being charged, it gives off explosive hydrogen gas.

• Don't use gasoline to wash your hands; there are excellent soaps available. Gasoline contains dangerous additives which can enter the body through a cut or through your pores. Gasoline also removes all the natural oils from the skin so that bone dry hands will suck up oil and grease.

• Don't service the air conditioning system unless you are equipped with the necessary tools and training. When liquid or compressed gas refrigerant is released to atmospheric pressure it will absorb heat from whatever it contacts. This will chill or freeze anything it touches. Although refrigerant is normally non-toxic, R-12 becomes a deadly poisonous gas in the presence of an open flame. One good whiff of the vapors from burning refrigerant can be fatal.

• Don't use screwdrivers for anything other than driving screws! A screwdriver used as an prying tool can snap when you least expect it, causing injuries. At the very least, you'll ruin a good screwdriver.

• Don't use a bumper or emergency jack (that little ratchet, scissors, or pantograph jack supplied with the vehicle) for anything other than changing a flat! These jacks are only intended for emergency use out on the road; they are NOT designed as a maintenance tool. If you are serious about maintaining your vehicle yourself, invest in a hydraulic floor jack of at least a 1½ ton capacity, and at least two sturdy jackstands.

FASTENERS, MEASUREMENTS AND CONVERSIONS

Bolts, Nuts and Other Threaded Retainers

▶ See Figures 20, 21, 22 and 23

Although there are a great variety of fasteners found in the modern car or truck, the most commonly used retainer is the threaded fastener (nuts, bolts, screws, studs, etc). Most threaded retainers may be reused, provided that they are not damaged in use or during the repair. Some retainers (such as stretch bolts or torque prevailing nuts) are designed to deform when tightened or in use and should not be reinstalled.

Whenever possible, we will note any special retainers which should be replaced during a procedure. But you should always inspect the condition of a retainer when it is removed and replace any that show signs of damage. Check all threads for rust or corrosion which can increase the torque necessary to achieve the desired clamp load for which that fastener was originally selected. Additionally, be sure that the driver surface of the fastener has not been compromised by rounding or other damage. In some cases a driver surface may become only partially

rounded, allowing the driver to catch in only one direction. In many of these occurrences, a fastener may be installed and tightened, but the driver would not be able to grip and loosen the fastener again. (This ould lead to frustration down the line should that component ever need to be disassembled again).

If you must replace a fastener, whether due to design or damage, you must ALWAYS be sure to use the proper replacement. In all cases, a retainer of the same design, material and strength should be used. Markings on the heads of most bolts will help determine the proper strength of the fastener. The same material, thread and pitch must be selected to assure proper installation and safe operation of the vehicle afterwards.

Thread gauges are available to help measure a bolt or stud's thread. Most automotive and hardware stores keep gauges available to help you select the proper size. In a pinch, you can use another nut or bolt for a thread gauge. If the bolt you are replacing is not too badly damaged, you can select a match by finding another bolt which will thread in its place. If you find a nut which threads properly onto the damaged bolt, then use that nut to help select the replacement bolt. If however, the bolt you are

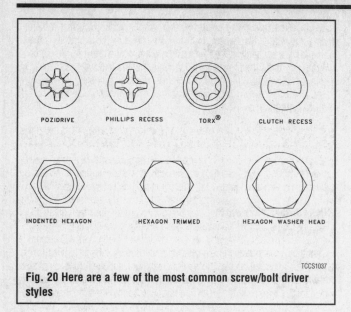

Fig. 20 Here are a few of the most common screw/bolt driver styles

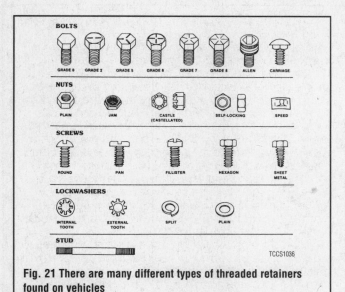

Fig. 21 There are many different types of threaded retainers found on vehicles

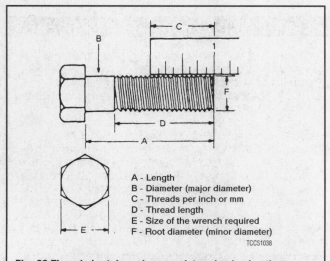

A - Length
B - Diameter (major diameter)
C - Threads per inch or mm
D - Thread length
E - Size of the wrench required
F - Root diameter (minor diameter)

Fig. 22 Threaded retainer sizes are determined using these measurements

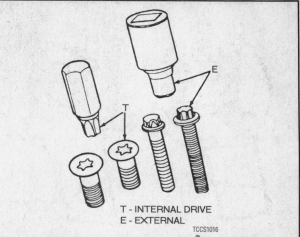

T - INTERNAL DRIVE
E - EXTERNAL

Fig. 23 Special fasteners such as these Torx® head bolts are used by manufacturers to discourage people from working on vehicles without the proper tools

replacing is so badly damaged (broken or drilled out) that its threads cannot be used as a gauge, you might start by looking for another bolt (from the same assembly or a similar location on your vehicle) which will thread into the damaged bolt's mounting. If so, the other bolt can be used to select a nut; the nut can then be used to select the replacement bolt.

In all cases, be absolutely sure you have selected the proper replacement. Don't be shy, you can always ask the store clerk for help.

❊❊ WARNING

Be aware that when you find a bolt with damaged threads, you may also find the nut or drilled hole it was threaded into has also been damaged. If this is the case, you may have to drill and tap the hole, replace the nut or otherwise repair the threads. NEVER try to force a replacement bolt to fit into the damaged threads.

Torque

Torque is defined as the measurement of resistance to turning or rotating. It tends to twist a body about an axis of rotation. A common example of this would be tightening a threaded retainer such as a nut, bolt or screw. Measuring torque is one of the most common ways to help assure that a threaded retainer has been properly fastened.

When tightening a threaded fastener, torque is applied in three distinct areas, the head, the bearing surface and the clamp load. About 50 percent of the measured torque is used in overcoming bearing friction. This is the friction between the bearing surface of the bolt head, screw head or nut face and the base material or washer (the surface on which the fastener is rotating). Approximately 40 percent of the applied torque is used in overcoming thread friction. This leaves only about 10 percent of the applied torque to develop a useful clamp load (the force which holds a joint together). This means that friction can account for as much as 90 percent of the applied torque on a fastener.

TORQUE WRENCHES

▶ See Figures 24, 25 and 26

In most applications, a torque wrench can be used to assure proper installation of a fastener. Torque wrenches come in various designs and most automotive supply stores will carry a variety to suit your needs. A torque wrench should be used any time we supply a specific torque value for a fastener. A torque wrench can also be used if you are following the

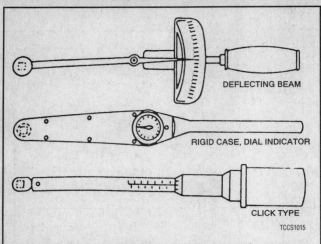

Fig. 24 Various styles of torque wrenches are usually available at your local automotive supply store

general guidelines in the accompanying charts. Keep in mind that because there is no worldwide standardization of fasteners, the charts are a general guideline and should be used with caution. Again, the general rule of "if you are using the right tool for the job, you should not have to strain to tighten a fastener" applies here.

Beam Type

◗ **See Figure 27**

The beam type torque wrench is one of the most popular types. It consists of a pointer attached to the head that runs the length of the flexible beam (shaft) to a scale located near the handle. As the wrench is pulled, the beam bends and the pointer indicates the torque using the scale.

Click (Breakaway) Type

◗ **See Figure 28**

Another popular design of torque wrench is the click type. To use the click type wrench you pre-adjust it to a torque setting. Once the torque is reached, the wrench has a reflex signaling feature that causes a momentary breakaway of the torque wrench body, sending an impulse to the operator's hand.

	Mark		Class		Mark	Class
Hexagon head bolt	Bolt head No.	4— 5— 6— 7— 8— 9— 10— 11—	4T 5T 6T 7T 8T 9T 10T 11T	Stud bolt	No mark	4T
		No mark	4T			
Hexagon flange bolt w/ washer hexagon bolt		No mark	4T		Grooved	6T
Hexagon head bolt		Two protruding lines	5T			
Hexagon flange bolt w/ washer hexagon bolt		Two protruding lines	6T	Welded bolt		
Hexagon head bolt		Three protruding lines	7T			4T
Hexagon head bolt		Four protruding lines	8T			

TCCS1240

Fig. 25 Determining bolt strength of metric fasteners—NOTE: this is a typical bolt marking system, but there is not a worldwide standard

Class	Diameter mm	Pitch mm	Specified torque					
			Hexagon head bolt			Hexagon flange bolt		
			N·m	kgf·cm	ft·lbf	N·m	kgf·cm	ft·lbf
4T	6	1	5	55	48 in.·lbf	6	60	52 in.·lbf
	8	1.25	12.5	130	9	14	145	10
	10	1.25	26	260	19	29	290	21
	12	1.25	47	480	35	53	540	39
	14	1.5	74	760	55	84	850	61
	16	1.5	115	1,150	83	—	—	—
5T	6	1	6.5	65	56 in.·lbf	7.5	75	65 in.·lbf
	8	1.25	15.5	160	12	17.5	175	13
	10	1.25	32	330	24	36	360	26
	12	1.25	59	600	43	65	670	48
	14	1.5	91	930	67	100	1,050	76
	16	1.5	140	1,400	101	—	—	—
6T	6	1	8	80	69 in.·lbf	9	90	78 in.·lbf
	8	1.25	19	195	14	21	210	15
	10	1.25	39	400	29	44	440	32
	12	1.25	71	730	53	80	810	59
	14	1.5	110	1,100	80	125	1,250	90
	16	1.5	170	1,750	127	—	—	—
7T	6	1	10.5	110	8	12	120	9
	8	1.25	25	260	19	28	290	21
	10	1.25	52	530	38	58	590	43
	12	1.25	95	970	70	105	1,050	76
	14	1.5	145	1,500	108	165	1,700	123
	16	1.5	230	2,300	166	—	—	—
8T	8	1.25	29	300	22	33	330	24
	10	1.25	61	620	45	68	690	50
	12	1.25	110	1,100	80	120	1,250	90
9T	8	1.25	34	340	25	37	380	27
	10	1.25	70	710	51	78	790	57
	12	1.25	125	1,300	94	140	1,450	105
10T	8	1.25	38	390	28	42	430	31
	10	1.25	78	800	58	88	890	64
	12	1.25	140	1,450	105	155	1,600	116
11T	8	1.25	42	430	31	47	480	35
	10	1.25	87	890	64	97	990	72
	12	1.25	155	1,600	116	175	1,800	130

TCCS1241

Fig. 26 Typical bolt torques for metric fasteners—WARNING: use only as a guide

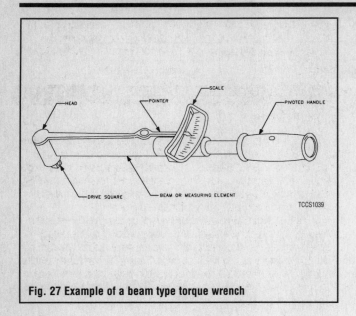

Fig. 27 Example of a beam type torque wrench

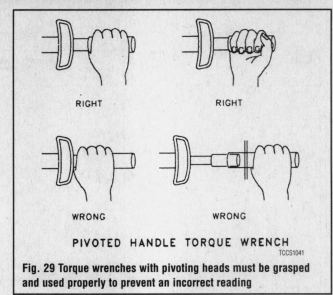

PIVOTED HANDLE TORQUE WRENCH

Fig. 29 Torque wrenches with pivoting heads must be grasped and used properly to prevent an incorrect reading

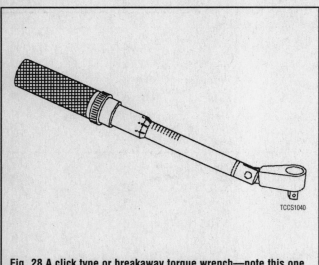

Fig. 28 A click type or breakaway torque wrench—note this one has a pivoting head

Pivot Head Type

▶ **See Figures 28 and 29**

Some torque wrenches (usually of the click type) may be equipped with a pivot head which can allow it to be used in areas of limited access. BUT, it must be used properly. To hold a pivot head wrench, grasp the handle lightly, and as you pull on the handle, it should be floated on the pivot point. If the handle comes in contact with the yoke extension during the process of pulling, there is a very good chance the torque readings will be inaccurate because this could alter the wrench loading point. The design of the handle is usually such as to make it inconvenient to deliberately misuse the wrench.

➡ **It should be mentioned that the use of any U-joint, wobble or extension will have an effect on the torque readings, no matter what type of wrench you are using. For the most accurate readings, install the socket directly on the wrench driver. If necessary, straight extensions (which hold a socket directly under the wrench driver) will have the least effect on the torque reading. Avoid any extension that alters the length of the wrench from the handle to the head/driving point (such as a crow's foot). U-joint or Wobble extensions can greatly affect the readings; avoid their use at all times.**

Rigid Case (Direct Reading)

▶ **See Figure 30**

A rigid case or direct reading torque wrench is equipped with a dial indicator to show torque values. One advantage of these wrenches is that they can be held at any position on the wrench without affecting accuracy. These wrenches are often preferred because they tend to be compact, easy to read and have a great degree of accuracy.

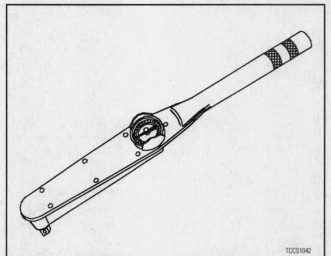

Fig. 30 The rigid case (direct reading) torque wrench uses a dial indicator to show torque

TORQUE ANGLE METERS

▶ **See Figure 31**

Because the frictional characteristics of each fastener or threaded hole will vary, clamp loads which are based strictly on torque will vary as well. In most applications, this variance is not significant enough to cause worry. But, in certain applications, a manufacturer's engineers may determine that more precise clamp loads are necessary (such is the case with many aluminum cylinder heads). In these cases, a torque angle method of installation would be specified. When installing fasteners which are torque angle tightened, a predetermined seating torque and standard torque wrench are

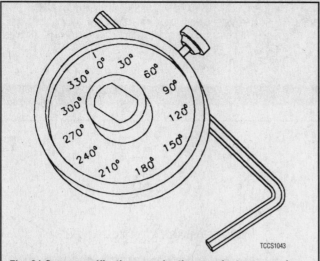

Fig. 31 Some specifications require the use of a torque angle meter (mechanical protractor)

usually used first to remove any compliance from the joint. The fastener is then tightened the specified additional portion of a turn measured in degrees. A torque angle gauge (mechanical protractor) is used for these applications.

Standard and Metric Measurements

▶ **See Figure 32**

Throughout this manual, specifications are given to help you determine the condition of various components on your vehicle, or to assist you in their installation. Some of the most common measurements include length (in. or cm/mm), torque (ft. lbs., inch lbs. or Nm) and pressure (psi, in. Hg, kPa or mm Hg). In most cases, we strive to provide the proper measurement as determined by the manufacturer's engineers.

Though, in some cases, that value may not be conveniently measured with what is available in your toolbox. Luckily, many of the measuring devices which are available today will have two scales so the Standard or Metric measurements may easily be taken. If any of the various measuring tools which are available to you do not contain the same scale as listed in the specifications, use the accompanying conversion factors to determine the proper value.

CONVERSION FACTORS

LENGTH–DISTANCE

Inches (in.)	x 25.4	= Millimeters (mm)	x .0394	= Inches
Feet (ft.)	x .305	= Meters (m)	x 3.281	= Feet
Miles	x 1.609	= Kilometers (km)	x .0621	= Miles

VOLUME

Cubic Inches (in3)	x 16.387	= Cubic Centimeters	x .061	= in3
IMP Pints (IMP pt.)	x .568	= Liters (L)	x 1.76	= IMP pt.
IMP Quarts (IMP qt.)	x 1.137	= Liters (L)	x .88	= IMP qt.
IMP Gallons (IMP gal.)	x 4.546	= Liters (L)	x .22	= IMP gal.
IMP Quarts (IMP qt.)	x 1.201	= US Quarts (US qt.)	x .833	= IMP qt.
IMP Gallons (IMP gal.)	x 1.201	= US Gallons (US gal.)	x .833	= IMP gal.
Fl. Ounces	x 29.573	= Milliliters	x .034	= Ounces
US Pints (US pt.)	x .473	= Liters (L)	x 2.113	= Pints
US Quarts (US qt.)	x .946	= Liters (L)	x 1.057	= Quarts
US Gallons (US gal.)	x 3.785	= Liters (L)	x .264	= Gallons

MASS–WEIGHT

Ounces (oz.)	x 28.35	= Grams (g)	x .035	= Ounces
Pounds (lb.)	x .454	= Kilograms (kg)	x 2.205	= Pounds

PRESSURE

Pounds Per Sq. In. (psi)	x 6.895	= Kilopascals (kPa)	x .145	= psi
Inches of Mercury (Hg)	x .4912	= psi	x 2.036	= Hg
Inches of Mercury (Hg)	x 3.377	= Kilopascals (kPa)	x .2961	= Hg
Inches of Water (H₂O)	x .07355	= Inches of Mercury	x 13.783	= H₂O
Inches of Water (H₂O)	x .03613	= psi	x 27.684	= H₂O
Inches of Water (H₂O)	x .248	= Kilopascals (kPa)	x 4.026	= H₂O

TORQUE

Pounds–Force Inches (in–lb)	x .113	= Newton Meters (N·m)	x 8.85	= in–lb
Pounds–Force Feet (ft–lb)	x 1.356	= Newton Meters (N·m)	x .738	= ft–lb

VELOCITY

Miles Per Hour (MPH)	x 1.609	= Kilometers Per Hour (KPH)	x .621	= MPH

POWER

Horsepower (Hp)	x .745	= Kilowatts	x 1.34	= Horsepower

FUEL CONSUMPTION*

Miles Per Gallon IMP (MPG)	x .354	= Kilometers Per Liter (Km/L)
Kilometers Per Liter (Km/L)	x 2.352	= IMP MPG
Miles Per Gallon US (MPG)	x .425	= Kilometers Per Liter (Km/L)
Kilometers Per Liter (Km/L)	x 2.352	= US MPG

*It is common to covert from miles per gallon (mpg) to liters/100 kilometers (1/100 km), where mpg (IMP) x 1/100 km = 282 and mpg (US) x 1/100 km = 235.

TEMPERATURE

Degree Fahrenheit (°F)	= (°C x 1.8) + 32
Degree Celsius (°C)	= (°F – 32) x .56

Fig. 32 Standard and metric conversion factors chart

The conversion factor chart is used by taking the given specification and multiplying it by the necessary conversion factor. For instance, looking at the first line, if you have a measurement in inches such as "free-play should be 2 in." but your ruler reads only in millimeters, multiply 2 in. by the conversion factor of 25.4 to get the metric equivalent of 50.8mm. Like-wise, if the specification was given only in a Metric measurement, for example in Newton Meters (Nm), then look at the center column first. If the measurement is 100 Nm, multiply it by the conversion factor of 0.738 to get 73.8 ft. lbs.

SERIAL NUMBER IDENTIFICATION

Vehicle Identification Number

▶ See Figures 33, 34, 35 and 36

The Vehicle Identification Number (VIN) is located on a plate which is attached to the left top side of the instrument panel. These numbers are visible from the outside of the vehicle. All Vehicle Identification Numbers contain 17 digits. The vehicle number is a code which tells country, make, vehicle type, engine, body and many other important characteristics of that specific vehicle.

There is also a vehicle information code plate which is riveted to the bulkhead in the engine compartment. The plate shows the VIN, model code, engine model, transaxle model and body color codes. The engine code used on this plate differs from the code letter used in the 8th position of the Vehicle Identification Number (VIN). Either code can be used to identify the particular engine in the vehicle. Since the vehicle owners card is usually carried, it may be easier to use the code letter in the VIN for engine reference. A second reason for referring to the VIN for engine identification is that code 4G63, located on the vehicle information code plate, does identify the engine as a 2.0L DOHC engine, but does not tell you if the engine is equipped with a turbocharger. If the 8th VIN number

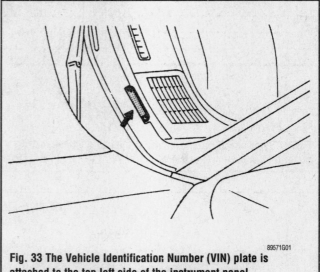

89571G01

Fig. 33 The Vehicle Identification Number (VIN) plate is attached to the top left side of the instrument panel

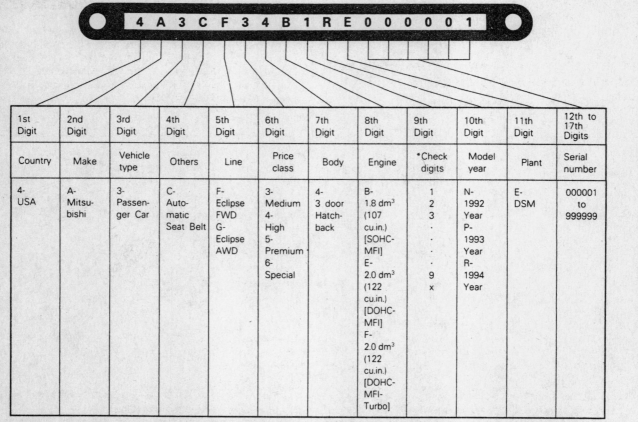

1st Digit	2nd Digit	3rd Digit	4th Digit	5th Digit	6th Digit	7th Digit	8th Digit	9th Digit	10th Digit	11th Digit	12th to 17th Digits
Country	Make	Vehicle type	Others	Line	Price class	Body	Engine	*Check digits	Model year	Plant	Serial number
4- USA	A- Mitsu-bishi	3- Passen-ger Car	C- Auto-matic Seat Belt	F- Eclipse FWD G- Eclipse AWD	3- Medium 4- High 5- Premium 6- Special	4- 3 door Hatch-back	B- 1.8 dm³ (107 cu.in.) [SOHC-MFI] E- 2.0 dm³ (122 cu.in.) [DOHC-MFI] F- 2.0 dm³ (122 cu.in.) [DOHC-MFI-Turbo]	1 2 3 . . . 9 x	N- 1992 Year P- 1993 Year R- 1994 Year	E- DSM	000001 to 999999

NOTE * "Check digit" means a single number or letter x used to verify the accuracy of transcription of vehicle identification number.

89571G02

Fig. 34 Example of the VIN breakdown

VEHICLE IDENTIFICATION CHART

		Engine Code					Model Year	
Code	Liters	Cu. In. (cc)	Cyl.	Fuel Sys.	Eng. Mfg.		Code	Year
T	1.8	107 (1755)	4	MFI	Mitsubishi		L	1990
B	1.8	107 (1755)	4	MFI	Mitsubishi		M	1991
R	2.0	122 (1997)	4	MFI	Mitsubishi		N	1992
E	2.0	122 (1997)	4	MFI	Mitsubishi		P	1993
Y	2.0	122 (1997)	4	MFI/SFI	Mitsubishi		R	1994
U	2.0	122 (1997)	4	MFI-Turbo	Mitsubishi		S	1995
F	2.0	122 (1997)	4	MFI-Turbo	Mitsubishi		T	1996
G	2.4	144 (2351)	4	MFI/SFI	Mitsubishi		V	1997
							W	1998

89571C03

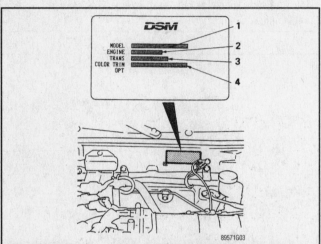

Fig. 35 The vehicle model, engine model, transaxle model, and body color code are all noted on the vehicle information code plate

is a U, there is no doubt that the engine in question is a 2.0L DOHC engine equipped with a turbocharger.

The engine codes found on the vehicle information code plate are as follows:

- 4G37—1.8L SOHC engine
- 420A—2.0L DOHC engine
- 4G63—2.0L DOHC engine
- 4G64—2.4L DOHC engine

A vehicle safety certification label is attached to the face of the left door pillar post. This label indicates the month and year of manufacture, Gross Vehicle Weight Rating (GRVW) front and rear, and Vehicle Identification Number (VIN).

Engine Identification Number

▶ See Figures 37, 38, 39, 40 and 41

The engine model number is stamped at the front side on the top edge of the cylinder block. The same 4 character code as on the vehicle information code plate is used. The engine serial number is also stamped near the engine model number. As mentioned above, the engine can also be identified by the 8th digit in the VIN number.

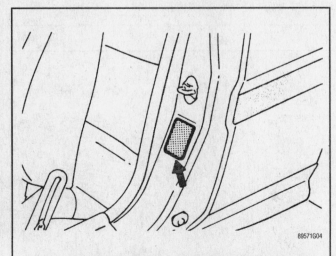

Fig. 36 Your car should have a vehicle safety certification label attached to the face of the left door pillar post

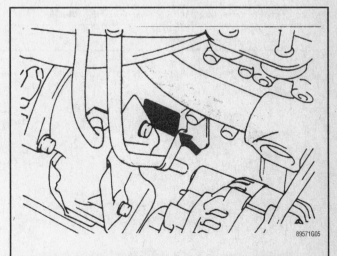

Fig. 37 The engine model stamp is located on the front side of the cylinder block—1990–94 vehicles

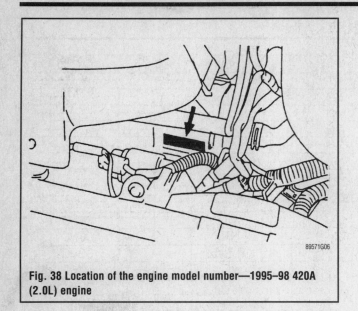

Fig. 38 Location of the engine model number—1995–98 420A (2.0L) engine

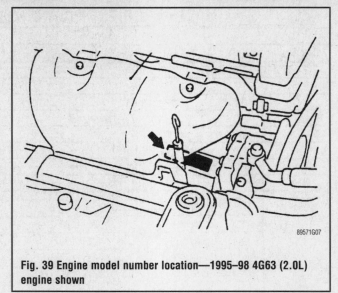

Fig. 39 Engine model number location—1995–98 4G63 (2.0L) engine shown

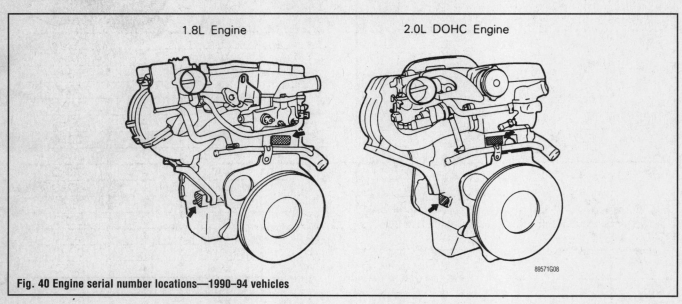

1.8L Engine

2.0L DOHC Engine

Fig. 40 Engine serial number locations—1990–94 vehicles

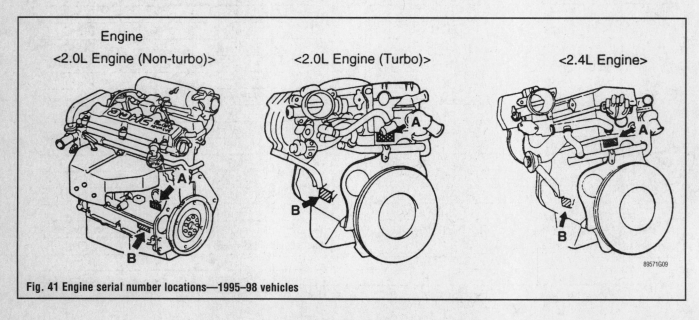

Engine

<2.0L Engine (Non-turbo)>

<2.0L Engine (Turbo)>

<2.4L Engine>

Fig. 41 Engine serial number locations—1995–98 vehicles

ENGINE IDENTIFICATION

Year	Model	Engine Displacement Liters (cc)	Engine Series (ID/VIN)	Fuel System	No. of Cylinders	Engine Type
1990	Eclipse	1.8 (1775)	T	MFI	4	SOHC
	Eclipse	2.0 (1997)	R	MFI	4	DOHC
	Eclipse	2.0 (1997)	U	MFI-Turbo	4	DOHC
	Laser	1.8 (1775)	T	MFI	4	SOHC
	Laser	2.0 (1997)	R	MFI	4	DOHC
	Laser	2.0 (1997)	U	MFI-Turbo	4	DOHC
	Talon	2.0 (1997)	R	MFI	4	DOHC
	Talon	2.0 (1997)	U	MFI-Turbo	4	DOHC
1991	Eclipse	1.8 (1775)	T	MFI	4	SOHC
	Eclipse	2.0 (1997)	R	MFI	4	DOHC
	Eclipse	2.0 (1997)	U	MFI-Turbo	4	DOHC
	Laser	1.8 (1775)	T	MFI	4	SOHC
	Laser	2.0 (1997)	R	MFI	4	DOHC
	Laser	2.0 (1997)	U	MFI-Turbo	4	DOHC
	Talon	2.0 (1997)	R	MFI	4	DOHC
	Talon	2.0 (1997)	U	MFI-Turbo	4	DOHC
1992	Eclipse	1.8 (1775)	T	MFI	4	SOHC
	Eclipse	2.0 (1997)	R	MFI	4	DOHC
	Eclipse	2.0 (1997)	U	MFI-Turbo	4	DOHC
	Laser	1.8 (1775)	T	MFI	4	SOHC
	Laser	2.0 (1997)	R	MFI	4	DOHC
	Laser	2.0 (1997)	U	MFI-Turbo	4	DOHC
	Talon	2.0 (1997)	R	MFI	4	DOHC
	Talon	2.0 (1997)	U	MFI-Turbo	4	DOHC
1993	Eclipse	1.8 (1775)	B	MFI	4	SOHC
	Eclipse	2.0 (1997)	E	MFI	4	DOHC
	Eclipse	2.0 (1997)	F	MFI-Turbo	4	DOHC
	Laser	1.8 (1775)	B	MFI	4	SOHC
	Laser	2.0 (1997)	E	MFI	4	DOHC
	Laser	2.0 (1997)	F	MFI-Turbo	4	DOHC
	Talon	1.8 (1775)	B	MFI	4	SOHC
	Talon	2.0 (1997)	E	MFI	4	DOHC
	Talon	2.0 (1997)	F	MFI	4	DOHC
1994	Eclipse	1.8 (1775)	B	MFI	4	SOHC
	Eclipse	2.0 (1997)	E	MFI	4	DOHC
	Eclipse	2.0 (1997)	F	MFI-Turbo	4	DOHC
	Laser	1.8 (1775)	B	MFI	4	SOHC
	Laser	2.0 (1997)	E	MFI	4	DOHC
	Laser	2.0 (1997)	F	MFI-Turbo	4	DOHC
	Talon	1.8 (1775)	B	MFI	4	SOHC
	Talon	2.0 (1997)	E	MFI	4	DOHC
	Talon	2.0 (1997)	F	MFI	4	DOHC
1995	Eclipse	2.0 (1997)	Y	MFI	4	DOHC
	Eclipse	2.0 (1997)	F	MFI-Turbo	4	DOHC
	Talon	2.0 (1997)	Y	MFI	4	DOHC
	Talon	2.0 (1997)	F	MFI-Turbo	4	DOHC
1996	Eclipse	2.0 (1997)	Y	MFI	4	DOHC
	Eclipse	2.0 (1997)	F	MFI-Turbo	4	DOHC
	Talon	2.0 (1997)	Y	MFI	4	DOHC
	Talon	2.0 (1997)	F	MFI-Turbo	4	DOHC

89571C04

ENGINE IDENTIFICATION

Year	Model	Engine Displacement Liters (cc)	Engine Series (ID/VIN)	Fuel System	No. of Cylinders	Engine Type
1997	Eclipse	2.0 (1997)	Y	MFI	4	DOHC
	Eclipse	2.0 (1997)	F	MFI-Turbo	4	DOHC
	Eclipse Spyder	2.0 (1997)	F	MFI	4	DOHC
	Eclipse Spyder	2.4 (2351)	G	MFI	4	SOHC
	Talon	2.0 (1997)	Y	MFI	4	DOHC
	Talon	2.0 (1997)	F	MFI-Turbo	4	DOHC
1998	Eclipse	2.0 (1997)	Y	MFI	4	DOHC
	Eclipse	2.0 (1997)	F	MFI-Turbo	4	DOHC
	Eclipse Spyder	2.0 (1997)	F	MFI	4	DOHC
	Eclipse Spyder	2.4 (2351)	G	MFI	4	SOHC
	Talon	2.0 (1997)	Y	MFI	4	DOHC
	Talon	2.0 (1997)	F	MFI-Turbo	4	DOHC

MFI - Multi-port Fuel Injection
SOHC - Single Over Head Cam
DOHC - Dual Over Head Cam

89571C05

Transaxle Identification

▶ **See Figures 42 and 43**

The transaxle model code is located on the vehicle information code plate. The transaxle identification number is etched on a boss located on the front upper portion of the case.

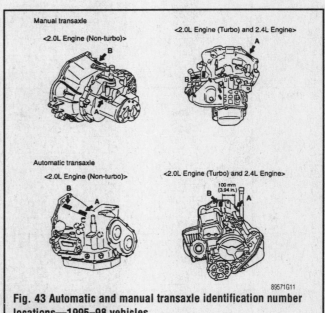

Fig. 43 Automatic and manual transaxle identification number locations—1995–98 vehicles

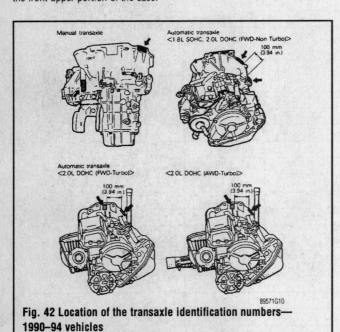

Fig. 42 Location of the transaxle identification numbers—1990–94 vehicles

MAINTENANCE COMPONENT LOCATIONS—NON-TURBO ENGINE

1. Power steering fluid reservoir
2. Accessory drive belt
3. Radiator fill cap
4. Engine oil level dipstick
5. Air cleaner assembly
6. Battery
7. Clutch master cylinder reservoir
8. Brake master cylinder reservoir
9. Windshield washer fluid reservoir
10. PCV valve
11. Spark plug wires
12. Vehicle information code label
13. Timing belt inspection cover
14. Coolant recovery reservoir

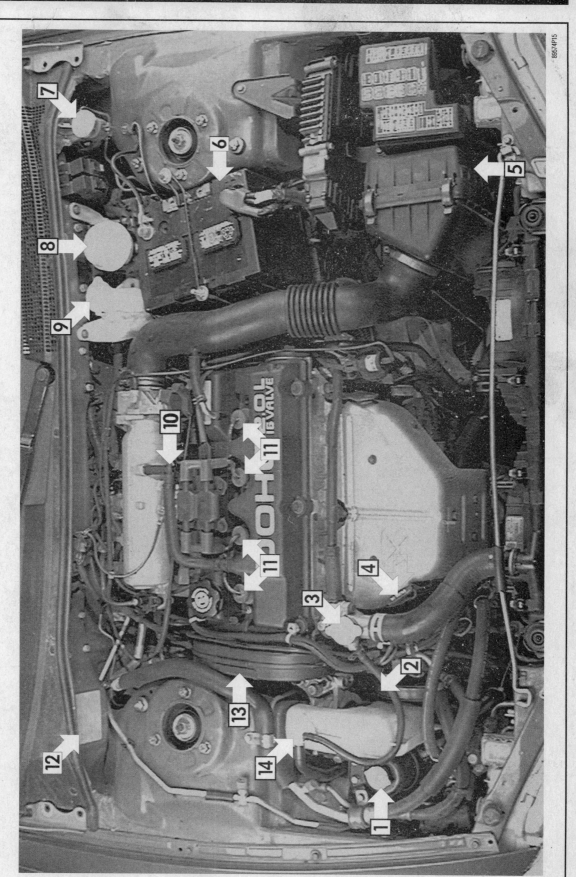

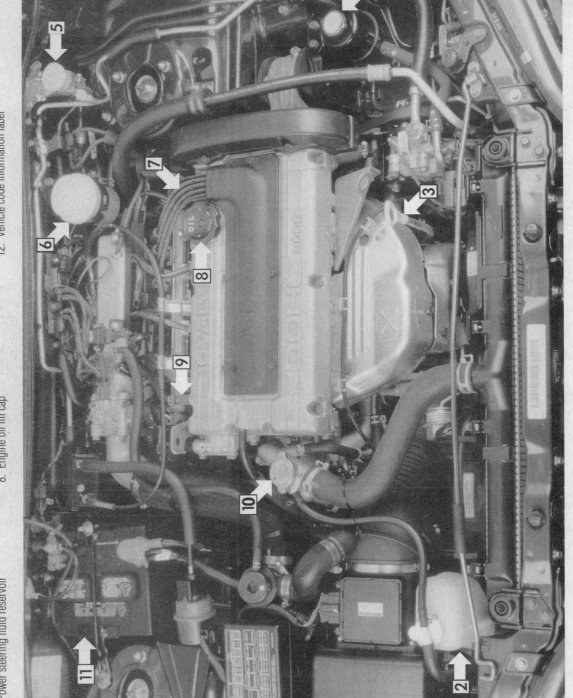

MAINTENANCE COMPONENT LOCATIONS—TURBO ENGINE

1. Air cleaner
2. Coolant recovery reservoir
3. Engine oil dipstick
4. Power steering fluid reservoir
5. Clutch master cylinder reservoir
6. Brake master cylinder reservoir
7. Spark plug wires
8. Engine oil fill cap
9. PCV valve
10. Radiator cap
11. Battery
12. Vehicle code information label

89571P04

Proper maintenance and tune-up is the key to long and trouble-free vehicle life, and the work can yield its own rewards. Studies have shown that a properly tuned and maintained vehicle can achieve better gas mileage than an out-of-tune vehicle. As a conscientious owner and driver, set aside a Saturday morning, say once a month, to check or replace items which could cause major problems later. Keep your own personal log to jot down which services you performed, how much the parts cost you, the date, and the exact odometer reading at the time. Keep all receipts for such items as engine oil and filters, so that they may be referred to in case of related problems or to determine operating expenses. As a do-it-yourselfer, these receipts are the only proof you have that the required maintenance was performed. In the event of a warranty problem, these receipts will be invaluable.

The literature provided with your vehicle when it was originally delivered includes the factory recommended maintenance schedule. If you no longer have this literature, replacement copies are usually available from the dealer. A maintenance schedule is provided later in this section, in case you do not have the factory literature.

Air Cleaner

REMOVAL & INSTALLATION

All vehicles covered in this manual are equipped with a disposable paper cartridge air cleaner element. At every tune-up or sooner, if the car is operated in a dusty area, remove the air filter element and inspect its condition. Check the element by holding a light up to the filter. If light can be seen through the filter, then it should be OK. Replace the filter if light can not be seen through the filter or if it appears extremely dirty. Loose dust can sometimes be removed by striking the filter against a hard surface several times or by blowing through it with compressed air from the inside out. The filter should be inspected at every oil changed and replaced as required. Before installing either the original or a replacement filter, wipe out the inside of the air cleaner housing with a clean rag or paper towel.

Except 2.0L Turbocharged Engine

▶ See Figures 44 thru 50

1. Disconnect the negative battery cable.
2. If equipped, detach the air flow sensor connector located on the top of the air cleaner cover.
3. Remove the air intake hose.
4. Unclamp the air cleaner cover.
5. Push the air intake hose backward and remove the air cleaner cover from the housing.

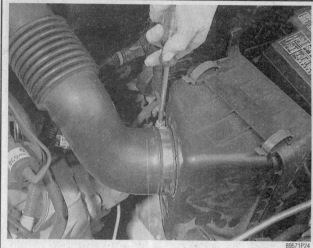

Fig. 45 Unfasten the screw that secures the air intake hose retaining clamp . . .

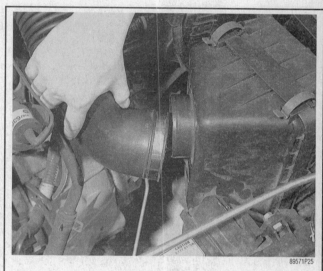

Fig. 46 . . . then detach the hose from the air cleaner housing

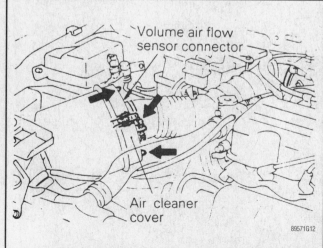

Fig. 44 Unplug the air flow sensor connector which is located on the top of the air cleaner cover

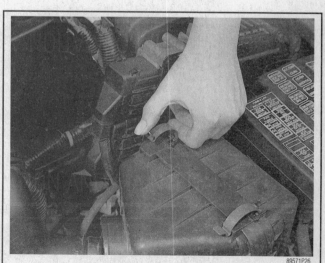

Fig. 47 Unlatch the air cleaner cover clamps. There are 2 on top and 2 on the bottom of the housing

Fig. 48 Route the hose out of the way, then pull the air cleaner cover off the housing

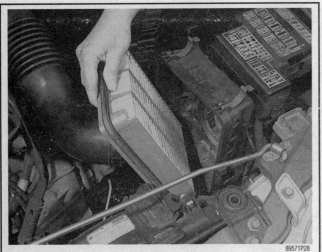

Fig. 49 Remove the air cleaner filter element from the housing and replace if necessary

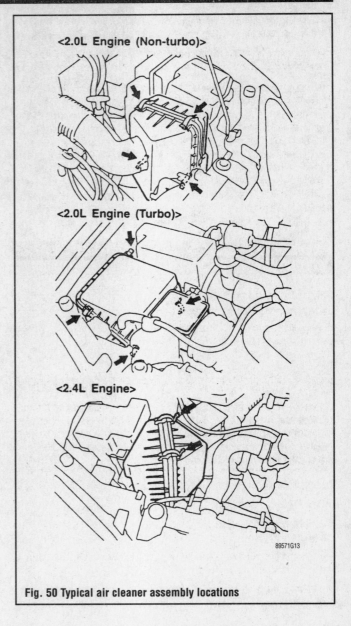

Fig. 50 Typical air cleaner assembly locations

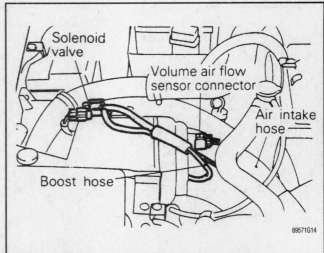

Fig. 51 Detach the air flow sensor connector, the boost hose and the solenoid valve connector

➡Care must be taken when removing the air cleaner cover from the housing. The air-flow sensor is attached to the cover and could be damaged during cover removal.

6. Remove the air cleaner element. Thoroughly clean the air cleaner housing prior to replacing the air filter.

To install:

7. Install the new air filter element into the housing.
8. Place the air cleaner cover into position and secure in place with the retaining clips.
9. Install the air intake hose.
10. Reattach the air flow sensor harness connector, if equipped.
11. Connect the negative battery cable.

2.0L Turbocharged Engine

▶ **See Figures 50 and 51**

1. Disconnect the negative battery cable.
2. Detach the air flow sensor connector.
3. Unfasten the boost hose.
4. Disconnect the solenoid valve with hoses.
5. Disconnect the air intake hose.

6. Unfasten the air cleaner retainer bolts and the air cleaner assembly.
7. Unclamp the cover and remove from the housing.

➡**Care must be taken when removing the air cleaner cover. The air flow sensor is attached and could be damaged during cover removal.**

8. Remove the air cleaner element. Thoroughly clean the air cleaner housing prior to replacing the air filter.

To install:

9. Install the new air cleaner element into the housing. Install and secure the cover in place.
10. Install the air cleaner assembly and the retainer bolts.
11. Connect the air intake hose.
12. Attach the solenoid valve.
13. Connect the boost hose.
14. Attach the air flow sensor connector.
15. Connect the negative battery cable.

Fuel Filter

REMOVAL & INSTALLATION

◆ **See Figures 52, 53, 54, 55 and 56**

On most vehicles covered by this manual, the fuel filter is located in the engine compartment, mounted to the firewall. On some 1996–98 2.0L non-turbo engines, the fuel filter is mounted to the fuel tank.

✳✳ CAUTION

Do not use conventional fuel filters, hoses or clamps when servicing fuel injection systems. They are not compatible with the injection system and could fail, causing personal injury or damage to the vehicle. Use only hoses and clamps specifically designed for fuel injection systems.

1. Properly relieve the fuel system pressure as outlined in Section 5 of this manual.
2. If not already done, disconnect the negative battery cable.
3. If necessary, raise and safely support the vehicle, then remove the fuel tank from the vehicle, as outlined in Section 5 of this manual.

➡**Wrap shop towels around the fitting that is being disconnected to absorb residual fuel in the lines.**

4. Cover the hose connection with shop towels to prevent any splash of fuel that could be caused by residual pressure in the fuel pipe line. Hold the fuel filter nut securely with a backup wrench, then remove the eye bolt. Disconnect the high-pressure fuel line from the filter. Remove and discard the gaskets.

5. While holding the fuel filter nut securely with a back-up wrench, loosen the main pipe flare nut. Separate the flare nut connection from the filter. Remove and discard the gaskets.

6. If equipped with a fuel tank mounted filter, perform the following:
   a. Remove the eye bolt, gasket and connector.
   b. Remove the pressure regulator.

7. Remove the mounting bolts and remove the fuel filter. If necessary, remove the fuel filter bracket.

To install:

8. Install the filter to its bracket only finger-tight. Movement of the filter will ease attachment of the fuel lines.

➡**Make sure new O-rings are installed prior to installation.**

9. Insert the main pipe at the connector part of the filter and manually screw in the main pipe's flare nut.
10. While holding the fuel filter nut with a back-up wrench, tighten the eye bolts to 22 ft. lbs. (30 Nm). Tighten the flare nut to 25 ft. lbs. (35 Nm), with a back-up wrench on the nut.
11. Tighten the filter mounting bolts to 10 ft. lbs. (14 Nm).

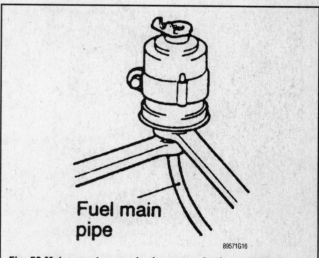

Fuel main pipe

89571G16

Fig. 53 Make sure to use a back-up wrench when unfastening the main fuel pipe also

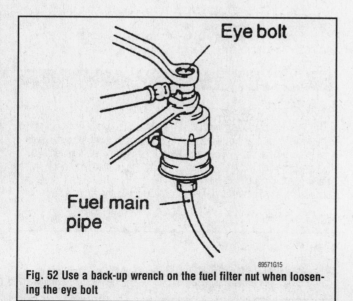

Eye bolt

Fuel main pipe

89571G15

Fig. 52 Use a back-up wrench on the fuel filter nut when loosening the eye bolt

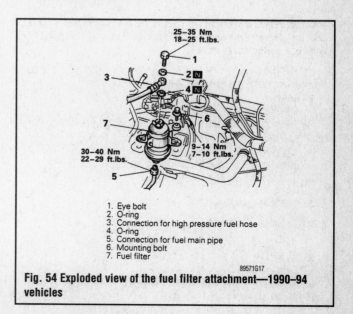

25–35 Nm
18–25 ft.lbs.

30–40 Nm
22–29 ft.lbs.

9–14 Nm
7–10 ft.lbs.

1. Eye bolt
2. O-ring
3. Connection for high pressure fuel hose
4. O-ring
5. Connection for fuel main pipe
6. Mounting bolt
7. Fuel filter

89571G17

Fig. 54 Exploded view of the fuel filter attachment—1990–94 vehicles

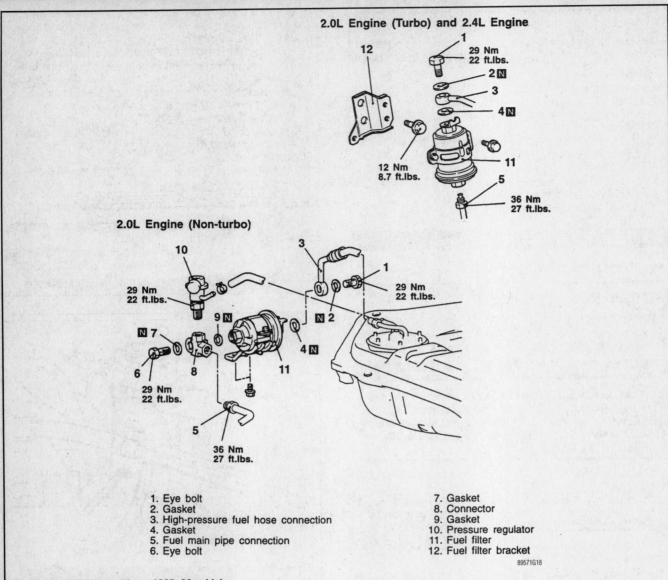

2.0L Engine (Turbo) and 2.4L Engine

2.0L Engine (Non-turbo)

1. Eye bolt
2. Gasket
3. High-pressure fuel hose connection
4. Gasket
5. Fuel main pipe connection
6. Eye bolt
7. Gasket
8. Connector
9. Gasket
10. Pressure regulator
11. Fuel filter
12. Fuel filter bracket

89571G18

Fig. 55 Fuel filter mounting—1995–98 vehicles

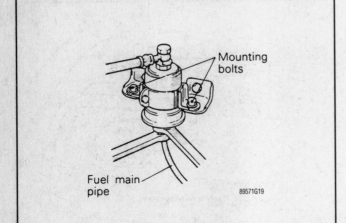

89571G19

Fig. 56 You must use back-up wrenches when tightening the fuel line fittings also

12. Connect the negative battery cable. Turn the key to the **ON** position to pressurize the fuel system and check for leaks.

13. If repairs of a leak are required, remember to release the fuel pressure before opening the fuel system.

PCV Valve

▶ **See Figure 57**

The Positive Crankcase Ventilation (PCV) valve is part of a system which is designed to protect the atmosphere from harmful vapors. Blow-by gas from the crankcase, as well as fumes from crankcase oil are diverted into the combustion chamber where they are burned during engine operation. Proper operation of this system will improve engine performance as well as decrease the amount of harmful vapors released into the atmosphere.

REMOVAL & INSTALLATION

▶ **See Figures 58 thru 65**

1. Disconnect the negative battery cable.
2. If necessary for access, remove the air intake hose and air cleaner assembly.

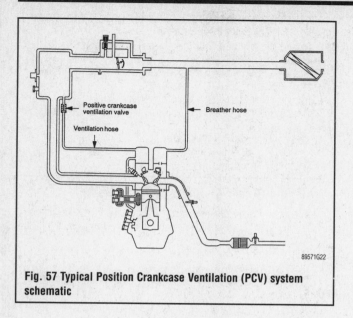

Fig. 57 Typical Position Crankcase Ventilation (PCV) system schematic

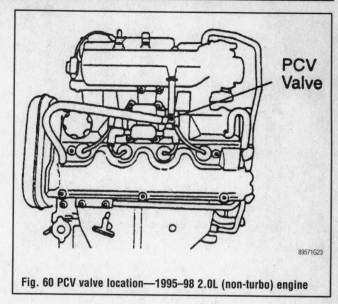

Fig. 60 PCV valve location—1995–98 2.0L (non-turbo) engine

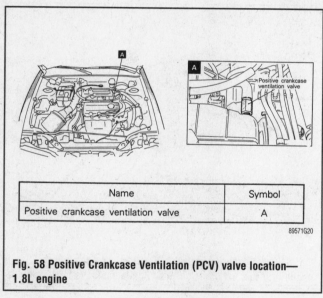

Name	Symbol
Positive crankcase ventilation valve	A

Fig. 58 Positive Crankcase Ventilation (PCV) valve location—1.8L engine

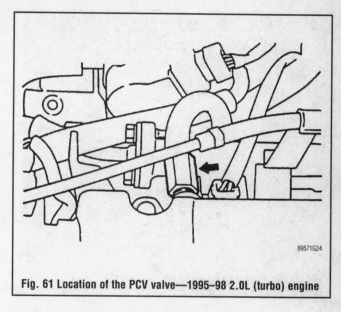

Fig. 61 Location of the PCV valve—1995–98 2.0L (turbo) engine

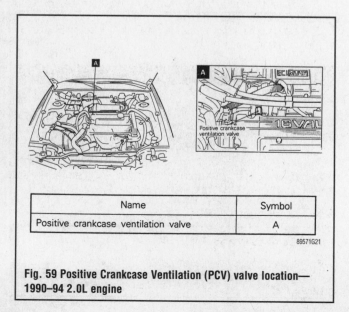

Name	Symbol
Positive crankcase ventilation valve	A

Fig. 59 Positive Crankcase Ventilation (PCV) valve location—1990–94 2.0L engine

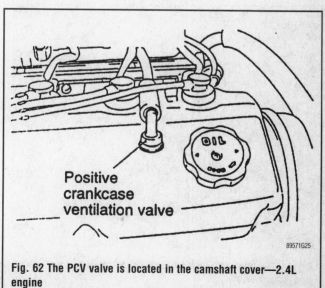

Fig. 62 The PCV valve is located in the camshaft cover—2.4L engine

Fig. 63 Use a pair of pliers to unfasten the PCV hose retaining clamps

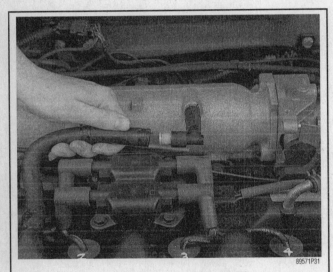

Fig. 64 Disconnect the valve cover-to-PCV valve hose . . .

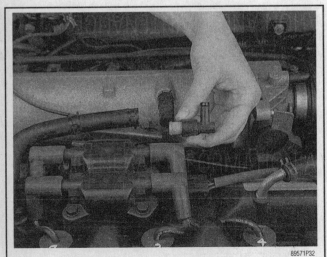

Fig. 65 . . . then unplug and remove the PCV valve from the vehicle

3. If necessary, unfasten the retaining clamp, then disconnect the ventilation hose from the PCV valve.

4. Remove the PCV valve from the camshaft (rocker) cover.

To install:

5. Install the PCV valve into the rocker cover. If the valve is threaded, tighten to 6–8.5 ft. lbs. (8–12 Nm) torque.

6. Reconnect the ventilation hose to the valve.

7. If removed, install the air intake hose and the air cleaner assembly.

8. Connect the negative battery cable.

FUNCTIONAL CHECKS

◆ **See Figures 66 and 67**

1. After disconnecting the ventilation hose from the PCV valve, remove the PCV valve from the cover and reconnect the PCV valve to the ventilation hose.

2. Run the engine at idle, then place your thumb over the end of the valve to check for vacuum.

3. If no vacuum exists, check for plugged hoses, manifold port vacuum at the throttle body or a defective PCV valve.

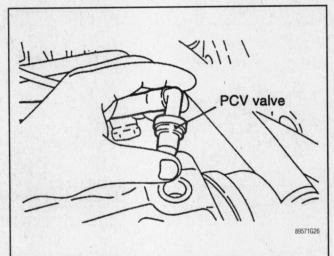

Fig. 66 Check for vacuum at the PCV valve by placing your thumb over the end of the valve while the engine is idling

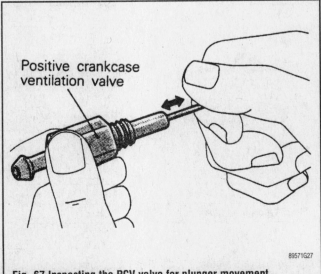

Fig. 67 Inspecting the PCV valve for plunger movement

4. Inspect the valve as follows:

a. Insert a thin stick into the positive ventilation valve from the threaded side to check that the plunger moves. If the plunger does not move, the PCV valve is clogged.

Evaporative Canister

SERVICING

▶ **See Figures 68 and 69**

The charcoal canister is part of the Evaporative Emission Control System. This system prevents the escape of raw gasoline vapors from the vehicle's fuel system to escape into the atmosphere.

The canister is designed to absorb fuel vapors under specific conditions. The canister is about the size of a coffee can and is located in the engine compartment. On some later model 2.0L (non-turbo) and 2.4L engines, the evaporative canister must be accessed through the passenger's side front wheel well.

The canister itself generally does not require replacement at a specific mileage however, the Evaporative Emission Control System does require a careful operations check at 50,000 miles or every 5 years, whichever comes first. Testing procedures are listed in Section 4 of this manual.

If removal does become necessary, prior to removing the canister assembly from the vehicle, label the vacuum hose connections at the top of the canister. For proper functioning of the system, it is essential that the hoses be returned to their original locations.

Battery

PRECAUTIONS

Always use caution when working on or near the battery. Never allow a tool to bridge the gap between the negative and positive battery terminals. Also, be careful not to allow a tool to provide a ground between the positive cable/terminal and any metal component on the vehicle. Either of these conditions will cause a short circuit, leading to sparks and possible personal injury.

Do not smoke, have an open flame or create sparks near a battery; the gases contained in the battery are very explosive and, if ignited, could cause severe injury or death.

All batteries, regardless of type, should be carefully secured by a battery hold-down device. If this is not done, the battery terminals or casing may crack from stress applied to the battery during vehicle operation. A battery which is not secured may allow acid to leak out, making it discharge faster; such leaking corrosive acid can also eat away at components under the hood.

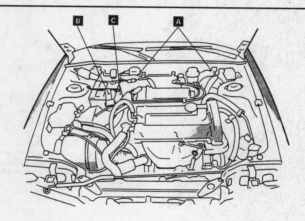

Name	Symbol
Evaporative emission canister	B
Evaporative emission purge solenoid	A
Purge control valve <Turbo>	C

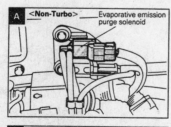
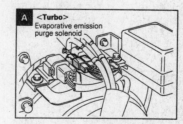
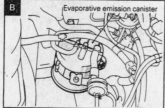
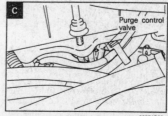

89571G28

Fig. 68 Location of the evaporative emission canister and related components—1990–94 2.0L engine shown

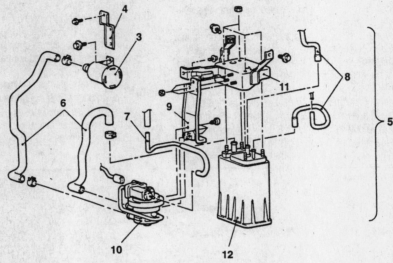

1. Suction hose fixing bolts
2. Pressure tube fixing bolt
3. Air filter
4. Air filter bracket
5. Evaporative emission canister and evaporative emission ventilation solenoid assembly
6. Vent hose
7. Vapor hose
8. Vapor hose
9. Evaporative emission ventilation solenoid bracket
10. Evaporative emission ventilation solenoid
11. Evaporative emission canister holder assembly
12. Evaporative emission canister assembly

89571G29

Fig. 69 On this 1997 2.0L (non-turbo) engine, the canister is located in the front corner of the engine compartment and must be accessed through the wheel well

Always visually inspect the battery case for cracks, leakage and corrosion. A white corrosive substance on the battery case or on nearby components would indicate a leaking or cracked battery. If the battery is cracked, it should be replaced immediately.

GENERAL MAINTENANCE

▶ **See Figure 70**

A battery that is not sealed must be checked periodically for electrolyte level. You cannot add water to a sealed maintenance-free battery (though not all maintenance-free batteries are sealed); however, a sealed battery must also be checked for proper electrolyte level, as indicated by the color of the built-in hydrometer "eye."

Always keep the battery cables and terminals free of corrosion. Check these components about once a year. Refer to the removal, installation and cleaning procedures outlined in this section.

Keep the top of the battery clean, as a film of dirt can help completely discharge a battery that is not used for long periods. A solution of baking soda and water may be used for cleaning, but be careful to flush this off with clear water. DO NOT let any of the solution into the filler holes. Baking soda neutralizes battery acid and will de-activate a battery cell.

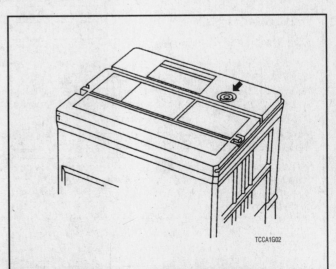

TCCA1G02

Fig. 70 A typical location for the built-in hydrometer on maintenance-free batteries

Batteries in vehicles which are not operated on a regular basis can fall victim to parasitic loads (small current drains which are constantly drawing current from the battery). Normal parasitic loads may drain a battery on a vehicle that is in storage and not used for 6–8 weeks. Vehicles that have additional accessories such as a cellular phone, an alarm system or other devices that increase parasitic load may discharge a battery sooner. If the vehicle is to be stored for 6–8 weeks in a secure area and the alarm system, if present, is not necessary, the negative battery cable should be disconnected at the onset of storage to protect the battery charge.

Remember that constantly discharging and recharging will shorten battery life. Take care not to allow a battery to be needlessly discharged.

BATTERY FLUID

Check the battery electrolyte level at least once a month, or more often in hot weather or during periods of extended vehicle operation. On non-sealed batteries, the level can be checked either through the case on translucent batteries or by removing the cell caps on opaque-cased types. The electrolyte level in each cell should be kept filled to the split ring inside each cell, or the line marked on the outside of the case.

If the level is low, add only distilled water through the opening until the level is correct. Each cell is separate from the others, so each must be checked and filled individually. Distilled water should be used, because the chemicals and minerals found in most drinking water are harmful to the battery and could significantly shorten its life.

If water is added in freezing weather, the vehicle should be driven several miles to allow the water to mix with the electrolyte. Otherwise, the battery could freeze.

Although some maintenance-free batteries have removable cell caps for access to the electrolyte, the electrolyte condition and level on all sealed maintenance-free batteries must be checked using the built-in hydrometer "eye." The exact type of eye varies between battery manufacturers, but most apply a sticker to the battery itself explaining the possible readings. When in doubt, refer to the battery manufacturer's instructions to interpret battery condition using the built-in hydrometer.

➡**Although the readings from built-in hydrometers found in sealed batteries may vary, a green eye usually indicates a properly charged battery with sufficient fluid level. A dark eye is normally an indicator of a battery with sufficient fluid, but one which may be low in charge. And a light or yellow eye is usually an indication that electrolyte supply has dropped below the necessary level for battery (and hydrometer) operation. In this last case, sealed batteries with an insufficient electrolyte level must usually be discarded.**

Checking the Specific Gravity

▶ **See Figures 71, 72 and 73**

A hydrometer is required to check the specific gravity on all batteries that are not maintenance-free. On batteries that are maintenance-free, the specific gravity is checked by observing the built-in hydrometer "eye" on the top of the battery case. Check with your battery's manufacturer for proper interpretation of its built-in hydrometer readings.

✳✳ CAUTION

Battery electrolyte contains sulfuric acid. If you should splash any on your skin or in your eyes, flush the affected area with plenty of clear water. If it lands in your eyes, get medical help immediately.

The fluid (sulfuric acid solution) contained in the battery cells will tell you many things about the condition of the battery. Because the cell plates must be kept submerged below the fluid level in order to operate, maintaining the fluid level is extremely important. And, because the specific gravity of the acid is an indication of electrical charge, testing the fluid can be an

Fig. 71 On non-maintenance-free batteries, the fluid level can be checked through the case on translucent models; the cell caps must be removed on other models

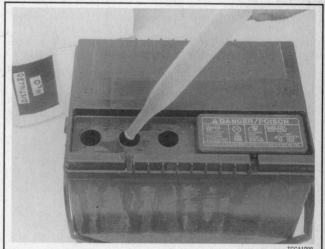

Fig. 72 If the fluid level is low, add only distilled water through the opening until the level is correct

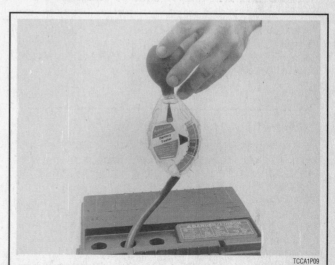

Fig. 73 Check the specific gravity of the battery's electrolyte with a hydrometer

aid in determining if the battery must be replaced. A battery in a vehicle with a properly operating charging system should require little maintenance, but careful, periodic inspection should reveal problems before they leave you stranded.

As stated earlier, the specific gravity of a battery's electrolyte level can be used as an indication of battery charge. At least once a year, check the specific gravity of the battery. It should be between 1.20 and 1.26 on the gravity scale. Most auto supply stores carry a variety of inexpensive battery testing hydrometers. These can be used on any non-sealed battery to test the specific gravity in each cell.

The battery testing hydrometer has a squeeze bulb at one end and a nozzle at the other. Battery electrolyte is sucked into the hydrometer until the float is lifted from its seat. The specific gravity is then read by noting the position of the float. If gravity is low in one or more cells, the battery should be slowly charged and checked again to see if the gravity has come up. Generally, if after charging, the specific gravity between any two cells varies more than 50 points (0.50), the battery should be replaced, as it can no longer produce sufficient voltage to guarantee proper operation.

CABLES

▶ **See Figures 74, 75, 76, 77 and 78**

Once a year (or as necessary), the battery terminals and the cable clamps should be cleaned. Loosen the clamps and remove the cables, negative cable first. On batteries with posts on top, the use of a puller specially made for this purpose is recommended. These are inexpensive and available in most auto parts stores. Side terminal battery cables are secured with a small bolt.

Clean the cable clamps and the battery terminal with a wire brush, until all corrosion, grease, etc., is removed and the metal is shiny. It is especially important to clean the inside of the clamp thoroughly (an old knife is useful here), since a small deposit of foreign material or oxidation there will prevent a sound electrical connection and inhibit either starting or charging. Special tools are available for cleaning these parts, one type for conventional top post batteries and another type for side terminal batteries. It is also a good idea to apply some dielectric grease to the terminal, as this will aid in the prevention of corrosion.

After the clamps and terminals are clean, reinstall the cables, negative cable last; DO NOT hammer the clamps onto battery posts. Tighten the clamps securely, but do not distort them. Give the clamps and terminals a thin external coating of grease after installation, to retard corrosion.

Check the cables at the same time that the terminals are cleaned. If

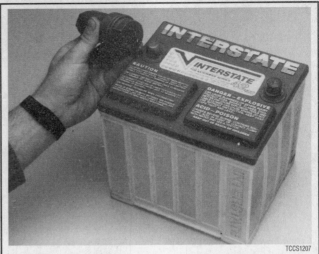
Fig. 75 The underside of this special battery tool has a wire brush to clean post terminals

Fig. 76 Place the tool over the battery posts and twist to clean until the metal is shiny

Fig. 74 Maintenance is performed with household items and with special tools like this post cleaner

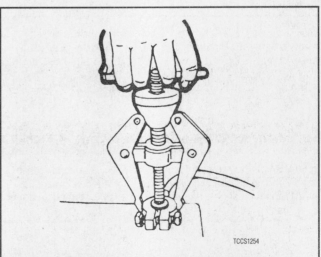
Fig. 77 A special tool is available to pull the clamp from the post

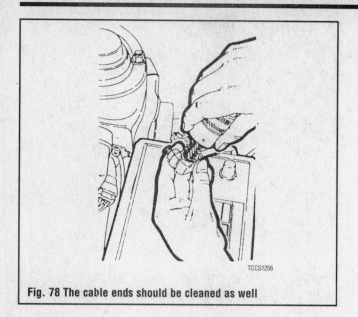

Fig. 78 The cable ends should be cleaned as well

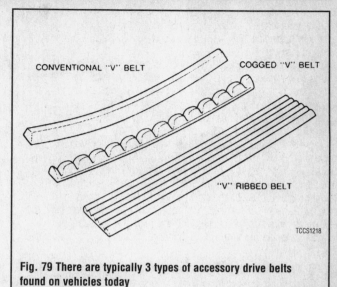

Fig. 79 There are typically 3 types of accessory drive belts found on vehicles today

the cable insulation is cracked or broken, or if the ends are frayed, the cable should be replaced with a new cable of the same length and gauge.

CHARGING

✳✳ CAUTION

The chemical reaction which takes place in all batteries generates explosive hydrogen gas. A spark can cause the battery to explode and splash acid. To avoid serious personal injury, be sure there is proper ventilation and take appropriate fire safety precautions when connecting, disconnecting, or charging a battery and when using jumper ables.

A battery should be charged at a slow rate to keep the plates inside from getting too hot. However, if some maintenance-free batteries are allowed to discharge until they are almost "dead," they may have to be charged at a high rate to bring them back to "life." Always follow the charger manufacturer's instructions on charging the battery.

REPLACEMENT

When it becomes necessary to replace the battery, select one with an amperage rating equal to or greater than the battery originally installed. Deterioration and just plain aging of the battery cables, starter motor, and associated wires makes the battery's job harder in successive years. The slow increase in electrical resistance over time makes it prudent to install a new battery with a greater capacity than the old.

Belts

INSPECTION

▶ **See Figures 79, 80, 81, 82 and 83**

Inspect the belts for signs of glazing or cracking. A glazed belt will be perfectly smooth from slippage, while a good belt will have a slight texture of fabric visible. Cracks will usually start at the inner edge of the belt and run outward. All worn or damaged drive belts should be replaced immediately. It is best to replace all drive belts at one time, as a preventive maintenance measure, during this service operation.

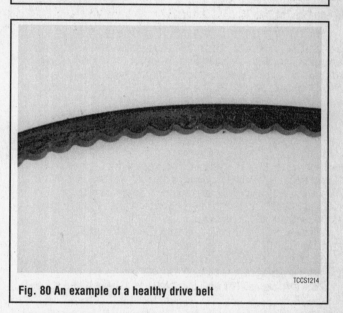

Fig. 80 An example of a healthy drive belt

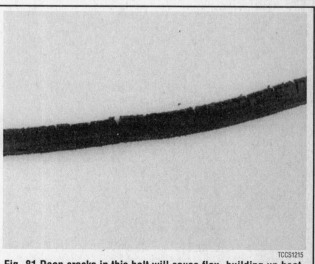

Fig. 81 Deep cracks in this belt will cause flex, building up heat that will eventually lead to belt failure

Fig. 82 The cover of this belt is worn, exposing the critical reinforcing cords to excessive wear

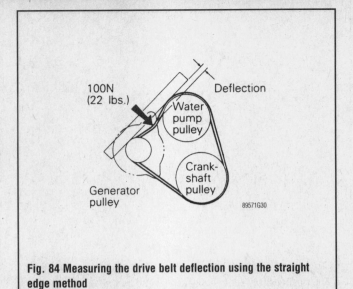

Fig. 84 Measuring the drive belt deflection using the straight edge method

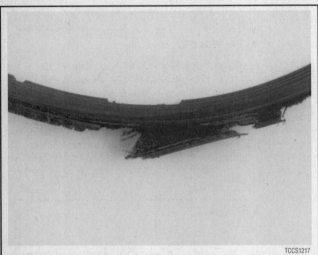

Fig. 83 Installing too wide a belt can result in serious belt wear and/or breakage

Fig. 85 Use a suitable tension gauge to check for correct belt tension

1990–94 Vehicles

▶ See Figures 84 and 85

Check the drive belts for cracks, fraying, wear and proper tension every 6,000 miles. It is recommended that the belts be replaced every 24 months or 24,000 miles.

1. Place a straight-edge along the top edge of the belt and across 2 pulleys. Allow both ends of the straight-edge to rest on top of each pulley for support.

2. Measure the deflection of the belt from the straight-edge with a force of about 22 lbs. (100 N) applied midway between the 2 pulleys. Deflection should measure as follows:

Air Conditioning Compressor Drive Belt
- 1.8L engine—0.160–0.200 in. (4.0–5.0mm)
- 2.0L engine—0.180–0.200 in. (4.5–5.0mm)

Alternator/Water Pump Drive Belt
- 1.8L engine—0.315–0.433 in. (8.0–11.0mm)
- 2.0L engine—0.354–0.453 in. (9.0–11.5mm)

3. Belt tension can also be checked with a tension gauge. Measure the belt tension between any 2 pulleys. The desired value should be 55–110 lbs. (250–500 N).

1995-98 Vehicles

▶ See Figures 86, 87, 88 and 89

1. Place a straight-edge along the top edge of the belt and across 2 pulleys. Allow both ends of the straight-edge to rest on top of each pulley for support.

2. Measure the deflection of the belt from the straight-edge with a force of about 22 lbs. (100 N) applied midway between the 2 pulleys. Deflection should measure as follows:

Alternator/Water Pump Drive Belt
- 2.0L non-turbo engine—0.35–0.47 in. (9.0–12.0mm)
- 2.0L turbo and 2.4L engines—0.35–0.45 in. (9.0–11.5mm)

Power Steering Pump Drive Belt
- 2.0L non-turbo engine—0.39–0.43 in. (10.0–11.0mm)
- 2.0L turbo and 2.4L engines—0.22–0.32 in. (5.5–8.0mm)

3. Belt tension can also be checked with a tension gauge. Measure the belt tension between any 2 pulleys. The desired tension value should be as follows:

Alternator/Water Pump Drive Belt
- 2.0L non-turbo engine—90–110 lbs. (400–490 N)
- 2.0L turbo and 2.4L engines—55.1–110.2 lbs. (245–490 N)

Power Steering Pump Drive Belt
- 2.0L non-turbo engine—92.6–114.6 lbs. (412–510mm)
- 2.0L turbo and 2.4L engines—55.1–110.2 lbs. (245–490 N)

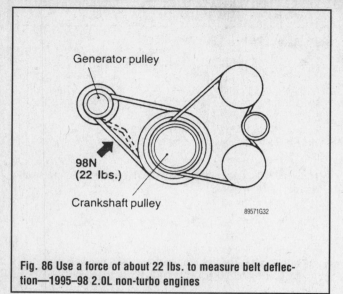

Fig. 86 Use a force of about 22 lbs. to measure belt deflection—1995–98 2.0L non-turbo engines

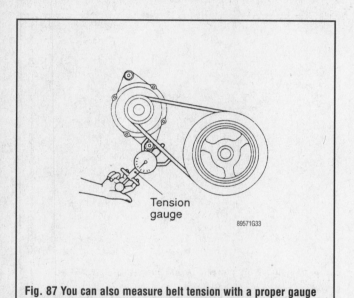

Fig. 87 You can also measure belt tension with a proper gauge

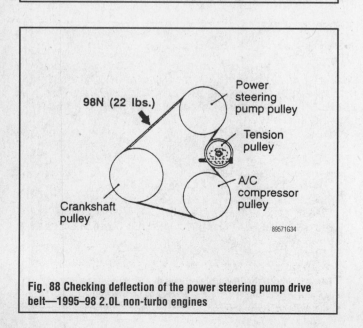

Fig. 88 Checking deflection of the power steering pump drive belt—1995–98 2.0L non-turbo engines

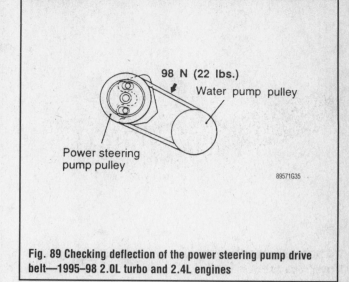

Fig. 89 Checking deflection of the power steering pump drive belt—1995–98 2.0L turbo and 2.4L engines

ADJUSTMENT

▶ **See Figures 90, 91, 92 and 93**

Excessive belt tension will cause damage to the alternator and water pump pulley bearings, while, on the other hand, loose belt tension will produce slip and premature wear on the belt. Therefore, be sure to adjust the belt tension to the proper level.

To adjust the tension on a drive belt, loosen the adjusting bolt or fixing bolt locknut on the alternator, alternator bracket or tension pulley. Then move the alternator or turn the adjusting bolt to adjust belt tension. Once the desired value is reached, secure the bolt or locknut and recheck tension.

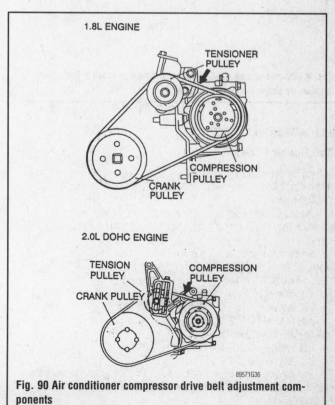

Fig. 90 Air conditioner compressor drive belt adjustment components

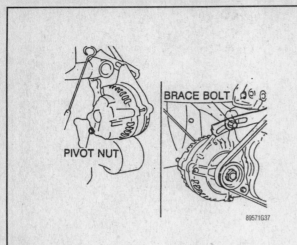

Fig. 91 Alternator assembly pivot and brace bolt location—1.8L engine shown

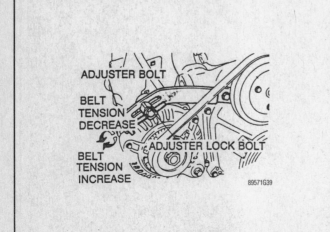

Fig. 92 Increasing the belt tension using prybar to apply pressure at stator part of alternator

Fig. 93 Alternator mounting and adjustment fasteners—2.0L engine shown

REMOVAL & INSTALLATION

▶ **See Figures 94 thru 106**

1. Disconnect the negative battery cable.
2. Loosen the adjusting bolt or fixing bolt locknut on the alternator, alternator bracket or tension pulley.
3. Move the alternator or turn the adjusting bolt to release the belt tension.
4. Take note of the exact routing of the belt prior to removal. Lift the drive belt from the pulleys and remove from the engine compartment.

➡ **If the belt being removed is located behind another belt, removal of the first belt is required.**

To install:
5. Position the replacement belt around the pulleys making sure belt routing is correct.
6. Adjust the belt until the correct tension is reached.
7. Once the desired tension is reached, secure the bolt or lock-nut and the pivot bolts. Recheck the belt tension and correct as required.

Fig. 94 Remove the power steering and A/C compressor lock bolt

Fig. 95 Loosen the power steering and A/C compressor adjusting screw . . .

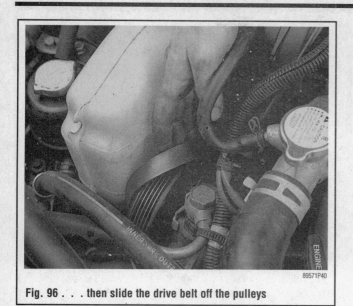

Fig. 96 . . . then slide the drive belt off the pulleys

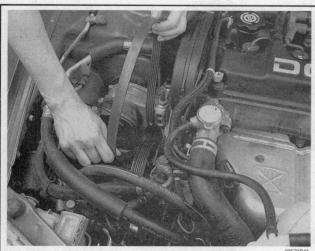

Fig. 97 Remove the power steering pump and A/C compressor belt from the vehicle

Fig. 98 For access to the alternator drive belt, unfasten the under cover side panel retaining bolts

Fig. 99 Remove undercover side panel screws

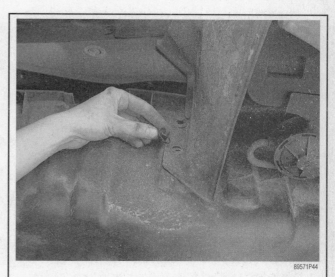

Fig. 100 Remove the under cover side panel trim retainers . . .

Fig. 101 . . . then pull the side panel from the wheel well

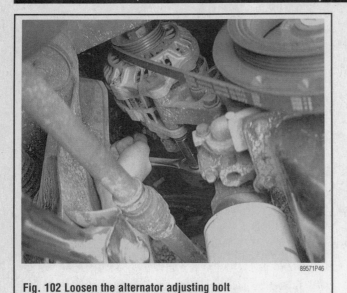

Fig. 102 Loosen the alternator adjusting bolt

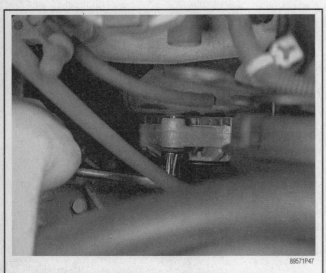

Fig. 103 Remove the alternator upper mounting bolt

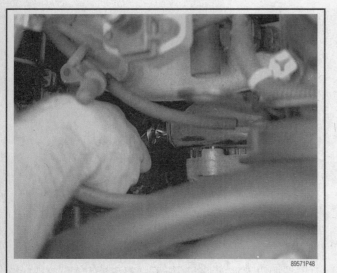

Fig. 104 Remove the alternator bracket side mounting bolt

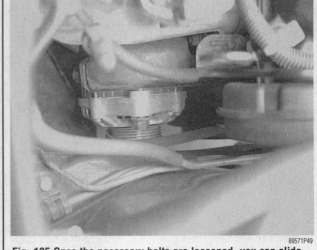

Fig. 105 Once the necessary bolts are loosened, you can slide the alternator belt off the pulley . . .

Fig. 106 . . . then pull the alternator belt up, and out of the vehicle

Timing Belts

INSPECTION

▶ **See Figures 107 thru 116**

All engines covered by this manual utilize timing belts to drive the camshaft from the crankshaft's turning motion and to maintain proper valve timing. Some manufacturer's schedule periodic timing belt replacement to assure optimum engine performance, to make sure the motorist is never stranded should the belt break (as the engine will stop instantly) and for some (manufacturer's with interference motors) to prevent the possibility of severe internal engine damage should the belt break.

Although the 1.8L engine is not listed as an interference motor (it is not listed by the manufacturer as a motor whose valves might contact the pistons if the camshaft was rotated separately from the crankshaft) the first 2 reasons for periodic replacement still apply and the timing belt should be replaced at 60,000 miles. The 2.0L and 2.4L engines are listed as interference motors, so the timing belt MUST be replaced at 60,000 miles to avoid severe engine damage if the belt should break.

Fig. 107 On some vehicles, you can unfasten the timing belt inspection cover retaining bolt . . .

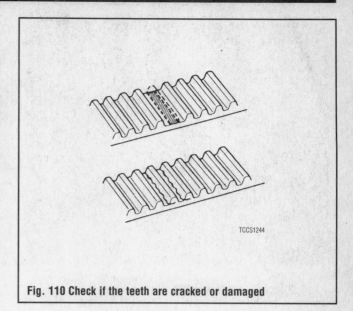

Fig. 110 Check if the teeth are cracked or damaged

Fig. 108 . . . then remove the inspection cover to check the cam timing and the condition of the timing belt

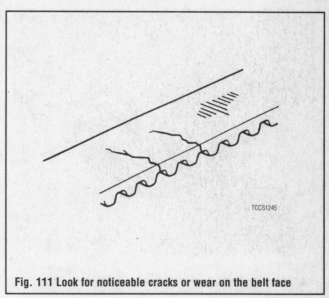

Fig. 111 Look for noticeable cracks or wear on the belt face

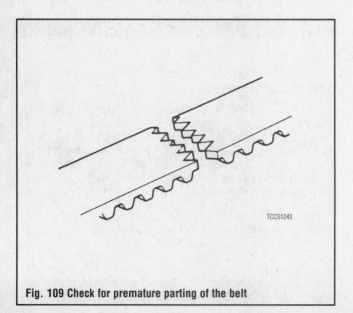

Fig. 109 Check for premature parting of the belt

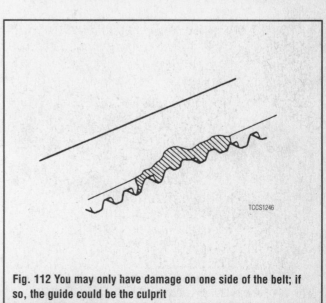

Fig. 112 You may only have damage on one side of the belt; if so, the guide could be the culprit

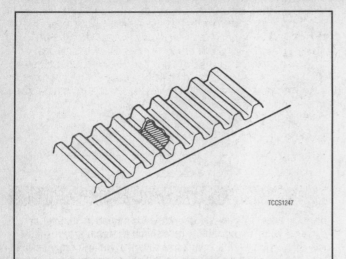

Fig. 113 Foreign materials can get in between the teeth and cause damage

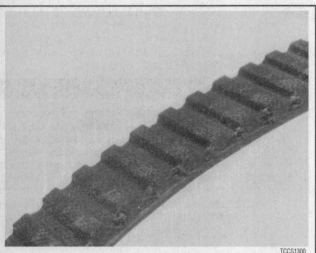

Fig. 114 Inspect the timing belt for cracks, fraying, glazing or damage of any kind

Fig. 115 Damage on only one side of the timing belt may indicate a faulty guide

Fig. 116 ALWAYS replace the timing belt at the interval specified by the manufacturer

But whether or not you decide to replace the timing belt in the manufacturer's schedule, you would be wise to check it periodically to make sure it has not become damaged or worn. Generally speaking, a severely worn belt may cause engine performance to drop dramatically, but a damaged belt (which could give out suddenly) may not give as much warning. In general, any time the engine timing cover(s) is(are) removed you should inspect the belt for premature parting, severe cracks or missing teeth. Also, an access plug is provided in the upper portion of the timing cover so that camshaft timing can be checked without cover removal. If timing is found to be off, cover removal and further belt inspection or replacement is necessary.

For the timing belt removal and installation procedure, please refer to Section 3 of this manual.

Hoses

INSPECTION

▶ **See Figures 117, 118, 119 and 120**

Upper and lower radiator hoses along with the heater hoses should be checked for deterioration, leaks and loose hose clamps at least every 15,000

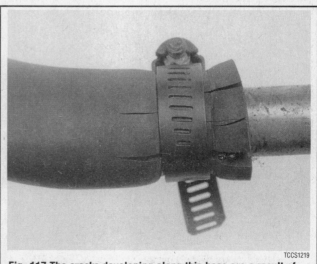

Fig. 117 The cracks developing along this hose are a result of age-related hardening

Fig. 118 A hose clamp that is too tight can cause older hoses to separate and tear on either side of the clamp

TCCS1220

Fig. 119 A soft spongy hose (identifiable by the swollen section) will eventually burst and should be replaced

TCCS1221

Fig. 120 Hoses are likely to deteriorate from the inside if the cooling system is not periodically flushed

TCCS1222

miles (24,000 km). It is also wise to check the hoses periodically in early spring and at the beginning of the fall or winter when you are performing other maintenance. A quick visual inspection could discover a weakened hose which might have left you stranded if it had remained unrepaired.

Whenever you are checking the hoses, make sure the engine and cooling system are cold. Visually inspect for cracking, rotting or collapsed hoses, and replace as necessary. Run your hand along the length of the hose. If a weak or swollen spot is noted when squeezing the hose wall, the hose should be replaced.

REMOVAL & INSTALLATION

1. Remove the radiator pressure cap.

> ❊❊ **CAUTION**
>
> **Never remove the pressure cap while the engine is running, or personal injury from scalding hot coolant or steam may result. if possible, wait until the engine has cooled to remove the pressure cap. If this is not possible, wrap a thick cloth around the pressure cap and turn it slowly to the stop. Step back while the pressure is released from the cooling system. When you are sure all the pressure has been released, use the cloth to turn and remove the cap.**

2. Position a clean container under the radiator and/or engine drain-cock or plug, then open the drain and allow the cooling system to drain to an appropriate level. For some upper hoses, only a little coolant must be drained. To remove hoses positioned lower on the engine, such as a lower radiator hose, the entire cooling system must be emptied.

> ❊❊ **CAUTION**
>
> **When draining coolant, keep in mind that cats and dogs are attracted by ethylene glycol antifreeze, and are quite likely to drink any that is left in an uncovered container or in puddles on the ground. This will prove fatal in sufficient quantity. Always drain coolant into a sealable container. Coolant may be reused unless it is contaminated or several years old.**

3. Loosen the hose clamps at each end of the hose requiring replacement. Clamps are usually either of the spring tension type (which require pliers to squeeze the tabs and loosen) or of the screw tension type (which require screw or hex drivers to loosen). Pull the clamps back on the hose away from the connection.
4. Twist, pull and slide the hose off the fitting, taking care not to damage the neck of the component from which the hose is being removed.

➡If the hose is stuck at the connection, do not try to insert a screwdriver or other sharp tool under the hose end in an effort to free it, as the connection and/or hose may become damaged. Heater connections especially may be easily damaged by such a procedure. If the hose is to be replaced, use a single-edged razor blade to make a slice along the portion of the hose which is stuck on the connection, perpendicular to the end of the hose. Do not cut deep so as to prevent damaging the connection. The hose can then be peeled from the connection and discarded.

5. Clean both hose mounting connections. Inspect the condition of the hose clamps and replace them, if necessary.
   To install:
6. Dip the ends of the new hose into clean engine coolant to ease installation.
7. Slide the clamps over the replacement hose, then slide the hose ends over the connections into position.
8. Position and secure the clamps at least ¼ in. (6.35mm) from the ends of the hose. Make sure they are located beyond the raised bead of the connector.
9. Close the radiator or engine drains and properly refill the cooling system with the clean drained engine coolant or a suitable mixture of ethylene glycol coolant and water.

10. If available, install a pressure tester and check for leaks. If a pressure tester is not available, run the engine until normal operating temperature is reached (allowing the system to naturally pressurize), then check for leaks.

☀ CAUTION

If you are checking for leaks with the system at normal operating temperature, BE EXTREMELY CAREFUL not to touch any moving or hot engine parts. Once temperature has been reached, shut the engine OFF, and check for leaks around the hose fittings and connections which were removed earlier.

CV-Boots

INSPECTION

▶ See Figures 121 and 122

The CV (Constant Velocity) boots should be checked for damage each time the oil is changed and any other time the vehicle is raised for service.

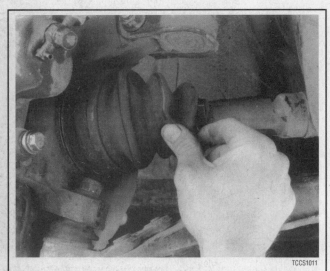

Fig. 121 CV-boots must be inspected periodically for damage

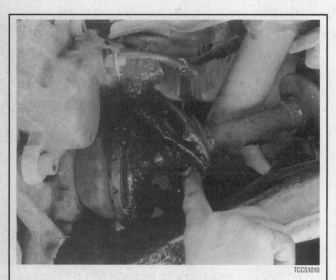

Fig. 122 A torn boot should be replaced immediately

These boots keep water, grime, dirt and other damaging matter from entering the CV-joints. Any of these could cause early CV-joint failure which can be expensive to repair. Heavy grease thrown around the inside of the front wheel(s) and on the brake caliper/drum can be an indication of a torn boot. Thoroughly check the boots for missing clamps and tears. If the boot is damaged, it should be replaced immediately. Please refer to Section 7 for procedures.

Spark Plugs

▶ See Figure 123

A typical spark plug consists of a metal shell surrounding a ceramic insulator. A metal electrode extends downward through the center of the insulator and protrudes a small distance. Located at the end of the plug and attached to the side of the outer metal shell is the side electrode. The side electrode bends in at a 90° angle so that its tip is just past and parallel to the tip of the center electrode. The distance between these two electrodes (measured in thousandths of an inch or hundredths of a millimeter) is called the spark plug gap.

The spark plug does not produce a spark but instead provides a gap across which the current can arc. The coil produces anywhere from 20,000 to 50,000 volts (depending on the type and application) which travels through the wires to the spark plugs. The current passes along the center electrode and jumps the gap to the side electrode, and in doing so, ignites the air/fuel mixture in the combustion chamber.

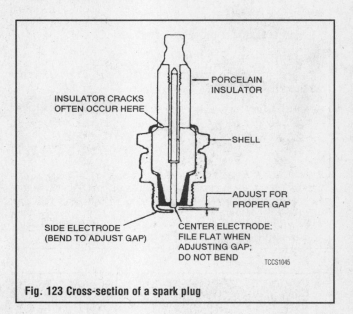

Fig. 123 Cross-section of a spark plug

SPARK PLUG HEAT RANGE

▶ See Figure 124

Spark plug heat range is the ability of the plug to dissipate heat. The longer the insulator (or the farther it extends into the engine), the hotter the plug will operate; the shorter the insulator (the closer the electrode is to the block's cooling passages) the cooler it will operate. A plug that absorbs little heat and remains too cool will quickly accumulate deposits of oil and carbon since it is not hot enough to burn them off. This leads to plug fouling and consequently to misfiring. A plug that absorbs too much heat will have no deposits but, due to the excessive heat, the electrodes will burn away quickly and might possibly lead to preignition or other ignition problems. Preignition takes place when plug tips get so hot that they glow sufficiently to ignite the air/fuel mixture before the actual spark occurs. This early ignition will usually cause a pinging during low speeds and heavy loads.

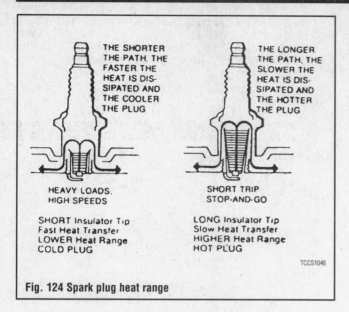

THE SHORTER THE PATH, THE FASTER THE HEAT IS DISSIPATED AND THE COOLER THE PLUG

THE LONGER THE PATH, THE SLOWER THE HEAT IS DISSIPATED AND THE HOTTER THE PLUG

HEAVY LOADS, HIGH SPEEDS

SHORT TRIP STOP-AND-GO

SHORT Insulator Tip
Fast Heat Transfer
LOWER Heat Range
COLD PLUG

LONG Insulator Tip
Slow Heat Transfer
HIGHER Heat Range
HOT PLUG

TCCS1046

Fig. 124 Spark plug heat range

89571P34

Fig. 126 . . . then unplug the wire from the spark plug by twisting and pulling on the boot

The general rule of thumb for choosing the correct heat range when picking a spark plug is: if most of your driving is long distance, high speed travel, use a colder plug; if most of your driving is stop and go, use a hotter plug. Original equipment plugs are generally a good compromise between the 2 styles and most people never have the need to change their plugs from the factory-recommended heat range.

REMOVAL & INSTALLATION

▶ **See Figures 125, 126, 127 and 128**

A set of spark plugs usually requires replacement after about 20,000–30,000 miles (32,000–48,000 km), depending on your style of driving. In normal operation plug gap increases about 0.001 in. (0.025mm) for every 2500 miles (4000 km). As the gap increases, the plug's voltage requirement also increases. It requires a greater voltage to jump the wider gap and about two to three times as much voltage to fire the plug at high speeds than at idle. The improved air/fuel ratio control of modern fuel injection combined with the higher voltage output of modern ignition systems will often allow an engine to run significantly longer on a set of standard spark plugs, but keep in mind that efficiency will drop as the gap widens (along with fuel economy and power).

89571P35

Fig. 127 Use a ratchet with a spark plug socket and extension to loosen the spark plug . . .

89571P33

Fig. 125 It may be easier to disconnect the plug wire by first detaching the wire from the ignition coil . . .

89571P36

Fig. 128 . . . then remove the spark plug from the cylinder head

When you're removing spark plugs, work on one at a time. Don't start by removing the plug wires all at once, because, unless you number them, they may become mixed up. Take a minute before you begin and number the wires with tape.

1. Disconnect the negative battery cable, and if the vehicle has been run recently, allow the engine to thoroughly cool.

2. If equipped, remove the center cover.

3. Carefully twist the spark plug wire boot to loosen it, then pull upward and remove the boot from the plug. Be sure to pull on the boot and not on the wire, otherwise the connector located inside the boot may become separated.

4. Using compressed air, blow any water or debris from the spark plug well to assure that no harmful contaminants are allowed to enter the combustion chamber when the spark plug is removed. If compressed air is not available, use a rag or a brush to clean the area.

➡**Remove the spark plugs when the engine is cold, if possible, to prevent damage to the threads. If removal of the plugs is difficult, apply a few drops of penetrating oil or silicone spray to the area around the base of the plug, and allow it a few minutes to work.**

5. Using a spark plug socket that is equipped with a rubber insert to properly hold the plug, turn the spark plug counterclockwise to loosen and remove the spark plug from the bore.

❋❋ WARNING

Be sure not to use a flexible extension on the socket. Use of a flexible extension may allow a shear force to be applied to the plug. A shear force could break the plug off in the cylinder head, leading to costly and frustrating repairs.

To install:

6. Inspect the spark plug boot for tears or damage. If a damaged boot is found, the spark plug wire must be replaced.

7. Using a wire feeler gauge, check and adjust the spark plug gap. When using a gauge, the proper size should pass between the electrodes with a slight drag. The next larger size should not be able to pass while the next smaller size should pass freely.

8. Carefully thread the plug into the bore by hand. If resistance is felt before the plug is almost completely threaded, back the plug out and begin threading again. In small, hard to reach areas, an old spark plug wire and boot could be used as a threading tool. The boot will hold the plug while you twist the end of the wire and the wire is supple enough to twist before it would allow the plug to crossthread.

❋❋ WARNING

Do not use the spark plug socket to thread the plugs. Always carefully thread the plug by hand or using an old plug wire to prevent the possibility of crossthreading and damaging the cylinder head bore.

9. Carefully tighten the spark plug. If the plug you are installing is equipped with a crush washer, seat the plug, then tighten about ¼ turn to crush the washer. If you are installing a tapered seat plug, tighten the plug to specifications provided by the vehicle or plug manufacturer.

10. Apply a small amount of silicone dielectric compound to the end of the spark plug lead or inside the spark plug boot to prevent sticking, then install the boot to the spark plug and push until it clicks into place. The click may be felt or heard, then gently pull back on the boot to assure proper contact.

INSPECTION & GAPPING

◆ **See Figures 129 thru 139**

Check the plugs for deposits and wear. If they are not going to be replaced, clean the plugs thoroughly. Remember that any kind of deposit will decrease the efficiency of the plug. Plugs can be cleaned on a spark

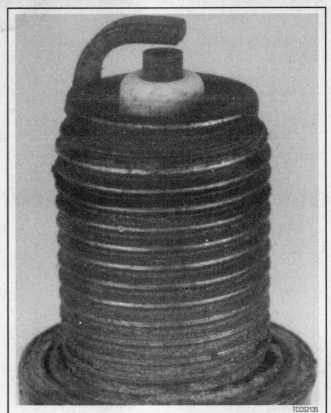
TCCS2135
Fig. 129 A normally worn spark plug should have light tan or gray deposits on the firing tip

TCCS2136
Fig. 130 A carbon fouled plug, identified by soft, sooty, black deposits, may indicate an improperly tuned vehicle. Check the air cleaner, ignition components and engine control system

plug cleaning machine, which can sometimes be found in service stations, or you can do an acceptable job of cleaning with a stiff brush. If the plugs are cleaned, the electrodes must be filed flat. Use an ignition points file, not an emery board or the like, which will leave deposits. The electrodes must be filed perfectly flat with sharp edges; rounded edges reduce the spark plug voltage by as much as 50%.

Check spark plug gap before installation. The ground electrode (the L-shaped one connected to the body of the plug) must be parallel to the center electrode and the specified size wire gauge (please refer to the Tune-Up Specifications chart for details) must pass between the electrodes with a slight drag.

➡**NEVER adjust the gap on a used platinum type spark plug.**

Always check the gap on new plugs as they are not always set correctly at the factory. Do not use a flat feeler gauge when measuring the gap on a used plug, because the reading may be inaccurate. A round-wire type gap-

Fig. 131 A variety of tools and gauges are needed for spark plug service

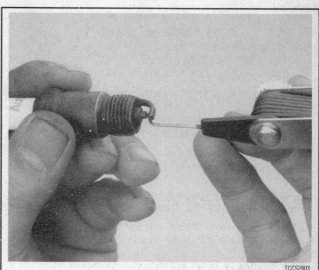

Fig. 133 Checking the spark plug gap with a feeler gauge

Fig. 132 A physically damaged spark plug may be evidence of severe detonation in that cylinder. Watch that cylinder carefully between services, as a continued detonation will not only damage the plug, but could also damage the engine

Fig. 134 An oil fouled spark plug indicates an engine with worn piston rings and/or bad valve seals allowing excessive oil to enter the chamber

ping tool is the best way to check the gap. The correct gauge should pass through the electrode gap with a slight drag. If you're in doubt, try one size smaller and one larger. The smaller gauge should go through easily, while the larger one shouldn't go through at all. Wire gapping tools usually have a bending tool attached. Use that to adjust the side electrode until the proper distance is obtained. Absolutely never attempt to bend the center electrode. Also, be careful not to bend the side electrode too far or too often as it may weaken and break off within the engine, requiring removal of the cylinder head to retrieve it.

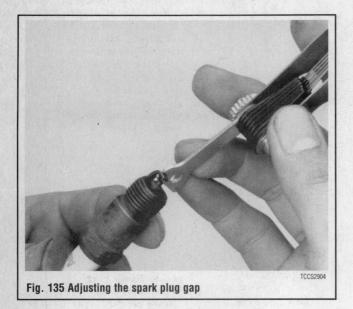

Fig. 135 Adjusting the spark plug gap

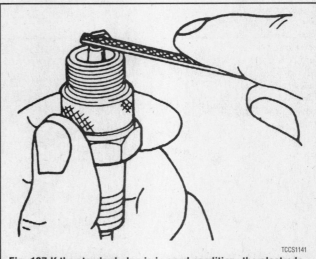

Fig. 137 If the standard plug is in good condition, the electrode may be filed flat—CAUTION: do not file platinum plugs

Fig. 136 This spark plug has been left in the engine too long, as evidenced by the extreme gap—Plugs with such an extreme gap can cause misfiring and stumbling accompanied by a noticeable lack of power

Fig. 138 A bridged or almost bridged spark plug, identified by a build-up between the electrodes caused by excessive carbon or oil build-up on the plug

Tracking Arc
High voltage arcs between a fouling deposit on the insulator tip and spark plug shell. This ignites the fuel/air mixture at some point along the insulator tip, retarding the ignition timing which causes a power and fuel loss.

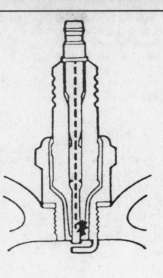

Wide Gap
Spark plug electrodes are worn so that the high voltage charge cannot arc across the electrodes. Improper gapping of electrodes on new or "cleaned" spark plugs could cause a similar condition. Fuel remains unburned and a power loss results.

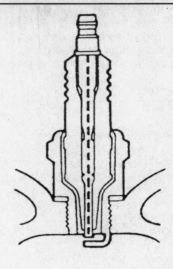

Flashover
A damaged spark plug boot, along with dirt and moisture, could permit the high voltage charge to short over the insulator to the spark plug shell or the engine. A buttress insulator design helps prevent high voltage flashover.

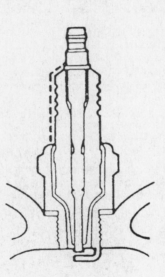

Fouled Spark Plug
Deposits that have formed on the insulator tip may become conductive and provide a "shunt" path to the shell. This prevents the high voltage from arcing between the electrodes. A power and fuel loss is the result.

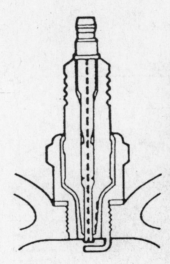

Bridged Electrodes
Fouling deposits between the electrodes "ground out" the high voltage needed to fire the spark plug. The arc between the electrodes does not occur and the fuel air mixture is not ignited. This causes a power loss and exhausting of raw fuel.

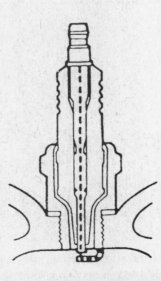

Cracked Insulator
A crack in the spark plug insulator could cause the high voltage charge to "ground out." Here, the spark does not jump the electrode gap and the fuel air mixture is not ignited. This causes a power loss and raw fuel is exhausted.

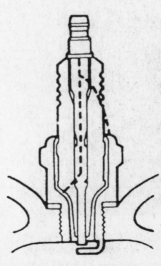

TCCS2001A

Fig. 139 Used spark plugs which show damage may indicate engine problems

Spark Plug Wires

Improper arrangement of the spark plug cables will induce voltage between the cables, causing misfiring and developing a surge at acceleration in high-speed operation. Therefore, be careful to arrange the spark plug cables properly.

TESTING

♦ See Figure 140

At every tune-up/inspection, visually check the spark plug cables for burns cuts, or breaks in the insulation. Check the boots and the nipples on the distributor cap and/or coil. Replace any damaged wiring.

Every 50,000 miles (80,000 Km) or 60 months, the resistance of the wires should be checked with an ohmmeter. Wires with excessive resistance will cause misfiring, and may make the engine difficult to start in damp weather.

1. Remove the spark plug cable from the engine.
2. Check the cap and the coating of the cable for cracks. Replace the cable if cracks are present.
3. Using a volt ohmmeter, measure the resistance of the wire. Compare the measured resistance to following the desired values:

1.8L Engine
- Spark plug cable No. 1—10.1K ohms
- Spark plug cable No. 2—11.5K ohms
- Spark plug cable No. 3—12.0K ohms
- Spark plug cable No. 4—13.0K ohms

1990–94 2.0L Engines
- Spark plug cable No. 1—5.8 ohms
- Spark plug cable No. 2—8.4 ohms
- Spark plug cable No. 3—10.6 ohms
- Spark plug cable No. 4—9.7 ohms

1995–98 2.0L Non-turbo Engines
- Spark plug cables No. 1–4—8K ohms.

1995–98 2.0L Turbo and 2.4L Engines
- Spark plug cables No. 1–4—22K ohms

4. If the measures resistance differs from the desired values, replace the spark plug cable. It is recommended that all cables be replaced if 1 wire need be replaced.

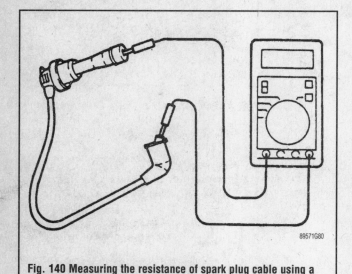

Fig. 140 Measuring the resistance of spark plug cable using a volt/ohmmeter

REMOVAL & INSTALLATION

➡To avoid confusion, always replace spark plugs one at a time.

1. Disconnect the negative battery cable.
2. If equipped, remove the center cover.

3. Remove the spark plug cable from the spark plug by holding the wire on the cap and twisting slightly while pulling the wire straight out.
4. With the cable removed from the spark plug, unfasten the wire from the retainers. Note the exact position of the wires to assure they are installed in the same position during installation.
5. Remove the cable end from the ignition coil or distributor cap, as applicable.

To install:

6. Install the cable over the spark plug and push until securely seated.
7. Install the cables securely in the retainers in the same position as removed. Make sure the cables are securely installed to avoid possible contact with metal parts. Install the cables neatly, ensuring that they are not too tight, loose, twisted or kinked.
8. Install the cable end onto terminal of the ignition coil or distributor cap, as equipped.
9. Repeat this procedure on the remaining spark plug cables until all have been replaced.
10. If equipped, install the center cover and tighten the fasteners to 2.5 ft. lbs. (3.5 Nm).
11. Connect the negative battery cable.

Distributor Cap and Rotor

REMOVAL & INSTALLATION

1.8L Engine

♦ See Figure 141

1. Disconnect the negative battery cable.
2. Label and unplug the spark plug wires from the distributor cap.
3. Remove the distributor cap retainers and lift the cap from the distributor housing.

➡Although most rotors can only be installed in one direction, it is still wise to note the position of the rotor before removal to assure proper installation and ignition timing.

4. Note the position of the rotor, unfasten the attaching screws (if necessary), then pull the rotor straight up and off the distributor assembly.
5. Inspect the cap and rotor, then replace any component that shows excess wear or damage.

To install:

6. Place the rotor on the distributor in the position from which is was removed. If necessary install the retaining screws.

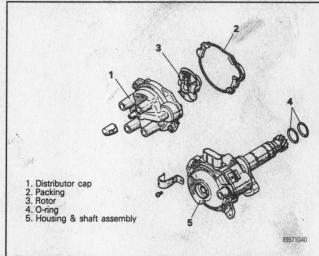

1. Distributor cap
2. Packing
3. Rotor
4. O-ring
5. Housing & shaft assembly

Fig. 141 Exploded view of the distributor cap and rotor and related components—1.8L engine

➡Prior to installing the cap onto the distributor housing, make sure the packing is in place.

7. Position the cap on the distributor and install the retainers.
8. Attach the spark plug wires to the cap, as tagged during removal.
9. Connect the negative battery cable.

INSPECTION

When inspecting a cap and rotor, look for signs of cracks, carbon tracking, burns and wear. The inside of the cap may be burnt or have wear on the carbon ends. On the rotor, look at the tip for burning and excessive wear.

Ignition Timing

INSPECTION & ADJUSTMENT

1.8L Engine

◆ See Figures 142, 143 and 144

1. Apply the parking brake and block the wheels. Run the engine until the coolant reaches normal operating temperature.
2. Make certain all lights, cooling fan and accessories are **OFF**.
3. Position the steering wheel in straight ahead position and the gear selector lever in **P** or **N**.
4. Connect a timing light to the engine.
5. Insert a paper clip into the CRC filter connector (3-pole connector), located in the engine compartment of the vehicle.
6. Connect a tachometer to the inserted clip.

➡During installation of the paper clip, do not separate the connector.

7. Check the curb idle speed. It should be 600–800 rpm.
8. Turn the engine **OFF**. Connect a jumper wire to the terminal for ignition-timing adjustment (located in the engine compartment), and ground it.
9. Start and run the engine at curb idle speed.
10. Check the basic ignition timing and adjust, if necessary. Basic ignition timing should be 5 degrees BTDC.
11. If the timing is not within specifications, loosen the distributor hold-down bolt and turn the distributor to bring the timing within specifications. Turning the distributor to the right retards timing, while turning to the left will advance timing.

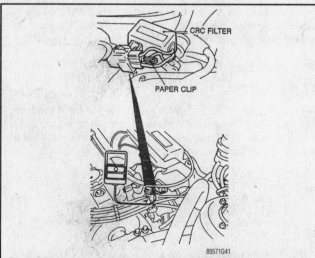

Fig. 142 Insert a paper clip into the CRC filter connector—1.8L engine

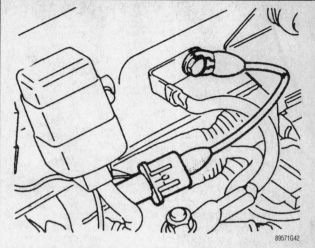

Fig. 143 Connect a jumper wire to the terminal for ignition timing adjustment—1.8L engine

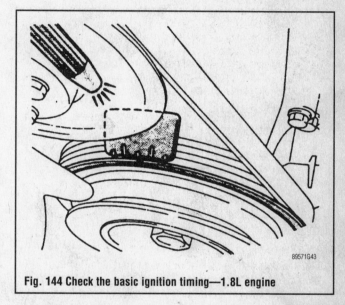

Fig. 144 Check the basic ignition timing—1.8L engine

12. Tighten the hold-down bolt after adjustment. Recheck the timing and adjust if necessary.
13. Stop the engine and remove the ground for the ignition timing connector.

➡Actual ignition timing may vary, depending on the control mode of the engine control unit. In such case, recheck the basic ignition timing. If there is no deviation, the ignition timing is functioning normally.

14. Start the engine and run at curb idle. Check the actual ignition timing. Actual ignition timing should be 10 degrees BTDC.

➡At altitudes more than approximately 2,300 ft. (701m) above sea level, the actual ignition timing is further advanced to ensure good combustion.

2.0L & 2.4L Engines

1990–94 VEHICLES

◆ See Figures 145, 146, 147 and 148

1. Apply the parking brake and block the wheels. Run the engine until it reaches normal operating temperature.

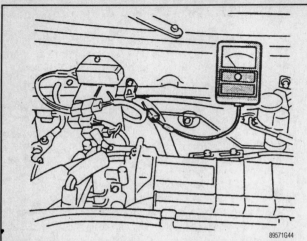

Fig. 145 Insert a paper clip into the engine revolution speed detection terminal and connect a tachometer to the inserted clip—1990–94 2.0L engines

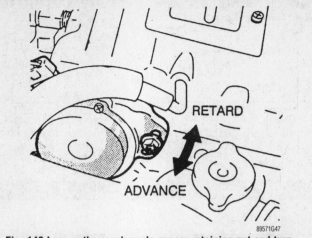

Fig. 148 Loosen the crank angle sensor retaining nut and turn the sensor to adjust the timing within specifications—1990–94 2.0L engines

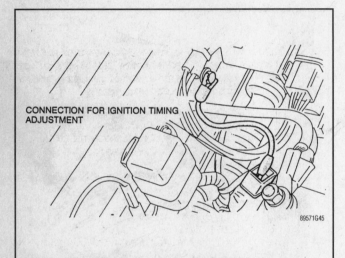

CONNECTION FOR IGNITION TIMING ADJUSTMENT

Fig. 146 Connect a jumper wire to the terminal for ignition-timing adjustment to ground—1990–94 2.0L engines

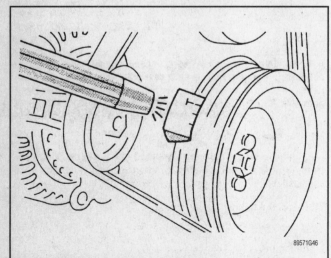

Fig. 147 Checking the basic ignition timing—1990–94 2.0L engines

2. Make certain all lights, cooling fan and accessories are **OFF**.

3. Position the steering wheel in straight ahead position and the gear selector lever in **P** or **N**.

4. Connect a timing light to the engine.

5. Insert a paper clip into the engine revolution speed detection terminal (in engine compartment) and connect a tachometer to the inserted clip.

6. Check the curb idle speed. Should be 650–850 rpm.

7. Stop the engine and connect a jumper wire to the terminal for ignition-timing adjustment to ground.

8. Start and run the engine at curb idle speed.

9. Check the basic ignition timing and adjust, if necessary. Basic ignition timing should be 5 degrees BTDC.

10. If the timing is not within specification, loosen the crank angle sensor retaining nut and turn the crank angel sensor to bring the timing within specs.

11. Tighten the sensor retaining nut after adjustment. Recheck the timing and adjust if necessary.

12. Stop the engine and remove the ground for the ignition timing connector.

13. Start the engine and run at curb idle. Check the actual ignition timing. Actual ignition timing should be 8 degrees BTDC.

➡Actual ignition timing may vary, depending on the control mode of the engine control unit. In such cases, recheck the basic ignition timing. If there is no deviation, the ignition timing is functioning normally. At altitudes more than approximately 2,300 ft. (701m) above sea level, the actual ignition timing is further advanced to ensure good combustion.

1995 VEHICLES

◆ See Figures 149, 150 and 151

➡This procedure is for 2.0L turbo engines only. For the non-turbo engines, it is not necessary to check the ignition timing using a timing light, as the crankshaft position is detected directly and the timing is controlled electronically.

1. Apply the parking brake and block the wheels.

2. Make certain all lights, cooling fan and accessories are **OFF**.

3. Position the steering wheel in straight ahead position and the gear selector lever in **P** or **N**.

4. Connect a timing light to the engine.

5. Insert a paper clip from the harness side into the 1-pin connector (blue) as shown in the accompanying figure. Attach a suitable tachometer to the paper clip. Do NOT use a scan tool to check or adjust the timing on these vehicles.

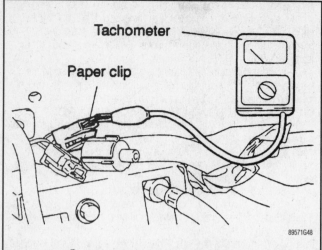

Fig. 149 Place a paper clip (from the harness side) into the 1-pin connector—1995 2.0L turbo engines

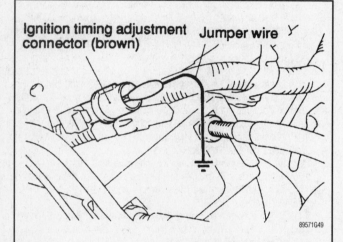

Fig. 150 Attach the jumper with the clip to the timing adjustment terminal and ground to the body

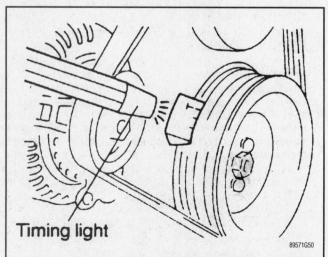

Fig. 151 Use a suitable timing light to check that the ignition timing is within specifications

6. Start the engine and let run until it reaches normal operating temperature.

7. Check that the idle speed is within specifications. The idle should be 650–850 rpm. For rpm, one-half of the actual engine rpm is indicated, so the actual engine rpm is 2 times the indicated valve shown by the tachometer.

8. Turn the ignition switch **OFF**.

9. Remove the waterproof connector from the ignition timing adjustment connector (brown).

10. Connect the jumper wire with the clip to the ignition timing adjustment terminal, and ground this to the body as shown in the accompanying figure. Grounding this terminal sets the engine to the basic ignition timing.

11. Start the engine and let it run at idle.

12. Check that the basic ignition timing is 2–8 degrees BTDC.

13. Turn the engine **OFF**, remove the jumper wire from the ignition timing adjustment connector, then return the connector to its original position.

14. Start the engine, then check to be sure the ignition timing is at the standard value.

15. The actual ignition timing is about 8 degrees BTDC; however ignition timing varies within about 7 degrees, even under normal operating conditions. Also, the timing is further advanced by around 5–8 degrees BTDC at higher altitudes.

1996–97 VEHICLES

◆ See Figure 151

➡ **This procedure is for 2.0L turbo and 2.4L engines only. For the 2.0L non-turbo engines, it is not necessary to check the ignition timing using a timing light, as the crankshaft position is detected directly and the timing is controlled electronically.**

1. Apply the parking brake and block the wheels. Run the engine until the coolant reaches normal operating temperature.

2. Make certain all lights, cooling fan and accessories are **OFF**.

3. Position the steering wheel in straight ahead position and the gear selector lever in **P** or **N**.

4. Turn the ignition switch to the **OFF** position, then connect a suitable scan tool to the data link connector.

5. Attach a timing light to the engine.

6. Start the engine and let it run at idle.

7. Select No. 22 of the SCAN TOOL DATA TEST.

8. Check that the engine idle speed is within 650–850 rpm.

9. Select No. 17 of the SCAN TOOL ACTUATOR TEST.

10. Check that the basic ignition timing is within 2–8 degrees BTDC. If the timing does not fall within the specified range, inspect the fuel injection system components.

11. Press the scan tool clear key (select a forced driving cancel mode) to release the actuator test. If the test is not canceled, a forced driving will continue for 27 minutes. Driving under this condition may damage the engine.

12. Check that the actual ignition timing is at the standard value, which is about 8 degrees BTDC. Keep in mind that ignition timing varies within about 7 degrees, even under normal operating conditions. Also, the timing is further advanced by around 5–8 degrees BTDC at higher altitudes.

Valve Lash

All of the engines covered by this manual are equipped with hydraulic valve adjusters. Because of this, there is no valve adjustment. Excess clearance between the tip of the valve and the rocker is taken up by engine oil pressure acting against a plunger in the adjuster.

1. If abnormal noise is heard from the lash adjusters check as follows:

a. Start the engine and allow to idle until normal operating temperature is reached. Shut the engine **OFF**.

b. While installed to the cylinder head, press the part of the rocker arm that contacts the lash adjuster. The part pressed will feel very hard if the lash adjuster condition is normal.

c. If, when pressed, it easily descends all the way downward, replace the lash adjuster.

d. If there is a spongy feeling when pressed, air is probably mixed in, and so the cause should be investigated. The cause is probably an insufficient amount of engine oil, or damage to the oil screen and/or gasket.

e. After finding the cause and taking the appropriate step, warm up the engine and drive at low speed for a short time. Then after stopping the engine and waiting a few minutes, drive again at low speed. Repeat this procedure a few times to bleed the air from the oil.

Idle Speed And Mixture Adjustments

The idle speed is factory set and usually no adjustments are ever necessary. If an adjustment becomes necessary, first check that the spark plugs, injectors, idle air control servo and compression pressure are all normal.

Data from various sensors and switches are used by the ECU to determine the proper fuel/air mixture for optimal engine performance. The mixture setting is not adjustable.

IDLE SPEED ADJUSTMENT

➡The idle speed is controlled electronically and adjustment is usually not necessary. If the throttle body has been replaced, check and adjust the idle speed as follows.

1.8L Engine

▶ See Figure 152

1990 VEHICLES

For this procedure, a multi-tester (scan tool) is required.

1. Warm the engine to operating temperature, leave lights, electric cooling fan and accessories **OFF**. The transaxle should be in **N** for manual transaxle or **P** for automatic transaxle. Place the steering wheel in a neutral (straight ahead) position for vehicles equipped with power steering.

2. Check the ignition timing and adjust, if necessary.

3. Connect a multi-use tester to the diagnostic (data link) connector, located beside the fuse block.

4. Turn the ignition switch to the **ON** position, without starting the engine, and hold it in that position for 15 seconds or more. With the ignition in this position, the idle speed control motor will retract to the idle position. Turn the ignition switch **OFF**.

5. Uncouple the connector of the idle speed control servo to secure the idle speed servo at this position.

6. In order to prevent the throttle valve from sticking, open it more than halfway 2 or 3 times and then release it to let it click shut. Loosen the fixed idle speed adjusting screw to allow for adjustment.

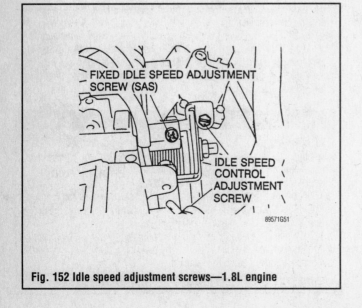

Fig. 152 Idle speed adjustment screws—1.8L engine

7. Start the engine and allow it to run at idle.

8. Check that the engine speed is at the desired reading of 650–750 rpm. The engine speed on a vehicle with 300 miles or less may be 20–100 rpm lower than specifications listed above, but adjustments may not be necessary.

9. If adjustment is required, turn the engine **OFF** and slacken the accelerator cable. Adjust the idle speed using the idle speed adjustment screw. When making the adjustment, use a hexagonal wrench in order to prevent play caused by backlash.

10. Once the engine rpm is set, screw in the fixed idle speed adjusting screw until the engine speed starts to rise. At this point return the fixed idle speed adjusting screw to find the point at which engine rpm does not change. Once at this point, turn the fixed idle speed adjusting screw in a half turn. Turn the engine **OFF**.

11. Switch the ignition to the **ON** position but do not start the engine.

12. Press code No. 14 on the scan tool and measure the output voltage of the throttle position sensor. Compare reading to the desired voltage of 0.48–0.52 volts. If the voltage is not correct, loosen the throttle position sensor mounting screws and turn the throttle position sensor to make the adjustment. Turn the ignition switch to the **OFF** position.

13. Adjust the play of the accelerator cable. Connect the idle speed control servo electrical connector. Start the engine and check that the engine idles at the correct speed.

14. Turn the engine off and disconnect the battery terminals for longer than 10 seconds, then reconnect. By doing this, the memory data will be erased.

15. Start the engine once again and let idle for about 5 minutes. Check to be sure the idling condition is normal and that the engine speed is correct.

1991–92 LASER AND TALON

1. Warm the engine to operating temperature, leave lights, electric cooling fan and accessories **OFF**. The transaxle should be in **N** for manual transaxle or **P** for automatic transaxle. Place the steering wheel in a neutral (straight ahead) position for vehicles equipped with power steering.

2. Connect a tachometer to the engine.

3. Connect a digital voltmeter between terminals 19 (throttle position sensor output voltage) and 24 (ground) of the engine control unit.

4. Turn the ignition to the **ON** position but do not start the engine. Keep in this position for at least 15 seconds. Turn the ignition to the **OFF** position.

5. Detach the idle speed control servo electrical connector. Back out the fixed idle speed adjusting screw enough to allow for adjustment.

6. Start the engine and run at idle.

7. Check that the engine speed is at the desired reading of 650–750 rpm. The engine speed on a vehicle with 300 miles or less may be 20–100 rpm lower than specifications listed above, but adjustments may not be necessary.

8. If adjustment is required, turn the engine **OFF** and slacken the accelerator cable. Adjust the idle speed using the idle speed adjustment screw. When making the adjustment, use a hexagonal wrench in order to prevent play caused by backlash.

9. Once the engine rpm is set, screw in the fixed idle speed adjusting screw until the engine speed starts to rise. At this point return the fixed idle speed adjusting screw to find the point at which engine rpm does not change. Once at this point, turn the fixed idle speed adjusting screw in a half turn. Turn the engine **OFF**.

10. Switch the ignition to the **ON** position, but do not start the engine.

11. Measure the output voltage of the throttle position sensor. Compare reading to the desired voltage of 0.48–0.52 volts. If the voltage is not correct, loosen the throttle position sensor mounting screws and turn the throttle position sensor to make the adjustment. Turn the ignition switch to the OFF position.

12. Adjust the play of the accelerator cable and remove the voltmeter. Connect the idle speed control servo electrical connector. Start the engine and check that the engine idles at the correct speed.

13. Turn the engine OFF and disconnect the battery terminals for longer than 10 seconds, then reconnect. By doing this, the memory data will be erased.

14. Start the engine once again and let idle for about 5 minutes. Check to be sure the idling condition is normal and that the engine speed is correct.

1991–93 ECLIPSE

For this procedure, a multi-tester (scan tool) is required.

1. Warm the engine to operating temperature, leave lights, electric cooling fan and accessories **OFF**. The transaxle should be in **N** for manual transaxle or **P** for automatic transaxle. Place the steering wheel in a neutral (straight ahead) position for vehicles equipped with power steering.

2. Slacken the accelerator cable to allow for adjustment. Connect the scan tool to the data link connector.

3. Switch the ignition to the **ON** position but do not start the engine. Leave in this position for 15 seconds or more. With the ignition in this position, the idle speed control motor will retract to the idle position. Turn the ignition switch **OFF**.

4. Uncouple the connector of the idle speed control servo to secure the idle speed servo at this position. In order to prevent the throttle valve from sticking, open it at least halfway 2 or more times and then release it so it will click shut.

5. Start the engine and let idle. Check the engine idle speed and compare to the desired specifications of 650–750 rpm.

6. If the idle speed is wrong, adjust with the idle speed control adjusting screw, using a hexagon wrench.

7. First loosen the fixed Speed Adjusting Screw (SAS). Then adjust the engine speed using the idle speed control adjusting screw until the desired engine speed is reached.

8. Once the engine rpm is set, screw in the fixed idle speed adjusting screw until the engine speed starts to rise. At this point return the fixed idle speed adjusting screw to find the point at which engine rpm does not change. Once at this point, turn the fixed idle speed adjusting screw in a half turn.

9. Turn the ignition switch **OFF**. Adjust the accelerator cable and the throttle position sensor.

10. Start the engine once again and let idle for about 5 minutes. Check to be sure the idling condition is normal and that the engine speed is correct.

1993 LASER AND TALON

For this procedure, a multi-tester (scan tool) is required.

1. Warm the engine to operating temperature, leave lights, electric cooling fan and accessories **OFF**. The transaxle should be in **N** for manual transaxle or **P** for automatic transaxle. Place the steering wheel in a neutral (straight ahead) position for vehicles equipped with power steering.

2. Slacken the accelerator cable to allow for adjustment. Connect the scan tool to the data link connector.

3. Switch the ignition to the **ON** position but do not start the engine. Leave in this position for 15 seconds or more. With the ignition in this position, the idle speed control motor will retract to the idle position. Turn the ignition switch **OFF**.

4. Uncouple the connector of the idle speed control servo to secure the idle speed servo at this position. In order to prevent the throttle valve from sticking, open it at least halfway 2 or more times and then release it so it will click shut.

5. Start the engine and let idle. Check the engine idle speed and compare to the desired specifications of 650–750 rpm.

6. If the idle speed is wrong, adjust with the idle speed control adjusting screw, using a hexagon wrench.

7. First loosen the fixed Speed Adjusting Screw (SAS). Then adjust the engine speed using the idle speed control adjusting screw until the desired engine speed is reached.

8. Once the engine rpm is set, screw in the fixed idle speed adjusting screw until the engine speed starts to rise. At this point return the fixed idle speed adjusting screw to find the point at which engine rpm does not change. Once at this point, turn the fixed idle speed adjusting screw in a half turn.

9. Turn the ignition switch **OFF**. Adjust the accelerator cable and the throttle position sensor.

10. Start the engine once again and let idle for about 5 minutes. Check to be sure the idling condition is normal and that the engine speed is correct.

2.0L and 2.4L Engines

1990–94 VEHICLES

♦ See Figures 153 and 154

1. Warm the engine to operating temperature, leave lights, electric cooling fan and accessories **OFF**. The transaxle should be in **N**. Place the steering wheel in a neutral position for vehicles with power steering.

2. Check the ignition timing and adjust, if necessary.

3. Attach a tachometer to the 1-pin connector under the hood.

4. Locate the self-diagnosis terminal under the dashboard and connect terminal No. **10** to ground with a jumper wire.

5. Disconnect the waterproof female connector used for ignition timing adjustment. Connect this terminal to ground using a jumper wire.

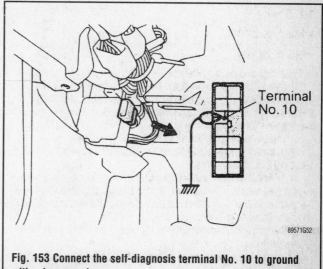

Fig. 153 Connect the self-diagnosis terminal No. 10 to ground with a jumper wire

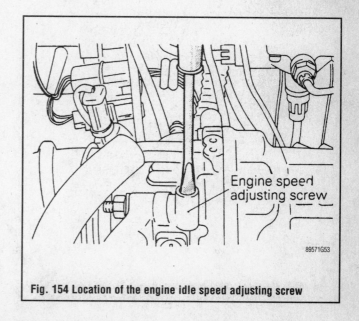

Fig. 154 Location of the engine idle speed adjusting screw

6. Start the engine and allow to idle. Check that the basic idle speed is 700–800 rpm. Be aware that on some vehicles, the rpm reading may be half of the actual engine rpm. Adjust the engine rpm using the speed adjusting screw. If the idle speed still is difficult to adjust or deviates from the specification, note the following:

a. A new engine will idle more slowly. Break-in should take approximately 300 miles.

b. If the vehicle stalls or has a very low idle speed, suspect a deposit buildup on the throttle valve which must be cleaned.

c. If the idle speed is high even though the speed adjusting screw is fully closed, check that the idle position switch (fixed speed adjusting screw) position has changed. If so, adjust the idle position switch.

d. If after all these checks the idle is still out of specification, it may be that there is leakage resulting from deterioration of the Fast-Idle Air Valve (FIAV).

7. Turn the ignition switch **OFF**. Disconnect the jumper wire from the diagnosis connector, disconnect the jumper wire from the ignition timing connector and reconnect the waterproof connector. Disconnect the tachometer.

8. Restart the engine, allow to run for 5 minutes and check for good idle quality and correct idle speed.

1995–96 VEHICLES

▶ See Figures 155, 156 and 157

1. Warm the engine to operating temperature, leave lights, electric cooling fan and accessories **OFF**. The transaxle should be in **N**. Place the steering wheel in a neutral position for vehicles with power steering.

2. Check the ignition timing and adjust, if necessary.

3. If available, connect a scan tool to the data link connector (16-pin connector). When the scan tool is connected, the diagnostic test mode control terminal should be grounded.

4. If you are not using a scan tool, proceed as follows:

a. Insert a paper clip into the 1-pin (blue) engine speed detection connector.

b. Attach a tachometer to the paper clip.

c. Use a diagnostic trouble code check harness to ground the diagnostic test mode control terminal (terminal 1) of the data link connector (16-pin connector).

5. Remove the waterproof female connector from the ignition timing adjustment connector.

6. Use a jumper wire to ground the ignition timing adjustment terminal.

7. Start the engine and allow it to run at idle. Check to see if the idle

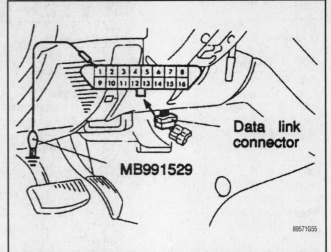

Fig. 156 Ground the diagnostic test mode control terminal of the data link connector

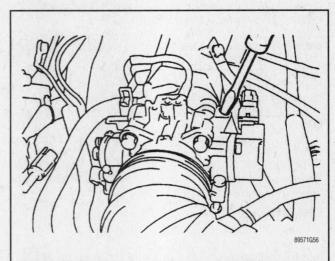

Fig. 157 If the idle speed is out of range, use a screwdriver to turn the engine speed adjusting screw to achieve the proper rpm

speed is within 700–800 rpm. For vehicles with less than 300 miles on the odometer, the engine speed may be 20–100 rpm lower than specifications, however no adjustment is necessary. If the engine stalls or the rpm is low even though the vehicle has been driven 300 or more miles, the throttle valve probably has accumulated deposits that need to be cleaned off.

8. If the idle is not within specifications, turn the engine speed adjusting screw to make the necessary adjustment.

9. Turn the ignition switch to the **OFF** position.

10. Disconnect the jumper wire from the ignition timing adjustment terminal and return the connector to its original condition.

11. Start the engine again and let it run at idle for about 10 minutes. Check to make sure the idling is normal.

1997–98 VEHICLES

▶ See Figure 157

1. Warm the engine to operating temperature, leave lights, electric cooling fan and accessories **OFF**. The transaxle should be in **N**. Place the steering wheel in a neutral position for vehicles with power steering.

2. Check the ignition timing and adjust, if necessary.

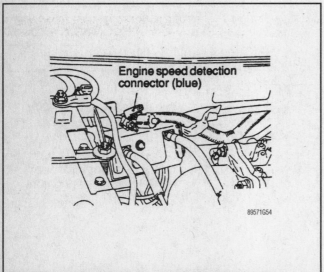

Fig. 155 Location of the engine speed detection connector

GASOLINE ENGINE TUNE-UP SPECIFICATIONS

Year	Engine ID/VIN	Engine Displacement Liters (cc)	Spark Plugs Gap (in.)	Ignition Timing (deg.)		Fuel Pump (psi)	Idle Speed (rpm)		Valve Clearance	
				MT	AT		MT	AT	In.	Ex.
1990	T	1.8 (1775)	0.039–0.043	5B	5B	38	750	750	HYD	HYD
	R	2.0 (1997)	0.039–0.043	5B	5B	38	750	750	HYD	HYD
	U	2.0 (1997)	0.028–0.031	5B	5B	27	750	750	HYD	HYD
1991	T	1.8 (1775)	0.039–0.043	5B	5B	38	750	750	HYD	HYD
	R	2.0 (1997)	0.039–0.043	5B	5B	38	750	750	HYD	HYD
	U	2.0 (1997)	0.028–0.031	5B	5B	27	750	750	HYD	HYD
1992	T	1.8 (1775)	0.039–0.043	5B	5B	38	750	750	HYD	HYD
	R	2.0 (1997)	0.039–0.043	5B	5B	38	750	750	HYD	HYD
	U	2.0 (1997)	0.028–0.031	5B	5B	27	750	750	HYD	HYD
1993	B	1.8 (1775)	0.039–0.043	5B	5B	38	750	750	HYD	HYD
	E	2.0 (1997)	0.039–0.043	5B	5B	38	750	750	HYD	HYD
	F	2.0 (1997)	0.028–0.031	5B	5B	27	750	750	HYD	HYD
1994	B	1.8 (1775)	0.039–0.043	5B	5B	38	750	750	HYD	HYD
	E	2.0 (1997)	0.039–0.043	5B	5B	38	750	750	HYD	HYD
	F	2.0 (1997)	0.028–0.031	5B	5B	①	750	750	HYD	HYD
1995	Y	2.0 (1997)	0.039–0.043	5B	5B	38	700	700	HYD	HYD
	F	2.0 (1997)	0.028–0.031	5B	5B	①	750	750	HYD	HYD
1996	Y	2.0 (1997)	0.039–0.043	5B	5B	38	700	700	HYD	HYD
	F	2.0 (1997)	0.028–0.031	5B	5B	①	750	750	HYD	HYD
1997	Y	2.0 (1997)	0.039–0.043	5B	5B	38	700	700	HYD	HYD
	F	2.0 (1997)	0.028–0.031	5B	5B	①	750	750	HYD	HYD
	G	2.4 (2351)	0.039–0.043	5B	5B	38	650–850	650–850	HYD	HYD
1998	Y	2.0 (1997)	0.039–0.043	5B	5B	38	700	700	HYD	HYD
	F	2.0 (1997)	0.028–0.031	5B	5B	①	750	750	HYD	HYD
	G	2.4 (2351)	0.039–0.043	5B	5B	38	650–850	650–850	HYD	HYD

HYD - Hydraulic

① Manual transmission: 36
  Automatic transmission: 43

89571C08

3. Connect a suitable scan tool to the data link connector (16-pin connector). When the scan tool is connected, the diagnostic test mode control terminal should be grounded.

4. Start the engine and allow it to run at idle.

5. Select item No. 30 of the SCAN TOOL (MUT-II) Actuator test.

➡This holds the IAC motor at the basic step to adjust the basic idle speed.

6. Check the idle speed. The proper specification is 700–800 rpm. For vehicles with less than 300 miles on the odometer, the engine speed may be 20–100 rpm lower than specifications, however no adjustment is necessary. If the engine stalls or the rpm is low even though the vehicle has been driven 300 or more miles, the throttle valve probably has accumulated deposits that need to be cleaned off.

7. If the idle is not within specifications, turn the engine speed adjusting screw to make the necessary adjustment.

8. Press the scan tool clear key, and release the IAC motor from the actuator test mode. Unless the IAC motor is released, the Actuator test mode will continue 27 minutes.

9. Turn the ignition to the OFF position.

10. Disconnect the scan tool.

11. Start the engine again and let it run at idle for about 10 minutes. Check to make sure the idling is normal.

Air Conditioning System

SYSTEM SERVICE & REPAIR

◆ See Figure 158

➡It is recommended that the A/C system be serviced by an EPA Section 609 certified automotive technician utilizing a refrigerant recovery/recycling machine.

The do-it-yourselfer should not service his/her own vehicle's A/C system for many reasons, including legal concerns, personal injury, environmental damage and cost. The following are some of the reasons why you may decide not to service your own vehicle's A/C system.

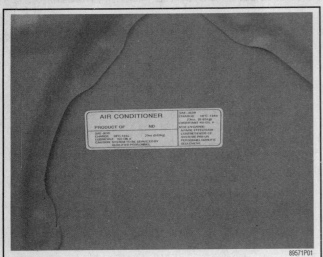

Fig. 158 Your vehicle should have an underhood sticker containing A/C system information

According to the U.S. Clean Air Act, it is a federal crime to service or repair (involving the refrigerant) a Motor Vehicle Air Conditioning (MVAC) system for money without being EPA certified. It is also illegal to vent R-12 and R-134a refrigerants into the atmosphere. Selling or distributing A/C system refrigerant (in a container which contains less than 20 pounds of refrigerant) to any person who is not EPA 609 certified is also not allowed by law.

State and/or local laws may be more strict than the federal regulations, so be sure to check with your state and/or local authorities for further information. For further federal information on the legality of servicing your A/C system, call the EPA Stratospheric Ozone Hotline.

➡**Federal law dictates that a fine of up to $25,000 may be levied on people convicted of venting refrigerant into the atmosphere. Additionally, the EPA may pay up to $10,000 for information or services leading to a criminal conviction of the violation of these laws.**

When servicing an A/C system you run the risk of handling or coming in contact with refrigerant, which may result in skin or eye irritation or frostbite. Although low in toxicity (due to chemical stability), inhalation of concentrated refrigerant fumes is dangerous and can result in death; cases of fatal cardiac arrhythmia have been reported in people accidentally subjected to high levels of refrigerant. Some early symptoms include loss of concentration and drowsiness.

➡**Generally, the limit for exposure is lower for R-134a than it is for R-12. Exceptional care must be practiced when handling R-134a.**

Also, refrigerants can decompose at high temperatures (near gas heaters or open flame), which may result in hydrofluoric acid, hydrochloric acid and phosgene (a fatal nerve gas).

R-12 refrigerant can damage the environment because it is a Chlorofluorocarbon (CFC), which has been proven to add to ozone layer depletion, leading to increasing levels of UV radiation. UV radiation has been linked with an increase in skin cancer, suppression of the human immune system, an increase in cataracts, damage to crops, damage to aquatic organisms, an increase in ground-level ozone, and increased global warming.

R-134a refrigerant is a greenhouse gas which, if allowed to vent into the atmosphere, will contribute to global warming (the Greenhouse Effect).

It is usually more economically feasible to have a certified MVAC automotive technician perform A/C system service on your vehicle. Some possible reasons for this are as follows:

• While it is illegal to service an A/C system without the proper equipment, the home mechanic would have to purchase an expensive refrigerant recovery/recycling machine to service his/her own vehicle.

• Since only a certified person may purchase refrigerant—according to the Clean Air Act, there are specific restrictions on selling or distributing

A/C system refrigerant—it is legally impossible (unless certified) for the home mechanic to service his/her own vehicle. Procuring refrigerant in an illegal fashion exposes one to the risk of paying a $25,000 fine to the EPA.

R-12 Refrigerant Conversion

If your vehicle still uses R-12 refrigerant, one way to save A/C system costs down the road is to investigate the possibility of having your system converted to R-134a. The older R-12 systems can be easily converted to R-134a refrigerant by a certified automotive technician by installing a few new components and changing the system oil.

The cost of R-12 is steadily rising and will continue to increase, because it is no longer imported or manufactured in the United States. Therefore, it is often possible to have an R-12 system converted to R-134a and recharged for less than it would cost to just charge the system with R-12.

If you are interested in having your system converted, contact local automotive service stations for more details and information.

PREVENTIVE MAINTENANCE

▶ **See Figures 159 and 160**

Although the A/C system should not be serviced by the do-it-yourselfer, preventive maintenance can be practiced and A/C system inspections can be performed to help maintain the efficiency of the vehicle's A/C system. For preventive maintenance, perform the following:

• The easiest and most important preventive maintenance for your A/C system is to be sure that it is used on a regular basis. Running the system for five minutes each month (no matter what the season) will help ensure that the seals and all internal components remain lubricated.

➡**Some newer vehicles automatically operate the A/C system compressor whenever the windshield defroster is activated. When running, the compressor lubricates the A/C system components; therefore, the A/C system would not need to be operated each month.**

• In order to prevent heater core freeze-up during A/C operation, it is necessary to maintain proper antifreeze protection. Use a hand-held coolant tester (hydrometer) to periodically check the condition of the antifreeze in your engine's cooling system.

➡**Antifreeze should not be used longer than the manufacturer specifies.**

• For efficient operation of an air conditioned vehicle's cooling system, the radiator cap should have a holding pressure which meets manufacturer's specifications. A cap which fails to hold these pressures should be replaced.

Fig. 159 A coolant tester can be used to determine the freezing and boiling levels of the coolant in your vehicle

GASKET

SEAL

TCCS1079

Fig. 160 To ensure efficient cooling system operation, inspect the radiator cap gasket and seal

• Any obstruction of or damage to the condenser configuration will restrict air flow which is essential to its efficient operation. It is, therefore, a good rule to keep this unit clean and in proper physical shape.

➡️**Bug screens which are mounted in front of the condenser (unless they are original equipment) are regarded as obstructions.**

• The condensation drain tube expels any water which accumulates on the bottom of the evaporator housing into the engine compartment. If this tube is obstructed, the air conditioning performance can be restricted and condensation buildup can spill over onto the vehicle's floor.

SYSTEM INSPECTION

◗ **See Figure 161**

Although the A/C system should not be serviced by the do-it-yourselfer, preventive maintenance can be practiced and A/C system inspections can be performed to help maintain the efficiency of the vehicle's A/C system. For A/C system inspection, perform the following:

The easiest and often most important check for the air conditioning system consists of a visual inspection of the system components. Visually inspect the air conditioning system for refrigerant leaks, damaged

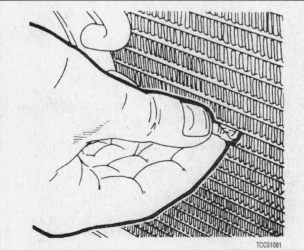

TCCS1081

Fig. 161 Periodically remove any debris from the condenser and radiator fins

compressor clutch, abnormal compressor drive belt tension and/or condition, plugged evaporator drain tube, blocked condenser fins, disconnected or broken wires, blown fuses, corroded connections and poor insulation.

A refrigerant leak will usually appear as an oily residue at the leakage point in the system. The oily residue soon picks up dust or dirt particles from the surrounding air and appears greasy. Through time, this will build up and appear to be a heavy dirt impregnated grease.

For a thorough visual and operational inspection, check the following:

• Check the surface of the radiator and condenser for dirt, leaves or other material which might block air flow.

• Check for kinks in hoses and lines. Check the system for leaks.

• Make sure the drive belt is properly tensioned. When the air conditioning is operating, make sure the drive belt is free of noise or slippage.

• Make sure the blower motor operates at all appropriate positions, then check for distribution of the air from all outlets with the blower on **HIGH** or **MAX**.

➡️**Keep in mind that under conditions of high humidity, air discharged from the A/C vents may not feel as cold as expected, even if the system is working properly. This is because vaporized moisture in humid air retains heat more effectively than dry air, thereby making humid air more difficult to cool.**

• Make sure the air passage selection lever is operating correctly. Start the engine and warm it to normal operating temperature, then make sure the temperature selection lever is operating correctly.

Windshield Wipers

ELEMENT (REFILL) CARE & REPLACEMENT

◗ **See Figures 162 thru 171**

For maximum effectiveness and longest element life, the windshield and wiper blades should be kept clean. Dirt, tree sap, road tar and so on will cause streaking, smearing and blade deterioration if left on the glass. It is advisable to wash the windshield carefully with a commercial glass cleaner at least once a month. Wipe off the rubber blades with the wet rag afterwards. Do not attempt to move wipers across the windshield by hand; damage to the motor and drive mechanism will result.

To inspect and/or replace the wiper blade elements, place the wiper switch in the **LOW** speed position and the ignition switch in the **ACC** position. When the wiper blades are approximately vertical on the windshield, turn the ignition switch to **OFF**.

Examine the wiper blade elements. If they are found to be cracked, broken or torn, they should be replaced immediately. Replacement intervals will vary with usage, although ozone deterioration usually limits element life to about one year. If the wiper pattern is smeared or streaked, or if the blade chatters across the glass, the elements should be replaced. It is easiest and most sensible to replace the elements in pairs.

If your vehicle is equipped with aftermarket blades, there are several different types of refills and your vehicle might have any kind. Aftermarket blades and arms rarely use the exact same type blade or refill as the original equipment. Here are some typical aftermarket blades; not all may be available for your vehicle:

The Anco® type uses a release button that is pushed down to allow the refill to slide out of the yoke jaws. The new refill slides back into the frame and locks in place.

Some Trico® refills are removed by locating where the metal backing strip or the refill is wider. Insert a small screwdriver blade between the frame and metal backing strip. Press down to release the refill from the retaining tab.

Other types of Trico® refills have two metal tabs which are unlocked by squeezing them together. The rubber filler can then be withdrawn from the frame jaws. A new refill is installed by inserting the refill into the front frame jaws and sliding it rearward to engage the remaining frame jaws. There are usually four jaws; be certain when installing that the refill is engaged in all of them. At the end of its travel, the tabs will lock into place on the front jaws of the wiper blade frame.

Another type of refill is made from polycarbonate. The refill has a simple locking device at one end which flexes downward out of the groove into which the jaws of the holder fit, allowing easy release. By sliding the new refill through all the jaws and pushing through the slight resistance when it reaches the end of its travel, the refill will lock into position.

To replace the Tridon® refill, it is necessary to remove the wiper blade. This refill has a plastic backing strip with a notch about 1 in. (25mm) from the end. Hold the blade (frame) on a hard surface so that the frame is tightly bowed. Grip the tip of the backing strip and pull up while twisting counter-clockwise. The backing strip will snap out of the retaining tab. Do this for the remaining tabs until the refill is free of the blade. The length of these refills is molded into the end and they should be replaced with identical types.

Regardless of the type of refill used, be sure to follow the part manufacturer's instructions closely. Make sure that all of the frame jaws are engaged as the refill is pushed into place and locked. If the metal blade holder and frame are allowed to touch the glass during wiper operation, the glass will be scratched.

TCCS1225

Fig. 164 Pylon® wiper blade and adaptor

TCCS1223

Fig. 162 Bosch® wiper blade and fit kit

TCCS1226

Fig. 165 Trico® wiper blade and fit kit

TCCS1224

Fig. 163 Lexor® wiper blade and fit kit

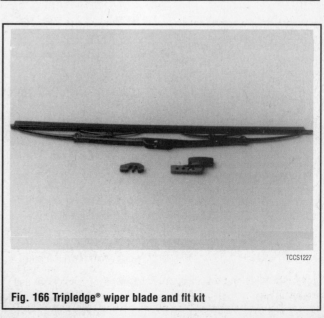

TCCS1227

Fig. 166 Tripledge® wiper blade and fit kit

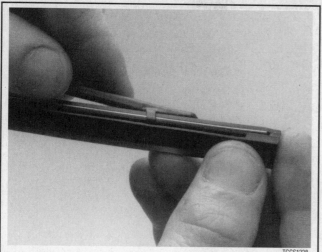

Fig. 167 To remove and install a Lexor® wiper blade refill, slip out the old insert and slide in a new one

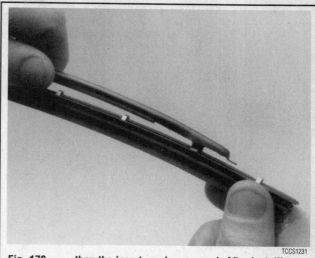

Fig. 170 . . . then the insert can be removed. After installing the replacement insert, bend the tab back

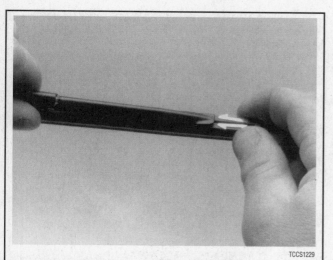

Fig. 168 On Pylon® inserts, the clip at the end has to be removed prior to sliding the insert off

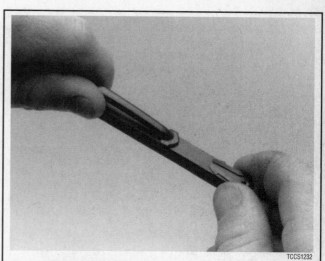

Fig. 171 The Tripledge® wiper blade insert is removed and installed using a securing clip

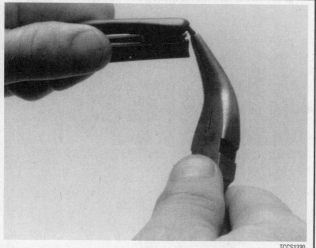

Fig. 169 On Trico® wiper blades, the tab at the end of the blade must be turned up . . .

Tires and Wheels

▶ **See Figure 172**

Common sense and good driving habits will afford maximum tire life. Fast starts, sudden stops and hard cornering are hard on tires and will shorten their useful life span. Make sure that you don't overload the vehicle or run with incorrect pressure in the tires. Both of these practices will increase tread wear.

➡**For optimum tire life, keep the tires properly inflated, rotate them often and have the wheel alignment checked periodically.**

Inspect your tires frequently. Be especially careful to watch for bubbles in the tread or sidewall, deep cuts or underinflation. Replace any tires with bubbles in the sidewall. If cuts are so deep that they penetrate to the cords, discard the tire. Any cut in the sidewall of a radial tire renders it unsafe. Also look for uneven tread wear patterns that may indicate the front end is out of alignment or that the tires are out of balance.

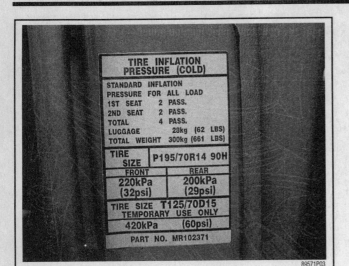

Fig. 172 Your vehicle probably has a tire information label located on the door jamb

Fig. 174 Unidirectional tires are identifiable by sidewall arrows and/or the word "rotation"

TIRE ROTATION

◆ See Figures 173 and 174

Tires must be rotated periodically to equalize wear patterns that vary with a tire's position on the vehicle. Tires will also wear in an uneven way as the front steering/suspension system wears to the point where the alignment should be reset.

Rotating the tires will ensure maximum life for the tires as a set, so you will not have to discard a tire early due to wear on only part of the tread. Regular rotation is required to equalize wear.

When rotating "unidirectional tires," make sure that they always roll in the same direction. This means that a tire used on the left side of the vehicle must not be switched to the right side and vice-versa. Such tires should only be rotated front-to-rear or rear-to-front, while always remaining on the same side of the vehicle. These tires are marked on the sidewall as to the direction of rotation; observe the marks when reinstalling the tire(s).

Some styled or "mag" wheels may have different offsets front to rear. In these cases, the rear wheels must not be used up front and vice-versa. Furthermore, if these wheels are equipped with unidirectional tires, they cannot be rotated unless the tire is remounted for the proper direction of rotation.

➡The compact or space-saver spare is strictly for emergency use. It must never be included in the tire rotation or placed on the vehicle for everyday use.

TIRE DESIGN

◆ See Figure 175

For maximum satisfaction, tires should be used in sets of four. Mixing of different types (radial, bias-belted, fiberglass belted) must be avoided. In most cases, the vehicle manufacturer has designated a type of tire on which the vehicle will perform best. Your first choice when replacing tires should be to use the same type of tire that the manufacturer recommends.

When radial tires are used, tire sizes and wheel diameters should be selected to maintain ground clearance and tire load capacity equivalent to the original specified tire. Radial tires should always be used in sets of four.

✳✳ CAUTION

Radial tires should never be used on only the front axle.

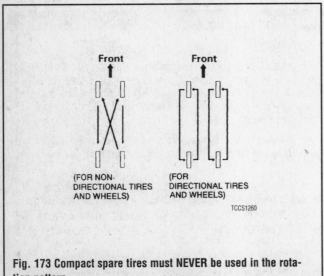

Fig. 173 Compact spare tires must **NEVER** be used in the rotation pattern

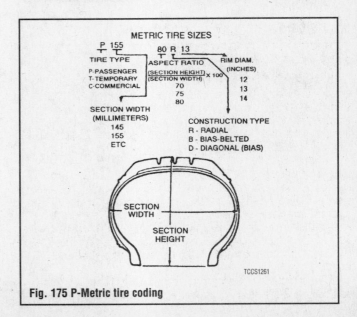

Fig. 175 P-Metric tire coding

When selecting tires, pay attention to the original size as marked on the tire. Most tires are described using an industry size code sometimes referred to as P-Metric. This allows the exact identification of the tire specifications, regardless of the manufacturer. If selecting a different tire size or brand, remember to check the installed tire for any sign of interference with the body or suspension while the vehicle is stopping, turning sharply or heavily loaded.

Snow Tires

Good radial tires can produce a big advantage in slippery weather, but in snow, a street radial tire does not have sufficient tread to provide traction and control. The small grooves of a street tire quickly pack with snow and the tire behaves like a billiard ball on a marble floor. The more open, chunky tread of a snow tire will self-clean as the tire turns, providing much better grip on snowy surfaces.

To satisfy municipalities requiring snow tires during weather emergencies, most snow tires carry either an M + S designation after the tire size stamped on the sidewall, or the designation "all-season." In general, no change in tire size is necessary when buying snow tires.

Most manufacturers strongly recommend the use of 4 snow tires on their vehicles for reasons of stability. If snow tires are fitted only to the drive wheels, the opposite end of the vehicle may become very unstable when braking or turning on slippery surfaces. This instability can lead to unpleasant endings if the driver can't counteract the slide in time.

Note that snow tires, whether 2 or 4, will affect vehicle handling in all non-snow situations. The stiffer, heavier snow tires will noticeably change the turning and braking characteristics of the vehicle. Once the snow tires are installed, you must re-learn the behavior of the vehicle and drive accordingly.

➡**Consider buying extra wheels on which to mount the snow tires. Once done, the "snow wheels" can be installed and removed as needed. This eliminates the potential damage to tires or wheels from seasonal removal and installation. Even if your vehicle has styled wheels, see if inexpensive steel wheels are available. Although the look of the vehicle will change, the expensive wheels will be protected from salt, curb hits and pothole damage.**

TIRE STORAGE

If they are mounted on wheels, store the tires at proper inflation pressure. All tires should be kept in a cool, dry place. If they are stored in the garage or basement, do not let them stand on a concrete floor; set them on strips of wood, a mat or a large stack of newspaper. Keeping them away from direct moisture is of paramount importance. Tires should not be stored upright, but in a flat position.

INFLATION & INSPECTION

▶ **See Figures 176 thru 183**

The importance of proper tire inflation cannot be overemphasized. A tire employs air as part of its structure. It is designed around the supporting strength of the air at a specified pressure. For this reason, improper inflation drastically reduces the tires's ability to perform as intended. A tire will lose some air in day-to-day use; having to add a few pounds of air periodically is not necessarily a sign of a leaking tire.

Two items should be a permanent fixture in every glove compartment: an accurate tire pressure gauge and a tread depth gauge. Check the tire pressure (including the spare) regularly with a pocket type gauge. Too often, the gauge on the end of the air hose at your corner garage is not accurate because it suffers too much abuse. Always check tire pressure when the tires are cold, as pressure increases with temperature. If you must move the vehicle to check the tire inflation, do not drive more than a mile before checking. A cold tire is generally one that has not been driven for more than three hours.

A plate or sticker is normally provided somewhere in the vehicle (door post, hood, tailgate or trunk lid) which shows the proper pressure for the

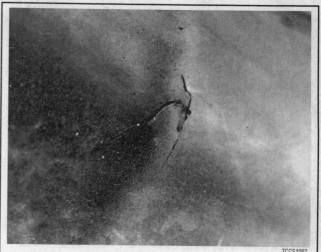
Fig. 176 Tires should be checked frequently for any sign of puncture or damage

Fig. 177 Tires with deep cuts, or cuts which show bulging should be replaced immediately

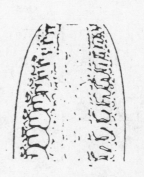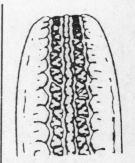
• DRIVE WHEEL HEAVY ACCELERATION
• OVERINFLATION

• HARD CORNERING
• UNDERINFLATION
• LACK OF ROTATION

Fig. 178 Examples of inflation-related tire wear patterns

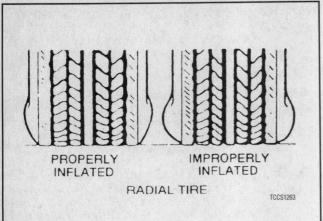

Fig. 179 Radial tires have a characteristic sidewall bulge; don't try to measure pressure by looking at the tire. Use a quality air pressure gauge

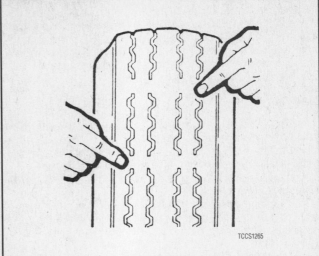

Fig. 181 Tread wear indicators will appear when the tire is worn

tires. Never counteract excessive pressure build-up by bleeding off air pressure (letting some air out). This will cause the tire to run hotter and wear quicker.

✳✳ CAUTION

Never exceed the maximum tire pressure embossed on the tire! This is the pressure to be used when the tire is at maximum loading, but it is rarely the correct pressure for everyday driving. Consult the owner's manual or the tire pressure sticker for the correct tire pressure.

Once you've maintained the correct tire pressures for several weeks, you'll be familiar with the vehicle's braking and handling personality. Slight adjustments in tire pressures can fine-tune these characteristics, but never change the cold pressure specification by more than 2 psi. A slightly softer tire pressure will give a softer ride but also yield lower fuel mileage. A slightly harder tire will give crisper dry road handling but can cause skidding on wet surfaces. Unless you're fully attuned to the vehicle, stick to the recommended inflation pressures.

All tires made since 1968 have built-in tread wear indicator bars that show up as ½ in. (13mm) wide smooth bands across the tire when 1⁄16 in.

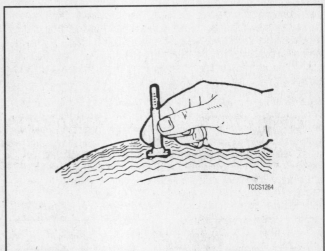

Fig. 182 Accurate tread depth indicators are inexpensive and handy

CONDITION	RAPID WEAR AT SHOULDERS	RAPID WEAR AT CENTER	CRACKED TREADS	WEAR ON ONE SIDE	FEATHERED EDGE	BALD SPOTS	SCALLOPED WEAR
EFFECT							
CAUSE	UNDER-INFLATION OR LACK OF ROTATION	OVER-INFLATION OR LACK OF ROTATION	UNDER-INFLATION OR EXCESSIVE SPEED*	EXCESSIVE CAMBER	INCORRECT TOE	UNBALANCED WHEEL OR TIRE DEFECT*	LACK OF ROTATION OF TIRES OR WORN OR OUT-OF-ALIGNMENT SUSPENSION.
CORRECTION	ADJUST PRESSURE TO SPECIFICATIONS WHEN TIRES ARE COOL ROTATE TIRES			ADJUST CAMBER TO SPECIFICATIONS	ADJUST TOE-IN TO SPECIFICATIONS	DYNAMIC OR STATIC BALANCE WHEELS	ROTATE TIRES AND INSPECT SUSPENSION

*HAVE TIRE INSPECTED FOR FURTHER USE.

Fig. 180 Common tire wear patterns and causes

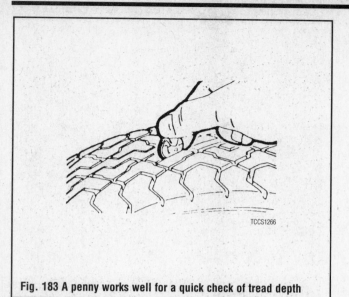

Fig. 183 A penny works well for a quick check of tread depth

(1.5mm) of tread remains. The appearance of tread wear indicators means that the tires should be replaced. In fact, many states have laws prohibiting the use of tires with less than this amount of tread.

You can check your own tread depth with an inexpensive gauge or by using a Lincoln head penny. Slip the Lincoln penny (with Lincoln's head upside-down) into several tread grooves. If you can see the top of Lincoln's head in 2 adjacent grooves, the tire has less than 1/16 in. (1.5mm) tread left and should be replaced. You can measure snow tires in the same manner by using the "tails" side of the Lincoln penny. If you can see the top of the Lincoln memorial, it's time to replace the snow tire(s).

CARE OF SPECIAL WHEELS

If you have invested money in magnesium, aluminum alloy or sport wheels, special precautions should be taken to make sure your investment is not wasted and that your special wheels look good for the life of the vehicle.

Special wheels are easily damaged and/or scratched. Occasionally check the rims for cracking, impact damage or air leaks. If any of these are found, replace the wheel. But in order to prevent this type of damage and the costly replacement of a special wheel, observe the following precautions:
• Use extra care not to damage the wheels during removal, installation, balancing, etc. After removal of the wheels from the vehicle, place them on a mat or other protective surface. If they are to be stored for any length of time, support them on strips of wood. Never store tires and wheels upright; the tread may develop flat spots.
• When driving, watch for hazards; it doesn't take much to crack a wheel.
• When washing, use a mild soap or non-abrasive dish detergent (keeping in mind that detergent tends to remove wax). Avoid cleansers with abrasives or the use of hard brushes. There are many cleaners and polishes for special wheels.
• If possible, remove the wheels during the winter. Salt and sand used for snow removal can severely damage the finish of a wheel.
• Make certain the recommended lug nut torque is never exceeded or the wheel may crack. Never use snow chains on special wheels; severe scratching will occur.

FLUIDS AND LUBRICANTS

Fluid Disposal

Used fluids such as engine oil, transmission fluid, antifreeze and brake fluid are hazardous wastes and must be disposed of properly. Before draining any fluids, consult with your local authorities; in many areas waste oil, etc. is being accepted as a part of recycling programs. A number of service stations and auto parts stores are also accepting waste fluids for recycling.

Be sure of the recycling center's policies before draining any fluids, as many will not accept different fluids that have been mixed together.

Fuel and Engine Oil Recommendations

▶ **See Figures 184 and 185**

All vehicles except those equipped with DOHC engines have been designed to run on unleaded fuel having a minimum octane rating of 87 or 91 RON (Research Octane Number).

Vehicles equipped with DOHC engines have been designed to run on unleaded fuel having a minimum octane rating of 91 or 95 RON (Research Octane Number).

The use of a fuel too low in octane (a measurement of anti-knock quality) will result in spark knock. Since many factors such as altitude, terrain, air temperature and humidity affect the operating efficiency, knocking may result even though the recommended fuel is being used. If persistent knocking occurs, it may be necessary to switch to a higher grade of fuel. Continuous or heavy knocking may result in engine damage and should be diagnosed, if continued.

Engine oil should be used which conforms to the requirements of the API classification "For Service SJ" or "For Service SJ/CD", and have the proper SAE grade number for the expected temperature range of vehicle operation.

✳✳ CAUTION

Non-detergent or straight mineral oil must never be used.

In order to improve fuel economy and conserve energy new, lower friction engine oils have been developed. These oils are readily available and can be identified by such labels as "Energy Conserving", "Energy Saving", "Improved Economy", etc.

A standard symbol appears on the top of oil containers and has 3 distinct areas for identifying various aspects of the oil. The top portion will indicate quality of the oil. The center portion will show SAE viscosity grade, such as SAE 10W-30. "Energy Conserving' shown in the lower portion, indicates that the oil has fuel-saving capabilities.

Fig. 184 Look for the API oil identification label when choosing your engine oil

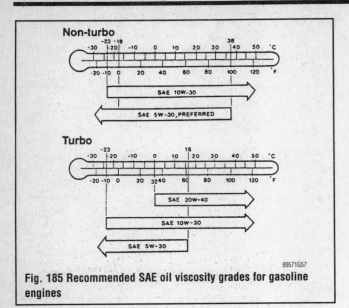

Fig. 185 Recommended SAE oil viscosity grades for gasoline engines

Fig. 187 The engine oil fill cap is located on the camshaft cover, next to the ignition coil

Engine

OIL LEVEL CHECK

▶ See Figures 186, 187, 188 and 189

1. Make sure the car is parked on level ground.
2. When checking the oil level, it is best for the engine to be at normal operating temperature, although checking the oil immediately after stopping will lead to a false reading. Wait a few minutes after turning off the engine to allow the oil to drain back into the crankcase.
3. Open the hood and locate the dipstick which will be in a guide tube mounted in the engine block. Pull the dipstick from its tube, wipe it clean (using a clean, lint free rag) and then reinsert it.
4. The oil dipstick has two marks to indicate the minimum (MIN) and maximum (MAX) oil level. If the oil is at or below the "MIN" mark on the dipstick, add oil of the proper viscosity through the capped opening in the top of the camshaft (valve) cover. See the oil and fuel recommendations listed earlier in this section for the proper viscosity and rating of oil to use. The oil level should be maintained in the safety margin, neither going above the "MAX" mark or below the "MIN" mark.

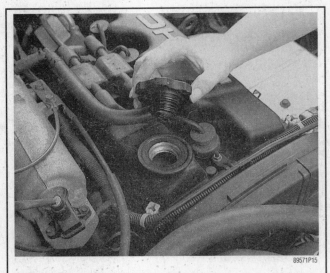

Fig. 188 Remove the engine oil fill cap . . .

Fig. 186 To check the engine oil level, pull the dipstick out of it's tube and wipe it clean with a lint free rag

Fig. 189 . . . then use a funnel to add the proper type and amount of engine oil

5. Insert the dipstick and check the oil level again after adding any oil. Approximately one quart of oil will raise the level from the MIN mark to the MAX mark. Be sure not to overfill the crankcase and waste the oil. Excess oil will generally be consumed at an accelerated rate.

✳✳ WARNING

DO NOT overfill the crankcase. It may result in oil-fouled spark plugs, oil leaks caused by oil seal failure or engine damage due to oil foaming.

OIL & FILTER CHANGE

▸ See Figures 190, 191, 192, 193 and 194

➡The manufacturer's recommended oil change interval is 7,500 miles (12,000 km) under normal operating conditions. We recommend and oil change interval of 3,000–3,500 miles (4,800–5,600 km) under normal conditions; more frequently under severe conditions such as when the average trip is less than 4 miles (6 km), engine is operated for extended periods at idle or low-speeds, when towing a trailer or operating in dusty areas. In addition, we recommend that the filter be replaced EVERY time the oil is changed.

1. Run the engine until it reaches normal operating temperature.
2. Raise the front of the vehicle and support it safely using a suitable pair of jackstands.
3. Slide a drain pan of a least 6 quarts capacity under the oil pan. Wipe the drain plug and surrounding area clean using an old rag.

✳✳ CAUTION

The EPA warns that prolonged contact with used engine oil may cause a number of skin disorders, including cancer! You should make every effort to minimize your exposure to used engine oil. Protective gloves should be worn when changing the oil. Wash your hands and any other exposed skin areas as soon as possible after exposure to used engine oil. Soap and water, or waterless hand cleaner should be used.

4. Loosen the drain plug using a ratchet, short extension and socket or a box-wrench. Turn the plug out by hand, using a rag to shield your fingers from the hot oil. By keeping an inward pressure on the plug as you unscrew it, oil won't escape past the threads and you can remove it without being burned by hot oil.

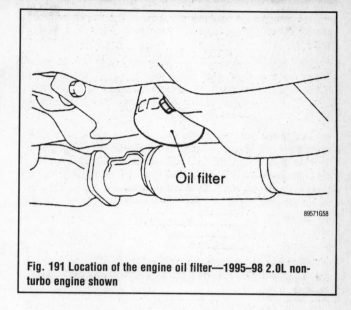

Fig. 191 Location of the engine oil filter—1995–98 2.0L non-turbo engine shown

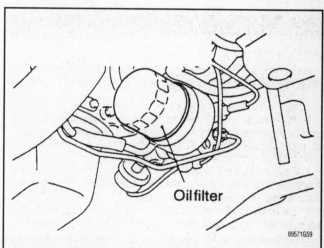

Fig. 192 Oil filter location—1995–98 2.0L turbo and 2.4L engines shown

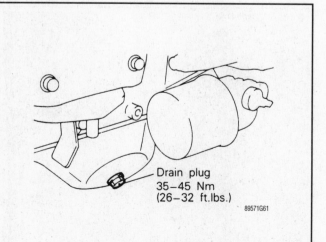

Fig. 190 Install the engine oil pan drain plug and tighten to specifications

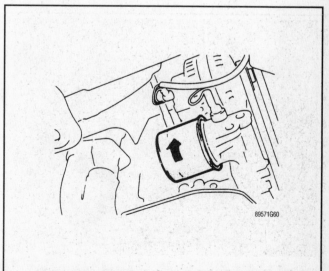

Fig. 193 Direction of rotation for removing the engine oil filter

➡️If the drain plug is equipped with a removable washer or gasket, check its condition and replace, if necessary, to provide a leakproof seal.

5. Quickly withdraw the plug and move your hands out of the way. Allow the oil to drain completely into the pan, then install and carefully tighten the drain plug to 26–32 ft. lbs. (35–45 Nm). Be careful not to over-tighten the drain plug, otherwise you'll be buying a new pan or a replacement plug for stripped threads.

➡️Although some manufacturers recommend changing the oil filter every other oil change, we recommend the filter be changed each time you change your oil. The old filter will contain up to a quart of dirty oil, which will contaminate the clean oil. Also, the benefit of clean oil is quickly lost if the old filter is clogged. The added protection for your engine far outweighs the few dollars saved by using an old filter.

6. Move the drain pan under the oil filter. Use a strap-type or cap-type filter wrench to loosen and remove the oil filter from the engine block. Keep in mind that it's holding about one quart of hot, dirty oil.

➡️Make sure the O-ring from the old oil filter is on the old oil filter. If a new oil filter is installed with the old O-ring stuck on the engine filter head, a severe oil leak will result. This, if not noticed, could result in engine damage. The quality of replacement filters vary widely. Only high quality filters should be used to assure most efficient service. Install only oil filters capable of withstanding a pressure of 256 psi.

7. Coat the O-ring on the top of the new oil filter lightly with clean engine oil. Thread the filter onto the oil filter head by hand. Tighten the oil filter as follows:
   a. For MD135737 filters: one full turn or 9–12 ft. lbs. (12–16 Nm).
   b. For MD136466 filters: ¾ turn or 10–14 ft. lbs. (13–20 Nm).
   c. For M05281090: ¾ turn or 15 ft. lbs. (20 Nm).

➡️Do NOT overtighten the oil filter.

8. Carefully lower the vehicle.
9. Refill the engine with the correct amount of fresh oil. Please refer to the Capacities chart in this section.
10. Check the oil level on the dipstick. It is normal for the level to be a bit above the full mark. Start the engine and allow it to idle for a few minutes.

✳✳ WARNING

Do not run the engine above idle speed until it has built up oil pressure, as indicated when the oil light goes out.

Fig. 194 Before installing a new oil filter, lightly coat the rubber gasket with clean oil

11. Shut off the engine and allow the oil to flow back to the crankcase for a minute, then recheck the oil level. Check around the filter and drain plug for any leaks, and correct as necessary.

Manual Transaxle

FLUID RECOMMENDATION

For all vehicles with manual transaxles, except 1995–98 2.0L non-turbo engine, use Hypoid gear oil SAE 75W-85W, or 75W-90W conforming to API specifications GL-4 or higher. For 1995–98 2.0L non turbo engines equipped with manual transaxles, use Texaco MTX fluid FM.

LEVEL CHECK

◆ **See Figures 195, 196, 197 and 198**

Inspect each component for leaking. Check the oil level by removing the filler plug. If the oil is contaminated, it is necessary to replace it with new oil. Check the oil level as follows:
1. Make sure the vehicle is parked on a level surface.

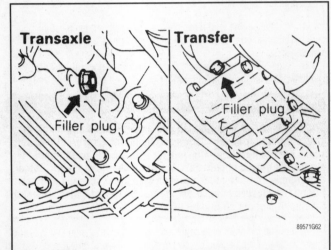

Fig. 195 Manual transaxle and transfer filler plugs—1990–94 vehicles

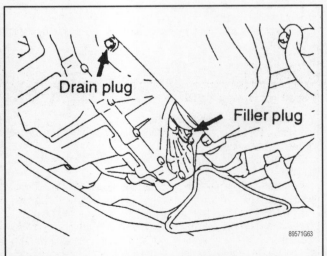

Fig. 196 Location of the manual transaxle drain and filler plugs—1995–98 2.0L non-turbo engine

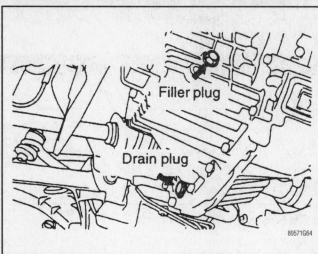

Fig. 197 Manual transaxle drain and filler plug location—1995–98 2.0L turbo and 2.4L engines

Fig. 199 Use a box-end wrench to loosen the manual transaxle drain plug . . .

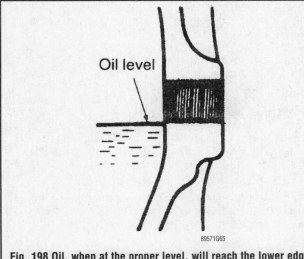

Fig. 198 Oil, when at the proper level, will reach the lower edge of the filler hole opening

Fig. 200 . . . then withdraw the plug and drain the manual transaxle oil into a suitable container

2. Remove the filler plug and make sure the oil level is up to the lower edge of the filler plug hole.

3. Check to be sure that the transaxle oil is not noticeably dirty and that it has a suitable viscosity.

DRAIN & REFILL

▶ **See Figures 199 and 200**

1. Make sure the vehicle is parked on a level surface.
2. Raise and safely support the vehicle. Place a suitable drain pan under the manual transaxle.
3. Remove the filler plug and the drain plug and allow the oil to drain completely.
4. Install the drain plug and tighten to 22 ft. lbs. (30 Nm) for 2.0L non-turbo engines, or to 24 ft. lbs. (33 Nm) for 2.0L turbo and 2.4L engines.
5. Refill the transaxle to the proper level, as shown in the Capacities chart, with Hypoid gear oil SAE 75W-85W/75W-90W conforming to API specifications GL-4 or higher or Texaco MTX fluid FM, as applicable. The oil level should be at the bottom of the oil filler hole.
6. When the oil reaches the proper level, install the filler plug and tighten to 22 ft. lbs. (30 Nm) for 2.0L non-turbo engines, or to 24 ft. lbs. (33 Nm) for 2.0L turbo and 2.4L engines.

Automatic Transaxle

FLUID RECOMMENDATIONS

When adding fluid or refilling the transaxle, use Mopar ATF plus (automatic transaxle fluid type 7176) or Diamond ATF SPII, or equivalent.

LEVEL CHECK

▶ **See Figures 201, 202, 203 and 204**

1. Drive the vehicle until normal operating temperature is reached.
2. Place vehicle on level surface.
3. Move the gear selector level into every position. Once this is done, position the shifter in NEUTRAL and apply the parking brake firmly.
4. Wipe the dirt from around the dipstick on the transaxle case. Remove the dipstick and check the condition of the fluid. The fluid should be changed if:
- The fluid smells burnt
- The fluid is discolored
- There is noticeable amounts of metal particles in the fluid

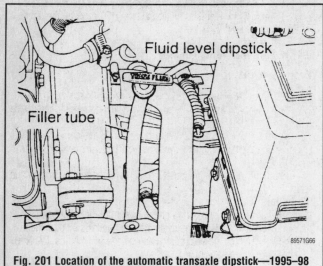

Fig. 201 Location of the automatic transaxle dipstick—1995–98 2.0l non-turbo engine shown

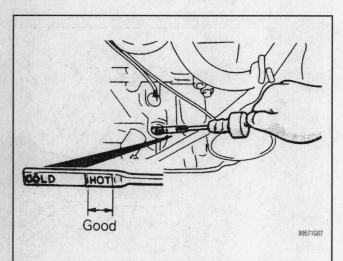

Fig. 202 Automatic transaxle dipstick location—1990–94 vehicles

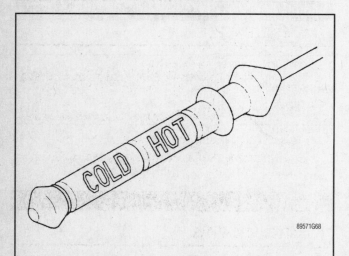

Fig. 203 The fluid level should be within the HOT range—1995–98 2.0L turbo and 2.4L engines shown

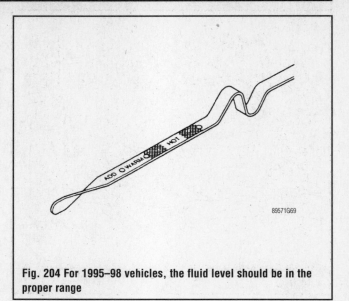

Fig. 204 For 1995–98 vehicles, the fluid level should be in the proper range

5. Wipe the fluid from the end of the dipstick and reinsert it into the transaxle assembly. Pull out the dipstick and inspect the fluid level on the stick.

6. On all vehicles, except 1995–98 2.0L non-turbo engines, the fluid level should be in the HOT range on the stick. If not, add the appropriate fluid to fill to specifications.

7. For 1995–98 2.0L non-turbo engines, if the vehicle has been driven for over 15 minutes before checking the level, the transaxle can be considered hot, and the reading should be above the warm mark. If the vehicle was running for under 15 minutes, but more than 60 seconds, the transaxle is warm and the reading should be above the ADD mark. Add fluid only is the level is below the ADD mark on the dipstick when the transaxle is warm.

8. Inspect the transaxle and related components for fluid leaks. Repair leaks as required.

➡When adding fluid to the transaxle, do not overfill the transaxle. Too much fluid could result in fluid aeration and cause slipping and eventual damage.

DRAIN & REFILL

Except 1995–98 2.0L Non-Turbo Engine

▶ **See Figures 205, 206 and 207**

1. Make sure the vehicle is parked on level ground. Raise and safely support the vehicle, if necessary for access to the drain plug.

2. Place a suitable drain pan with a large opening under the automatic transaxle fluid pan.

3. Remove the drain plug(s) and allow the fluid to drain completely.

4. Unfasten the retainers, then remove the transaxle oil pan.

5. Check the oil filter for damage or restrictions and replace as required.

6. Clean the inside of the pan and the magnets. Make sure the magnets are positioned to the concave part of the oil pan.

7. Clean all gasket mating surfaces.

To install:

8. Install the oil pan with new gasket in place. Install and tighten the retaining bolts to 8 ft. lbs. (12 Nm).

9. Install the oil drain plug with new gasket in place. Tighten the plug to 25 ft. lbs. (35 Nm).

10. Fill the transaxle assembly through the dipstick hole, adding 8.5 pints of specified ATF.

11. Start the engine and allow to idle for 2 minutes. Cycle the gear selector lever through all gears and then position in NEUTRAL. Add sufficient ATF to the transaxle to fill to the lower mark.

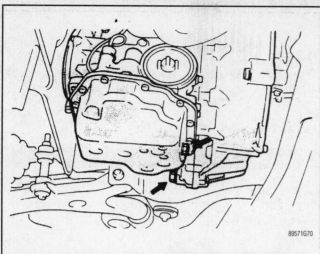

Fig. 205 Automatic transaxle drain plug locations—1990–94 vehicles

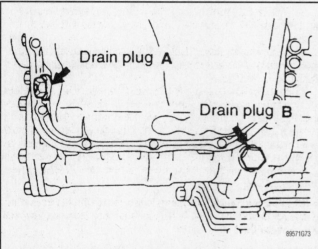

Fig. 206 The 1995–98 2.0L turbo and 2.4L engine have 2 drain plugs

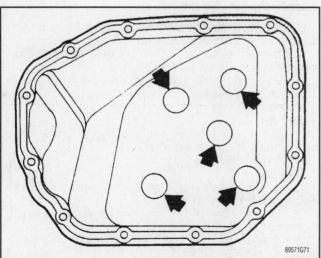

Fig. 207 Positioning of magnets inside of the automatic transaxle oil pan—1990–94 vehicles

12. Allow the engine to reach normal operating temperature. Recheck the fluid level and add until fluid registers at the HOT mark on the dipstick.

13. Inspect for fluid leaks.

1995–98 2.0L Non-Turbo Engines

▶ **See Figure 208**

1. Raise and safely support the vehicle, for access to the fluid pan.
2. Place a suitable drain pan, with a large opening, under the transaxle oil pan.
3. Loosen the fluid pan bolts, then tap the pan at one corner to brake it loose, allowing the fluid to drain. Once the fluid is done draining, remove the pan.
4. Thoroughly clean all the gasket mating surfaces and the oil pan and magnet.

To install:

5. Install a new filter and o-ring on the bottom of the valve body.
6. Apply Loctite® 18718 or equivalent to the transaxle oil pan, then install the pan. Tighten the fluid pan retaining bolts to 14 ft. lbs. (19 Nm).
7. Carefully lower the vehicle.
8. Add 8.0 pts. of the specified fluid through the transaxle fluid dipstick/filler tube.
9. Check the fluid level, as outlined earlier.

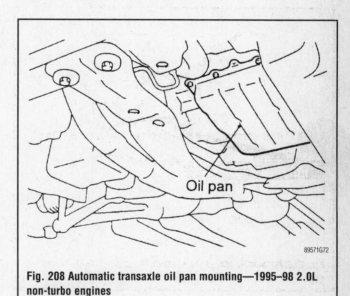

Fig. 208 Automatic transaxle oil pan mounting—1995–98 2.0L non-turbo engines

PAN & FILTER SERVICE

1. Drain and remove the transaxle oil pan.
2. Remove the oil filter retainers and the filter noting exact positioning of both.

To install:

3. Install the oil filter in the exact positioning as removed and secure with the retainers.
4. Install the transaxle oil pan.
5. Refill the transaxle assembly with the correct amount of ATF.
6. Inspect for fluid leaks.

Transfer Case

FLUID RECOMMENDATIONS

When adding fluid or refilling the transfer case, use Hypoid gear oil SAE 75W-85W or 75W-90W conforming to API specifications GL-4 or higher.

LEVEL CHECK

▶ See Figure 209

Inspect each component for leaking. Check the oil level by removing the filler plug. If the oil is contaminated, it is necessary to replace it with new oil.

1. Park the vehicle on level surface.
2. Remove the filler plug and make sure the oil level reaches the lower edge of the filler plug hole.
3. Check to be sure that the oil is not noticeably dirty and that it has the proper viscosity.
4. If necessary, add oil through the filler hole until is runs out of the hole.

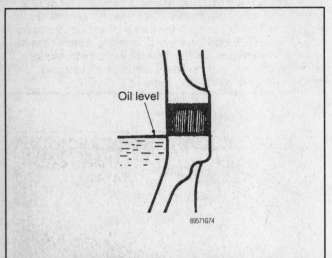

89571G74

Fig. 209 Check to be sure the fluid reaches the bottom edge of the transfer case filler plug hole

DRAIN & REFILL

▶ See Figure 210

1. Raise and safely support the vehicle, for access to the transfer case.
2. Place a suitable drain pan under the transfer case fluid drain plug.

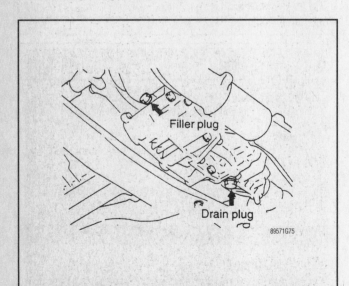

89571G75

Fig. 210 Location of the transfer case filler and drain plugs

3. Remove the filler and the drain plug and allow the oil to drain into the drain pan.
4. After the fluid has drained completely, install the drain plug and tighten to 24 ft. lbs. (32 Nm).
5. Refill the transfer case to the proper level with Hypoid gear oil SAE 75W-85W/75W-90W conforming to API specifications GL-4 or higher. The oil level should reach the bottom edge of the oil filler hole.
6. Install the transfer case filler plug and tighten to 24 ft. lbs. (32 Nm).
7. Carefully lower the vehicle.

Rear Axle

FLUID RECOMMENDATIONS

▶ See Figure 211

Since fluid viscosity range may vary depending on specific temperature range of operation, please refer to the accompanying chart for the proper fluid for your vehicle.

Lubricant	API classification GL-5 or higher
Anticipated temperature range	Viscosity range
Above −23°C (−10°F)	SAE 90 SAE 85W-90 SAE 80W-90
−23°C to −34°C (−10°F to −30°F)	SAE 80W, SAE 80W-90
Below −34°C (−30°F)	SAE 75W

89571G76

Fig. 211 Rear axle lubricant application chart

LEVEL CHECK

1. Make sure the vehicle is parked on level ground.
2. Remove the oil fill plug to check the oil level.
3. The oil level is sufficient if it reaches the lower portion of the filler plug hole. If the fluid is low, add as required through the filler plug.

DRAIN & REFILL

▶ See Figure 212

1. Position the vehicle on a flat surface or raise and safely support the vehicle in a level position.
2. Place a suitable drain pan under the rear axle.
3. Remove the filler and the drain plugs and allow the oil to drain completely into the pan.
4. Install the drain plug and tighten to 24 ft. lbs. (32 Nm).
5. Refill the rear axle with the proper type and amount of fluid. The level should reach the bottom of the oil filler hole.
6. Install the filler plug and tighten to 24 ft. lbs. (32 Nm).
7. If raised, carefully lower the vehicle.

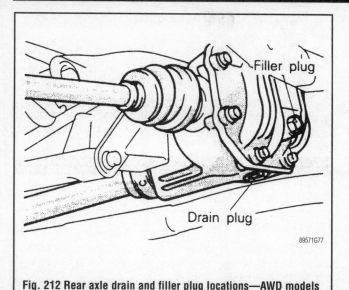

Fig. 212 Rear axle drain and filler plug locations—AWD models

Cooling System

♦ See Figure 213

✳✳ CAUTION

When draining the coolant, keep in mind that cats and dogs are attracted by ethylene glycol antifreeze, and are quite likely to drink any that is left in an uncovered container or in puddles on the ground. This will prove fatal in sufficient quantity. Always drain the coolant into a sealable container. Coolant should be reused unless it is contaminated or several years old (in which case it should be taken to a recycling facility such as a service station).

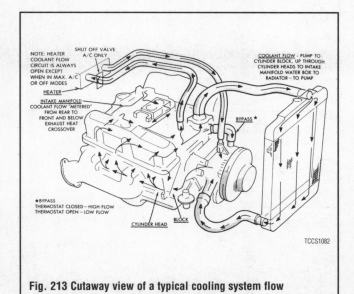

Fig. 213 Cutaway view of a typical cooling system flow

FLUID RECOMMENDATIONS

The cooling fluid or antifreeze normally should be changed every 30,000 miles (48,000 km) or 24 months. When replacing the fluid, use a mixture of 50% water and 50% ethylene glycol antifreeze.

LEVEL CHECK

♦ See Figures 214, 215 and 216

Check the coolant level every 3,000 miles or once a month. In hot weather operation, it may be a good idea to check the level once a week. Check for loose connections and signs of deterioration of the coolant hoses. Check the coolant level in the reservoir when the engine is cold, making sure the level is at the FULL or MAX mark. If the bottle is empty, check the level in the radiator and refill as necessary. Then fill the bottle up to the FULL or MAX level.

✳✳ CAUTION

Never remove the radiator cap when the vehicle is hot or over-heated. Wait until it has cooled. Place a thick cloth over the radiator cap to shield yourself from the heat and turn the radiator cap, SLIGHTLY, until the sound of escaping pressure can be heard. DO NOT turn any more; allow the pressure to release gradually. When no more pressure can be heard escaping, remove the cap with the heavy cloth, CAUTIOUSLY.

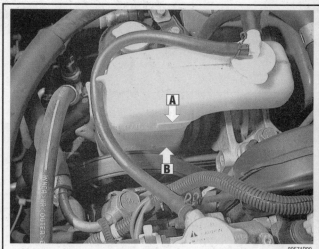

Fig. 214 The coolant reservoir has FULL (A) and LOW (B) marks located on the tank

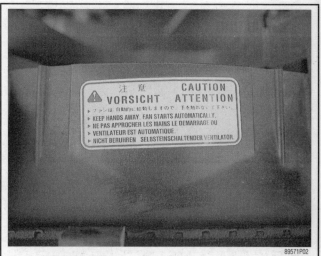

Fig. 215 Be EXTREMELY careful when working around the electric cooling fan

Fig. 216 Add the proper water/coolant mixture to the reservoir until the fluid reaches the proper level

➡**Never add cold water to an overheated engine.**

After filling the radiator, run the engine until it reaches normal operating temperature, to make sure that the thermostat has opened and all the air is bled from the system.

DRAIN & REFILL

▶ **See Figures 217 thru 223**

✻✻ CAUTION

Do not remove a radiator cap while the engine and radiator are still hot. Danger of burns by scalding fluid and steam under pressure may result!

1. Make sure the vehicle is parked on a level surface.
2. Remove the coolant recovery reservoir fill cap.
3. With a cool engine, slowly rotate the radiator cap counterclockwise to the detent without pressing down on the cap.
4. Wait until any remaining pressure is relieved by listening for a hissing sound.

Fig. 217 NEVER remove the radiator cap when the engine is hot!

5. After all the pressure is relieved, press down on the cap and continue to rotate the radiator cap counterclockwise.
6. With a suitable container to catch the fluid under the radiator, open the radiator drain cock.
7. If equipped, remove the engine block drain plugs. This will help to drain the coolant from the block.
8. Loosen or slide the recovery tank hose clamp at the radiator filler neck overflow tube and remove the hose. Holding the hose down to the drain pan, allow the recovery tank to empty. Attach the hose to the filler neck overflow and tighten the clamp.

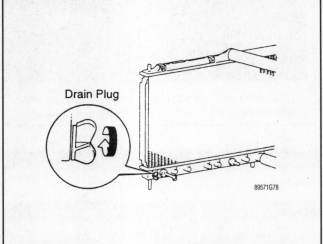

Fig. 218 The radiator drain cock is located at the bottom corner of the radiator

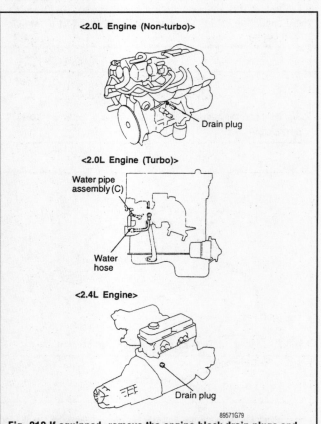

Fig. 219 If equipped, remove the engine block drain plugs and let the coolant drain into a suitable container

Fig. 220 Refill the system by adding coolant through the radiator filler neck

Fig. 221 Cooling systems should be pressure tested for leaks periodically

TOOL C-4080

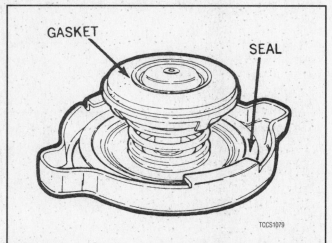

GASKET

SEAL

Fig. 222 Be sure the rubber gasket on the radiator cap has a tight seal

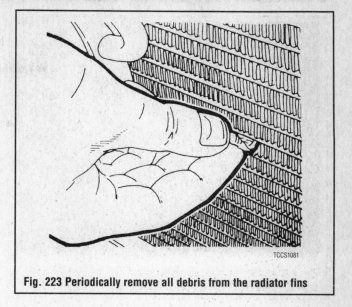

Fig. 223 Periodically remove all debris from the radiator fins

9. Close the radiator drain cock and install the engine block drain plug.

10. Add enough coolant mixture to fill the system to a level just below the radiator neck. Fill the reservoir assembly to the FULL mark.

➡ **Fill the cooling system with a 50/50 mixture of water and Ethylene Glycol antifreeze.**

11. Firmly set the parking brake. Run the engine with the radiator cap OFF, until normal operating temperature is reached.

✳✳ CAUTION

Under some conditions, ethylene glycol is flammable. To avoid being burned when adding engine coolant, do not spill it on the exhaust system or on hot engine parts.

12. With the engine idling, add engine coolant to the radiator until the level reaches the bottom of the radiator fill neck. Install the cap assembly.

➡ **Never add cold water to an overheated engine.**

13. Add coolant to the recovery tank, as necessary.

14. After filling the radiator and recovery tank, run the engine until it reaches normal operating temperature, to make sure that the thermostat has opened and all the air is bled from the system.

FLUSHING & CLEANING THE SYSTEM

1. Drain the cooling system. Close the petcock slightly.

2. Remove the thermostat from the engine. Disconnect the upper radiator hose at the radiator neck.

3. Install a high pressure hose into the thermostat housing and allow the water pressure to back-flush the system.

4. Continue this procedure until the water coming from the hose is clean.

5. Reverse the removal procedure and refill the cooling system with fresh coolant.

Brake Master Cylinder

FLUID RECOMMENDATIONS

▶ **See Figure 224**

When adding fluid to the brake master cylinder, use a quality brake fluid of the DOT 3 or DOT 4 specifications. Never reuse old brake fluid.

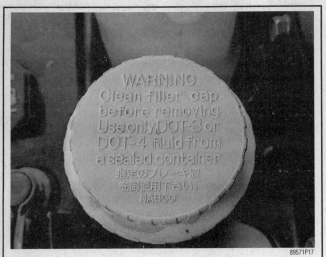

Fig. 224 If it becomes necessary to add brake fluid, make sure to use the proper type

✳✳ CAUTION

Be careful to avoid spilling any brake fluid on painted surfaces, because the paint coat will become discolored or damaged.

LEVEL CHECK

▶ See Figures 225, 226 and 227

Check the levels of brake fluid in the brake master cylinder reservoir once a month or every 3,000 miles (4,800 km). The fluid level should be maintained to a level between the MAX and the MIN lines on the master cylinder reservoir. Never add a mixture of fluid. Any sudden decrease in the level in the reservoir indicates a leak in the brake system and should be checked out immediately. A slight gradual decrease in the fluid level in the master cylinder is normal due to brake pad wear.

Fig. 225 Make sure the master cylinder reservoir cap is clean, then unscrew the cap from the reservoir

Fig. 226 Remove the lid from the brake master cylinder fluid reservoir . . .

Fig. 227 When adding brake fluid, always use fluid from a fresh, sealed container

Clutch Master Cylinder

FLUID RECOMMENDATIONS

When adding or changing the fluid in the systems, use a quality brake fluid conforming to DOT 3 specifications. Never reuse old brake fluid.

LEVEL CHECK

▶ See Figures 228, 229 and 230

1. If necessary, remove the air cleaner assembly to gain access to the clutch master cylinder cap.
2. Wipe the clutch master cylinder reservoir cap and the surrounding area clean with a shop towel.
3. Inspect the fluid in the reservoir, making sure fluid is between the MAX and the MIN marks.
4. If required, remove the clutch master cylinder reservoir lid, then add fresh fluid to fill to the top full mark on the reservoir.

Fig. 228 The clutch master cylinder has MAX (A) and MIN (B) fill lines on the reservoir

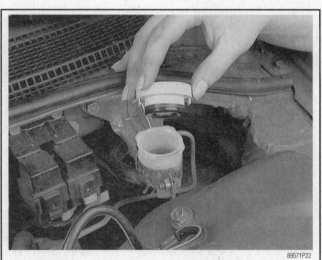

Fig. 229 Remove the clutch master cylinder lid by pulling it straight up and off the reservoir

Fig. 230 If the fluid is low, add until it reaches the proper level on the side of the reservoir

✳✳ CAUTION

Be careful to avoid spilling any brake fluid on painted surfaces, because the paint coat will become discolored or damaged.

5. Reinstall the lid onto the clutch master cylinder.
6. If removed, install the air cleaner assembly.

Power Steering Pump

FLUID RECOMMENDATIONS

When adding or changing the power steering fluid, use Dexron®II ATF (Automatic Transmission Fluid). The system uses approximately 0.95 qts. of fluid.

LEVEL CHECK

▶ **See Figures 231, 232, 233 and 234**

Like all other general maintenance items, check every 3,000 miles (4,800 km) or once a month. Inspect the oil level in the reservoir by check-

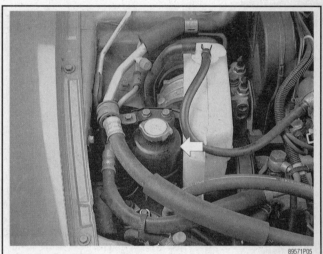

Fig. 231 The power steering fluid reservoir can be found in the right front of the engine compartment

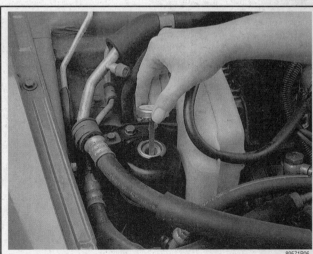

Fig. 232 Twist the reservoir cap, then lift up on the integral cap/dipstick assembly

Fig. 233 Make sure the fluid lines are between the MIN (A) and MAX (B) lines on the dipstick

Fig. 234 If the power steering level is low, use a funnel to add fluid until the proper level is reached

ing the position of the fluid against the mark on the dipstick. Add fluid to the reservoir if the fluid does not reach the appropriate full line.

Chassis Greasing

On most models, the manufacturer doesn't install lubrication fittings on lube points on the steering linkage or suspension. However, if the lubrication point does have a grease fitting, lubricate with multipurpose NLGI No. 2 (Lithium base) grease.

Body Lubrication and Maintenance

Body hinges and latches should be lubricated as needed to maintain smooth operation of doors, hoods and latches. When required, lubricate the hood lock latch, door lock strikers, seat adjusters, liftgate lock and the parking brake control cable mechanism with multipurpose NLGI No. 2 (Lithium base) grease. Wipe area to be lubricated clean with a shop rag and inspect for damage or misalignment. Adjust the component, if required, prior to lubrication.

Keeping your vehicle clean extends the beauty and the life of your vehicle. When washing your car with high pressure car washing equipment or steam car washing equipment, be sure to stay back away from the vehicle. Be sure to maintain the spray nozzle at a distance of at least 12 in. (300mm) from any plastic parts and all opening parts such as doors, luggage compartment, hood, etc. Do not clean aluminum wheels with pressure or steam cleaners or damage to the finish will occur.

Wheel Bearings

REPACKING

The wheel bearings used on these vehicles are sealed units and do not require routine maintenance. For removal and installation instructions, please refer to Section 7 (for rear bearings) or Section 8 (for front bearings).

TRAILER TOWING

General Recommendations

Your vehicle was primarily designed to carry passengers and cargo. It is important to remember that towing a trailer will place additional loads on your vehicles engine, drivetrain, steering, braking and other systems. However, if you decide to tow a trailer, using the prior equipment is a must.

Local laws may require specific equipment such as trailer brakes or fender mounted mirrors. Check your local laws.

Trailer Weight

The weight of the trailer is the most important factor. A good weight-to-horsepower ratio is about 35:1, 35 lbs. of Gross Combined Weight (GCW) for every horsepower your engine develops. Multiply the engine's rated horsepower by 35 and subtract the weight of the vehicle passengers and luggage. The number remaining is the approximate ideal maximum weight you should tow, although a numerically higher axle ratio can help compensate for heavier weight.

Hitch (Tongue) Weight

▶ See Figure 235

Calculate the hitch weight in order to select a proper hitch. The weight of the hitch is usually 9–11% of the trailer gross weight and should be measured with the trailer loaded. Hitches fall into various categories: those that mount on the frame and rear bumper, the bolt-on type, or the weld-on distribution type used for larger trailers. Axle mounted or clamp-on bumper hitches should never be used.

Check the gross weight rating of your trailer. Tongue weight is usually figured as 10% of gross trailer weight. Therefore, a trailer with a maximum gross weight of 2000 lbs. will have a maximum tongue weight of 200 lbs. Class I trailers fall into this category. Class II trailers are those with a gross weight rating of 2000–3000 lbs., while Class III trailers fall into the 3500–6000 lbs. category. Class IV trailers are those over 6000 lbs. and are for use with fifth wheel trucks, only.

When you've determined the hitch that you'll need, follow the manufacturer's installation instructions, exactly, especially when it comes to fastener

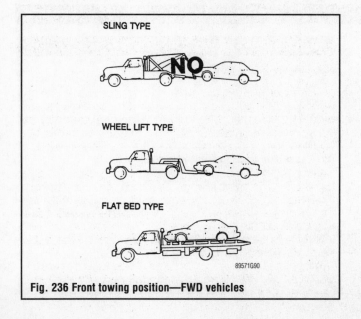

Fig. 235 Calculating proper tongue weight for your trailer

torques. The hitch will subjected to a lot of stress and good hitches come with hardened bolts. Never substitute an inferior bolt for a hardened bolt.

Cooling

ENGINE

Aftermarket engine oil coolers are helpful for prolonging engine oil life and reducing overall engine temperatures. Both of these factors increase engine life. While not absolutely necessary in towing Class I and some Class II trailers, they are recommended for heavier Class II and all Class III towing. Engine oil cooler systems usually consist of an adapter, screwed on in place of the oil filter, a remote filter mounting and a multi-tube, finned

TOWING THE VEHICLE

Front Wheel Drive Models

▶ **See Figures 236 and 237**

To prevent the bumper from deforming, these vehicles cannot be towed by a wrecker using sling-type equipment. If these vehicles require towing,

heat exchanger, which is mounted in front of the radiator or air conditioning condenser.

TRANSAXLE

An automatic transaxle is usually recommended for trailer towing. Modern automatics have proven reliable and, of course, easy to operate, in trailer towing. The increased load of a trailer, however, causes an increase in the temperature of the automatic transaxle fluid. Heat is the worst enemy of an automatic transaxle. As the temperature of the fluid increases, the life of the fluid decreases.

It is essential, therefore, that you install an automatic transaxle cooler. The cooler, which consists of a multi-tube, finned heat exchanger, is usually installed in front of the radiator or air conditioning compressor, and hooked in-line with the transaxle cooler tank inlet line. Follow the cooler manufacturer's installation instructions.

Select a cooler of at least adequate capacity, based upon the combined gross weights of the vehicle and trailer.

Cooler manufacturers recommend that you use an aftermarket cooler in addition to, and not instead of, the present cooling tank in your radiator. If you do want to use it in place of the radiator cooling tank, get a cooler at least two sizes larger than normally necessary.

➡**A transaxle cooler can, sometimes, cause slow or harsh shifting in the transaxle during cold weather, until the fluid has a chance to come up to normal operating temperature. Some coolers can be purchased with or retrofitted with a temperature bypass valve which will allow fluid flow through the cooler only when the fluid has reached above a certain operating temperature.**

Handling A Trailer

Towing a trailer with ease and safety requires a certain amount of experience. It's a good idea to learn the feel of a trailer by practicing turning, stopping and backing in an open area such as an empty parking lot.

use a wheel lift or flat bed equipment. It is recommended that the vehicle be towed from the front if a flat bed is not available.

Manual transaxle vehicles may be towed from the rear provided that the transaxle is in Neutral and the driveline has not been damaged. The steering wheel must be clamped in the straight-ahead position with a steering wheel clamping device designed for towing service use.

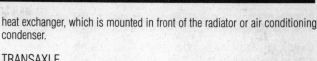

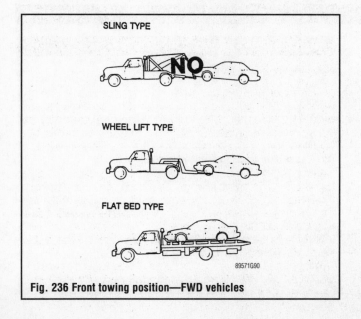

Fig. 236 Front towing position—FWD vehicles

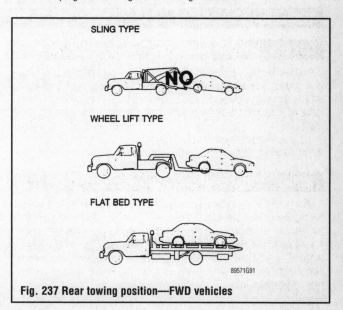

Fig. 237 Rear towing position—FWD vehicles

✳✳ CAUTION

Do not use the steering column lock to secure the front wheel position for towing.

Automatic transaxle vehicles may be towed on the front wheels at speeds not to exceed 30 mph (50 km/h) for a distance not to exceed 18 miles (30 km). If these limits can not be met, then the front wheels must be placed on a tow dolly.

All Wheel Drive Models

▶ See Figure 238

All Wheel Drive vehicles should only be towed with all 4 wheels on the ground or lifted from the road surface. This means that the vehicle is to be towed either with flatbed equipment, with all wheels on dollies or flat towed. Damage to the viscous coupling may result if the vehicle is towed with only 2 wheels on the ground.

Towing methods	Remarks
If a tow truck is used Lifting method for 4 wheels—**Good**	• For 4WD models, the basic principle is that all four wheels are to be raised before towing. • The shift lever should be set to 1st gear and the parking brake should be applied.
Front wheels lifted—**No good**	• The vehicle must not be towed by placing only its front wheels or only the rear wheels on a rolling dolly, because to do so will result in deterioration of the viscous coupling and result in the viscous coupling causing the vehicle to jump forward suddenly.
Front wheels lifted—**No good**	• If only the front wheels or only the rear wheels are lifted for towing, the bumper will be damaged. In addition, lifting of the rear wheels causes the oil to flow forward, and may result in heat damage to the rear bushing of the transfer, and so should never be done.
Rear wheels lifted—**No good**	
Towing by rope or cable—**Good**	• The front and rear wheels must rotate normally. • The various mechanisms must function normally. • The shift lever must be set to the neutral position and the ignition key must be set to "ACC".

89571G92

Fig. 238 Towing instructions—AWD models

JUMP STARTING A DEAD BATTERY

▶ See Figure 239

Whenever a vehicle is jump started, precautions must be followed in order to prevent the possibility of personal injury. Remember that batteries contain a small amount of explosive hydrogen gas which is a by-product of battery charging. Sparks should always be avoided when working around batteries, especially when attaching jumper cables. To minimize the possibility of accidental sparks, follow the procedure carefully.

✳✳ CAUTION

NEVER hook the batteries up in a series circuit or the entire electrical system will go up in smoke, including the starter!

Vehicles equipped with a diesel engine may utilize two 12 volt batteries. If so, the batteries are connected in a parallel circuit (positive terminal to positive terminal, negative terminal to negative terminal). Hooking the batteries up in parallel circuit increases battery cranking power without increasing total battery voltage output. Output remains at 12 volts. On the other hand, hooking two 12 volt batteries up in a series circuit (positive terminal to negative terminal, positive terminal to negative terminal) increases total battery output to 24 volts (12 volts plus 12 volts).

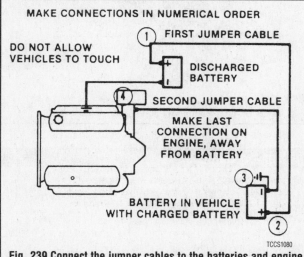

Fig. 239 Connect the jumper cables to the batteries and engine in the order shown

Jump Starting Precautions

- Be sure that both batteries are of the same voltage. Vehicles covered by this manual and most vehicles on the road today utilize a 12 volt charging system.
- Be sure that both batteries are of the same polarity (have the same terminal, in most cases NEGATIVE grounded).
- Be sure that the vehicles are not touching or a short could occur.
- On serviceable batteries, be sure the vent cap holes are not obstructed.
- Do not smoke or allow sparks anywhere near the batteries.
- In cold weather, make sure the battery electrolyte is not frozen. This can occur more readily in a battery that has been in a state of discharge.
- Do not allow electrolyte to contact your skin or clothing.

Jump Starting Procedure

1. Make sure that the voltages of the 2 batteries are the same. Most batteries and charging systems are of the 12 volt variety.
2. Pull the jumping vehicle (with the good battery) into a position so the jumper cables can reach the dead battery and that vehicle's engine. Make sure that the vehicles do NOT touch.
3. Place the transmissions/transaxles of both vehicles in **Neutral** (MT) or **P** (AT), as applicable, then firmly set their parking brakes.

➡If necessary for safety reasons, the hazard lights on both vehicles may be operated throughout the entire procedure without significantly increasing the difficulty of jumping the dead battery.

4. Turn all lights and accessories OFF on both vehicles. Make sure the ignition switches on both vehicles are turned to the **OFF** position.
5. Cover the battery cell caps with a rag, but do not cover the terminals.
6. Make sure the terminals on both batteries are clean and free of corrosion or proper electrical connection will be impeded. If necessary, clean the battery terminals before proceeding.
7. Identify the positive (+) and negative (–) terminals on both batteries.
8. Connect the first jumper cable to the positive (+) terminal of the dead battery, then connect the other end of that cable to the positive (+) terminal of the booster (good) battery.
9. Connect one end of the other jumper cable to the negative (–) terminal on the booster battery and the final cable clamp to an engine bolt head, alternator bracket or other solid, metallic point on the engine with the dead battery. Try to pick a ground on the engine that is positioned away from the battery in order to minimize the possibility of the 2 clamps touching should one loosen during the procedure. DO NOT connect this clamp to the negative (–) terminal of the bad battery.

✳✳ CAUTION

Be very careful to keep the jumper cables away from moving parts (cooling fan, belts, etc.) on both engines.

10. Check to make sure that the cables are routed away from any moving parts, then start the donor vehicle's engine. Run the engine at moderate speed for several minutes to allow the dead battery a chance to receive some initial charge.
11. With the donor vehicle's engine still running slightly above idle, try to start the vehicle with the dead battery. Crank the engine for no more than 10 seconds at a time and let the starter cool for at least 20 seconds between tries. If the vehicle does not start in 3 tries, it is likely that something else is also wrong or that the battery needs additional time to charge.
12. Once the vehicle is started, allow it to run at idle for a few seconds to make sure that it is operating properly.
13. Turn ON the headlights, heater blower and, if equipped, the rear defroster of both vehicles in order to reduce the severity of voltage spikes and subsequent risk of damage to the vehicles' electrical systems when the cables are disconnected. This step is especially important to any vehicle equipped with computer control modules.
14. Carefully disconnect the cables in the reverse order of connection. Start with the negative cable that is attached to the engine ground, then the negative cable on the donor battery. Disconnect the positive cable from the donor battery and finally, disconnect the positive cable from the formerly dead battery. Be careful when disconnecting the cables from the positive terminals not to allow the alligator clips to touch any metal on either vehicle or a short and sparks will occur.

JACKING

▶ **See Figures 240 and 241**

Your vehicle was supplied with a jack for emergency road repairs. This jack is fine for changing a flat tire or other short term procedures not requiring you to go beneath the vehicle. If it is used in an emergency situation, carefully follow the instructions provided either with the jack or in your owner's manual. Do not attempt to use the jack on any portions of the vehicle other than specified by the vehicle manufacturer. Always block the diagonally opposite wheel when using a jack.

Jack receptacles are located at the body sills to accept the scissors jack supplied with the vehicle. Always block the opposite wheels and jack the vehicle on a level surface.

❈❈ CAUTION

Climbing under a car supported by just the jack is extremely dangerous and should NEVER be done.

A more convenient way of jacking is the use of a garage or floor jack. You may use the floor jack in the following locations:
Front:
- FWD—Under the mid point of the crossmember
- AWD—Under the mid point of the crossmember
Rear:
- FWD—Under the jack up bracket of the rear floor pan
- AWD—Under the rear differential
Never place the jack under the radiator, engine or transmission components. Severe and expensive damage will result when the jack is raised. Additionally, never jack under the floorpan or bodywork; the metal will deform.

Whenever you plan to work under the vehicle, you must support it on jackstands or ramps. Never use cinder blocks or stacks of wood to support the vehicle, even if you're only going to be under it for a few minutes. Never crawl under the vehicle when it is supported only by the tire-changing jack or other floor jack.

➡**Always position a block of wood or small rubber pad on top of the jack or jackstand to protect the lifting point's finish when lifting or supporting the vehicle.**

Small hydraulic, screw, or scissors jacks are satisfactory for raising the vehicle. Drive-on trestles or ramps are also a handy and safe way to both raise and support the vehicle. Be careful though, some ramps may be too steep to drive your vehicle onto without scraping the front bottom panels. Never support the vehicle on any suspension member (unless specifically instructed to do so by a repair manual) or by an underbody panel.

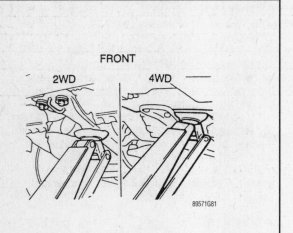

Fig. 240 Floor jack positioning on the front of the vehicle

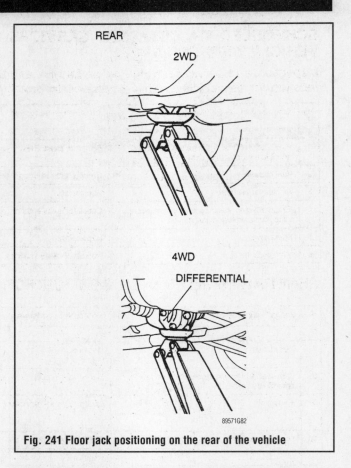

Fig. 241 Floor jack positioning on the rear of the vehicle

Jacking Precautions

The following safety points cannot be overemphasized:
- Always block the opposite wheel or wheels to keep the vehicle from rolling off the jack.
- When raising the front of the vehicle, firmly apply the parking brake.
- When the drive wheels are to remain on the ground, leave the vehicle in gear to help prevent it from rolling.
- Always use jackstands to support the vehicle when you are working underneath. Place the stands beneath the vehicle's jacking brackets. Before climbing underneath, rock the vehicle a bit to make sure it is firmly supported.
- Never use a jack at the lateral rod or the rear suspension assembly on a FWD vehicle.
- In order to prevent scaring of the centermember on FWD vehicle, or crossmember on AWD vehicle, place a piece of cloth or rubber pad on the jack's contact surface. This will prevent the formation of corrosion caused by damage to the protective coating.
- A floor jack must never be used on any part of the underbody.
- Do not attempt to raise one entire side of the vehicle by placing the jack midway between he front and the rear wheels. This practice may result in permanent damage to the body.

SCHEDULED MAINTENANCE TABLE

SCHEDULED MAINTENANCE SERVICES FOR EMISSION CONTROL AND PROPER VEHICLE PERFORMANCE

Inspection and services should be performed any time a malfunction is observed or suspected. Retain receipts for all vehicle emission services to protect your emission warranty.

No.	Emission control system maintenance	Service to be performed	Kilometers in thousands	24	48	72	96	120	144	168
			Mileage in thousands	15	30	45	60	75	90	105
1	Fuel system (Tank, pipe line and connection, and fuel tank filler tube cap)	Check for leaks Every 5 years or					×			
2	Fuel hoses	Check condition Every 2 years or			×		×		×	
3	Air cleaner element	Replace at			×		×		×	
4	Evaporative emission control system (except evaporative emission canister)	Check for leaks and clogging Every 5 years or					×			
5	Spark plugs	Replace at			×		×		×	
6	Ignition cables	Replace Every 5 years or					×			

GENERAL MAINTENANCE SERVICE FOR PROPER VEHICLE PERFORMANCE

No.	General maintenance		Service to be performed	Kilometers in thousands	24	48	72	96	120	144	168
				Mileage in thousands	15	30	45	60	75	90	105
7	Timing belts		Replace at					×* 1		160,000 km*2 (100,000 miles)	
8	Drive belt (for generator, water pump, power steering pump)		Check condition at			×		×		×	
9	Engine oil	Non-turbo	Change Every 6 months or	Every 12,000 km (7,500 miles)							
		Turbo		Every 8,000 km (5,000 miles)							
10	Engine oil filter	Non-turbo	Replace Every Year*3 or	×	×	×	×	×	×	×	×
		Turbo	Replace Every Year or	Every 16,000 km (10,000 miles)							
11	Manual transaxle oil		Check oil level at			×		×		×	
12	Automatic transaxle fluid		Check fluid level Every year or	×	×	×	×	×	×	×	×
13	Transfer oil		Check oil level at			×		×		×	
14	Engine coolant		Change Every 2 years or			×		×		×	
15	Disc brake pads		Check for wear Every year or	×	×	×	×	×	×	×	×
16	Rear drum brake linings and rear wheel cylinders (vehicles without disc brakes for all wheels)		Check for wear and leaks Evety 2 years or			×		×		×	
17	Brake hoses		Check for deterioration or leaks Every year or	×	×	×	×	×	×	×	×
18	Ball joint and steering linkage seals		Check for grease leaks and damage Every 2 years or			×		×		×	
19	Drive shaft boots		Check for grease leaks and damage Every year or	×	×	×	×	×	×	×	×
20	Rear axle oil		Check oil level at			×		×		×	
21	SRS*4 system		Check system	At 10 years							
22	Exhaust system (connection portion of muffler, pipings and converter heat shields)		Check and service as required Every 2 years or			×		×		×	

NOTES
*1: For California, this maintenance is recommended but not required
*2: Not required if belt was previously changed.
*3: If the mileage is less than 12,000 km (7,500 miles) each year, the oil filter should be replaced at every oil change.
*4: Supplemental Restraint system

89571C01

SCHEDULED MAINTENANCE UNDER SEVERE USAGE CONDITIONS

The maintenance items should be performed according to the following table:

No.	Maintenance item	Service to be performed	Kilometers in thousands	24	48	72	96	120	144	168	Severe usage conditions
			Mileage in Thousands	15	30	45	60	75	90	105	
3	Air cleaner element	Replace		×	×	×	×	×	×	×	A and E
5	Spark plugs	Replace		×	×	×	×	×	×	×	B and D
9	Engine oil	Change Every 3 months or	Every 4,800 km (3,000 miles)								A, B, C, D and G
10	Engine oil filter	Replace Every 6 months or	Every 9,600 km (6,000 miles)								A, B, C, D and G
11	Manual transaxle oil	Change oil*1			×		×		×		B, G and H
12	Automatic transaxle fluid	Change fluid			×		×		×		B, G and H
13	Transfer oil	Change oil			×		×		×		B, G and H
15	Disc brake pads	Check for wear Every 6 months or	Every 9,600km (6,000 miles)								A and F
16	Rear drum brake linings and rear wheel cylinders (vehicles without disc brakes for all wheels)	Check for wear and leaks Every 12 months or	Every 24,000km (15,000 miles)								A and F

*1: Vehicles with turbocharger.

Severe usage conditions

A – Driving in dusty conditions
B – Trailer towing or police, taxi, or commercial type operation
C – Extensive idling, driving in stop and go traffic
D – Short-trip operation at freezing temperatures (engine not throughly warmed up)

E – Driving in sandy areas
F – Driving in salty areas
G – More than 50% operation in heavy city traffic or at sustained high speeds during hot weather above 32°C (90°F)
H – Driving on off-road

89571C02

CAPACITIES

Year	Model	Engine ID/VIN	Engine Displacement Liters (cc)	Engine Oil with Filter	Transmission (pts.)		Transfer Case (pts.)	Drive Axle		Fuel Tank (gal.)	Cooling System (qts.)
					5-Spd	Auto.		Front (pts.)	Rear (pts.)		
1990	Eclipse	T	1.8 (1775)	4.1	3.8	12.8	—	—	—	15.9	6.6
	Eclipse	R	2.0 (1997)	4.6	3.8	12.8	—	—	—	15.9	7.6
	Eclipse	U	2.0 (1997)	4.6	①	12.8	1.3	—	1.5	15.9	7.6
	Laser	T	1.8 (1775)	4.1	3.8	12.8	—	—	—	15.9	6.6
	Laser	R	2.0 (1997)	4.6	3.8	12.8	—	—	—	15.9	7.6
	Laser	U	2.0 (1997)	4.6	①	12.8	1.3	—	1.5	15.9	7.6
	Talon	R	2.0 (1997)	4.6	3.8	12.8	—	—	—	15.9	7.6
	Talon	U	2.0 (1997)	4.6	①	12.8	1.3	—	1.5	15.9	7.6
1991	Eclipse	T	1.8 (1775)	4.1	3.8	12.8	—	—	—	15.9	6.6
	Eclipse	R	2.0 (1997)	4.6	3.8	12.8	—	—	—	15.9	7.6
	Eclipse	U	2.0 (1997)	4.6	①	12.8	1.3	—	1.5	15.9	7.6
	Laser	T	1.8 (1775)	4.1	3.8	12.8	—	—	—	15.9	6.6
	Laser	R	2.0 (1997)	4.6	3.8	12.8	—	—	—	15.9	7.6
	Laser	U	2.0 (1997)	4.6	①	12.8	1.3	—	1.5	15.9	7.6
	Talon	R	2.0 (1997)	4.6	3.8	12.8	—	—	—	15.9	7.6
	Talon	U	2.0 (1997)	4.6	①	12.8	1.3	—	1.5	15.9	7.6
1992	Eclipse	T	1.8 (1775)	4.1	3.8	12.8	—	—	—	15.9	6.6
	Eclipse	R	2.0 (1997)	4.6	3.8	12.8	—	—	—	15.9	7.6
	Eclipse	U	2.0 (1997)	4.6	①	12.8	1.3	—	1.5	15.9	7.6
	Laser	T	1.8 (1775)	4.1	3.8	12.8	—	—	—	15.9	6.6
	Laser	R	2.0 (1997)	4.6	3.8	12.8	—	—	—	15.9	7.6
	Laser	U	2.0 (1997)	4.6	①	12.8	1.3	—	1.5	15.9	7.6
	Talon	R	2.0 (1997)	4.6	3.8	12.8	—	—	—	15.9	7.6
	Talon	U	2.0 (1997)	4.6	①	12.8	1.3	—	1.5	15.9	7.6
1993	Eclipse	B	1.8 (1775)	4.1	3.8	12.8	—	—	—	15.9	6.6
	Eclipse	E	2.0 (1997)	4.6	3.8	12.8	—	—	—	15.9	7.6
	Eclipse	F	2.0 (1997)	4.8	4.8	14.8	1.3	—	1.5	15.9	7.6
	Laser	B	1.8 (1775)	4.1	3.8	12.8	—	—	—	15.9	6.6
	Laser	E	2.0 (1997)	4.6	3.8	12.8	—	—	—	15.9	7.6
	Laser	F	2.0 (1997)	4.8	4.8	14.8	1.3	—	1.5	15.9	7.6
	Talon	B	1.8 (1775)	4.1	3.8	12.8	—	—	—	15.9	7.6
	Talon	E	2.0 (1997)	4.6	3.8	12.8	—	—	—	15.9	7.6
	Talon	F	2.0 (1997)	4.8	4.8	14.8	1.3	—	1.5	15.9	7.6
1994	Eclipse	B	1.8 (1775)	4.1	3.8	12.8	—	—	—	15.9	6.6
	Eclipse	E	2.0 (1997)	4.6	3.8	12.8	—	—	—	15.9	7.6
	Eclipse	F	2.0 (1997)	4.8	4.8	14.8	1.3	—	1.5	15.9	7.6
	Laser	B	1.8 (1775)	4.1	3.8	12.8	—	—	—	15.9	6.6
	Laser	E	2.0 (1997)	4.6	3.8	12.8	—	—	—	15.9	7.6
	Laser	F	2.0 (1997)	4.8	4.8	14.8	1.3	—	1.5	15.9	7.6
	Talon	B	1.8 (1775)	4.1	3.8	12.8	—	—	—	15.9	7.6
	Talon	E	2.0 (1997)	4.6	3.8	12.8	—	—	—	15.9	7.6
	Talon	F	2.0 (1997)	4.8	4.8	14.8	1.3	—	1.5	15.9	7.6
1995	Eclipse	Y	2.0 (1997)	4.5	4.2	18.2	—	—	—	15.9	7.4
	Eclipse	F	2.0 (1997)	5.0	②	14.2	1.1	—	1.8	15.9	7.4
	Talon	Y	2.0 (1997)	4.5	4.2	18.2	—	—	—	15.9	7.4
	Talon	F	2.0 (1997)	5.0	②	14.2	1.1	—	1.8	15.9	7.4
1996	Eclipse	Y	2.0 (1997)	4.5	4.2	18.2	—	—	—	15.9	7.4
	Eclipse	F	2.0 (1997)	5.0	②	14.2	1.1	—	1.8	15.9	7.4
	Talon	Y	2.0 (1997)	4.5	4.2	18.2	—	—	—	15.9	7.4
	Talon	F	2.0 (1997)	5.0	②	14.2	1.1	—	1.8	15.9	7.4

89571C06

CAPACITIES

Year	Model	Engine ID/VIN	Engine Displacement Liters (cc)	Engine Oil with Filter	Transmission (pts.) 5-Spd	Transmission (pts.) Auto.	Transfer Case (pts.)	Drive Axle Front (pts.)	Drive Axle Rear (pts.)	Fuel Tank (gal.)	Cooling System (qts.)
1997	Eclipse	Y	2.0 (1997)	4.5	4.2	18.2	—	—	—	17.0	7.4
	Eclipse	F	2.0 (1997)	4.5	②	14.2	1.1	—	1.8	17.0	7.4
	Eclipse Spyder	F	2.0 (1997)	4.5	4.2	14.2	—	—	—	17.0	7.4
	Eclipse Spyder	G	2.4 (2351)	4.5	4.2	12.8	—	—	—	17.0	7.4
	Talon	Y	2.0 (1997)	4.5	4.2	18.2	—	—	—	17.0	7.4
	Talon	F	2.0 (1997)	4.5	②	14.2	1.1	—	1.8	17.0	7.4
1998	Eclipse	Y	2.0 (1997)	4.5	4.2	18.2	—	—	—	17.0	7.4
	Eclipse	F	2.0 (1997)	4.5	②	14.2	1.1	—	1.8	17.0	7.4
	Eclipse Spyder	F	2.0 (1997)	4.5	4.2	14.2	—	—	—	17.0	7.4
	Eclipse Spyder	G	2.4 (2351)	4.5	4.2	12.8	—	—	—	17.0	7.4
	Talon	Y	2.0 (1997)	4.5	4.2	18.2	—	—	—	17.0	7.4
	Talon	F	2.0 (1997)	4.5	②	14.2	1.1	—	1.8	17.0	7.4

NOTE: All capacities are approximate. Add fluid gradually and check to be sure a proper fluid level is reached.

① FWD vehicles: 4.6 pts.
   AWD vehicles: 4.8 pts.
② FWD vehicles: 4.2 pts.
   AWD vehicles: 4.6 pts.

89571C07

ENGLISH TO METRIC CONVERSION: MASS (WEIGHT)

Current **mass** measurement is expressed in pounds and ounces (lbs. & ozs.). The metric unit of mass (or weight) is the kilogram (kg). Even although this table does not show conversion of masses (weights) larger than 15 lbs, it is easy to calculate larger units by following the data immediately below.

To convert ounces (oz.) to grams (g): multiply th number of ozs. by 28
To convert grams (g) to ounces (oz.): multiply the number of grams by .035

To convert pounds (lbs.) to kilograms (kg): multiply the number of lbs. by .45
To convert kilograms (kg) to pounds (lbs.): multiply the number of kilograms by 2.2

lbs	kg	lbs	kg	oz	kg	oz	kg
0.1	0.04	0.9	0.41	0.1	0.003	0.9	0.024
0.2	0.09	1	0.4	0.2	0.005	1	0.03
0.3	0.14	2	0.9	0.3	0.008	2	0.06
0.4	0.18	3	1.4	0.4	0.011	3	0.08
0.5	0.23	4	1.8	0.5	0.014	4	0.11
0.6	0.27	5	2.3	0.6	0.017	5	0.14
0.7	0.32	10	4.5	0.7	0.020	10	0.28
0.8	0.36	15	6.8	0.8	0.023	15	0.42

ENGLISH TO METRIC CONVERSION: TEMPERATURE

To convert Fahrenheit (°F) to Celsius (°C): take number of °F and subtract 32; multiply result by 5; divide result by 9

To convert Celsius (°C) to Fahrenheit (°F): take number of °C and multiply by 9; divide result by 5; add 32 to total

Fahrenheit (F)		Celsius (C)		Fahrenheit (F)		Celsius (C)		Fahrenheit (F)		Celsius (C)	
°F	°C	°C	°F	°F	°C	°C	°F	°F	°C	°C	°F
−40	−40	−38	−36.4	80	26.7	18	64.4	215	101.7	80	176
−35	−37.2	−36	−32.8	85	29.4	20	68	220	104.4	85	185
−30	−34.4	−34	−29.2	90	32.2	22	71.6	225	107.2	90	194
−25	−31.7	−32	−25.6	95	35.0	24	75.2	230	110.0	95	202
−20	−28.9	−30	−22	100	37.8	26	78.8	235	112.8	100	212
−15	−26.1	−28	−18.4	105	40.6	28	82.4	240	115.6	105	221
−10	−23.3	−26	−14.8	110	43.3	30	86	245	118.3	110	230
−5	−20.6	−24	−11.2	115	46.1	32	89.6	250	121.1	115	239
0	−17.8	−22	−7.6	120	48.9	34	93.2	255	123.9	120	248
1	−17.2	−20	−4	125	51.7	36	96.8	260	126.6	125	257
2	−16.7	−18	−0.4	130	54.4	38	100.4	265	129.4	130	266
3	−16.1	−16	3.2	135	57.2	40	104	270	132.2	135	275
4	−15.6	−14	6.8	140	60.0	42	107.6	275	135.0	140	284
5	−15.0	−12	10.4	145	62.8	44	112.2	280	137.8	145	293
10	−12.2	−10	14	150	65.6	46	114.8	285	140.6	150	302
15	−9.4	−8	17.6	155	68.3	48	118.4	290	143.3	155	311
20	−6.7	−6	21.2	160	71.1	50	122	295	146.1	160	320
25	−3.9	−4	24.8	165	73.9	52	125.6	300	148.9	165	329
30	−1.1	−2	28.4	170	76.7	54	129.2	305	151.7	170	338
35	1.7	0	32	175	79.4	56	132.8	310	154.4	175	347
40	4.4	2	35.6	180	82.2	58	136.4	315	157.2	180	356
45	7.2	4	39.2	185	85.0	60	140	320	160.0	185	365
50	10.0	6	42.8	190	87.8	62	143.6	325	162.8	190	374
55	12.8	8	46.4	195	90.6	64	147.2	330	165.6	195	383
60	15.6	10	50	200	93.3	66	150.8	335	168.3	200	392
65	18.3	12	53.6	205	96.1	68	154.4	340	171.1	205	401
70	21.1	14	57.2	210	98.9	70	158	345	173.9	210	410
75	23.9	16	60.8	212	100.0	75	167	350	176.7	215	414

TCCS1C01

ENGLISH TO METRIC CONVERSION: LENGTH

To convert inches (ins.) to millimeters (mm): multiply number of inches by 25.4

To convert millimeters (mm) to inches (ins.): multiply number of millimeters by .04

Inches	Decimals	Milli-meters	Inches to millimeters: inches	mm	Inches	Decimals	Milli-meters	Inches to millimeters: inches	mm
1/64	0.051625	0.3969	0.0001	0.00254	33/64	0.515625	13.0969	0.6	15.24
1/32	0.03125	0.7937	0.0002	0.00508	17/32	0.53125	13.4937	0.7	17.78
3/64	0.046875	1.1906	0.0003	0.00762	35/64	0.546875	13.8906	0.8	20.32
1/16	0.0625	1.5875	0.0004	0.01016	9/16	0.5625	14.2875	0.9	22.86
5/64	0.078125	1.9844	0.0005	0.01270	37/64	0.578125	14.6844	1	25.4
3/32	0.09375	2.3812	0.0006	0.01524	19/32	0.59375	15.0812	2	50.8
7/64	0.109375	2.7781	0.0007	0.01778	39/64	0.609375	15.4781	3	76.2
1/8	0.125	3.1750	0.0008	0.02032	5/8	0.625	15.8750	4	101.6
9/64	0.140625	3.5719	0.0009	0.02286	41/64	0.640625	16.2719	5	127.0
5/32	0.15625	3.9687	0.001	0.0254	21/32	0.65625	16.6687	6	152.4
11/64	0.171875	4.3656	0.002	0.0508	43/64	0.671875	17.0656	7	177.8
3/16	0.1875	4.7625	0.003	0.0762	11/16	0.6875	17.4625	8	203.2
13/64	0.203125	5.1594	0.004	0.1016	45/64	0.703125	17.8594	9	228.6
7/32	0.21875	5.5562	0.005	0.1270	23/32	0.71875	18.2562	10	254.0
15/64	0.234375	5.9531	0.006	0.1524	47/64	0.734375	18.6531	11	279.4
1/4	0.25	6.3500	0.007	0.1778	3/4	0.75	19.0500	12	304.8
17/64	0.265625	6.7469	0.008	0.2032	49/64	0.765625	19.4469	13	330.2
9/32	0.28125	7.1437	0.009	0.2286	25/32	0.78125	19.8437	14	355.6
19/64	0.296875	7.5406	0.01	0.254	51/64	0.796875	20.2406	15	381.0
5/16	0.3125	7.9375	0.02	0.508	13/16	0.8125	20.6375	16	406.4
21/64	0.328125	8.3344	0.03	0.762	53/64	0.828125	21.0344	17	431.8
11/32	0.34375	8.7312	0.04	1.016	27/32	0.84375	21.4312	18	457.2
23/64	0.359375	9.1281	0.05	1.270	55/64	0.859375	21.8281	19	482.6
3/8	0.375	9.5250	0.06	1.524	7/8	0.875	22.2250	20	508.0
25/64	0.390625	9.9219	0.07	1.778	57/64	0.890625	22.6219	21	533.4
13/32	0.40625	10.3187	0.08	2.032	29/32	0.90625	23.0187	22	558.8
27/64	0.421875	10.7156	0.09	2.286	59/64	0.921875	23.4156	23	584.2
7/16	0.4375	11.1125	0.1	2.54	15/16	0.9375	23.8125	24	609.6
29/64	0.453125	11.5094	0.2	5.08	61/64	0.953125	24.2094	25	635.0
15/32	0.46875	11.9062	0.3	7.62	31/32	0.96875	24.6062	26	660.4
31/64	0.484375	12.3031	0.4	10.16	63/64	0.984375	25.0031	27	690.6
1/2	0.5	12.7000	0.5	12.70					

ENGLISH TO METRIC CONVERSION: TORQUE

To convert foot-pounds (ft. lbs.) to Newton-meters: multiply the number of ft. lbs. by 1.3

To convert inch-pounds (in. lbs.) to Newton-meters: multiply the number of in. lbs. by .11

in lbs	N-m	in lbs	N-m	in lbs	N-m	in lbs	N-m	in lbs	N-m
0.1	0.01	1	0.11	10	1.13	19	2.15	28	3.16
0.2	0.02	2	0.23	11	1.24	20	2.26	29	3.28
0.3	0.03	3	0.34	12	1.36	21	2.37	30	3.39
0.4	0.04	4	0.45	13	1.47	22	2.49	31	3.50
0.5	0.06	5	0.56	14	1.58	23	2.60	32	3.62
0.6	0.07	6	0.68	15	1.70	24	2.71	33	3.73
0.7	0.08	7	0.78	16	1.81	25	2.82	34	3.84
0.8	0.09	8	0.90	17	1.92	26	2.94	35	3.95
0.9	0.10	9	1.02	18	2.03	27	3.05	36	4.0

TCCS1C02

ENGLISH TO METRIC CONVERSION: TORQUE

Torque is now expressed as either foot-pounds (ft./lbs.) or inch-pounds (in./lbs.). The metric measurement unit for torque is the Newton-meter (Nm). This unit—the Nm—will be used for all SI metric torque references, both the present ft./lbs. and in./lbs.

ft lbs	N-m	ft lbs	N-m	ft lbs	N-m	ft lbs	N-m
0.1	0.1	33	44.7	74	100.3	115	155.9
0.2	0.3	34	46.1	75	101.7	116	157.3
0.3	0.4	35	47.4	76	103.0	117	158.6
0.4	0.5	36	48.8	77	104.4	118	160.0
0.5	0.7	37	50.7	78	105.8	119	161.3
0.6	0.8	38	51.5	79	107.1	120	162.7
0.7	1.0	39	52.9	80	108.5	121	164.0
0.8	1.1	40	54.2	81	109.8	122	165.4
0.9	1.2	41	55.6	82	111.2	123	166.8
1	1.3	42	56.9	83	112.5	124	168.1
2	2.7	43	58.3	84	113.9	125	169.5
3	4.1	44	59.7	85	115.2	126	170.8
4	5.4	45	61.0	86	116.6	127	172.2
5	6.8	46	62.4	87	118.0	128	173.5
6	8.1	47	63.7	88	119.3	129	174.9
7	9.5	48	65.1	89	120.7	130	176.2
8	10.8	49	66.4	90	122.0	131	177.6
9	12.2	50	67.8	91	123.4	132	179.0
10	13.6	51	69.2	92	124.7	133	180.3
11	14.9	52	70.5	93	126.1	134	181.7
12	16.3	53	71.9	94	127.4	135	183.0
13	17.6	54	73.2	95	128.8	136	184.4
14	18.9	55	74.6	96	130.2	137	185.7
15	20.3	56	75.9	97	131.5	138	187.1
16	21.7	57	77.3	98	132.9	139	188.5
17	23.0	58	78.6	99	134.2	140	189.8
18	24.4	59	80.0	100	135.6	141	191.2
19	25.8	60	81.4	101	136.9	142	192.5
20	27.1	61	82.7	102	138.3	143	193.9
21	28.5	62	84.1	103	139.6	144	195.2
22	29.8	63	85.4	104	141.0	145	196.6
23	31.2	64	86.8	105	142.4	146	198.0
24	32.5	65	88.1	106	143.7	147	199.3
25	33.9	66	89.5	107	145.1	148	200.7
26	35.2	67	90.8	108	146.4	149	202.0
27	36.6	68	92.2	109	147.8	150	203.4
28	38.0	69	93.6	110	149.1	151	204.7
29	39.3	70	94.9	111	150.5	152	206.1
30	40.7	71	96.3	112	151.8	153	207.4
31	42.0	72	97.6	113	153.2	154	208.8
32	43.4	73	99.0	114	154.6	155	210.2

TCCS1C03

ENGLISH TO METRIC CONVERSION: FORCE

Force is presently measured in pounds (lbs.). This type of measurement is used to measure spring pressure, specifically how many pounds it takes to compress a spring. Our present force unit (the pound) will be replaced in SI metric measurements by the Newton (N). This term will eventually see use in specifications for electric motor brush spring pressures, valve spring pressures, etc.

To convert pounds (lbs.) to Newton (N): multiply the number of lbs. by 4.45

lbs	N	lbs	N	lbs	N	oz	N
0.01	0.04	21	93.4	59	262.4	1	0.3
0.02	0.09	22	97.9	60	266.9	2	0.6
0.03	0.13	23	102.3	61	271.3	3	0.8
0.04	0.18	24	106.8	62	275.8	4	1.1
0.05	0.22	25	111.2	63	280.2	5	1.4
0.06	0.27	26	115.6	64	284.6	6	1.7
0.07	0.31	27	120.1	65	289.1	7	2.0
0.08	0.36	28	124.6	66	293.6	8	2.2
0.09	0.40	29	129.0	67	298.0	9	2.5
0.1	0.4	30	133.4	68	302.5	10	2.8
0.2	0.9	31	137.9	69	306.9	11	3.1
0.3	1.3	32	142.3	70	311.4	12	3.3
0.4	1.8	33	146.8	71	315.8	13	3.6
0.5	2.2	34	151.2	72	320.3	14	3.9
0.6	2.7	35	155.7	73	324.7	15	4.2
0.7	3.1	36	160.1	74	329.2	16	4.4
0.8	3.6	37	164.6	75	333.6	17	4.7
0.9	4.0	38	169.0	76	338.1	18	5.0
1	4.4	39	173.5	77	342.5	19	5.3
2	8.9	40	177.9	78	347.0	20	5.6
3	13.4	41	182.4	79	351.4	21	5.8
4	17.8	42	186.8	80	355.9	22	6.1
5	22.2	43	191.3	81	360.3	23	6.4
6	26.7	44	195.7	82	364.8	24	6.7
7	31.1	45	200.2	83	369.2	25	7.0
8	35.6	46	204.6	84	373.6	26	7.2
9	40.0	47	209.1	85	378.1	27	7.5
10	44.5	48	213.5	86	382.6	28	7.8
11	48.9	49	218.0	87	387.0	29	8.1
12	53.4	50	224.4	88	391.4	30	8.3
13	57.8	51	226.9	89	395.9	31	8.6
14	62.3	52	231.3	90	400.3	32	8.9
15	66.7	53	235.8	91	404.8	33	9.2
16	71.2	54	240.2	92	409.2	34	9.4
17	75.6	55	244.6	93	413.7	35	9.7
18	80.1	56	249.1	94	418.1	36	10.0
19	84.5	57	253.6	95	422.6	37	10.3
20	89.0	58	258.0	96	427.0	38	10.6

TCCS1C04

ENGLISH TO METRIC CONVERSION: LIQUID CAPACITY

Liquid or fluid capacity is presently expressed as pints, quarts or gallons, or a combination of all of these. In the metric system the liter (l) will become the basic unit. Fractions of a liter would be expressed as deciliters, centiliters, or most frequently (and commonly) as milliliters.

To convert pints (pts.) to liters (l): multiply the number of pints by .47
To convert liters (l) to pints (pts.): multiply the number of liters by 2.1
To convert quarts (qts.) to liters (l): multiply the number of quarts by .95

To convert liters (l) to quarts (qts.): multiply the number of liters by 1.06
To convert gallons (gals.) to liters (l): multiply the number of gallons by 3.8
To convert liters (l) to gallons (gals.): multiply the number of liters by .26

gals	liters	qts	liters	pts	liters
0.1	0.38	0.1	0.10	0.1	0.05
0.2	0.76	0.2	0.19	0.2	0.10
0.3	1.1	0.3	0.28	0.3	0.14
0.4	1.5	0.4	0.38	0.4	0.19
0.5	1.9	0.5	0.47	0.5	0.24
0.6	2.3	0.6	0.57	0.6	0.28
0.7	2.6	0.7	0.66	0.7	0.33
0.8	3.0	0.8	0.76	0.8	0.38
0.9	3.4	0.9	0.85	0.9	0.43
1	3.8	1	1.0	1	0.5
2	7.6	2	1.9	2	1.0
3	11.4	3	2.8	3	1.4
4	15.1	4	3.8	4	1.9
5	18.9	5	4.7	5	2.4
6	22.7	6	5.7	6	2.8
7	26.5	7	6.6	7	3.3
8	30.3	8	7.6	8	3.8
9	34.1	9	8.5	9	4.3
10	37.8	10	9.5	10	4.7
11	41.6	11	10.4	11	5.2
12	45.4	12	11.4	12	5.7
13	49.2	13	12.3	13	6.2
14	53.0	14	13.2	14	6.6
15	56.8	15	14.2	15	7.1
16	60.6	16	15.1	16	7.6
17	64.3	17	16.1	17	8.0
18	68.1	18	17.0	18	8.5
19	71.9	19	18.0	19	9.0
20	75.7	20	18.9	20	9.5
21	79.5	21	19.9	21	9.9
22	83.2	22	20.8	22	10.4
23	87.0	23	21.8	23	10.9
24	90.8	24	22.7	24	11.4
25	94.6	25	23.6	25	11.8
26	98.4	26	24.6	26	12.3
27	102.2	27	25.5	27	12.8
28	106.0	28	26.5	28	13.2
29	110.0	29	27.4	29	13.7
30	113.5	30	28.4	30	14.2

TCCS1C05

ENGLISH TO METRIC CONVERSION: PRESSURE

The basic unit of pressure measurement used today is expressed as pounds per square inch (psi). The metric unit for psi will be the kilopascal (kPa). This will apply to either fluid pressure or air pressure, and will be frequently seen in tire pressure readings, oil pressure specifications, fuel pump pressure, etc.

To convert pounds per square inch (psi) to kilopascals (kPa): multiply the number of psi by 6.89

Psi	kPa	Psi	kPa	Psi	kPa	Psi	kPa
0.1	0.7	37	255.1	82	565.4	127	875.6
0.2	1.4	38	262.0	83	572.3	128	882.5
0.3	2.1	39	268.9	84	579.2	129	889.4
0.4	2.8	40	275.8	85	586.0	130	896.3
0.5	3.4	41	282.7	86	592.9	131	903.2
0.6	4.1	42	289.6	87	599.8	132	910.1
0.7	4.8	43	296.5	88	606.7	133	917.0
0.8	5.5	44	303.4	89	613.6	134	923.9
0.9	6.2	45	310.3	90	620.5	135	930.8
1	6.9	46	317.2	91	627.4	136	937.7
2	13.8	47	324.0	92	634.3	137	944.6
3	20.7	48	331.0	93	641.2	138	951.5
4	27.6	49	337.8	94	648.1	139	958.4
5	34.5	50	344.7	95	655.0	140	965.2
6	41.4	51	351.6	96	661.9	141	972.2
7	48.3	52	358.5	97	668.8	142	979.0
8	55.2	53	365.4	98	675.7	143	985.9
9	62.1	54	372.3	99	682.6	144	992.8
10	69.0	55	379.2	100	689.5	145	999.7
11	75.8	56	386.1	101	696.4	146	1006.6
12	82.7	57	393.0	102	703.3	147	1013.5
13	89.6	58	399.9	103	710.2	148	1020.4
14	96.5	59	406.8	104	717.0	149	1027.3
15	103.4	60	413.7	105	723.9	150	1034.2
16	110.3	61	420.6	106	730.8	151	1041.1
17	117.2	62	427.5	107	737.7	152	1048.0
18	124.1	63	434.4	108	744.6	153	1054.9
19	131.0	64	441.3	109	751.5	154	1061.8
20	137.9	65	448.2	110	758.4	155	1068.7
21	144.8	66	455.0	111	765.3	156	1075.6
22	151.7	67	461.9	112	772.2	157	1082.5
23	158.6	68	468.8	113	779.1	158	1089.4
24	165.5	69	475.7	114	786.0	159	1096.3
25	172.4	70	482.6	115	792.9	160	1103.2
26	179.3	71	489.5	116	799.8	161	1110.0
27	186.2	72	496.4	117	806.7	162	1116.9
28	193.0	73	503.3	118	813.6	163	1123.8
29	200.0	74	510.2	119	820.5	164	1130.7
30	206.8	75	517.1	120	827.4	165	1137.6
31	213.7	76	524.0	121	834.3	166	1144.5
32	220.6	77	530.9	122	841.2	167	1151.4
33	227.5	78	537.8	123	848.0	168	1158.3
34	234.4	79	544.7	124	854.9	169	1165.2
35	241.3	80	551.6	125	861.8	170	1172.1
36	248.2	81	558.5	126	868.7	171	1179.0

TCCS1C06

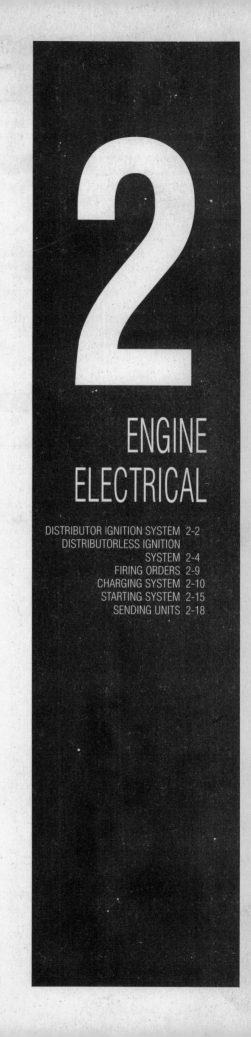

2

ENGINE ELECTRICAL

DISTRIBUTOR IGNITION SYSTEM

➡For information on understanding electricity and troubleshooting electrical circuits, please refer to Section 6 of this manual.

General Information

The ignition system on the 1.8L engine uses a pointless type distributor, whose advance mechanism is controlled by the Engine Control Unit (ECU). The distributor houses a built in crankshaft position sensor, camshaft position sensor, ignition coil and ignition power transistor.

When the ignition switch is turned **ON**, battery voltage is applied to the ignition coil primary winding. As the shaft of the distributor rotates, signals are transmitted from the multi-port injection control unit to the ignition power transistor. These signals activate the power transistor to cause ignition coil primary winding current flow from the ignition coil negative terminal through the power transistor to ground repeatedly. This interruption induces high voltage in the ignition coil secondary windings, which is diverted through the distributor, spark plug cable and spark plug to ground, thus causing ignition in each cylinder.

Diagnosis and Testing

SERVICE PRECAUTIONS

• Always turn the key **OFF** and isolate both ends of a circuit whenever testing for short or continuity.
• Always disconnect solenoids and switches from the harness before measuring for continuity, resistance or energizing by way of a 12 volts source.
• When disengaging connectors, inspect for damaged or pushed-out pins, corrosion, loose wires, etc. Service if required.

TROUBLESHOOTING HINTS

1. Engine cranks, but won't start:
   a. Spark is insufficient or does not occur at all, at spark plug:
   Check ignition coil.
   Check distributor.
   Check power transistor.
   Check spark plugs.
   b. Spark is good:
   Check the ignition timing.
2. Engine Idles Roughly or Stalls:
   Check spark plugs.
   Check ignition timing.
   Check ignition coil.
   Check spark plug cables.
3. Poor Acceleration:
   Check ignition timing.
   Check ignition coil.
   Check spark plug cables.
4. Engine overheats or consumes excessive fuel:
   Check ignition timing.

SECONDARY SPARK TEST

The best way to perform this procedure is to use a spark tester (available at most automotive parts stores). Two types of spark testers are commonly available. The neon bulb type is connected to the spark plug wire and flashes with each ignition pulse. The air gap type must be adjusted to the individual spark plug gap specified for the engine. This type of tester allows the user to not only detect the presence of spark, but also the intensity (orange/yellow is weak, blue is strong).

1. Disconnect a spark plug wire at the spark plug end.
2. Connect the plug wire to the spark tester and ground the tester to a good ground on the engine.
3. Crank the engine and check for spark at the tester.
4. If spark exists at the tester, the ignition system is functioning properly.
5. If spark does not exist at the spark plug wire, remove the distributor cap and ensure the rotor is turning when the engine is cranked.
6. If the rotor is turning, perform the spark test again using the ignition coil wire.
7. If spark does not exist at the ignition coil wire, test the ignition coil, power transistor and related wiring. Repair or replace components as necessary.

Ignition Coil

TESTING

▶ See Figure 1

➡The ignition coil is an integral part of the distributor.

1. Measure the resistance of the primary ignition coil as follows:
   a. Unplug the electrical connector at the distributor. Using an ohmmeter, measure the resistance between terminal **1** and terminal **2** of the distributor connector.
   b. Compare the measured reading with the desired reading of 0.9–1.2 ohms.
   c. If the actual reading differs from the desired specification, replace the ignition coil.
   d. If the measured value is within standard allowance, there are no broken wires or short circuits.
2. Measure the resistance of the secondary ignition coil as follows:
   a. Insert one of the test leads into the secondary ignition coil terminal on top of the distributor cap.
   b. Touch the second test lead to terminal **1** or terminal **2** of the distributor connector.
   c. Measure the resistance and compare to the desired specifications of 19–27 kilo-ohms.
   d. If the measured value is within standard allowance, there are no broken wires or short circuits.
   e. If the actual reading differs from the desired specification, replace the ignition coil.

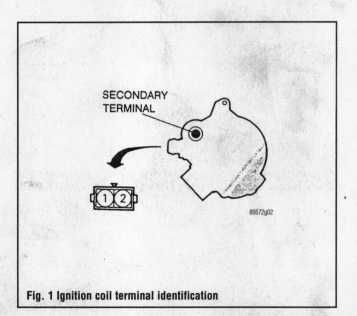

SECONDARY TERMINAL

89572g02

Fig. 1 Ignition coil terminal identification

Power Transistor (Ignition Module)

TESTING

▶ **See Figure 2**

➡**When testing the power transistor(s), an analog-type circuit tester should be used.**

1. Connect the negative terminal of a 1.5V power source to terminal **5** of the power transistor connector.
2. Check whether there is continuity between terminal **5** and terminal **8** when terminal **6** and the positive terminal are connected and disconnected.

➡**Connect the negative probe of the tester to terminal 8 of the power transistor connector.**

3. With terminal **6** and the positive terminal connected, there should be continuity between terminal **5** and terminal **8** of the connector.
4. With terminal **6** and the positive terminal disconnected, there should be no continuity between terminal **5** and terminal **8** of the connector.
5. If the results of the test are not as specified above, replace the power transistor.

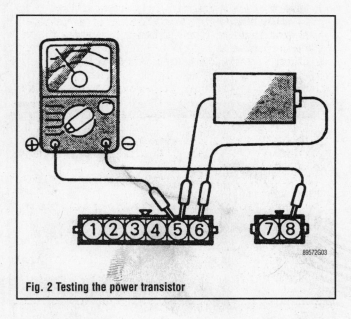

Fig. 2 Testing the power transistor

REMOVAL & INSTALLATION

1. Disconnect negative battery cable.
2. Unplug the electrical connector from the transistor.
3. Remove the coil as required.
4. Remove the transistor mounting bolts and remove from the engine.
5. Installation is the reverse of the removal procedure.

Distributor

REMOVAL

▶ **See Figure 3**

1. Disconnect the negative battery cable. Remove the ignition wire cover, if equipped.
2. Tag and disconnect the spark plug wires from the distributor cap.
3. Position the engine so No. 1 piston is at TDC on its compression stroke. Disconnect the negative battery cable.

4. Detach the distributor harness electrical connector.
5. Unscrew the distributor cap hold-down screws or release the clips and lift off the distributor cap with all ignition wires still connected. Remove the coil wire, if necessary.
6. Matchmark the rotor to the distributor housing and the distributor housing to the engine.

➡**Do not crank the engine during this procedure. If the engine is cranked, the matchmark must be disregarded.**

7. Remove the hold-down nut.
8. Carefully remove the distributor from the engine.

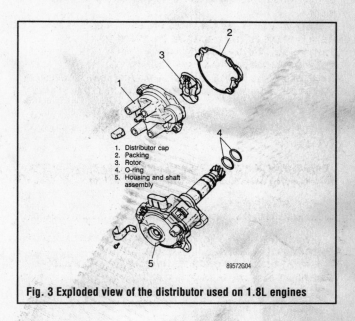

1. Distributor cap
2. Packing
3. Rotor
4. O-ring
5. Housing and shaft assembly

Fig. 3 Exploded view of the distributor used on 1.8L engines

INSTALLATION

▶ **See Figures 4 and 5**

➡**Some engines may be sensitive to the routing of the distributor sensor wires. If routed near the high-voltage coil wire or the spark plug wires, the electromagnetic field surrounding the high voltage wires could generate an occasional disruption of the ignition system operation.**

Timing Not Disturbed

1. Install a new distributor housing O-ring and lubricate with clean oil.
2. Install the distributor in the engine so the rotor is aligned with the matchmark on the housing and the housing is aligned with the matchmark on the engine. Make sure the distributor is fully seated and the distributor shaft is fully engaged.
3. Install the hold-down nut.
4. Engage the distributor harness connectors.
5. Make sure the sealing O-ring is in place, install the distributor cap and tighten the screws or secure the clips.
6. Connect the negative battery cable.
7. Adjust the ignition timing and tighten the hold-down nut.

Timing Disturbed

1. Install a new distributor housing O-ring and lubricate with clean oil.
2. Position the engine so the No. 1 piston is at TDC of its compression stroke and the mark on the vibration damper is aligned with **0** on the timing indicator.
3. Align the distributor housing and gear mating marks. Install the distributor in engine so the slot or groove of the distributor's installation flange aligns with the distributor installation stud in the engine block. Make sure

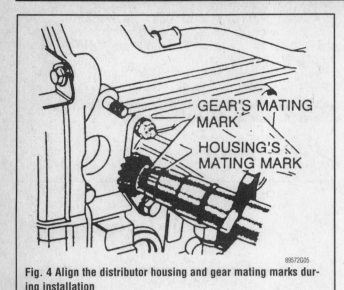

Fig. 4 Align the distributor housing and gear mating marks during installation

Fig. 5 Install the distributor in engine so the slot or groove of the installation flange aligns with the distributor installation stud in the engine block

the distributor is fully seated. Inspect alignment of the distributor rotor making sure the rotor is aligned with the position of the No. 1 ignition wire in the distributor cap.

➥Make sure the rotor is pointing to where the No. 1 runner originates inside the cap, if equipped, and not where the No. 1 ignition wire plugs into the cap.

4. Install the hold-down nut.
5. Engage the distributor harness connectors.
6. Make sure the sealing O-ring is in place, install the distributor cap and tighten the screws or secure the clips.
7. Connect the negative battery cable.
8. Adjust the ignition timing and tighten the hold-down bolt.

DISTRIBUTORLESS IGNITION SYSTEM

General Information

◆ **See Figure 6**

The ignition system found on the 2.0L and 2.4L engines is a distributorless type. The advance of this system, like the distributor type ignition system on the 1.8L engine, is controlled by the Engine Control Unit (ECU) or Powertrain Control Module (PCM). The distributorless ignition system contains a crank angle/position sensor which detects the crank angle or position to each cylinder and converts this data into pulse signals. These signals are sent to the ECU/PCM, which will calculate the engine rpm and regulate the fuel injection and ignition timing accordingly. The system also contains a top dead center sensor which detects the top dead center position of each cylinder and converts this data into pulse signals. These signals are then sent to the ECU/PCM, which will calculate the sequence of fuel injection and engine rpm. Both sensors are located in a common housing on the cylinder head opposite the timing belt side. The power and ground for both sensors is supplied by the ECU/PCM.

When the ignition switch is turned **ON**, battery voltage is applied to the ignition coil primary winding. As the crank angle sensor shaft rotates, ignition signals are transmitted from the multi port injection control unit to the power transistor. These signals activate the power transistor to cause ignition coil primary winding current to flow from the ignition coil negative terminal through the power transistor to ground or be interrupted, repeatedly. This action induces high voltage in the secondary winding of the ignition coil. From the ignition coil, the secondary winding current produced flows through the spark plug to ground, thus causing ignition in each cylinder.

Ignition Coil Pack

SECONDARY SPARK TEST

The best way to perform this procedure is to use a spark tester (available at most automotive parts stores). Two types of spark testers are commonly available. The neon bulb type is connected to the spark plug wire and flashes with each ignition pulse. The air gap type must be adjusted to the individual spark plug gap specified for the engine. This type of tester allows the user to not only detect the presence of spark, but also the intensity (orange/yellow is weak, blue is strong).

1. Disconnect a spark plug wire at the spark plug end.
2. Connect the plug wire to the spark tester and ground the tester to a good ground on the engine.
3. Crank the engine and check for spark at the tester.
4. If spark exists at the tester, the ignition system is functioning properly.
5. If spark does not exist at the spark plug wire, remove the distributor cap and ensure the rotor is turning when the engine is cranked.

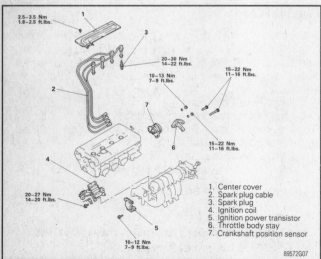

1. Center cover
2. Spark plug cable
3. Spark plug
4. Ignition coil
5. Ignition power transistor
6. Throttle body stay
7. Crankshaft position sensor

Fig. 6 Distributorless ignition system components found on 1990–94 2.0L engines; others similar

6. If the rotor is turning, perform the spark test again using the ignition coil wire.

7. If spark does not exist at the ignition coil wire, test the ignition coil, power transistor and related wiring. Repair or replace components as necessary.

COIL TESTING

1990 2.0L Engines

▶ **See Figure 7**

1. Disconnect the negative battery cable and ignition coil harness connector.

2. Measure the primary coil resistance as follows:

   a. Measure the resistance between terminals **4** and **2** (coils at the No. 1 and No. 4 cylinder sides) of the ignition coil, and between terminals **4** and **1** (coils at the No. 2 and No. 3 cylinder sides).

   b. Compare reading to the desired primary coil resistance of 0.77–0.95 ohms.

3. Measure the coil secondary resistance as follows:

   a. Disconnect the connector of the ignition coil.

   b. Measure the resistance between the high-voltage terminals for the No. 1 and No. 4 cylinders, and between the high-voltage terminals for the No. 2 and No. 3 cylinders.

   c. Compare the measured resistance to the desired secondary coil resistance of 10.3–13.9 kilo-ohms.

4. If the readings are not within the specified value, replace the ignition coil.

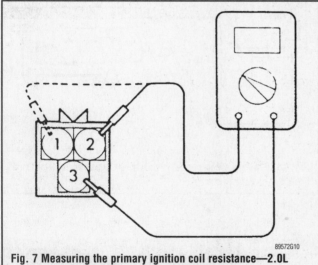

Fig. 7 Measuring the primary ignition coil resistance—2.0L engines, except 1995–98 non-turbo engines

1991–98 2.0L Engines

EXCEPT 1995–98 2.0L NON-TURBO ENGINES

▶ **See Figure 8**

1. Disconnect the negative battery cable and ignition coil harness connector.

2. Measure the primary coil resistance as follows:

   a. Measure the resistance between terminals **3** and **2** (coils at the No. 1 and No. 4 cylinder sides) of the ignition coil, and between terminals **3** and **1** (coils at the No. 2 and No. 3 cylinder sides).

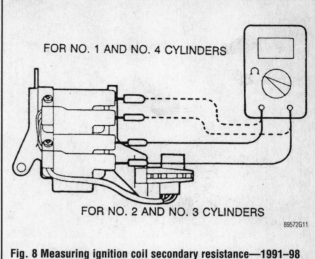

Fig. 8 Measuring ignition coil secondary resistance—1991–98 2.0L engines, except 1995–98 2.0L non-turbo

   b. Compare reading to the desired primary coil resistance of 0.70–0.86 ohms.

3. Measure the coil secondary resistance as follows:

   a. Detach the connector from the ignition coil.

   b. Measure the resistance between the high-voltage terminals for the No. 1 and No. 4 cylinders, and between the high-voltage terminals for the No. 2 and No. 3 cylinders.

   c. The desired secondary coil resistance is 11.3–15.3 kilo-ohms.

4. If the readings are not within the specified value, replace the ignition coil.

1995–98 2.0L NON-TURBO ENGINES

▶ **See Figures 9, 10 and 11**

1. Disconnect the negative battery cable.

2. To check the primary coil resistance, perform the following:

   a. Detach the electrical connector from the coil pack.

   b. Measure the primary resistance of each coil. At the coil, connect an ohmmeter between the B+ pin and the pin corresponding to the questionable cylinder.

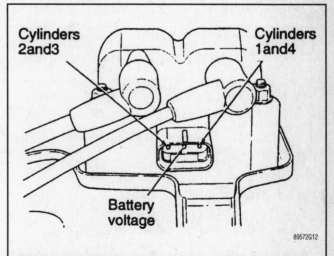

Fig. 9 Terminal identification for measuring primary coil resistance—1995–98 2.0L non-turbo engine

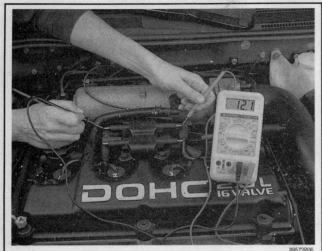

Fig. 10 Measuring the secondary ignition coil resistance between the No. 1 and No. 4 cylinders

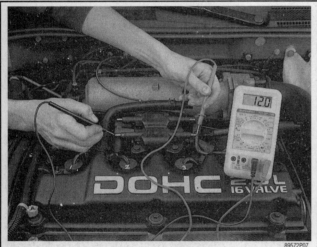

Fig. 11 Measuring the secondary ignition coil resistance between the No. 2 and No. 3 cylinders

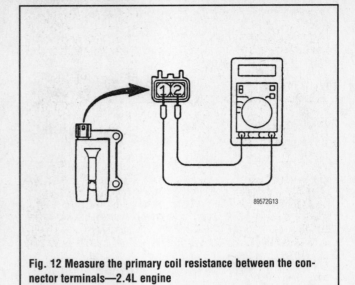

Fig. 12 Measure the primary coil resistance between the connector terminals—2.4L engine

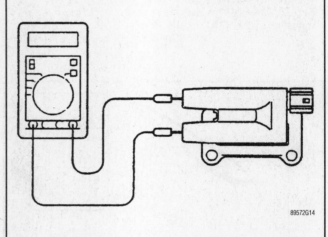

Fig. 13 Measure the secondary resistance between the towers of the coil—2.4L engine

c. If the resistance is not between 0.51–0.61 ohms, replace the ignition coil.
3. To check the secondary coil resistance, perform the following:
    a. Tag and disconnect the spark plug wires from the ignition coil.
    b. Measure the secondary resistance of the coil between the towers of each individual coil.
    c. If the resistance is not between 11.5–13.5 kilo-ohms, replace the ignition coil.

2.4L Engines

▶ **See Figures 12 and 13**

1. Disconnect the negative battery cable.
2. To check the primary coil resistance, perform the following:
    a. Detach the electrical connector from the coil pack.
    b. Measure the primary resistance between the ignition coil connector terminals.
    c. If the resistance is not between 0.74–0.90 ohms, replace the ignition coil.
3. To check the secondary coil resistance, perform the following:
    a. Tag and disconnect the spark plug wires from the ignition coil.

b. Measure the secondary resistance of the coil between the towers of each individual coil.
c. If the resistance is not between 20.1–27.3 kilo-ohms, replace the ignition coil.

REMOVAL & INSTALLATION

▶ **See Figures 14 thru 19**

1. Disconnect the negative battery cable.
2. Tag and disconnect the spark plug wires from the ignition coil. When pulling the wire from the coil, grip the boot and not the cable.
3. If necessary, pull up on the electrical connector locking tab, then unplug the coil connector.
4. Unfasten the ignition coil mounting bolts/screws, then remove the coil from the engine.
5. Installation is the reverse of the removal procedure.
6. Tighten the ignition coil mounting bolts to the following specifications:
    a. 1990–94 2.0L engines: 14–20 ft. lbs. (20–27 Nm).
    b. 1995–98 2.0L non-turbo engines: 9 ft. lbs. (12 Nm).
    c. 1995–98 2.0L turbo and 2.4L engines: 10 ft. lbs. (14 Nm).

Fig. 14 The ignition coil has the corresponding cylinder numbers stamped into it

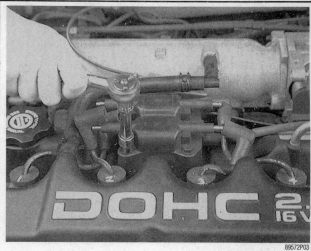

Fig. 17 Use an extension to better access the ignition coil mounting bolts

Fig. 15 Tag and disconnect the spark plug wires from the ignition coil

Fig. 18 Remove the ignition coil mounting bolts . . . .

Fig. 16 Pull up on the connector locking tab, then unplug the ignition coil electrical connector

Fig. 19 . . . then remove the ignition coil assembly from the vehicle

Power Transistor (Ignition Module)

TESTING

➡ When testing the power transistor(s), an analog-type circuit tester should be used.

2.0L Engine

1990 VEHICLES

◆ **See Figure 20**

1. To test the No. 1 and 4 cylinders:
   a. Select the ohm range on the analog tester and connect the tester between terminals 1 and 3.
   b. Connect the positive (+) lead of a 1.5 volt dry cell battery between terminal 2 and the negative lead to terminal 3.
   c. Continuity should be indicated when the dry cell is connected. No continuity should be indicated when the dry cell is disconnected.
2. To test the No. 2 and 3 cylinders:
   a. Select the ohm range on the analog tester and connect the tester between terminals 6 and 3.
   b. Connect a 1.5 volt dry cell battery between terminals 3 and 5. The positive (+) lead connects to terminal 5 and the negative (-) to terminal 3.
   c. Continuity should be indicated when the dry cell is connected. No continuity should be indicated when the dry cell is disconnected.
3. If the results of the tests are not as indicated above, replace the power transistor.

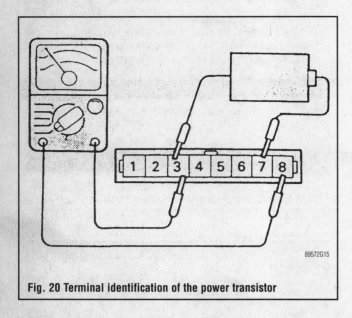

Fig. 20 Terminal identification of the power transistor

1991 VEHICLES

◆ **See Figures 21 and 22**

1. To test the No. 1 and 4 cylinders:
   a. Connect the negative terminal of a 1.5 volt dry cell battery to terminal 3 of the power transistor; then check whether there is continuity between terminals 7 and 3 when terminal 6 and the positive (+) terminal are connected and disconnected.

➡ Connect the negative probe of the tester to terminal 7 of the power transistor.

   b. With terminal 6 and the positive (+) lead connected, there should be continuity between terminal 7 and terminal 3. With terminal 6 and the positive (+) lead disconnected, there should be no continuity between terminal 7 and terminal 3.

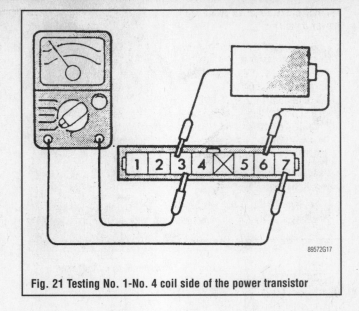

Fig. 21 Testing No. 1-No. 4 coil side of the power transistor

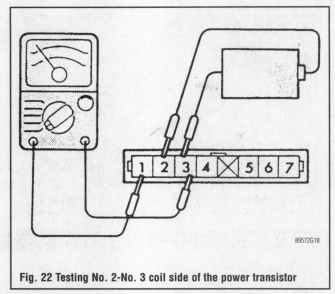

Fig. 22 Testing No. 2-No. 3 coil side of the power transistor

2. To test the No. 2 and 3 cylinders:
   a. Connect the negative terminal of a 1.5 volts dry cell to terminal 3 of the power transistor; then check whether there is continuity between terminals 1 and 3 when terminal 2 and the positive (+) terminal are connected and disconnected.

➡ Connect the negative probe of the tester to terminal 1 of the power transistor.

   b. With terminal 2 and the positive (+) lead connected, there should be continuity between terminal 1 and terminal 3. With terminal 2 and the positive (+) lead disconnected, there should be no continuity between terminal 1 and terminal 3.
3. If the results of the tests are not as indicated above, replace the power transistor.

1992–93 VEHICLES

◆ **See Figures 23 and 24**

1. To test the No. 1 and 4 cylinders:
   a. Connect the negative terminal of a 1.5 volt dry cell battery to terminal 3 of the power transistor; then check whether there is continuity between terminals 8 and 3 when terminal 7 and the positive (+) terminal are connected and disconnected.

→Connect the negative probe of the tester to terminal 8 of the power transistor.

b. With terminal 7 and the positive (+) lead connected, there should be continuity between terminal 8 and terminal 3. With terminal 7 and the positive (+) lead disconnected, there should be no continuity between terminal 8 and terminal 3.

2. To test the No. 2 and 3 cylinders:

a. Connect the negative terminal of a 1.5 volt dry cell battery to terminal 3 of the power transistor; then check whether there is continuity between terminals 1 and 3 when terminal 2 and the positive (+) terminal are connected and disconnected.

→Connect the negative probe of the tester to terminal 1 of the power transistor.

b. With terminal 2 and the positive (+) lead connected, there should be continuity between terminal 1 and terminal 3. With terminal 2 and the

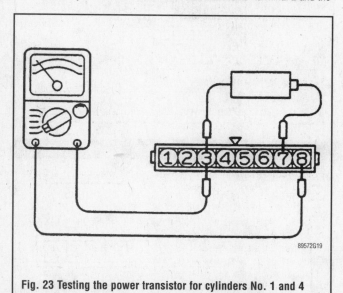

Fig. 23 Testing the power transistor for cylinders No. 1 and 4

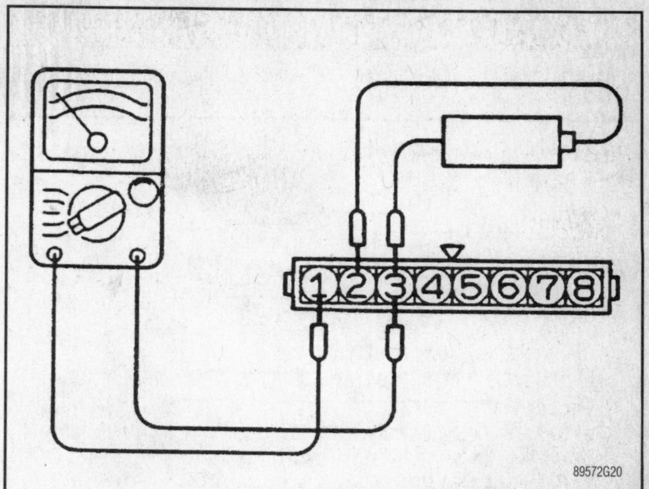

89572G19

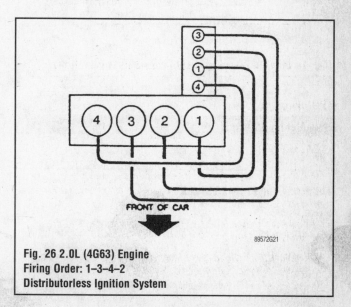

Fig. 24 Testing the power transistor for cylinders No. 2 and 3

89572G20

positive (+) lead disconnected, there should be no continuity between terminal 1 and terminal 3.

3. If the results of the tests are not as indicated above, replace the power transistor.

REMOVAL & INSTALLATION

1. Disconnect the negative battery cable.
2. Tag and disconnect the wires from the power transistor.
3. Remove the retaining screws and lift the power transistor from the engine.
4. Installation is the reverse of the removal procedure.

Crankshaft and Camshaft Position Sensors

For general information, testing and removal and installation of these sensors, please refer to Section 4 of this manual.

FIRING ORDERS

♦ See Figures 25, 26, 27 and 28

→To avoid confusion, remove and tag the spark plug wires one at a time, for replacement.

If a distributor is not keyed for installation with only one orientation, it could have been removed previously and rewired. The resultant wiring would hold the correct firing order, but could change the relative placement

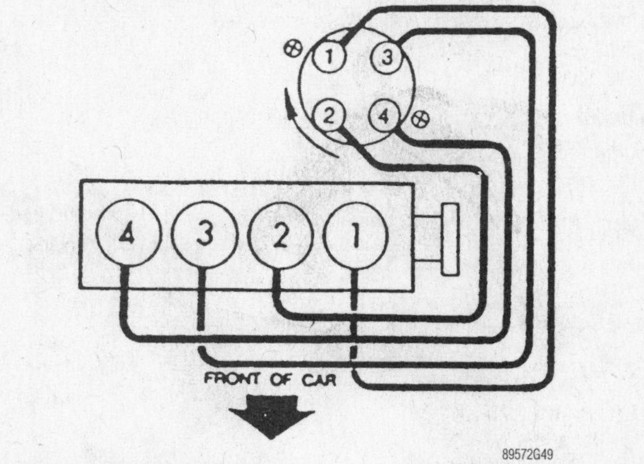

Fig. 25 1.8L (4G37)Engine
Firing Order: 1–3–4–2
Distributor Rotation: Clockwise

89572G49

Fig. 26 2.0L (4G63) Engine
Firing Order: 1–3–4–2
Distributorless Ignition System

89572G21

of the plug towers in relation to the engine. For this reason it is imperative that you label all wires before disconnecting any of them. Also, before removal, compare the current wiring with the accompanying illustrations. If the current wiring does not match, make notes in your book to reflect how your engine is wired.

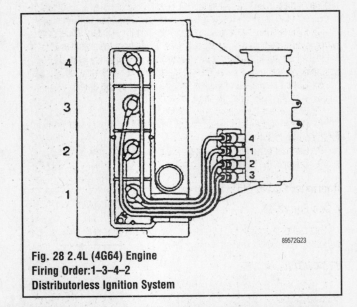

**Fig. 27 2.0L (420A) Engine
Firing Order:1–3–4–2
Distributorless Ignition System**

**Fig. 28 2.4L (4G64) Engine
Firing Order:1–3–4–2
Distributorless Ignition System**

CHARGING SYSTEM

Alternator Precautions

Several precautions must be observed with alternator-equipped vehicles to avoid damage to the unit.

• If the battery is removed for any reason, make sure it is reconnected with the correct polarity. Reversing the battery connections may result in damage to the 1-way rectifiers.

• When utilizing a booster battery as a starting aid, always connect the positive to positive terminals and the negative terminal from the booster battery to a good engine ground on the vehicle being started.

• Never use a fast charger as a booster to start vehicles.

• Disconnect the battery cables when charging the battery with a fast charger.

• Never attempt to polarize the alternator.

• Do not use test lamps of more than 12 volts when checking diode continuity.

• Do not short across or ground any of the alternator terminals.

• The polarity of the battery, alternator and regulator must be matched and considered before making any electrical connections within the system.

• Never separate the alternator on an open circuit. Make sure all connections within the circuit are clean and tight.

• Disconnect the battery ground terminal when performing any service on electrical components.

• Disconnect the battery if arc welding is to be done on the vehicle.

Alternator

TESTING

Alternator Output Wire Voltage Drop

▸ **See Figure 29**

This test will determine whether or not the wiring (including the fusible link) between the alternator **B** terminal and the battery positive terminal is sound by voltage drop method. A clamp type ammeter that can measure current without disconnecting the harness is preferred for this test.

TEST PREPARATION

1. Turn the ignition **OFF** .
2. Disconnect the battery ground cable.
3. Disconnect the alternator output lead from the alternator **B** terminal.
4. Connect the positive lead of an ammeter to the **B** terminal and the negative lead to the disconnected output wire.
5. Connect a digital voltmeter between the alternator **B** terminal and the battery positive terminal. Connect the positive lead wire of the voltmeter to the **B** terminal and the negative lead wire to the battery positive terminal.
6. Connect the battery ground cable.
7. Leave the hood to the engine compartment open.

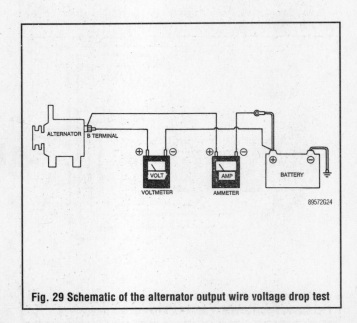

Fig. 29 Schematic of the alternator output wire voltage drop test

TEST PROCEDURE

1. Start the engine.

2. Turn the headlamps and small lamps **ON** and adjust the engine speed so that the ammeter reads 20A. Note the voltmeter indication under this condition.

3. It is OK if the voltmeter reads the standard value of 0.2V max.

4. If the voltmeter indicates a value larger than the standard value, poor wiring is suspected, in which case check the wiring from the alternator **B** terminal to the fuse link to battery positive terminal. Check for loose connection, color change due to overheating hardness, etc. and correct before testing again.

5. Upon completion of the test, set the engine speed at idle.

6. Turn the lights and the ignition switch **OFF**.

7. Disconnect the battery ground cable.

8. Disconnect the ammeter and the voltmeter that have been connected for the purpose of the test.

9. Connect the alternator output wire to the alternator **B** terminal.

10. Connect the battery ground cable.

Alternator Output Current Test

♦ See Figure 30

This test is designed to judge whether or not the alternator gives an output current that is equivalent to the nominal output.

TEST PREPARATION

1. Check the battery that installed in the vehicle, making sure it is in good sound state. Test the battery as required to assure this. The battery used to check output current should be one that has been rather discharged. With a fully discharged battery, the test may not be conducted correctly due to an insufficient load.

2. Check the alternator drive belt for proper tension, as outlined in Section 1.

3. Make sure the ignition switch is turned **OFF**. Disconnect the battery ground cable.

4. Disconnect the alternator output lead from the alternator **B** terminal.

5. Connect the positive lead of an ammeter to the **B** terminal and the negative lead to the disconnected output wire.

➡ **Tighten each connection by bolt and nuts securely as a heavy current will flow through the wire. Do not rely on clips.**

6. Connect a voltmeter between the **B** terminal and ground. Connect the positive lead wire to the alternator **B** terminal and the negative lead wire to a sound ground.

7. Connect the battery ground cable.

8. Leave the hood open.

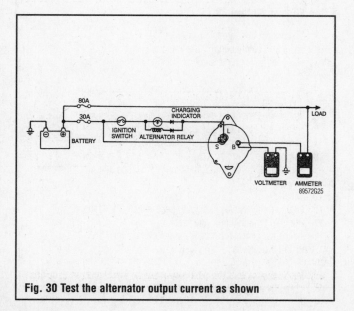

Fig. 30 Test the alternator output current as shown

TEST PROCEDURE

1. Check to see that the voltmeter reads the same value as the battery voltage. If the voltmeter reads 0 volts, an open circuit in the wire between the alternator **B** terminal and the battery negative terminal, a blown fuse link, or poor grounding is suspected.

2. Turn the headlight switch on and start the engine.

3. Set the headlights at high beam and the heater blower switch at high, quickly increase the engine speed to 2,500 rpm and read the maximum output current value indicated by the ammeter.

➡ **After engine start up, the charging current drops quickly, therefore, above operation must be done quickly to read the maximum current value correctly.**

4. The ammeter reading must be higher than the limit value. If it is lower than the limit value but the alternator output wire is normal, remove the alternator from the vehicle and check it further. The limit values are as follows:

- 65A alternator—45.5A minimum
- 75A alternator—52.5A minimum

➡ **The nominal output current value is shown on the nameplate affixed to the alternator body. The output current value changes with the electrical load and the temperature of the alternator itself. Therefore, the nominal output current may not be obtained if the vehicle electrical load at the time of the test is small. In such case, keep the headlights on to cause discharge of the battery to increase the electrical load. The nominal output current may not be obtained if the temperature of the alternator itself or ambient temperature is too high.**

5. Upon completion of the test, lower the engine speed to idle and turn the ignition switch **OFF**.

6. Disconnect the battery ground cable.

7. Disconnect and remove the engine tachometer, voltmeter and ammeter connected for the purpose of this test.

8. Connect the alternator output wire.

9. Connect the battery ground cable.

Regulated Voltage Test

♦ See Figure 31

The purpose of this test is to determine that the electronic voltage regulator controls the voltage correctly.

TEST PREPARATION

1. Check the battery that installed in the vehicle, making sure it is in good sound state. Test the battery as required to assure this. The battery must be fully charged.

2. Check the alternator drive belt for proper tension as outlined in Section 1.

3. Make sure the ignition switch is turned **OFF**. Disconnect the battery ground cable.

4. Connect a digital voltmeter between the **S** terminal of the alternator and the alternator. inserting from the wire side of the 2-way connector. Connect the negative test lead to a sound ground or negative battery terminal.

5. Disconnect the alternator output lead from the alternator **B** terminal.

6. Connect the positive lead of an ammeter to the **B** terminal and the negative lead to the disconnected output wire.

7. Connect the battery ground cable.

8. Leave the hood open.

TEST PROCEDURE

1. Turn the ignition switch **ON**. Check to see that the voltmeter reads the same value as the battery voltage. If the voltmeter reads 0 volts, an open circuit in the wire between the alternator **S** terminal and the battery positive terminal or the fuse link is blown.

2. Start the engine and keep all lights and accessories off.

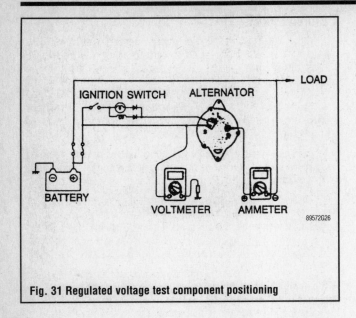

Fig. 31 Regulated voltage test component positioning

3. Run the engine at 2,500 rpm and read the voltmeter when the alternator output current drops to 10A or less.

4. If the voltmeter readings agree with the desired readings listed below, the voltage regulator is functioning properly. If the measured reading disagrees with the desired value, the voltage regulator or the alternator is faulty. The desired voltages are as follows:

• Voltage regulator ambient temperature at 68°F (20°C)—13.9–14.9 volts

• Voltage regulator ambient temperature at 140°F (68°C)—13.4–14.6 volts

• Voltage regulator ambient temperature at 176°F (80°C)—13.1–14.5 volts

5. Upon completion of test, set the engine speed at idle and turn the ignition switch **OFF**.

6. Disconnect the negative battery terminal.

7. Disconnect all test meters installed for this test procedure.

8. Connect the alternator output wire to the alternator **B** terminal.

9. Connect the negative battery terminal.

REMOVAL & INSTALLATION

1990–94 Vehicles

◆ See Figure 32

1. Disconnect the negative battery cable.

2. Raise and safely support the vehicle. Remove the left wheel and tire assembly.

3. For 2.0L engines, remove the left side undercover from the vehicle.

4. If equipped with A/C, remove the condenser electric fan motor and shroud assembly.

5. Remove the alternator, water pump and air conditioner compressor drive belts.

6. Remove both of the water pump pulleys.

7. Remove the alternator top brace.

8. Disconnect the alternator wiring, then remove the alternator from the vehicle.

To install:

9. Manuever the alternator into position, then connect the electrical harness.

10. Install the alternator top brace to the engine and tighten the mounting bolt to 20 ft. lbs. (27 Nm).

11. Install the alternator mounting bolt loosely.

12. Install the water pump pulleys and tighten retainer bolts to 7 ft. lbs. (10 Nm).

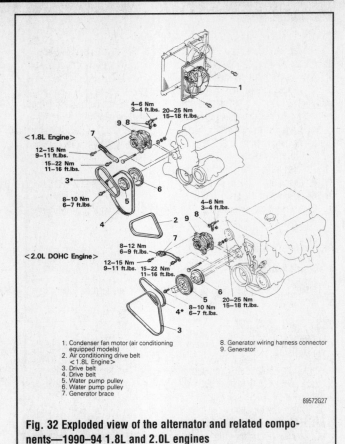

1. Condenser fan motor (air conditioning equipped models)
2. Air conditioning drive belt <1.8L Engine>
3. Drive belt
4. Drive belt
5. Water pump pulley
6. Water pump pulley
7. Generator brace
8. Generator wiring harness connector
9. Generator

Fig. 32 Exploded view of the alternator and related components—1990–94 1.8L and 2.0L engines

13. Install the drive belts and adjust until the proper tension is achieved. Secure the lower alternator through-bolt nut to 18 ft. lbs. (25 Nm) and the upper alternator lock bolt to 11 ft. lbs. (15 Nm).

14. Install the condenser electric fan motor and shroud assembly.

15. Install the left side undercover from the vehicle, if removed.

16. Connect the negative battery cable. Start the engine and check the alternator for proper operation.

1995–98 Vehicles

2.0L NON-TURBO ENGINE

◆ See Figures 33 thru 38

1. Disconnect the negative battery cable.

2. Raise and safely support the vehicle.

3. Remove the left side wheel and tire assembly. Remove the under cover side panel.

4. For 2.0L non-turbo engines equipped with auto-cruise control, remove the speed control assembly.

5. Remove the alternator drive belt, as outlined in Section 1 of this manual.

6. Detach the alternator harness connector(s).

7. Remove the lower alternator bracket.

8. Remove the alternator adjusting bolt.

9. Remove the mounting bolts, then remove the alternator from the vehicle.

To install:

10. Install the alternator brace and secure with the retainers.

11. Position the alternator and bracket.

12. Attach the alternator harness connectors.

13. Install the alternator drive belt. Adjust the tension as outlined in Section 1 of this manual.

14. Install the under cover side panel and the wheel and tire assembly.

15. Carefully lower the vehicle, then connect the negative battery cable.

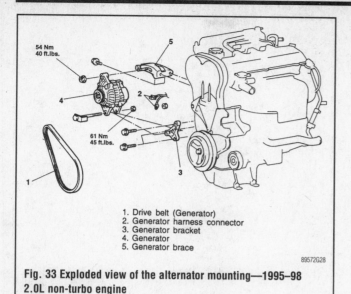

1. Drive belt (Generator)
2. Generator harness connector
3. Generator bracket
4. Generator
5. Generator brace

54 Nm
40 ft.lbs.

61 Nm
45 ft.lbs.

89572G28

Fig. 33 Exploded view of the alternator mounting—1995–98 2.0L non-turbo engine

89572P12

Fig. 36 Unfasten the BAT terminal retaining nut from the rear of the alternator

89572P10

Fig. 34 There are two electrical connections found on the back of the alternator

89572P15

Fig. 37 Remove the alternator adjusting bolt

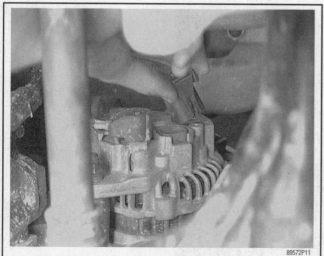

89572P11

Fig. 35 With the vehicle raised and supported, unplug the electrical connector from the rear of the alternator

89572P13

Fig. 38 Remove the alternator mounting bolts, then carefully lower the alternator and remove it from vehicle

2.0L TURBO AND 2.4L ENGINES

▶ See Figures 39, 40, 41 and 42

1. Disconnect the negative battery cable.
2. If necessary, partially raise and support the vehicle.
3. Remove the left side wheel and tire assembly. Remove the under cover side panel.
4. Remove the alternator drive belt.
5. Unplug the alternator harness connector(s).
6. For the 2.0L turbo engine, perform the following:

➡**Do NOT disconnect the oil pump hose.**

a. Remove the mounting bolt of the power steering oil pump, and hold the pump above the engine mount bracket. Use a rag to prevent scratching of the rocker cover.
b. With the alternator facing as shown in the accompanying figure, lift upward and remove the alternator from the vehicle.
7. For the 2.4L engine, perform the following:
a. Remove the oil pressure switch terminal.
b. Remove the alternator from the underside of the vehicle.
8. If necessary to remove the alternator brace, perform the following:

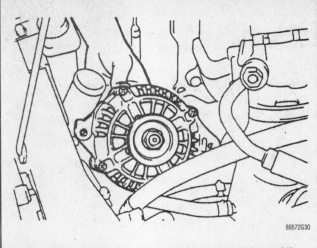

Fig. 41 On the 2.0L engine, lift the alternator up and out of the vehicle

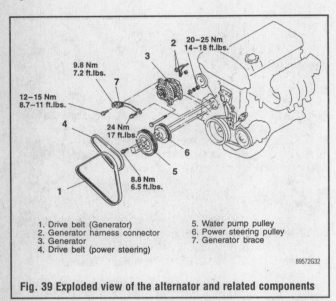

1. Drive belt (Generator)
2. Generator harness connector
3. Generator
4. Drive belt (power steering)
5. Water pump pulley
6. Power steering pulley
7. Generator brace

Fig. 39 Exploded view of the alternator and related components

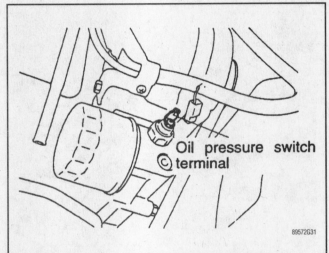

Fig. 42 On the 2.4L engine, you must remove the oil pressure switch terminal for room to remove the alternator

a. Remove the power steering drive belt.
b. Remove the water pump pulley.
c. Remove the power steering pump pulley.
d. Remove the alternator brace from the vehicle.

To install:

9. Installation is the reverse of the removal.
10. Note that the alternator is installed from the top of the engine for the 2.0L turbo engine and from underneath the vehicle on the 2.4L engine.
11. During installation, make sure to tighten all retainers to the specifications shown in the accompanying figures.
12. Install the undercover side panel, then carefully lower the vehicle.
13. Connect the negative battery cable.

Regulator

All models use a regulator that is integral with the alternator. If the regulator is defective, replace the alternator.

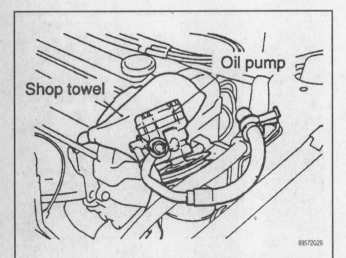

Fig. 40 Position the power steering pump aside with a rag underneath

STARTING SYSTEM

Starter

TESTING

If the starter motor does not operate at all, inspect the following:
Check the starter coil
Check for poor contact at the battery terminal
1. If the starter motor does not stop, inspect the following:
Check the starter magnetic switch

Magnetic Switch Pull-In Test

▶ See Figure 43

1. Disconnect the negative battery cable.
2. Remove the starter assembly from the vehicle.
3. Disconnect the field coil wire from the M-terminal of the magnetic switch.
4. Connect a 12V battery between S-terminal and M-terminal on the magnetic switch of the starter.

❈❈ CAUTION

The test must be performed quickly, in less than 10 seconds, to prevent the coil from burning.

5. If the pinion moves out, the pull-in coil is functioning properly. If it doesn't, replace the magnetic switch.

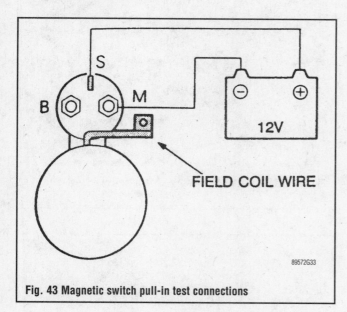

Fig. 43 Magnetic switch pull-in test connections

Magnetic Switch Hold-In Test

▶ See Figure 44

1. Disconnect the negative battery cable.
2. Remove the starter assembly from the vehicle.
3. Disconnect the field coil wire from the M-terminal of the magnetic switch.
4. Connect a 12V battery between S-terminal and body.

❈❈ CAUTION

The test must be performed quickly, in less than 10 seconds, to prevent the coil from burning.

5. If the pinion remains out, everything is in order. If the pinion moves in, the hold-in circuit is open. Replace the magnetic switch.

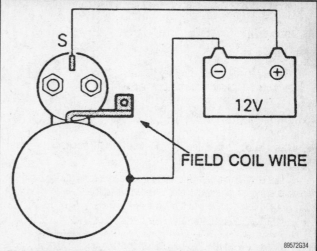

Fig. 44 Starter motor terminal identification for the magnetic switch hold-in test

Free Running Test

▶ See Figure 45

1. Disconnect the negative battery cable.
2. Remove the starter assembly from the vehicle.
3. Place the starter assembly into a vise with soft jaws. Connect a fully charged 12 volt battery to the starter motor as follows:
   a. Connect a test ammeter with 100 ampere scale and a carbon pile rheostat in series with battery positive post and starter motor terminal.
   b. Connect a voltmeter across the starter motor.
   c. Rotate the carbon pile to full-resistance position.
   d. Connect the battery cable from the negative battery post to the starter motor body.
   e. Adjust the rheostat until the battery voltage shown by the voltmeter is 11.5V for direct drive type starter, which are normally installed in 1.8L engines. On reduction-drive starters, which are normally installed in 2.0L engines, adjust the rheostat until the battery voltage shown by the voltmeter is 11.0 V.
   f. Confirm that the maximum amperage is within the specifications listed below and the starter turns freely.

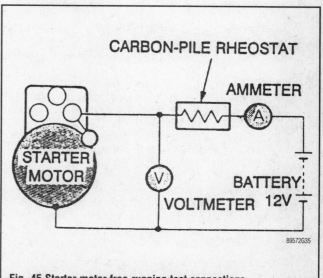

Fig. 45 Starter motor free-running test connections

Direct drive starter—60 Amps maximum
Reduction drive starter—90 Amps maximum
4. If the starter is not within specifications, replace the unit.

Magnetic Switch Return Test

▶ See Figure 46

1. Disconnect the negative battery cable.
2. Remove the starter assembly from the vehicle.
3. Disconnect the field coil wire from the M-terminal of the magnetic switch.
4. Connect a 12 volt battery between the M-terminal of the starter and the starter body.

➡ **This test must be done quickly, in less than 10 seconds, to prevent coil from burning.**

5. Pull the pinion out and then release it. If the pinion quickly returns to its original position, everything is in order. If it doesn't, replace the magnetic switch.

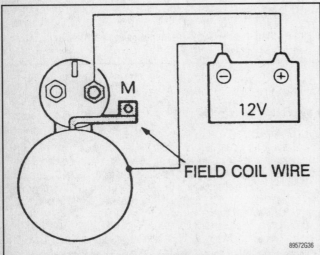

Fig. 46 Starter motor terminal identification—magnetic switch return test

REMOVAL & INSTALLATION

▶ See Figures 47 thru 52

1. Disconnect the negative, then the positive battery cables from the battery.
2. For 1990–94 vehicles, remove the battery and battery tray from the engine compartment.
3. For 1990–94 vehicles, detach the speedometer cable connector from the transaxle.
4. For 1995–98 2.0L turbo engines, remove the air hose.
5. For 1995–98 2.4L engines, remove the air cleaner and air intake hose.
6. If equipped with 1.8L engine, remove the bracket on the lower side if the intake manifold.
7. Detach the starter motor electrical connections.
8. Unfasten the starter motor mounting bolts, then remove the starter from the vehicle.

To install:

9. Clean both surfaces of starter motor flange and rear plate. Install the starter motor onto the engine and secure with the retainer bolts. Tighten the retainers to the specifications shown in the accompanying figure.
10. Attach the electrical harness connector(s) to the starter.
11. If removed, install the intake manifold stay and tighten the retainers to 18 ft. lbs. (25 Nm).
12. For 1995–98 2.4L engines, install the air cleaner and air intake hose.

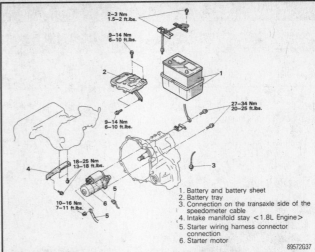

Fig. 47 Exploded view of the starter motor and related components—1990–94 vehicles, others similar

1. Battery and battery sheet
2. Battery tray
3. Connection on the transaxle side of the speedometer cable
4. Intake manifold stay <1.8L Engine>
5. Starter wiring harness connector connection
6. Starter motor

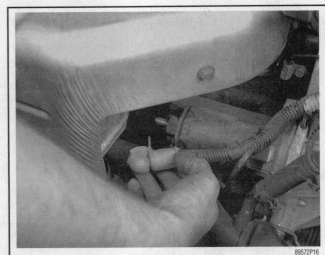

Fig. 48 Unfasten the BAT terminal connector from the starter motor

Fig. 49 Unplug the starter motor electrical connector

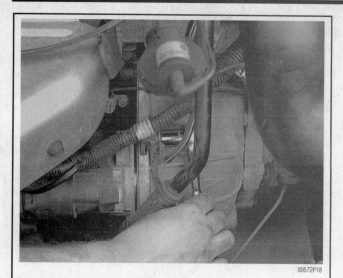

Fig. 50 Unfasten the starter mounting bolts

Fig. 51 Remove all of the starter mounting bolts . . .

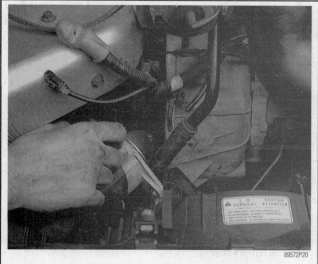

Fig. 52 . . . then remove the starter motor from the vehicle

13. For 1995–98 2.0L turbo engines, install the air hose.

14. For 1990–94 vehicles, attach the speedometer cable to the transaxle. Install the battery tray and battery.

15. Connect the positive, then the negative battery cables.

16. Operate the starter to assure proper operation.

Starter Relay

REMOVAL & INSTALLATION

▶ **See Figure 53**

1. If equipped, disable the air bag system, as outlined in Section 6 of this manual.

2. Remove the retainers and the knee protector from the vehicle.

3. Remove the starter relay from the underside of the relay box.

4. To test the relay, perform the following:

a. Connect battery voltage to terminal 2 and check continuity between the terminals with terminal 4 grounded.

With power supplied to terminal 2 and terminal 4 is grounded—there is no continuity between terminal 1 and 3.

When no power is supplied to terminal 2—there is continuity between terminals 1 and 3 and also between terminals 2 and 4.

b. If the test results differ from the results listed above, replace the starter relay.

To install:

5. Install the starter relay in the underside of the relay box.

6. Position the knee protector, then install the retainers.

7. If equipped, enable the air bag system, as outlined in Section 6 of this manual.

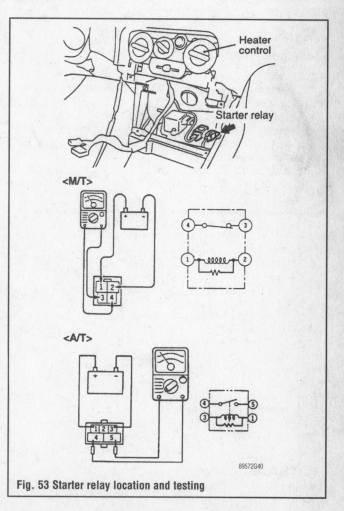

Fig. 53 Starter relay location and testing

SENDING UNITS

➡This section describes the operating principles of sending units, warning lights and gauges. Sensors which provide information to the Electronic Control Module (ECM) are covered in Section 4 of this manual.

Instrument panels contain a number of indicating devices (gauges and warning lights). These devices are composed of two separate components. One is the sending unit, mounted on the engine or other remote part of the vehicle, and the other is the actual gauge or light in the instrument panel.

Several types of sending units exist, however most can be characterized as being either a pressure type or a resistance type. Pressure type sending units convert liquid pressure into an electrical signal which is sent to the gauge. Resistance type sending units are most often used to measure temperature and use variable resistance to control the current flow back to the indicating device. Both types of sending units are connected in series by a wire to the battery (through the ignition switch). When the ignition is turned **ON**, current flows from the battery through the indicating device and on to the sending unit.

Engine Coolant Temperature

TESTING

The coolant temperature sensor is used to operate the temperature gauge. Do not confuse this sensor with the other switches or sensors used to signal the engine control unit or air conditioning regarding temperature of the coolant. Usually, these other units are mounted near the coolant temperature sensor used for engine control.

Gauge Check

♦ **See Figures 54 and 55**

1. Detach the engine coolant gauge sensor electrical connector.
2. Connect a suitable test light (12V–3.4W) between the harness side connector and the ground.
3. Turn the ignition switch to the **ON** position.
4. Check the condition of the test light and gauge as follows:
   a. If all components are operating properly, the test light should illuminate and the gauge needle should move.
   b. If the test light is illuminates and the gauge needle does not moving, replace the coolant temperature gauge.

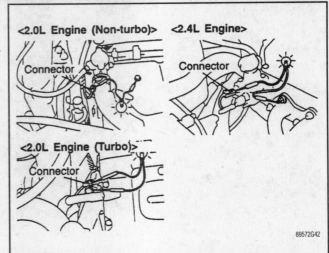

Fig. 55 Engine coolant temperature gauge unit connector locations—1995–98 vehicles

c. If the test light is illuminated and the gauge needle, check the fuse for a broken wire, or resistance between the gauge terminals
d. If the test light is not illuminated and the gauge is not moving, check, then replace the wiring harness, if necessary.

Sender Check

♦ **See Figure 56**

1. Drain the engine coolant to a level below the coolant temperature sensor.
2. Disconnect the sensor wiring harness and remove the coolant temperature sensor.
3. Place the sensor tip in a pan of warm water. Use a thermometer to measure the water temperature.
4. Measure the resistance across the sensor terminals while the sensor is in the water.
5. Note the ohm reading and compare to the following specifications:

Water temperature of 68°F (20°C)—2.21–2.69 kilo-ohms resistance

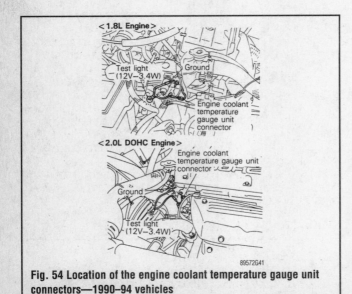

Fig. 54 Location of the engine coolant temperature gauge unit connectors—1990–94 vehicles

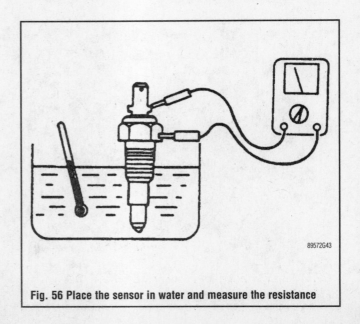

Fig. 56 Place the sensor in water and measure the resistance

Water temperature of 158°F (70°C)—90.5–117.5 ohms resistance
Water temperature of 176°F (80°C)—264–328 ohms resistance.
If the resistance is not approximately accurate for the temperature, the sensor must be replaced.

REMOVAL & INSTALLATION

▶ See Figures 57 and 58

1. Disconnect the negative battery cable.
2. Position a suitable drain pan under the radiator.
3. Drain the engine coolant a level below the coolant temperature sensor.
4. Disconnect the sensor wiring harness, then remove the coolant temperature sensor from the engine.

To install:

5. Coat the sensor threads with a suitable thread sealant.
6. Install the engine coolant temperature gauge sensor into the bore in the engine and tighten to 7–8 ft. lbs. (10–12 Nm).
7. Attach the electrical harness connector to the sensor.
8. Fill the cooling system to the proper level. Connect the negative battery cable.

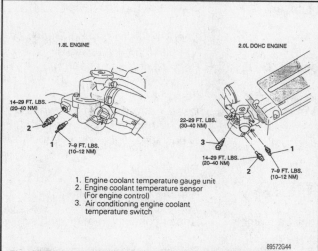

Fig. 57 Typical locations of the engine coolant temperature gauge unit and related components

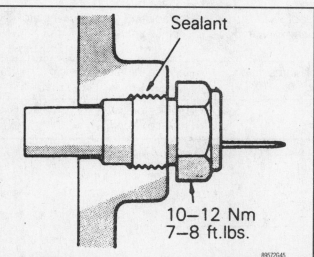

Fig. 58 Before installing the sensor, coat the threads with a suitable sealant

Oil Pressure Switch

TESTING

Gauge Check

▶ See Figure 59

1. Disconnect the oil pressure gauge unit electrical connector.
2. Use a suitable test light (12V–3.4W) to ground the harness side connector.
3. Turn the ignition to the **ON** position.
4. Check the condition of the test light and gauge as follows:
   a. If all components are operating properly, the test light will flash or light steadily and the oil pressure gauge needle will move.
   b. If the test light flashes or lights steadily and but the gauge does not move, the gauge must be replaced.
   c. If neither the test light or the gauge operated, check the oil pressure gauge circuit and replace, if necessary.

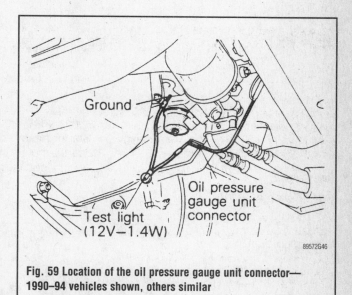

Fig. 59 Location of the oil pressure gauge unit connector—1990–94 vehicles shown, others similar

Sender Check

1. Remove the electrical harness connector from the switch and remove the switch from the oil filter head.
2. Connect an ohmmeter between the terminal and the sensor body cavity and check for conductivity. If there is no conductivity, replace the switch.
3. Next, insert a very thin wedge through the oil hole in the end of the sensor. Push the wedge in slightly and measure resistance. There should be no conductivity.
4. If there is conductivity, even when wedge is pushed, replace the switch.
5. If there is no conductivity when a 71 psi pressure is placed through the oil hole, the switch is operating properly.
6. Check to see that there is no air pressure leakage through the switch. If there is air pressure leakage, the diaphragm is broken and the switch will require replacement.

REMOVAL & INSTALLATION

1. Disconnect the negative battery cable.
2. Raise and support the vehicle safely.
3. Detach the electrical harness connector from the switch, then remove the unit from the oil filter head.

To install:

4. Apply a thin bead of sealant to the threaded portion of the oil pressure sensor. Do not allow sealer to contact the end of the threaded portion of the sensor.

5. Install the sensor and tighten to 8 ft. lbs. (12 Nm). Do not overtighten the sensor.

6. Attach the electrical harness connector to the sensor.

7. Carefully lower the vehicle, then connect the negative battery cable.

Troubleshooting Basic Starting System Problems

Problem	Cause	Solution
Starter motor rotates engine slowly	• Battery charge low or battery defective	• Charge or replace battery
	• Defective circuit between battery and starter motor	• Clean and tighten, or replace cables
	• Low load current	• Bench-test starter motor. Inspect for worn brushes and weak brush springs.
	• High load current	• Bench-test starter motor. Check engine for friction, drag or coolant in cylinders. Check ring gear-to-pinion gear clearance.
Starter motor will not rotate engine	• Battery charge low or battery defective	• Charge or replace battery
	• Faulty solenoid	• Check solenoid ground. Repair or replace as necessary.
	• Damaged drive pinion gear or ring gear	• Replace damaged gear(s)
	• Starter motor engagement weak	• Bench-test starter motor
	• Starter motor rotates slowly with high load current	• Inspect drive yoke pull-down and point gap, check for worn end bushings, check ring gear clearance
	• Engine seized	• Repair engine
Starter motor drive will not engage (solenoid known to be good)	• Defective contact point assembly	• Repair or replace contact point assembly
	• Inadequate contact point assembly ground	• Repair connection at ground screw
	• Defective hold-in coil	• Replace field winding assembly
Starter motor drive will not disengage	• Starter motor loose on flywheel housing	• Tighten mounting bolts
	• Worn drive end busing	• Replace bushing
	• Damaged ring gear teeth	• Replace ring gear or driveplate
	• Drive yoke return spring broken or missing	• Replace spring
Starter motor drive disengages prematurely	• Weak drive assembly thrust spring	• Replace drive mechanism
	• Hold-in coil defective	• Replace field winding assembly
Low load current	• Worn brushes	• Replace brushes
	• Weak brush springs	• Replace springs

TCCS2C01

3

ENGINE AND ENGINE OVERHAUL

ENGINE MECHANICAL

GENERAL ENGINE SPECIFICATIONS

Year	Engine ID/VIN	Engine Displacement Liters (cc)	Fuel System Type	Net Horsepower @ rpm	Net Torque @ rpm (ft. lbs.)	Bore x Stroke (In.)	Compression Ratio	Oil Pressure @ rpm
1990	T	1.8 (1775)	MFI	92 @ 5000	105 @ 3200	3.17 x 3.39	9.0:1	11.5 @ 750
	R	2.0 (1997)	MFI	135 @ 6000	125 @ 5000	3.35 x 3.47	9.0:1	11.5 @ 750
	U	2.0 (1997)	MFI-Turbo	190 @ 6000	203 @ 3000	3.35 x 3.47	8.7:1	11.5 @ 750
1991	T	1.8 (1775)	MFI	92 @ 5000	105 @ 3200	3.17 x 3.39	9.0:1	11.5 @ 750
	R	2.0 (1997)	MFI	135 @ 6000	125 @ 5000	3.35 x 3.47	9.0:1	11.5 @ 750
	U	2.0 (1997)	MFI-Turbo	190 @ 6000	203 @ 3000	3.35 x 3.47	8.7:1	11.5 @ 750
1992	T	1.8 (1775)	MFI	92 @ 5000	105 @ 3200	3.17 x 3.39	9.0:1	11.5 @ 750
	R	2.0 (1997)	MFI	135 @ 6000	125 @ 5000	3.35 x 3.47	9.0:1	11.5 @ 750
	U	2.0 (1997)	MFI-Turbo	190 @ 6000	203 @ 3000	3.35 x 3.47	8.7:1	11.5 @ 750
1993	B	1.8 (1775)	MFI	92 @ 5000	105 @ 3200	3.17 x 3.39	9.0:1	11.5 @ 750
	E	2.0 (1997)	MFI	135 @ 6000	125 @ 5000	3.35 x 3.47	9.0:1	11.5 @ 750
	F	2.0 (1997)	MFI-Turbo	190 @ 6000	203 @ 3000	3.35 x 3.47	8.7:1	11.5 @ 750
1994	B	1.8 (1775)	MFI	92 @ 5000	105 @ 3200	3.17 x 3.39	9.0:1	①
	E	2.0 (1997)	MFI	135 @ 6000	125 @ 5000	3.35 x 3.47	9.0:1	①
	F	2.0 (1997)	MFI-Turbo	190 @ 6000	203 @ 3000	3.35 x 3.47	8.7:1	①
1995	Y	2.0 (1997)	MFI	②	③	3.35 X 3.46	8.5:1	①
	F	2.0 (1997)	MFI-Turbo	140 @ 6000	131 @ 4800	3.44 X 3.27	9.6:1	④
1996	Y	2.0 (1997)	MFI	②	③	3.35 X 3.46	8.5:1	①
	F	2.0 (1997)	MFI-Turbo	140 @ 6000	131 @ 4800	3.44 X 3.27	9.6:1	④
1997	Y	2.0 (1997)	MFI	②	③	3.35 X 3.46	8.5:1	①
	F	2.0 (1997)	MFI-Turbo	140 @ 6000	131 @ 4800	3.44 x 3.27	9.6:1	④
	G	2.4 (2351)	MFI	⑤	140 @ 3000	3.41 X 3.94	9.5:1	41 @ 2000
1998	Y	2.0 (1997)	MFI	②	③	3.35 X 3.46	8.5:1	①
	F	2.0 (1997)	MFI-Turbo	140 @ 6000	131 @ 4800	3.44 x 3.27	9.6:1	④
	G	2.4 (2351)	MFI	⑤	140 @ 3000	3.41 X 3.94	9.5:1	41 @ 2000

① 11.4 psi or more at curb idle speed
② Manual transmission: 210 @ 6000 rpm
  Automatic transmission: 205 @ 6000 rpm
③ Manual transmission: 214 @ 3000 rpm
  Automatic transmission: 220 @ 3000
④ 4 psi or more at curb idle speed
⑤ California: 138 @ 5500
  Except California: 141 @ 5500

89573C01

1.8L ENGINE SPECIFICATIONS

Description	English	Metric
Type	Inline Single Overhead Cam (SOHC)	
Displacement	107.1 in.	1.8 (1,755mm)
Number of Cylinders	4	
Bore	3.17 in.	80.6mm
Stroke	3.39 in.	86mm
Compression ratio	9.0:1	
Cylinder bore		
Diameter	3.173 in.	80.6mm
Out-of-round and taper (max.)	0.0004 in.	0.01mm
Flatness of gasket surface	0.0019 in.	0.05mm
Pistons		
Clearance to bore	0.0008-0.0016 in.	0.02-0.04mm
Outside diameter	3.173 in.	80.6mm
Piston ring		
Ring groove width		
No. 1	0.0598-0.0606 in.	1.52-1.54mm
No. 2	0.0594-0.0602 in.	1.51-1.53mm
Oil	0.1581-0.1593 in.	4.015-4.045mm
Side Clearance		
No. 1	0.0018-0.0033 in.	0.045-0.085mm
No. 2	0.0008-0.0024 in.	0.02-0.06mm
End gap		
No. 1	0.0118-0.177 in.	0.30-0.45mm
No. 2	0.0079-0.217 in.	0.20-0.55mm
Oil ring side rail	0.0079-0.0276 in.	0.20-0.70mm
Camshaft		
Camshaft height		
Intake	1.4138 in.	35.91mm
Exhaust	1.4138 in.	35.91mm
Journal outside diameter	1.3360-1.3366 in.	33.935-33.950mm
Bearing oil clearance	0.0020-0.0035 in.	0.05-0.09mm
End play	0.004-0.008 in.	0.1-0.2mm
Crankshaft and connecting rods		
Connecting rod bearing		
Oil clearance	0.0008-0.0020 in.	0.02-0.05mm
Crankshaft main bearing		
Oil clearance	0.0008-0.0020 in.	0.02-0.05mm
Crankshaft		
Pin outside diameter	1.77 in.	45mm
Journal outside diameter	2.24mm	57mm
Out-of-round (max.)	0.0006 in.	0.015mm
Taper (max.)	0.0002 in.	0.005mm
End Play	0.0020-0.0070 in.	0.05-0.18mm
Valves and valve springs		
Valve stem-to-guide clearance		
Intake	0.0012-0.0024 in.	0.03-0.06mm
Exhaust	0.0020-0.0035 in.	0.05-0.09mm
Valve guide length		
Intake	1.73 in.	44mm
Exhaust	1.89 in.	48mm
Valve seat		
Width of seat contact	0.0354-0.0512 in.	0.9-1.3mm
Seat angle	44-44.5°	
Valve spring		
Free length	1.937 in.	49.2mm
Load at installed height	68 lbs. @ 1.469 in.	310 N @ 37.3mm
Valve length		
Intake	3.866 in.	98.2mm
Exhaust	3.760 in.	95.5mm
Stem outside diameter	0.31 in.	8mm
Face angle	45-45.5°	
Thickness of valve head		
Intake	0.047 in.	1.2mm
Exhaust	0.059 in.	1.5mm
Oil Pump		
Pressure @ curb idle speed	11.4 psi @ 167-194°F	80 kPa @ 75-90°C
Tip clearance	0.0016-0.0047 in.	0.04-0.12mm
Side clearance	0.0024-0.0047 in.	0.06-0.12mm
Body clearance	0.0039-0.0063	0.10-0.16mm

89573C06

1990-94 2.0L ENGINE SPECIFICATIONS

Description	English	Metric
Type	Inline Double Overhead Cam (DOHC)	
Displacement	122 cu. in.	2.0L (1997cc)
Number of Cylinders	4	
Bore	3.35 in.	85mm
Stroke	3.46 in.	88mm
Compression ratio		
Non-turbo	9.0:1	
Turbo	7.8:1	
Cylinder block		
Cylinder bore	3.3465 in.	85mm
Out-of-round and taper (max.)	0.0004 in.	0.010mm
Flatness of gasket surface	0.0020 in.	0.05mm
Cylinder head		
Flatness of gasket surface	0.0020 in.	0.05mm
Overall height	5.197 in.	132mm
Camshaft		
Cam height		
Intake		
Non-turbo, Turbo M/T	1.3974 in.	35.493mm
Turbo A/T	1.3858 in.	35.200mm
Exhaust		
Non-turbo, Turbo A/T	1.3858 in.	35.200mm
Turbo A/T	1.3974 in.	35.493mm
Journal Diameter	1.0217-1.0224 in.	25.951-25.970mm
Bearing oil clearance	0.0020-0.0035 in.	0.05-0.09mm
End-play clearance	0.004-0.008 in.	0.1-0.2mm
Pistons		
Outside diameter	3.3465 in.	85mm
Piston-to-cylinder clearance		
Non-turbo	0.0008-0.0016 in.	0.02-0.04mm
Turbo	0.0012-0.0020 in.	0.03-0.05mm
Ring groove width	0.8664-0.8666 in.	22.008-22.012mm
No. 1		
Non-turbo	0.0476-0.0484 in.	1.21-1.23mm
Turbo	0.480-0.488 in.	1.22-1.24mm
No. 2	0.0598-0.0606 in.	1.52-1.54mm
Oil	0.1185-0.1193 in.	3.01-3.03mm
Piston rings		
Side clearance		
No. 1, No. 2	0.0012-0.0028	0.03-0.07mm
End gap		
No. 1	0.0098-0.0157 in.	0.25-0.40mm
No. 2	0.0177-0.0236 in.	0.45-0.60mm
Oil ring side rail	0.0079-0.0276mm	0.20-0.70mm
Crankshaft and connecting rods		
Connecting rod big end-to-crankshaft side clearance	0.0040-0.0098 in.	0.10-0.25mm
Connecting rod bearing oil clearance	0.0008-0.0020 in.	0.02-0.05mm
Crankshaft main bearing oil clearance	0.0008-0.0016 in.	0.02-0.04mm
Crankshaft pin outside diameter	1.7709-1.7715 in.	44.980-44.995mm
Crankshaft journal outside diameter	2.2433-2.2439 in.	56.980-56.995mm
Out-of-roundness of journal and pin	0.0006 in.	0.015mm
Taper of journal and pin	0.0002 in.	0.005mm
End play	0.0020-0.0070 in.	0.05-0.18mm

89573C08

1990-94 2.0L ENGINE SPECIFICATIONS

Description	English	Metric
Oil pump		
Oil pressure @ curb idle speed	11.4 psi @ 167-194°F	80 kPa @75-90°C
Oil pump side clearance		
Drive gear	0.0031-0.0055 in.	0.08-0.14mm
Driven gear	0.0024-0.0047 in.	0.06-0.12mm
Valves and springs		
Valve length		
Intake	4.311 in.	109.5mm
Exhaust	4.319 in.	109.7mm
Stem outer diameter		
Intake	0.2585-0.2591	6.565-6.580mm
Exhaust	0.2571-0.2579 in.	6.530-6.550mm
Face angle	45-45.5°	
Thickness of valve head		
Intake	0.0008-0.0019 in.	0.02-0.047mm
Exhaust	0.0020-0.0033 in.	0.05-0.085mm
Valve guide length		
Intake	1.791 in.	45.5mm
Exhaust	1.988 in.	50.5mm
Valve seat		
Width of seat contact	0.035-0.051 in.	0.9-1.3mm
Seat angle	44-44.5°	
Valve spring		
Free length	1.902 in.	48.3mm
Load at installed height	66 lbs.	300 N

89573C09

1995-98 2.0L NON-TURBO ENGINE SPECIFICATIONS

Description	English	Metric
Type	Inline Double Overhead Cam (DOHC)	
Displacement	122 cu. in.	2.0L (1997cc)
Number of Cylinders	4	
Bore	3.445 in.	87.5mm
Stroke	3.267 in.	83.0mm
Compression ratio	9.6:1	
Cylinder head and valve		
Flatness of gasket surface	0.004 in.	0.1mm
Valve seat angle	44.5-45°	
Valve seat runout (max.)	0.002 in.	0.050mm
Valve seat width (finish)	0.035-0.051 in.	0.9-1.3mm
Valve seat guide bore diameter	0.4330-0.4338 in.	11.00-11.02mm
Intake valve seat diameter	1.358 in.	34.50mm
Exhaust valve diameter	1.161 in.	29.50mm
Valve face angle	45-45.5°	
Valve head diameter		
Intake	1.364-1.375 in.	34.67-34.93mm
Exhaust	1.195-1.205 in.	30.37-30.63mm
Valve margin		
Intake	0.050-0.063 in.	1.285-1.615mm
Exhaust	0.038-0.051 in.	0.985-1.315mm
Valve length (overall)		
Intake	4.389-4.409 in.	111.49-111.99mm
Exhaust	4.314-4.334 in.	109.59-110.09mm
Valve stem tip height		
Intake	1.891 in.	48.04mm
Exhaust	1.889 in.	47.99mm
Valve stem diameter		
Intake	0.233-0.234 in.	5.934-5.952mm
Exhaust	0.232-0.233 in.	5.906-5.924mm
Valve stem-to-guide clearance		
Intake	0.0019-0.0026 in.	0.048-0.066mm
Exhaust	0.0029-0.0037 in.	0.074-0.094mm
Valve guide inner diameter	0.2352-0.2362 in.	5.975-6.000mm
Valve spring free length	1.811 in.	46mm
Valve spring tension		
Valve closed	55-60 lbs. @ 1.496 in.	246-270 N @ 38mm
Valve open	123-137 lbs. @ 1.153 in.	549-611 N @ 38mm
Valve spring number of coils	—	7.35mm
Valve spring wire diameter	0.148 in.	3.76mm
Valve spring installed height	1.496 in.	38.00mm
Oil Pump		
Oil pump clearance over rotors	0.004 in	0.102mm
Oil pump cver out of flat	0.003 in.	0.076mm
Oil pump inner rotor thickness	0.301 in.	7.64mm
Oil pump outer rotor clearance	0.015 in.	0.39mm
Oil pump outer rotor diameter	3.148 in.	79.95mm
Oil pump outer rotor thickness	0.301 in.	7.64mm
Oil pump tip clearance between rotors	0.0008 in.	0.02mm
Oil pressure @ curb idle speed	4 psi	25 kPa

89573C10

1995-98 2.0L NON-TURBO ENGINE SPECIFICATIONS

Description	English	Metric
Piston, connecting rod and cylinder block		
Standard piston size	3.4434-3.4441 in.	87.463-87.481mm
Piston-to-bore clearance	0.005-0.0017 in.	0.012-0.044mm
From bottom of skirt	0.0005-0.0017 in.	0.012-0.044mm
Land clearance (diametrical)	0.29-0.32 in.	0.740-0.803mm
Piston length	2.513 in.	63.82mm
Piston ring groove depth		
Top upper compression ring	0.157-0.163 in.	3.983-4.132mm
Intermediate compression ring	0.175-0.181 in.	4.456-4.605mm
Oil control (steel) ring	0.151-0.160 in.	3.841-4.075mm
Piston pin clearance in piston	0.0003-0.0008 in.	0.008-0.020mm
Piston pin in rod interference	0.0007-0.0017 in.	0.018-0.043mm
Piston pin diameter	0.8267-0.8269 in.	20.998-21.003mm
Piston pin length	2.943-2.963 in.	74.75-75.25mm
Piston ring gap		
Top upper compression ring	0.009-0.020 in.	0.23-0.52mm
Intermediate compression ring	0.019-0.031 in.	0.49-0.78mm
Oil control (steel) ring	0.009-0.026 in.	0.23-0.66mm
Piston ring side clearance		
Top upper and intermediate compression ring	0.0010-0.0026 in.	0.025-0.065mm
Oil control (pack) ring	0.0002-0.0070 in.	0.004-0.178mm
Piston ring width		
Top upper and intermediate compression ring	0.046-0.047 in.	1.17-1.19mm
Oil control (pack) ring	0.1124-0.1184 in.	2.854-3.008mm
Cylinder block cylinder ore diameter	3.445 in.	87.5mm
Cylinder block cylinder bore out-of-round	0.002 in.	0.051mm
Cylinder block cylinder bore taper	0.002 in.	0.051mm
Connecting rod bearing oil clearance	0.0010-0.0023 in.	0.026-0.059mm
Connecting rod piston pin bore diameter	0.8252-0.8260 in.	20.96-20.98mm
Connecting rod large end bore diameter	2.0075-2.0081 in.	50.991-51.005mm
Connecting rod side clearance	0.0051-0.0150 in.	0.13-0.18mm
Main bearing journal diameter	2.0469-2.0475 in.	51.9924-52.0076
Main bearing journal out-of-round	0.0001 in.	0.00035mm
Main bearing journal taper	0.0001 in.	0.0038mm
Crankshaft		
Crankshaft connecting rod journal diameter	1.8894-1.8900 in.	47.9924-48.0076mm
Crankshaft out-of-round	0.0001 in.	0.0035mm
Crankshaft tape	0.0001 in.	0.0038mm
Crankshaft main bearing diameter clearance	0.0008-0.0024 in.	0.022-0.062mm
Crankshaft end play	0.0035-0.0094 in.	0.09-0.24mm

89573C11

1995-98 2.0L TURBO ENGINE SPECIFICATIONS

Description	English	Metric
Type	Inline Double Overhead Cam (DOHC)	
Displacement	122 cu. in.	2.0L (1997cc)
Number of Cylinders	4	
Bore	3.35 in.	85.0mm
Stroke	3.46 in.	88.0mm
Compression ratio	8.5:1	
Rocker arms and camshaft		
Camshaft cam height		
Intake	1.37 in.	34.91mm
Exhaust	1.37 in.	34.91mm
Camshaft journal outside diameter	1.02 in.	25.96mm
Cylinder head and valve		
Flatness of gasket surface	0.0020 in.	0.05mm
Cylinder head overall height	5.193-5.201 in.	131.9-132.1mm
Cylinder head bolt shank length	3.91 in.	99.4mm
Valve thickness of valve head (margin)		
Intake	0.039 in.	1.0mm
Exhaust	0.059 in.	1.5mm
Valve overall height		
Intake	4.3110 in.	109.50mm
Exhaust	4.3189 in.	109.70mm
Valve thickness-to-valve guide clearance		
Intake	0.0008-0.0020 in.	0.02-0.05mm
Exhaust	0.0020-0.0035 in.	0.05-0.09mm
Valve face angle	45-45.5°	
Valve spring free length	1.85 in.	47mm
Valve spring load/installed height	54 lbs. @ 1.57 in.	245 N @ 40mm
Valve spring out of squareness	Max. 1.5°	
Valve seat valve contact width	0.035-0.051 in.	0.9-1.3mm
Valve guide inside diameter	0.260 in.	6.6mm
Valve guide outside diameter	0.476 in.	12.1mm
Valve guide projection from cylinder head upper surface	0.77 in.	19.5mm
Valve stem projection		
Intake	1.9370 in.	49.20mm
Exhaust	1.9055 in.	48.40mm
Front case, oil pump and oil pan		
Oil pump side clearance		
Drive gear	0.0031-0.0055 in.	0.08-0.14mm
Driven gear	0.0024-0.0047 in.	0.06-0.12mm
Oil cooler bypass valve dimension	1.36 in.	34.5mm
Oil cooler bypass hole closing temperature	1.57 in.	40mm
Oil pressure @ curb idle speed	11.4 psi @ 167-194°F	80 kPa @ 75-90°C
Piston and connecting rod		
Piston outside diameter	3.334 in.	84.98mm
Piston ring side clearance		
No. 1	0.0016-0.0031 in.	0.04-0.08mm
No. 2	0.0008-0.0024 in.	0.02-0.06mm
Piston ring end gap		
No. 1	0.0098-0.138 in.	0.25-0.35mm
No. 2	0.0157-0.0217 in.	0.40-0.55mm
Oil	0.0039-0.0157 in.	0.10-0.40mm
Piston pin outside diameter	0.83 in.	21mm
Crankshaft pin oil clearance	0.0008-0.0020 in.	0.02-0.05mm
Connecting rod big end side clearance	0.0039-0.0098 in.	0.10-0.25mm
Crankshaft, flywheel and drive plate		
Bearing cap bolt shank length	2.80 in.	71.1mm
Crankshaft end play	0.0020-0.0071 in.	0.05-0.18mm
Crankshaft journal outside diameter	2.24 in.	57mm
Crankshaft pin outside diameter	1.77 in.	42mm
Crankshaft journal oil clearance	0.0008-0.0020 in.	0.02-0.05mm
Piston-to-cylinder clearance	0.0012-0.0020 in.	0.03-0.05mm
Cylinder block flatness of gasket surface	0.0020 in.	0.05mm
Cylinder block overall height	11.177-11.185 in.	283.9-284.1mm
Cylinder block inside diameter	3.35 in.	85mm

89573C12

2.4L ENGINE SPECIFICATIONS

Description	English	Metric
Type	Inline Single Overhead Cam (SOHC)	
Displacement	143.4 in.	2.4L (2351cc)
Number of Cylinders	4	
Bore	3.41 in.	86.5mm
Stroke	3.94 in.	100mm
Compression ratio	9.5:1	
Rocker arms and camshaft		
Camshaft cam height		
Intake	1.4720 in.	37.39mm
Exhaust	1.4752 in.	37.47mm
Camshaft journal outside diameter	1.77 in.	45mm
Cylinder head and valve		
Flatness of gasket surface	0.0020 in.	0.05mm
Cylinder head overall height	4.720-4.728 in.	119.9-120.1mm
Cylinder head bolt shank length	3.91 in.	99.4mm
Valve thickness of valve head (margin)		
Intake	0.039 in.	1.0mm
Exhaust	0.47 in.	1.2mm
Valve overall height		
Intake	4.4213 in.	112.30mm
Exhaust	4.4925 in.	114.11m
Valve thickness-to-valve guide clearance		
Intake	0.0008-0.0020 in.	0.02-0.05mm
Exhaust	0.0012-0.0028 in.	0.03-0.07mm
Valve face angle	45-45.5°	
Valve spring free length	2.008 in.	51mm
Valve spring load/installed height	60 lbs. @ 1.74 in.	267 N @ 44.2mm
Valve spring out of squareness	2° or less	
Valve seat valve contact width	0.035-0.051 in.	0.9-1.3mm
Valve guide inside diameter	0.236 in.	6mm
Valve guide projection from cylinder head upper surface	0.55 in.	14.0mm
Valve stem projection	1.9409 in.	49.30mm
Front case, oil pump and oil pan		
Oil pump side clearance		
Drive gear	0.0031-0.0055 in.	0.08-0.14mm
Driven gear	0.0024-0.0047 in.	0.06-0.12mm
Oil pressure @ curb idle speed	11.4 psi @ 167-194°F	78 kPa @ 75-90°C
Piston and connecting rod		
Piston outside diameter	3.41 in.	86.5mm
Piston ring side clearance		
No. 1	0.0012-0.0028 in.	0.03-0.07mm
No. 2	0.0012-0.0028 in.	0.03-0.07mm
Piston ring end gap		
No. 1	0.0098-0.0138 in.	0.25-0.35mm
No. 2	0.0157-0.0217 in.	0.40-0.55mm
Oil ring side rail	0.0039-0.0157 in.	0.10-0.40mm
Piston pin outside diameter	0.87 in.	22mm
Crankshaft pin oil clearance	0.0008-0.0020 in.	0.02-0.05mm
Connecting rod big end side clearance	0.0039-0.0098	0.10-0.25mm
Crankshaft, flywheel and drive plate		
Bearing cap bolt shank length	2.80 in.	71.1mm
Crankshaft end play	0.0020-0.0071 in.	0.05-0.18mm
Crankshaft journal outside diameter	2.24 in.	57mm
Crankshaft pin outside diameter	1.77 in.	45mm
Crankshaft journal oil clearance	0.0008-0.0016 in.	0.02-0.04mm
Piston-to-cylinder clearance	0.0008-0.0016 in.	0.02-0.04mm
Cylinder block flatness of gasket surface	0.0020 in.	0.05mm
Cylinder block overall height	11.413-11.421 in.	289.9-290.1mm
Cylinder block inside diameter	3.4055 in.	86.50mm
Cylindricity	0.0004 in.	0.01mm

89573C14

Engine

REMOVAL & INSTALLATION

In the process of removing the engine, you will come across a number of steps which call for the removal of a separate component or system, such as "disconnect the exhaust system" or "remove the radiator." In most instances, a detailed removal procedure can be found elsewhere in this manual.

It is virtually impossible to list each individual wire and hose which must be disconnected, simply because so many different model and engine combinations have been manufactured. Careful observation and common sense are the best possible approaches to any repair procedure.

Removal and installation of the engine can be made easier if you follow these basic points:

- If you have to drain any of the fluids, use a suitable container.
- Always tag any wires or hoses and, if possible, the components they came from before disconnecting them.
- Because there are so many bolts and fasteners involved, store and label the retainers from components separately in muffin pans, jars or coffee cans. This will prevent confusion during installation.
- After unbolting the transmission or transaxle, always make sure it is properly supported.
- If it is necessary to disconnect the air conditioning system, have this service performed by a qualified technician using a recovery/recycling station. If the system does not have to be disconnected, unbolt the compressor and set it aside.
- When unbolting the engine mounts, always make sure the engine is properly supported. When removing the engine, make sure that any lifting devices are properly attached to the engine. It is recommended that if your engine is supplied with lifting hooks, your lifting apparatus be attached to them.
- Lift the engine from its compartment slowly, checking that no hoses, wires or other components are still connected.
- After the engine is clear of the compartment, place it on an engine stand or workbench.
- After the engine has been removed, you can perform a partial or full teardown of the engine using the procedures outlined in this manual.

The following procedure can be used on all vehicles. Slight variations may occur due to extra connections, etc., but the basic procedure covers all models.

1. Relieve the fuel system pressure.
2. If not already done, disconnect the negative battery cable.
3. If equipped, remove the engine under cover.
4. Matchmark the hood and hinges and remove the hood assembly. Remove the air cleaner assembly and all adjoining air intake duct work.
5. Drain the engine coolant into a suitable container, then remove the radiator assembly, coolant reservoir and intercooler.
6. If equipped with AWD, remove the transaxle and transfer case.
7. Tag and detach the following components: accelerator cable, heater hoses, brake vacuum hose, connection for vacuum hoses, high pressure fuel line, fuel return line, oxygen sensor connection, coolant temperature gauge connection, coolant temperature sensor connector, connection for thermo switch sensor, if equipped with automatic transaxle, the connection for the idle speed control, motor position sensor connector, throttle position sensor connector, EGR temperature sensor connection (California vehicles), fuel injector connectors, power transistor connector, ignition coil connector, condenser and noise filter connector, distributor and control harness, connections for the alternator and oil pressure switch wires.
8. If equipped, with A/C, remove the A/C drive belt and the compressor. Leave the A/C lines attached. Do NOT discharge the system. Wire the compressor aside.
9. Remove the power steering pump and wire aside.
10. Remove the exhaust manifold-to-head pipe nuts. Discard the gasket and replace with a new one during installation.
11. Attach a hoist to the engine and take up the engine weight. Remove the engine mount bracket. Remove any torque control brackets (roll stoppers). Note that some engine mount pieces have arrows on them for proper assembly. Double check that all cables, hoses, harness connectors, etc., are disconnected from the engine. Lift the engine slowly from the engine compartment.

To install:

12. Install the engine and secure in position. The front lower mount through-bolt nut should not be tigthened until the full weight of the engine is on the mount.
    a. Tigthen the engine mount bolts as specified in the engine torque chart, located in this section.
13. Install the exhaust pipe, power steering pump and A/C compressor.
14. Checking the tags installed during removal, reconnect all electrical and vacuum connections.
15. Install the transaxle to the vehicle and tighten the upper mounting bolts to 65 ft. lbs. (90 Nm). Install the starter assembly and tighten both mounting bolts to 54–65 ft. lbs. (75–90 Nm).
16. Install the radiator assembly and intercooler.
17. Install the air cleaner assembly. Install all control brackets, if not already done.
18. Fill the engine with the proper amount of engine oil. Connect the negative battery cable.
19. Refill the cooling system. Start the engine, allow it to reach normal operating temperature. Check for leaks.
20. Check the ignition timing and adjust, if necessary.
21. Install the hood making sure to align the matchmarks made during disassembly.
22. Road test the vehicle and check all functions for proper operation.

Valve Cover

REMOVAL & INSTALLATION

1.8L Engine

▶ See Figures 1, 2 and 3

1. Relieve the fuel system pressure.
2. If not already done, disconnect the negative battery cable.
3. Disconnect the air intake and breather hoses.
4. Remove the PCV hose from the valve.
5. Disconnect the accelerator cable. If equipped, with cruise control there will be 2 cables.
6. Tag and disconnect the spark plug wires, then remove the spark plugs from the cylinder head.
7. Disconnect the vacuum line for the brake booster.
8. Remove the clamp that holds the power steering pressure hose to the engine mounting bracket, if required.

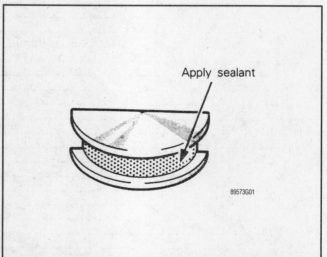

Fig. 1 Apply sealant to the area shown on the semi-circular packing

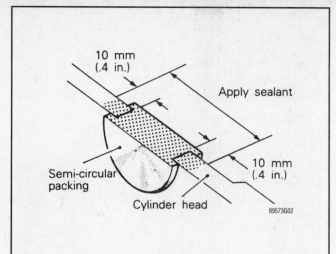

Fig. 2 Install the semi-circular packing into the cylinder head, then apply sealant to its top surface

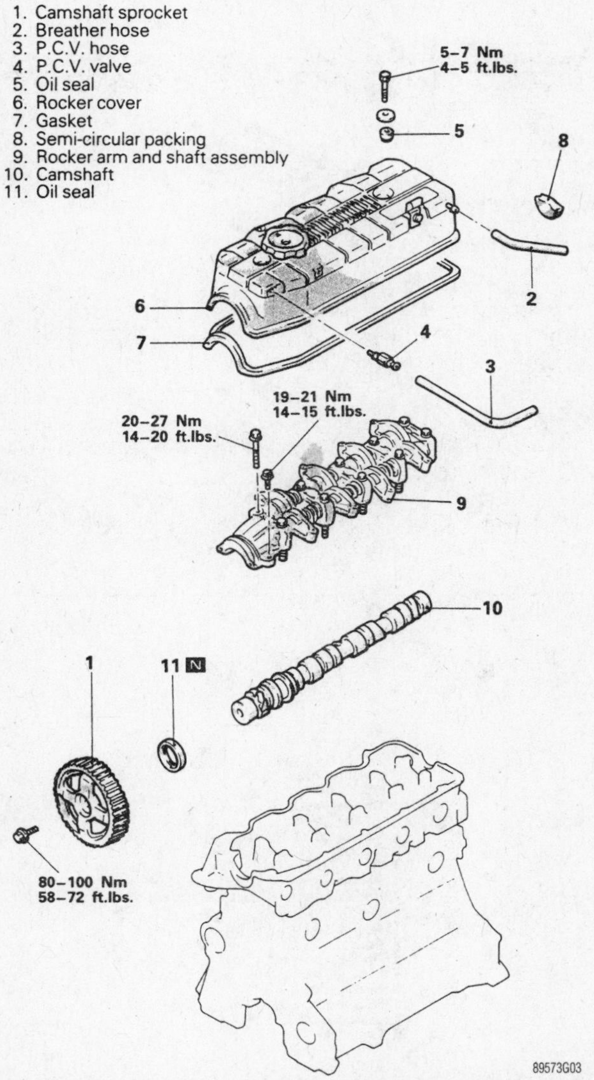

1. Camshaft sprocket
2. Breather hose
3. P.C.V. hose
4. P.C.V. valve
5. Oil seal
6. Rocker cover
7. Gasket
8. Semi-circular packing
9. Rocker arm and shaft assembly
10. Camshaft
11. Oil seal

Fig. 3 Exploded view of the valve (rocker) and related components

9. Remove the valve cover mounting bolts.
10. Remove the valve cover, gasket and half-round seal from the engine.
11. Clean all mating surfaces.

To install:

12. Apply sealer to the perimeter of the half-round seal and position in position in the cylinder head. Install a new valve cover gasket.

13. Install the valve cover to the engine and tighten the retaining bolts to 5 ft. lbs. (7 Nm). Make sure the gasket remains in position during cover installation.

14. Attach or install all previously disconnected hoses, cables and electrical connections. Adjust the throttle cable(s).

15. Install the air intake hose. Connect the breather hose and PCV hose.

16. Connect the negative battery cable, then start the engine and let idle. Inspect for leaks.

17. Check and adjust the idle speed as required.

2.0L and 2.4L Engines

▶ **See Figures 4 thru 10**

1. Relieve the fuel system pressure.
2. If not already done, disconnect the negative battery cable.
3. Disconnect the accelerator cable. There will be 2 cables if equipped with cruise-control.

Fig. 4 Unfasten the retaining clamp, then disconnect the PCV hose

Fig. 5 On some vehicles, such as this 1996 2.0L non-turbo, the ignition coil must be removed first

Fig. 6 Reposition any wires that block access to the valve cover retainers

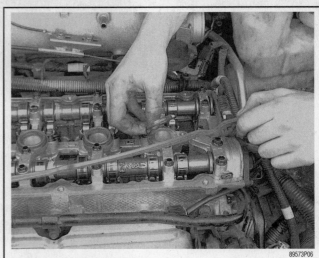

Fig. 9 Remove the gasket and seals, check for damage and replace if necessary

Fig. 7 Unfasten the valve cover retaining bolts . . .

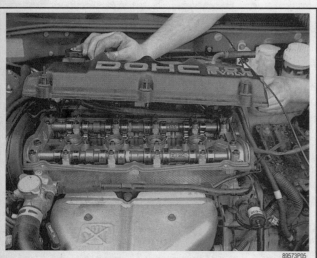

Fig. 8 . . . then lift the valve cover up and away from the cylinder head

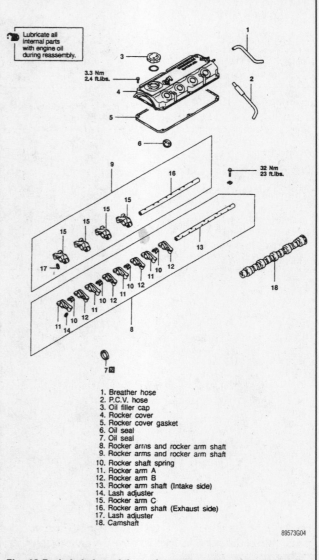

Lubricate all internal parts with engine oil during reassembly.

3.3 Nm
2.4 ft.lbs.

32 Nm
23 ft.lbs.

1. Breather hose
2. P.C.V. hose
3. Oil filler cap
4. Rocker cover
5. Rocker cover gasket
6. Oil seal
7. Oil seal
8. Rocker arms and rocker arm shaft
9. Rocker arms and rocker arm shaft
10. Rocker shaft spring
11. Rocker arm A
12. Rocker arm B
13. Rocker arm shaft (Intake side)
14. Lash adjuster
15. Rocker arm C
16. Rocker arm shaft (Exhaust side)
17. Lash adjuster
18. Camshaft

Fig. 10 Exploded view of the rocker arm cover, rocker arms and related components—2.4L engine shown

4. Remove the air cleaner with the air intake hose.

5. If equipped, remove the spark plug cable center cover and remove the spark plug cable.

6. Reposition the electrical harness and vacuum hoses as not to interfere with valve cover removal. Remove the PCV hose, as required. Disconnect the brake booster vacuum hose.

7. If necessary for removal of the valve cover bolts, remove the ignition coil.

8. Re-route any wires in the way of the valve cover retaining bolts

9. Remove the valve cover retaining screws/bolts.

10. Remove the valve cover, half-round seal and gasket from the engine.

11. Clean all gasket mating surfaces.

To install:

12. Apply sealer to the perimeter of the half-round seal and to the lower edges of the half-round portions of the belt-side of the new gasket. Install the valve cover.

13. Tigthen the retainers evenly to 3 ft. lbs. (3.5 Nm).

14. Connect or install all previously disconnected hoses, cables and electrical connections. Adjust the throttle cable(s).

15. Install the spark plug cable center cover.

16. Install the air cleaner and intake hose. Connect the breather hose.

17. Connect the negative battery cable, run the vehicle until the thermostat opens and inspect for leaks.

18. Check and adjust the idle speed, as required.

Rocker Arm/Shafts

REMOVAL & INSTALLATION

➡ **The DOHC engines do not use rocker shafts. To remove the arms, the camshaft must first be removed. It is recommended that all rocker arms and lash adjusters are replaced together.**

1.8L Engine

▸ **See Figures 11, 12, 13 and 14**

1. Disconnect the negative battery cable.

2. Remove the valve cover. Install lash adjuster retainer tools MD998443 or equivalent, to the rocker arm. If this tool is not available, rubber bands can be used.

3. Remove the distributor extension, if necessary.

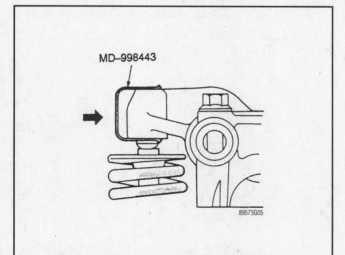

Fig. 11 Install the retainer tools to hold the lash adjusters in place. Rubber bands can be used if this tool is not available

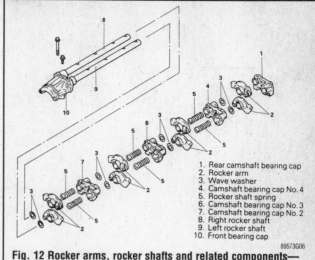

1. Rear camshaft bearing cap
2. Rocker arm
3. Wave washer
4. Camshaft bearing cap No. 4
5. Rocker shaft spring
6. Camshaft bearing cap No. 3
7. Camshaft bearing cap No. 2
8. Right rocker shaft
9. Left rocker shaft
10. Front bearing cap

Fig. 12 Rocker arms, rocker shafts and related components— 1.8L engine

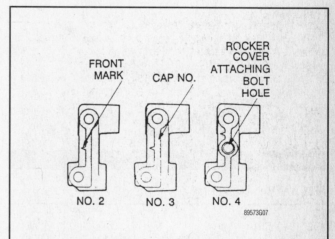

Fig. 13 No. 2, No. 3 and No. 4 caps look alike. Install correct 1 at correct position. They can be identified by the front mark, cap number and rocker cover attaching bolt hole—1.8L engine

4. Have a helper hold the rear of the camshaft down. If not, the timing belt will dislodge and valve timing will be lost.

5. Loosen the camshaft cap retaining bolts but don't remove them from the caps. Remove the rear bearing cap.

6. Loosen the remaining camshaft cap retaining bolts but don't remove them from the caps. Do not loosen the forward most camshaft bearing cap bolt.

7. At this point, the shafts can be removed as an assembly for service or service of individual components can be made by sliding component to be replaced off back end of shafts. If the later method of replacement is used, only disassembly as far as needed and keep all parts in order of removal. Installation of parts in the same location and orientation is necessary.

8. To remove the shafts as an assembly, remove bearing caps Nos. 2, 3 and 4, rocker arms, rocker shafts and bolts. It is essential that all parts be kept in the same order and orientation for reinstallation. Remove the lash adjuster tools to replace the adjuster(s) as required. Inspect the roller surfaces of the rockers. Replace if there are any signs of damage or if the roller does not turn smoothly. Check the inside bore of the rockers and lifter for wear.

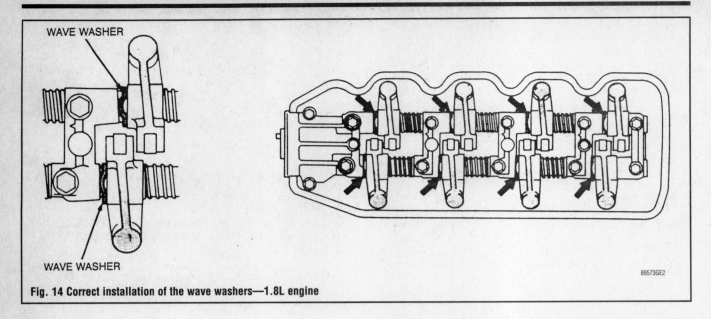

Fig. 14 Correct installation of the wave washers—1.8L engine

To install:

9. Apply a drop of sealant to the rear edges of the end caps.

10. Install the assembly into the front bearing cap making sure the notches in the rocker shafts are facing up. Insert the installation bolt but do not tighten at this point.

11. Install the remaining cap bolts. Tighten all bolts evenly and gradually to 15 ft. lbs. (20 Nm). Remove the lash adjuster retainers.

12. Install the distributor extension, if removed.

13. Install the valve cover with a new gasket in place.

14. Connect the negative battery cable.

Thermostat

REMOVAL & INSTALLATION

1990–94 Vehicles

▶ **See Figures 15, 16 and 17**

1. Disconnect the negative battery cable.
2. Drain the cooling system into a suitable container.

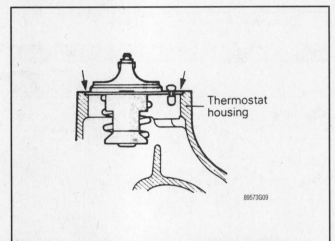

Fig. 16 Install the thermostat so its flange seats tightly in the machined recess in the thermostat housing—1990–94 1.8L engine

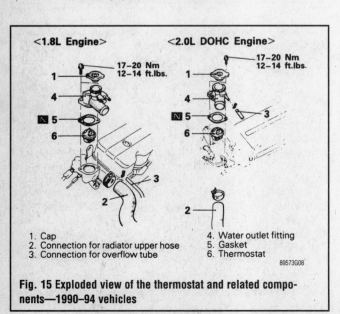

1. Cap
2. Connection for radiator upper hose
3. Connection for overflow tube
4. Water outlet fitting
5. Gasket
6. Thermostat

Fig. 15 Exploded view of the thermostat and related components—1990–94 vehicles

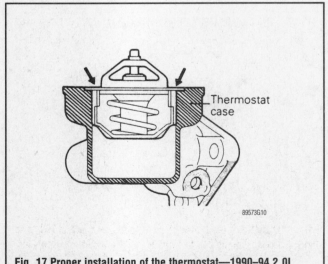

Fig. 17 Proper installation of the thermostat—1990–94 2.0L engine

3. Disconnect the upper radiator hose and overflow hose from the thermostat housing.

4. Remove the thermostat housing and gasket.

5. Remove the thermostat taking note of its original position in the housing.

To install:

6. Install the thermostat so its flange seats tightly in the machined recess in the thermostat housing. Refer to its location prior to removal.

7. Use a new gasket and reinstall the thermostat housing. Tighten the housing mounting bolts to 12–14 ft. lbs. (17–20 Nm).

8. Attach the hoses and fill the system with coolant.

9. Connect the negative battery cable, run the vehicle until the thermostat opens and fill the radiator completely.

10. Once the vehicle has cooled, recheck the coolant level.

1995–98 Vehicles

◆ **See Figures 18 thru 25**

1. Disconnect the negative battery cable.
2. Drain the cooling system into a suitable container.
3. For the 2.0L turbo engine, disconnect the air hose.
4. Matchmark the position of the upper or lower radiator hose for installation purposes.

5. For the 2.0L non-turbo engine, disconnect the radiator upper hose connection.

6. For the 2.0L turbo and 2.4L engines disconnect the radiator lower hose connector.

7. Unfasten the retaining bolt(s), then remove the water outlet or inlet fitting, as applicable.

8. If equipped, remove gasket, then remove the thermostat from the vehicle.

9. Thoroughly clean the gasket mating surfaces.

To install:

10. Install the thermostat so that the jiggle valve is facing straight up and is aligned with the mark on the thermostat case as shown in the accompanying figure.

➡**Make sure that no oil sticks to the rubber ring of the thermostat. Also, make sure not to fold or scratch the ring when inserting the thermostat.**

11. Position the water inlet or outlet fitting, then secure using the retaining bolt(s). For 2.0L non-turbo engines, tighten the bolt to 16 ft. lbs. (22 Nm). Tighten the bolts to 9.4 ft. lbs. (13 Nm) for 2.0L turbo and 2.4L engines.

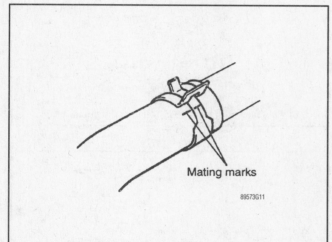

Fig. 18 Before disconnecting the radiator hose, matchmark for installation purposes—1995–98 vehicles

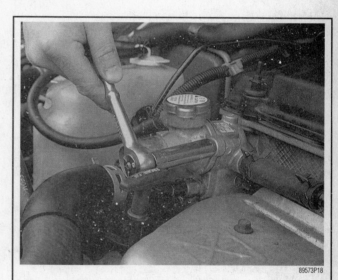

Fig. 20 Unfasten the thermostat housing retaining bolts

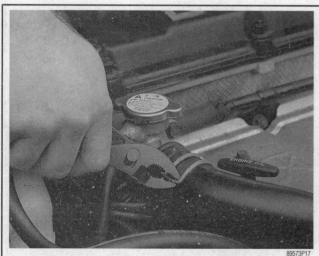

Fig. 19 Use a pair of pliers to unfasten the upper hose retaining clamp, then disconnect the hose

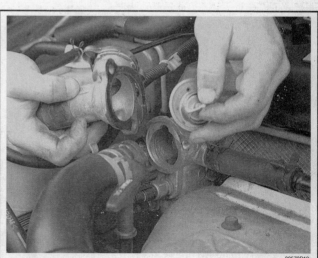

Fig. 21 Pull the fitting away, then remove the themostat from the vehicle

12. Insert the radiator upper or lower hose as far as the projection of the water outlet or inlet fitting.

13. Align the mating marks on the radiator hose and hose clamp, then connect the radiator hose.

14. For the 2.0L turbo engine, connect the air hose.

15. Fill the cooling system with the proper type and amount of coolant.

16. Connect the negative battery cable, then start the engine and check for leaks. Check the coolant level, and add if necessary.

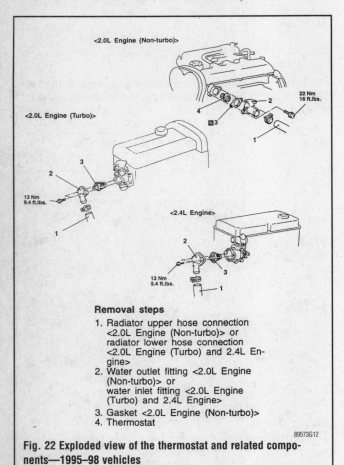

Removal steps

1. Radiator upper hose connection <2.0L Engine (Non-turbo)> or radiator lower hose connection <2.0L Engine (Turbo) and 2.4L Engine>
2. Water outlet fitting <2.0L Engine (Non-turbo)> or water inlet fitting <2.0L Engine (Turbo) and 2.4L Engine>
3. Gasket <2.0L Engine (Non-turbo)>
4. Thermostat

89573G12

Fig. 22 Exploded view of the thermostat and related components—1995–98 vehicles

89573P20

Fig. 23 Position the thermostat in the housing

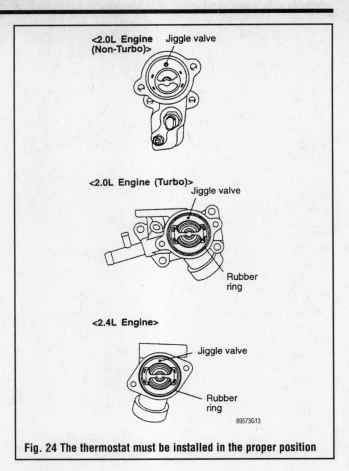

89573G13

Fig. 24 The thermostat must be installed in the proper position

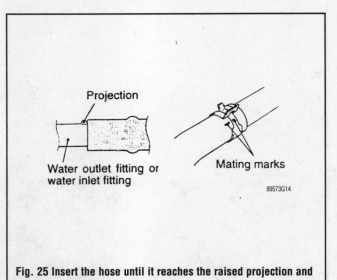

89573G14

Fig. 25 Insert the hose until it reaches the raised projection and align the mating marks

Intake Manifold

REMOVAL & INSTALLATION

1990–94 Vehicles

▶ See Figure 26

1. Relieve the fuel system pressure.
2. Disconnect the negative battery cable.

3. Drain the cooling system into a suitable container.

4. Disconnect the accelerator cable, breather hose and air intake hose.

5. Detach the upper radiator hose, heater hose and water bypass hose.

6. Remove all vacuum hoses and pipes as necessary, including the brake booster vacuum line.

7. Disconnect the high pressure fuel line, fuel return hose and remove throttle control cable brackets.

8. Tag and detach the electrical connectors from the oxygen sensor, coolant temperature sensor, thermo switch, idle speed control connection, EGR temperature sensor, spark plug wires, etc. that may interfere with the manifold removal procedure.

9. Remove the fuel rail, fuel injectors, pressure regulator and insulators from the engine.

10. If equipped with 1989–91 engines, remove the distributor from the engine if it passes through the manifold. Matchmark the distributor shaft to the housing and the housing to the head or nearest accessory prior to removal.

11. If equipped with 2.0L engine, remove the ignition coil. Remove the intake manifold bracket.

12. Detach the water hose connections at the throttle body, water inlet, and heater assembly.

13. If the thermostat housing is preventing removal of the intake manifold, remove it.

14. Detach the vacuum connection at the power brake booster and the PCV valve if still connected.

15. Remove the intake manifold mounting bolts and remove the intake manifold assembly. Disassemble the manifold from the intake plenum on a work bench if required.

To install:

16. Assemble the intake manifold assembly using all new gaskets. Starting from the center and working outwards, tighten the air intake plenum bolts to 11–14 ft. lbs. (15–19 Nm).

17. Clean all gasket material from the cylinder head intake mounting surface and intake manifold assembly. Check both surfaces for cracks or other damage. Check the intake manifold water passages and jet air passages for clogging. Clean if necessary.

18. Install a new intake manifold gasket to the head and install the manifold. Tighten the manifold in a crisscross pattern, starting from the inside and working outwards to 11–14 ft. lbs. (15–19 Nm).

19. Install the fuel delivery pipe, injectors and pressure regulator from the engine. Tighten the retaining bolts to 7–9 ft. lbs. (10–13 Nm).

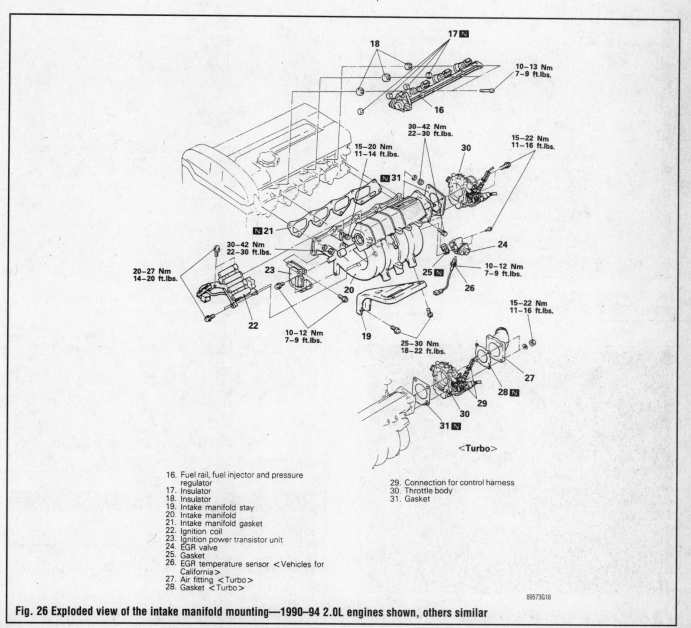

16. Fuel rail, fuel injector and pressure regulator
17. Insulator
18. Insulator
19. Intake manifold stay
20. Intake manifold
21. Intake manifold gasket
22. Ignition coil
23. Ignition power transistor unit
24. EGR valve
25. Gasket
26. EGR temperature sensor <Vehicles for California>
27. Air fitting <Turbo>
28. Gasket <Turbo>
29. Connection for control harness
30. Throttle body
31. Gasket

Fig. 26 Exploded view of the intake manifold mounting—1990–94 2.0L engines shown, others similar

20. Install the thermostat housing, intake manifold brace bracket, distributor and throttle body stay bracket.

21. Attach or install all hoses, cables and electrical connectors that were removed or disconnected during the removal procedure.

22. Fill the system with coolant.

23. Connect the negative battery cable, run the vehicle until the thermostat opens, fill the radiator completely. Check for leaks.

24. Adjust the accelerator cable. Check and adjust the idle speed as required.

25. Once the vehicle has cooled, recheck the coolant level.

1995–98 Vehicles

▶ **See Figures 27 thru 43**

1. Properly relieve the fuel system pressure.
2. Disconnect the negative battery cable.
3. Drain the cooling system into a suitable container.
4. For 2.0L non-turbo engines, if equipped, remove the auto-cruise reservoir.
5. For 2.0L turbo and 2.4L engines, disconnect the positive cable, then remove the battery.
6. Disconnect the air intake and breather hoses.

7. Detach the accelerator cable connection.
8. For 2.0L non-turbo engines, detach the connectors from the following components:
   a. MAP sensor
   b. Charge temperature sensor
   c. Throttle position sensor
   d. AIS sensor
9. For 2.0L turbo and 2.4L engines, detach the connectors from the following components:
   a. Fuel injectors
   b. Ignition coil
   c. Manifold differential pressure sensor connector
   d. Capacitor connector
   e. Throttle position sensor
   f. Knock sensor
   g. Engine coolant temperature sensor
   h. IAC motor
   i. Camshaft position sensor
   j. Crankshaft position sensor
   k. A/C compressor
10. Remove the control wiring harness clip.
11. Unplug the vacuum hose connection.

Fig. 27 Remove the accelerator cable connection

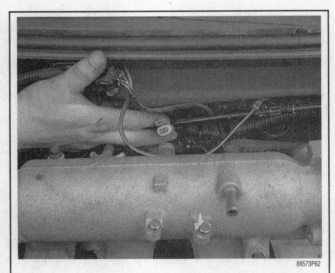

Fig. 29 Unplug the charge air temperature electrical connector

Fig. 28 Detach the MAP sensor electrical connector

Fig. 30 Unfasten the bolt, then position the control wiring harness aside

Fig. 31 Unfasten the hose retaining clamp . . .

12. Unfasten the retainer, then remove the control wiring harness.

13. For 2.0L non-turbo engines, detach the alternator wiring harness connector.

14. Disconnect the PCV hose assembly and the brake booster vacuum hose connection.

15. For 2.0L turbo and 2.4L engines, detach the spark plug cable connection and fuel return hose connection.

16. For 2.0L non-turbo engines, detach the EGR pipe connection.

17. For 2.4L engines, remove the evaporative emission purge solenoid valve connector.

18. For 2.0L turbo and 2.4L engines, disconnect the following:

a. Vacuum hose connection and vacuum pipe.

b. Brake booster vacuum hose connection.

c. Heater hose connections.

19. As outlined in Section 5, disconnect the high-pressure fuel hose connection.

20. If equipped, remove the intake manifold stay.

21. Remove the engine hanger.

22. For 2.0L non-turbo engine, perform the following:

a. Detach the injector connector, then remove the throttle body from the vehicle.

Fig. 32 . . . then disconnect the brake vacuum hose connection

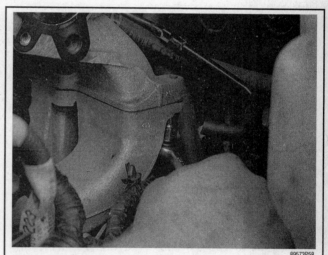

Fig. 34 Unfasten the plenum-to-lower manifold retaining bolts . . .

Fig. 33 Unfasten the retaining bolts, and separate the EGR pipe connection

Fig. 35 . . . then remove the upper intake manifold from the vehicle

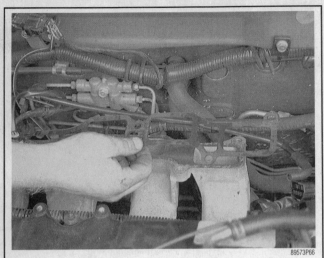

Fig. 36 Remove the intake plenum gaskets and replace with new ones during installation

23. Unfasten the retaining bolts, remove the intake manifold plenum, then remove and discard the plenum gasket.

24. Remove the fuel rail, fuel injector and pressure regulator assembly, as outlined in Section 5 of this manual.

25. If equipped, remove the insulators.

26. For the 2.0L turbo and 2.4L engines perform the following:
    a. Ignition power transistor
    b. Ignition coil
    c. EGR valve
    d. Intake manifold stay
    e. Engine hanger

27. Unfasten the retaining bolts, then remove the intake manifold from the vehicle. Remove and discard the gasket.

28. For 2.0L turbo engines, perform the following, if replacing the intake manifold:
    a. Remove the manifold differential pressure sensor.
    b. Remove the charge air cooler fitting.
    c. Remove the throttle body from the vehicle.

29. For 2.4L engines, perform the following if replacing the intake manifold:
    a. Remove the throttle body.
    b. Remove the EGR valve.

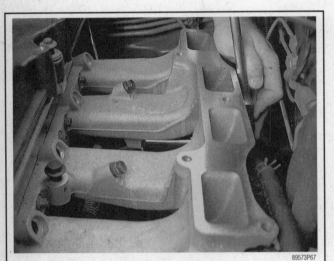

Fig. 37 Use a ratchet with an extension to remove the rear intake manifold mounting bolts

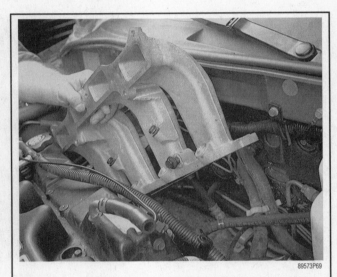

Fig. 39 . . . then remove the intake manifold from the vehicle

Fig. 38 Remove the remaining intake manifold mounting bolts . . .

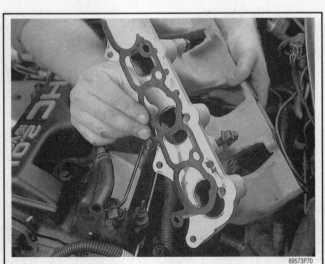

Fig. 40 Remove and discard the intake manifold gaskets, and thoroughly clean the mating surfaces

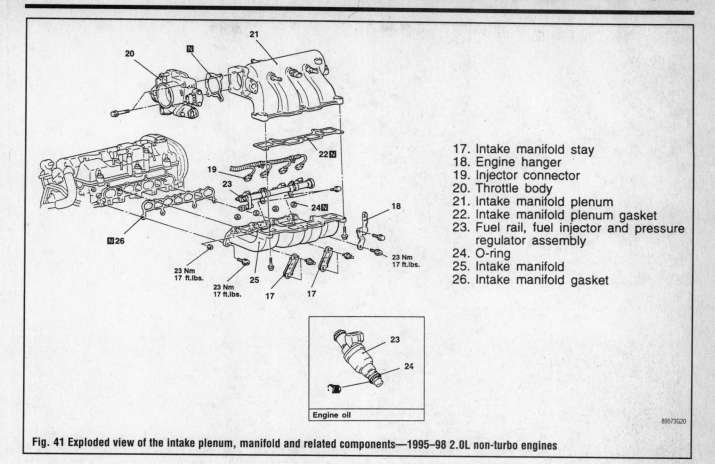

17. Intake manifold stay
18. Engine hanger
19. Injector connector
20. Throttle body
21. Intake manifold plenum
22. Intake manifold plenum gasket
23. Fuel rail, fuel injector and pressure regulator assembly
24. O-ring
25. Intake manifold
26. Intake manifold gasket

Engine oil

89573G20

Fig. 41 Exploded view of the intake plenum, manifold and related components—1995–98 2.0L non-turbo engines

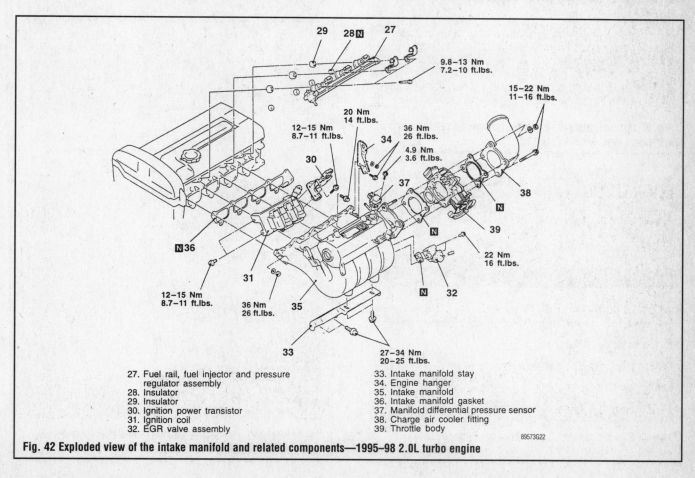

27. Fuel rail, fuel injector and pressure regulator assembly
28. Insulator
29. Insulator
30. Ignition power transistor
31. Ignition coil
32. EGR valve assembly
33. Intake manifold stay
34. Engine hanger
35. Intake manifold
36. Intake manifold gasket
37. Manifold differential pressure sensor
38. Charge air cooler fitting
39. Throttle body

89573G22

Fig. 42 Exploded view of the intake manifold and related components—1995–98 2.0L turbo engine

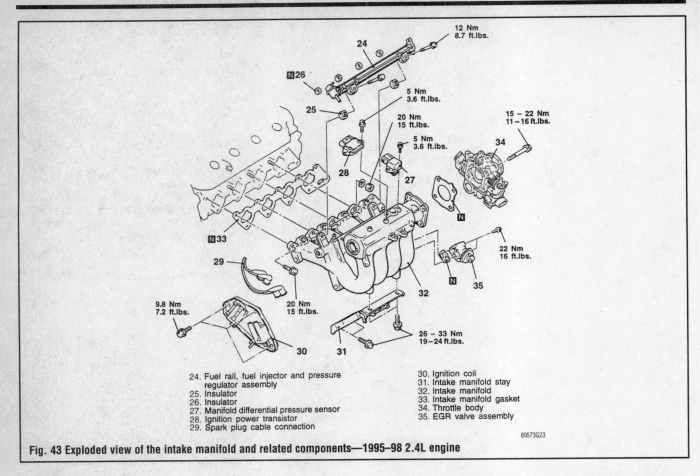

Fig. 43 Exploded view of the intake manifold and related components—1995–98 2.4L engine

24. Fuel rail, fuel injector and pressure regulator assembly
25. Insulator
26. Insulator
27. Manifold differential pressure sensor
28. Ignition power transistor
29. Spark plug cable connection
30. Ignition coil
31. Intake manifold stay
32. Intake manifold
33. Intake manifold gasket
34. Throttle body
35. EGR valve assembly

89573G23

To install:

30. Position a new gasket, then install the intake manifold. Tighten the retaining bolts to the specifications shown in the accompanying figures. Use a crisscross pattern starting from the center and work outwards.

31. Install new O-rings, then install the fuel rail assembly.

32. Place a new plenum gasket on the manifold, then install the intake manifold plenum. Tighten the bolts to the specifications shown in the accompanying figure.

33. Install the remaining components in the reverse order of the removal procedure.

34. Attach or install all hoses, cables and electrical connectors that were removed or disconnected during the removal procedure.

35. Fill the system with coolant.

36. Connect the negative battery cable, run the vehicle until the thermostat opens, fill the radiator completely. Check for leaks.

37. Adjust the accelerator cable. Check and adjust the idle speed as required.

38. Once the vehicle has cooled, recheck the coolant level.

Exhaust Manifold

REMOVAL & INSTALLATION

Non-Turbocharged Vehicles

1990–94 1.8L AND 2.0L ENGINES

▶ See Figure 44

1. Disconnect the negative battery cable.

2. For 2.0L engines equipped with A/C, remove the condenser fan motor.

3. For 1.8L engines, remove the engine oil level dipstick and O-ring.

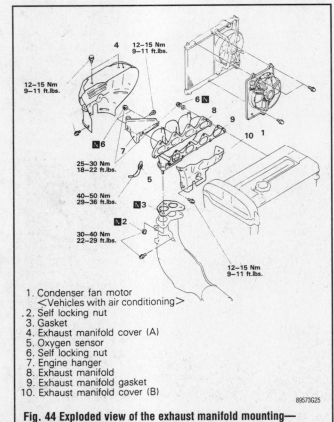

1. Condenser fan motor
   <Vehicles with air conditioning>
2. Self locking nut
3. Gasket
4. Exhaust manifold cover (A)
5. Oxygen sensor
6. Self locking nut
7. Engine hanger
8. Exhaust manifold
9. Exhaust manifold gasket
10. Exhaust manifold cover (B)

89573G25

Fig. 44 Exploded view of the exhaust manifold mounting—1990–94 2.0L engines

4. If necessary for access, raise and safely support the vehicle.

5. Remove the exhaust pipe-to-manifold self-locking nut. Separate the exhaust pipe from the manifold, then remove and discard the gasket.

6. Carefully lower the vehicle.

7. For 2.0L engines, remove the outer heat shield assembly.

8. Remove the oxygen sensor.

9. For 1.8L engines, remove the outer heat shield assembly.

10. For 2.0L engines, remove the engine hanger self locking nut.

11. Remove the engine hanger.

12. Remove the exhaust manifold mounting bolts, the exhaust manifold and the inner heat shield from the engine. Remove and discard the gaskets.

To install:

13. Clean all gasket material from the mating surfaces and check the manifold for damage or cracking.

14. Install a new gasket and install the manifold. Tighten the nuts to in a crisscross pattern to:

    1.8L engine —11–14 ft. lbs. (15–20 Nm).
    2.0L engine —18–22 ft. lbs. (25–30 Nm).

15. Install the heat shields.

16. Connect EGR components.

17. Install the electric cooling fan assembly, dipstick tube and alternator, as required.

18. Install a new flange gasket and connect the exhaust pipe.

19. Connect the negative battery cable and check for exhaust leaks.

1995–98 2.0L ENGINES

▶ See Figures 45 thru 56

1. Disconnect the negative battery cable. Drain the cooling system into a suitable container.

2. Detach the air intake hose.

3. Disconnect the upper radiator hose.

4. Remove the retaining clamp, then unfasten the air hose connector.

5. Detach the control wiring harness connection.

6. Disconnect the water pipe assembly.

7. If necessary for clearance, remove the engine oil level gauge.

8. Remove the exhaust manifold heat shield.

9. Unfasten the retaining bolts, then remove the engine hanger.

10. Remove the retainers, then unfasten the front exhaust pipe connection.

11. Unfasten the retaining bolts/nuts, then remove the exhaust manifold from the vehicle. Remove the exhaust manifold from the vehicle. Remove and discard the gasket.

12. Thoroughly clean the gasket mating surfaces.

Fig. 46 Remove the retainer, then disconnect the water pipe assembly

Fig. 47 Unfasten the water pipe bracket retaining bolt

Fig. 45 Unfasten the retaining clamp and disconnect the upper radiator hose

Fig. 48 Remove the heat shield retaining bolts . . .

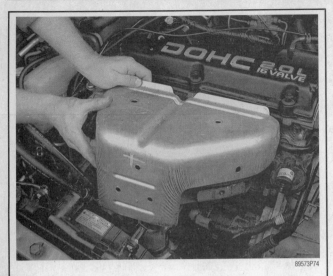

Fig. 49 . . . then remove the heat shield from the manifold

Fig. 52 From under the vehicle, unfasten the retaining bolts and separate the front exhaust pipe

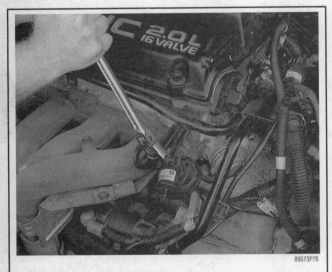

Fig. 50 Unfasten the retaining bolts . . .

Fig. 53 Remove and discard the front exhaust pipe gasket

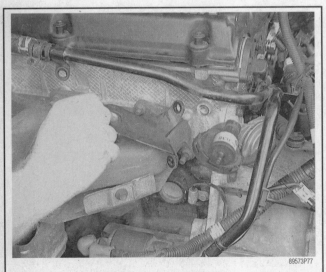

Fig. 51 . . . then remove the engine hanger

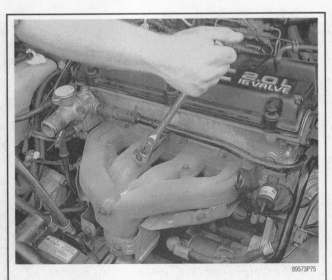

Fig. 54 Unfasten the exhaust manifold retaining bolts . . .

Fig. 55 . . . then remove the exhaust manifold and gasket from the vehicle

To install:

13. Using a new gasket, position the exhaust manifold on the cylinder head, then install the retainers and tighten to the specifications shown in the accompanying figure.
14. Attach the front exhaust pipe connection and secure with the retainers.
15. Install the engine hanger and retaining bolts.
16. Install the exhaust manifold heat shield.
17. Install the engine oil level gauge.
18. Connect the water pipe assembly.
19. Attach the control wiring harness connection.
20. Attach the air hose connector, then secure with the retaining clamp.
21. Connect the upper radiator hose.
22. Attach the air intake hose.
23. Fill the cooling system with the proper type and amount of coolant.
24. Connect the negative battery cable, then start the engine and check for leaks.

1995–98 2.4L ENGINES

▶ See Figure 57

1. Disconnect the negative battery cable.
2. Unfasten the retainers, then separate the front exhaust pipe connection. Remove and discard the gasket.
3. Remove the exhaust manifold heat shield.
4. Unfasten the retaining nuts, then remove the engine hanger.
5. Remove the retainer, then remove the exhaust manifold from the vehicle. Remove and discard the exhaust manifold gasket.

To install:

6. Using a new gasket, install the exhaust manifold and secure with the retainers. Tighten to the specifications shown in the accompanying figure.
7. Install the engine hanger and secure with the retaining nuts.
8. Install the exhaust manifold heat shield.
9. Position the front exhaust pipe connection and install the retainers.
10. Connect the negative battery cable.

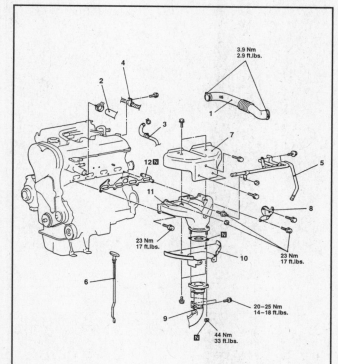

1. Air intake hose
2. Radiator upper hose connection
3. Air hose connection
4. Control wiring harness connection
5. Water pipe assembly
6. Engine oil level gauge
7. Heat protector
8. Engine hanger
9. Front exhaust pipe connection
10. Heat protector
11. Exhaust manifold
12. Exhaust manifold gasket

Fig. 56 Exploded view of the exhaust manifold and related components—1995–98 2.0L

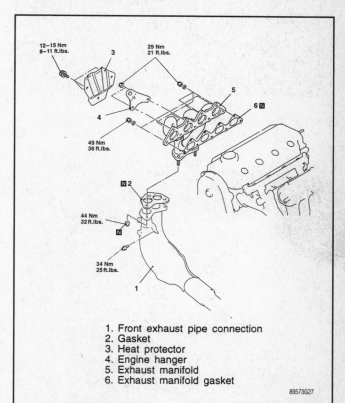

1. Front exhaust pipe connection
2. Gasket
3. Heat protector
4. Engine hanger
5. Exhaust manifold
6. Exhaust manifold gasket

Fig. 57 Exploded view of the exhaust manifold and related components—1995–98 2.4L engines

Turbocharged Engines

▶ **See Figures 58 and 59**

1. Disconnect the negative battery cable. Drain the cooling system into a suitable container.

2. If equipped with A/C, remove the condenser cooling fan from the vehicle. Remove the power steering pump and bracket and position aside.

3. Detach the oxygen sensor electrical harness.

4. Raise the vehicle and support safely.

5. Drain the oil from the crankcase and remove the oil level indicator and tube.

6. For 1990–94 vehicles, perform the following:

a. Detach the air intake hose connection.

b. Tag and disconnect the necessary vacuum hoses.

c. Detach the connector air hose A.

7. For 1995–98 vehicles, perform the following:

a. Remove the air cleaner and air intake hose assembly.

b. Disconnect the air hose.

c. Detach the water hose connections and the oil pipe connection from the turbocharger.

8. Remove the upper exhaust manifold and turbocharger heat shields.

9. For the 1990–94 vehicles, unbolt the power steering pump and position it aside. Do NOT disconnect the power steering fluid lines. Remove the power steering oil pump bracket.

10. Remove the self-locking nut, then remove the engine hanger.

11. For 1990–94 vehicles, perform the following:

a. Remove the eye bolt and gaskets.

b. Detach the connections for the water hose and water pipe from the turbocharger.

c. Unfasten the self-locking nut, then separate the exhaust pipe. Remove and discard the gasket.

12. For 1995–98 vehicles, perform the following:

a. Unfasten the retainers, then separate the front exhaust pipe connection

b. Remove the flange bolts and nut.

c. Remove the coned disc spring.

13. Remove the exhaust manifold mounting nuts. Remove the exhaust manifold and gasket from the engine. Discard the gasket.

To install:

14. Clean all gasket material from the mating surfaces and check the manifold for damage.

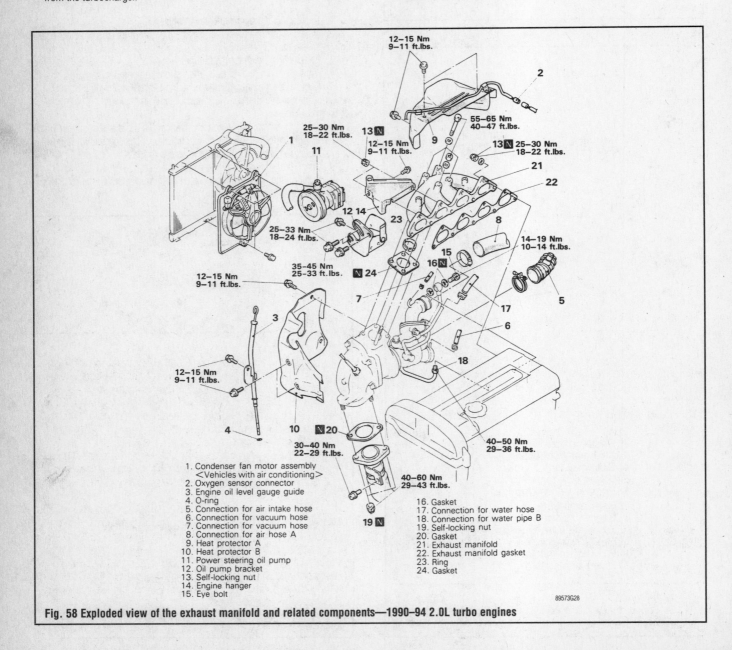

1. Condenser fan motor assembly <Vehicles with air conditioning>
2. Oxygen sensor connector
3. Engine oil level gauge guide
4. O-ring
5. Connection for air intake hose
6. Connection for vacuum hose
7. Connection for vacuum hose
8. Connection for air hose A
9. Heat protector A
10. Heat protector B
11. Power steering oil pump
12. Oil pump bracket
13. Self-locking nut
14. Engine hanger
15. Eye bolt
16. Gasket
17. Connection for water hose
18. Connection for water pipe B
19. Self-locking nut
20. Gasket
21. Exhaust manifold
22. Exhaust manifold gasket
23. Ring
24. Gasket

89573G28

Fig. 58 Exploded view of the exhaust manifold and related components—1990–94 2.0L turbo engines

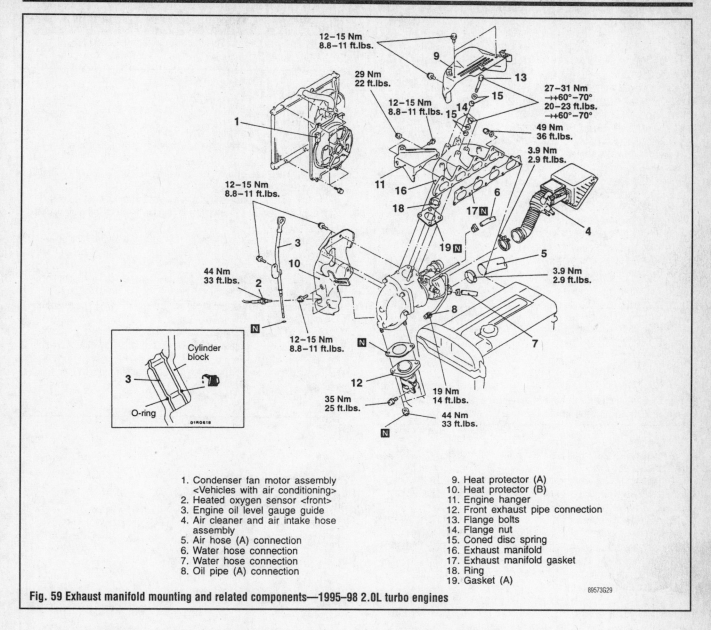

Fig. 59 Exhaust manifold mounting and related components—1995–98 2.0L turbo engines

1. Condenser fan motor assembly
   <Vehicles with air conditioning>
2. Heated oxygen sensor <front>
3. Engine oil level gauge guide
4. Air cleaner and air intake hose assembly
5. Air hose (A) connection
6. Water hose connection
7. Water hose connection
8. Oil pipe (A) connection
9. Heat protector (A)
10. Heat protector (B)
11. Engine hanger
12. Front exhaust pipe connection
13. Flange bolts
14. Flange nut
15. Coned disc spring
16. Exhaust manifold
17. Exhaust manifold gasket
18. Ring
19. Gasket (A)

89573G29

15. Install new gaskets and install the manifold. Tighten the manifold to head nuts in a crisscross pattern to the specifications shown in the accompanying figures. Tighten the manifold-to-turbo nut and bolts as shown in the accompanying figures.

16. Install the engine hanger, water and oil lines to the turbocharger.

17. Install the heat shields.

18. Use a new gasket, then connect the exhaust pipe.

19. Install the condenser cooling fan and power steering pump. Connect the oxygen sensor harness.

20. Install the oil level indicator and tube replacing O-ring as required.

21. Fill the crankcase with clean oil and refill the cooling system.

22. Connect the negative battery cable and check for exhaust leaks.

Turbocharger

REMOVAL & INSTALLATION

▶ **See Figure 60**

Many turbocharger failures are due to oil supply problems. Heat soak after hot shutdown can cause the engine oil in the turbocharger and oil lines to "coke." Often the oil feed lines will become partially or completely blocked with hardened particles of carbon, blocking oil flow. Check the oil feed pipe and oil return line for clogging. Clean these tubes well. Always use new gaskets above and below the oil feed eyebolt fitting. Do not allow particles of dirt or old gasket material to enter the oil passage hole and that no portion of the new gasket blocks the passage.

1. Disconnect the negative battery cable.

2. Drain the engine oil, cooling system and remove the radiator. On vehicles equipped with A/C, remove the condenser fan assembly with the radiator.

3. Disconnect the oxygen sensor connector and remove the sensor.

4. Remove the oil dipstick and tube.

5. Remove the air intake bellows hose, the wastegate vacuum hose, the connections for the air outlet hose, and the upper and lower heat shield.

6. Unbolt the power steering pump and bracket assembly and leaving the hoses connected, wire it aside.

7. Remove the self-locking exhaust manifold nuts, the triangular engine hanger bracket, the eyebolt and gaskets that connect the oil feed line to the turbo center section and the water cooling lines. The water line under the turbo has a threaded connection.

8. Remove the exhaust pipe nuts and gasket and lift off the exhaust manifold. Discard the gasket.

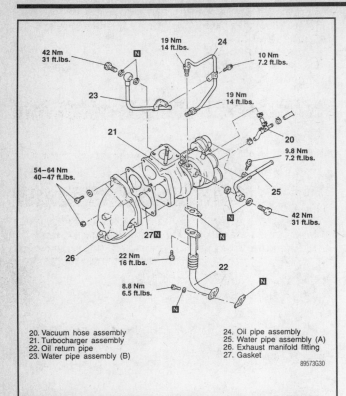

20. Vacuum hose assembly
21. Turbocharger assembly
22. Oil return pipe
23. Water pipe assembly (B)
24. Oil pipe assembly
25. Water pipe assembly (A)
26. Exhaust manifold fitting
27. Gasket

89573G30

Fig. 60 Exploded view of the turbocharger assembly—1995–98 vehicles shown, earlier models similar

9. Remove the 2 through bolts and 2 nuts that hold the exhaust manifold to the turbocharger.

10. Remove the 2 capscrews from the oil return line (under the turbo). Discard the gasket. Separate the turbo from the exhaust manifold. The 2 water pipes and oil feed line can still be attached.

11. Visually check the turbine wheel (hot side) and compressor wheel (cold side) for cracking or other damage. Check whether the turbine wheel and the compressor wheel can be easily turned by hand. Check for oil leakage. Check whether or not the wastegate valve remains open. If any problem is found, replace the part. Inspect oil passages for restriction or deposits and clean as required.

12. The wastegate can be checked with a pressure tester. Apply approximately 9 psi to the actuator and make sure the rod moves. Do not apply more than 10.3 psi or the diaphragm in the wastegate may be damaged. Vacuum applied to the wastegate actuator should be maintained, replace if leaks vacuum. Do not attempt to adjust the wastegate valve.

To install:

13. Prime the oil return line with clean engine oil. Replace all locking nuts. Before installing the threaded connection for the water inlet pipe, apply light oil to the inner surface of the pipe flange. Assemble the turbocharger and exhaust manifold.

14. Install the exhaust manifold using a new gasket.

15. Connect the water cooling lines, oil feed line and engine hanger.

16. If removed, install the power steering pump and bracket.

17. Install the heat shields, air outlet hose, wastegate hose and air intake bellows.

18. Install the oil dipstick tube and dipstick. Install the oxygen sensor.

19. Install the radiator assembly.

20. Fill the engine with oil, fill the cooling system and reconnect the negative battery cable.

Charge Air Cooler

REMOVAL & INSTALLATION

1990–94 Vehicles

◆ **See Figure 61**

1. Disconnect the negative battery cable.

2. Label and disconnect the vacuum hoses at the turbocharger by-pass valve.

3. Remove the air intake hoses and the air cleaner assembly from the engine compartment.

4. Remove the splash shield and extension from the inside of the right front wheel well. Disconnect and remove any remaining air plumbing.

5. Remove the charge air cooler mounting bolts and the charge air cooler from the vehicle.

To install:

6. Install the charge air cooler and the charge air cooler mounting bolts Tighten bolts to 11 ft. lbs. (15 Nm).

7. Install the lower air plumbing and the splash shield and extension inside of the right front wheel well.

8. Install the air cleaner assembly and the air intake hoses.

9. Connect the vacuum hoses at the turbocharged by-pass valve and the negative battery cable.

10. Confirm that all air hoses are securely installed and the connections are tight.

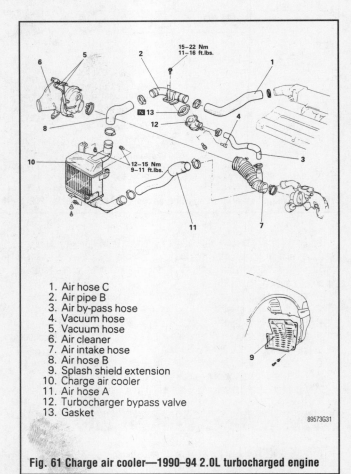

1. Air hose C
2. Air pipe B
3. Air by-pass hose
4. Vacuum hose
5. Vacuum hose
6. Air cleaner
7. Air intake hose
8. Air hose B
9. Splash shield extension
10. Charge air cooler
11. Air hose A
12. Turbocharger bypass valve
13. Gasket

89573G31

Fig. 61 Charge air cooler—1990–94 2.0L turbocharged engine

1995–98 Vehicles

▶ See Figure 62

1. Disconnect the negative battery cable.
2. Remove the front bumper for access to the charge air cooler.
3. Remove the air cleaner assembly.
4. Remove the relay box.

✳✳ CAUTION

Do not allow any foreign matter to get into the hoses while they are disconnected.

5. Disconnect the air bypass and air intake hoses from the air cleaner assembly.
6. Disconnect the air hose and turbocharger bypass valve from the charge air cooler air hose assembly.
7. Detach the air hose from the charge air cooler.
8. Unfasten the duct from the charge air cooler.
9. Remove the charge air cooler from the vehicle, detaching it from the remaining air hose.
10. Inspect the charge air cooler fins for bends, damage or foreign matter and check the hoses for damage. Replace any necessary components.

To install:

11. Position the charge air cooler in the vehicle.
12. Attach the duct work and hoses disconnected during removal.

➡ **When connecting the air hoses and pipes, align the paint marks on the hoses with the projections and indentations on the pipe.**

13. Installation of the remaining components is the reverse of the removal procedure.
14. Install the front bumper on the vehicle.
15. The connect the negative battery cable, then start the engine and check for proper operation.

Radiator

REMOVAL & INSTALLATION

▶ See Figures 63 thru 71

✳✳ CAUTION

Allow the cooling system to completely cool before attempting any repair or draining the system. Injury from scalding could result if radiator cap or hose connections are removed while system is hot.

1. Disconnect the negative battery cable.
2. Drain the cooling system into a suitable container.
3. Detach the overflow tube. Some vehicles may also require removal of the overflow tank.
4. Disconnect upper and lower radiator hoses. Matchmark the upper radiator hose to assure installation in the proper orientation.
5. Tag and detach the electrical connectors for cooling fan and air conditioning condenser fan, if equipped. Remove the fan assembly from the engine compartment.

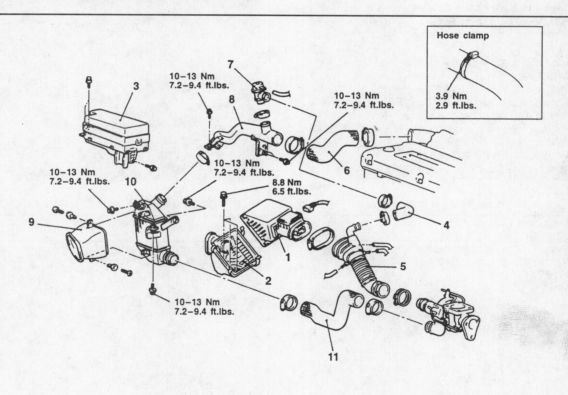

1. Air cleaner assembly
2. Air duct assembly (B)
3. Relay box
4. Air bypass hose
5. Air intake hose
6. Air hose (C)
7. Turbocharger bypass valve
8. Air hose (B)
9. Charge air cooler duct
10. Charge air cooler
11. Air hose (A)

NOTE
Align the mating marks on the hoses and pipes, and remove them.

89573G32

Fig. 62 Charge air cooler removal and installation—1995–98 2.0L turbocharged engines

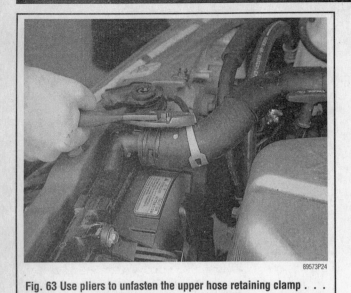

Fig. 63 Use pliers to unfasten the upper hose retaining clamp . . .

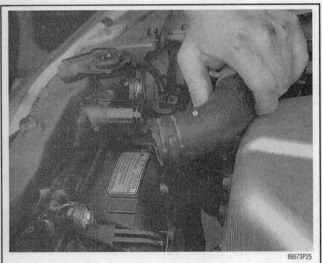

Fig. 64 . . . then disconnect the upper radiator hose

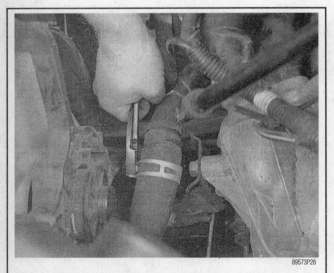

Fig. 65 Slide the retaining clamp back on the lower hose . . .

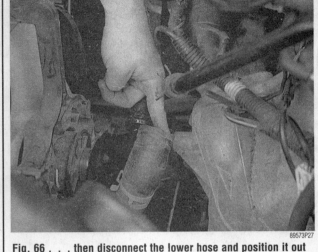

Fig. 66 . . . then disconnect the lower hose and position it out of the way

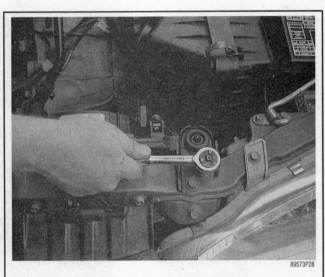

Fig. 67 Unfasten the radiator upper mount retaining bolts . . .

Fig. 68 . . . then remove the upper mounts

Fig. 69 Carefully lift the radiator, up and out of the vehicle

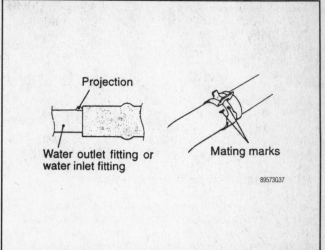

Fig. 71 During installation, make sure to position the hose to align the matchmarks, and insert far enough to reach the projections

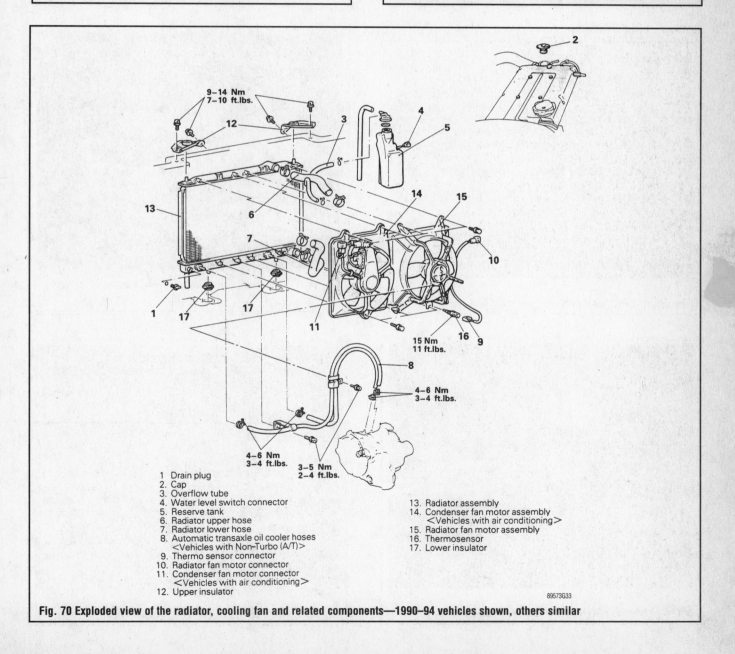

1. Drain plug
2. Cap
3. Overflow tube
4. Water level switch connector
5. Reserve tank
6. Radiator upper hose
7. Radiator lower hose
8. Automatic transaxle oil cooler hoses
   <Vehicles with Non-Turbo (A/T)>
9. Thermo sensor connector
10. Radiator fan motor connector
11. Condenser fan motor connector
    <Vehicles with air conditioning>
12. Upper insulator
13. Radiator assembly
14. Condenser fan motor assembly
    <Vehicles with air conditioning>
15. Radiator fan motor assembly
16. Thermosensor
17. Lower insulator

Fig. 70 Exploded view of the radiator, cooling fan and related components—1990–94 vehicles shown, others similar

6. Disconnect the thermo sensor wires.

7. If equipped with an automatic transaxle, detach and plug the automatic transaxle cooler lines.

8. Remove the upper radiator mounts and lift out the radiator assembly.

9. Service the lower mounts, as required.

To install:

10. Install the radiator and fan assembly, if removed, as an assembly.

11. Attach the automatic transaxle cooler lines, if disconnected.

12. Connect the thermo wires.

13. Install the fan, if removed separately.

14. Install the radiator hoses. Make sure to position the upper radiator hose so the matchmarks made during disassembly are in proper alignment.

15. Install the overflow tube and reservoir, if removed.

16. Fill the system with coolant.

17. Connect the negative battery cable, run the vehicle until the thermostat opens, fill the radiator completely and check the automatic transaxle fluid level, if equipped.

18. Once the vehicle has cooled, recheck the coolant level.

Engine Fan

REMOVAL & INSTALLATION

▶ **See Figures 70, 72, 73 and 74**

1. Disconnect the negative battery cable.

2. If necessary for access, remove the coolant recovery reservoir.

3. If equipped with an automatic transaxle, disconnect and plug the transaxle cooler lines.

4. Detach the electrical connector from the coolant fan motor.

5. Remove the mounting bolts, fan and shroud assembly from the vehicle.

6. Remove the fan blade retainer nut from the shaft on the fan motor and separate the fan from the motor.

7. If motor replacement is necessary, remove the motor-to-shroud attaching screws, then separate the motor from the shroud.

To install:

8. If removed, position the motor to the shroud and secure with the mounting bolts.

9. Install the fan to the motor shaft and secure with the retainer nut.

10. Install the fan and shroud assembly into the engine compartment and secure to the radiator.

11. Attach the fan motor electrical connector.

Fig. 72 Unplug the cooling fan electric connector

Fig. 73 Unfasten the electric fan mounting bolts . . .

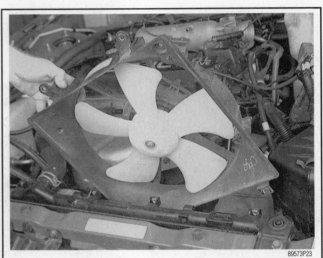

Fig. 74 . . . then pull the fan assembly up and out of the vehicle

12. If equipped with an automatic transaxle, unplug and connect the transaxle cooler lines.

13. If removed, install the coolant recovery reservoir.

14. Connect the negative battery cable and inspect the cooling fan for proper operation.

TESTING

▶ **See Figures 75, 76 and 77**

1. Disconnect the negative battery cable.

2. Check to be sure the radiator fan rotates when spun by hand.

3. For 1990–94 vehicles proceed as follows:

a. Connect 1 end of a jumper wire to terminal **4** of the coolant fan motor connector. Connect the other end of the jumper wire to the negative battery terminal.

b. Connect 1 end of another jumper wire to terminal **2** of the coolant fan motor connector. Momentarily connect the other end of the jumper wire to the positive battery terminal.

4. To test the cooling fan for 1995–98 vehicles, attach the jumper wire as shown in the accompanying figures.

5. The fan motor should run. Listen for abnormal noise while the motor is turning. If present, replace the coolant fan motor.

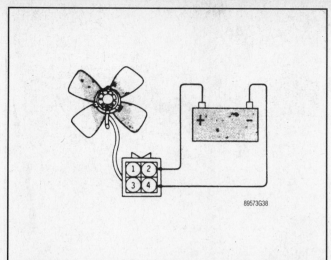

Fig. 75 Engine cooling fan testing connections—1990–94 vehicles

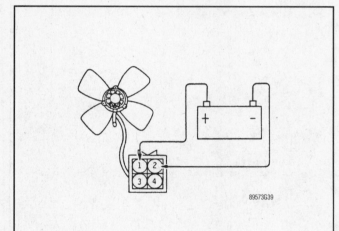

Fig. 76 Testing the engine cooling fan—1995–98 2.0L non-turbo engines

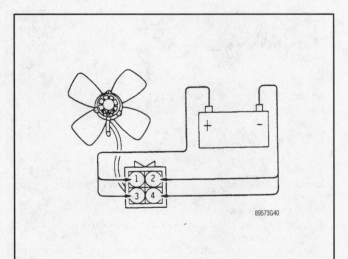

Fig. 77 Test connections for the engine cooling fan—1995–98 2.0L turbo and 2.4L engines

Water Pump

REMOVAL & INSTALLATION

1990–94 Vehicles

▶ See Figure 78

1. Disconnect the negative battery cable.
2. Drain the cooling system into a suitable container.
3. Remove the accessory drive belts, as outlined in Section 1.
4. Remove the engine undercover.
5. Remove the clamp bolt from the power steering hose. Remove the tensioner pulley bracket.
6. Support the engine with the appropriate equipment, then remove the engine mount bracket.
7. Remove both the outer and the inner timing belts from the front of the engine. If reusing old belt, mark the direction of rotation on the outer belt surface. This will assure belt rotation in the original direction and extend belt life.
8. Remove the alternator brace from the front of the water pump.
9. Unfasten the retaining bolts, then remove the water pump and gasket from the engine. Discard the gasket.
10. Remove the O-ring where the water inlet pipe(s) joins the pump. Clean all mating surfaces and inspect for cracks or other damage. Replace components that are damaged or cracked.

To install:

11. Thoroughly clean and dry both gasket surfaces of the water pump and block.
12. Install a new O-ring into the groove on the front end of the water inlet pipe. Do not apply oils or grease to the O-ring. Wet with water only.
13. Install the gasket and pump assembly and tighten the bolts. Note the marks on the bolt heads. Those marked **4** should be tigthened to 9–11 ft. lbs. (12–15 Nm). Those bolts marked **7** should be tigthened from 15–19 ft. lbs. (20–27 Nm).
14. Connect the hoses to the pump.
15. Reinstall the timing belt and related parts.
16. Install the engine undercover.
17. Fill the system with coolant.
18. Connect the negative battery cable, run the vehicle until the thermostat opens and fill the radiator completely.
19. Once the vehicle has cooled, recheck the coolant level.

1995–98 Vehicles

▶ See Figures 79 thru 88

1. Disconnect the negative battery cable.
2. Drain the engine coolant into a suitable container.
3. Remove the timing belt, as outlined later in this section.
4. If necessary, remove the alternator brace from the water pump.
5. Unfasten the retainers, then remove any brackets for access to the rear cover.
6. If necessary, remove the timing belt rear cover.
7. Remove the water pump mounting bolts.
8. Remove the water pump, gasket and O-ring. Discard the gasket and O-ring and replace with new ones during installation.

To install:

9. Install a new O-ring on the water inlet pipe. Coat the O-ring with water or coolant. Do not allow oil or other grease to contact the O-ring.
10. Use a new gasket and install the water pump to the engine block. Tighten the mounting bolts to 8.7–11 ft. lbs. (12–15 Nm). Install the alternator brace on the water pump. Tighten the brace pivot bolt to 17 ft. lbs. (24 Nm).
11. If removed, install the timing belt rear cover.
12. Install the timing belt.
13. Install the remaining components.
14. Refill the engine with coolant.
15. Connect the negative battery cable, start the engine and check for leaks.

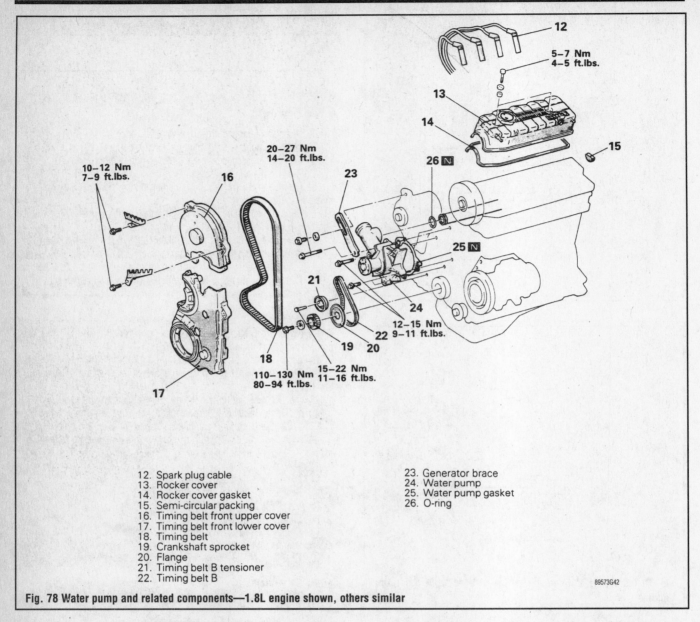

12. Spark plug cable
13. Rocker cover
14. Rocker cover gasket
15. Semi-circular packing
16. Timing belt front upper cover
17. Timing belt front lower cover
18. Timing belt
19. Crankshaft sprocket
20. Flange
21. Timing belt B tensioner
22. Timing belt B

23. Generator brace
24. Water pump
25. Water pump gasket
26. O-ring

Fig. 78 Water pump and related components—1.8L engine shown, others similar

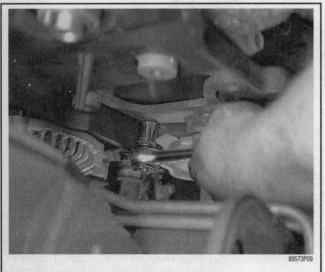

Fig. 79 Remove the bracket retaining bolts . . .

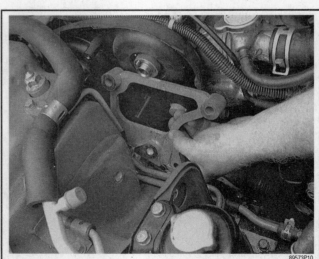

Fig. 80 . . . then remove the bracket for access to the rear cover

Fig. 81 Remove the rear timing belt cover retaining bolts . . .

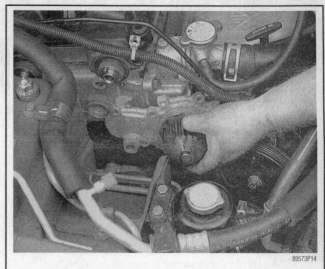

Fig. 84 Remove the water pump assembly from the vehicle

Fig. 82 . . . then remove the rear timing belt cover in order to access the water pump

Fig. 85 Remove and discard the water pump gasket

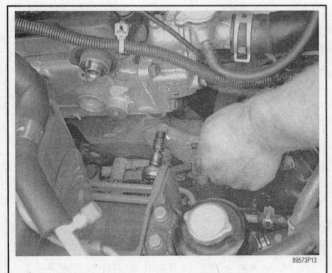

Fig. 83 Unfasten the water pump mounting bolts

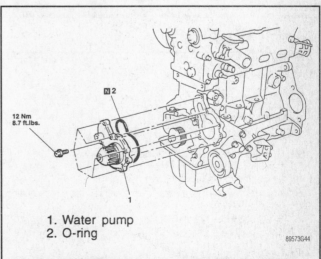

1. Water pump
2. O-ring

Fig. 86 Exploded view of the water pump mounting—1995–98 2.0L non-turbo engine

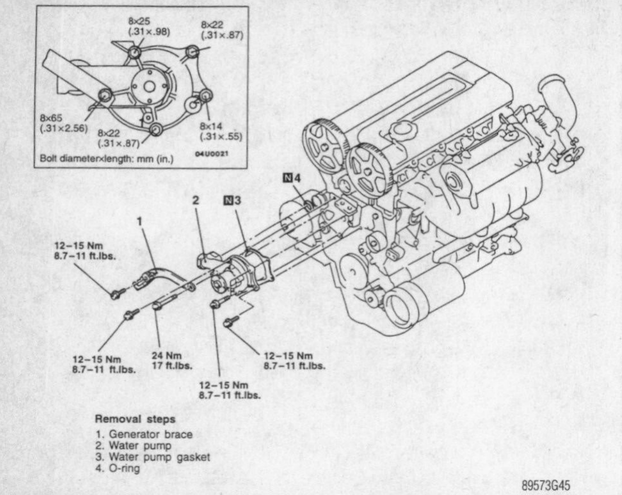

Fig. 87 Exploded view of the water pump mounting—1995–98 2.0L turbo and 2.4L engines

9. Tag and unplug the spark plug cables. Make sure not to pull on the cable, only on the boot, when removing the spark plug wire.

10. Detach and plug the fuel return line.

11. Disconnect the vacuum line for the brake booster.

12. Tag and detach the electrical connections for the oxygen sensor, engine coolant temperature gauge unit and the water temperature sensor.

13. Detach the electrical connections for the idle speed control motor, Throttle Position Sensor (TPS), distributor, motor position sensor connector, fuel injectors, EGR temperature sensor (California vehicles), power transistor, condenser and engine ground cable.

14. Disconnect the engine control wiring harness.

15. Remove the clamp that holds the power steering pressure hose to the engine mounting bracket.

16. Place a suitable floor jack and wood block under the oil pan and carefully lift just enough to take the weight off the engine mounting bracket. Then remove the bracket.

17. Remove the valve cover, gasket and half-round seal. Remove the timing belt front upper cover.

18. If possible, rotate the crankshaft clockwise until the timing marks on the cam sprocket and belt align. This should position the engine so No. 1 piston is at top dead center of it's compression stroke.

![Photo of hands installing water pump gasket](Fig. 88)

Fig. 88 When installing a new water pump gasket, make sure to position it properly to avoid leakage

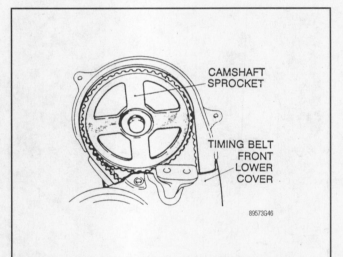

Fig. 89 Remove the camshaft sprocket with the belt attached, then place on top of timing belt front lower cover—1.8L engine

Cylinder Head

REMOVAL & INSTALLATION

1990–94 Vehicles

1.8L ENGINE

▶ See Figures 89, 90, 91 and 92

1. Relieve the fuel system pressure.

2. If not already done, disconnect the negative battery cable.

3. Drain the cooling system into a suitable container.

4. Remove the air intake hose and the breather hose.

5. Disconnect the accelerator cable. There will be 2 cables, if equipped with cruise-control.

6. Place a shop towel around the high pressure fuel line to absorb any residual fuel remaining in the system. Disconnect the high pressure fuel line.

7. Remove the upper radiator hose, the water breather hose, the water bypass hose and the heater hose.

8. Disconnect the PCV hose.

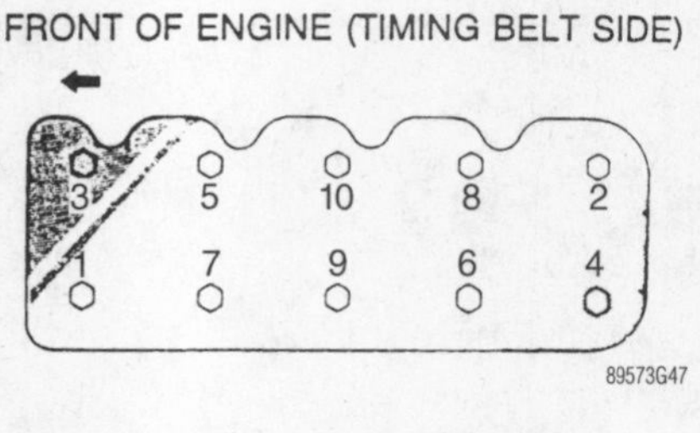

FRONT OF ENGINE (TIMING BELT SIDE)

Fig. 90 The cylinder head bolts must be removed in the proper sequence—1.8L engine

19. Remove the camshaft sprocket retainer bolt. Remove the camshaft sprocket with the timing belt attached, and allow to rest on the timing belt front lower cover. Do not allow the tension of the belt to slacken or engine timing may be lost.

20. Remove the timing belt rear upper cover. Remove the exhaust pipe self-locking nuts and separate the exhaust pipe from the exhaust manifold. Discard the gasket.

21. Loosen the cylinder head mounting bolts in 3 steps, starting from the outside and working inward. Lift off the cylinder head assembly and remove the head gasket.

To install:

22. Thoroughly clean and dry the mating surfaces of the head and block. Check the cylinder head for cracks, damage or engine coolant leakage. Remove scale, sealing compound and carbon. Clean oil passages thoroughly. Check the head for flatness. End to end, the head should be within 0.002 in. normally with 0.008 in. the maximum allowed out of true. The total thickness allowed to be removed from the head and block is 0.008 in. maximum.

23. Place a new head gasket on the cylinder block with the identification marks facing upward. Make sure the gasket has the proper identification mark for the engine. Do not use sealer on the gasket.

24. Carefully install the cylinder head on the block. Using 3 even Steps, Tighten the head bolts in sequence to 51–54 ft. lbs. (70–75 Nm).

25. Install a new exhaust pipe gasket and connect the exhaust pipe to the manifold. Install the upper rear timing cover.

26. Align the timing marks and install the cam sprocket. Tighten the retaining bolt to 58–72 ft. lbs. (80–100 Nm). Check the belt tension and adjust, if necessary. Install the outer timing cover.

27. Apply sealer to the perimeter of the half-round seal. Install a new valve cover gasket. Install the valve cover.

28. Install the engine mount bracket. Once secure, remove the jack.

29. Install the clamp that holds the power steering pressure hose to the engine mounting bracket.

30. Connect or install all previously disconnected hoses, cables and electrical connections. Adjust the throttle cable(s).

31. Replace the O-rings and connect the fuel lines.

32. Install the air intake hose. Connect the breather hose.

33. Change the engine oil and oil filter.

34. Fill the system with coolant.

35. Connect the negative battery cable, run the vehicle until the thermostat opens, fill the radiator completely.

36. Check and adjust the idle speed and ignition timing.

37. Once the vehicle has cooled, recheck the coolant level.

2.0L ENGINE

▶ **See Figures 93, 94, 95 and 96**

1. Relieve the fuel system pressure.

2. If not already done, disconnect the negative battery cable.

3. Drain the cooling system into a suitable container.

4. Disconnect the accelerator cable. There will be 2 cables if equipped with cruise-control.

5. Remove the air cleaner with the air intake hose.

6. Disconnect the oxygen sensor, engine coolant temperature sensor, the engine coolant temperature gauge unit and the engine coolant temperature switch on vehicles with air conditioning.

7. Detach the ISC motor, throttle position sensor, crankshaft angle sensor, fuel injectors, ignition coil, power transistor, noise filter, knock sensor on turbocharged engines, EGR temperature sensor (California vehicles), ground cable and engine control wiring harness.

8. Disconnect the upper radiator hose and the overflow tube.

9. Remove the spark plug cable center cover, then tag and disconnect the spark plug cables.

10. Disconnect and plug the high pressure fuel line.

11. Tag and disconnect the small vacuum hoses.

12. Detach the heater hose and water bypass hose.

13. Remove the PCV hose.

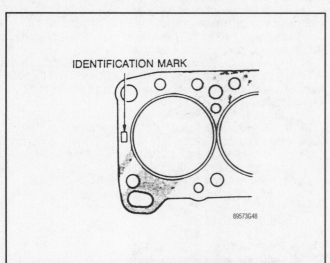

Fig. 91 Place a new head gasket on the cylinder block with the identification marks facing upward—1.8L engine

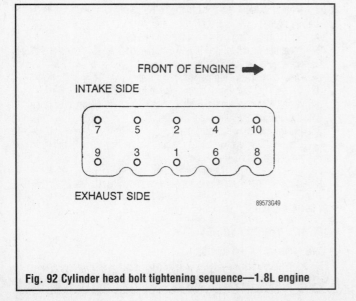

Fig. 92 Cylinder head bolt tightening sequence—1.8L engine

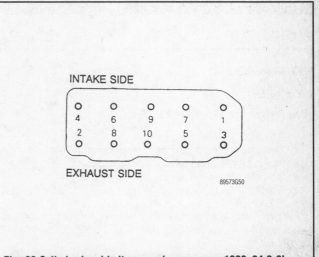

Fig. 93 Cylinder head bolt removal sequence—1990–94 2.0L engines

14. If turbocharged, remove the vacuum hoses, water line and eyebolt connection for the oil line for the turbocharger.

15. Disconnect and plug the fuel return hose.

16. Detach the brake booster vacuum hose.

17. Remove the timing belt, as outlined later in this section.

18. Remove the valve cover and the half-round seal.

19. On non-turbocharged engines, remove the exhaust pipe self-locking nuts and separate the exhaust pipe from the exhaust manifold. Discard the gasket.

20. On turbocharged engines, remove the sheet metal heat protector and remove the bolts that attach the turbocharger to the exhaust manifold.

21. Loosen the cylinder head mounting bolts in 3 steps, starting from the outside and working inward. Lift off the cylinder head assembly and remove the head gasket.

To install:

22. Thoroughly clean and dry the mating surfaces of the head and block. Check the cylinder head for cracks, damage or engine coolant leakage. Remove scale, sealing compound and carbon. Clean oil passages thoroughly. Check the head for flatness. End to end, the head should be within 0.002 in. normally with 0.008 in. the maximum allowed out of true. The total thickness allowed to be removed from the head and block is 0.008 in. maximum.

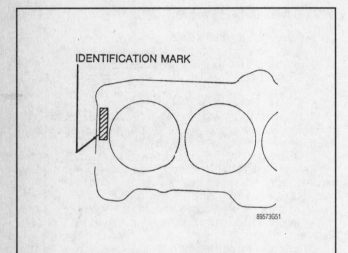

Fig. 94 Place a new head gasket on the cylinder block with the identification marks facing upward—1990–94 2.0L engine

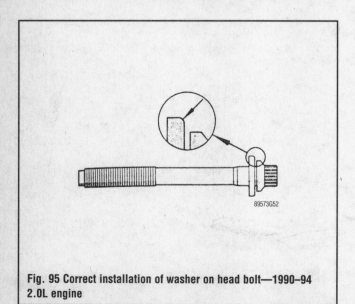

Fig. 95 Correct installation of washer on head bolt—1990–94 2.0L engine

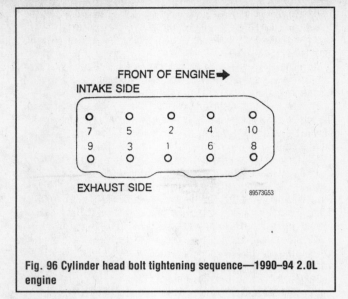

Fig. 96 Cylinder head bolt tightening sequence—1990–94 2.0L engine

23. Place a new head gasket on the cylinder block with the identification marks at the front top (upward) position. Make sure the gasket has the proper identification mark for the engine. Do not use sealer on the gasket. Replace the turbo gasket and ring, if equipped.

24. If equipped with 1993 vehicle, inspect the cylinder head bolts shank length prior to installation. If the length exceeds 3.79 in. (96.4mm), the bolt must be replaced. Install the washer onto the bolt so the chamfer on the washer faces towards the head of the bolt.

25. Carefully install the cylinder head on the block.

26. On 1990–92 models, tighten the cylinder head bolts using 3 even steps, in sequence to 65–72 ft. lbs. (90–100 Nm). This torque applies to a cold engine. If checking cylinder head bolt torque on hot engine, the desired specification is 72–80 ft. lbs. (100–110 Nm).

27. On 1993–94 models, tighten the cylinder head bolts as follows:

   a. Following the proper tightening sequence, tighten the cylinder head bolts to 54 ft. lbs. (75 Nm).

   b. Loosen all bolts completely.

   c. Tigthen the bolts to 15 ft. lbs. (20 Nm).

   d. Tigthen the bolts an additional ¼ turn.

   e. Tigthen the bolts an additional ¼ turn.

28. On turbocharged engine, install the heat shield. On non-turbocharged engine, install a new exhaust pipe gasket and connect the exhaust pipe to the manifold.

29. Apply sealer to the perimeter of the half-round seal and to the lower edges of the half-round portions of the belt-side of the new gasket. Install the valve cover.

30. Install the timing belt and all related items.

31. Attach or install all previously disconnected hoses, cables and electrical connections. Adjust the throttle cable(s).

32. Install the spark plug cable center cover.

33. Replace the O-rings and connect the fuel lines.

34. Install the air cleaner and intake hose. Connect the breather hose.

35. Change the engine oil and oil filter.

36. Fill the system with coolant.

37. Connect the negative battery cable, run the vehicle until the thermostat opens, fill the radiator completely.

38. Check and adjust the idle speed and ignition timing.

39. Once the vehicle has cooled, recheck the coolant level.

1995–98 Vehicles

2.0L NON-TURBO ENGINES

▶ See Figures 97, 98 and 99

1. Relieve the fuel system pressure.

2. Disconnect the negative battery cable.

3. Drain the engine coolant and oil into suitable containers.

4. Remove the air cleaner and air intake duct.

5. Tag and detach the connectors from the following components:

  a. A/C compressor

  b. Power steering pressure switch

  c. Heated oxygen sensor

  d. Engine coolant temperature gauge sender

  e. Engine coolant temperature sensor

  f. MAP sensor

  g. Intake air temperature sensor

  h. Throttle position sensor

  i. Idle air control (IAC) motor

  j. Injector harness

  k. Ignition coil

  l. Camshaft position sensor

  m. EGR solenoid valve

6. Disconnect the accelerator cable from the throttle body.

7. Detach the heater hoses from the rear of the engine.

8. Disconnect the fuel lines from the fuel supply rail.

9. Detach the purge air hose and the brake booster vacuum hose connections.

10. Unfasten the overflow tube connection.

11. Mark the position of the clamp on the hose and disconnect the upper radiator hose and the water hose connections.

12. Remove the timing belt, as outlined later in this section.

13. Remove the intake manifold stay.

14. Remove the intake and exhaust camshafts.

15. Disconnect the exhaust pipe connection from the exhaust manifold.

16. Unfasten the cylinder head mounting bolts, then remove the cylinder head from the vehicle.

To install:

17. Thoroughly clean the cylinder head and engine block sealing surfaces. Check the deck and the cylinder head for warpage.

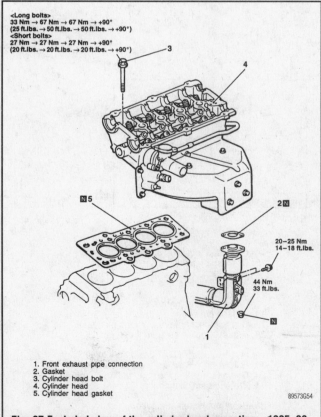

<Long bolts>
33 Nm → 67 Nm → 67 Nm →+90°
(25 ft.lbs. → 50 ft.lbs. → 50 ft.lbs. →+90°)
<Short bolts>
27 Nm → 27 Nm → 27 Nm →+90°
(20 ft.lbs. → 20 ft.lbs. → 20 ft.lbs. →+90°)

20–25 Nm
14–18 ft.lbs.

44 Nm
33 ft.lbs.

1. Front exhaust pipe connection
2. Gasket
3. Cylinder head bolt
4. Cylinder head
5. Cylinder head gasket

89573G54

Fig. 97 Exploded view of the cylinder head mounting—1995–98 2.0L non-turbo engines

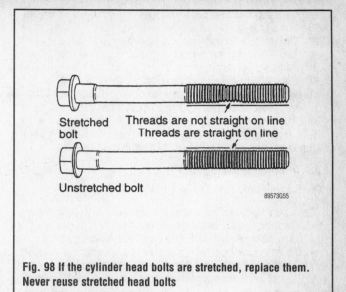

Stretched bolt

Threads are not straight on line
Threads are straight on line

Unstretched bolt

89573G55

Fig. 98 If the cylinder head bolts are stretched, replace them. Never reuse stretched head bolts

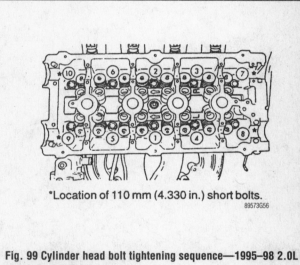

*Location of 110 mm (4.330 in.) short bolts.

89573G56

Fig. 99 Cylinder head bolt tightening sequence—1995–98 2.0L non-turbo engine

18. Clean the cylinder head bolts and inspect them for stretching. If the bolt appears to by stretched, replace it.

19. Place a new head gasket on the engine block and carefully place the cylinder head on the engine.

20. Coat the threads of the bolts with clean engine oil and install the bolts finger tight in the engine block. The short bolts go in the corners.

21. Tigthen the cylinder head bolts as follows:

  a. Tigthen the center bolts 1 through 6 to 25 ft. lbs. (33 Nm) then Tighten the outer bolts 7 through 10 to 20 ft. lbs. (27 Nm)

  b. Tigthen the center bolts 1 through 6 to 50 ft. lbs. (67 Nm) then Tighten the outer bolts 7 through 10 to 20 ft. lbs. (27 Nm)

  c. Tigthen the center bolts 1 through 6 to 50 ft. lbs. (67 Nm) then Tighten the outer bolts 7 through 10 to 20 ft. lbs. (27 Nm)

  • Turn all fasteners 1 through 10 ¼ turn (90°) more in sequence. Do not use a torque wrench for this step.

22. Use a new gasket and connect the front exhaust pipe to the exhaust manifold.

23. Install the camshafts.

24. Install the timing belts.

25. Install the intake manifold stay.

26. Connect the upper radiator hose. Install the clamp in the original position.

27. Attach the water hose to the water pipe.
28. Connect the overflow tube.
29. Attach the brake booster vacuum hose and purge air hose connection.
30. Use a new O-ring and connect the fuel lines to the fuel supply rail.
31. Connect the heater hose.
32. Attach all electrical connectors, as tagged during removal.
33. Install and adjust the accelerator cable.
34. Install the air intake duct and the air cleaner assembly.
35. Refill the engine with oil and coolant. Replace the oil filter.
36. Turn the ignition to the **ON** position and check for fuel leaks. Then start the engine and check for coolant leaks and proper operation.

2.0L TURBO ENGINES

▶ See Figures 100, 101, 102 and 103

1. Properly relieve the fuel system pressure.
2. If not already done, disconnect the negative battery cable.
3. Drain the engine coolant and engine oil into suitable containers.
4. Disconnect the accelerator cable and remove the mounting bracket.
5. Detach the intake air duct (hose) from the throttle body.
6. Tag and detach the electrical connector from the following components:

a. Idle air control (IAC) motor
b. Knock sensor
c. Heated oxygen sensor
d. Engine coolant temperature gauge sender
e. Engine coolant temperature sensor
f. Ignition module (power transistor)
g. Throttle position sensor
h. Condenser
i. Manifold differential pressure sensor
j. Fuel injectors
k. Ignition coil
l. Camshaft position sensor
m. Crankshaft position sensor
n. A/C compressor
o. Engine control wiring harness

7. Remove the engine center cover. Tag and disconnect the spark plug wires.
8. Disconnect the brake booster vacuum hose.
9. Detach the fuel lines from the fuel supply rail.
10. Disconnect the by-pass hose and the water hose connections.
11. Disconnect the vacuum hoses, breather hose and the PCV hose.
12. Remove the timing belt, as outlined later in this section.

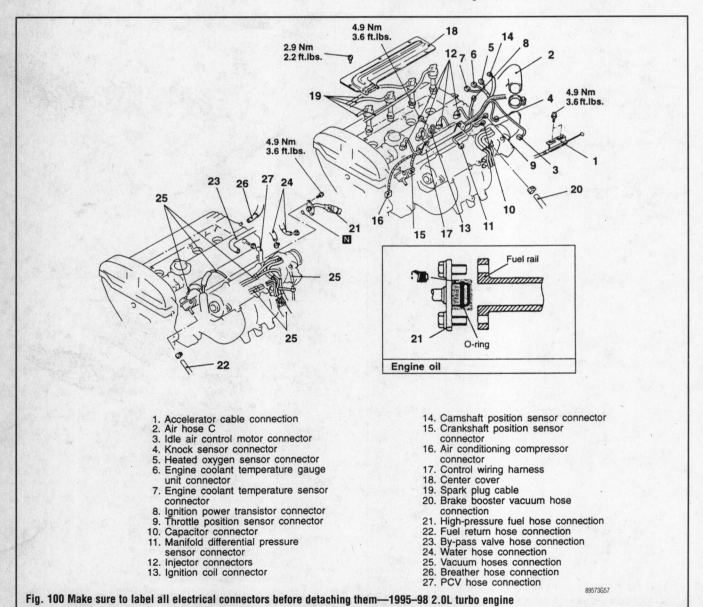

1. Accelerator cable connection
2. Air hose C
3. Idle air control motor connector
4. Knock sensor connector
5. Heated oxygen sensor connector
6. Engine coolant temperature gauge unit connector
7. Engine coolant temperature sensor connector
8. Ignition power transistor connector
9. Throttle position sensor connector
10. Capacitor connector
11. Manifold differential pressure sensor connector
12. Injector connectors
13. Ignition coil connector
14. Camshaft position sensor connector
15. Crankshaft position sensor connector
16. Air conditioning compressor connector
17. Control wiring harness
18. Center cover
19. Spark plug cable
20. Brake booster vacuum hose connection
21. High-pressure fuel hose connection
22. Fuel return hose connection
23. By-pass valve hose connection
24. Water hose connection
25. Vacuum hoses connection
26. Breather hose connection
27. PCV hose connection

Fig. 100 Make sure to label all electrical connectors before detaching them—1995–98 2.0L turbo engine

89573G57

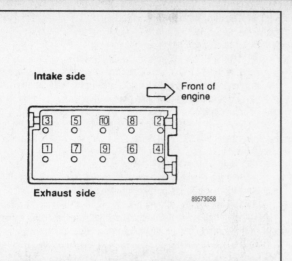

Intake side

Front of engine

Exhaust side

89573G58

Fig. 101 Cylinder head bolt removal sequence—1995–98 2.0L turbo engine

13. Remove the power steering pump.

14. Remove the cylinder head cover and the semi-circular packing.

15. Remove the heat protector.

16. Mark the position of the hose clamps on the hoses and disconnect the water hoses and the radiator hoses.

17. Remove the thermostat housing and the O-ring.

18. Remove the intake manifold stay.

19. Remove the turbocharger assembly from the exhaust manifold.

20. Gradually loosen the cylinder head bolts in two or three steps using the specified sequence and remove the bolts.

21. Remove the cylinder head and the gasket. Discard the gasket and replace with a new one during installation.

To install:

22. Thoroughly clean the deck surface of the engine block and the sealing surface of the cylinder head. Check the cylinder head for warpage.

23. Measure the length of the cylinder head bolts from below the head to the end, if the bolt measures more than 3.913 in. (99.4 mm), replace the bolt.

24. Install a new gasket on the engine block with the identification mark facing upwards.

25. Carefully place the cylinder head on the engine. Apply clean engine oil to the bolts and install the bolts finger tight.

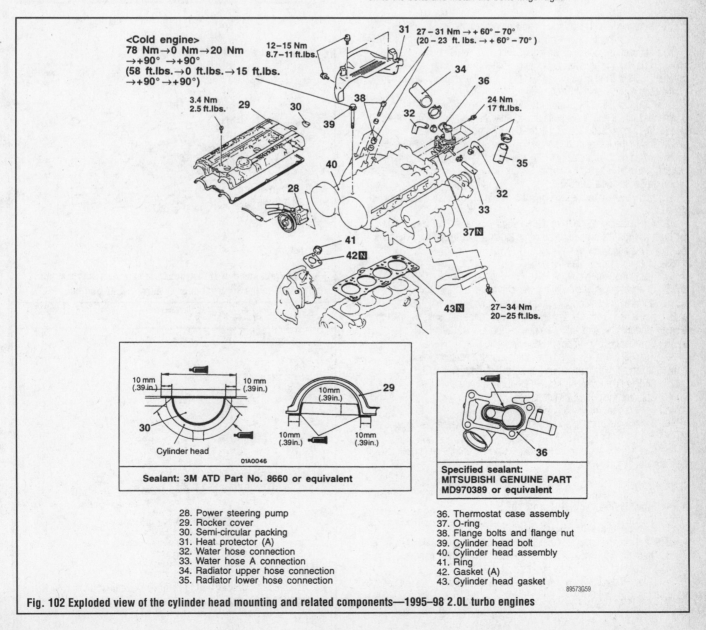

28. Power steering pump
29. Rocker cover
30. Semi-circular packing
31. Heat protector (A)
32. Water hose connection
33. Water hose A connection
34. Radiator upper hose connection
35. Radiator lower hose connection
36. Thermostat case assembly
37. O-ring
38. Flange bolts and flange nut
39. Cylinder head bolt
40. Cylinder head assembly
41. Ring
42. Gasket (A)
43. Cylinder head gasket

Sealant: 3M ATD Part No. 8660 or equivalent

Specified sealant: MITSUBISHI GENUINE PART MD970389 or equivalent

89573G59

Fig. 102 Exploded view of the cylinder head mounting and related components—1995–98 2.0L turbo engines

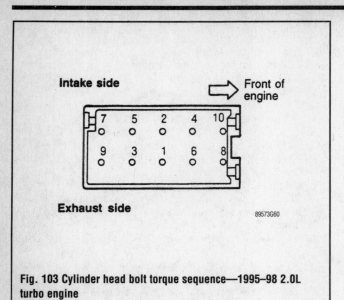

Intake side

Front of engine

Exhaust side

89573G60

Fig. 103 Cylinder head bolt torque sequence—1995–98 2.0L turbo engine

26. Tighten the bolts using the following procedure:
   a. Tighten the bolts in sequence to 58 ft. lbs. (78 Nm).
   b. Loosen the bolts completely in the reverse order.
   c. Tighten the bolts in sequence to 15 ft. lbs. (20 Nm).
   d. Make a paint mark on the head of the bolt and the cylinder head at the same spot. Tighten the bolt 90° or ¼ turn from the mark.
   e. Tighten the bolt an additional 90° or ¼ turn so that the mark on the head of the bolt is opposite the original mark on the cylinder head.
27. Use a new gasket and install the turbocharger to the exhaust manifold.
28. Install the intake manifold stay.
29. Install the thermostat housing and connect the hoses. Align the matchmarks and install the clamps.
30. Install the heat protector.
31. Apply sealant to the semi-circular packing and install it on the cylinder head.
32. Apply sealant at the front of the cylinder head where the camshaft oil seal retainer and the cylinder head come together and install the cylinder head cover using a new gasket.
33. Install the power steering pump.
34. Install the timing belt.
35. Connect the PCV, breather and vacuum hoses.
36. Connect the water hose and the by-pass hose.
37. Use a new O-ring and connect the lines to the fuel supply rail. Apply a small amount of engine oil to the new O-ring.
38. Connect the brake booster vacuum hose.
39. Connect the spark plug wires and install the center cover.
40. Attach all of the connectors, as tagged during removal.
41. Connect the intake air hose to the throttle body.
42. Connect and adjust the accelerator cable.
43. Refill the engine with coolant.
44. Replace the oil filter and refill the engine with the proper amount of oil.
45. Connect the negative battery cable, start the engine and check for fuel, coolant and oil leaks.

2.4L ENGINE

▶ **See Figures 104, 105, 106 and 107**

1. Properly relieve the fuel system pressure.
2. If not already done, disconnect the negative battery cable.
3. Drain the engine coolant and engine oil into suitable containers.
4. Disconnect the air intake hose.
5. Detach the accelerator cable. Remove cable mounting brackets and position the cable aside.
6. Remove the breather hose.

7. At the throttle body, tag and disconnect the three small vacuum hoses, the coolant hoses, and the brake booster vacuum hose.
8. Disconnect and plug the high pressure fuel line.
9. Disconnect and plug the fuel return hose.
10. Tag and detach the connectors from the following components: the oxygen sensor, engine coolant temperature sensor, the engine coolant temperature gauge unit and the engine coolant temperature switch on vehicles with air conditioning.
11. Disconnect the ISC motor, throttle position sensor, distributor, fuel injectors, noise filter, EGR temperature sensor, ground cable and engine control wiring harness.
12. Tag and remove the spark plug cables.
13. At the thermostat case assembly, remove the coolant hoses and unbolt the thermostat case from the engine.
14. Remove the upper timing belt cover. Align all timing marks.
15. Secure the timing belt to the camshaft sprocket using a piece of cord so the position of the camshaft sprocket does not move.

❋❋ **WARNING**

After removing the camshaft sprocket, do NOT rotation the crankshaft.

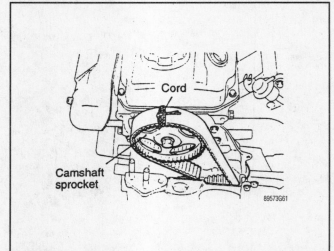

Cord

Camshaft sprocket

89573G61

Fig. 104 Tie a piece of cord around the camshaft sprocket and timing belt so the sprocket doesn't move—2.4L engine

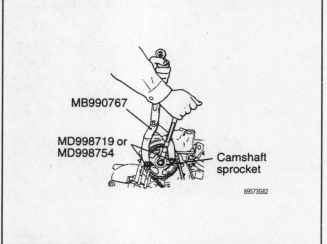

MB990767

MD998719 or MD998754

Camshaft sprocket

89573G62

Fig. 105 Use the proper tool to remove the camshaft sprocket with the belt attached—2.4L engine

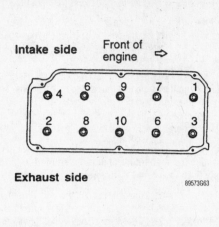

Fig. 106 Cylinder head bolt removal sequence—2.4L engine

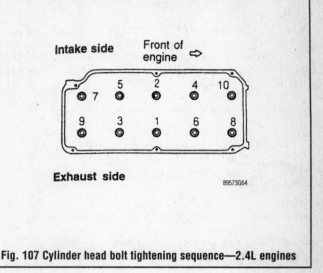

Fig. 107 Cylinder head bolt tightening sequence—2.4L engines

16. Use the special tool shown in the accompanying figure to remove the camshaft sprocket with the timing belt attached.

17. Remove the valve cover and the half-round seal.

18. Disconnect the intake manifold stay bracket from the intake manifold.

19. Remove the exhaust pipe self-locking nuts and separate the exhaust pipe from the exhaust manifold. Discard the gasket.

20. Loosen the cylinder head mounting bolts in 3 steps, starting from the outside and working inward, as shown in the accompanying figure. Lift off the cylinder head assembly and remove the head gasket.

To install:

21. Thoroughly clean and dry the mating surfaces of the head and block. Check the cylinder head for cracks, damage or engine coolant leakage. Remove scale, sealing compound and carbon. Clean oil passages thoroughly. Check the head for flatness.

22. Place a new head gasket on the cylinder block with the identification marks at the front top (upward) position. Make sure the gasket has the proper identification mark for the engine. Do not use sealer on the gasket.

23. Inspect the cylinder head bolts shank length prior to installation. If the length exceeds 3.91 in. (99.4mm), the bolt must be replaced. Install the washer onto the bolt so the chamfer on the washer faces towards the head of the bolt.

24. Carefully install the cylinder head on the block and tighten the cylinder head bolts as follows:

   a. Following the proper tightening sequence, tighten the cylinder head bolts to 58 ft. lbs. (78 Nm).

   b. Loosen all bolts completely.

   c. Torque bolts to 15 ft. lbs. (20 Nm).

   d. Tigthen bolts an additional ¼ turn.

   e. Tigthen bolts an additional ¼ turn.

25. Install the new exhaust pipe gasket and connect the exhaust pipe to the manifold. Tighten the self-locking bolts to 33 ft. lbs. (44 Nm).

26. Install the thermostat case and tighten the mounting bolts to 18 ft. lbs. (24 Nm).

27. Connect the coolant hoses to the thermostat case.

28. Apply sealer to the perimeter of the half-round seal and to the lower edges of the half-round portions of the belt-side of the new gasket. Install the valve cover.

29. Connect the intake manifold stay and tighten the mounting bolts to 22 ft. lbs. (30 Nm).

30. Install the timing belt and all related items.

31. Connect or install all previously disconnected hoses, cables and electrical connections, as tagged during removal.

32. Install the spark plug cable center cover.

33. Replace the O-rings and connect the fuel lines.

34. Install the air cleaner and intake hose. Connect the breather hose.

35. Replace the engine oil and oil filter.

36. Fill the system with coolant.

37. Connect the negative battery cable, run the vehicle until the thermostat opens, fill the radiator completely.

38. Check and adjust the idle speed and ignition timing.

39. Check for leaks and road test for proper operation.

Oil Pan

REMOVAL & INSTALLATION

1990–94 Vehicles

♦ **See Figures 108, 109 and 110**

1. Disconnect the negative battery cable.

2. Raise and safely support the vehicle.

3. Remove the oil pan drain plug and drain the engine oil into a suitable container.

4. After the oil has drained completely, install the drain plug and tighten to 33 ft. lbs. (45 Nm).

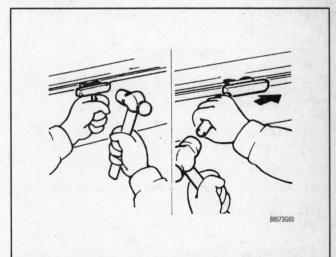

Fig. 108 Remove the oil pan by placing a brass bar at the corner of the tool and tap with a hammer

5. Disconnect and lower the exhaust pipe from the engine manifold.

6. Using the appropriate equipment, support the weight of the engine.

7. On FWD models, remove the retainer bolts and the center crossmember and AWD models, remove the left member.

8. Unfasten the oil pan bolts. Carefully the special tool or a thin prybar between the engine block and the oil pan. Lower and remove the oil pan from the vehicle.

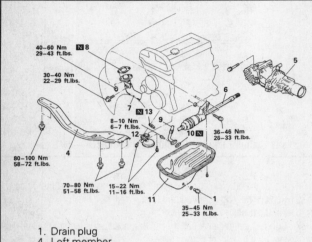

1. Drain plug
4. Left member
5. Transfer assembly
6. Drive shaft
7. Exhaust pipe connection
8. Gasket
9. Oil return pipe connection
10. Gasket
11. Oil pan
12. Oil screen
13. Gasket

89473G68

Fig. 109 Exploded view of the oil pan and related components— 1990–94 2.0L AWD engines, others similar

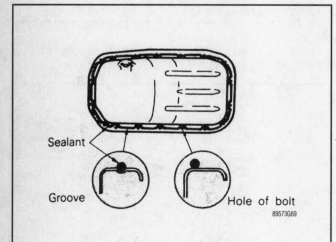

89573G69

Fig. 110 Proper application of sealant on the oil pan gasket mating surfaces—1990–94 vehicles

➡ **Do not use a chisel, screwdriver or similar tool when removing the oil pan. Damage to engine components may occur.**

9. Inspect the oil pan for damage and cracks. Replace if faulty. While the pan is removed, inspect the oil screen for clogging, damage and cracks. Replace if faulty.

To install:

10. Using a wire brush or other tool, scrape clean all gasket surfaces of the cylinder block and the oil pan so that all loose material is removed. Clean sealing surfaces of all dirt and oil.

11. Apply sealant around the gasket surfaces of the oil pan in such a manner that all bolt holes are circled and there is a continuous bead of sealer around the entire perimeter of the oil pan.

➡ **The continuous bead of sealer should be applied in a bead approximately 0.16 in. (4mm) in diameter.**

12. Install the oil pan onto the cylinder block within 15 minutes after applying sealant. Install the fasteners and tighten to 4–6 ft. lbs. (6–8 Nm).

13. On FWD models, install the crossmember and tighten the crossmember mounting bolts to 72 ft. lbs. (100 Nm).

14. On AWD models, install the left member and tighten the forward retainer bolts to 72 ft. lbs. (100 Nm). Tighten the rearward left member bolts to 58 ft. lbs. (80 Nm).

15. Connect the exhaust pipe from the engine manifold with new gasket in place. Tighten the exhaust pipe to manifold flange nuts to 29 ft. lbs. (40 Nm). Install and tighten the support bolt to 29 ft. lbs. (40 Nm).

16. Lower the vehicle and fill the crankcase to the proper level with clean engine oil.

17. Connect the negative battery cable. Start the engine and check for leaks.

1995–98 Vehicles

2.0L NON-TURBO ENGINE

▶ **See Figure 111**

1. Disconnect the negative battery cable.
2. Raise and safely support the vehicle.
3. Drain the engine oil into a suitable container.
4. Once the oil has completely drained, install the plug and tighten to 25 ft. lbs. (34 Nm).
5. Remove the front exhaust pipe.
6. Remove the engine oil dipstick and tube assembly.
7. Remove the front plate.
8. Unfasten the oil pan mounting bolts, then remove the oil pan and gasket.

To install:

9. Apply sealant at the point where the engine block meets the oil pump.
10. Use a new gasket and install the oil pan. Tighten the mounting bolts to 8.9 ft. lbs. (12 Nm).
11. Install the front plate.
12. Install the front exhaust pipe.
13. Install the dipstick and tube assembly.
14. Safely lower the vehicle to the floor.
15. Refill the crankcase with oil to the proper level.
16. Connect the negative battery cable.
17. Start the engine and check for leaks.

2.0L TURBO ENGINE

▶ **See Figures 108, 112 and 113**

1. Disconnect the negative battery cable.
2. Safely raise and support the vehicle.
3. Remove the front exhaust pipe.
4. Remove the exhaust pipe and muffler assembly.

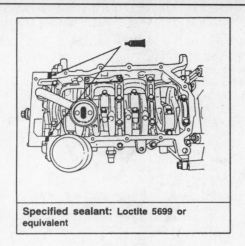

Specified sealant: Loctite 5699 or equivalent

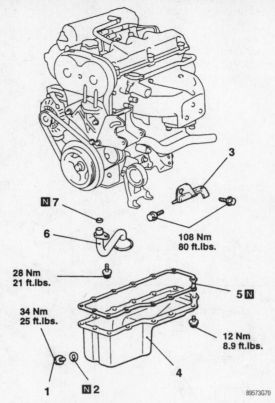

108 Nm
80 ft.lbs.

N 7

6

28 Nm
21 ft.lbs.

34 Nm
25 ft.lbs.

5 N

12 Nm
8.9 ft.lbs.

1. Drain plug
2. Gasket
3. Front plate
4. Oil pan
5. Oil pan gasket
6. Oil screen
7. O-ring

1   N 2   4

89573G70

Fig. 111 Exploded view of the oil pan and related components—1995–98 2.0L non-turbo engine

5. Drain the engine oil into a suitable container. Once the oil has drained completely, tighten the plug to 29 ft. lbs. (39 Nm).

6. Remove the dipstick and tube.

7. For AWD vehicles, remove the transfer case assembly as follows:

a. With the propeller shaft still installed, remove the transfer mounting bolt.

b. Insert a suitable prytool in between the transfer case and transaxle, then remove the transfer case from the center shaft.

c. Remove the transfer case from the center shaft. Do NOT tilt the transfer assembly to the rear or oil will leak out.

d. After removing the transfer assembly, insert tool MB991193 or equivalent, to prevent the oil from leaking out. Use a piece of wire to suspend the transfer case from the body.

8. Remove the bell housing cover.

9. Disconnect the oil return pipe from the oil pan.

10. Remove the oil pan mounting bolts. Tap the oil pan seal breaker MB998727 or equivalent between the oil pan and the engine block to break the seal and remove the oil pan.

To install:

11. Clean the sealing surface on the oil pan and engine block. Apply a continuous bead of sealant MD970389 or equivalent to the oil pan.

12. Clean the oil pan mounting bolt holes in the oil seal case.

13. Install the oil pan to the engine block. Tighten the mounting bolts to 5.1 ft. lbs. (6.9 Nm).

14. Use a new gasket and connect the oil return pipe to the oil pan.

15. Install the bell housing cover.

16. If equipped with AWD, install the transfer case assembly.

17. Install the dipstick and tube assembly.

18. Install the front exhaust pipe.

19. Install the exhaust pipe and muffler.

20. Install a new oil filter.

21. Safely lower the vehicle to the floor and add five quarts of oil to the crankcase.

22. Connect the negative battery cable.

23. Start the engine and check for leaks.

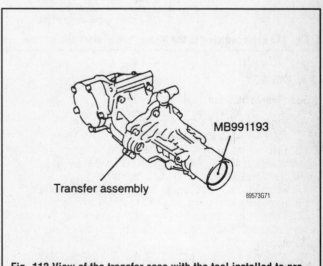

MB991193

Transfer assembly

89573G71

Fig. 112 View of the transfer case with the tool installed to prevent oil from leaking out—1995–98 2.0L turbo engines

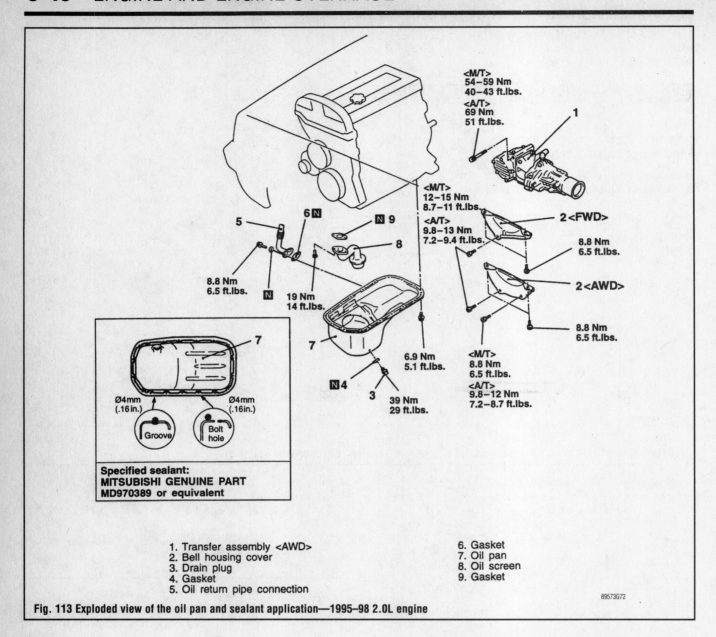

<M/T>
54–59 Nm
40–43 ft.lbs.
<A/T>
69 Nm
51 ft.lbs.

1

<M/T>
12–15 Nm
8.7–11 ft.lbs.
<A/T>
9.8–13 Nm
7.2–9.4 ft.lbs.

5

6 N

N 9

8

2 <FWD>

8.8 Nm
6.5 ft.lbs.

2 <AWD>

8.8 Nm
6.5 ft.lbs.

8.8 Nm
6.5 ft.lbs.

N

19 Nm
14 ft.lbs.

7

7

6.9 Nm
5.1 ft.lbs.

<M/T>
8.8 Nm
6.5 ft.lbs.
<A/T>
9.8–12 Nm
7.2–8.7 ft.lbs.

N 4

3

39 Nm
29 ft.lbs.

Ø4mm
(.16 in.)

Ø4mm
(.16 in.)

Groove

Bolt hole

Specified sealant:
MITSUBISHI GENUINE PART
MD970389 or equivalent

1. Transfer assembly <AWD>
2. Bell housing cover
3. Drain plug
4. Gasket
5. Oil return pipe connection
6. Gasket
7. Oil pan
8. Oil screen
9. Gasket

89573G72

Fig. 113 Exploded view of the oil pan and sealant application—1995–98 2.0L engine

2.4L ENGINE

▶ See Figures 108 and 114

1. Remove the negative battery cable.
2. Raise and safely support the vehicle.
3. Drain the engine oil into a suitable container. When the oil has completely drained, install the plug and tighten to 29 ft. lbs. (39 Nm).
4. Remove the engine dipstick and tube assembly.
5. Remove the front exhaust pipe.
6. Remove the bell housing inspection cover.
7. Unfasten the bolts attaching the oil pan to the cylinder block, then using special tool, remove the oil pan assembly from the vehicle.

To install:

8. Make sure that the oil pan and cylinder block mating surfaces are free of any old sealing material. Apply the specified sealant or the equivalent.
9. Install the oil pan to the cylinder block and tighten the bolts to 5 ft. lbs. (7 Nm).
10. Reinstall the bell housing inspection cover. Tighten the bolts to 7 ft. lbs. (9 Nm).
11. Install the front exhaust pipe.
12. Reinstall the engine dipstick and tube assembly using a new O-ring.

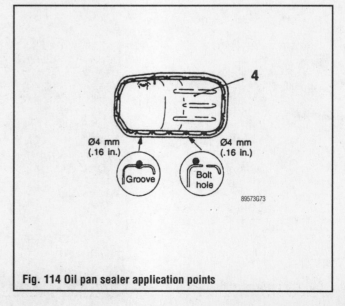

4

Ø4 mm
(.16 in.)

Ø4 mm
(.16 in.)

Groove

Bolt hole

89573G73

Fig. 114 Oil pan sealer application points

13. Carefully lower the vehicle.

14. Refill the engine with oil. Reconnect the negative battery cable. Start the engine and check for leaks.

Oil Pump

REMOVAL & INSTALLATION

▶ **See Figures 109, 110, 111, 112 and 113**

➡**Whenever the oil pump is disassembled or the cover removed, the gear cavity must be filled with petroleum jelly for priming purposes. Do not use grease. Also, these procedures require the use of several special tools. Do not attempt without the proper tools.**

1990–94 Vehicles

1.8L ENGINE

▶ **See Figure 115**

1. Disconnect the negative battery cable.

2. Remove the front engine mount bracket and accessory drive belts. Make sure to support the engine using the proper equipment prior to removing the front engine mount.

3. Remove timing belt upper and lower covers.

4. Remove the timing belt and crankshaft sprocket.

5. Drain the engine oil. Once the oil is completely drained, install the drain plug and tighten to specifications.

6. Remove the oil pan, as outlined earlier in this section.

7. Remove the oil screen and gasket.

8. Remove the retainer bolts from the oil pump cover. Remove the oil pump cover from the front engine case cover.

9. Remove the flange bolt and the oil pump drive and oil pump driven gears.

10. Clean all mating surfaces of gasket material.

11. After disassembling the oil pump, clean all components.

12. Assemble the oil pump gears into the front case and rotate them to ensure smooth rotation and no looseness. Make sure there is no ridge wear on the contact surface between the front case and the gear surface of the oil pump front cover. Replace if any components are worn.

13. Measure the oil pump gears clearances as follows:

a. With the drive and driven gears installed in the front case, measure the tip clearance of the gears. The distance between the tips of the drive gear's teeth and the case should be 0.0039–0.0079 in. with a limit of 0.071 in. The distance between the tips of the driven gear's teeth and the case should also be 0.0039–0.0079 in. with a limit of 0.071 in.

b. Next measure the oil pump gear end-play. The end-play is checked by placing a straight-edge across the machined cover surface and measuring with a feeler gauge. The end-play for each gear should be 0.0024–0.0047 in. with a limit of 0.008 in.

14. If any measurement is beyond specification, replace the entire pump assembly.

To install:

15. Align the timing mark on the oil pump drive gear with that on the driven gear and install them into the engine front cover. Apply engine oil to the gears.

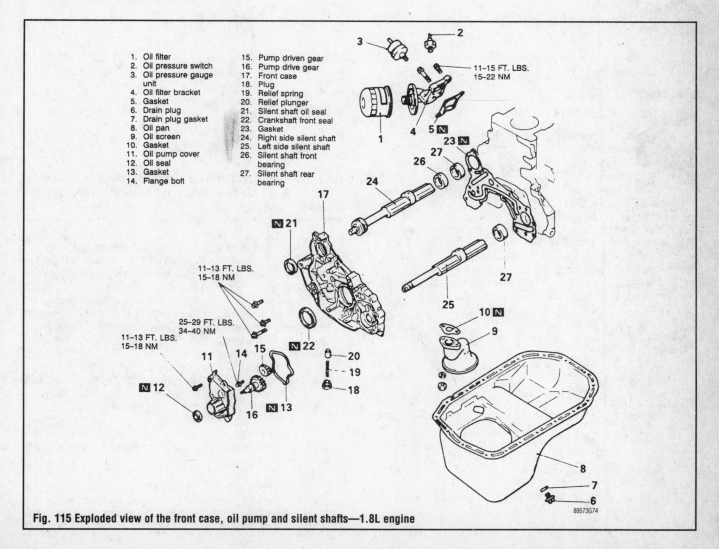

1. Oil filter	15. Pump driven gear
2. Oil pressure switch	16. Pump drive gear
3. Oil pressure gauge unit	17. Front case
	18. Plug
4. Oil filter bracket	19. Relief spring
5. Gasket	20. Relief plunger
6. Drain plug	21. Silent shaft oil seal
7. Drain plug gasket	22. Crankshaft front seal
8. Oil pan	23. Gasket
9. Oil screen	24. Right side silent shaft
10. Gasket	25. Left side silent shaft
11. Oil pump cover	26. Silent shaft front bearing
12. Oil seal	27. Silent shaft rear bearing
13. Gasket	
14. Flange bolt	

11–15 FT. LBS.
15–22 NM

11–13 FT. LBS.
15–18 NM

25–29 FT. LBS.
34–40 NM

11–13 FT. LBS.
15–18 NM

Fig. 115 Exploded view of the front case, oil pump and silent shafts—1.8L engine

89573G74

16. Insert a Phillips screwdriver with a shank diameter of 0.032 in. (8mm) into the plug hole on the left side of the cylinder to block the silent shaft. Tighten the flange bolt to 29 ft. lbs. (40 Nm).

17. Install a new oil pump gasket into the groove in the front case. When installing the gasket, face the round side to the oil pump cover.

18. Install a new oil seal into the oil pump cover, making sure the lip of the seal is in the correct direction.

19. Install the oil pump cover onto the engine front case and tighten the bolts to 13 ft. lbs. (18 Nm).

20. Install the oil screen in position with new gasket in place.

21. Clean both mating surfaces of the oil pan and the cylinder block. Apply sealant in the groove in the oil pan flange, keeping towards the inside of the bolt holes. The width of the sealant bead applied is to be about 0.016 in. (4mm) wide.

➡**After applying sealant to the oil pan, do not exceed 15 minutes before installing the oil pan.**

22. Install the oil pan to the engine and secure with the retainers. Tighten bolts to 6 ft. lbs. (8 Nm).

23. Install the oil filter bracket to the engine with new gasket in place. Tighten the retainer bolts to 15 ft. lbs. (22 Nm).

24. Install the oil pressure sending unit as follows:

   a. Apply a thin bead of sealant to the threaded portion of the oil pressure sensor. Do not allow sealer to contact the end of the threaded portion of the sensor.

   b. Install the sensor and tighten to 8 ft. lbs. (12 Nm). Do not overtigthen the sensor.

   c. Connect the electrical harness connector to the sensor.

25. Lubricate the sealing ring on the oil filter with a small amount of clean engine oil. Install new oil filter, filled with clean oil, onto the filter bracket.

26. Fill the engine to the correct level with clean engine oil.

27. Connect the negative battery cable and start the engine. Check the oil pressure, making sure it is at the correct reading. Inspect for leaks.

2.0L ENGINE

▶ **See Figures 116, 117, 118 and 119**

1. Disconnect the negative battery cable. Rotate the engine so No. 1 plug is on Top Dead Center (TDC) of it's compression stroke. The timing marks should be aligned at this point.

2. Raise and safely support the vehicle.

3. Drain the engine oil. Once the oil is completely drained, install the drain plug and tighten to specifications.

4. Carefully lower the vehicle.

5. Using the proper equipment, support the weight of the engine. Remove the front engine mount bracket and accessory drive belts.

6. Remove timing belt upper and lower covers.

7. Remove the timing belt and crankshaft sprocket.

8. Disconnect the electrical connector from the oil pressure sending unit. Remove the oil pressure sensor using special removal tool MD998054. Remove the oil filter and the oil filter bracket.

9. Remove the oil pan, oil screen and gasket.

10. Using special tool MD998162, remove the plug cap in the engine front cover. If the plug is too tight, hit the plug head with a hammer a few times and the plug should be easier to loosen.

11. Remove the plug on the side of the engine block. Insert a Phillips screwdriver with a shank diameter of 0.32 in. (8mm) into the plug hole. This will hold the silent shaft.

12. Remove the driven gear bolt that secures the oil pump driven gear to the silent shaft.

13. Remove and tag the front cover mounting bolts. Note the lengths of the mounting bolts as they are removed for proper installation.

14. Remove the front case cover and oil pump assembly. If necessary, the silent shaft can come out with the cover assembly.

15. Remove the oil pump cover, located on the back of the engine front cover. Remove the oil pump drive and driven gears.

16. After disassembling the oil pump, clean all components.

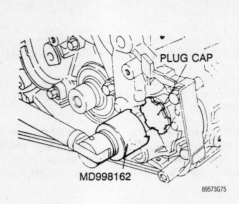

Fig. 116 Using special tool MD998162, remove the plug cap in the engine front cover—1990–94 2.0L engine

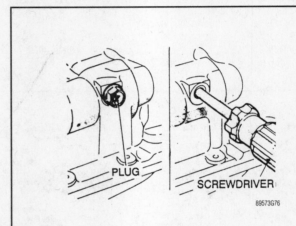

Fig. 117 Insert a Phillips screwdriver with a shank diameter of 0.32 in. (8mm) into the plug hole on the side of the engine block—1990–94 2.0L engine

17. Assemble the oil pump gears into the front case and rotate it to ensure smooth rotation and no looseness. Make sure there is no ridge wear on the contact surface between the front case and the gear surface of the oil pump front cover.

18. The gear side clearance should be checked using the following procedure:

   a. With the drive and driven gears installed in the front case, measure the tip clearance of the gears. The distance between the tips of the drive gear's teeth and the case should be 0.0063–0.0083 in. with a limit of 0.0098 in. The distance between the tips of the driven gear's teeth and the case should be 0.0051–0.0071 in. with a limit of 0.0098 in.

   b. Measure each oil pump gears end-play. The end-play is checked by placing a straight-edge across the machined cover surface and measuring with a feeler gauge. The end-play for the drive gear should be 0.0031–0.0055 in. with a limit of 0.0098 in. The end-play for the driven gear is 0.0024–0.0047 in. with a limit of 0.0098 in.

19. If any measurement is beyond specification, replace the entire pump assembly.

To install:

20. Align the timing mark on the oil pump drive gear with that on the driven gear and install them into the engine front case. Apply engine oil to the gears.

21. Install the oil pump cover and tighten the retainer bolts to 13 ft. lbs. (18 Nm).

22. Using the appropriate driver, install a new crankshaft seal into the front case.

23. Position new front case gasket in place. Set seal guide tool MD998285 on the front end of the crankshaft to protect the seal from damage. Apply a thin coat of oil to the outer circumference of the seal pilot tool.

24. Install the front case assembly through a new front case gasket and temporarily tighten the flange bolts.

25. Mount the oil filter on the bracket with new oil filter bracket gasket in place. Install the 4 bolts with washers and tighten to 25 ft. lbs. (34 Nm).

26. Insert a Phillips screwdriver into a hole in the left side of the engine block to lock the silent shaft in place.

27. Secure the oil pump drive gear onto the left silent shaft by installing and tightening the driven gear bolt to 29 ft. lbs. (40 Nm).

28. Install new O-ring to the groove in the front case and install the plug cap. Using the special tool MD998162, tighten the cap to 20 ft. lbs. (27 Nm).

29. Install the oil screen in position with new gasket in place.

30. Clean both mating surfaces of the oil pan and the cylinder block. Apply sealant in the groove in the oil pan flange, keeping towards the inside of the bolt holes. The width of the sealant bead applied is to be about 0.016 in. (4mm) wide.

➡**After applying sealant to the oil pan, do not exceed 15 minutes before installing the oil pan.**

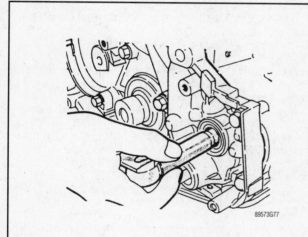

Fig. 118 Remove the driven gear bolt that secures the oil pump driven gear to the silent shaft—1990–94 2.0L engine

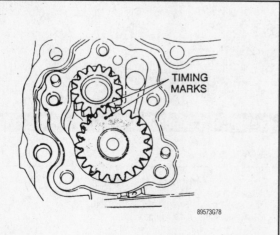

Fig. 119 Install the 2 oil pump gears into the case; make sure to align the timing marks—1990–94 2.0L engine

31. Install the oil pan to the engine and secure with the retainers. Tighten bolts to 9 ft. lbs. (12 Nm).

32. Install the oil pressure gauge unit and the oil pressure switch. Connect the electrical harness connector.

33. Install the oil cooler secure with oil cooler bolt tigthened to 33 ft. lbs. (45 Nm).

34. Install new oil filled with clean engine oil.

35. Connect the negative battery cable and start the engine. Check the oil pressure, making sure it is at the correct reading. Inspect for leaks.

1995–98 Vehicles

2.0L NON-TURBO ENGINES

▶ See Figures 120, 121 and 122

1. Disconnect the negative battery cable.
2. Raise the safely support the vehicle.
3. Drain the engine oil into a suitable container. When the oil is completely drained, install the drain plug.
4. Remove the rear plate.
5. Remove the oil filter and adapter.
6. Remove the oil pan.
7. Remove the oil pick-up tube.
8. Remove the timing belt.
9. Using tool MB995027 or equivalent, remove the crankshaft sprocket.

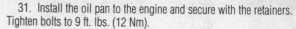

Do not nick the crankshaft sealing surface or the seal bore.

10. Using tool MB995020 or equivalent, remove the crankshaft oil seal.

11. Unfasten the oil pump mounting bolts, then remove the oil pump from the vehicle.

To install:

12. Apply a bead of the specified sealant to the sealing surface of the oil pump and install a new O-ring into the counter bore on the oil pump discharge passage.

13. Carefully install the oil pump on the crankshaft until seated to the engine block. Tighten the bolts to 17 ft. lbs. (23 Nm).

14. Install a new crankshaft oil seal in the oil pump.

15. Install the crankshaft sprocket using the proper installation tools.

16. Install the timing belt and related components.

17. Install the oil pick-up tube.

18. Apply Loctite®18718 or equivalent at the point where the oil pump meets the engine block.

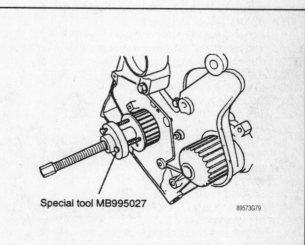

Fig. 120 Use the proper tool to remove the crankshaft sprocket—1995–98 2.0L non-turbo engine

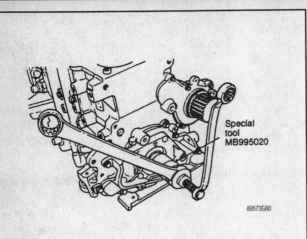

Fig. 121 Removing the front crankshaft oil seal—1995–98 2.0L non-turbo engine

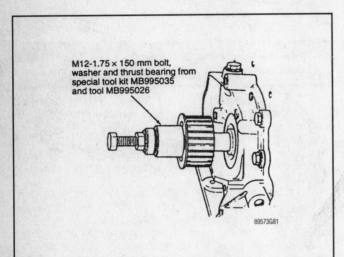

M12-1.75 × 150 mm bolt, washer and thrust bearing from special tool kit MB995035 and tool MB995026

Fig. 122 Install the crankshaft sprocket using the proper installation—1995–98 2.0L non-turbo engine

19. Install the oil pan using a new gasket. Tighten the mounting bolts to 9 ft. lbs. (12 Nm).

20. Use a new O-ring and install the oil filter adapter to the engine. Made sure the roll pin aligns with the hole. Tighten the assembly to 40 ft. lbs. (55 Nm).

21. Install a new oil filter.

22. Install the rear plate.

23. Safely lower the vehicle to the floor.

24. Refill the engine with the proper amount of oil.

25. Start the engine and check for leaks.

2.0L TURBO AND 2.4L ENGINES

1. Disconnect the negative battery cable. Rotate the engine so No. 1 cylinder is on Top Dead Center (TDC) of its compression stroke. The timing marks should be aligned at this point.

2. Raise and safely support the vehicle.

3. Drain the engine oil. Lower the vehicle.

4. Using the proper equipment, support the weight of the engine. Remove the front engine mount bracket and accessory drive belts.

5. Remove timing belt upper and lower covers.

6. Remove the timing belt and crankshaft sprocket.

7. Disconnect the electrical connector from the oil pressure sending unit and remove the oil pressure sensor. Remove the oil filter and the oil filter bracket.

8. Remove the oil pan, oil screen and gasket.

9. Using special tool MD998162, remove the plug cap in the engine front cover.

10. Remove the plug on the side of the engine block. Insert a Phillips screwdriver with a shank diameter of 0.32 in. (8mm) into the plug hole. This will hold the silent shaft.

11. Remove the driven gear bolt that secures the oil pump driven gear to the silent shaft.

12. Remove and tag the front cover mounting bolts. Note the lengths of the mounting bolts as they are removed for proper installation.

13. Remove the front case cover and oil pump assembly. If necessary, the silent shaft can come out with the cover assembly.

14. Remove the oil pump cover, located on the back of the engine front cover. Remove the oil pump drive and driven gears.

15. After disassembling the oil pump, clean all components and remove gasket material from mating surfaces.

16. Assemble the oil pump gears into the front case and rotate it to ensure smooth rotation and no looseness. Make sure there is no ridge wear on the contact surface between the front case and the gear surface of the oil pump front cover.

To install:

17. Align the timing mark on the oil pump drive gear with that on the driven gear and install them into the engine front case. Apply engine oil to the gears.

18. Install the oil pump cover and tighten the retainer bolts to 13 ft. lbs. (18 Nm).

19. Using the appropriate driver, install a new crankshaft seal into the front case.

20. Position new front case gasket in place. Set seal guide tool MD998285 on the front end of the crankshaft to protect the seal from damage. Apply a thin coat of oil to the outer circumference of the seal pilot tool.

21. Install the front case assembly through a new front case gasket and temporarily tighten the flange bolts.

22. Mount the oil filter on the bracket with new oil filter bracket gasket in place. Install the bolts with washers and tighten to 4 ft. lbs. (19 Nm).

23. Insert a Phillips screwdriver into a hole in the left side of the engine block to lock the silent shaft in place.

24. Secure the oil pump drive gear onto the left silent shaft by installing and tightening the driven gear bolt to 27 ft. lbs. (37 Nm).

25. Install a new O-ring to the groove in the front case and install the plug cap. Using the special tool MD998162, tighten the cap to 17 ft. lbs. (24 Nm).

26. Install the oil screen in position with new gasket in place.

27. Clean both mating surfaces of the oil pan and the cylinder block. Apply sealant in the groove in the oil pan flange, keeping towards the inside of the bolt holes. The width of the sealant bead applied is to be about 0.016 in. (4mm) wide.

➡**After applying sealant to the oil pan, do not exceed 15 minutes before installing the oil pan.**

28. Install the oil pan to the engine and secure with the retainers.

29. Install the oil pressure gauge unit and the oil pressure switch. Connect the electrical harness connector.

30. Install the oil cooler. Secure with oil cooler bolt tigthened to 31 ft. lbs. (43 Nm).

31. Install a new oil filter. Refill the crankcase.

32. Connect the negative battery cable and start the engine. Verify oil pressure. Inspect for leaks.

Crankshaft Damper Pulley

REMOVAL & INSTALLATION

◆ **See Figures 123, 124, 125, 126 and 127**

1. Disconnect the negative battery cable.

2. Remove the engine undercover.

3. For all engines, except the 1995(en dash)98 2.0L non-turbo engines, use the proper equipment to slightly raise the engine to take the weight off of the side engine mount. Support the engine in this position. Remove the engine mount bracket.

4. Remove the accessory drive belts.
5. Unfasten the retaining bolt, then remove the crankshaft pulley.
6. Use a jawed puller or tools MB995055 and MB995057 to remove the crankshaft pulley from the shaft.

To install:

7. Install the crankshaft pulley, adapter and/or damper pulley. For 1995–98 2.0L non-turbo engines, install the crankshaft pulley using MB995035, or equivalent.
8. Install the mounting bolt(s) and tighten as follows:
    a. 1.8L engine: 13 ft. lbs. (18 Nm)
    b. 1990–94 2.0L engine: 22 ft. lbs. (30 Nm).
    c. 1995–98 2.0L non-turbo engine: 105 ft. lbs. (142 Nm), using tool MB990767, or equivalent.
    d. 1995–98 2.0L turbo and 2.4L engines: 18 ft. lbs. (25 Nm).
9. Install the accessory drive belts and adjust to the correct tension.
10. If removed, install the engine mount bracket. Tighten the bolts as follows:
Engine mount bracket through bolt—58 ft. lbs. (80 Nm)
Upper mount bracket mounting nuts (2)—47 ft. lbs. (65 Nm)
Upper mount bracket mounting bolt—47 ft. lbs. (65 Nm)
11. Install the clamp for the power steering pressure hose.
12. Install the engine under cover.
13. Connect the negative battery cable.

Fig. 125 . . . then pull the damper pulley from the hub

Fig. 123 With the engine undercover removed, loosen the crankshaft pulley retaining bolt

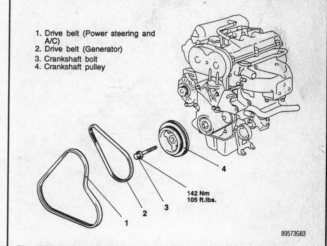

1. Drive belt (Power steering and A/C)
2. Drive belt (Generator)
3. Crankshaft bolt
4. Crankshaft pulley

142 Nm
105 ft.lbs.

Fig. 126 Exploded view of the crankshaft pulley and related components—1995–98 2.0L non-turbo engine shown

Fig. 124 Install a suitable jawed puller to the crankshaft pulley . . .

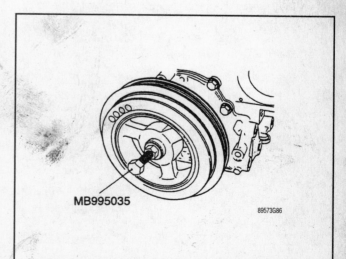

MB995035

Fig. 127 Installing the crankshaft pulley on the 1995–98 2.0L non-turbo engine

Timing Belt Cover and Seal

REMOVAL & INSTALLATION

◗ See Figures 128 thru 142

1. Disconnect the negative battery cable.
2. Remove the engine undercover.
3. Remove the crankshaft pulley, as outlined later in this section.
4. Using the proper equipment, slightly raise the engine to take the weight off of the side engine mount. Support the engine in this position.
5. Remove the engine mount bracket.
6. If not already done, remove the drive belts, tension pulley brackets, water pump pulley and crankshaft pulley.

➡On the 2.0L engine, take notice of the locations of each timing belt cover fastener during the removal procedure. Due to the difference in lengths, it is important that they are installed in their original locations. Refer to the illustration.

Fig. 130 Make sure to remove all of the engine mount retaining bolts

Fig. 128 With the engine supported, unfasten the top engine mount bracket retaining bolts

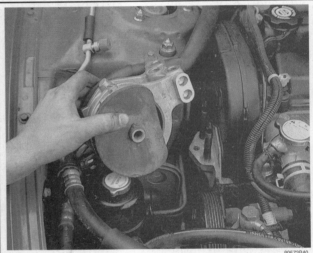

Fig. 131 Remove the engine mount bracket

Fig. 129 Remove the bracket side retaining bolts

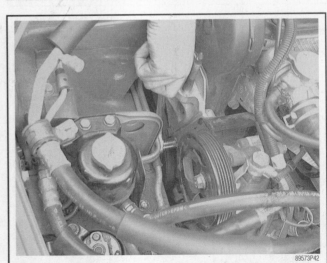

Fig. 132 Remove the power steering pump pulley and bracket mounting bolts

Fig. 133 Remove the engine mount-to-timing cover retaining bolts . . .

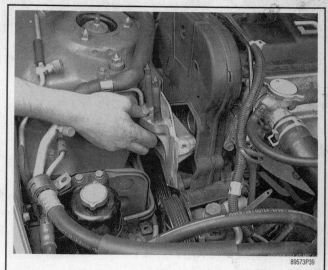

Fig. 134 . . . then remove the engine mount bracket

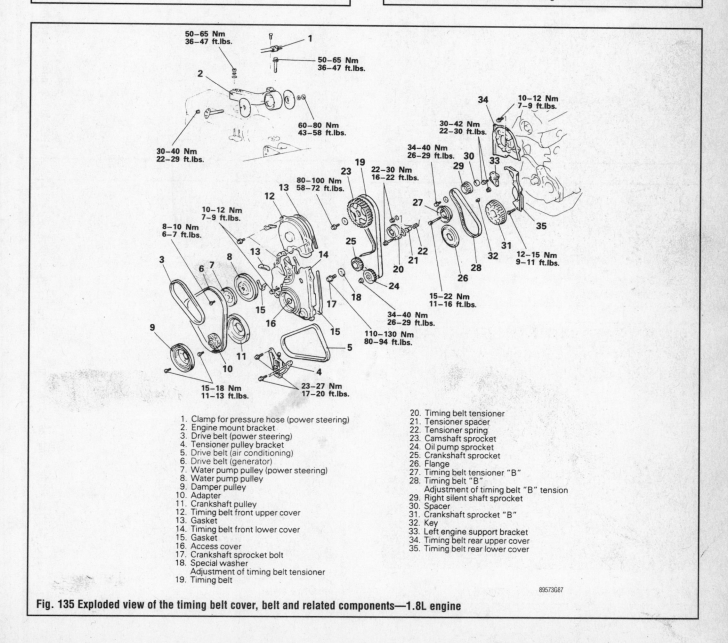

Fig. 135 Exploded view of the timing belt cover, belt and related components—1.8L engine

1. Clamp for pressure hose (power steering)
2. Engine mount bracket
3. Drive belt (power steering)
4. Tensioner pulley bracket
5. Drive belt (air conditioning)
6. Drive belt (generator)
7. Water pump pulley (power steering)
8. Water pump pulley
9. Damper pulley
10. Adapter
11. Crankshaft pulley
12. Timing belt front upper cover
13. Gasket
14. Timing belt front lower cover
15. Gasket
16. Access cover
17. Crankshaft sprocket bolt
18. Special washer
    Adjustment of timing belt tensioner
19. Timing belt

20. Timing belt tensioner
21. Tensioner spacer
22. Tensioner spring
23. Camshaft sprocket
24. Oil pump sprocket
25. Crankshaft sprocket
26. Flange
27. Timing belt tensioner "B"
28. Timing belt "B"
    Adjustment of timing belt "B" tension
29. Right silent shaft sprocket
30. Spacer
31. Crankshaft sprocket "B"
32. Key
33. Left engine support bracket
34. Timing belt rear upper cover
35. Timing belt rear lower cover

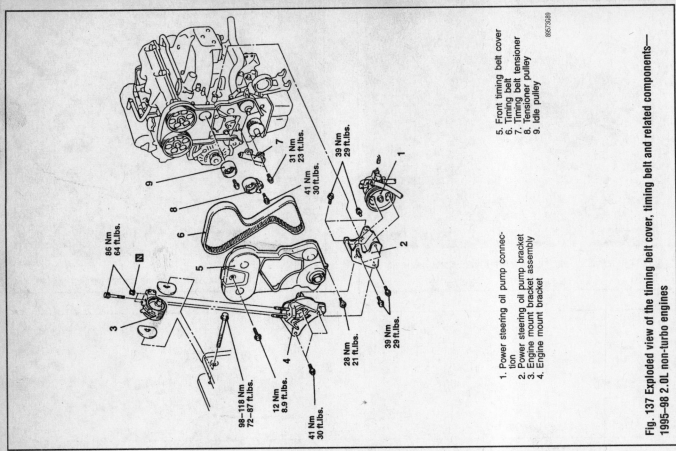

Fig. 137 Exploded view of the timing belt cover, timing belt and related components—1995–98 2.0L non-turbo engines

1. Power steering oil pump connection
2. Power steering oil pump bracket
3. Engine mount bracket assembly
4. Engine mount bracket
5. Front timing belt cover
6. Timing belt
7. Timing belt tensioner
8. Tensioner pulley
9. Idle pulley

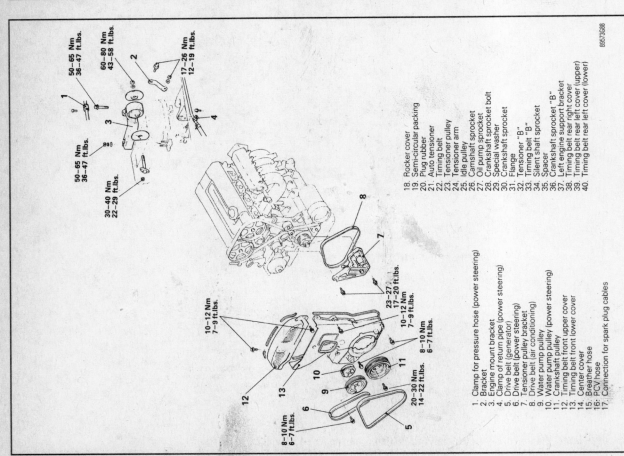

Fig. 136 Timing belt cover, belt and related components—1990–94 2.0L engines

1. Clamp for pressure hose (power steering)
2. Bracket
3. Engine mount bracket
4. Clamp of return pipe (power steering)
5. Drive belt (generator)
6. Drive belt (power steering)
7. Tensioner pulley bracket
8. Drive belt (air conditioning)
9. Water pump pulley
10. Water pump pulley (power steering)
11. Crankshaft pulley
12. Timing belt front upper cover
13. Timing belt front lower cover
14. Center cover
15. Breather hose
16. PCV hose
17. Connection for spark plug cables
18. Rocker cover
19. Semi-circular packing
20. Plug rubber
21. Auto tensioner
22. Timing belt
23. Tensioner pulley
24. Tensioner arm
25. Idle pulley
26. Camshaft sprocket
27. Oil pump sprocket
28. Crankshaft sprocket bolt
29. Special washer
30. Crankshaft sprocket
31. Flange
32. Tensioner "B"
33. Timing belt "B"
34. Silent shaft sprocket
35. Spacer
36. Crankshaft sprocket "B"
37. Left engine support bracket
38. Timing belt rear right cover
39. Timing belt rear left cover (upper)
40. Timing belt rear left cover (lower)

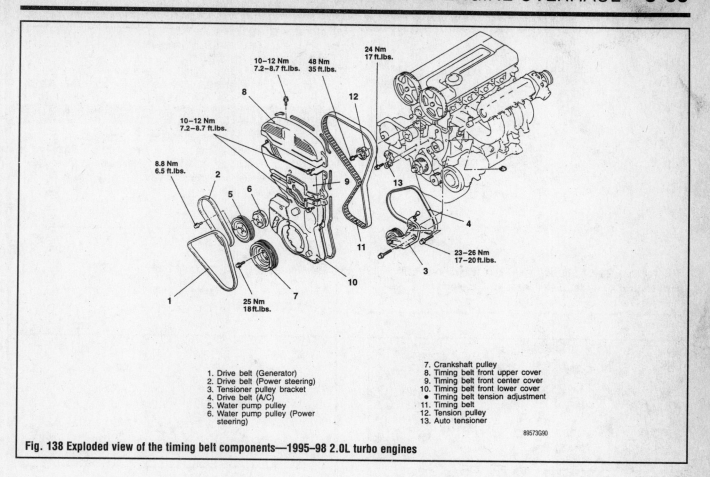

1. Drive belt (Generator)
2. Drive belt (Power steering)
3. Tensioner pulley bracket
4. Drive belt (A/C)
5. Water pump pulley
6. Water pump pulley (Power steering)

7. Crankshaft pulley
8. Timing belt front upper cover
9. Timing belt front center cover
10. Timing belt front lower cover
   • Timing belt tension adjustment
11. Timing belt
12. Tension pulley
13. Auto tensioner

89573G90

Fig. 138 Exploded view of the timing belt components—1995–98 2.0L turbo engines

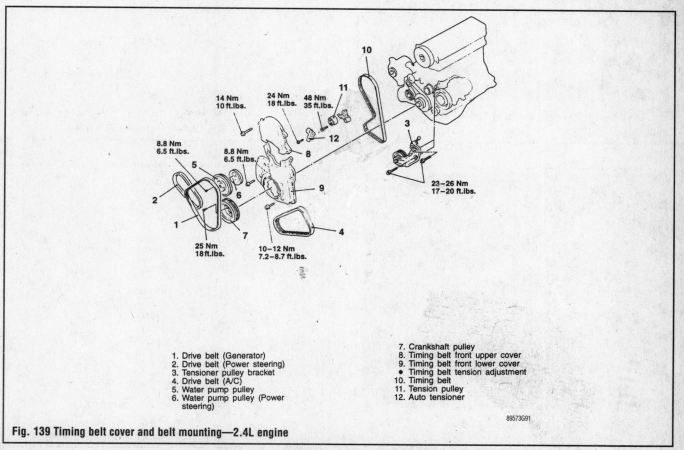

1. Drive belt (Generator)
2. Drive belt (Power steering)
3. Tensioner pulley bracket
4. Drive belt (A/C)
5. Water pump pulley
6. Water pump pulley (Power steering)

7. Crankshaft pulley
8. Timing belt front upper cover
9. Timing belt front lower cover
   • Timing belt tension adjustment
10. Timing belt
11. Tension pulley
12. Auto tensioner

89573G91

Fig. 139 Timing belt cover and belt mounting—2.4L engine

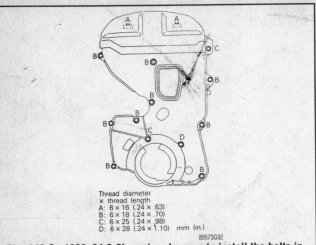

Thread diameter
x thread length
A: 6 × 16 (.24 × .63)
B: 6 × 18 (.24 × .70)
C: 6 × 25 (.24 × .98)
D: 6 × 28 (.24 × 1.10) mm (in.)

89573G92

Fig. 140 On 1990–94 2.0L engine, be sure to install the bolts in their original locations. Their dimensions differ according to their locations

89573P37

Fig. 141 Unfasten the lower timing belt cover retaining bolts . . .

89573P38

Fig. 142 . . . then pull the timing belt cover up and out of the engine

7. Remove all attaching screws and remove the upper and lower timing belt covers. If equipped with 2.0L engine, take note of the original locations of the cover fasteners prior to removal.

8. The installation is the reverse of the removal procedure. Make sure all pieces of packing are positioned in the inner grooves of the covers when installing.

Timing Belt and Sprockets

It is recommended that the timing belt be replaced periodically to assure correct engine performance. Because of their composition, timing belts wear over a period of time and mileage. To avoid vehicle break down and possible engine damage, the manufacturer recommends timing belt replacement at 60,000 miles.

REMOVAL & INSTALLATION

1.8L Engine

▶ See Figures 135, 143, 144 and 145

1. If possible, position the engine so the No. 1 piston is at TDC.
2. Disconnect the negative battery cable.

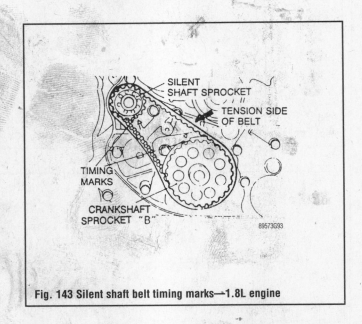

89573G93

Fig. 143 Silent shaft belt timing marks—1.8L engine

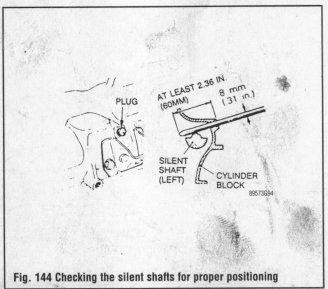

89573G94

Fig. 144 Checking the silent shafts for proper positioning

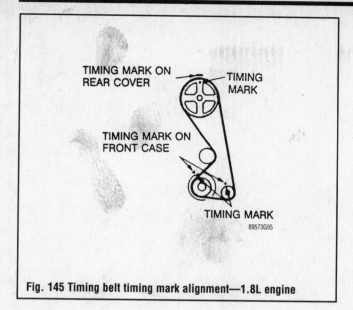

Fig. 145 Timing belt timing mark alignment—1.8L engine

3. Remove the timing belt covers.

4. Remove the timing (outer) belt tensioner and remove the outer timing belt.

5. Remove the outer crankshaft sprocket and flange.

6. Remove the silent shaft (inner) belt tensioner and remove the belt.

To install:

7. Align the timing marks of the silent shaft sprockets and the crankshaft sprocket with the timing marks on the front case. Wrap the timing belt around the sprockets so there is no slack in the upper span of the belt and the timing marks are still aligned.

8. Install the tensioner pulley and move the pulley by hand so the long side of the belt deflects about ¼ in.

9. Hold the pulley tightly so the pulley cannot rotate when the bolt is tightened. Tighten the bolt to 15 ft. lbs. (20 Nm) and recheck the deflection amount.

10. Install the timing belt tensioner fully toward the water pump and tighten the bolts. Place the upper end of the spring against the water pump body.

11. Align the timing marks of the camshaft, crankshaft and oil pump sprockets with their corresponding marks on the front case or rear cover.

➥There is a possibility to align all timing marks and have the oil pump sprocket and silent shaft out of time, causing an engine vibration during operation. If the following step is not followed exactly, there is a 50 percent chance that the silent shaft alignment will be 180 degrees off.

12. Before installing the timing belt, ensure that the left side (rear) silent shaft (oil pump sprocket) is in the correct position as follows:

 a. Remove the plug from the rear side of the block and insert a tool with shaft diameter of 0.31 in. (8mm) into the hole.

 b. With the timing marks still aligned, the shaft of the tool must be able to go in at least 2 1/2 in. If the tool can only go in about 1 in., the shaft is not in the correct orientation and will cause a vibration during engine operation. Remove the tool from the hole and turn the oil pump sprocket 1 complete revolution. Realign the timing marks and insert the tool. The shaft of the tool must go in at least 2 1/3 in.

 c. Recheck and realign the timing mark.

 d. Leave the tool in place to hold the silent shaft while continuing.

13. Install the belt to the crankshaft sprocket, oil pump sprocket, then camshaft sprocket, in that order. While doing so, make sure there is no slack between the sprocket except where the tensioner is installed.

14. Recheck the timing marks' alignment. If all are aligned, loosen the tensioner mounting bolt and allow the tensioner to apply tension to the belt.

15. Remove the tool that is holding the silent shaft and rotate the crankshaft a distance equal to 2 teeth on the camshaft sprocket. This will allow the tensioner to automatically apply the proper tension on the belt. Do not manually overtighten the belt or it will howl.

16. Tighten the lower mounting bolt first, then the upper spacer bolt.

17. To verify correct belt tension, check that the deflection at the longest span of the belt is about ½ in.

18. Install the timing belt covers and all related items.

19. Connect the negative battery cable.

2.0L Engine

1990–94 VEHICLES

◆ See Figures 136, 146, 147, 148 and 149

1. Disconnect the negative battery cable.

2. Remove the timing belt upper and lower covers.

3. Rotate the crankshaft clockwise and align the timing marks so No. 1 piston will be at TDC of the compression stroke. At this time the timing marks on the camshaft sprocket and the upper surface of the cylinder head should coincide, and the dowel pin of the camshaft sprocket should be at the upper side.

➥Always rotate the crankshaft in a clockwise direction. Make a mark on the back of the timing belt indicating the direction of rotation so it may be reassembled in the same direction if it is to be reused.

4. Remove the auto tensioner and remove the outermost timing belt.

5. Remove the timing belt tensioner pulley, tensioner arm, idler pulley, oil pump sprocket, special washer, flange and spacer.

6. Remove the silent shaft (inner) belt tensioner and remove the belt.

7. Remove the crankshaft retaining bolts, then remove the pulley.

8. Remove the crankshaft sprocket retainer bolt and washer from the sprocket, if used, and remove the sprocket. If the sprocket is hard to removed, the proper puller may be used. If no bolts are used on the sprocket. Use the correct puller to remove.

9. Hold the camshaft stationary using the hexagon cast between journals No. 2 and 3 and remove the retainer bolt. Remove the sprocket from the camshaft.

To install:

10. Install the sprockets to their appropriate shafts. Install the retainer bolts and tighten the camshaft sprocket bolt to 65 ft. lbs. (90 Nm).

11. Check both tensioner and idler pulley for bearing wear, and replace if needed.

12. Align the timing marks on the crankshaft sprocket and the silent shaft sprocket. Fit the inner timing belt over the crankshaft and silent shaft sprocket. Ensure that there is no slack in the belt.

13. While holding the inner timing belt tensioner with your fingers, adjust the timing belt tension by applying a force towards the center of the belt, until the tension side of the belt is taut. Tighten the tensioner bolt.

➥When tightening the bolt of the tensioner, ensure that the tensioner pulley shaft does not rotate with the bolt. Allowing it to rotate with the bolt can cause excessive tension on the belt.

14. Check belt for proper tension by depressing the belt on its' long side with your finger and noting the belt deflection. The desired reading is 0.20–0.28 in. (5–7mm). If tension is not correct, readjust and check belt deflection.

15. Install the flange, crankshaft and washer to the crankshaft. The flange on the crankshaft sprocket must be installed towards the inner timing belt sprocket. Tighten bolt to 80–94 ft. lbs. (110–130 Nm).

16. To install the oil pump sprocket, insert a Phillips screwdriver with a shaft 0.31 in. (8mm) in diameter into the plug hole in the left side of the cylinder block to hold the left silent shaft. Tighten the nut to 36–43 ft. lbs. (50–60 Nm).

17. Using a wrench, hold the camshaft at its' hexagon between journal No. 2 and 3 and tighten camshaft sprocket mounting bolt, if removed, to

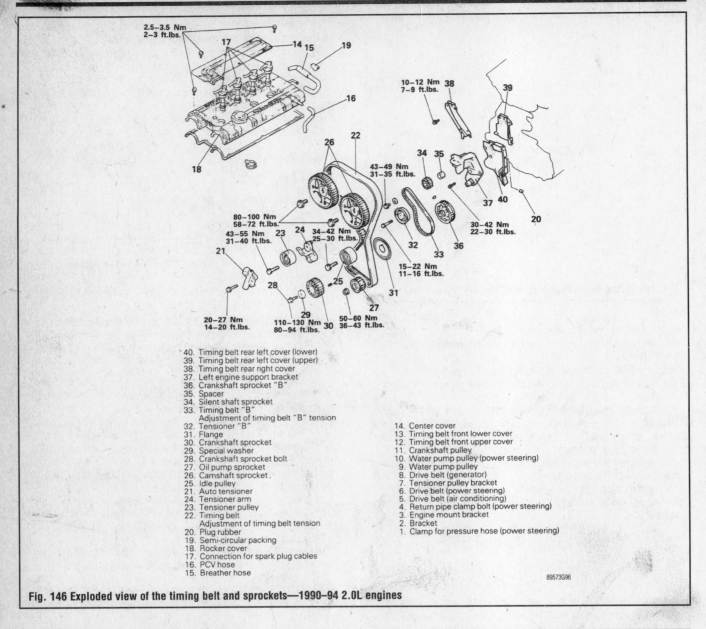

40. Timing belt rear left cover (lower)
39. Timing belt rear left cover (upper)
38. Timing belt rear right cover
37. Left engine support bracket
36. Crankshaft sprocket "B"
35. Spacer
34. Silent shaft sprocket
33. Timing belt "B"
    Adjustment of timing belt "B" tension
32. Tensioner "B"
31. Flange
30. Crankshaft sprocket
29. Special washer
28. Crankshaft sprocket bolt
27. Oil pump sprocket
26. Camshaft sprocket
25. Idle pulley
21. Auto tensioner
24. Tensioner arm
23. Tensioner pulley
22. Timing belt
    Adjustment of timing belt tension
20. Plug rubber
19. Semi-circular packing
18. Rocker cover
17. Connection for spark plug cables
16. PCV hose
15. Breather hose

14. Center cover
13. Timing belt front lower cover
12. Timing belt front upper cover
11. Crankshaft pulley
10. Water pump pulley (power steering)
 9. Water pump pulley
 8. Drive belt (generator)
 7. Tensioner pulley bracket
 6. Drive belt (power steering)
 5. Drive belt (air conditioning)
 4. Return pipe clamp bolt (power steering)
 3. Engine mount bracket
 2. Bracket
 1. Clamp for pressure hose (power steering)

89573G96

Fig. 146 Exploded view of the timing belt and sprockets—1990–94 2.0L engines

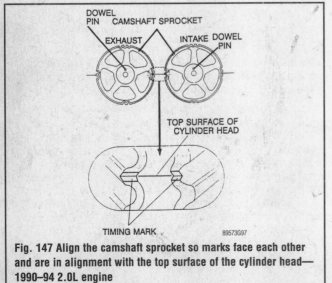

89573G97

Fig. 147 Align the camshaft sprocket so marks face each other and are in alignment with the top surface of the cylinder head—1990–94 2.0L engine

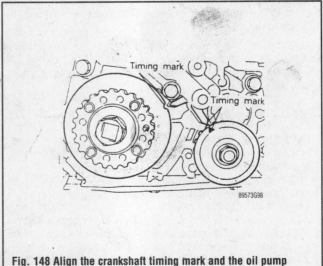

89573G98

Fig. 148 Align the crankshaft timing mark and the oil pump sprocket timing mark—1990–94 2.0L engine

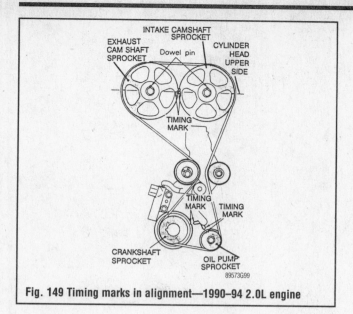

Fig. 149 Timing marks in alignment—1990-94 2.0L engine

58-72 ft. lbs. (80-100 Nm). If no hexagon is present between journal No. 2 and 3, hold the sprocket stationary with a spanner wrench while tightening the sprocket retainer bolt.

18. Carefully push the auto tensioner rod in until the set hole in the rod aligned up with the hole in the cylinder. Place a wire into the hole to retain the rod.

19. Install the tensioner pulley onto the tensioner arm. Locate the pin-hole in the tensioner pulley shaft to the left of the center bolt. Then, tighten the center bolt finger-tight.

20. When installing the timing belt, turn the 2 camshaft sprockets so their dowel pins are located on top. Align the timing marks facing each other and with the top surface of the cylinder head. When you let go of the exhaust camshaft sprocket, it will rotate 1 tooth in the counterclockwise direction. This should be taken into account when installing the timing belts on the sprocket.

➡**Both camshaft sprockets are used for the intake and exhaust camshafts and are provided with 2 timing marks. When the sprocket is mounted on the exhaust camshaft, use the timing mark on the right with the dowel pin hole on top. For the intake camshaft sprocket, use the 1 on the left with the dowel pin hole on top.**

21. Align the crankshaft sprocket and oil pump sprocket timing marks.

22. After alignment of the oil pump sprocket timing marks, remove the plug on the cylinder block and insert a Phillips screwdriver with a shaft diameter of 0.31 in. (8mm) through the hole. If the shaft can be inserted 2.4 in. deep, the silent shaft is in the correct position. If the shaft of the tool can only be inserted 0.8-1.0 in. (20-25mm) deep, turn the oil pump sprocket 1 turn and realign the marks. Reinsert the tool making sure it is inserted 2.4 in. deep. Keep the tool inserted in hole for the remainder of this procedure.

➡**The above step assures that the oil pump socket is in correct orientation to the silent shafts. This step must not be skipped or a vibration may develop during engine operation.**

23. Install the timing belt as follows:

a. Install the timing belt around the intake camshaft sprocket and retain it with 2 spring clips or binder clips.

b. Install the timing belt around the exhaust sprocket, aligning the timing marks with the cylinder head top surface using 2 wrenches. Retain the belt with 2 spring clips.

c. Install the timing belt around the idler pulley, oil pump sprocket, crankshaft sprocket and the tensioner pulley. Remove the 2 spring clips.

d. Lift upward on the tensioner pulley in a clockwise direction and tighten the center bolt. Make sure all timing marks are aligned.

e. Rotate the crankshaft ¼ turn counterclockwise. Then, turn in clockwise until the timing marks are aligned again.

24. To adjust the timing (outer) belt, turn the crankshaft ¼ turn counterclockwise, then turn it clockwise to move No. 1 cylinder to TDC.

25. Loosen the center bolt. Using tool MD998738 or equivalent and a torque wrench, apply a torque of 1.88-2.03 ft. lbs. (2.6-2.8 Nm). Tighten the center bolt.

26. Screw the special tool into the engine left support bracket until its end makes contact with the tensioner arm. At this point, screw the special tool in some more and remove the set wire attached to the auto tensioner, if the wire was not previously removed. Then remove the special tool.

27. Rotate the crankshaft 2 complete turns clockwise and let it sit for approximately 15 minutes. Then, measure the auto tensioner protrusion (the distance between the tensioner arm and auto tensioner body) to ensure that it is within 0.15-0.18 in. (3.8-4.5mm). If out of specification, repeat Step 1-4 until the specified value is obtained.

28. If the timing belt tension adjustment is being performed with the engine mounted in the vehicle, and clearance between the tensioner arm and the auto tensioner body cannot be measured, the following alternative method can be used:

a. Screw in special tool MD998738 or equivalent, until its end makes contact with the tensioner arm.

b. After the special tool makes contact with the arm, screw it in some more to retract the auto tensioner pushrod while counting the number of turns the tool makes until the tensioner arm is brought into contact with the auto tensioner body. Make sure the number of turns the special tool makes conforms with the standard value of 2½-3 turns.

c. Install the rubber plug to the timing belt rear cover.

29. Install the timing belt covers and all related items.

30. Connect the negative battery cable.

1995-98 NON-TURBO ENGINES

▶ **See Figures 137 and 150 thru 167**

1. Disconnect the negative battery cable.
2. Remove the accessory drive belts.
3. Remove the power steering pump from the bracket and position it out of the way. Do not disconnect the hoses.
4. Remove the power steering pump bracket from the engine.
5. Remove the crankshaft pulley.
6. Use a floor jack with a piece of wood on it and jack up the engine to take the weight off of the engine mount.
7. Remove the engine mount and bracket.
8. Unfasten the retainers, then remove the front timing belt cover.

➡**If the timing belt is going to be reused, mark the direction of rotation on the belt with an arrow. Install the belt in the same direction.**

Fig. 150 Unfasten the power steering pump retaining bolts

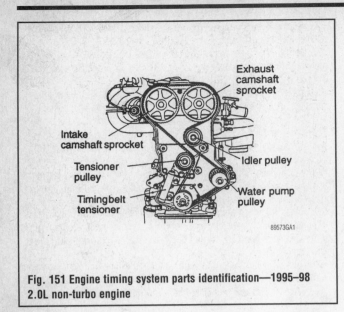

Fig. 151 Engine timing system parts identification—1995–98 2.0L non-turbo engine

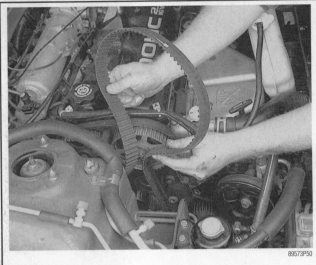

Fig. 154 . . . then remove the timing belt from the engine

Fig. 152 If you are going to reinstall the old belt, mark the direction of rotation for installation purposes

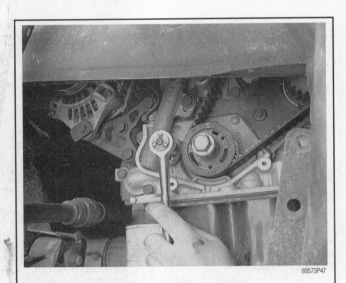

Fig. 155 Unfasten the tensioner retaining bolts . . .

Fig. 153 Loosen the timing belt tensioner bolts (see arrows) . . .

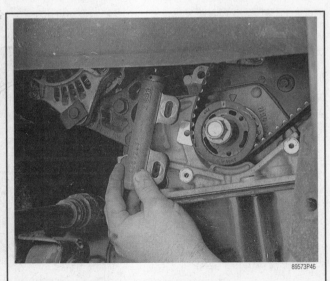

Fig. 156 Remove the timing belt tensioner

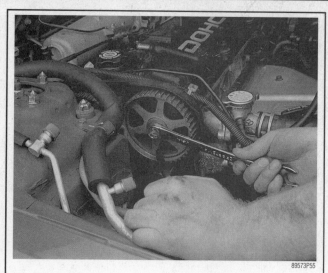

Fig. 157 Remove the camshaft sprocket retaining bolt . . .

Fig. 158 . . . then remove the camshaft sprocket from the vehicle

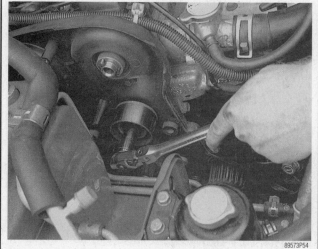

Fig. 159 If necessary to remove the idle pulley, unfasten the retaining bolt

Fig. 160 . . . then remove the idle pulley, if necessary

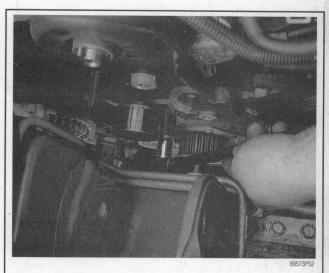

Fig. 161 Unfasten the tensioner pulley retaining bolt . . .

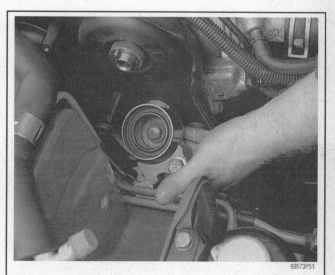

Fig. 162 . . . then remove the tensioner pulley

9. Rotate the crankshaft sprocket clockwise until the timing marks are aligned. Loosen the timing belt tensioner and remove the timing belt.

10. Use tool MB995027 or equivalent to hold the crankshaft sprocket while removing the mounting bolt in the center.

11. If available, you can use end yoke holder tool MB990767 or equivalent to hold the camshaft sprocket while removing the mounting bolt in the center.

✳✳ WARNING

Do not rotate the crankshaft or the camshafts while the belt is removed.

12. If necessary, unfasten the retainers, then remove the idle and tensioner pulleys.

To install:

13. Use the special tool to hold the camshaft sprocket and install the center bolt. Tighten the bolt to 75 ft. lbs. (101 Nm).

14. Use tool MB995038 and MB995026 or equivalent, to install the crankshaft sprocket.

15. Using a vise, slowly compress the plunger into the body of the tensioner and install a pin through the body of the tensioner to retain the plunger.

Fig. 165 Use the vise to carefully compress the plunger into the body

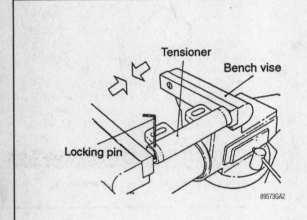

Fig. 163 Compress the tensioner in a vise—1995–98 2.0L non-turbo engine

Fig. 166 When the plunger of the tensioner is fully compressed, insert a pin through the body to hold it

Fig. 164 Once the tensioner is removed from the vehicle, place it in a suitable vise

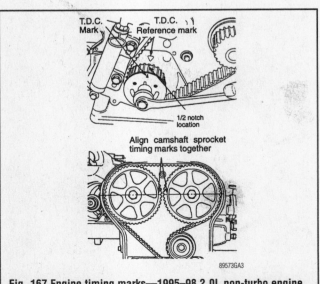

Fig. 167 Engine timing marks—1995–98 2.0L non-turbo engine

16. Make sure the timing marks are still aligned, if not, align the camshaft sprocket timing marks facing each other. Align the crankshaft sprocket timing mark with the mark on the oil pump housing, then turn the crankshaft sprocket backward ½ notch.

17. Install the timing belt starting at the crankshaft, go around the water pump sprocket, idler pulley, camshaft sprockets and then around the tensioner pulley.

18. Turn the crankshaft sprocket ½ notch to TDC to take up the slack in the belt.

19. Install the tensioner on the engine but do not tighten the bolts.

20. Place a torque wrench on the tensioner pulley and apply 21 ft. lbs. (28 Nm) of torque in the direction of the water pump. Push the tensioner up against the tensioner pulley and Tighten the mounting bolts to 23 ft. lbs. (31 Nm).

21. Pull the pin out of the tensioner. Belt tension is correct when the pin can be removed and installed.

22. Rotate the crankshaft two revolutions and check the timing marks for alignment. Repeat the previous steps if necessary.

23. Install the timing belt cover.

24. Install the crankshaft pulley.

25. Install the engine mount and bracket. Remove the jack from under the engine.

26. Install the power steering pump bracket and pump.

27. Install the drive belts.

28. Connect the negative battery cable.

1995–98 TURBO ENGINES

♦ **See Figures 138 and 168 thru 173**

1. Disconnect the negative battery cable.
2. Remove the engine undercover.
3. Remove the engine mount bracket.
4. Remove the drive belts.
5. Remove the belt tensioner pulley.
6. Remove the water pump pulleys.
7. Remove the crankshaft pulley.
8. Remove the stud bolt from the engine support bracket and remove the timing belt covers.
9. Rotate the crankshaft clockwise to line up the camshaft timing marks. Always turn the crankshaft in the forward direction only.
10. Loosen the tension pulley center bolt.

➥If the timing belt is to be reused, mark the direction of rotation on the flat side of the belt with an arrow.

11. Move the tension pulley towards the water pump and remove the timing belt.

12. Remove the crankshaft sprocket center bolt using special tool MB990767 to hold the crankshaft sprocket while removing the center bolt. Then use MB998778 or equivalent puller to remove the sprocket.

13. Mark the direction of rotation on the timing belt B with a arrow.

14. Loosen the center bolt on the tensioner and remove the belt.

15. To remove the camshaft sprocket, remove the cylinder head cover. Use a wrench to hold the hexagonal part of the camshaft and remove the sprocket mounting bolt.

❈❈ WARNING

Do not rotate the camshafts or the crankshaft while the timing belt is removed.

To install:

16. Use a wrench to hold the camshaft and install the sprocket and mounting bolt. Tighten the bolt(s) to 65 ft. lbs. (88 Nm).

17. Install the cylinder head cover.

18. Place the crankshaft sprocket on the crankshaft. Use tool MB990767 or equivalent to hold the crankshaft sprocket while tightening the center bolt. Tighten the center bolt to 80–94 ft. lbs. (108–127 Nm).

19. Align the timing marks on the crankshaft sprocket B and the balance shaft.

20. Install timing belt B on the sprockets. Position the center of the tensioner pulley to the left and above the center of the mounting bolt.

21. Push the pulley clockwise toward the crankshaft to apply tension to the belt and tighten the mounting bolt to 14 ft. lbs. (19 Nm). Do not let the pulley turn when tightening the bolt because it will cause excessive tension on the belt. The belt should deflect 0.20–0.28 in. (5–7 mm) when finger pressure is applied between the pulleys.

22. Install the crankshaft sensing blade and the crankshaft sprocket. Apply engine oil to the mounting bolt and Tighten the bolt to 80–94 ft. lbs. (108–127 Nm).

23. Use a press or vise to compress the auto tensioner pushrod. Insert a set pin when the holed are lined up.

❈❈ WARNING

Do not compress the pushrod too quickly, damage to the pushrod can occur.

24. Install the auto tensioner on the engine.

25. Align the timing marks on the camshaft sprocket, crankshaft sprocket and the oil pump sprocket.

26. After aligning the mark on the oil pump sprocket, remove the cylinder block plug and insert a Phillips screwdriver in the hole to check the

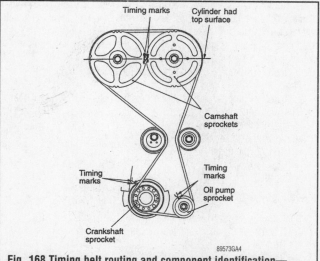

Fig. 168 Timing belt routing and component identification— 1995–98 2.0L turbo engine

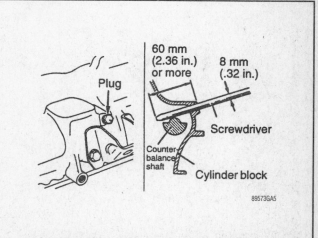

Fig. 169 After the timing mark on the oil pump sprocket is lined up, remove the block plug and insert a screwdriver to assure proper alignment

position of the counter balance shaft. The screwdriver should go in at least 2.36 in. or more, if not, rotate the oil pump sprocket once and realign the timing mark so the screwdriver goes in. Do not remove the screwdriver until the timing belt is installed.

27. Install the timing belt on the intake camshaft and secure it with a clip.

28. Install the timing belt on the exhaust camshaft. Align the timing marks with the cylinder head top surface using two wrenches. Secure the belt with another clip.

29. Install the belt around the idler pulley, oil pump sprocket, crankshaft sprocket and the tensioner pulley.

30. Turn the tension pulley so the pinholes are at the bottom. Press the pulley lightly against the timing belt.

31. Screw the special tool into the left engine support bracket until it contacts the tensioner arm, then screw the tool in a little more and remove the pushrod pin from the auto tensioner. Remove the special tool and Tighten the center bolt to 35 ft. lbs. (48 Nm).

32. Turn the crankshaft ¼ turn counterclockwise and then clockwise until the timing marks are aligned.

33. Loosen the center bolt. Install special tool MD998767 on the tension pulley. Turn the tension pulley counterclockwise with a torque of 2.6 ft. lbs. (3.5 Nm) and tighten the center bolt to 35 ft. lbs. (48 Nm). Do not let the tension pulley turn with the bolt.

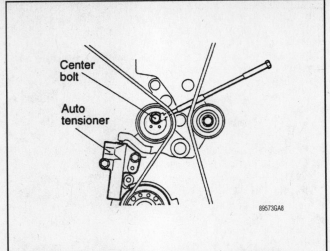

Fig. 172 Use a torque wrench and adapter to apply tension to the timing belt—1995–98 2.0L turbo engine

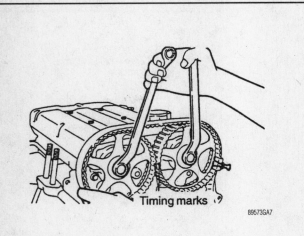

Fig. 170 Keep the timing belt in position using a bulldog clip

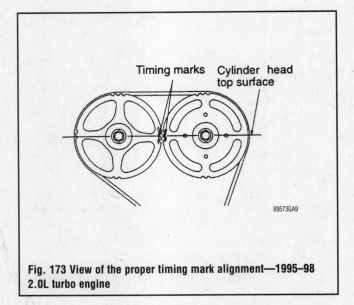

Fig. 173 View of the proper timing mark alignment—1995–98 2.0L turbo engine

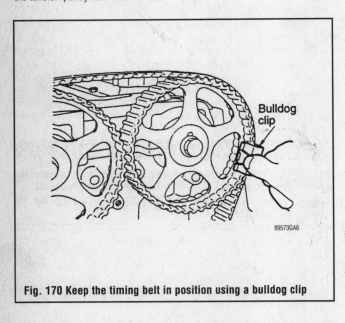

Fig. 171 Use 2 wrenches to align the marks with the top of the cylinder head

34. Turn the crankshaft two revolutions to the right and align the timing marks. After 15 minutes, measure the protrusion of the pushrod on the auto tensioner. The standard measurement is 0.150–0.177 in (3.8–4.5 mm). If the protrusion is out of specification, loosen the tension pulley, apply the proper torque to the belt and retighten the center bolt.

35. Install the crankshaft pulley. Tighten the mounting bolts to 18 ft. lbs. (25 Nm).

36. Install the water pump. Tighten the mounting bolts to 6.5 ft. lbs. (8.8 Nm).

37. Install and adjust the drive belts.

38. Install the engine mount bracket.

39. Install the engine undercover.

40. Connect the negative battery cable.

2.4L Engine

▶ See Figures 139 and 174 thru 178

1. If possible, position the engine so the No. 1 piston is at TDC.

2. Disconnect the negative battery cable.

3. Remove the splash shield under the engine.

4. Safely support the weight of the engine and remove the engine mount and bracket assembly.

5. Remove the drive belts and the timing belt covers.

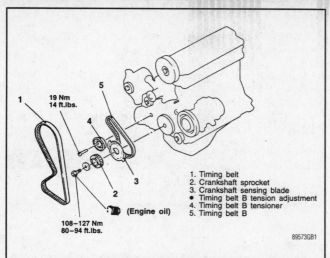

Fig. 174 Exploded view of the inner (B) timing belt and related components—2.4L engine

1. Timing belt
2. Crankshaft sprocket
3. Crankshaft sensing blade
● Timing belt B tension adjustment
4. Timing belt B tensioner
5. Timing belt B

19 Nm
14 ft.lbs.

108–127 Nm
80–94 ft.lbs.

(Engine oil)

89573GB1

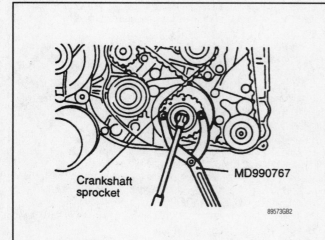

Fig. 175 You will probably have to use a special tool to remove the crankshaft pulley bolt—2.4L engine

Crankshaft sprocket

MD990767

89573GB2

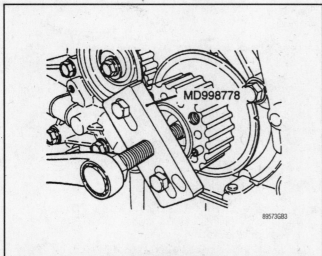

Fig. 176 If you're having trouble removing the sprocket, you may have to use a suitable puller

MD998778

89573GB3

➡If timing belts are going to be reused, mark the direction of rotation on the belt. This will ensure the belt is reinstalled in same direction, extending belt life.

6. To loosen the timing (outer) belt tensioner, install special tool MD998738 or equivalent, to the slot and screw inward to move tensioner toward the water pump. Once the tension has been relieved, remove the outer timing belt.

7. If tensioner replacement is required, align the pin hole in the tensioner rod to the hole in the tensioner cylinder. Insert a 0.055 inch (1.4 mm) wire in the hole and remove the special tool from the slot. With the cylinder tension relieved, remove the auto tensioner cylinder assembly two mounting bolts.

8. Remove the outer crankshaft sprocket and flange.

9. Loosen the silent shaft (inner) belt tensioner and remove the belt. If pulley replacement is required, remove the center adjusting bolt.

10. Remove the crankshaft pulley retainer bolts and remove the pulley.

11. Remove the crankshaft sprocket retainer bolt and washer from the sprocket, if used, and remove sprocket. If sprocket is difficult to remove, the appropriate puller may be used. If no bolts are used on the sprocket, use the appropriate puller to remove.

12. Hold the camshaft stationary using the hexagon cast between journals No. 2 and 3 and remove the retainer bolt. Remove the sprocket from the camshaft.

To install:

13. Install the sprockets to their appropriate shafts. Install the retainer bolts and Tighten the camshaft sprocket bolt to 65 ft. lbs. (90 Nm)

Inspect the timing belts in detail for any flaw or wear. Check the sprockets and tensioner for wear. The sprocket teeth should be well defined, not rounded and the valleys between the teeth should be clean. Turn both tensioner pulleys and check for any signs of bearing wear. If sprockets or pulleys show any sign of wear, they must be replaced.

✷✷ WARNING

Do not spray or immerse the sprockets or tensioners in cleaning solvent. The sprocket may absorb the solvent and transfer it to the belt. The tensioners are internally lubricated and the solvent will dilute or dissolve the lubricant.

14. Align the timing marks of the silent shaft sprockets and the crankshaft sprocket with the timing marks on the front case. Wrap the timing belt around the sprockets so there is no slack in the upper span of the belt and the timing marks are still aligned.

15. Install the tensioner pulley and move the pulley by hand so the long side of the belt deflects about ¼ inch.

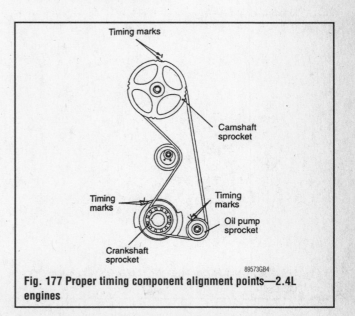

Fig. 177 Proper timing component alignment points—2.4L engines

Timing marks

Camshaft sprocket

Timing marks

Oil pump sprocket

Crankshaft sprocket

89573GB4

16. Hold the pulley tightly so the pulley cannot rotate when the bolt is tigthened. Tighten the bolt to 14 ft. lbs. (19 Nm) and recheck the deflection amount.

17. Align the timing marks of the camshaft, crankshaft and oil pump sprockets with their corresponding marks on the front case or rear cover.

➡**There is a possibility to align all timing marks and have the oil pump sprocket and silent shaft out of time, causing an engine vibration during operation. If the following step is not followed exactly, there is a 50 percent chance that the silent shaft alignment will be 180 degrees off.**

18. Before installing the timing belt, ensure that the left side (rear) silent shaft (oil pump sprocket) is in the correct position as follows:

   a. Remove the plug from the rear side of the block and insert a tool with shaft diameter of 0.31 inches. (8mm) into the hole.

   b. With the timing marks still aligned, the shaft of the tool must be able to go in at least 2 ½ inches. If the tool can only go in about 1 in., the shaft is not in the correct orientation and will cause a vibration during engine operation. Remove the tool from the hole and turn the oil pump sprocket 1 complete revolution. Realign the timing marks and insert the tool. The shaft of the tool must go in at least 2 ¼ inches.

   c. Recheck and realign the timing mark.

   d. Leave the tool in place to hold the silent shaft while continuing.

19. If the camshaft belt tensioner was removed, use a vise to carefully push the auto tensioner rod in until the set hole in the rod aligned up with the hole in the cylinder. Place a wire into the hole to retain the rod. Mount the tensioner to the engine block and tighten the mounting bolt to 17 ft. lbs. (23 Nm).

20. Install the belt to the crankshaft sprocket, oil pump sprocket, then camshaft sprocket, in that order. While doing so, make sure there is no slack between the sprocket except where the tensioner is installed.

21. To adjust the timing (outer) belt perform the following steps:

   a. Turn the crankshaft ¼ turn counterclockwise, then turn it clockwise to move No. 1 cylinder to TDC.

   b. Loosen the center bolt. Using tool MD998752 or equivalent and a torque wrench, apply a torque of 2.6 ft. lbs. (3.6 Nm). Tighten the center bolt.

   c. Screw the special tool into the engine left support bracket until its end makes contact with the tensioner arm. At this point, screw the special tool in some more and remove the set wire attached to the auto tensioner, if the wire was not previously removed. Then remove the special tool.

   d. Rotate the crankshaft two complete turns clockwise and let it sit for approximately 15 minutes. Then, measure the auto tensioner protrusion (the distance between the tensioner arm and auto tensioner body) to ensure that it is within 0.15–0.18 inch (3.8–4.5mm). If out of specification, repeat Step 1–4 until the specified value is obtained.

➡**Do not manually overtigthen the belt or it will howl.**

22. Install the upper and lower timing belt covers. Tighten the bolts to the specifications shown in the accompanying figure.

23. Install the drive belts and properly adjust.

24. Reinstall the engine mount and bracket assembly and safely lower the engine.

25. Install the splash shield.

26. Connect the negative battery cable. Start the engine and let it idle.

27. Run engine until thermostat opens. Check and adjust ignition timing.

Camshaft

REMOVAL & INSTALLATION

1.8L Engine

▶ **See Figure 179**

1. Disconnect the negative battery cable. Remove the air intake hose and the PCV hose.

2. Remove the valve covers and timing belt.

3. Install auto lash adjuster retainer tools MD998443 or equivalent, on the rocker arm. If this tool is not available, rubber bands may be used.

4. Remove the camshaft bearing caps but do not remove the bolts from the carrier.

5. Remove the rocker arms, rocker shafts and bearing caps from the engine as an assembly.

6. Remove the camshaft from the cylinder head.

7. Inspect the bearing journals on the camshaft for excess wear or damage. Measure the cam lobe height and compare to the desired readings. Inspect the bearing surfaces in the cylinder head. Replace any components that is damaged or shows signs of excess wear.

   To install:

8. Lubricate the camshaft journals and camshaft with clean engine oil and install the camshaft in the cylinder head.

9. Align the camshaft bearing caps with the arrow mark depending on cylinder numbers and install in numerical order.

10. Apply sealer at the ends of the bearing caps and install the assembly.

11. Tigthen the bearing cap bolts in the following sequence: No. 3, No. 2, No. 1 and No. 4 to 85 inch lbs. (10 Nm).

12. Repeat the sequence increasing the torque to 15 ft. lbs. (20 Nm).

13. Install the distributor extension if it was removed.

14. Install the timing belt, valve cover and all related parts.

15. Connect the negative battery cable and check for leaks.

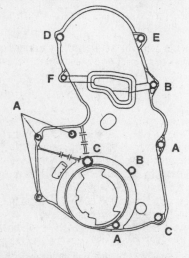

Thread diameter × thread length mm (in.)		Bolt classification	Tightening torque Nm (ft.lbs.)
A	6 × 18 (.24 × .71)	Flange bolt	10−12 (7.2−8.7)
B	6 × 25 (.24 × .98)	Flange bolt	10−12 (7.2−8.7)
C	6 × 25 (.24 × .98)	Washer assembled bolt	8.8 (6.5)
D	8 × 50 (.31 × 1.97)	Flange bolt	14 (10)
E	8 × 28 (.31 × 1.10)	Flange bolt	14 (10)
F	8 × 35 (.31 × 1.38)	Flange bolt	14 (10)

89573GB5

Fig. 178 Timing belt cover retainer specifications—2.4L engine

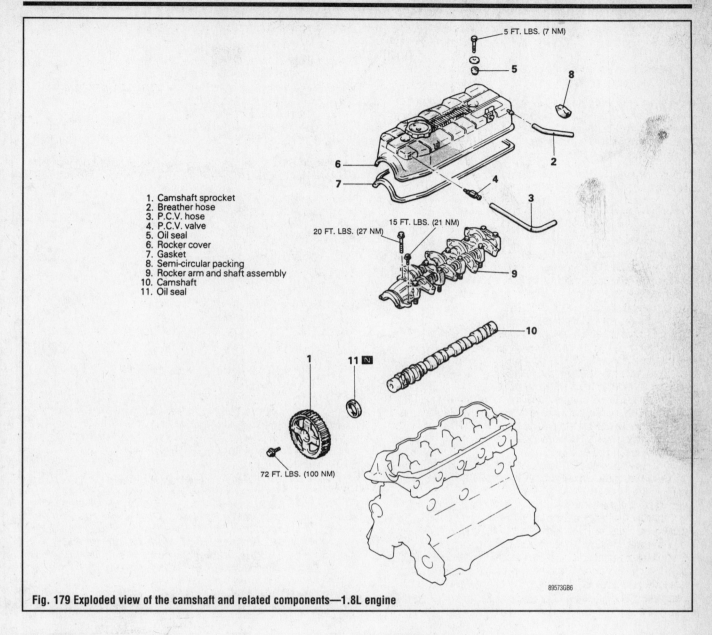

5 FT. LBS. (7 NM)

1. Camshaft sprocket
2. Breather hose
3. P.C.V. hose
4. P.C.V. valve
5. Oil seal
6. Rocker cover
7. Gasket
8. Semi-circular packing
9. Rocker arm and shaft assembly
10. Camshaft
11. Oil seal

20 FT. LBS. (27 NM)

15 FT. LBS. (21 NM)

72 FT. LBS. (100 NM)

89573GB6

Fig. 179 Exploded view of the camshaft and related components—1.8L engine

2.0L Engine

1990–94 VEHICLES

▶ See Figure 180

1. Relieve the fuel system pressure.
2. Disconnect the accelerator cable from the throttle body and position aside.
3. Remove the timing belt cover and timing belt.
4. Label and disconnect the spark plug cable.
5. Remove the center cover, breather and PCV hose.
6. Remove the rocker cover, semi-circular packing, throttle body stay, crankshaft angle sensor, both camshaft sprockets, and oil seal.
7. Loosen the bearing cap bolts in 2–3 steps. Label and remove all camshaft bearing caps.

➡If the bearing caps are difficult to remove, use a plastic hammer to gently tap the rear part of the camshaft.

8. Remove the intake and exhaust camshafts.
9. Check the camshaft journals for wear or damage. Check the cam lobes for damage. Also, check the cylinder head oil holes for clogging.

To install:

10. Lubricate the camshafts with heavy engine oil and position the camshafts on the cylinder head.

➡Do not confuse the intake camshaft with the exhaust camshaft. The intake camshaft has a split on its rear end for driving the crank angle sensor.

11. Make sure the dowel pin on both camshaft sprocket ends are located on the top.
12. Install the bearing caps. Tighten the caps in sequence and in 2 or 3 steps. No. 2 and 5 caps are of the same shape. Check the markings on the caps to identify the cap number and intake/exhaust symbol. Only **L** (intake) or **R** (exhaust) is stamped on No. 1 bearing cap. Also, make sure the rocker arm is correctly mounted on the lash adjuster and the valve stem end. Tighten the retaining bolts to 15 ft. lbs. (20 Nm).
13. Apply a coating of engine oil to the oil seal. Using tool MD998307 or equivalent, press-fit the seal into the cylinder head.
14. Align the punch mark on the crank angle sensor housing with the notch in the plate. With the dowel pin on the sprocket side of the intake camshaft at top, install the crank angle sensor on the cylinder head.

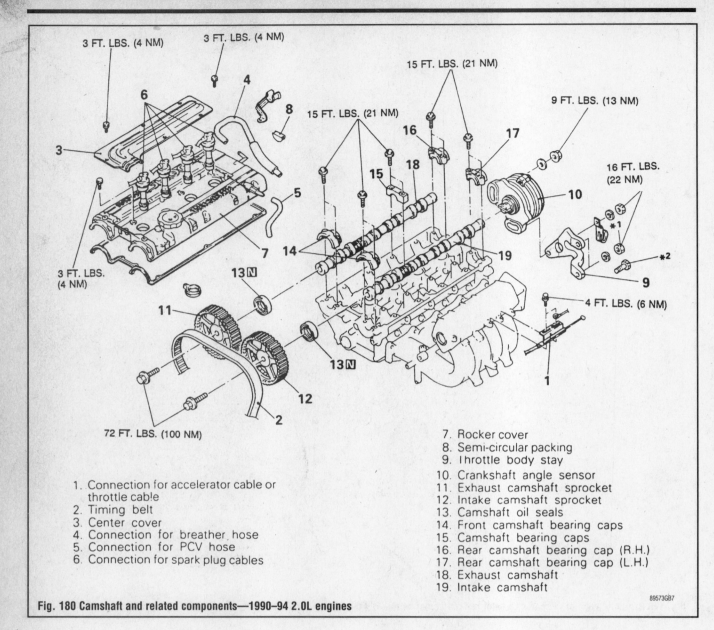

Fig. 180 Camshaft and related components—1990–94 2.0L engines

1. Connection for accelerator cable or throttle cable
2. Timing belt
3. Center cover
4. Connection for breather hose
5. Connection for PCV hose
6. Connection for spark plug cables
7. Rocker cover
8. Semi-circular packing
9. Throttle body stay
10. Crankshaft angle sensor
11. Exhaust camshaft sprocket
12. Intake camshaft sprocket
13. Camshaft oil seals
14. Front camshaft bearing caps
15. Camshaft bearing caps
16. Rear camshaft bearing cap (R.H.)
17. Rear camshaft bearing cap (L.H.)
18. Exhaust camshaft
19. Intake camshaft

➡ Do not position the crank angle sensor with the punch mark positioned opposite the notch; this position will result in incorrect fuel injection and ignition timing.

15. Install the timing belt, valve cover and all related parts.
16. Connect the negative battery cable and check for leaks.

1995–98 NON-TURBO ENGINES

♦ See Figures 181, 182, 183 and 184

1. Disconnect the negative battery cable.
2. Remove the ignition coil pack.
3. Disconnect the PCV hose and the breather hose from the cylinder head cover.
4. Remove the semi-circular packing from the rear of the head.
5. Remove the camshaft position sensor.
6. Remove the timing belt.
7. Use tool MB990767 and MB998719 or equivalent to hold the camshaft sprockets and remove the sprocket mounting bolt and the sprocket.
8. Remove the bracket and the rear timing belt cover.
9. Remove the outside camshaft bearing cap.

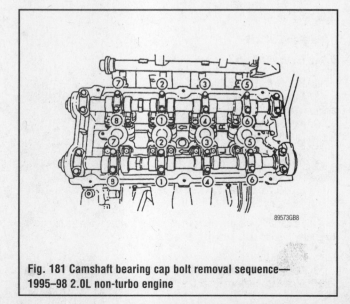

Fig. 181 Camshaft bearing cap bolt removal sequence—1995–98 2.0L non-turbo engine

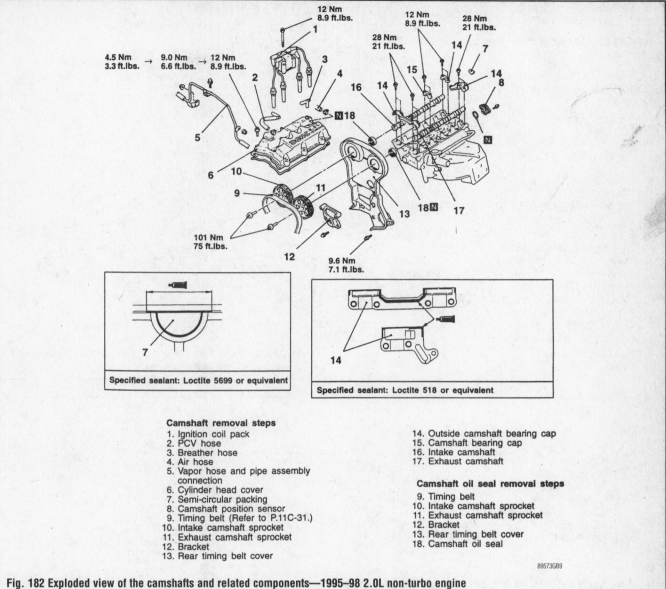

Camshaft removal steps
1. Ignition coil pack
2. PCV hose
3. Breather hose
4. Air hose
5. Vapor hose and pipe assembly connection
6. Cylinder head cover
7. Semi-circular packing
8. Camshaft position sensor
9. Timing belt (Refer to P.11C-31.)
10. Intake camshaft sprocket
11. Exhaust camshaft sprocket
12. Bracket
13. Rear timing belt cover

14. Outside camshaft bearing cap
15. Camshaft bearing cap
16. Intake camshaft
17. Exhaust camshaft

Camshaft oil seal removal steps
9. Timing belt
10. Intake camshaft sprocket
11. Exhaust camshaft sprocket
12. Bracket
13. Rear timing belt cover
18. Camshaft oil seal

89573GB9

Fig. 182 Exploded view of the camshafts and related components—1995–98 2.0L non-turbo engine

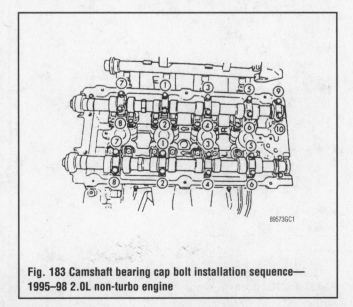

89573GC1

Fig. 183 Camshaft bearing cap bolt installation sequence—1995–98 2.0L non-turbo engine

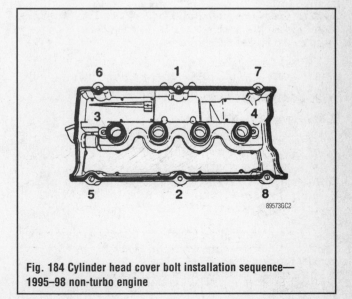

89573GC2

Fig. 184 Cylinder head cover bolt installation sequence—1995–98 non-turbo engine

10. Gradually loosen the camshaft bearing caps in sequence, one camshaft at a time and remove the bearing caps.

➡**Keep the bearing caps in order. They must be installed in the location that they were removed from.**

11. Mark the camshafts for later identification and remove the camshafts. The camshafts are not interchangeable.

To install:

12. Apply engine oil or assembly lube to the camshaft and install the camshafts.

13. Install the bearing caps. Torque the bolts evenly and in sequence.

14. Apply Loctite 518® to the outside camshaft bearing caps and install them.

15. Install the camshaft oil seal.

16. Install the rear timing belt cover and the bracket.

17. Use the special tools and install the camshaft sprockets.

18. Install the timing belt.

19. Apply Loctite 5699® or equivalent to the semi-circular packing and install it in the rear of the cylinder head.

20. Install the camshaft position sensor.

21. Install the cylinder head cover. Torque the bolts in the proper sequence, evenly as follows:
   a. Step 1: 3.3 ft. lbs. (4.5 Nm).
   b. Step 2: 6.6 ft. lbs. (9.0 Nm).
   c. Step 3: 8.9 ft. lbs. (12 Nm).

22. Install the air, breather and PCV hoses.

23. Install the coil pack.

24. Connect the negative battery cable.

1995–98 TURBO ENGINES

▸ See Figures 185, 186, 187 and 188

1. Disconnect the negative battery cable.
2. Disconnect the accelerator cable from the throttle body and remove the cable bracket from the intake plenum.

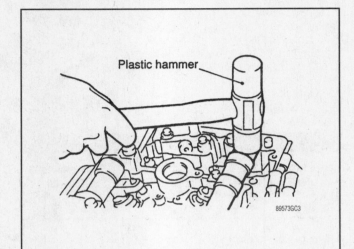

Fig. 185 Tap the camshaft with a plastic hammer to loosen the bearing caps—1995–98 2.0L turbo engine

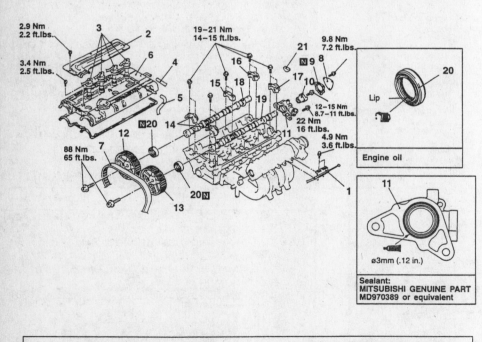

1. Accelerator cable connection
2. Center cover
3. Spark plug cable
4. Breather hose
5. PCV hose
6. Rocker cover
7. Timing belt
8. Cover
9. Gasket
10. Camshaft position sensing cylinder
11. Camshaft position sensor support
12. Exhaust camshaft sprocket
13. Intake camshaft sprocket
14. Front camshaft bearing cap
15. Camshaft bearing cap
16. Rear camshaft bearing cap (R.H.)
17. Rear camshaft bearing cap (L.H.)
18. Exhaust camshaft
19. Intake camshaft
20. Camshaft oil seal
21. Semi-circular packing

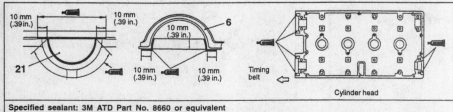

Fig. 186 Exploded view of the camshafts and related components—1995–98 2.0L turbo engines

3. Remove the engine center cover.

4. Disconnect the spark plug cables from the spark plugs. Label them if necessary.

5. Disconnect the breather hose and the PCV hose from the rocker cover.

6. Remove the rocker cover.

7. Position the No. 1 cylinder at TDC on compression.

8. Remove the timing belt.

9. Use a wrench on the hex shaped part of the camshaft to hold the cam and remove the camshaft sprockets.

10. Loosen the bearing cap bolts in two or three steps and remove the bearing caps. If the bearing caps are hard to remove, tap the rear of the camshaft with a plastic hammer.

11. Remove the camshaft(s) and the oil seals.

To install:

12. Apply engine oil or assembly lube to the camshafts and install them on the cylinder head.

✳✳ WARNING

If new camshaft(s) are being installed, remove the rocker arms and install the camshaft(s) and the bearing caps. Make sure the camshaft(s) can be turned by hand. After checking, remove the camshafts and install the rocker arms.

➡ Bearing caps and rocker arms must be installed in the same location that they were remove from.

13. Install the bearing caps and torque the bolts evenly in two or three steps to specifications.

14. Apply engine oil to the lip of the seal. Using MB998713, install the front oil seal.

15. Install the camshaft sprockets.

16. Install the timing belt.

17. Apply sealant to the semi-circular packing and install it in the cylinder head.

18. Apply sealant to the lower part of the front and rear bearing caps where they meet the cylinder head. Use a new gasket and install the rocker cover.

19. Connect the PCV hose and the breather hose.

20. Connect the spark plug wires.

21. Install the center cover.

22. Install the adjust the accelerator cable.

23. Connect the negative battery cable.

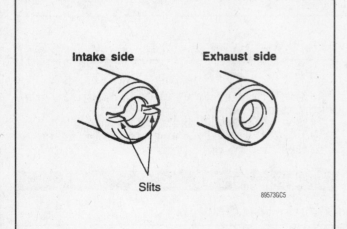

Fig. 187 During installation, make sure not to confuse the intake and exhaust camshafts

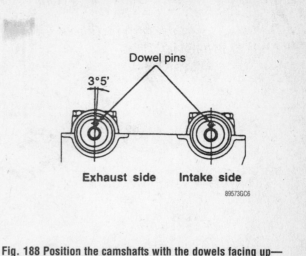

Fig. 188 Position the camshafts with the dowels facing up— 1995–98 2.0L turbo engine

2.4L Engines

▶ See Figures 189 and 190

1. Disconnect and remove the battery.

2. Remove the accelerator cable bracket and position the cable aside.

3. Remove the air intake hose.

4. Remove the breather hose and disconnect the PCV hose.

5. Label and disconnect the spark plug cables.

6. Remove the rocker cover.

7. Install lash adjuster retainer tools MD998443 or equivalent, to the rocker arm.

8. Remove the timing belt covers and the timing belt assembly.

9. While holding camshaft stationary, with an appropriate spanner wrench, remove the camshaft sprocket retainer bolt. Remove the sprocket from the shaft.

10. Remove the camshaft oil seal.

11. Remove both rocker arm shaft assemblies from the head. Do not disassembly rocker arms and rocker arm shaft assemblies.

12. Remove the camshaft from the cylinder head.

13. Inspect the bearing journals on the camshaft, cylinder head, and bearing caps.

To install:

14. Lubricate the camshaft journals and camshaft with clean engine oil and install the camshaft in the cylinder head.

15. Install the rocker arm and shaft assemblies. Tighten the rocker arm shaft retainer bolts to 21–25 ft. lbs. (29–35 Nm).

16. Apply a coating of engine oil to the oil seal. Using the proper size driver, press-fit the seal into the cylinder head.

17. Install the camshaft sprocket and retainer bolt and tighten to 65 ft. lbs. (90 Nm).

18. Install the timing belt and belt covers.

19. Remove the lash adjuster retaining tools.

20. Install the rocker cover using new gasket material on mating surfaces.

21. Connect the spark plug cables.

22. Reinstall the air intake hose.

23. Install the breather hose and connect the PCV hose.

24. Install the battery.

25. Run the engine at idle until normal operating temperature is reached. Check idle speed and ignition timing; adjust as required.

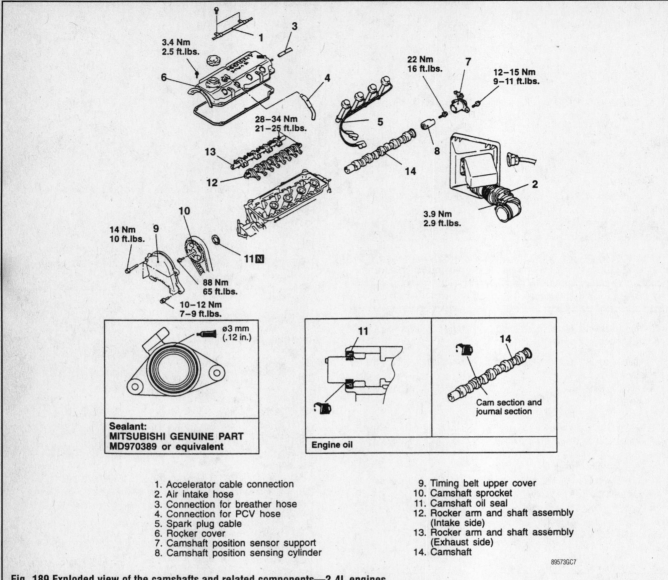

3.4 Nm
2.5 ft.lbs.

22 Nm
16 ft.lbs.

12–15 Nm
9–11 ft.lbs.

28–34 Nm
21–25 ft.lbs.

3.9 Nm
2.9 ft.lbs.

14 Nm
10 ft.lbs.

88 Nm
65 ft.lbs.

10–12 Nm
7–9 ft.lbs.

ø3 mm
(.12 in.)

Sealant:
MITSUBISHI GENUINE PART
MD970389 or equivalent

Cam section and
journal section

Engine oil

1. Accelerator cable connection
2. Air intake hose
3. Connection for breather hose
4. Connection for PCV hose
5. Spark plug cable
6. Rocker cover
7. Camshaft position sensor support
8. Camshaft position sensing cylinder
9. Timing belt upper cover
10. Camshaft sprocket
11. Camshaft oil seal
12. Rocker arm and shaft assembly (Intake side)
13. Rocker arm and shaft assembly (Exhaust side)
14. Camshaft

89573GC7

Fig. 189 Exploded view of the camshafts and related components—2.4L engines

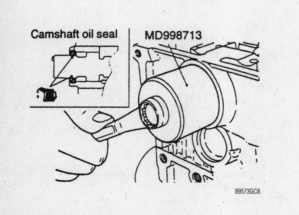

Camshaft oil seal   **MD998713**

89573GC8

Fig. 190 Installation of the camshaft oil seal using the proper tool—2.4L engines

INSPECTION

◆ **See Figures 191 and 192**

1. Check the camshaft journal surfaces for wear and/or damage. If any is found, replace the camshaft.
2. Inspect the camshafts for excessive wear and damage, then replaced if found. Measure the camshaft lobe height and replace if not within the specifications given in the chart in this section.

Silent (Balance) Shaft

REMOVAL & INSTALLATION

1.8L Engine

◆ **See Figure 193**

➡A special oil seal guide MD998285 or equivalent, is needed to complete this operation.

1. Disconnect the negative battery cable.

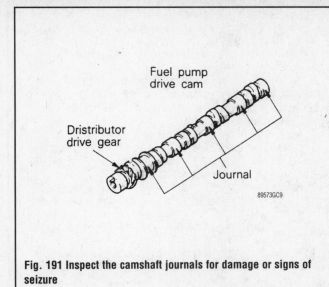

Fig. 191 Inspect the camshaft journals for damage or signs of seizure

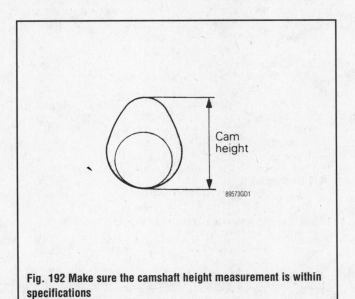

Fig. 192 Make sure the camshaft height measurement is within specifications

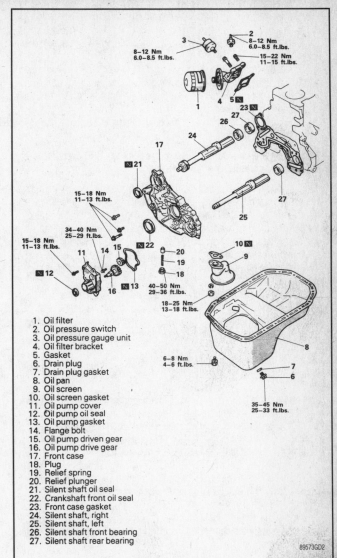

1. Oil filter
2. Oil pressure switch
3. Oil pressure gauge unit
4. Oil filter bracket
5. Gasket
6. Drain plug
7. Drain plug gasket
8. Oil pan
9. Oil screen
10. Oil screen gasket
11. Oil pump cover
12. Oil pump oil seal
13. Oil pump gasket
14. Flange bolt
15. Oil pump driven gear
16. Oil pump drive gear
17. Front case
18. Plug
19. Relief spring
20. Relief plunger
21. Silent shaft oil seal
22. Crankshaft front oil seal
23. Front case gasket
24. Silent shaft, right
25. Silent shaft, left
26. Silent shaft front bearing
27. Silent shaft rear bearing

Fig. 193 Exploded view of the silent shaft and related components—1.8L engines

2. Remove the oil filter, oil pressure switch, oil gauge sending unit, oil filter mounting bracket and gasket.

3. Raise and safely support the vehicle. Drain engine oil. Remove engine oil pan, oil screen and gasket.

4. Lower the vehicle. Remove the timing belts.

5. Remove the front engine cover. Different length bolts are used. Take note of their locations. If the cover sticks to the block, look for a special slot provided and pry with a flat bladed tool. Discard the shaft seal and gasket.

6. Remove the oil pump driven gear flange bolt. When loosening this bolt, first insert a tool approximately ⅜ in. diameter into the plug hole on the left side of the cylinder block to hold the silent shaft. Remove the oil pump gears and remove the front case assembly. Remove the threaded plug, the oil pressure relief spring and plunger.

7. Remove the silent shaft oil seals, the crankshaft oil seal and front case gasket.

8. Remove the silent shafts and inspect as follows:

a. Check the oil holes in the shaft for clogging.

b. Check journals of the shaft for seizure, damage and contact with bearing. If there is anything wrong with the journal, replace the silent shaft bearing, silent shaft or front case.

c. Check the silent shaft oil clearance. If the clearance is beyond the specifications, replace the silent shaft bearing, silent shaft or front case. The specifications for oil clearances are as follows:

Right shaft
Front—0.0008–0.0024 in. (0.02–0.06mm)
Rear—0.0020–0.0036 in. (0.05–0.09mm)

Left shaft
Front—0.0008–0.0021 in. (0.02–0.05mm)
Rear—0.0020–0.0036 in. (0.05–0.09mm)

9. If bearing replacement is required, remove the front bearing from the engine block by using tool MD998282–01.

10. To remove the rear silent shaft bearing from the engine block, use tool MD998283–01.

To install:

11. Install the rear silent shaft bearing into the cylinder block as follows:

a. Apply clean engine oil to the rear bearing outer circumference and bearing hole in the cylinder block.

b. Using bearing installation tool MD998286–01 and a hammer, drive the rear bearing into the cylinder block.

➡ **Make sure the bearing oil holes align with the oil holes in the block, once the bearings are installed.**

12. Install the front silent shaft bearing into the cylinder block as follows:

   a. Install 2 guide pins, normally included in the special tool set with bearing installer MD998289–01, to the threaded holes in the cylinder block.

   b. Set the front baring on the installation tool so that the ratchet ball of the tool fits in the hole in the bearing.

   c. Apply engine oil to the bearing outer circumference and the bearing hole in the cylinder block.

   d. Set the installation tool on the guide pins and, using a hammer, drive the bearing into the cylinder block.

➡**Make sure the bearing oil holes align with the oil holes in the block, once the bearings are installed.**

13. Lubricate the bearing surface of the shaft and the bearing journals with clean engine oil. Carefully install the silent shafts to the block.

14. Clean the gasket material from the mating surface of the cylinder block and the engine front cover. Install new gasket in place.

15. Using seal installation tool MD998304–01 or equivalent, install the crankshaft oil seal into the front engine cover.

16. Using the proper size socket wrench, press in the silent shaft oil seal into the front case.

17. Place pilot tool MD998285–01 or equivalent, onto the nose of the crankshaft. Apply clean engine oil to the outer circumference of the pilot tool.

18. Install the front case onto the engine block and install the retainer bolts in their original positions. Tighten retainers evenly to 12 ft. lbs. (17 Nm).

19. Install the oil pump relief plunger and spring into the bore in the front case and tighten to 33 ft. lbs. (45 Nm). Make sure a new gasket is in place.

20. Install the oil pimp drive gear and driven gear to the front case, lining up the timing marks. Lubricate the gears with clean engine oil.

21. Inspect the orientation of the silent shaft as outlined in the timing belt section of this chapter. Insert the Phillips screwdriver into the hole on the side of the engine block. Install and tighten the flange bolt to 27 ft. lbs. (37 Nm).

22. Install a new oil pump cover gasket in the groove of the front case. When installing the gasket, make sure the round side of the gasket is towards the oil pump cover.

23. Install the oil pump seal into the oil pump cover, making sure the lip is facing the correct direction. The lip of the seal should be installed against the oil it is to stop.

➡**The timing of the oil pump sprocket and connected silent shaft can be incorrect, even with the timing mark aligned. Incorrect orientation of the silent shaft will result in engine vibration during operation. Follow the alignment procedure in the timing belt section of this chapter.**

24. Install the timing belts and all related items. Make sure the timing and the orientation of the silent shafts is correct, using alignment tool in the hole in the left side of the engine block, as specified in the timing belt section of this chapter.

25. Install the oil pan, oil filter mounting bracket, oil switches and new oil filter to the engine. Fill the crankcase to the proper level with clean engine oil.

26. Connect the negative battery cable and start the engine. Check for proper timing and inspect for leaks.

2.0L Engine

♦ **See Figure 194**

➡**A special oil seal guide MD998285 and a plug cap socket tool MD998162 or exact equivalents are needed to complete this operation.**

1. Disconnect the negative battery cable.

2. Remove the oil filter, oil pressure switch, oil gauge sending unit, oil filter mounting bracket and gasket. If equipped with turbocharged engine, remove the oil cooler bolt and oil cooler from the oil filter bracket.

3. Raise and safely support the vehicle. Drain engine oil. Remove engine oil pan, oil screen and gasket. Remove the relief plug, gasket, relief spring and relief plunger.

4. Lower the vehicle. Using the proper equipment, support the weight of the engine.

5. Remove the front engine mount bracket and accessory drive belt.

6. Disconnect the electrical connector from the oil pressure sending unit. Remove the oil pressure sensor using special removal tool MD998054. Remove the oil filter and the oil filter bracket.

7. Remove the oil pan, oil screen and gasket.

8. Using special tool MD998162, remove the plug cap in the engine front cover. If the plug is too tight, hit the plug head with a hammer a few times and the plug should be easier to loosen.

9. Remove the plug on the side of the engine block. Insert a Phillips screwdriver with a shank diameter of 0.32 in. (8mm) into the plug hole. This will hold the silent shaft.

10. Remove the driven gear bolt that secures the oil pump driven gear to the silent shaft.

11. Remove and tag the front cover mounting bolts. Note the lengths of the mounting bolts as they are removed for proper installation.

12. Remove the front case cover and oil pump assembly. If necessary, the silent shaft can come out with the cover assembly.

13. Remove the silent shaft oil seals, the crankshaft oil seal and front case gasket.

14. Remove the silent shafts and inspect as follows:

   a. Check the oil holes in the shaft for clogging.

   b. Check journals of the shaft for seizure, damage and contact with bearing. If there is anything wrong with the journal, replace the silent shaft bearing, silent shaft or front case.

   c. Check the silent shaft oil clearance. If the clearance is beyond the specifications, replace the silent shaft bearing, silent shaft or front case. The specifications for oil clearances are as follows:

   Right shaft
   Front—0.0012–0.0024 in. (0.03–0.06mm)
   Rear—0.0008–0.0021 in. (0.02–0.05mm)
   Left shaft
   Front—0.0020–0.0036 in. (0.05–0.09mm)
   Rear—0.0017–0.0033 in. (0.04–0.08mm)

15. If bearing replacement is required, remove the front bearing from the engine block by using tool MD998371.

16. To remove the rear silent shaft bearing from the engine block, use tool MD998372 and guide plate MD998374.

To install:

17. Clean all mating surfaces of gasket material.

18. Install the rear silent shaft bearing into the cylinder block as follows:

   a. If installing the left rear bearing, install the guide plate MD9983774 to the cylinder block.

   b. Apply clean engine oil to the rear bearing outer circumference and bearing hole in the cylinder block.

   c. Using bearing installation tool MD998374, MD998373 and a hammer, drive the rear bearing into the cylinder block.

➡**The left rear bearing has no oil holes. Make sure the oil hole in the right bearing align with the oil hole in the block, once the bearing is installed.**

19. Install the front silent shaft bearings into the cylinder block, using installation tool as follows:

20. Apply clean engine oil to the rear bearing outer circumference and bearing hole in the cylinder block.

21. Using bearing installation tool MD998373 and a hammer, drive the rear bearing into the cylinder block.

➡**Make sure the bearing oil holes align with the oil holes in the block, once the bearings are installed. Also, make sure that the clinch of the bearing is in the upper most position.**

22. Lubricate the bearing surface of the shaft and the bearing journals with clean engine oil. Carefully install the silent shafts to the block.

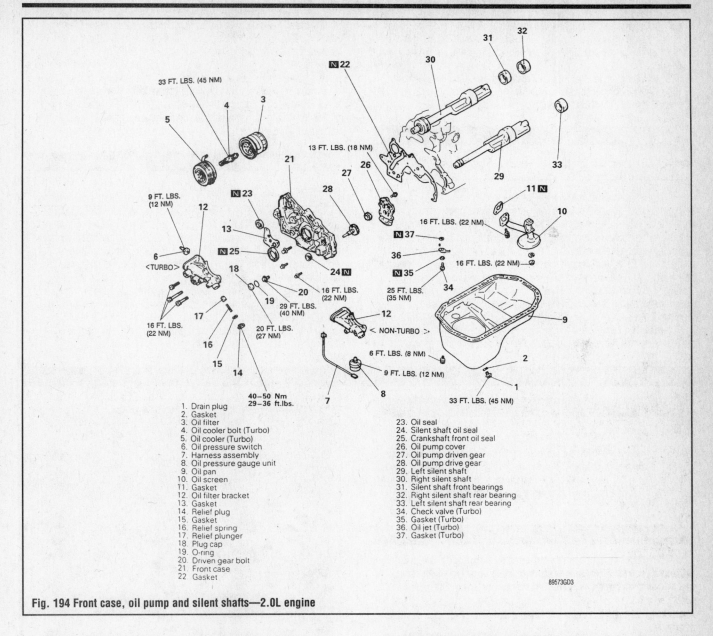

Fig. 194 Front case, oil pump and silent shafts—2.0L engine

1. Drain plug
2. Gasket
3. Oil filter
4. Oil cooler bolt (Turbo)
5. Oil cooler (Turbo)
6. Oil pressure switch
7. Harness assembly
8. Oil pressure gauge unit
9. Oil pan
10. Oil screen
11. Gasket
12. Oil filter bracket
13. Gasket
14. Relief plug
15. Gasket
16. Relief spring
17. Relief plunger
18. Plug cap
19. O-ring
20. Driven gear bolt
21. Front case
22. Gasket

23. Oil seal
24. Silent shaft oil seal
25. Crankshaft front oil seal
26. Oil pump cover
27. Oil pump driven gear
28. Oil pump drive gear
29. Left silent shaft
30. Right silent shaft
31. Silent shaft front bearings
32. Right silent shaft rear bearing
33. Left silent shaft rear bearing
34. Check valve (Turbo)
35. Gasket (Turbo)
36. Oil jet (Turbo)
37. Gasket (Turbo)

89573GD3

23. Clean the gasket material from the mating surface of the cylinder block and the engine front cover. Install new gasket in place.

24. Install the oil pump drive gear and driven gear to the front case, lining up the timing marks. Lubricate the gears with clean engine oil. Install the oil pump cover, with new gasket in place and tighten the mounting bolts to 13 ft. lbs. (18 Nm).

25. Using seal installation tool C–3095–A or equivalent, install the crankshaft oil seal into the front engine case.

26. Using the proper size socket wrench, press in the silent shaft oil seal into the front case.

27. Place pilot tool MD998285 or equivalent, onto the nose of the crankshaft. Apply clean engine oil to the outer circumference of the pilot tool.

28. Install the front case onto the engine block and temporarily tighten the flange bolts (other than those for tightening the filter bracket). Mount the oil filter bracket with new gasket in place. Install the 4 bolts with washers and tighten to 16 ft. lbs. (22 Nm).

29. Insert the Phillips screwdriver into the hole on the side of the engine block. Secure the oil pump driven gear onto the left silent shaft by tightening the driven gear flange bolt to 29 ft. lbs. (40 Nm).

30. Install a new O-ring onto the groove in the front case. Using special socket tool, install and tighten the plug cap to 20 ft. lbs. (27 Nm).

31. Install the oil pump relief plunger and spring into the bore in the oil filter bracket and tighten to 36 ft. lbs. (50 Nm). Make sure a new gasket is in place.

32. Clean both mating surfaces of the oil pan and the cylinder block. Apply sealant in the groove in the oil pan flange, keeping towards the inside of the bolt holes. The width of the sealant bead applied is to be about 0.016 in. (4mm) wide.

➡**After applying sealant to the oil pan, do not exceed 15 minutes before installing the oil pan.**

33. Install the oil pan to the engine and secure with the retainers. Tighten bolts to 6 ft. lbs. (8 Nm).

34. Install the oil pressure gauge unit and the oil pressure switch. Connect the electrical harness connector.

35. Install the oil cooler secure with oil cooler bolt tigthened to 33 ft. lbs. (45 Nm).

36. Install new oil filled with clean engine oil.

➡**The timing of the oil pump sprocket and connected silent shaft can be incorrect, even with the timing mark aligned. Incorrect orientation of the silent shaft will result in engine vibration during operation. Follow the alignment procedure in the timing belt section of this chapter.**

37. Install the timing belts and all related items. Make sure the timing and orientation of the silent shafts is correct by inserting the alignment tool in the hole in the left side of the engine block, as specified in the timing belt section of this chapter.

38. Install any remaining components removed during disassembly.

39. Connect the negative battery cable and start the engine. Check for proper timing and inspect for leaks.

Rear Main Seal

REMOVAL & INSTALLATION

1. Disconnect the negative battery cable.

2. Remove the transaxle and transfer case, if equipped, from the vehicle.

3. If equipped with automatic transaxle, remove the flywheel/ring gear assembly from the crankshaft.

4. If equipped with manual transaxle, remove the rear engine plate and the bellhousing cover.

5. If the crankshaft rear oil seal case is leaking, remove it. Otherwise, just remove the oil seal. Some engines have a separator that should also be removed.

To install:

6. Lubricate the inner diameter of the new seal with clean engine oil.

7. Install the oil seal in the crankshaft rear oil seal case using tool MD998376 or equivalent. Press the seal all the way in without tilting it. Force the oil separator into the oil seal case so the oil hole in the separator is downward.

8. Install the seal case to the crankshaft with a new gasket, if removed.

9. Install the flywheel or drive plate, transfer and transaxle.

10. Connect the negative battery cable and check for leaks.

11. Fill the crankcase with clean oil to the proper level. Start the engine and check for leaks.

Flywheel and Ring Gear

REMOVAL & INSTALLATION

1. If equipped with a manual transaxle, refer to the Clutch, Removal and Installation procedures in Chapter 7, then remove the transaxle and the clutch assembly. If equipped with an automatic transaxle, refer to the Automatic Transaxle, Removal and Installation procedures in Chapter 7, then remove the transaxle and the torque converter.

2. For manual transaxles, remove the flywheel-to-crankshaft bolts and the flywheel. For automatic transaxles, remove the drive plate-to-crankshaft bolts and the drive plate.

3. To install, reverse the removal procedures. Tighten the flywheel-to-crankshaft bolts to specifications.

EXHAUST SYSTEM

Inspection

▶ **See Figures 195 thru 201**

➡Safety glasses should be worn at all times when working on or near the exhaust system. Older exhaust systems will almost always be covered with loose rust particles which will shower you when disturbed. These particles are more than a nuisance and could injure your eye.

❊❊ CAUTION

Do NOT perform exhaust repairs or inspection with the engine or exhaust hot. Allow the system to cool completely before attempting any work. Exhaust systems are noted for sharp

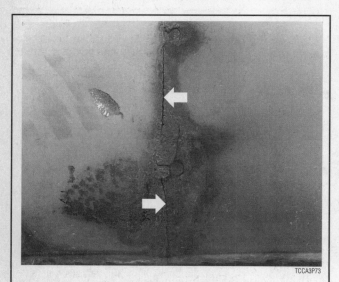

TCCA3P73

Fig. 195 Cracks in the muffler are a guaranteed leak

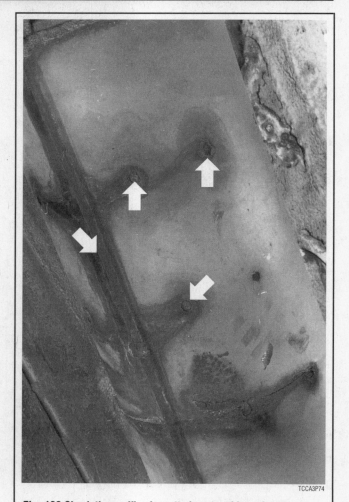

TCCA3P74

Fig. 196 Check the muffler for rotted spot welds and seams

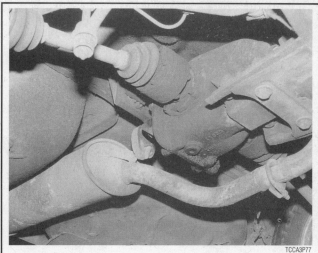

Fig. 197 Make sure the exhaust components are not contacting the body or suspension

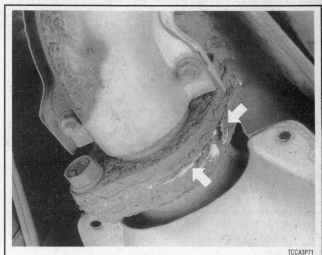

Fig. 200 Inspect flanges for gaskets that have deteriorated and need replacement

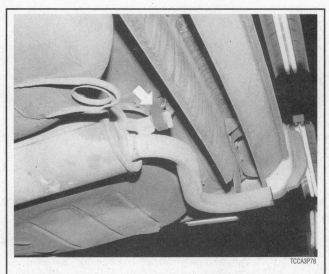

Fig. 198 Check for overstreached or torn exhaust hangers

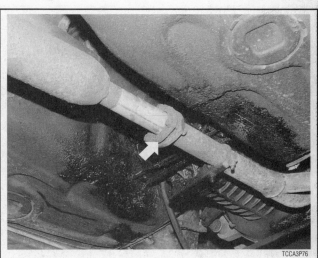

Fig. 201 Some systems, like this one, use large O-rings (donuts) in between the flanges

Fig. 199 Example of a badly deteriorated exhaust pipe

edges, flaking metal and rusted bolts. Gloves and eye protection are required. A healthy supply of penetrating oil and rags is highly recommended.

Your vehicle must be raised and supported safely to inspect the exhaust system properly. By placing 4 safety stands under the vehicle for support should provide enough room for you to slide under the vehicle and inspect the system completely. Start the inspection at the exhaust manifold or turbocharger pipe where the header pipe is attached and work your way to the back of the vehicle. On dual exhaust systems, remember to inspect both sides of the vehicle. Check the complete exhaust system for open seams, holes loose connections, or other deterioration which could permit exhaust fumes to seep into the passenger compartment. Inspect all mounting brackets and hangers for deterioration, some models may have rubber O-rings that can be overstretched and non-supportive. These components will need to be replaced if found. It has always been a practice to use a pointed tool to poke up into the exhaust system where the deterioration spots are to see whether or not they crumble. Some models may have heat shield covering certain parts of the exhaust system, it will be necessary to remove these shields to have the exhaust visible for inspection also.

REPLACEMENT

◆ See Figures 202 thru 209

There are basically two types of exhaust systems. One is the flange type where the component ends are attached with bolts and a gasket in-between. The other exhaust system is the slip joint type. These components slip into one another using clamps to retain them together.

❋❋ CAUTION

Allow the exhaust system to cool sufficiently before spraying a solvent exhaust fasteners. Some solvents are highly flammable and could ignite when sprayed on hot exhaust components.

Before removing any component of the exhaust system, ALWAYS squirt a liquid rust dissolving agent onto the fasteners for ease of removal. A lot of knuckle skin will be saved by following this rule. It may even be wise to spray the fasteners and allow them to sit overnight.

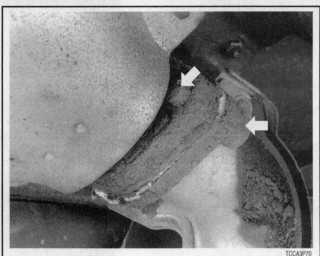

TCCA3P70

Fig. 202 Nuts and bolts will be extremely difficult to remove when deteriorated with rust

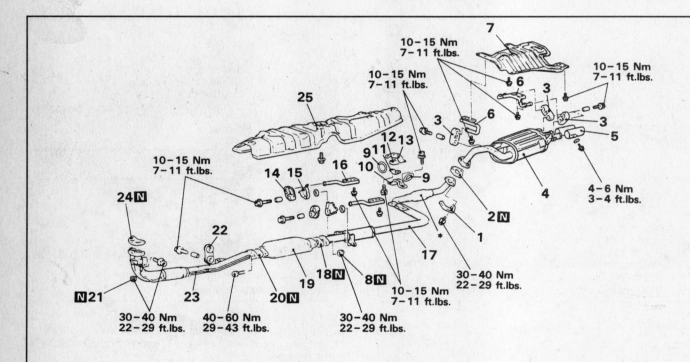

1. Protector
2. Gasket
3. Hanger
4. Main muffler
5. Moulding <2.0L DOHC engine (Non-Turbo)>
6. Hanger bracket
7. Rear heat protector panel
8. Self locking nut
9. O-ring
10. Hook
11. Bracket
12. Stopper
13. Hanger bracket
14. Hanger
15. Protector

16. Hanger bracket
17. Center exhaust pipe
18. Gasket
19. Catalytic converter
20. Gasket
21. Self locking nut
22. Hanger
23. Front exhaust pipe
24. Gasket
25. Front floor heat protector panel

89573GD4

Fig. 203 Exhaust system components—1990–94 1.8L engine and 1990–94 2.0L non-turbo engines

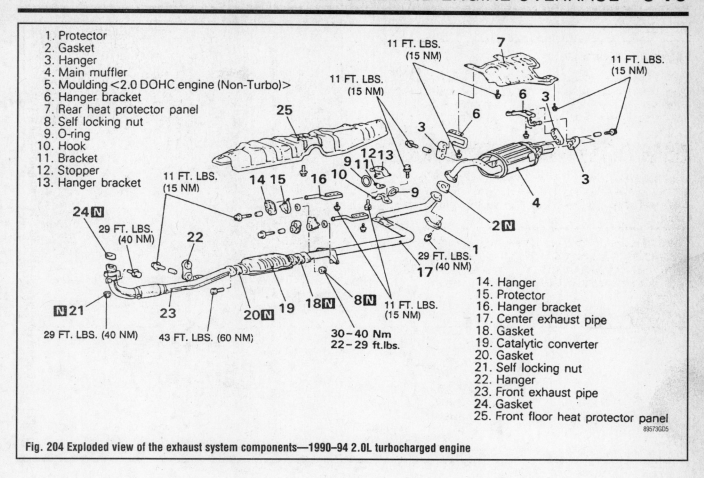

1. Protector
2. Gasket
3. Hanger
4. Main muffler
5. Moulding <2.0 DOHC engine (Non-Turbo)>
6. Hanger bracket
7. Rear heat protector panel
8. Self locking nut
9. O-ring
10. Hook
11. Bracket
12. Stopper
13. Hanger bracket

14. Hanger
15. Protector
16. Hanger bracket
17. Center exhaust pipe
18. Gasket
19. Catalytic converter
20. Gasket
21. Self locking nut
22. Hanger
23. Front exhaust pipe
24. Gasket
25. Front floor heat protector panel

11 FT. LBS. (15 NM)
11 FT. LBS. (15 NM)
11 FT. LBS. (15 NM)
11 FT. LBS. (15 NM)
29 FT. LBS. (40 NM)
29 FT. LBS. (40 NM)
29 FT. LBS. (40 NM)
43 FT. LBS. (60 NM)
30–40 Nm
22–29 ft.lbs.

89573GD5

Fig. 204 Exploded view of the exhaust system components—1990–94 2.0L turbocharged engine

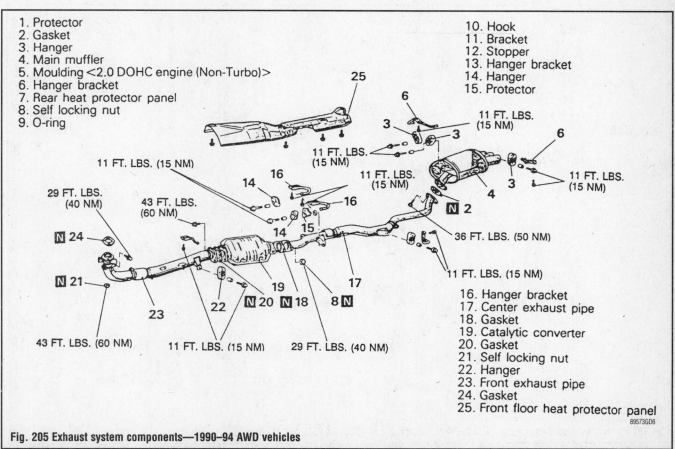

1. Protector
2. Gasket
3. Hanger
4. Main muffler
5. Moulding <2.0 DOHC engine (Non-Turbo)>
6. Hanger bracket
7. Rear heat protector panel
8. Self locking nut
9. O-ring

10. Hook
11. Bracket
12. Stopper
13. Hanger bracket
14. Hanger
15. Protector

16. Hanger bracket
17. Center exhaust pipe
18. Gasket
19. Catalytic converter
20. Gasket
21. Self locking nut
22. Hanger
23. Front exhaust pipe
24. Gasket
25. Front floor heat protector panel

11 FT. LBS. (15 NM)
11 FT. LBS. (15 NM)
11 FT. LBS. (15 NM)
11 FT. LBS. (15 NM)
29 FT. LBS. (40 NM)
43 FT. LBS. (60 NM)
36 FT. LBS. (50 NM)
11 FT. LBS. (15 NM)
43 FT. LBS. (60 NM)
11 FT. LBS. (15 NM)
29 FT. LBS. (40 NM)

89573GD6

Fig. 205 Exhaust system components—1990–94 AWD vehicles

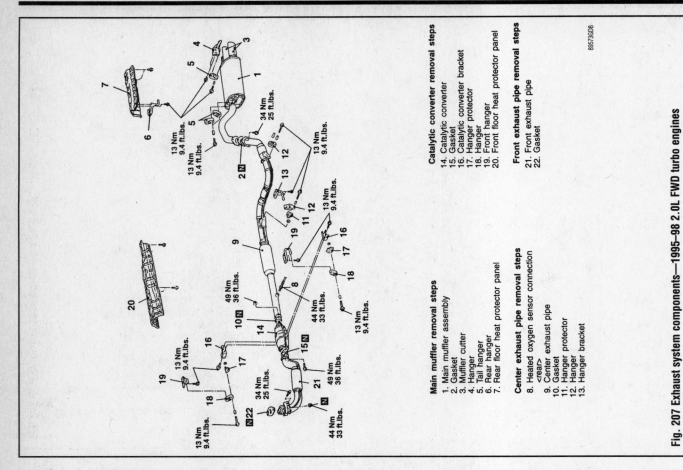

Catalytic converter removal steps
14. Catalytic converter
15. Gasket
16. Catalytic converter bracket
17. Hanger protector
18. Hanger
19. Front hanger
20. Rear floor heat protector panel

Front exhaust pipe removal steps
21. Front exhaust pipe
22. Gasket

Main muffler removal steps
1. Main muffler assembly
2. Gasket
3. Muffler cutter
4. Hanger
5. Tail hanger
6. Rear hanger
7. Rear floor heat protector panel

Center exhaust pipe removal steps
8. Heated oxygen sensor connection
<rear>
9. Center exhaust pipe
10. Gasket
11. Hanger protector
12. Hanger
13. Hanger bracket

Fig. 207 Exhaust system components—1995–98 2.0L FWD turbo engines

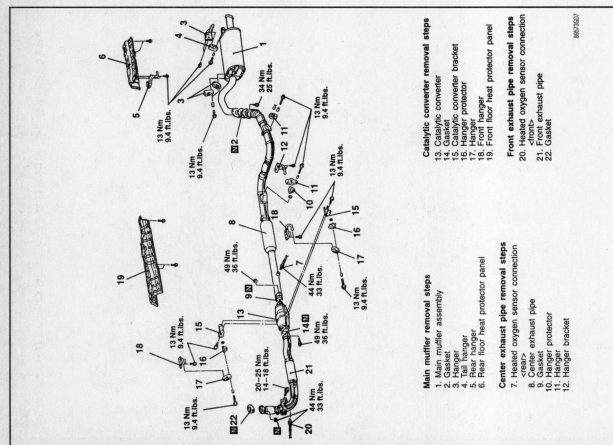

Catalytic converter removal steps
13. Catalytic converter
14. Gasket
15. Catalytic converter bracket
16. Hanger protector
17. Hanger
18. Front hanger
19. Front floor heat protector panel

Front exhaust pipe removal steps
20. Heated oxygen sensor connection
<front>
21. Front exhaust pipe
22. Gasket

Main muffler removal steps
1. Main muffler assembly
2. Gasket
3. Hanger
4. Tail hanger
5. Rear hanger
6. Rear floor heat protector panel

Center exhaust pipe removal steps
7. Heated oxygen sensor connection
<rear>
8. Center exhaust pipe
9. Gasket
10. Hanger protector
11. Hanger
12. Hanger bracket

Fig. 206 Exploded view of the exhaust system components—1995–98 2.0L non-turbo engines

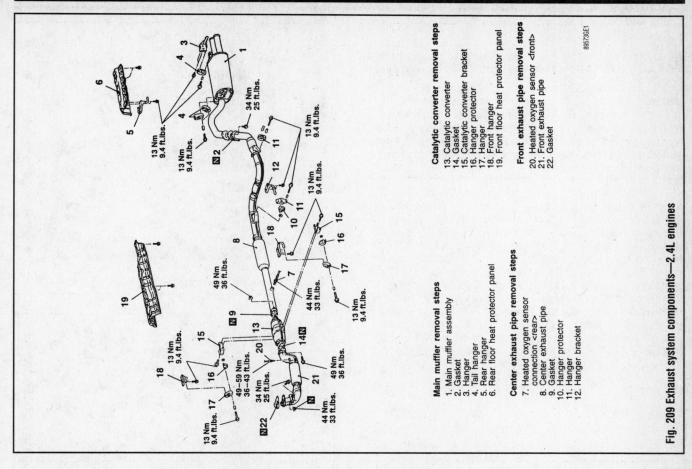

Catalytic converter removal steps

13. Catalytic converter
14. Gasket
15. Catalytic converter bracket
16. Hanger protector
17. Hanger
18. Front hanger
19. Front floor heat protector panel

Front exhaust pipe removal steps

20. Heated oxygen sensor <front>
21. Front exhaust pipe
22. Gasket

Main muffler removal steps

1. Main muffler assembly
2. Gasket
3. Hanger
4. Tail hanger
5. Rear hanger
6. Rear floor heat protector panel

Center exhaust pipe removal steps

7. Heated oxygen sensor connection <rear>
8. Center exhaust pipe
9. Gasket
10. Hanger protector
11. Hanger
12. Hanger bracket

Fig. 209 Exhaust system components—2.4L engines

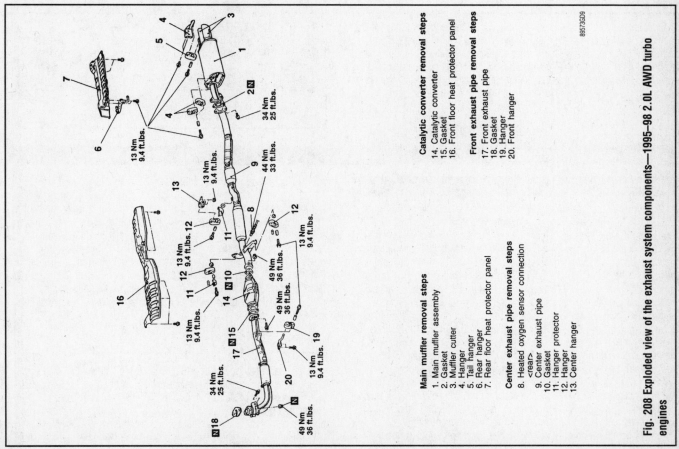

Main muffler removal steps

1. Main muffler assembly
2. Gasket
3. Muffler cutter
4. Hanger
5. Tail hanger
6. Rear hanger
7. Rear floor heat protector panel

Center exhaust pipe removal steps

8. Heated oxygen sensor connection <rear>
9. Center exhaust pipe
10. Gasket
11. Hanger protector
12. Hanger
13. Center hanger

Catalytic converter removal steps

14. Catalytic converter
15. Gasket
16. Front floor heat protector panel

Front exhaust pipe removal steps

17. Front exhaust pipe
18. Gasket
19. Hanger
20. Front hanger

Fig. 208 Exploded view of the exhaust system components—1995–98 2.0L AWD turbo engines

Flange Type

▶ See Figure 210

> ✳✳ **CAUTION**
>
> Do NOT perform exhaust repairs or inspection with the engine or exhaust hot. Allow the system to cool completely before attempting any work. Exhaust systems are noted for sharp edges, flaking metal and rusted bolts. Gloves and eye protection are required. A healthy supply of penetrating oil and rags is highly recommended. Never spray liquid rust dissolving agent onto a hot exhaust component.

Before removing any component on a flange type system, ALWAYS squirt a liquid rust dissolving agent onto the fasteners for ease of removal. Start by unbolting the exhaust piece at both ends (if required). When unbolting the headpipe from the manifold, make sure that the bolts are free before trying to remove them. if you snap a stud in the exhaust manifold, the stud will have to be removed with a bolt extractor, which often means removal of the manifold itself. Next, disconnect the component from the mounting; slight twisting and turning may be required to remove the component completely from the vehicle. You may need to tap on the component with a rubber mallet to loosen the component. If all else fails, use a hacksaw to separate the parts. An oxy-acetylene cutting torch may be faster but the sparks are DANGEROUS near the fuel tank, and at the very least, accidents could happen, resulting in damage to the under-car parts, not to mention yourself.

Slip Joint Type

▶ See Figure 211

Before removing any component on the slip joint type exhaust system, ALWAYS squirt a liquid rust dissolving agent onto the fasteners for ease of removal. Start by unbolting the exhaust piece at both ends (if required). When unbolting the headpipe from the manifold, make sure that the bolts are free before trying to remove them. if you snap a stud in the exhaust manifold, the stud will have to be removed with a bolt extractor, which often means removal of the manifold itself. Next, remove the mounting U-bolts from around the exhaust pipe you are extracting from the vehicle. Don't be surprised if the U-bolts break while removing the nuts. Loosen the exhaust pipe from any mounting brackets retaining it to the floor pan and separate the components.

TCCA3P72

Fig. 210 Example of a flange type exhaust system joint

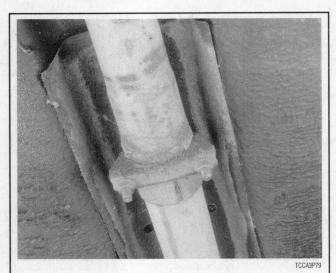

TCCA3P79

Fig. 211 Example of a common slip joint type system

ENGINE RECONDITIONING

Determining Engine Condition

Anything that generates heat and/or friction will eventually burn or wear out (ie. a light bulb generates heat, therefore its life span is limited). With this in mind, a running engine generates tremendous amounts of both; friction is encountered by the moving and rotating parts inside the engine and heat is created by friction and combustion of the fuel. However, the engine has systems designed to help reduce the effects of heat and friction and provide added longevity. The oiling system reduces the amount of friction encountered by the moving parts inside the engine, while the cooling system reduces heat created by friction and combustion. If either system is not maintained, a break-down will be inevitable. Therefore, you can see how regular maintenance can affect the service life of your vehicle. If you do not drain, flush and refill your cooling system at the proper intervals, deposits will begin to accumulate in the radiator, thereby reducing the amount of heat it can extract from the coolant. The same applies to your oil and filter; if it is not changed often enough it becomes laden with contaminates and is unable to properly lubricate the engine. This increases friction and wear.

There are a number of methods for evaluating the condition of your engine. A compression test can reveal the condition of your pistons, piston rings, cylinder bores, head gasket(s), valves and valve seats. An oil pressure test can warn you of possible engine bearing, or oil pump failures. Excessive oil consumption, evidence of oil in the engine air intake area and/or bluish smoke from the tail pipe may indicate worn piston rings, worn valve guides and/or valve seals. As a general rule, an engine that uses no more than one quart of oil every 1000 miles is in good condition. Engines that use one quart of oil or more in less than 1000 miles should first be checked for oil leaks. If any oil leaks are present, have them fixed before determining how much oil is consumed by the engine, especially if blue smoke is not visible at the tail pipe.

COMPRESSION TEST

A noticeable lack of engine power, excessive oil consumption and/or poor fuel mileage measured over an extended period are all indicators of internal engine wear. Worn piston rings, scored or worn cylinder bores, blown head gaskets, sticking or burnt valves, and worn valve seats are all possible culprits. A check of each cylinder's compression will help locate the problem.

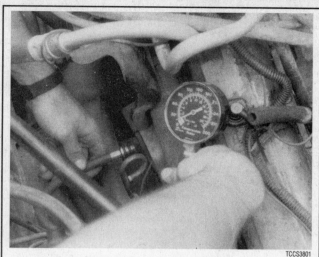

TCCS3801

A screw-in type compression gauge is more accurate and easier to use without an assistant

→A screw-in type compression gauge is more accurate than the type you simply hold against the spark plug hole. Although it takes slightly longer to use, it's worth the effort to obtain a more accurate reading.

1. Make sure that the proper amount and viscosity of engine oil is in the crankcase, then ensure the battery is fully charged.

2. Warm-up the engine to normal operating temperature, then shut the engine **OFF**.

3. Disable the ignition system.

4. Label and disconnect all of the spark plug wires from the plugs.

5. Thoroughly clean the cylinder head area around the spark plug ports, then remove the spark plugs.

6. Set the throttle plate to the fully open (wide-open throttle) position. You can block the accelerator linkage open for this, or you can have an assistant fully depress the accelerator pedal.

7. Install a screw-in type compression gauge into the No. 1 spark plug hole until the fitting is snug.

✳✳ WARNING

Be careful not to crossthread the spark plug hole.

8. According to the tool manufacturer's instructions, connect a remote starting switch to the starting circuit.

9. With the ignition switch in the **OFF** position, use the remote starting switch to crank the engine through at least five compression strokes (approximately 5 seconds of cranking) and record the highest reading on the gauge.

10. Repeat the test on each cylinder, cranking the engine approximately the same number of compression strokes and/or time as the first.

11. Compare the highest readings from each cylinder to that of the others. The indicated compression pressures are considered within specifications if the lowest reading cylinder is within 75 percent of the pressure recorded for the highest reading cylinder. For example, if your highest reading cylinder pressure was 150 psi (1034 kPa), then 75 percent of that would be 113 psi (779 kPa). So the lowest reading cylinder should be no less than 113 psi (779 kPa).

12. If a cylinder exhibits an unusually low compression reading, pour a tablespoon of clean engine oil into the cylinder through the spark plug hole and repeat the compression test. If the compression rises after adding oil, it means that the cylinder's piston rings and/or cylinder bore are damaged or worn. If the pressure remains low, the valves may not be seating properly (a valve job is needed), or the head gasket may be blown near that cylinder. If compression in any two adjacent cylinders is low, and if the addition of oil doesn't help raise compression, there is leakage past the head gasket. Oil

and coolant in the combustion chamber, combined with blue or constant white smoke from the tail pipe, are symptoms of this problem. However, don't be alarmed by the normal white smoke emitted from the tail pipe during engine warm-up or from cold weather driving. There may be evidence of water droplets on the engine dipstick and/or oil droplets in the cooling system if a head gasket is blown.

OIL PRESSURE TEST

Check for proper oil pressure at the sending unit passage with an externally mounted mechanical oil pressure gauge (as opposed to relying on a factory installed dash-mounted gauge). A tachometer may also be needed, as some specifications may require running the engine at a specific rpm.

1. With the engine cold, locate and remove the oil pressure sending unit.

2. Following the manufacturer's instructions, connect a mechanical oil pressure gauge and, if necessary, a tachometer to the engine.

3. Start the engine and allow it to idle.

4. Check the oil pressure reading when cold and record the number. You may need to run the engine at a specified rpm, so check the specifications chart located earlier in this section.

5. Run the engine until normal operating temperature is reached (upper radiator hose will feel warm).

6. Check the oil pressure reading again with the engine hot and record the number. Turn the engine **OFF**.

7. Compare your hot oil pressure reading to that given in the chart. If the reading is low, check the cold pressure reading against the chart. If the cold pressure is well above the specification, and the hot reading was lower than the specification, you may have the wrong viscosity oil in the engine. Change the oil, making sure to use the proper grade and quantity, then repeat the test.

Low oil pressure readings could be attributed to internal component wear, pump related problems, a low oil level, or oil viscosity that is too low. High oil pressure readings could be caused by an overfilled crankcase, too high of an oil viscosity or a faulty pressure relief valve.

Buy or Rebuild?

Now that you have determined that your engine is worn out, you must make some decisions. The question of whether or not an engine is worth rebuilding is largely a subjective matter and one of personal worth. Is the engine a popular one, or is it an obsolete model? Are parts available? Will it get acceptable gas mileage once it is rebuilt? Is the car it's being put into worth keeping? Would it be less expensive to buy a new engine, have your engine rebuilt by a pro, rebuild it yourself or buy a used engine from a salvage yard? Or would it be simpler and less expensive to buy another car? If you have considered all these matters and more, and have still decided to rebuild the engine, then it is time to decide how you will rebuild it.

→**The editors at Chilton feel that most engine machining should be performed by a professional machine shop. Don't think of it as wasting money, rather, as an assurance that the job has been done right the first time. There are many expensive and specialized tools required to perform such tasks as boring and honing an engine block or having a valve job done on a cylinder head. Even inspecting the parts requires expensive micrometers and gauges to properly measure wear and clearances. Also, a machine shop can deliver to you clean, and ready to assemble parts, saving you time and aggravation. Your maximum savings will come from performing the removal, disassembly, assembly and installation of the engine and purchasing or renting only the tools required to perform the above tasks. Depending on the particular circumstances, you may save 40 to 60 percent of the cost doing these yourself.**

A complete rebuild or overhaul of an engine involves replacing all of the moving parts (pistons, rods, crankshaft, camshaft, etc.) with new ones and machining the non-moving wearing surfaces of the block and heads. Unfortunately, this may not be cost effective. For instance, your crankshaft may have been damaged or worn, but it can be machined undersize for a minimal fee.

So, as you can see, you can replace everything inside the engine, but, it is wiser to replace only those parts which are really needed, and, if possible, repair the more expensive ones. Later in this section, we will break the engine down into its two main components: the cylinder head and the engine block. We will discuss each component, and the recommended parts to replace during a rebuild on each.

Engine Overhaul Tips

Most engine overhaul procedures are fairly standard. In addition to specific parts replacement procedures and specifications for your individual engine, this section is also a guide to acceptable rebuilding procedures. Examples of standard rebuilding practice are given and should be used along with specific details concerning your particular engine.

Competent and accurate machine shop services will ensure maximum performance, reliability and engine life. In most instances it is more profitable for the do-it-yourself mechanic to remove, clean and inspect the component, buy the necessary parts and deliver these to a shop for actual machine work.

Much of the assembly work (crankshaft, bearings, piston rods, and other components) is well within the scope of the do-it-yourself mechanic's tools and abilities. You will have to decide for yourself the depth of involvement you desire in an engine repair or rebuild.

TOOLS

The tools required for an engine overhaul or parts replacement will depend on the depth of your involvement. With a few exceptions, they will be the tools found in a mechanic's tool kit (see Section 1 of this manual). More in-depth work will require some or all of the following:

- A dial indicator (reading in thousandths) mounted on a universal base
- Micrometers and telescope gauges
- Jaw and screw-type pullers
- Scraper
- Valve spring compressor
- Ring groove cleaner
- Piston ring expander and compressor
- Ridge reamer
- Cylinder hone or glaze breaker
- Plastigage®
- Engine stand

The use of most of these tools is illustrated in this section. Many can be rented for a one-time use from a local parts jobber or tool supply house specializing in automotive work.

Occasionally, the use of special tools is called for. See the information on Special Tools and the Safety Notice in the front of this book before substituting another tool.

OVERHAUL TIPS

Aluminum has become extremely popular for use in engines, due to its low weight. Observe the following precautions when handling aluminum parts:

- Never hot tank aluminum parts (the caustic hot tank solution will eat the aluminum.
- Remove all aluminum parts (identification tag, etc.) from engine parts prior to the tanking.
- Always coat threads lightly with engine oil or anti-seize compounds before installation, to prevent seizure.
- Never overtigthen bolts or spark plugs especially in aluminum threads.

When assembling the engine, any parts that will be exposed to frictional contact must be prelubed to provide lubrication at initial start-up. Any product specifically formulated for this purpose can be used, but engine oil is not recommended as a prelube in most cases.

When semi-permanent (locked, but removable) installation of bolts or nuts is desired, threads should be cleaned and coated with Loctite® or another similar, commercial non-hardening sealant.

CLEANING

Before the engine and its components are inspected, they must be thoroughly cleaned. You will need to remove any engine varnish, oil sludge and/or carbon deposits from all of the components to insure an accurate inspection. A crack in the engine block or cylinder head can easily become overlooked if hidden by a layer of sludge or carbon.

Most of the cleaning process can be carried out with common hand tools and readily available solvents or solutions. Carbon deposits can be chipped away using a hammer and a hard wooden chisel. Old gasket material and varnish or sludge can usually be removed using a scraper and/or cleaning solvent. Extremely stubborn deposits may require the use of a power drill with a wire brush. If using a wire brush, use extreme care around any critical machined surfaces (such as the gasket surfaces, bearing saddles, cylinder bores, etc.). USE OF A WIRE BRUSH IS NOT RECOMMENDED ON ANY ALUMINUM COMPONENTS. Always follow any safety recommendations given by the manufacturer of the tool and/or solvent. You should always wear eye protection during any cleaning process involving scraping, chipping or spraying of solvents.

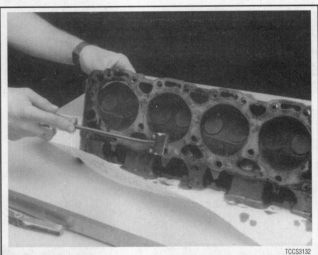

TCCS3132

Use a gasket scraper to remove the old gasket material from the mating surfaces

TCCS3211

Use a ring expander tool to remove the piston rings

An alternative to the mess and hassle of cleaning the parts yourself is to drop them off at a local garage or machine shop. They will, more than likely, have the necessary equipment to properly clean all of the parts for a nominal fee.

✱✱ CAUTION

Always wear eye protection during any cleaning process involving scraping, chipping or spraying of solvents.

Remove any oil galley plugs, freeze plugs and/or pressed-in bearings and carefully wash and degrease all of the engine components including the fasteners and bolts. Small parts such as the valves, springs, etc., should be placed in a metal basket and allowed to soak. Use pipe cleaner type brushes, and clean all passageways in the components. Use a ring expander and remove the rings from the pistons. Clean the piston ring grooves with a special tool or a piece of broken ring. Scrape the carbon off of the top of the piston. You should never use a wire brush on the pistons. After preparing all of the piston assemblies in this manner, wash and degrease them again.

✱✱ WARNING

Use extreme care when cleaning around the cylinder head valve seats. A mistake or slip may cost you a new seat.

When cleaning the cylinder head, remove carbon from the combustion chamber with the valves installed. This will avoid damaging the valve seats.

REPAIRING DAMAGED THREADS

◆ See Figures 212, 213, 214, 215 and 216

Several methods of repairing damaged threads are available. Heli-Coil® (shown here), Keenserts® and Microdot® are among the most widely used. All involve basically the same principle—drilling out stripped threads, tapping the hole and installing a prewound insert—making welding, plugging and oversize fasteners unnecessary.

Two types of thread repair inserts are usually supplied: a standard type for most inch coarse, inch fine, metric course and metric fine thread sizes and a spark lug type to fit most spark plug port sizes. Consult the individual tool manufacturer's catalog to determine exact applications. Typical thread repair kits will contain a selection of prewound threaded inserts, a tap (corresponding to the outside diameter threads of the insert) and an installation tool. Spark plug inserts usually differ because they require a tap equipped with pilot threads and a combined reamer/tap section. Most manufacturers also supply blister-packed thread repair inserts separately in addition to a master kit containing a variety of taps and inserts plus installation tools.

Clean the piston ring grooves using a ring groove cleaner tool, or . . .

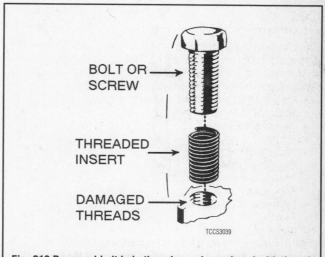

Fig. 212 Damaged bolt hole threads can be replaced with thread repair inserts

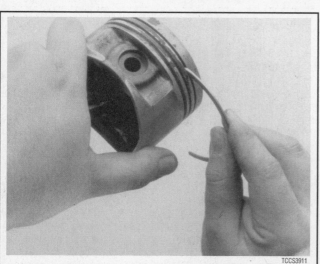

. . . use a piece of an old ring to clean the grooves. Be careful, the ring can be quite sharp

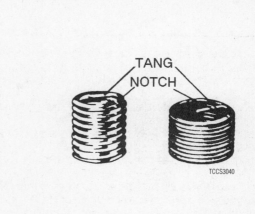

Fig. 213 Standard thread repair insert (left), and spark plug thread insert

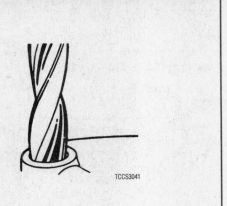

Fig. 214 Drill out the damaged threads with the specified size bit. Be sure to drill completely through the hole or to the bottom of a blind hole

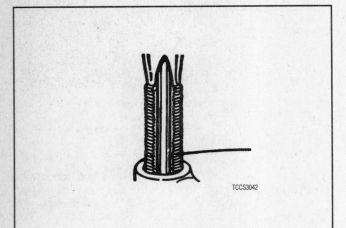

Fig. 215 Using the kit, tap the hole in order to receive the thread insert. Keep the tap well oiled and back it out frequently to avoid clogging the threads

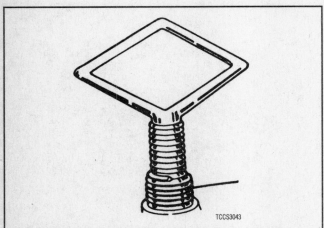

Fig. 216 Screw the insert onto the installer tool until the tang engages the slot. Thread the insert into the hole until it is ¼–½ turn below the top surface, then remove the tool and break off the tang using a punch

Before attempting to repair a threaded hole, remove any snapped, broken or damaged bolts or studs. Penetrating oil can be used to free frozen threads. The offending item can usually be removed with locking pliers or using a screw/stud extractor. After the hole is clear, the thread can be repaired, as shown in the series of accompanying illustrations and in the kit manufacturer's instructions.

Engine Preparation

To properly rebuild an engine, you must first remove it from the vehicle, then disassemble and diagnose it. Ideally you should place your engine on an engine stand. This affords you the best access to the engine components. Follow the manufacturer's directions for using the stand with your particular engine. Remove the flywheel or flexplate before installing the engine to the stand.

Now that you have the engine on a stand, and assuming that you have drained the oil and coolant from the engine, it's time to strip it of all but the necessary components. Before you start disassembling the engine, you may want to take a moment to draw some pictures, or fabricate some labels or containers to mark the locations of various components and the bolts and/or studs which fasten them. Modern day engines use a lot of little brackets and clips which hold wiring harnesses and such, and these holders are often mounted on studs and/or bolts that can be easily mixed up. The manufacturer spent a lot of time and money designing your vehicle, and they wouldn't have wasted any of it by haphazardly placing brackets, clips or fasteners on the vehicle. If it's present when you disassemble it, put it back when you assemble, you will regret not remembering that little bracket which holds a wire harness out of the path of a rotating part.

You should begin by unbolting any accessories still attached to the engine, such as the water pump, power steering pump, alternator, etc. Then, unfasten any manifolds (intake or exhaust) which were not removed during the engine removal procedure. Finally, remove any covers remaining on the engine such as the rocker arm, front or timing cover and oil pan. Some front covers may require the vibration damper and/or crank pulley to be removed beforehand. The idea is to reduce the engine to the bare necessities (cylinder head(s), valve train, engine block, crankshaft, pistons and connecting rods), plus any other `in block' components such as oil pumps, balance shafts and auxiliary shafts.

Finally, remove the cylinder head(s) from the engine block and carefully place on a bench. Disassembly instructions for each component follow later in this section.

Cylinder Head

There are two basic types of cylinder heads used on today's automobiles: the Overhead Valve (OHV) and the Overhead Camshaft (OHC). The latter can also be broken down into two subgroups: the Single Overhead Camshaft (SOHC) and the Dual Overhead Camshaft (DOHC). Generally, if there is only a single camshaft on a head, it is just referred to as an OHC head. Also, an engine with a OHV cylinder head is also known as a pushrod engine.

Most cylinder heads these days are made of an aluminum alloy due to its light weight, durability and heat transfer qualities. However, cast iron was the material of choice in the past, and is still used on many vehicles today. Whether made from aluminum or iron, all cylinder heads have valves and seats. Some use two valves per cylinder, while the more hi-tech engines will utilize a multi-valve configuration using 3, 4 and even 5 valves per cylinder. When the valve contacts the seat, it does so on precision machined surfaces, which seals the combustion chamber. All cylinder heads have a valve guide for each valve. The guide centers the valve to the seat and allows it to move up and down within it. The clearance between the valve and guide can be critical. Too much clearance and the engine may consume oil, lose vacuum and/or damage the seat. Too little, and the valve can stick in the guide causing the engine to run poorly if at all, and possibly causing severe damage. The last component all cylinder heads have are valve springs. The spring holds the valve against its seat. It also returns the valve to this position when the valve has been opened by the valve train or camshaft. The spring is fastened to the valve by a retainer and valve locks (sometimes called keepers). Aluminum heads will also have a valve spring shim to keep the spring from wearing away the aluminum.

An ideal method of rebuilding the cylinder head would involve replacing all of the valves, guides, seats, springs, etc. with new ones. However, depending on how the engine was maintained, often this is not necessary. A major cause of valve, guide and seat wear is an improperly tuned engine. An engine that is running too rich, will often wash the lubricating oil out of the guide with gasoline, causing it to wear rapidly. Conversely, an engine which is running too lean will place higher combustion temperatures on the valves and seats allowing them to wear or even burn. Springs fall victim to the driving habits of the individual. A driver who often runs the engine rpm to the redline will wear out or break the springs faster then one that stays well below it. Unfortunately, mileage takes it toll on all of the parts. Generally, the valves, guides, springs and seats in a cylinder head can be machined and re-used, saving you money. However, if a valve is burnt, it may be wise to replace all of the valves, since they were all operating in the same environment. The same goes for any other component on the cylinder head. Think of it as an insurance policy against future problems related to that component.

Unfortunately, the only way to find out which components need replacing, is to disassemble and carefully check each piece. After the cylinder head(s) are disassembled, thoroughly clean all of the components.

DISASSEMBLY

Whether it is a single or dual overhead camshaft cylinder head, the disassembly procedure is relatively unchanged. One aspect to pay attention to is careful labeling of the parts on the dual camshaft cylinder head. There will be an intake camshaft and followers as well as an exhaust camshaft and followers and they must be labeled as such. In some cases, the components are identical and could easily be installed incorrectly. DO NOT MIX THEM UP! Determining which is which is very simple; the intake camshaft and components are on the same side of the head as was the intake manifold. Conversely, the exhaust camshaft and components are on the same side of the head as was the exhaust manifold.

TCCA3P62

Example of a multivalve cylinder head. Note how it has 2 intake and 2 exhaust valve ports

CUP TYPE CAMSHAFT FOLLOWERS

Most cylinder heads with cup type camshaft followers will have the valve spring, retainer and locks recessed within the follower's bore. You will need a C-clamp style valve spring compressor tool, an OHC spring removal tool (or equivalent) and a small magnet to disassemble the head.

1. If not already removed, remove the camshaft(s) and/or followers. Mark their positions for assembly.

2. Position the cylinder head to allow use of a C-clamp style valve spring compressor tool.

TCCA3P54

Exploded view of a valve, seal, spring, retainer and locks from an OHC cylinder head

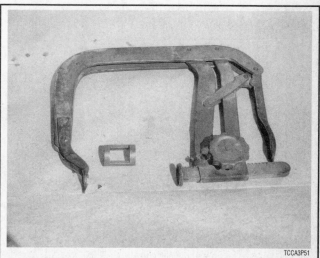

TCCA3P51

C-clamp type spring compressor and an OHC spring removal tool (center) for cup type followers

➡️It is preferred to position the cylinder head gasket surface facing you with the valve springs facing the opposite direction and the head laying horizontal.

3. With the OHC spring removal adapter tool positioned inside of the follower bore, compress the valve spring using the C-clamp style valve spring compressor.

4. Remove the valve locks. A small magnetic tool or screwdriver will aid in removal.

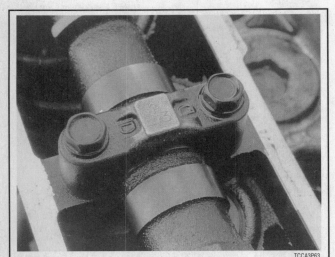

TCCA3P63

Most cup type follower cylinder heads retain the camshaft using bolt-on bearing caps

TCCA3P65

Position the OHC spring tool in the follower bore, then compress the spring with a C-clamp type tool

5. Release the compressor tool and remove the spring assembly.

6. Withdraw the valve from the cylinder head.

7. If equipped, remove the valve seal.

➡️**Special valve seal removal tools are available. Regular or needle nose type pliers, if used with care, will work just as well. If using ordinary pliers, be sure not to damage the follower bore. The follower and its bore are machined to close tolerances and any damage to the bore will effect this relationship.**

8. If equipped, remove the valve spring shim. A small magnetic tool or screwdriver will aid in removal.

9. Repeat Steps 3 through 8 until all of the valves have been removed.

ROCKER ARM TYPE CAMSHAFT FOLLOWERS

Most cylinder heads with rocker arm-type camshaft followers are easily disassembled using a standard valve spring compressor. However, certain models may not have enough open space around the spring for the standard tool and may require you to use a C-clamp style compressor tool instead.

1. If not already removed, remove the rocker arms and/or shafts and the camshaft. If applicable, also remove the hydraulic lash adjusters. Mark their positions for assembly.

2. Position the cylinder head to allow access to the valve spring.

TCCA3P53

Example of the shaft mounted rocker arms on some OHC heads

TCCA3P61

Another example of the rocker arm type OHC head. This model uses a follower under the camshaft

3. Use a valve spring compressor tool to relieve the spring tension from the retainer.

➡**Due to engine varnish, the retainer may stick to the valve locks. A gentle tap with a hammer may help to break it loose.**

4. Remove the valve locks from the valve tip and/or retainer. A small magnet may help in removing the small locks.
5. Lift the valve spring, tool and all, off of the valve stem.
6. If equipped, remove the valve seal. If the seal is difficult to remove with the valve in place, try removing the valve first, then the seal. Follow the steps below for valve removal.
7. Position the head to allow access for withdrawing the valve.

➡**Cylinder heads that have seen a lot of miles and/or abuse may have mushroomed the valve lock grove and/or tip, causing difficulty in removal of the valve. If this has happened, use a metal file to carefully remove the high spots around the lock grooves and/or tip. Only file it enough to allow removal.**

8. Remove the valve from the cylinder head.
9. If equipped, remove the valve spring shim. A small magnetic tool or screwdriver will aid in removal.
10. Repeat Steps 3 though 9 until all of the valves have been removed.

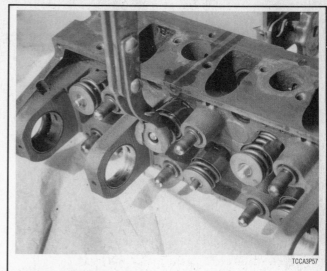
Compress the valve spring . . .

Before the camshaft can be removed, all of the followers must first be removed . . .

. . . then remove the valve locks from the valve stem and spring retainer

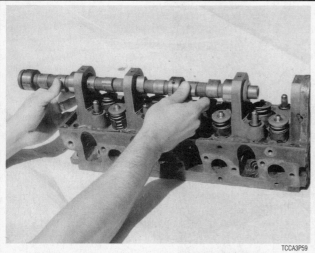
. . . then the camshaft can be removed by sliding it out (shown), or unbolting a bearing cap (not shown)

Remove the valve spring and retainer from the cylinder head

Remove the valve seal from the guide. Some gentle prying or pliers may help to remove stubborn ones

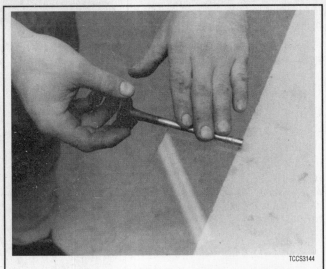

Valve stems may be rolled on a flat surface to check for bends

All aluminum and some cast iron heads will have these valve spring shims. Remove all of them as well

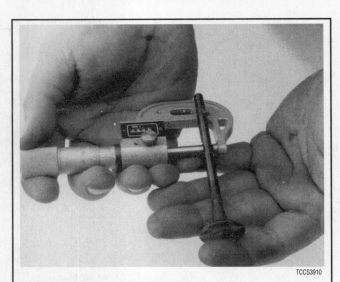

Use a micrometer to check the valve stem diameter

INSPECTION

Now that all of the cylinder head components are clean, it's time to inspect them for wear and/or damage. To accurately inspect them, you will need some specialized tools:

- A 0–1 inch micrometer for the valves
- A dial indicator or inside diameter gauge for the valve guides
- A spring pressure test gauge

If you do not have access to the proper tools, you may want to bring the components to a shop that does.

Valves

The first thing to inspect are the valve heads. Look closely at the head, margin and face for any cracks, excessive wear or burning. The margin is the best place to look for burning. It should have a squared edge with an even width all around the diameter. When a valve burns, the margin will look melted and the edges rounded. Also inspect the valve head for any signs of tulipping. This will show as a lifting of the edges or dishing in the center of the head and will usually not occur to all of the valves. All of the heads should look the same, any that seem dished more than others are

probably bad. Next, inspect the valve lock grooves and valve tips. Check for any burrs around the lock grooves, especially if you had to file them to remove the valve. Valve tips should appear flat, although slight rounding with high mileage engines is normal. Slightly worn valve tips will need to be machined flat. Last, measure the valve stem diameter with the micrometer. Measure the area that rides within the guide, especially towards the tip where most of the wear occurs. Take several measurements along its length and compare them to each other. Wear should be even along the length with little to no taper. If no minimum diameter is given in the specifications, then the stem should not read more than 0.001 in. (0.025mm) below the specification. Any valves that fail these inspections should be replaced.

Springs, Retainers and Valve Locks

The first thing to check is the most obvious, broken springs. Next check the free length and squareness of each spring. If applicable, insure to distinguish between intake and exhaust springs. Use a ruler and/or carpenters square to measure the length. A carpenters square should be used to check the springs for squareness. If a spring pressure test gauge is available, check each springs rating and compare to the specifications chart. Check the readings against the specifications given. Any springs that fail these inspections should be replaced.

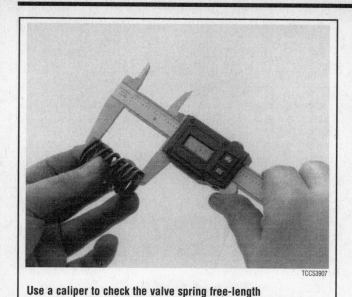

TCCS3907

Use a caliper to check the valve spring free-length

TCCS3142

A dial gauge may be used to check valve stem-to-guide clearance; read the gauge while moving the valve stem

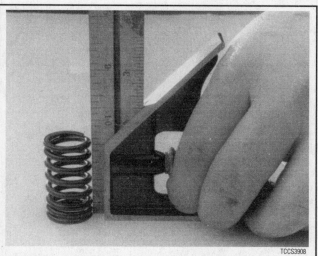

TCCS3908

Check the valve spring for squareness on a flat surface; a carpenter's square can be used

The spring retainers rarely need replacing, however they should still be checked as a precaution. Inspect the spring mating surface and the valve lock retention area for any signs of excessive wear. Also check for any signs of cracking. Replace any retainers that are questionable.

Valve locks should be inspected for excessive wear on the outside contact area as well as on the inner notched surface. Any locks which appear worn or broken and its respective valve should be replaced.

Cylinder Head

There are several things to check on the cylinder head: valve guides, seats, cylinder head surface flatness, cracks and physical damage.

VALVE GUIDES

Now that you know the valves are good, you can use them to check the guides, although a new valve, if available, is preferred. Before you measure

anything, look at the guides carefully and inspect them for any cracks, chips or breakage. Also if the guide is a removable style (as in most aluminum heads), check them for any looseness or evidence of movement. All of the guides should appear to be at the same height from the spring seat. If any seem lower (or higher) from another, the guide has moved. Mount a dial indicator onto the spring side of the cylinder head. Lightly oil the valve stem and insert it into the cylinder head. Position the dial indicator against the valve stem near the tip and zero the gauge. Grasp the valve stem and wiggle towards and away from the dial indicator and observe the readings. Mount the dial indicator 90 degrees from the initial point and zero the gauge and again take a reading. Compare the two readings for a out of round condition. Check the readings against the specifications given. An Inside Diameter (I.D.) gauge designed for valve guides will give you an accurate valve guide bore measurement. If the I.D. gauge is used, compare the readings with the specifications given. Any guides that fail these inspections should be replaced or machined.

VALVE SEATS

A visual inspection of the valve seats should show a slightly worn and pitted surface where the valve face contacts the seat. Inspect the seat carefully for severe pitting or cracks. Also, a seat that is badly worn will be recessed into the cylinder head. A severely worn or recessed seat may need to be replaced. All cracked seats must be replaced. A seat concentricity gauge, if available, should be used to check the seat run-out. If run-out exceeds specifications the seat must be machined (if no specification is given use 0.002 in. or 0.051mm).

CYLINDER HEAD SURFACE FLATNESS

After you have cleaned the gasket surface of the cylinder head of any old gasket material, check the head for flatness.

Place a straigthedge across the gasket surface. Using feeler gauges, determine the clearance at the center of the straigthedge and across the cylinder head at several points. Check along the centerline and diagonally on the head surface. If the warpage exceeds 0.003 in. (0.076mm) within a 6.0 in. (15.2cm) span, or 0.006 in. (0.152mm) over the total length of the head, the cylinder head must be resurfaced. After resurfacing the heads of a V-type engine, the intake manifold flange surface should be checked, and if necessary, milled proportionally to allow for the change in its mounting position.

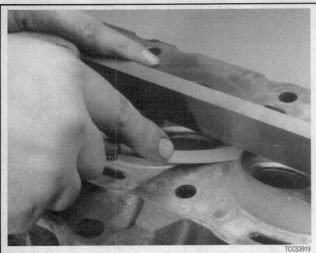

Check the head for flatness across the center of the head surface using a straigthedge and feeler gauge

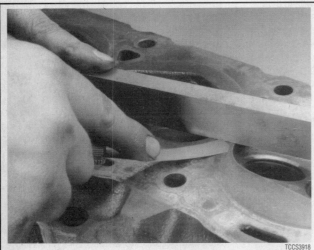

Checks should also be made along both diagonals of the head surface

CRACKS AND PHYSICAL DAMAGE

Generally, cracks are limited to the combustion chamber, however, it is not uncommon for the head to crack in a spark plug hole, port, outside of the head or in the valve spring/rocker arm area. The first area to inspect is always the hottest: the exhaust seat/port area.

A visual inspection should be performed, but just because you don't see a crack does not mean it is not there. Some more reliable methods for inspecting for cracks include Magnaflux®, a magnetic process or Zyglo®, a dye penetrant. Magnaflux® is used only on ferrous metal (cast iron) heads. Zyglo® uses a spray on fluorescent mixture along with a black light to reveal the cracks. It is strongly recommended to have your cylinder head checked professionally for cracks, especially if the engine was known to have overheated and/or leaked or consumed coolant. Contact a local shop for availability and pricing of these services.

Physical damage is usually very evident. For example, a broken mounting ear from dropping the head or a bent or broken stud and/or bolt. All of these defects should be fixed or, if unrepairable, the head should be replaced.

Camshaft and Followers

Inspect the camshaft(s) and followers as described earlier in this section.

REFINISHING & REPAIRING

Many of the procedures given for refinishing and repairing the cylinder head components must be performed by a machine shop. Certain steps, if the inspected part is not worn, can be performed yourself inexpensively. However, you spent a lot of time and effort so far, why risk trying to save a couple bucks if you might have to do it all over again?

Valves

Any valves that were not replaced should be refaced and the tips ground flat. Unless you have access to a valve grinding machine, this should be done by a machine shop. If the valves are in extremely good condition, as well as the valve seats and guides, they may be lapped in without performing machine work.

It is a recommended practice to lap the valves even after machine work has been performed and/or new valves have been purchased. This insures a positive seal between the valve and seat.

LAPPING THE VALVES

➡️**Before lapping the valves to the seats, read the rest of the cylinder head section to insure that any related parts are in acceptable enough condition to continue.**

➡️**Before any valve seat machining and/or lapping can be performed, the guides must be within factory recommended specifications.**

1. Invert the cylinder head.
2. Lightly lubricate the valve stems and insert them into the cylinder head in their numbered order.
3. Raise the valve from the seat and apply a small amount of fine lapping compound to the seat.
4. Moisten the suction head of a hand-lapping tool and attach it to the head of the valve.
5. Rotate the tool between the palms of both hands, changing the position of the valve on the valve seat and lifting the tool often to prevent grooving.
6. Lap the valve until a smooth, polished circle is evident on the valve and seat.
7. Remove the tool and the valve. Wipe away all traces of the grinding compound and store the valve to maintain its lapped location.

✳️✳️ WARNING

Do not get the valves out of order after they have been lapped. They must be put back with the same valve seat they were lapped with.

Springs, Retainers and Valve Locks

There is no repair or refinishing possible with the springs, retainers and valve locks. If they are found to be worn or defective, they must be replaced with new (or known good) parts.

Cylinder Head

Most refinishing procedures dealing with the cylinder head must be performed by a machine shop. Read the sections below and review your inspection data to determine whether or not machining is necessary.

VALVE GUIDE

➡️**If any machining or replacements are made to the valve guides, the seats must be machined.**

Unless the valve guides need machining or replacing, the only service to perform is to thoroughly clean them of any dirt or oil residue.

There are only two types of valve guides used on automobile engines: the replaceable-type (all aluminum heads) and the cast-in integral-type (most cast iron heads). There are four recommended methods for repairing worn guides.

- Knurling
- Inserts
- Reaming oversize
- Replacing

Knurling is a process in which metal is displaced and raised, thereby reducing clearance, giving a true center, and providing oil control. It is the least expensive way of repairing the valve guides. However, it is not necessarily the best, and in some cases, a knurled valve guide will not stand up for more than a short time. It requires a special knurlizer and precision reaming tools to obtain proper clearances. It would not be cost effective to purchase these tools, unless you plan on rebuilding several of the same cylinder head.

Installing a guide insert involves machining the guide to accept a bronze insert. One style is the coil-type which is installed into a threaded guide. Another is the thin-walled insert where the guide is reamed oversize to accept a split-sleeve insert. After the insert is installed, a special tool is then run through the guide to expand the insert, locking it to the guide. The insert is then reamed to the standard size for proper valve clearance.

Reaming for oversize valves restores normal clearances and provides a true valve seat. Most cast-in type guides can be reamed to accept an valve with an oversize stem. The cost factor for this can become quite high as you will need to purchase the reamer and new, oversize stem valves for all guides which were reamed. Oversizes are generally 0.003 to 0.030 in. (0.076 to 0.762mm), with 0.015 in. (0.381mm) being the most common.

To replace cast-in type valve guides, they must be drilled out, then reamed to accept replacement guides. This must be done on a fixture which will allow centering and leveling off of the original valve seat or guide, otherwise a serious guide-to-seat misalignment may occur making it impossible to properly machine the seat.

Replaceable-type guides are pressed into the cylinder head. A hammer and a stepped drift or punch may be used to install and remove the guides. Before removing the guides, measure the protrusion on the spring side of the head and record it for installation. Use the stepped drift to hammer out the old guide from the combustion chamber side of the head. When installing, determine whether or not the guide also seals a water jacket in the head, and if it does, use the recommended sealing agent. If there is no water jacket, grease the valve guide and its bore. Use the stepped drift, and hammer the new guide into the cylinder head from the spring side of the cylinder head. A stack of washers the same thickness as the measured protrusion may help the installation process.

VALVE SEATS

➡Before any valve seat machining can be performed, the guides must be within factory recommended specifications.

➡If any machining or replacements were made to the valve guides, the seats must be machined.

If the seats are in good condition, the valves can be lapped to the seats, and the cylinder head assembled. See the valves section for instructions on lapping.

If the valve seats are worn, cracked or damaged, they must be serviced by a machine shop. The valve seat must be perfectly centered to the valve guide, which requires very accurate machining.

CYLINDER HEAD SURFACE

If the cylinder head is warped, it must be machined flat. If the warpage is extremely severe, the head may need to be replaced. In some instances, it may be possible to straigthen a warped head enough to allow machining. In either case, contact a professional machine shop for service.

➡Any OHC cylinder head that shows excessive warpage should have the camshaft bearing journals align bored after the cylinder head has been resurfaced.

✳✳ WARNING

Failure to align bore the camshaft bearing journals could result in severe engine damage including but not limited to: valve and piston damage, connecting rod damage, camshaft and/or crankshaft breakage.

CRACKS AND PHYSICAL DAMAGE

Certain cracks can be repaired in both cast iron and aluminum heads. For cast iron, a tapered threaded insert is installed along the length of the crack. Aluminum can also use the tapered inserts, however welding is the preferred method. Some physical damage can be repaired through brazing or welding. Contact a machine shop to get expert advice for your particular dilemma.

ASSEMBLY

The first step for any assembly job is to have a clean area in which to work. Next, thoroughly clean all of the parts and components that are to be assembled. Finally, place all of the components onto a suitable work space and, if necessary, arrange the parts to their respective positions.

OHV Engines

1. Lightly lubricate the valve stems and insert all of the valves into the cylinder head. If possible, maintain their original locations.
2. If equipped, install any valve spring shims which were removed.
3. If equipped, install the new valve seals, keeping the following in mind:
- If the valve seal presses over the guide, lightly lubricate the outer guide surfaces.
- If the seal is an O-ring type, it is installed just after compressing the spring but before the valve locks.
4. Place the valve spring and retainer over the stem.
5. Position the spring compressor tool and compress the spring.
6. Assemble the valve locks to the stem.
7. Relieve the spring pressure slowly and insure that neither valve lock becomes dislodged by the retainer.
8. Remove the spring compressor tool.
9. Repeat Steps 2 through 8 until all of the springs have been installed.

OHC Engines

CUP TYPE CAMSHAFT FOLLOWERS

To install the springs, retainers and valve locks on heads which have these components recessed into the camshaft follower's bore, you will need a small screwdriver-type tool, some clean white grease and a lot of patience. You will also need the C-clamp style spring compressor and the OHC tool used to disassemble the head.

1. Lightly lubricate the valve stems and insert all of the valves into the cylinder head. If possible, maintain their original locations.
2. If equipped, install any valve spring shims which were removed.
3. If equipped, install the new valve seals, keeping the following in mind:
- If the valve seal presses over the guide, lightly lubricate the outer guide surfaces.
- If the seal is an O-ring type, it is installed just after compressing the spring but before the valve locks.
4. Place the valve spring and retainer over the stem.
5. Position the spring compressor and the OHC tool, then compress the spring.
6. Using a small screwdriver as a spatula, fill the valve stem side of the lock with white grease. Use the excess grease on the screwdriver to fasten the lock to the driver.
7. Carefully install the valve lock, which is stuck to the end of the screwdriver, to the valve stem then press on it with the screwdriver until the grease squeezes out. The valve lock should now be stuck to the stem.

Once assembled, check the valve clearance and correct as needed

8. Repeat Steps 6 and 7 for the remaining valve lock.
9. Relieve the spring pressure slowly and insure that neither valve lock becomes dislodged by the retainer.
10. Remove the spring compressor tool.
11. Repeat Steps 2 through 10 until all of the springs have been installed.
12. Install the followers, camshaft(s) and any other components that were removed for disassembly.

ROCKER ARM TYPE CAMSHAFT FOLLOWERS

1. Lightly lubricate the valve stems and insert all of the valves into the cylinder head. If possible, maintain their original locations.
2. If equipped, install any valve spring shims which were removed.
3. If equipped, install the new valve seals, keeping the following in mind:
• If the valve seal presses over the guide, lightly lubricate the outer guide surfaces.
• If the seal is an O-ring type, it is installed just after compressing the spring but before the valve locks.
4. Place the valve spring and retainer over the stem.
5. Position the spring compressor tool and compress the spring.
6. Assemble the valve locks to the stem.
7. Relieve the spring pressure slowly and insure that neither valve lock becomes dislodged by the retainer.
8. Remove the spring compressor tool.
9. Repeat Steps 2 through 8 until all of the springs have been installed.
10. Install the camshaft(s), rockers, shafts and any other components that were removed for disassembly.

Engine Block

GENERAL INFORMATION

A thorough overhaul or rebuild of an engine block would include replacing the pistons, rings, bearings, timing belt/chain assembly and oil pump. For OHV engines also include a new camshaft and lifters. The block would then have the cylinders bored and honed oversize (or if using removable cylinder sleeves, new sleeves installed) and the crankshaft would be cut undersize to provide new wearing surfaces and perfect clearances. However, your particular engine may not have everything worn out. What if only the piston rings have worn out and the clearances on everything else are still within factory specifications? Well, you could just replace the rings and put it back together, but this would be a very rare example. Chances are, if one component in your engine is worn, other components are sure to follow, and soon. At the very least, you should always replace the rings, bearings and oil pump. This is what is commonly called a "freshen up".

Cylinder Ridge Removal

Because the top piston ring does not travel to the very top of the cylinder, a ridge is built up between the end of the travel and the top of the cylinder bore.

Pushing the piston and connecting rod assembly past the ridge can be difficult, and damage to the piston ring lands could occur. If the ridge is not removed before installing a new piston or not removed at all, piston ring breakage and piston damage may occur.

➡ **It is always recommended that you remove any cylinder ridges before removing the piston and connecting rod assemblies. If you know that new pistons are going to be installed and the engine block will be bored oversize, you may be able to forego this step. However, some ridges may actually prevent the assemblies from being removed, necessitating its removal.**

There are several different types of ridge reamers on the market, none of which are inexpensive. Unless a great deal of engine rebuilding is anticipated, borrow or rent a reamer.
1. Turn the crankshaft until the piston is at the bottom of its travel.
2. Cover the head of the piston with a rag.
3. Follow the tool manufacturers instructions and cut away the ridge, exercising extreme care to avoid cutting too deeply.
4. Remove the ridge reamer, the rag and as many of the cuttings as possible. Continue until all of the cylinder ridges have been removed.

DISASSEMBLY

The engine disassembly instructions following assume that you have the engine mounted on an engine stand. If not, it is easiest to disassemble the engine on a bench or the floor with it resting on the bellhousing or transmission mounting surface. You must be able to access the connecting rod fasteners and turn the crankshaft during disassembly. Also, all engine covers (timing, front, side, oil pan, whatever) should have already been removed. Engines which are seized or locked up may not be able to be completely disassembled, and a core (salvage yard) engine should be purchased.

If not done during the cylinder head removal, remove the timing chain/belt and/or gear/sprocket assembly. Remove the oil pick-up and pump assembly and, if necessary, the pump drive. If equipped, remove any balance or auxiliary shafts. If necessary, remove the cylinder ridge from the top of the bore. See the cylinder ridge removal procedure earlier in this section.

Rotate the engine over so that the crankshaft is exposed. Use a number punch or scribe and mark each connecting rod with its respective cylinder number. The cylinder closest to the front of the engine is always number 1. However, depending on the engine placement, the front of the engine could

Place rubber hose over the connecting rod studs to protect the crankshaft and cylinder bores from damage

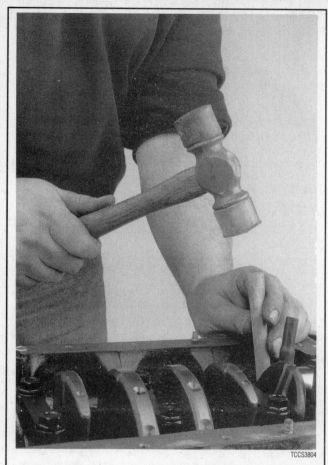

TCCS3804

Carefully tap the piston out of the bore using a wooden dowel

either be the flywheel or damper/pulley end. Generally the front of the engine faces the front of the vehicle. Use a number punch or scribe and also mark the main bearing caps from front to rear with the front most cap being number 1 (if there are five caps, mark them 1 through 5, front to rear).

✳✳ WARNING

Take special care when pushing the connecting rod up from the crankshaft because the sharp threads of the rod bolts/studs will score the crankshaft journal. Insure that special plastic caps are installed over them, or cut two pieces of rubber hose to do the same.

Again, rotate the engine, this time to position the number one cylinder bore (head surface) up. Turn the crankshaft until the number one piston is at the bottom of its travel, this should allow the maximum access to its connecting rod. Remove the number one connecting rods fasteners and cap and place two lengths of rubber hose over the rod bolts/studs to protect the crankshaft from damage. Using a sturdy wooden dowel and a hammer, push the connecting rod up about 1 in. (25mm) from the crankshaft and remove the upper bearing insert. Continue pushing or tapping the connecting rod up until the piston rings are out of the cylinder bore. Remove the piston and rod by hand, put the upper half of the bearing insert back into the rod, install the cap with its bearing insert installed, and hand-tigthen the cap fasteners. If the parts are kept in order in this manner, they will not get lost and you will be able to tell which bearings came form what cylinder if any problems are discovered and diagnosis is necessary. Remove all the other piston assemblies in the same manner. On V-style engines, remove all of the pistons from one bank, then reposition the engine with the other cylinder bank head surface up, and remove that banks piston assemblies.

The only remaining component in the engine block should now be the crankshaft. Loosen the main bearing caps evenly until the fasteners can be turned by hand, then remove them and the caps. Remove the crankshaft from the engine block. Thoroughly clean all of the components.

INSPECTION

Now that the engine block and all of its components are clean, it's time to inspect them for wear and/or damage. To accurately inspect them, you will need some specialized tools:
  • Two or three separate micrometers to measure the pistons and crankshaft journals
  • A dial indicator
  • Telescoping gauges for the cylinder bores
  • A rod alignment fixture to check for bent connecting rods

If you do not have access to the proper tools, you may want to bring the components to a shop that does.

Generally, you shouldn't expect cracks in the engine block or its components unless it was known to leak, consume or mix engine fluids, it was severely overheated, or there was evidence of bad bearings and/or crankshaft damage. A visual inspection should be performed on all of the components, but just because you don't see a crack does not mean it is not there. Some more reliable methods for inspecting for cracks include Magnaflux®, a magnetic process or Zyglo®, a dye penetrant. Magnaflux® is used only on ferrous metal (cast iron). Zyglo® uses a spray on fluorescent mixture along with a black light to reveal the cracks. It is strongly recommended to have your engine block checked professionally for cracks, especially if the engine was known to have overheated and/or leaked or consumed coolant. Contact a local shop for availability and pricing of these services.

Engine Block

ENGINE BLOCK BEARING ALIGNMENT

Remove the main bearing caps and, if still installed, the main bearing inserts. Inspect all of the main bearing saddles and caps for damage, burrs or high spots. If damage is found, and it is caused from a spun main bearing, the block will need to be align-bored or, if severe enough, replacement. Any burrs or high spots should be carefully removed with a metal file.

Place a straigthedge on the bearing saddles, in the engine block, along the centerline of the crankshaft. If any clearance exists between the straigthedge and the saddles, the block must be align-bored.

Align-boring consists of machining the main bearing saddles and caps by means of a flycutter that runs through the bearing saddles.

DECK FLATNESS

The top of the engine block where the cylinder head mounts is called the deck. Insure that the deck surface is clean of dirt, carbon deposits and old gasket material. Place a straigthedge across the surface of the deck along its centerline and, using feeler gauges, check the clearance along several points. Repeat the checking procedure with the straigthedge placed along both diagonals of the deck surface. If the reading exceeds 0.003 in. (0.076mm) within a 6.0 in. (15.2cm) span, or 0.006 in. (0.152mm) over the total length of the deck, it must be machined.

CYLINDER BORES

The cylinder bores house the pistons and are slightly larger than the pistons themselves. A common piston-to-bore clearance is 0.0015–0.0025 in. (0.0381mm–0.0635mm). Inspect and measure the cylinder bores. The bore should be checked for out-of-roundness, taper and size. The results of this inspection will determine whether the cylinder can be used in its existing size and condition, or a rebore to the next oversize is required (or in the case of removable sleeves, have replacements installed).

The amount of cylinder wall wear is always greater at the top of the cylinder than at the bottom. This wear is known as taper. Any cylinder that has a taper of 0.0012 in. (0.305mm) or more, must be rebored. Measurements are taken at a number of positions in each cylinder: at the top, mid-

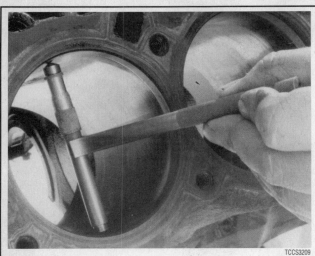

Use a telescoping gauge to measure the cylinder bore diameter—take several readings within the same bore

TCCS3209

dle and bottom and at two points at each position; that is, at a point 90 degrees from the crankshaft centerline, as well as a point parallel to the crankshaft centerline. The measurements are made with either a special dial indicator or a telescopic gauge and micrometer. If the necessary precision tools to check the bore are not available, take the block to a machine shop and have them mike it. Also if you don't have the tools to check the cylinder bores, chances are you will not have the necessary devices to check the pistons, connecting rods and crankshaft. Take these components with you and save yourself an extra trip.

For our procedures, we will use a telescopic gauge and a micrometer. You will need one of each, with a measuring range which covers your cylinder bore size.

1. Position the telescopic gauge in the cylinder bore, loosen the gauges lock and allow it to expand.

➡ **Your first two readings will be at the top of the cylinder bore, then proceed to the middle and finally the bottom, making a total of six measurements.**

2. Hold the gauge square in the bore, 90 degrees from the crankshaft centerline, and gently tigthen the lock. Tilt the gauge back to remove it from the bore.

3. Measure the gauge with the micrometer and record the reading.

4. Again, hold the gauge square in the bore, this time parallel to the crankshaft centerline, and gently tigthen the lock. Again, you will tilt the gauge back to remove it from the bore.

5. Measure the gauge with the micrometer and record this reading. The difference between these two readings is the out-of-round measurement of the cylinder.

6. Repeat steps 1 through 5, each time going to the next lower position, until you reach the bottom of the cylinder. Then go to the next cylinder, and continue until all of the cylinders have been measured.

The difference between these measurements will tell you all about the wear in your cylinders. The measurements which were taken 90 degrees from the crankshaft centerline will always reflect the most wear. That is because at this position is where the engine power presses the piston against the cylinder bore the hardest. This is known as thrust wear. Take your top, 90 degree measurement and compare it to your bottom, 90 degree measurement. The difference between them is the taper. When you measure your pistons, you will compare these readings to your piston sizes and determine piston-to-wall clearance.

Crankshaft

Inspect the crankshaft for visible signs of wear or damage. All of the journals should be perfectly round and smooth. Slight scores are normal for a used crankshaft, but you should hardly feel them with your fingernail.

When measuring the crankshaft with a micrometer, you will take readings at the front and rear of each journal, then turn the micrometer 90 degrees and take two more readings, front and rear. The difference between the front-to-rear readings is the journal taper and the first-to-90 degree reading is the out-of-round measurement. Generally, there should be no taper or out-of-roundness found, however, up to 0.0005 in. (0.0127mm) for either can be overlooked. Also, the readings should fall within the factory specifications for journal diameters.

If the crankshaft journals fall within specifications, it is recommended that it be polished before being returned to service. Polishing the crankshaft insures that any minor burrs or high spots are smoothed, thereby reducing the chance of scoring the new bearings.

Pistons and Connecting Rods

PISTONS

The piston should be visually inspected for any signs of cracking or burning (caused by hot spots or detonation), and scuffing or excessive wear on the skirts. The wristpin attaches the piston to the connecting rod. The piston should move freely on the wrist pin, both sliding and pivoting. Grasp the connecting rod securely, or mount it in a vise, and try to rock the piston back and forth along the centerline of the wristpin. There should not be any excessive play evident between the piston and the pin. If there are C-clips retaining the pin in the piston then you have wrist pin bushings in the rods. There should not be any excessive play between the wrist pin and the rod bushing. Normal clearance for the wrist pin is approx. 0.001–0.002 in. (0.025mm–0.051mm).

Use a micrometer and measure the diameter of the piston, perpendicular to the wrist pin, on the skirt. Compare the reading to its original cylinder measurement obtained earlier. The difference between the two readings is the piston-to-wall clearance. If the clearance is within specifications, the piston may be used as is. If the piston is out of specification, but the bore is not, you will need a new piston. If both are out of specification, you will need the cylinder rebored and oversize pistons installed. Generally if two or more pistons/bores are out of specification, it is best to rebore the entire block and purchase a complete set of oversize pistons.

Measure the piston's outer diameter, perpendicular to the wrist pin, with a micrometer

TCCS3210

CONNECTING ROD

You should have the connecting rod checked for straightness at a machine shop. If the connecting rod is bent, it will unevenly wear the bearing and piston, as well as place greater stress on these components. Any bent or twisted connecting rods must be replaced. If the rods are straight and the wrist pin clearance is within specifications, then only the bearing end of the rod need be checked. Place the connecting rod into a vice, with the bearing inserts in place, install the cap to the rod and torque the fasteners to specifications. Use a telescoping gauge and carefully measure the inside diameter of the bearings. Compare this reading to the rods original crankshaft journal diameter measurement. The difference is the oil clearance. If the oil clearance is not within specifications, install new bearings in the rod and take another measurement. If the clearance is still out of specifications, and the crankshaft is not, the rod will need to be reconditioned by a machine shop.

➡**You can also use Plastigage® to check the bearing clearances. The assembling section has complete instructions on its use.**

Camshaft

Inspect the camshaft and lifters/followers as described earlier in this section.

Bearings

All of the engine bearings should be visually inspected for wear and/or damage. The bearing should look evenly worn all around with no deep scores or pits. If the bearing is severely worn, scored, pitted or heat blued, then the bearing, and the components that use it, should be brought to a machine shop for inspection. Full-circle bearings (used on most camshafts, auxiliary shafts, balance shafts, etc.) require specialized tools for removal and installation, and should be brought to a machine shop for service.

Oil Pump

➡**The oil pump is responsible for providing constant lubrication to the whole engine and so it is recommended that a new oil pump be installed when rebuilding the engine.**

Completely disassemble the oil pump and thoroughly clean all of the components. Inspect the oil pump gears and housing for wear and/or damage. Insure that the pressure relief valve operates properly and there is no binding or sticking due to varnish or debris. If all of the parts are in proper working condition, lubricate the gears and relief valve, and assemble the pump.

REFINISHING

Almost all engine block refinishing must be performed by a machine shop. If the cylinders are not to be rebored, then the cylinder glaze can be removed with a ball hone. When removing cylinder glaze with a ball hone, use a light or penetrating type oil to lubricate the hone. Do not allow the hone to run dry as this may cause excessive scoring of the cylinder bores

Use a ball type cylinder hone to remove any glaze and provide a new surface for seating the piston rings

and wear on the hone. If new pistons are required, they will need to be installed to the connecting rods. This should be performed by a machine shop as the pistons must be installed in the correct relationship to the rod or engine damage can occur.

Pistons and Connecting Rods

Only pistons with the wrist pin retained by C-clips are serviceable by the home-mechanic. Press fit pistons require special presses and/or heaters to remove/install the connecting rod and should only be performed by a machine shop.

All pistons will have a mark indicating the direction to the front of the engine and the must be installed into the engine in that manner. Usually it is a notch or arrow on the top of the piston, or it may be the letter F cast or stamped into the piston.

Most pistons are marked to indicate positioning in the engine (usually a mark means the side facing the front)

ASSEMBLY

Before you begin assembling the engine, first give yourself a clean, dirt free work area. Next, clean every engine component again. The key to a good assembly is cleanliness.

Mount the engine block into the engine stand and wash it one last time using water and detergent (dishwashing detergent works well). While washing it, scrub the cylinder bores with a soft bristle brush and thoroughly clean all of the oil passages. Completely dry the engine and spray the entire assembly down with an anti-rust solution such as WD-40® or similar product. Take a clean lint-free rag and wipe up any excess anti-rust solution from the bores, bearing saddles, etc. Repeat the final cleaning process on the crankshaft. Replace any freeze or oil galley plugs which were removed during disassembly.

Crankshaft

1. Remove the main bearing inserts from the block and bearing caps.
2. If the crankshaft main bearing journals have been refinished to a definite undersize, install the correct undersize bearing. Be sure that the bearing inserts and bearing bores are clean. Foreign material under inserts will distort bearing and cause failure.
3. Place the upper main bearing inserts in bores with tang in slot.

➡**The oil holes in the bearing inserts must be aligned with the oil holes in the cylinder block.**

4. Install the lower main bearing inserts in bearing caps.
5. Clean the mating surfaces of block and rear main bearing cap.

6. Carefully lower the crankshaft into place. Be careful not to damage bearing surfaces.

7. Check the clearance of each main bearing by using the following procedure:

a. Place a piece of Plastigage® or its equivalent, on bearing surface across full width of bearing cap and about ¼ in. off center.

b. Install cap and tigthen bolts to specifications. Do not turn crankshaft while Plastigage® is in place.

c. Remove the cap. Using the supplied Plastigage® scale, check width of Plastigage® at widest point to get maximum clearance. Difference between readings is taper of journal.

d. If clearance exceeds specified limits, try a 0.001 in. or 0.002 in. undersize bearing in combination with the standard bearing. Bearing clearance must be within specified limits. If standard and 0.002 in. undersize bearing does not bring clearance within desired limits, refinish crankshaft journal, then install undersize bearings.

8. Install the rear main seal.

9. After the bearings have been fitted, apply a light coat of engine oil to the journals and bearings. Install the rear main bearing cap. Install all bearing caps except the thrust bearing cap. Be sure that main bearing caps are installed in original locations. Tigthen the bearing cap bolts to specifications.

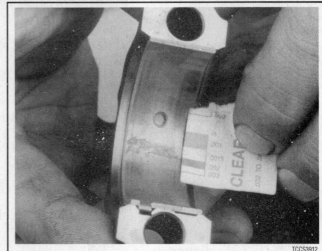

TCCS3912

After the cap is removed again, use the scale supplied with the gauging material to check the clearance

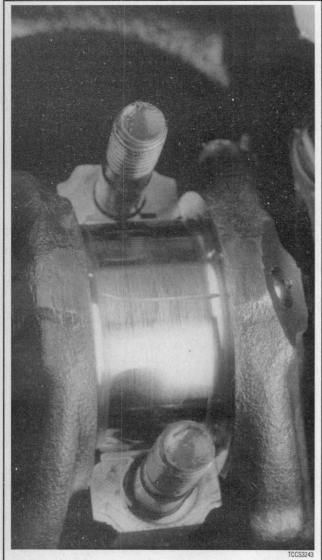

TCCS3243

Apply a strip of gauging material to the bearing journal, then install and torque the cap

TCCS3805

A dial gauge may be used to check crankshaft end-play

TCCS3806

Carefully pry the crankshaft back and forth while reading the dial gauge for end-play

10. Install the thrust bearing cap with bolts finger-tight.

11. Pry the crankshaft forward against the thrust surface of upper half of bearing.

12. Hold the crankshaft forward and pry the thrust bearing cap to the rear. This aligns the thrust surfaces of both halves of the bearing.

13. Retain the forward pressure on the crankshaft. Tigthen the cap bolts to specifications.

14. Measure the crankshaft end-play as follows:

a. Mount a dial gauge to the engine block and position the tip of the gauge to read from the crankshaft end.

b. Carefully pry the crankshaft toward the rear of the engine and hold it there while you zero the gauge.

c. Carefully pry the crankshaft toward the front of the engine and read the gauge.

d. Confirm that the reading is within specifications. If not, install a new thrust bearing and repeat the procedure. If the reading is still out of specifications with a new bearing, have a machine shop inspect the thrust surfaces of the crankshaft, and if possible, repair it.

15. Rotate the crankshaft so as to position the first rod journal to the bottom of its stroke.

Pistons and Connecting Rods

1. Before installing the piston/connecting rod assembly, oil the pistons, piston rings and the cylinder walls with light engine oil. Install connecting rod bolt protectors or rubber hose onto the connecting rod bolts/studs. Also perform the following:

a. Select the proper ring set for the size cylinder bore.

b. Position the ring in the bore in which it is going to be used.

c. Push the ring down into the bore area where normal ring wear is not encountered.

d. Use the head of the piston to position the ring in the bore so that the ring is square with the cylinder wall. Use caution to avoid damage to the ring or cylinder bore.

e. Measure the gap between the ends of the ring with a feeler gauge. Ring gap in a worn cylinder is normally greater than specification. If the ring gap is greater than the specified limits, try an oversize ring set.

f. Check the ring side clearance of the compression rings with a feeler gauge inserted between the ring and its lower land according to specification. The gauge should slide freely around the entire ring circumference without binding. Any wear that occurs will form a step at the inner portion of the lower land. If the lower lands have high steps, the piston should be replaced.

2. Unless new pistons are installed, be sure to install the pistons in the cylinders from which they were removed. The numbers on the connecting rod and bearing cap must be on the same side when installed in the cylinder bore. If a connecting rod is ever transposed from one engine or cylinder to another, new bearings should be fitted and the connecting rod should be numbered to correspond with the new cylinder number. The notch on the piston head goes toward the front of the engine.

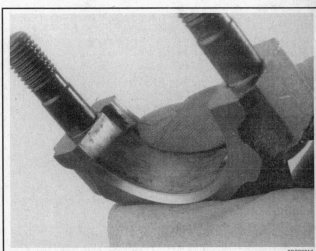

TCCS3917

The notch on the side of the bearing cap matches the tang on the bearing insert

TCCS3923

Checking the piston ring-to-ring groove side clearance using the ring and a feeler gauge

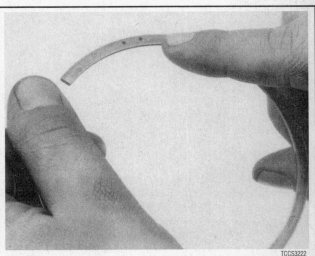

TCCS3222

Most rings are marked to show which side of the ring should face up when installed to the piston

Install the piston and rod assembly into the block using a ring compressor and the handle of a hammer

TCCS3914

3. Install all of the rod bearing inserts into the rods and caps.

4. Install the rings to the pistons. Install the oil control ring first, then the second compression ring and finally the top compression ring. Use a piston ring expander tool to aid in installation and to help reduce the chance of breakage.

5. Make sure the ring gaps are properly spaced around the circumference of the piston. Fit a piston ring compressor around the piston and slide the piston and connecting rod assembly down into the cylinder bore, pushing it in with the wooden hammer handle. Push the piston down until it is only slightly below the top of the cylinder bore. Guide the connecting rod onto the crankshaft bearing journal carefully, to avoid damaging the crankshaft.

6. Check the bearing clearance of all the rod bearings, fitting them to the crankshaft bearing journals. Follow the procedure in the crankshaft installation above.

7. After the bearings have been fitted, apply a light coating of assembly oil to the journals and bearings.

8. Turn the crankshaft until the appropriate bearing journal is at the bottom of its stroke, then push the piston assembly all the way down until the connecting rod bearing seats on the crankshaft journal. Be careful not to allow the bearing cap screws to strike the crankshaft bearing journals and damage them.

9. After the piston and connecting rod assemblies have been installed, check the connecting rod side clearance on each crankshaft journal.

10. Prime and install the oil pump and the oil pump intake tube.

11. Install the auxiliary/balance shaft(s)/assembly(ies).

12. Install the cylinder head(s) using new gaskets.

13. Install the timing sprockets/gears and the belt/chain assemblies.

Install the timing cover(s) and oil pan. Refer to your notes and drawings made prior to disassembly and install all of the components that were removed. Install the engine into the vehicle.

Engine Start-up and Break-in

STARTING THE ENGINE

Now that the engine is installed and every wire and hose is properly connected, go back and double check that all coolant and vacuum hoses are connected. Check that you oil drain plug is installed and properly tightened. If not already done, install a new oil filter onto the engine. Fill the crankcase with the proper amount and grade of engine oil. Fill the cooling system with a 50/50 mixture of coolant/water.

1. Connect the vehicle battery.

2. Start the engine. Keep your eye on your oil pressure indicator; if it does not indicate oil pressure within 10 seconds of starting, turn the vehicle off.

✳✳ WARNING

Damage to the engine can result if it is allowed to run with no oil pressure. Check the engine oil level to make sure that it is full. Check for any leaks and if found, repair the leaks before continuing. If there is still no indication of oil pressure, you may need to prime the system.

3. Confirm that there are no fluid leaks (oil or other).

4. Allow the engine to reach normal operating temperature (the upper radiator hose will be hot to the touch).

5. If necessary, set the ignition timing.

6. Install any remaining components such as the air cleaner (if removed for ignition timing) or body panels which were removed.

BREAKING IT IN

Make the first miles on the new engine, easy ones. Vary the speed but do not accelerate hard. Most importantly, do not lug the engine, and avoid sustained high speeds until at least 100 miles. Check the engine oil and coolant levels frequently. Expect the engine to use a little oil until the rings seat. Change the oil and filter at 500 miles, 1500 miles, then every 3000 miles past that.

KEEP IT MAINTAINED

Now that you have just gone through all of that hard work, keep yourself from doing it all over again by thoroughly maintaining it. Not that you may not have maintained it before, heck you could have had one to two hundred thousand miles on it before doing this. However, you may have bought the vehicle used, and the previous owner did not keep up on maintenance. Which is why you just went through all of that hard work. See?

TORQUE SPECIFICATIONS

Component	ft. lbs.	inch lbs.	Nm
Accelerator cable adjusting bolts			
1.8L engine	3-4		4-6
2.0L engine	3-4		4-6
Camshaft sprocket			
1.8L and 1990-94 2.0L engines	58-72		80-100
2.0L engine			
1995-98 non-turbo engine	75		101
1995-98 turbo engine	65		90
2.4L Engine	65		90
Camshaft bearing cap bolt			
1.8L engine			
6x20 bolts	14-20		20-27
8x65 bolts	14-15		19-20
2.0L engine			
1990-94 vehicles (plus an additional 1/4 turn)	18		25
1995-98 non-turbo engines			
Outside bearing cap bolts	21		28
Inside bearing cap bolts	8.9		12
2.4L Engine	21-25		28-34
Connecting rod bearing cap			
1.8L engine	24-25		32-35
2.0L engine			
1990-94 vehicles (plus an additional 1/4 turn)	14.5		20
1995-98 vehicles			
Non-turbo (plus an additional 1/4 turn)	20		27
Turbo	14.5		20
2.4L engine (plus an additional 1/4 turn)	14.5		20
Crankshaft sprocket			
1.8L and 1990-94 2.0L engines	80-94		110-130
Crankshaft pulley			
1.8L engine	11-13		15-18
2.0L engine			
1990-94 vehicles	14-22		20-30
1995-98 non-turbo engines	105		142
1995-98 turbo engines	87		120
2.4L Engines	87		120
Crankshaft damper pulley			
1.8L engine	11-13		15-18
2.0L engine			
1990-94 vehicles (plus an additional 1/4 turn)	18		25
Crankshaft bearing cap			
1.8L engine	37-39		50-55
2.0L engine			
1990-94 vehicles (plus an additional 1/4 turn)	18		25
1995-98 turbo engines (plus an additional 1/4 turn)	18		25
Cylinder head			
1.8L engine	51-54		70-75
2.0L engine			
1990-94 vehicles (plus 2 additional 1/4 turns)	14		20
1995-98 vehicles (plus an additional 1/4 turn)			
Non-turbo			
Short bolts	20		28
Long bolts	48		67
Turbo (plus 2 additional 1/4 turns)	14.5		20

89573C02

TORQUE SPECIFICATIONS

Component	ft. lbs.	inch lbs.	Nm
2.4L Engine			
Step 1:	58		78
Step 2:		Loosen completely	
Step 3: (plus an additional 1/4 turn)	14.5		20
Engine mount insulator nut			
1.8L and 1990-94 2.0L engines			
Large	43-58		60-80
Small	22-29		30-40
Engine mount bracket nut or bolt			
1.8L and 1990-94 engines	36-47		50-65
2.0L engines			
1995-98 non-turbo engines	30		41
Engine support bracket bolt			
1995-98 2.0L turbo engines			
Left and right support bracket bolt	33		45
Front support bracket bolt	43		60
Exhaust manifold			
1.8L Engine			
Front exhaust pipe-to-manifold bolts	22-29		30-40
Exhaust manifold-to-engine bolts	11-14		15-20
2.0L non-turbo engine			
1990-94 vehicles			
Front exhaust pipe-to-manifold	22-29		30-40
Exhaust manifold-to-engine	11-14		15-20
1995-98 vehicles			
Front exhaust pipe-to-manifold nuts	33		44
Exhaust manifold-to-engine bolts	17		23
2.0L turbo engine			
1990-94 vehicles			
Front exhaust pipe-to manifold nuts	22-29		30-40
Exhaust manifold-to-engine bolts	18-22		25-30
1995-98 vehicles			
Engine hanger-to-exhaust pipe nuts	22		29
Exhaust manifold-to-engine nuts	36		49
2.4L engine			
M8 bolts	20		28
M10 bolts	22		30
Flywheel			
1.8L engine	94-101		130-140
2.0L engine			
1990-94 vehicles	22		30
1995-98 turbo engines	98		135
2.4L engine	98		135
Intake manifold			
1.8L engine			
Intake manifold-to-engine	11-14		15-20
Intake plenum-to-manifold	11-14		15-20
2.0L engine			
1990-94 vehicles			
Intake manifold-to-engine			
M8 bolts	11-14		15-20
M10 bolts	22-30		30-42
1995-98 non-turbo engines			
Intake manifold-to-engine	17		23

89573C03

TORQUE SPECIFICATIONS

Component				ft. lbs.	inch lbs.	Nm
	1995-98 turbo engines					
		Intake manifold bolt		14		20
		Intake manifold nut		26		36
		Intake manifold plenum retainers		20		28
	2.4L engine			13		18
Oil pan						
	1.8L engine					
		Bolts		4-6		6-8
		Nuts		3.5-5		5-7
	2.0L engine					
		1990-94 vehicles				
			Bolts	4-6		6-8
			Nuts	3.5-5		5-7
		1995-98 non-turbo engines		9		12
		1995-98 turbo engines		5		7
	2.4L engine			5		7
Oil pump						
	1.8L engine					
		Cover		11-13		15-18
		Driven gear		25-29		34-40
	2.0L engine					
		1990-94 vehicles				
			Cover	11-13		15-18
			Sprocket	36-43		50-60
			Driven gear	25-29		34-40
		1995-98 non-turbo engines				
			Cover	9		12
			Pump mounting bolts	17		23
		1995-98 turbo engines				
			Cover	12		17
	2.4L engine					
		Cover screw		7		10
		Cover bolt		12		17
Rocker arm (valve) cover bolts						
	1.8L engine			13-18		18-25
	2.0L engine					
		1990-94 vehicles		2-3		2.5-3.5
		1995-98 non-turbo engines		2.5		3.4
	2.4L engine			2.4		3.3
Rocker arm nuts/bolts						
	1.8L engine					
		Long bolts		14-20		20-27
		Short bolts		14-15		19-21
	2.4L engine			23		32
Thermostat housing retainers						
	1.8L engine			12-14		17-20
	2.0L engines					
		1990-94 vehicles		12-14		17-20
		1995-98 non-turbo engines		16		22
		1995-98 turbo engines		9.4		13
	2.4L engines			18		24

89573C04

TORQUE SPECIFICATIONS

Component			ft. lbs.	inch lbs.	Nm
Timing belt (front) cover					
1.8L engine			7-9		10-12
2.0L engines					
	1990-94 vehicles				
		Bolts	7-9		10-12
		Washer assembled bolt	6-7		8-10
	1995-98 non-turbo engines				
		Inspection cover bolt	8.9		12
		Bottom cover bolt	21		28
	1995-98 turbo engines		7.2-8.7		10.12
2.4L engine					
	M6 flange bolts		8		11
	M6 washer assembled bolt		7		9
	M8 bolts		10		48
Timing belt tensioner					
1.8L engine			16-22		22-30
2.0L engine					
	1990-94 vehicles				
		Tensioner pulley	31-40		43-55
		Idle pulley	25-30		34-42
	1995-98 non-turbo engines				
		Tensioner bolts	23		31
		Tensioner pulley bolts	30		41
	1995-98 turbo engines				
		Tensioner pulley bolt	35		49
		Tensioner arm bolt	16		22
		Auto tensioner bolt	17		24
		Idler pulley bolt	27		38
		Tensioner B bolt	14		19
2.4L engine	Tensioner arm		15		21
	Auto tensioner		17		24
	Idler pulley		26		36
	Tensioner B		14		19
Water pump					
1.8L engine					
	Pump-to-engine bolts		9-11		12-15
	Alternator brace-to-pump through bolt		14-20		20-27
2.0L Engine					
	1990-94 vehicles				
		Pump-to-engine bolts	9-11		12-15
		Alternator brace-to-pump through bolt	14-20		20-27
	1995-98 non-turbo engines		8.7		12
		Pump-to-engine bolts	8.7-11		12-15
		Alternator brace-to-pump through bolt	17		24
2.4L engine			10		14
Water pump pulley					
1.8L engine			6-7		8-10
2.0L engine					
	1990-94 vehicles		6-7		8-10
	1995-98 turbo engines		6.5		8.8
2.4L engine			8		11

89573C05

USING A VACUUM GAUGE

White needle = steady needle   *Dark needle = drifting needle*

The vacuum gauge is one of the most useful and easy-to-use diagnostic tools. It is inexpensive, easy to hook up, and provides valuable information about the condition of your engine.

Indication: Normal engine in good condition

Gauge reading: Steady, from 17–22 in./Hg.

Indication: Sticking valve or ignition miss

Gauge reading: Needle fluctuates from 15–20 in./Hg. at idle

Indication: Late ignition or valve timing, low compression, stuck throttle valve, leaking carburetor or manifold gasket.

Gauge reading: Low (15–20 in./Hg.) but steady

Indication: Improper carburetor adjustment, or minor intake leak at carburetor or manifold

NOTE: Bad fuel injector O-rings may also cause this reading.

Gauge reading: Drifting needle

Indication: Weak valve springs, worn valve stem guides, or leaky cylinder head gasket (vibrating excessively at all speeds).

NOTE: A plugged catalytic converter may also cause this reading.

Gauge reading: Needle fluctuates as engine speed increases

Indication: Burnt valve or improper valve clearance. The needle will drop when the defective valve operates.

Gauge reading: Steady needle, but drops regularly

Indication: Choked muffler or obstruction in system. Speed up the engine. Choked muffler will exhibit a slow drop of vacuum to zero.

Gauge reading: Gradual drop in reading at idle

Indication: Worn valve guides

Gauge reading: Needle vibrates excessively at idle, but steadies as engine speed increases

TCCS3C01

Troubleshooting Engine Mechanical Problems

Problem	Cause	Solution
External oil leaks	• Cylinder head cover RTV sealant broken or improperly seated	• Replace sealant; inspect cylinder head cover sealant flange and cylinder head sealant surface for distortion and cracks
	• Oil filler cap leaking or missing	• Replace cap
	• Oil filter gasket broken or improperly seated	• Replace oil filter
	• Oil pan side gasket broken, improperly seated or opening in RTV sealant	• Replace gasket or repair opening in sealant; inspect oil pan gasket flange for distortion
	• Oil pan front oil seal broken or improperly seated	• Replace seal; inspect timing case cover and oil pan seal flange for distortion
	• Oil pan rear oil seal broken or improperly seated	• Replace seal; inspect oil pan rear oil seal flange; inspect rear main bearing cap for cracks, plugged oil return channels, or distortion in seal groove
	• Timing case cover oil seal broken or improperly seated	• Replace seal
	• Excess oil pressure because of restricted PCV valve	• Replace PCV valve
	• Oil pan drain plug loose or has stripped threads	• Repair as necessary and tighten
	• Rear oil gallery plug loose	• Use appropriate sealant on gallery plug and tighten
	• Rear camshaft plug loose or improperly seated	• Seat camshaft plug or replace and seal, as necessary
Excessive oil consumption	• Oil level too high	• Drain oil to specified level
	• Oil with wrong viscosity being used	• Replace with specified oil
	• PCV valve stuck closed	• Replace PCV valve
	• Valve stem oil deflectors (or seals) are damaged, missing, or incorrect type	• Replace valve stem oil deflectors
	• Valve stems or valve guides worn	• Measure stem-to-guide clearance and repair as necessary
	• Poorly fitted or missing valve cover baffles	• Replace valve cover
	• Piston rings broken or missing	• Replace broken or missing rings
	• Scuffed piston	• Replace piston
	• Incorrect piston ring gap	• Measure ring gap, repair as necessary
	• Piston rings sticking or excessively loose in grooves	• Measure ring side clearance, repair as necessary
	• Compression rings installed upside down	• Repair as necessary
	• Cylinder walls worn, scored, or glazed	• Repair as necessary

TCCS3C02

Troubleshooting Engine Mechanical Problems

Problem	Cause	Solution
Excessive oil consumption (cont.)	• Piston ring gaps not properly staggered	• Repair as necessary
	• Excessive main or connecting rod bearing clearance	• Measure bearing clearance, repair as necessary
No oil pressure	• Low oil level	• Add oil to correct level
	• Oil pressure gauge, warning lamp or sending unit inaccurate	• Replace oil pressure gauge or warning lamp
	• Oil pump malfunction	• Replace oil pump
	• Oil pressure relief valve sticking	• Remove and inspect oil pressure relief valve assembly
	• Oil passages on pressure side of pump obstructed	• Inspect oil passages for obstruction
	• Oil pickup screen or tube obstructed	• Inspect oil pickup for obstruction
	• Loose oil inlet tube	• Tighten or seal inlet tube
Low oil pressure	• Low oil level	• Add oil to correct level
	• Inaccurate gauge, warning lamp or sending unit	• Replace oil pressure gauge or warning lamp
	• Oil excessively thin because of dilution, poor quality, or improper grade	• Drain and refill crankcase with recommended oil
	• Excessive oil temperature	• Correct cause of overheating engine
	• Oil pressure relief spring weak or sticking	• Remove and inspect oil pressure relief valve assembly
	• Oil inlet tube and screen assembly has restriction or air leak	• Remove and inspect oil inlet tube and screen assembly. (Fill inlet tube with lacquer thinner to locate leaks.)
	• Excessive oil pump clearance	• Measure clearances
	• Excessive main, rod, or camshaft bearing clearance	• Measure bearing clearances, repair as necessary
High oil pressure	• Improper oil viscosity	• Drain and refill crankcase with correct viscosity oil
	• Oil pressure gauge or sending unit inaccurate	• Replace oil pressure gauge
	• Oil pressure relief valve sticking closed	• Remove and inspect oil pressure relief valve assembly
Main bearing noise	• Insufficient oil supply	• Inspect for low oil level and low oil pressure
	• Main bearing clearance excessive	• Measure main bearing clearance, repair as necessary
	• Bearing insert missing	• Replace missing insert
	• Crankshaft end-play excessive	• Measure end-play, repair as necessary
	• Improperly tightened main bearing cap bolts	• Tighten bolts with specified torque
	• Loose flywheel or drive plate	• Tighten flywheel or drive plate attaching bolts
	• Loose or damaged vibration damper	• Repair as necessary

TCCS3C03

Troubleshooting Engine Mechanical Problems

Problem	Cause	Solution
Connecting rod bearing noise	• Insufficient oil supply	• Inspect for low oil level and low oil pressure
	• Carbon build-up on piston	• Remove carbon from piston crown
	• Bearing clearance excessive or bearing missing	• Measure clearance, repair as necessary
	• Crankshaft connecting rod journal out-of-round	• Measure journal dimensions, repair or replace as necessary
	• Misaligned connecting rod or cap	• Repair as necessary
	• Connecting rod bolts tightened improperly	• Tighten bolts with specified torque
Piston noise	• Piston-to-cylinder wall clearance excessive (scuffed piston)	• Measure clearance and examine piston
	• Cylinder walls excessively tapered or out-of-round	• Measure cylinder wall dimensions, rebore cylinder
	• Piston ring broken	• Replace all rings on piston
	• Loose or seized piston pin	• Measure piston-to-pin clearance, repair as necessary
	• Connecting rods misaligned	• Measure rod alignment, straighten or replace
	• Piston ring side clearance excessively loose or tight	• Measure ring side clearance, repair as necessary
	• Carbon build-up on piston is excessive	• Remove carbon from piston
Valve actuating component noise	• Insufficient oil supply	• Check for: (a) Low oil level (b) Low oil pressure (c) Wrong hydraulic tappets (d) Restricted oil gallery (e) Excessive tappet to bore clearance
	• Rocker arms or pivots worn	• Replace worn rocker arms or pivots
	• Foreign objects or chips in hydraulic tappets	• Clean tappets
	• Excessive tappet leak-down	• Replace valve tappet
	• Tappet face worn	• Replace tappet; inspect corresponding cam lobe for wear
	• Broken or cocked valve springs	• Properly seat cocked springs; replace broken springs
	• Stem-to-guide clearance excessive	• Measure stem-to-guide clearance, repair as required
	• Valve bent	• Replace valve
	• Loose rocker arms	• Check and repair as necessary
	• Valve seat runout excessive	• Regrind valve seat/valves
	• Missing valve lock	• Install valve lock
	• Excessive engine oil	• Correct oil level

TCCS3C04

Troubleshooting Engine Performance

Problem	Cause	Solution
Hard starting (engine cranks normally)	• Faulty engine control system component	• Repair or replace as necessary
	• Faulty fuel pump	• Replace fuel pump
	• Faulty fuel system component	• Repair or replace as necessary
	• Faulty ignition coil	• Test and replace as necessary
	• Improper spark plug gap	• Adjust gap
	• Incorrect ignition timing	• Adjust timing
	• Incorrect valve timing	• Check valve timing; repair as necessary
Rough idle or stalling	• Incorrect curb or fast idle speed	• Adjust curb or fast idle speed (If possible)
	• Incorrect ignition timing	• Adjust timing to specification
	• Improper feedback system operation	• Refer to Chapter 4
	• Faulty EGR valve operation	• Test EGR system and replace as necessary
	• Faulty PCV valve air flow	• Test PCV valve and replace as necessary
	• Faulty TAC vacuum motor or valve	• Repair as necessary
	• Air leak into manifold vacuum	• Inspect manifold vacuum connections and repair as necessary
	• Faulty distributor rotor or cap	• Replace rotor or cap (Distributor systems only)
	• Improperly seated valves	• Test cylinder compression, repair as necessary
	• Incorrect ignition wiring	• Inspect wiring and correct as necessary
	• Faulty ignition coil	• Test coil and replace as necessary
	• Restricted air vent or idle passages	• Clean passages
	• Restricted air cleaner	• Clean or replace air cleaner filter element
Faulty low-speed operation	• Restricted idle air vents and passages	• Clean air vents and passages
	• Restricted air cleaner	• Clean or replace air cleaner filter element
	• Faulty spark plugs	• Clean or replace spark plugs
	• Dirty, corroded, or loose ignition secondary circuit wire connections	• Clean or tighten secondary circuit wire connections
	• Improper feedback system operation	• Refer to Chapter 4
	• Faulty ignition coil high voltage wire	• Replace ignition coil high voltage wire (Distributor systems only)
	• Faulty distributor cap	• Replace cap (Distributor systems only)
Faulty acceleration	• Incorrect ignition timing	• Adjust timing
	• Faulty fuel system component	• Repair or replace as necessary
	• Faulty spark plug(s)	• Clean or replace spark plug(s)
	• Improperly seated valves	• Test cylinder compression, repair as necessary
	• Faulty ignition coil	• Test coil and replace as necessary

TCCS3C05

Troubleshooting Engine Performance

Problem	Cause	Solution
Faulty acceleration (cont.)	• Improper feedback system operation	• Refer to Chapter 4
Faulty high speed operation	• Incorrect ignition timing • Faulty advance mechanism	• Adjust timing (if possible) • Check advance mechanism and repair as necessary (Distributor systems only)
	• Low fuel pump volume • Wrong spark plug air gap or wrong plug • Partially restricted exhaust manifold, exhaust pipe, catalytic converter, muffler, or tailpipe • Restricted vacuum passages • Restricted air cleaner	• Replace fuel pump • Adjust air gap or install correct plug • Eliminate restriction • Clean passages • Cleaner or replace filter element as necessary
	• Faulty distributor rotor or cap	• Replace rotor or cap (Distributor systems only)
	• Faulty ignition coil • Improperly seated valve(s)	• Test coil and replace as necessary • Test cylinder compression, repair as necessary
	• Faulty valve spring(s)	• Inspect and test valve spring tension, replace as necessary
	• Incorrect valve timing	• Check valve timing and repair as necessary
	• Intake manifold restricted	• Remove restriction or replace manifold
	• Worn distributor shaft	• Replace shaft (Distributor systems only)
	• Improper feedback system operation	• Refer to Chapter 4
Misfire at all speeds	• Faulty spark plug(s) • Faulty spark plug wire(s) • Faulty distributor cap or rotor	• Clean or relace spark plug(s) • Replace as necessary • Replace cap or rotor (Distributor systems only)
	• Faulty ignition coil • Primary ignition circuit shorted or open intermittently • Improperly seated valve(s)	• Test coil and replace as necessary • Troubleshoot primary circuit and repair as necessary • Test cylinder compression, repair as necessary
	• Faulty hydraulic tappet(s) • Improper feedback system operation • Faulty valve spring(s)	• Clean or replace tappet(s) • Refer to Chapter 4 • Inspect and test valve spring tension, repair as necessary
	• Worn camshaft lobes • Air leak into manifold	• Replace camshaft • Check manifold vacuum and repair as necessary
	• Fuel pump volume or pressure low • Blown cylinder head gasket • Intake or exhaust manifold passage(s) restricted	• Replace fuel pump • Replace gasket • Pass chain through passage(s) and repair as necessary
Power not up to normal	• Incorrect ignition timing • Faulty distributor rotor	• Adjust timing • Replace rotor (Distributor systems only)

Troubleshooting Engine Performance

Problem	Cause	Solution
Power not up to normal (cont.)	• Incorrect spark plug gap	• Adjust gap
	• Faulty fuel pump	• Replace fuel pump
	• Faulty fuel pump	• Replace fuel pump
	• Incorrect valve timing	• Check valve timing and repair as necessary
	• Faulty ignition coil	• Test coil and replace as necessary
	• Faulty ignition wires	• Test wires and replace as necessary
	• Improperly seated valves	• Test cylinder compression and repair as necessary
	• Blown cylinder head gasket	• Replace gasket
	• Leaking piston rings	• Test compression and repair as necessary
	• Improper feedback system operation	• Refer to Chapter 4
Intake backfire	• Improper ignition timing	• Adjust timing
	• Defective EGR component	• Repair as necessary
	• Defective TAC vacuum motor or valve	• Repair as necessary
Exhaust backfire	• Air leak into manifold vacuum	• Check manifold vacuum and repair as necessary
	• Faulty air injection diverter valve	• Test diverter valve and replace as necessary
	• Exhaust leak	• Locate and eliminate leak
Ping or spark knock	• Incorrect ignition timing	• Adjust timing
	• Distributor advance malfunction	• Inspect advance mechanism and repair as necessary (Distributor systems only)
	• Excessive combustion chamber deposits	• Remove with combustion chamber cleaner
	• Air leak into manifold vacuum	• Check manifold vacuum and repair as necessary
	• Excessively high compression	• Test compression and repair as necessary
	• Fuel octane rating excessively low	• Try alternate fuel source
	• Sharp edges in combustion chamber	• Grind smooth
	• EGR valve not functioning properly	• Test EGR system and replace as necessary
Surging (at cruising to top speeds)	• Low fuel pump pressure or volume	• Replace fuel pump
	• Improper PCV valve air flow	• Test PCV valve and replace as necessary
	• Air leak into manifold vacuum	• Check manifold vacuum and repair as necessary
	• Incorrect spark advance	• Test and replace as necessary
	• Restricted fuel filter	• Replace fuel filter
	• Restricted air cleaner	• Clean or replace air cleaner filter element
	• EGR valve not functioning properly	• Test EGR system and replace as necessary
	• Improper feedback system operation	• Refer to Chapter 4

Troubleshooting the Serpentine Drive Belt

Problem	Cause	Solution
Tension sheeting fabric failure (woven fabric on outside circumference of belt has cracked or separated from body of belt)	• Grooved or backside idler pulley diameters are less than minimum recommended • Tension sheeting contacting (rubbing) stationary object • Excessive heat causing woven fabric to age • Tension sheeting splice has fractured	• Replace pulley(s) not conforming to specification • Correct rubbing condition • Replace belt • Replace belt
Noise (objectional squeal, squeak, or rumble is heard or felt while drive belt is in operation)	• Belt slippage • Bearing noise • Belt misalignment • Belt-to-pulley mismatch • Driven component inducing vibration • System resonant frequency inducing vibration	• Adjust belt • Locate and repair • Align belt/pulley(s) • Install correct belt • Locate defective driven component and repair • Vary belt tension within specifications. Replace belt.
Rib chunking (one or more ribs has separated from belt body)	• Foreign objects imbedded in pulley grooves • Installation damage • Drive loads in excess of design specifications • Insufficient internal belt adhesion	• Remove foreign objects from pulley grooves • Replace belt • Adjust belt tension • Replace belt
Rib or belt wear (belt ribs contact bottom of pulley grooves)	• Pulley(s) misaligned • Mismatch of belt and pulley groove widths • Abrasive environment • Rusted pulley(s) • Sharp or jagged pulley groove tips • Rubber deteriorated	• Align pulley(s) • Replace belt • Replace belt • Clean rust from pulley(s) • Replace pulley • Replace belt
Longitudinal belt cracking (cracks between two ribs)	• Belt has mistracked from pulley groove • Pulley groove tip has worn away rubber-to-tensile member	• Replace belt • Replace belt
Belt slips	• Belt slipping because of insufficient tension • Belt or pulley subjected to substance (belt dressing, oil, ethylene glycol) that has reduced friction • Driven component bearing failure • Belt glazed and hardened from heat and excessive slippage	• Adjust tension • Replace belt and clean pulleys • Replace faulty component bearing • Replace belt
"Groove jumping" (belt does not maintain correct position on pulley, or turns over and/or runs off pulleys)	• Insufficient belt tension • Pulley(s) not within design tolerance • Foreign object(s) in grooves	• Adjust belt tension • Replace pulley(s) • Remove foreign objects from grooves

TCCS3C09

Troubleshooting the Serpentine Drive Belt

Problem	Cause	Solution
"Groove jumping" (belt does not maintain correct position on pulley, or turns over and/or runs off pulleys)	• Excessive belt speed • Pulley misalignment • Belt-to-pulley profile mismatched • Belt cordline is distorted	• Avoid excessive engine acceleration • Align pulley(s) • Install correct belt • Replace belt
Belt broken (Note: identify and correct problem before replacement belt is installed)	• Excessive tension • Tensile members damaged during belt installation • Belt turnover • Severe pulley misalignment • Bracket, pulley, or bearing failure	• Replace belt and adjust tension to specification • Replace belt • Replace belt • Align pulley(s) • Replace defective component and belt
Cord edge failure (tensile member exposed at edges of belt or separated from belt body)	• Excessive tension • Drive pulley misalignment • Belt contacting stationary object • Pulley irregularities • Improper pulley construction • Insufficient adhesion between tensile member and rubber matrix	• Adjust belt tension • Align pulley • Correct as necessary • Replace pulley • Replace pulley • Replace belt and adjust tension to specifications
Sporadic rib cracking (multiple cracks in belt ribs at random intervals)	• Ribbed pulley(s) diameter less than minimum specification • Backside bend flat pulley(s) diameter less than minimum • Excessive heat condition causing rubber to harden • Excessive belt thickness • Belt overcured • Excessive tension	• Replace pulley(s) • Replace pulley(s) • Correct heat condition as necessary • Replace belt • Replace belt • Adjust belt tension

TCCS3C10

Troubleshooting the Cooling System

Problem	Cause	Solution
High temperature gauge indication—overheating	• Coolant level low • Improper fan operation • Radiator hose(s) collapsed • Radiator airflow blocked • Faulty pressure cap • Ignition timing incorrect • Air trapped in cooling system • Heavy traffic driving • Incorrect cooling system component(s) installed • Faulty thermostat • Water pump shaft broken or impeller loose • Radiator tubes clogged • Cooling system clogged • Casting flash in cooling passages • Brakes dragging • Excessive engine friction • Antifreeze concentration over 68% • Missing air seals • Faulty gauge or sending unit • Loss of coolant flow caused by leakage or foaming • Viscous fan drive failed	• Replenish coolant • Repair or replace as necessary • Replace hose(s) • Remove restriction (bug screen, fog lamps, etc.) • Replace pressure cap • Adjust ignition timing • Purge air • Operate at fast idle in neutral intermittently to cool engine • Install proper component(s) • Replace thermostat • Replace water pump • Flush radiator • Flush system • Repair or replace as necessary. Flash may be visible by removing cooling system components or removing core plugs. • Repair brakes • Repair engine • Lower antifreeze concentration percentage • Replace air seals • Repair or replace faulty component • Repair or replace leaking component, replace coolant • Replace unit
Low temperature indication—undercooling	• Thermostat stuck open • Faulty gauge or sending unit	• Replace thermostat • Repair or replace faulty component
Coolant loss—boilover	• Overfilled cooling system • Quick shutdown after hard (hot) run • Air in system resulting in occasional "burping" of coolant • Insufficient antifreeze allowing coolant boiling point to be too low • Antifreeze deteriorated because of age or contamination • Leaks due to loose hose clamps, loose nuts, bolts, drain plugs, faulty hoses, or defective radiator	• Reduce coolant level to proper specification • Allow engine to run at fast idle prior to shutdown • Purge system • Add antifreeze to raise boiling point • Replace coolant • Pressure test system to locate source of leak(s) then repair as necessary

TCCS3C11

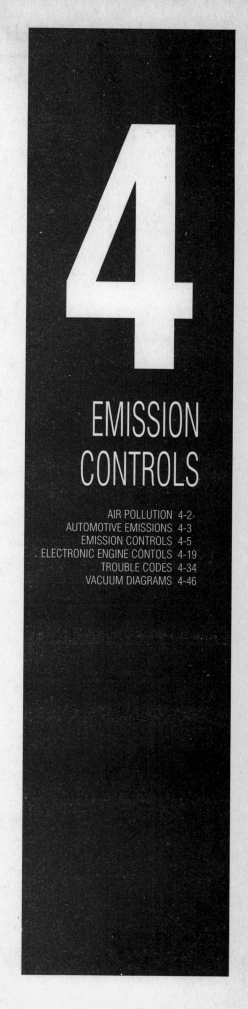

4

EMISSION CONTROLS

AIR POLLUTION

The earth's atmosphere, at or near sea level, consists approximately of 78 percent nitrogen, 21 percent oxygen and 1 percent other gases. If it were possible to remain in this state, 100 percent clean air would result. However, many varied sources allow other gases and particulates to mix with the clean air, causing our atmosphere to become unclean or polluted.

Some of these pollutants are visible while others are invisible, with each having the capability of causing distress to the eyes, ears, throat, skin and respiratory system. Should these pollutants become concentrated in a specific area and under certain conditions, death could result due to the displacement or chemical change of the oxygen content in the air. These pollutants can also cause great damage to the environment and to the many man made objects that are exposed to the elements.

To better understand the causes of air pollution, the pollutants can be categorized into 3 separate types, natural, industrial and automotive.

Natural Pollutants

Natural pollution has been present on earth since before man appeared and continues to be a factor when discussing air pollution, although it causes only a small percentage of the overall pollution problem. It is the direct result of decaying organic matter, wind born smoke and particulates from such natural events as plain and forest fires (ignited by heat or lightning), volcanic ash, sand and dust which can spread over a large area of the countryside.

Such a phenomenon of natural pollution has been seen in the form of volcanic eruptions, with the resulting plume of smoke, steam and volcanic ash blotting out the sun's rays as it spreads and rises higher into the atmosphere. As it travels into the atmosphere the upper air currents catch and carry the smoke and ash, while condensing the steam back into water vapor. As the water vapor, smoke and ash travel on their journey, the smoke dissipates into the atmosphere while the ash and moisture settle back to earth in a trail hundreds of miles long. In some cases, lives are lost and millions of dollars of property damage result.

Industrial Pollutants

Industrial pollution is caused primarily by industrial processes, the burning of coal, oil and natural gas, which in turn produce smoke and fumes. Because the burning fuels contain large amounts of sulfur, the principal ingredients of smoke and fumes are sulfur dioxide and particulate matter. This type of pollutant occurs most severely during still, damp and cool weather, such as at night. Even in its less severe form, this pollutant is not confined to just cities. Because of air movements, the pollutants move for miles over the surrounding countryside, leaving in its path a barren and unhealthy environment for all living things.

Working with Federal, State and Local mandated regulations and by carefully monitoring emissions, big business has greatly reduced the amount of pollutant introduced from its industrial sources, striving to obtain an acceptable level. Because of the mandated industrial emission clean up, many land areas and streams in and around the cities that were formerly barren of vegetation and life, have now begun to move back in the direction of nature's intended balance.

Automotive Pollutants

The third major source of air pollution is automotive emissions. The emissions from the internal combustion engines were not an appreciable problem years ago because of the small number of registered vehicles and the nation's small highway system. However, during the early 1950's, the trend of the American people was to move from the cities to the surrounding suburbs. This caused an immediate problem in transportation because the majority of suburbs were not afforded mass transit conveniences. This lack of transportation created an attractive market for the automobile manufacturers, which resulted in a dramatic increase in the number of vehicles produced and sold, along with a marked increase in highway construction

between cities and the suburbs. Multi-vehicle families emerged with a growing emphasis placed on an individual vehicle per family member. As the increase in vehicle ownership and usage occurred, so did pollutant levels in and around the cities, as suburbanites drove daily to their businesses and employment, returning at the end of the day to their homes in the suburbs.

It was noted that a smoke and fog type haze was being formed and at times, remained in suspension over the cities, taking time to dissipate. At first this "smog," derived from the words "smoke" and "fog," was thought to result from industrial pollution but it was determined that automobile emissions shared the blame. It was discovered that when normal automobile emissions were exposed to sunlight for a period of time, complex chemical reactions would take place.

It is now known that smog is a photo chemical layer which develops when certain oxides of nitrogen (NOx) and unburned hydrocarbons (HC) from automobile emissions are exposed to sunlight. Pollution was more severe when smog would become stagnant over an area in which a warm layer of air settled over the top of the cooler air mass, trapping and holding the cooler mass at ground level. The trapped cooler air would keep the emissions from being dispersed and diluted through normal air flows. This type of air stagnation was given the name "Temperature Inversion."

TEMPERATURE INVERSION

In normal weather situations, surface air is warmed by heat radiating from the earth's surface and the sun's rays. This causes it to rise upward, into the atmosphere. Upon rising it will cool through a convection type heat exchange with the cooler upper air. As warm air rises, the surface pollutants are carried upward and dissipated into the atmosphere.

When a temperature inversion occurs, we find the higher air is no longer cooler, but is warmer than the surface air, causing the cooler surface air to become trapped. This warm air blanket can extend from above ground level to a few hundred or even a few thousand feet into the air. As the surface air is trapped, so are the pollutants, causing a severe smog condition. Should this stagnant air mass extend to a few thousand feet high, enough air movement with the inversion takes place to allow the smog layer to rise above ground level but the pollutants still cannot dissipate. This inversion can remain for days over an area, with the smog level only rising or lowering from ground level to a few hundred feet high. Meanwhile, the pollutant levels increase, causing eye irritation, respiratory problems, reduced visibility, plant damage and in some cases, even disease.

This inversion phenomenon was first noted in the Los Angeles, California area. The city lies in terrain resembling a basin and with certain weather conditions, a cold air mass is held in the basin while a warmer air mass covers it like a lid.

Because this type of condition was first documented as prevalent in the Los Angeles area, this type of trapped pollution was named Los Angeles Smog, although it occurs in other areas where a large concentration of automobiles are used and the air remains stagnant for any length of time.

HEAT TRANSFER

Consider the internal combustion engine as a machine in which raw materials must be placed so a finished product comes out. As in any machine operation, a certain amount of wasted material is formed. When we relate this to the internal combustion engine, we find that through the input of air and fuel, we obtain power during the combustion process to drive the vehicle. The by-product or waste of this power is, in part, heat and exhaust gases with which we must dispose.

The heat from the combustion process can rise to over 4000°F (2204°C). The dissipation of this heat is controlled by a ram air effect, the use of cooling fans to cause air flow and a liquid coolant solution surrounding the combustion area to transfer the heat of combustion through the cylinder walls and into the coolant. The coolant is then directed to a thin-finned, multi-tubed radiator, from which the excess heat is transferred to the atmosphere by 1 of the 3 heat transfer methods, conduction, convection or radiation.

The cooling of the combustion area is an important part in the control of exhaust emissions. To understand the behavior of the combustion and transfer of its heat, consider the air/fuel charge. It is ignited and the flame front burns progressively across the combustion chamber until the burning charge reaches the cylinder walls. Some of the fuel in contact with the walls is not hot enough to burn, thereby snuffing out or quenching the combustion process. This leaves unburned fuel in the combustion chamber. This unburned fuel is then forced out of the cylinder and into the exhaust system, along with the exhaust gases.

Many attempts have been made to minimize the amount of unburned fuel in the combustion chambers due to quenching, by increasing the coolant temperature and lessening the contact area of the coolant around the combustion area. However, design limitations within the combustion chambers prevent the complete burning of the air/fuel charge, so a certain amount of the unburned fuel is still expelled into the exhaust system, regardless of modifications to the engine.

AUTOMOTIVE EMISSIONS

Before emission controls were mandated on internal combustion engines, other sources of engine pollutants were discovered along with the exhaust emissions. It was determined that engine combustion exhaust produced approximately 60 percent of the total emission pollutants, fuel evaporation from the fuel tank and carburetor vents produced 20 percent, with the final 20 percent being produced through the crankcase as a by-product of the combustion process.

Exhaust Gases

The exhaust gases emitted into the atmosphere are a combination of burned and unburned fuel. To understand the exhaust emission and its composition, we must review some basic chemistry.

When the air/fuel mixture is introduced into the engine, we are mixing air, composed of nitrogen (78 percent), oxygen (21 percent) and other gases (1 percent) with the fuel, which is 100 percent hydrocarbons (HC), in a semi-controlled ratio. As the combustion process is accomplished, power is produced to move the vehicle while the heat of combustion is transferred to the cooling system. The exhaust gases are then composed of nitrogen, a diatomic gas (N_2), the same as was introduced in the engine, carbon dioxide (CO_2), the same gas that is used in beverage carbonation, and water vapor (H_2O). The nitrogen (N_2), for the most part, passes through the engine unchanged, while the oxygen (O_2) reacts (burns) with the hydrocarbons (HC) and produces the carbon dioxide (CO_2) and the water vapors (H_2O). If this chemical process would be the only process to take place, the exhaust emissions would be harmless. However, during the combustion process, other compounds are formed which are considered dangerous. These pollutants are hydrocarbons (HC), carbon monoxide (CO), oxides of nitrogen (NOx) oxides of sulfur (SOx) and engine particulates.

HYDROCARBONS

Hydrocarbons (HC) are essentially fuel which was not burned during the combustion process or which has escaped into the atmosphere through fuel evaporation. The main sources of incomplete combustion are rich air/fuel mixtures, low engine temperatures and improper spark timing. The main sources of hydrocarbon emission through fuel evaporation on most vehicles used to be the vehicle's fuel tank and carburetor float bowl.

To reduce combustion hydrocarbon emission, engine modifications were made to minimize dead space and surface area in the combustion chamber. In addition, the air/fuel mixture was made more lean through the improved control which feedback carburetion and fuel injection offers and by the addition of external controls to aid in further combustion of the hydrocarbons outside the engine. Two such methods were the addition of air injection systems, to inject fresh air into the exhaust manifolds and the installation of catalytic converters, units that are able to burn traces of hydrocarbons without affecting the internal combustion process or fuel economy.

To control hydrocarbon emissions through fuel evaporation, modifications were made to the fuel tank to allow storage of the fuel vapors during periods of engine shut-down. Modifications were also made to the air intake system so that at specific times during engine operation, these vapors may be purged and burned by blending them with the air/fuel mixture.

CARBON MONOXIDE

Carbon monoxide is formed when not enough oxygen is present during the combustion process to convert carbon (C) to carbon dioxide (CO_2). An increase in the carbon monoxide (CO) emission is normally accompanied by an increase in the hydrocarbon (HC) emission because of the lack of oxygen to completely burn all of the fuel mixture.

Carbon monoxide (CO) also increases the rate at which the photo chemical smog is formed by speeding up the conversion of nitric oxide (NO) to nitrogen dioxide (NO_2). To accomplish this, carbon monoxide (CO) combines with oxygen (O_2) and nitric oxide (NO) to produce carbon dioxide (CO_2) and nitrogen dioxide (NO_2). ($CO + O_2 + NO = CO_2 + NO_2$).

The dangers of carbon monoxide, which is an odorless and colorless toxic gas are many. When carbon monoxide is inhaled into the lungs and passed into the blood stream, oxygen is replaced by the carbon monoxide in the red blood cells, causing a reduction in the amount of oxygen supplied to the many parts of the body. This lack of oxygen causes headaches, lack of coordination, reduced mental alertness and, should the carbon monoxide concentration be high enough, death could result.

NITROGEN

Normally, nitrogen is an inert gas. When heated to approximately 2500°F (1371°C) through the combustion process, this gas becomes active and causes an increase in the nitric oxide (NO) emission.

Oxides of nitrogen (NOx) are composed of approximately 97–98 percent nitric oxide (NO). Nitric oxide is a colorless gas but when it is passed into the atmosphere, it combines with oxygen and forms nitrogen dioxide (NO_2). The nitrogen dioxide then combines with chemically active hydrocarbons (HC) and when in the presence of sunlight, causes the formation of photochemical smog.

Ozone

To further complicate matters, some of the nitrogen dioxide (NO_2) is broken apart by the sunlight to form nitric oxide and oxygen. ($NO_2 + $ sunlight $= NO + O$). This single atom of oxygen then combines with diatomic (meaning 2 atoms) oxygen (O_2) to form ozone (O_3). Ozone is one of the smells associated with smog. It has a pungent and offensive odor, irritates the eyes and lung tissues, affects the growth of plant life and causes rapid deterioration of rubber products. Ozone can be formed by sunlight as well as electrical discharge into the air.

The most common discharge area on the automobile engine is the secondary ignition electrical system, especially when inferior quality spark plug cables are used. As the surge of high voltage is routed through the secondary cable, the circuit builds up an electrical field around the wire, which acts upon the oxygen in the surrounding air to form the ozone. The faint glow along the cable with the engine running that may be visible on a dark night, is called the "corona discharge." It is the result of the electrical field passing from a high along the cable, to a low in the surrounding air, which forms the ozone gas. The combination of corona and ozone has been a major cause of cable deterioration. Recently, different and better quality insulating materials have lengthened the life of the electrical cables.

Although ozone at ground level can be harmful, ozone is beneficial to the earth's inhabitants. By having a concentrated ozone layer called the "ozonosphere," between 10 and 20 miles (16–32 km) up in the atmosphere, much of the ultra violet radiation from the sun's rays are absorbed and screened. If this ozone layer were not present, much of the earth's surface would be burned, dried and unfit for human life.

OXIDES OF SULFUR

Oxides of sulfur (SOx) were initially ignored in the exhaust system emissions, since the sulfur content of gasoline as a fuel is less than $\frac{1}{10}$ of 1 percent. Because of this small amount, it was felt that it contributed very little to the overall pollution problem. However, because of the difficulty in solving the sulfur emissions in industrial pollutions and the introduction of catalytic converter to the automobile exhaust systems, a change was mandated. The automobile exhaust system, when equipped with a catalytic converter, changes the sulfur dioxide (SO_2) into sulfur trioxide (SO_3).

When this combines with water vapors (H_2O), a sulfuric acid mist (H_2SO_4) is formed and is a very difficult pollutant to handle since it is extremely corrosive. This sulfuric acid mist that is formed, is the same mist that rises from the vents of an automobile battery when an active chemical reaction takes place within the battery cells.

When a large concentration of vehicles equipped with catalytic converters are operating in an area, this acid mist may rise and be distributed over a large ground area causing land, plant, crop, paint and building damage.

PARTICULATE MATTER

A certain amount of particulate matter is present in the burning of any fuel, with carbon constituting the largest percentage of the particulates. In gasoline, the remaining particulates are the burned remains of the various other compounds used in its manufacture. When a gasoline engine is in good internal condition, the particulate emissions are low but as the engine wears internally, the particulate emissions increase. By visually inspecting the tail pipe emissions, a determination can be made as to where an engine defect may exist. An engine with light gray or blue smoke emitting from the tail pipe normally indicates an increase in the oil consumption through burning due to internal engine wear. Black smoke would indicate a defective fuel delivery system, causing the engine to operate in a rich mode. Regardless of the color of the smoke, the internal part of the engine or the fuel delivery system should be repaired to prevent excess particulate emissions.

Diesel and turbine engines emit a darkened plume of smoke from the exhaust system because of the type of fuel used. Emission control regulations are mandated for this type of emission and more stringent measures are being used to prevent excess emission of the particulate matter. Electronic components are being introduced to control the injection of the fuel at precisely the proper time of piston travel, to achieve the optimum in fuel ignition and fuel usage. Other particulate after-burning components are being tested to achieve a cleaner emission.

Good grades of engine lubricating oils should be used, which meet the manufacturers specification. Cut-rate oils can contribute to the particulate emission problem because of their low flash or ignition temperature point. Such oils burn prematurely during the combustion process causing emission of particulate matter.

The cooling system is an important factor in the reduction of particulate matter. The optimum combustion will occur, with the cooling system operating at a temperature specified by the manufacturer. The cooling system must be maintained in the same manner as the engine oiling system, as each system is required to perform properly in order for the engine to operate efficiently for a long time.

Crankcase Emissions

Crankcase emissions are made up of water, acids, unburned fuel, oil fumes and particulates. These emissions are classified as hydrocarbons (HC) and are formed by the small amount of unburned, compressed air/fuel mixture entering the crankcase from the combustion area (between the cylinder walls and piston rings) during the compression and power strokes. The head of the compression and combustion help to form the remaining crankcase emissions.

Since the first engines, crankcase emissions were allowed into the atmosphere through a road draft tube, mounted on the lower side of the engine block. Fresh air came in through an open oil filler cap or breather. The air passed through the crankcase mixing with blow-by gases. The motion of the vehicle and the air blowing past the open end of the road draft tube caused a low pressure area (vacuum) at the end of the tube. Crankcase emissions were simply drawn out of the road draft tube into the air.

To control the crankcase emission, the road draft tube was deleted. A hose and/or tubing was routed from the crankcase to the intake manifold so the blow-by emission could be burned with the air/fuel mixture. However, it was found that intake manifold vacuum, used to draw the crankcase emissions into the manifold, would vary in strength at the wrong time and not allow the proper emission flow. A regulating valve was needed to control the flow of air through the crankcase.

Testing, showed the removal of the blow-by gases from the crankcase as quickly as possible, was most important to the longevity of the engine. Should large accumulations of blow-by gases remain and condense, dilution of the engine oil would occur to form water, soots, resins, acids and lead salts, resulting in the formation of sludge and varnishes. This condensation of the blow-by gases occurs more frequently on vehicles used in numerous starting and stopping conditions, excessive idling and when the engine is not allowed to attain normal operating temperature through short runs.

Evaporative Emissions

Gasoline fuel is a major source of pollution, before and after it is burned in the automobile engine. From the time the fuel is refined, stored, pumped and transported, again stored until it is pumped into the fuel tank of the vehicle, the gasoline gives off unburned hydrocarbons (HC) into the atmosphere. Through the redesign of storage areas and venting systems, the pollution factor was diminished, but not eliminated, from the refinery standpoint. However, the automobile still remained the primary source of vaporized, unburned hydrocarbon (HC) emissions.

Fuel pumped from an underground storage tank is cool but when exposed to a warmer ambient temperature, will expand. Before controls were mandated, an owner might fill the fuel tank with fuel from an underground storage tank and park the vehicle for some time in warm area, such as a parking lot. As the fuel would warm, it would expand and should no provisions or area be provided for the expansion, the fuel would spill out of the filler neck and onto the ground, causing hydrocarbon (HC) pollution and creating a severe fire hazard. To correct this condition, the vehicle manufacturers added overflow plumbing and/or gasoline tanks with built in expansion areas or domes.

However, this did not control the fuel vapor emission from the fuel tank. It was determined that most of the fuel evaporation occurred when the vehicle was stationary and the engine not operating. Most vehicles carry 5–25 gallons (19–95 liters) of gasoline. Should a large concentration of vehicles be parked in one area, such as a large parking lot, excessive fuel vapor emissions would take place, increasing as the temperature increases.

To prevent the vapor emission from escaping into the atmosphere, the fuel systems were designed to trap the vapors while the vehicle is stationary, by sealing the system from the atmosphere. A storage system is used to collect and hold the fuel vapors from the carburetor (if equipped) and the fuel tank when the engine is not operating. When the engine is started, the storage system is then purged of the fuel vapors, which are drawn into the engine and burned with the air/fuel mixture.

EMISSION COMPONENT LOCATIONS—2.0L NON-TURBO

1. ECT sensor
2. MAP sensor
3. IAT sensor
4. PCV valve
5. Knock sensor (mounted in cylinder head)
6. IAC valve
7. TP sensor
8. ECM
9. CMP sensor
10. EGR valve (under air cleaner duct)
11. Electric EGR transducer solenoid
12. Front heated oxygen sensor (rear mounted in exhaust pipe)

89574P15

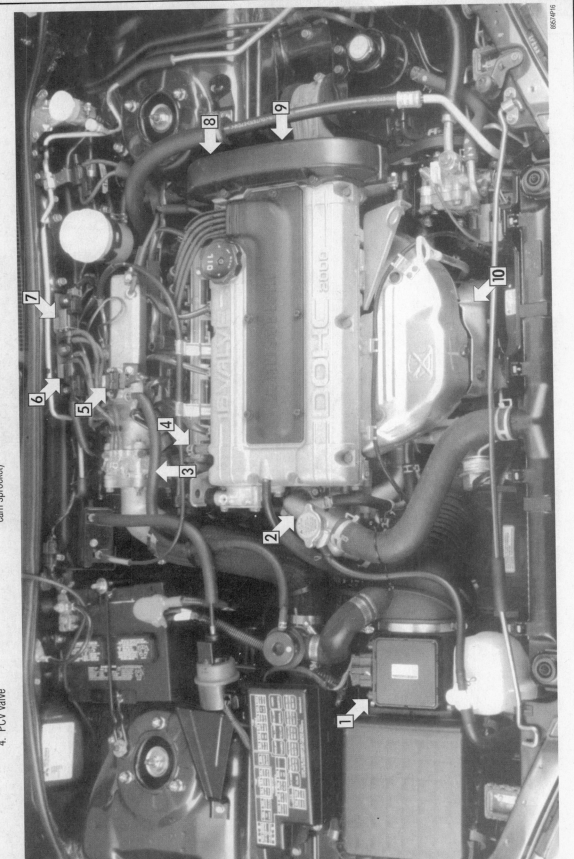

EMISSION COMPONENT LOCATIONS—2.0L TURBO

1. Volume air flow sensor (includes IAT sensor and barometric pressure sensor)
2. ECT sensor
3. TP sensor
4. PCV valve
5. MDP sensor
6. EGR solenoid
7. Evaporative emission purge solenoid
8. CMP sensor (mounted behind intake cam sprocket)
9. CKP sensor (mounted near crankshaft sprocket)
10. Front heated oxygen sensor

89574P16

Crankcase Ventilation System

OPERATION

▶ **See Figures 1, 2, 3 and 4**

All engines are equipped with the Positive Crankcase Ventilation (PCV) system. The PCV system vents crankcase gases into the engine air intake where they are burned with the fuel and air mixture. The PCV system keeps pollutants from being released into the atmosphere. It also helps to keep the engine oil clean, by ridding the crankcase of moisture and corrosive fumes. The PCV system consists of the PCV valve, the nipple in the air intake and the connecting hoses.

Incorrect operation of the PCV system can cause multiple driveability symptoms.

A plugged valve or hose may cause:
- Rough idle
- Stalling or slow idle speed
- Oil leaks
- Sludge in engine

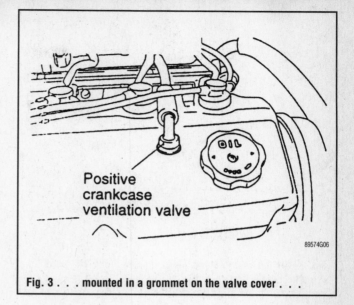

Fig. 3 . . . mounted in a grommet on the valve cover . . .

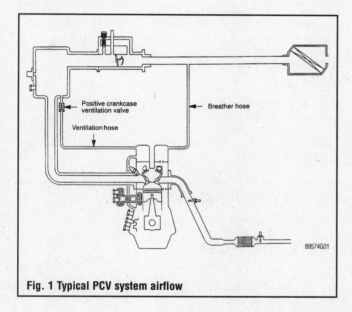

Fig. 1 Typical PCV system airflow

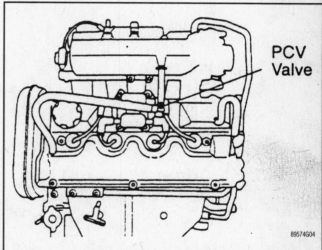

Fig. 4 . . . or in the hose between the valve cover and intake plenum

A leaking valve or hose would cause:
- Rough idle
- Stalling
- High idle speed

COMPONENT TESTING

▶ **See Figures 5 and 6**

1. Disconnect the ventilation hose from the PCV valve. Remove the PCV valve from the engine. Once removed, reconnect the ventilation hose to the valve.

2. Start the engine and allow to idle. Place a finger over open end of the PCV valve. Make sure intake manifold vacuum is felt on finger.

3. If vacuum is not felt, the PCV valve may be restricted.

4. Turn the engine **OFF** and remove the PCV valve from the hose.

5. Insert a thin stick into the threaded end of the PCV valve. Push on the inner plunger and inspect for movement.

6. If plunger inside the PCV valve is not free to move back and forth, the valve is clogged and will require replacement.

➡ **It is possible to clean the valve using the appropriate solvent, but replacement is recommended.**

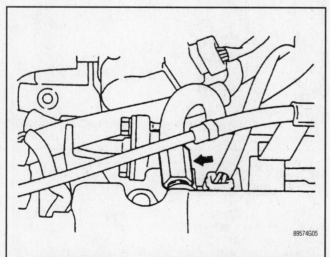

Fig. 2 The PCV valve can be found either threaded to the valve cover, . . .

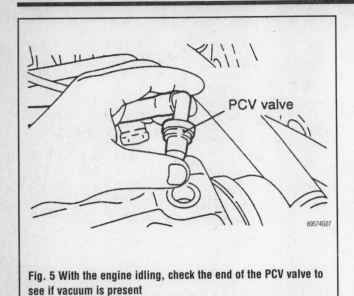

Fig. 5 With the engine idling, check the end of the PCV valve to see if vacuum is present

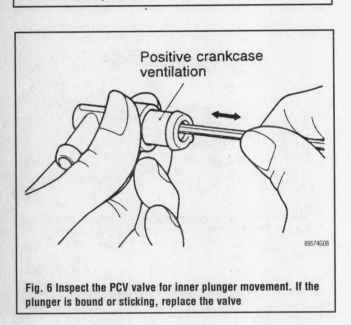

Fig. 6 Inspect the PCV valve for inner plunger movement. If the plunger is bound or sticking, replace the valve

REMOVAL & INSTALLATION

For PCV valve removal and installation, please refer to Section 1 of this manual.

Evaporative Emission Control System

OPERATION

▶ **See Figure 7**

The function of this control system is to prevent the emissions of gasoline vapors from the fuel tank into the atmosphere. When fuel evaporates in the fuel tank, the vapors pass through vent hoses or tubes to a charcoal canister. There they are temporarily held until they can be drawn into the intake manifold when the engine is running and burned the combustion process during engine operation. This action prevents excessive pressure buildup in the fuel tank.

The system also prevents fuel spillage in the event of an accidental roll over of the vehicle. All vehicles have a roll over (two-way) valve installed

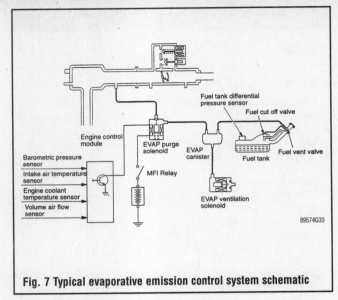

Fig. 7 Typical evaporative emission control system schematic

in-line above the tank to release fuel tank pressure to the canister and to prevent fuel from leaking in the event of an accidental vehicle roll over.

Charcoal Canister

▶ **See Figure 8**

A sealed, maintenance free charcoal canister is used on all vehicles. The fuel tank vents lead to the canister. Fuel vapors are temporarily held in the canister's activated charcoal until they can be drawn into the intake manifold and burned in the combustion chamber. There is no scheduled maintenance interval on the charcoal canister.

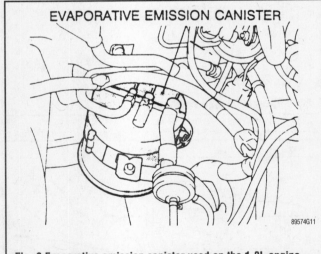

Fig. 8 Evaporative emission canister used on the 1.8L engine—other models similar

Purge Control System

▶ **See Figures 9, 10, 11 and 12**

The canister is connected to the engine via a purge control solenoid; a purge control valve is added to the system on turbo engines. The purge control solenoid is located as follows:
• 1.8L engine—on the firewall just to the right of the brake fluid reservoir.
• 1990–94 2.0L non-turbo engine—on the firewall, slightly right of center.

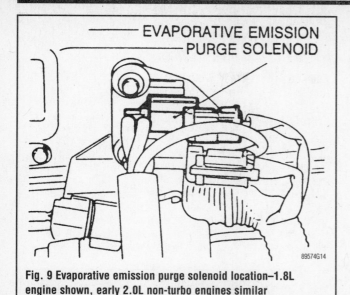

Fig. 9 Evaporative emission purge solenoid location—1.8L engine shown, early 2.0L non-turbo engines similar

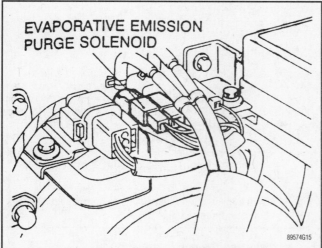

Fig. 10 Location of the evaporative emission purge solenoid—1990–94 2.0L turbo engine shown, later models similar

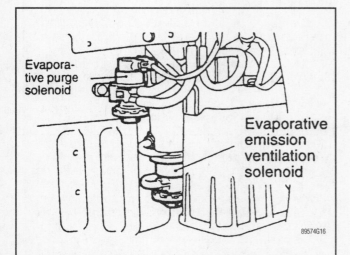

Fig. 11 Evaporative emission purge and ventilation solenoid locations—1995–98 2.0L non-turbo engine

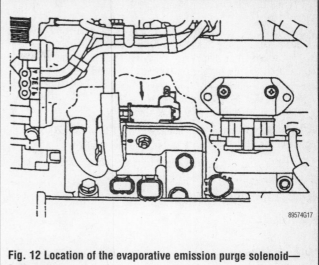

Fig. 12 Location of the evaporative emission purge solenoid—2.4L engine

- 1990–94 2.0L turbo engine—the innermost solenoid in the solenoid cluster at the left rear corner of the engine compartment.
- 1995–98 2.0L non-turbo engine—mounted to the evaporative canister.
- 1995–98 2.0L turbo engines—on the firewall, to the left of the brake fluid reservoir.

COMPONENT TESTING

Purge Control System Check

1990–94 NON-TURBO ENGINES

1. Disconnect the red striped vacuum hose from the throttle body and connect it to a hand held vacuum pump.
2. Plug the open nipple on the throttle body.
3. Using the hand pump, apply vacuum while the engine is idling. Check that vacuum is maintained or released as outlined below:
   a. With the engine coolant at 140°F (60°C) or less—14.8 in. Hg of vacuum is maintained.
   b. With the coolant at 158°F (70°C) or higher—14.8 in. Hg of vacuum is maintained.
4. With the engine coolant at 158°F (70°C) or higher, run the engine at 3000 rpm within 3 minutes of starting vehicle. Try to apply vacuum using the hand held pump. Vacuum should leak.
5. With the engine coolant at 158°F (70°C) or higher, run the engine at 3000 rpm after 3 minutes have elapsed after starting vehicle. Apply 14.8 in. Hg of vacuum. The vacuum should be maintained momentarily, after which it should leak.

➡ **The vacuum will leak continuously if the altitude is 7,200 ft. or higher, or the intake air temperature is 122°F (50°C) or higher.**

6. If the test results differ from the desired results, the purge control system is not operating properly.

1990–92 TURBO ENGINES

1. Disconnect the purge air hose from the intake hose and plug the air intake hose.
2. Connect a hand vacuum pump to the purge air hose.
3. Under various engine conditions, inspect the system operation:
   a. Allow the engine to cool to a temperature of 140°F (60°C) or below.
   b. Start the engine and run at idle.
   c. Using the hand pump, apply 14.8 in. Hg of vacuum. In this condition, the vacuum should be maintained.
   d. Raise the engine speed to 3000 rpm.
   e. Using the hand pump, apply 14.8 in. Hg of vacuum. In this condition, the vacuum should be maintained.

4. Run the engine until the coolant temperature reaches 158°F (70°C). Inspect system operations as follows:

    a. Using the hand pump, apply 14.8 in. Hg of vacuum with the engine at idle. In this condition, vacuum should be maintained.

    b. Increase the engine speed to 3000 rpm within 3 minutes of starting the engine. Try applying vacuum. The vacuum should leak.

    c. After 3 minutes have elapsed after starting engine, raise the engine speed to 3000 rpm. Apply 14.8 in. Hg of vacuum. Vacuum should be maintained momentarily, after which it will leak.

➡**The vacuum will leak continuously if the altitude is 7200 ft. or higher or the air temperature is 122°F (50°C) or higher.**

5. If the results of either test differs from specifications, the system is not functioning properly and will require further diagnosis.

1993–94 TURBO ENGINES

▶ **See Figure 13**

1. Disconnect red striped vacuum hose from the throttle body and connect it to a hand-held vacuum pump.

2. Plug nipple from which the vacuum hose was disconnected.

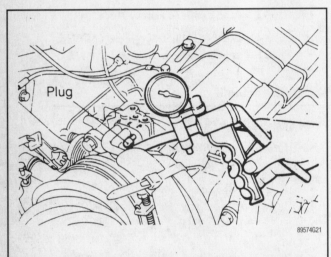

Fig. 13 To test the purge control operation, connect the vacuum hose from the throttle body to a vacuum pump

3. Allow the engine coolant to cool below 104°F (60°C) or below. Check system operation as follows:

    a. Start the engine and run at idle speed. Apply 14.8 in. Hg of vacuum. The vacuum should be maintained.

    b. Run the engine at 3000 rpm. Apply 14.8 in. Hg of vacuum. The vacuum should be maintained.

4. Run the engine until the coolant temperature reaches 158°F (70°C) of above. Inspect system operation as follows:

    a. With the engine at idle, apply 14.8 in. Hg of vacuum using the hand pump. The vacuum should be maintained.

    b. Run the engine at 3000 rpm within 3 minutes after starting the engine, and try applying vacuum. The vacuum should leak.

    c. Run the engine at 3000 rpm after 3 minutes have elapsed after starting the vehicle and apply 14.8 in Hg of vacuum. Vacuum will be maintained momentarily, then it will leak.

➡**The vacuum will leak continuously if the altitude is 7200 ft. or higher or the air temperature is 122°F (50°C) or higher.**

5. If any of the test results differ from the specifications, there is a fault in the operation of the system and further diagnosis is required.

1995–98 2.0L NON-TURBO ENGINES

▶ **See Figure 14**

1. Disconnect the vacuum hose from the throttle body, then connect it to a hand-held vacuum pump.

2. Plug the nipple where the vacuum hose was disconnected. Start the engine.

3. When the engine reaches operating temperature, coolant 176° F (80°C or higher), apply 15.7 in. Hg (53 kPa) of vacuum at idle to check the condition of the engine and vacuum as follows:

    a. Right after the engine is started, the vacuum should be maintained.

    b. After ten or more seconds, the vacuum should leak.

4. If any of the test results differ from the specifications, there is a fault in the operation of the system and further diagnosis is required.

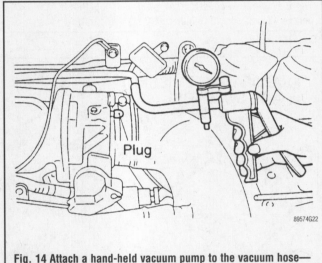

Fig. 14 Attach a hand-held vacuum pump to the vacuum hose—1995–98 2.0L non-turbo engine

1995–98 2.0L TURBO AND 2.4L ENGINES

▶ **See Figure 15**

➡**This test requires the use of a special purge flow indicator tool, MB991700, or equivalent.**

1. Disconnect the purge hose form the EVAP canister, then connect Purge Flow Indicator MB991700, or equivalent between the canister and the purge hose.

2. The engine should be warmed up to operating temperature, 170–203°F. (80–95°C), with all lights, fans and accessories off. The transaxle should be in Park for automatics or Neutral for manuals.

3. Run the engine at idle for at least 3–4 minutes.

4. Check the purge flow volume when the brake is depressed suddenly a few times. The reading should be 2.5 SCFH (20cm/sec.)

5. If the volume is less than the standard value, check it again with the vacuum hose disconnected from the canister. If the purge flow volume is less than the standard, check for blockages in the vacuum port and vacuum hose, and also inspect the evaporative emission purge solenoid and purge control valve.

6. If the purge flow volume is at the standard value, replace the EVAP canister.

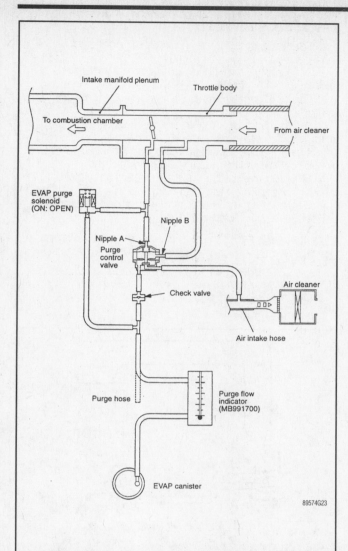

Fig. 15 Purge control system check—1995–98 2.0L turbo engine shown, 2.4L similar

Purge Control Valve

1990–94 2.0L TURBO ENGINE

▶ See Figure 16

1. The purge control valve is located to the right side of the battery. Remove the purge control valve from the engine compartment.

2. Connect a hand vacuum pump to the vacuum nipple of the purge control valve.

3. Apply 15.7 in. Hg of vacuum and check air tightness. Blow in air lightly from the evaporative emission canister side nipple and check conditions as follows:

If there is no vacuum applied to the valve—air will not pass.

When 8.0 in. Hg of vacuum is applied to the valve—air will pass through.

4. Connect a hand vacuum pump to the positive pressure nipple of the purge control valve.

5. Apply a vacuum of 15.7 in. Hg and check for air tightness. The valve should be air tight.

6. If the results differ from the desired outcomes, replace the purge control valve.

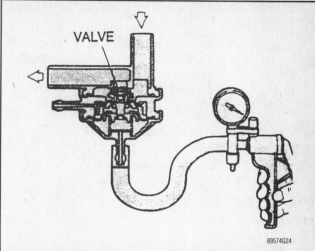

Fig. 16 Attach a hand vacuum pump to the nipple on the purge control valve

Evaporative Emission Purge Solenoid

1990–94 NON-TURBO AND 1993–94 TURBO ENGINES

▶ See Figures 17, 18, 19 and 20

1. Label and disconnect the 2 vacuum hoses from the purge control solenoid valve.

2. Disconnect the electrical harness connector from the solenoid.

3. Connect a hand vacuum pump to the nipple which the red striped vacuum hose was connected.

4. Check air tightness by applying a vacuum with voltage applied directly from the battery to the evaporative emission purge solenoid and without applying voltage. The desired results are as follows:

   —With battery voltage applied—vacuum should leak

   —With battery voltage not applied—vacuum should be maintained

5. Measure the resistance across the terminals of the solenoid. The desired reading is 36–44 ohms when at 68°F (20°C).

6. If any of the test results differ from the desired outcomes, replace the purge control solenoid.

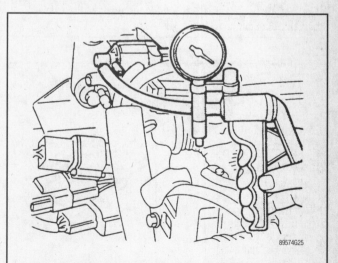

Fig. 17 Apply vacuum to the purge solenoid to check for air-tightness with and without voltage—1.8L engine

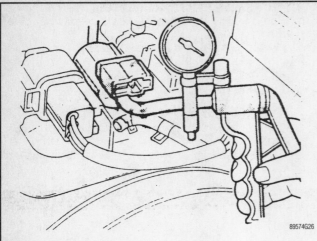

Fig. 18 Using a hand-held vacuum gauge to check for air-tightness—1990-94 2.0L non-turbo and 1993-94 2.0L turbo engines

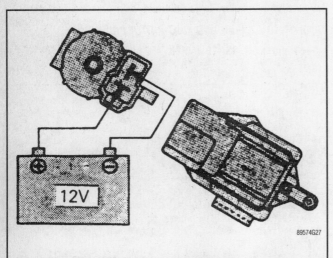

Fig. 19 Battery voltage applied to the terminals of the evaporative emission purge solenoid

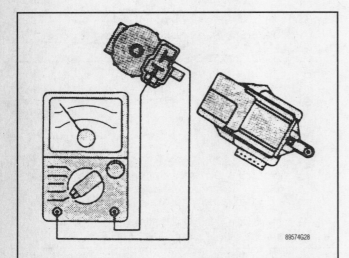

Fig. 20 Measuring the resistance between the terminals of the evaporative emission purge solenoid

1990-92 2.0L TURBO ENGINE

1. Label and disconnect the 2 vacuum hoses from the purge control solenoid valve.
2. Disconnect the electrical harness connector from the solenoid.
3. Connect a hand vacuum pump to the nipple which the red striped vacuum hose was connected.
4. Check air tightness by applying a vacuum with voltage applied directly from the battery to the evaporative emission purge solenoid and without applying voltage. With battery voltage applied, vacuum should be maintained. Without voltage, vacuum should leak
5. Measure the resistance across the terminals of the solenoid. The desired reading is 36-44 ohms when at 68°F (20°C).
6. If any of the test results differ from the specifications, replace the emission purge control solenoid.

1995-98 VEHICLES

▶ **See Figures 21, 22, 23 and 24**

1. Tag and disconnect the vacuum hoses from the solenoid valve.
2. Detach the harness connector.

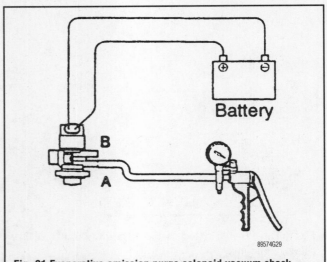

Fig. 21 Evaporative emission purge solenoid vacuum check—1995-98 2.0L non-turbo engine

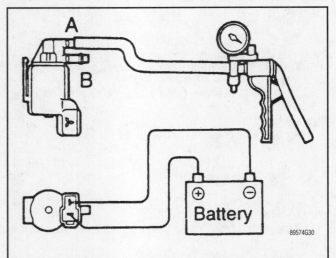

Fig. 22 Purge solenoid valve test connections—1995-98 2.0L turbo engine

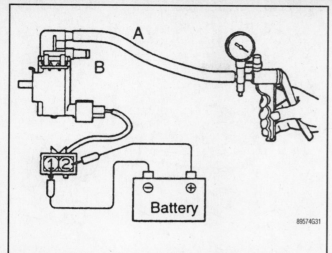

Fig. 23 Test connections for the evaporative purge solenoid—2.4L engine

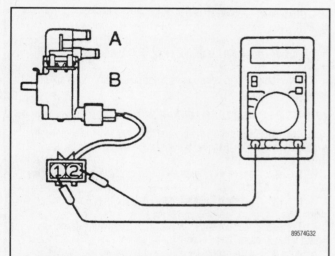

Fig. 24 Measure the resistance across the terminal of the solenoid valve—2.4L engine shown, others similar

3. Attach a hand-held vacuum pump to the nipple (A) of the solenoid valve, as shown in the accompanying figures.

4. Check air tightness by applying a vacuum with voltage applied directly from the battery to the evaporative emission purge solenoid and without applying voltage. The desired results are as follows:
—With battery voltage applied—vacuum should be maintained
—With battery voltage not applied—vacuum should leak

5. Measure the resistance across the terminals of the solenoid. The standard values are as follows:
   a. 2.0L non-turbo engines: 25–35 ohms when at 68°F (20°C).
   b. 2.0L turbo and 2.4L engines: 34–44 ohms when at 68°F (20°C).

6. If any of the test results differ from the specifications, replace the emission purge control solenoid.

REMOVAL & INSTALLATION

Evaporative Canister

▶ **See Figure 8**

1. Disconnect the negative battery cable.
2. If necessary, raise and safely support the vehicle, remove the front passengers side wheel, then remove the splash shield.
3. If necessary, remove the battery from the vehicle.

4. Tag and disconnect all necessary vacuum lines.
5. Unfasten and retaining bolts and/or straps, then remove the canister from the vehicle
6. Installation is the reverse of the removal procedure.

Solenoid Valves

▶ **See Figures 9, 10, 11 and 12**

1. Disconnect the negative battery cable.
2. Label and remove the vacuum and electrical harness connections from the purge control solenoid.
3. Remove the solenoid and mounting bracket from the engine compartment.
4. Installation is the reverse of the removal procedure.

Exhaust Gas Recirculation System

OPERATION

▶ **See Figure 25**

The Exhaust Gas Recirculation (EGR) system is used to reduce Oxides of Nitrogen (NOx) in the engine exhaust. This is accomplished by allowing a predetermined amount of hot exhaust gas to recirculate and dilute the incoming air and fuel mixture. This process reduces peak flame temperature during combustion. The system uses a vacuum-controlled Exhaust Gas Recirculation (EGR) valve, in order to modulate exhaust gas flow from the exhaust manifold into the intake manifold.

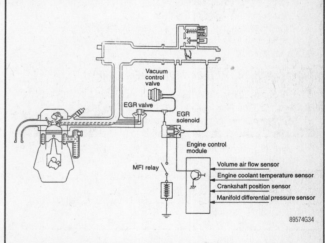

Fig. 25 Typical EGR system schematic—2.4L engine shown, others similar

COMPONENT TESTING

EGR Valve

▶ **See Figure 26**

1. Remove the EGR valve from the vehicle. Check for sticking of plunger caused by excess carbon deposits. If such a condition exists, clean with appropriate solvent so the valve seats correctly.
2. Connect a vacuum pump to the valve and apply 20 in. Hg (67 kPa) of vacuum.
3. Check for air tightness. If the valve has 2 vacuum ports; pick one and plug the other. The vacuum must be retained.
4. For 1990–94 vehicles, blow air from 1 passage of the EGR to check condition as follows:
   a. With 1.8 in. Hg (6 kPa) of vacuum or less applied to the valve, air should not pass through the valve.

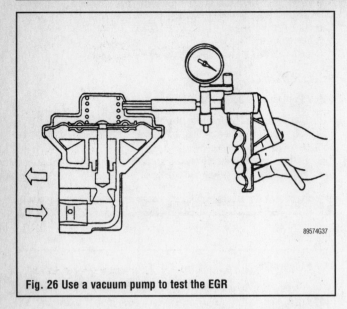

Fig. 26 Use a vacuum pump to test the EGR

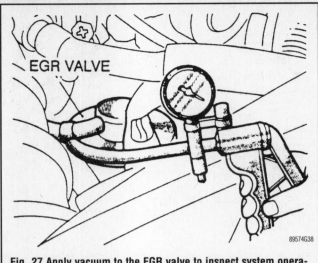

Fig. 27 Apply vacuum to the EGR valve to inspect system operation

b. With 8.5 in. Hg (28.7 kPa) of vacuum or more applied to the valve, air should pass through the valve.

5. For 1995–98 vehicles, apply vacuum (specified below) and check the passage of air by blowing through either side of the EGR passages, as follows:

a. With 1.6 in. Hg or less of vacuum applied to the valve, air should blow out of the opposite passage.

b. With 8.7 in. Hg or more of vacuum applies to the valve, air should not blow out of the opposite passage.

6. If the results are not as described, replace the EGR valve.

System Operation

1990–94 FEDERAL AND CANADIAN VEHICLES

1. Disconnect the green striped vacuum hose from the throttle body, then connect a hand-held vacuum pump to the vacuum hose.

2. Plug the nipple from which the vacuum hose was disconnected.

3. Under the engine conditions listed below, inspect the system operation by applying vacuum from a hand held vacuum pump.

4. With the engine temperature cold, 104°F (40°C) or below, the response should be as follows:

a. Engine at idle—vacuum should leak

5. With the engine at temperature of 176°F (80°C) or higher, the response should be as follows:

a. With 1.8 in. Hg (6 kPa) of vacuum applied—the engine should idle and vacuum should be maintained.

b. With 8.5 in. Hg (29 kPa) of vacuum applied—the engine should change from idling to slightly unstable and the vacuum should be maintained.

6. If the test results differ from those listed, thoroughly inspect the EGR system components.

1990–94 CALIFORNIA VEHICLES

▶ See Figure 27

1. Disconnect the green striped vacuum hose from the EGR valve and connect a hand vacuum pump through a 3-way connector. The pump will now be installed in the line.

2. With engine cold (below 68°F), test system operation as follows:

a. Race the engine by rapidly operating the accelerator.

b. Measure the pressure reading on the pump. The negative pressure at the valve should not change.

3. With the engine warm (68°F or more), test system operation as follows:

a. Race the engine by rapidly operating the accelerator

b. The negative pressure at the gauge rises to 3.9 in. Hg (13 kPa) or more.

4. Disconnect the 3-way terminal and connect a hand vacuum pump to the EGR valve.

5. When a negative pressure of 8.5 in. Hg (29 kPa) is applied during engine idling, check that the engine stops or the idle becomes unstable.

6. Inspect the system components if test results differ from specifications listed above.

1995–98 2.0L NON-TURBO ENGINES

1. Check the EGR control system and the valve with the engine fully warmed up running. The engine coolant temperature should be over 170°F (76°C.)

2. With the transaxle in Neutral, and the throttle close, let the engine idle for about 70 seconds.

3. Quickly accelerate the engine to about 2,000 rpm, but do not go over 3000 rpm.

4. The EGR valve stem should move when accelerating the engine. Repeat the test several times to confirm movement.

5. If the EGR valve stem moves, the control system is operating normally.

6. Disconnect and plug the vacuum hose from the EGR valve.

7. Connect a vacuum pump to the EGR valve. Check to see if the engine stalls or if the idle is unstable when a vacuum of 3.5 in. Hg (12 kPa) or higher is applied while the engine is idling.

1995–98 2.0L TURBO AND 2.4L ENGINES

▶ See Figures 28 and 29

1. Disconnect the vacuum hose (the 2.0L turbo has a green stripe and the 2.4L engine has a white stripe), then connect a hand-held vacuum pump to the 3-way terminal.

2. Check the condition of the vacuum when the engine has been raced rapidly, as follows:

a. When the engine is cold, coolant temperature at 68°F (20°C) or less, and the throttle is opened quickly, no vacuum should generate (it should remain as barometric pressure).

b. When the engine is hot, coolant temperature at 176°F (80°C) or higher, and the throttle quickly opened, the vacuum should momentarily rise over 3.9 in. Hg (13 kPa).

3. Disconnect the 3-way terminal.

4. Connect the vacuum pump right to the EGR valve.

5. Check to see if the engine stalls or if the idle is unstable when a vacuum of 7.9 in. Hg or higher is applied while the engine is idling.

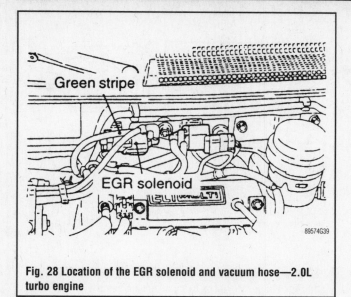

Fig. 28 Location of the EGR solenoid and vacuum hose—2.0L turbo engine

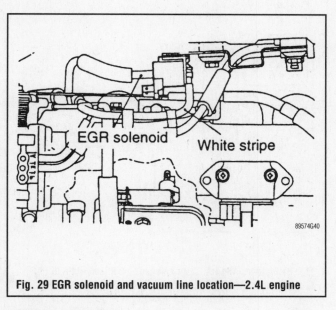

Fig. 29 EGR solenoid and vacuum line location—2.4L engine

EGR Temperature Sensor

▶ See Figure 30

The EGR temperature sensor is used on California vehicles only. The EGR temperature sensor detects the temperature of the gas passing through the EGR control valve. It converts the detected temperature into an electrical voltage signal which is sent the vehicles Engine Control Unit (ECU). If the circuit of the EGR temperature sensor is broken, the warning light will come on.

1. Remove the EGR temperature sensor from the engine.
2. Place the EGR sensor into water. While increasing the temperature of the water, measure the sensor resistance. Compare the values to following specifications:
    a. 122°F (50°C)—60–83 k.ohms resistance
    b. 212°F (100°C)—11–14 k.ohms resistance
3. If the resistance obtained varies significantly from specifications, replace the sensor.

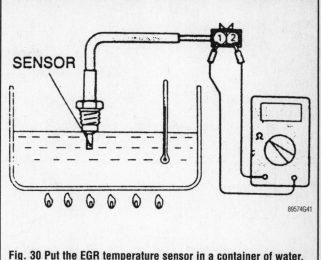

Fig. 30 Put the EGR temperature sensor in a container of water, then measure resistance as the water temperature is increased

Thermal Vacuum Valve

1992–94 FEDERAL AND CANADIAN 2.0L ENGINES

▶ See Figure 31

1. Label and disconnect the vacuum hose at the thermo valve.
2. Connect a hand held vacuum pump to the vacuum hose on the thermo valve.
3. Apply vacuum and check the air passage through the thermo valve. Compare results to the following specifications:
    a. Engine coolant temperature of 122°F (50°C) or less—vacuum leaks
    b. Engine coolant temperature of 176°F (80°C) or more—vacuum is maintained
4. If the results differ from the desired specifications, replace the valve.

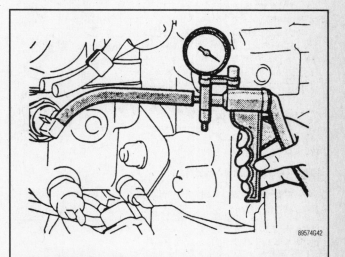

Fig. 31 Testing the thermal vacuum valve—2.0L engine (Federal) shown, others similar

EGR Port Vacuum Check

▶ **See Figures 32 and 33**

1. Disconnect the vacuum hose from the throttle body EGR vacuum nipple. Connect a hand-held vacuum pump to the nipple.

2. Start the engine, then slowly raise the speed and compare with the following specifications.

    a. For 1990–94 vehicles, check to be sure the vacuum raised proportionally with the rise in engine speed.

    b. For 1995–98 vehicles, the vacuum reading on the pump should remain constant.

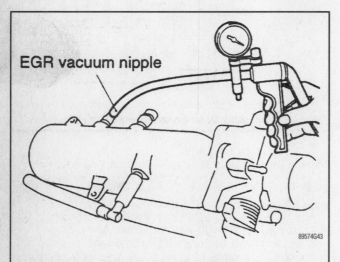

Fig. 32 Connect a vacuum pump to the EGR vacuum nipple on the throttle body—1995–98 2.0L non-turbo engine shown

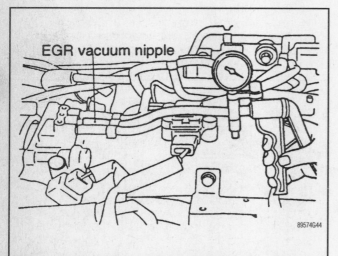

Fig. 33 Location of the throttle body EGR valve vacuum nipple—2.4L engine shown

EGR Solenoid

1990–94 VEHICLES

▶ **See Figures 34 and 35**

1. Label and disconnect the yellow and green striped vacuum hose from the EGR solenoid.

2. Disconnect the electrical harness connector.

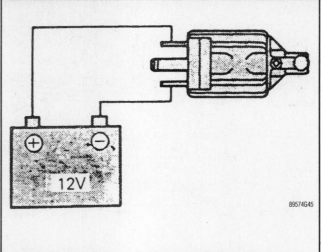

Fig. 34 Apply voltage to the EGR solenoid using jumper wires and check for air-tightness using a vacuum pump

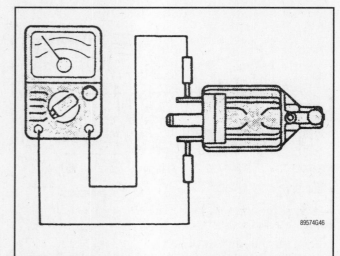

Fig. 35 Measure the resistance between the terminals of the EGR solenoid

3. Connect a hand vacuum pump to the nipple to which the green-striped vacuum hose was connected.

4. Apply a vacuum and check for air-tightness when voltage is applied and discontinued. When voltage is applied, the vacuum should be maintained. When voltage is discontinued, vacuum should leak.

5. Measure the resistance between the terminals of the solenoid valve. The resistance should be 36–44 ohms at 68°F (20°C).

6. If the test results differ from the specifications, replace the EGR solenoid.

1995–98 2.0L NON-TURBO ENGINE

▶ **See Figure 36**

➡On these engines, the solenoid is referred to as an electric EGR transducer solenoid.

1. Disconnect the vacuum hose from the electric EGR transducer.

2. Detach the harness connector.

3. Plug nipple A, then connect a hand vacuum pump to nipple B.

4. Use a jumper wire to connect the solenoid terminal to the battery terminal.

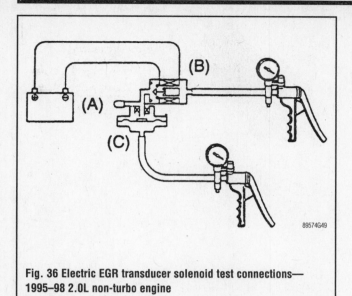

Fig. 36 Electric EGR transducer solenoid test connections— 1995–98 2.0L non-turbo engine

5. Turn on and off the negative battery terminal side under wire and apply vacuum and positive pressure to check the air tightness. Compare with the following specifications:

    a. With the jumper wire disconnected and pressure not applied, vacuum should leak.

    b. With the jumper wire disconnected and pressure applied, the vacuum should be maintained.

    c. With the jumper wire connected and pressure not applied, vacuum should be maintained.

6. Measure the resistance between the terminals of the solenoid. The resistance should be 25–35 ohms at 68°F (20°C).

7. If the test results differ from the specifications, replace the solenoid.

1995–98 2.0L TURBO AND 2.4L ENGINES

◗ **See Figures 37 and 38**

➡**Before disconnecting the vacuum hoses, tag them to assure proper connection during installation**

1. Tag and disconnect the vacuum hose (2.0L turbo engine: yellow stripe, white and green stripe, 2.4L engine: yellow stripe and white stripe) from the solenoid valve.

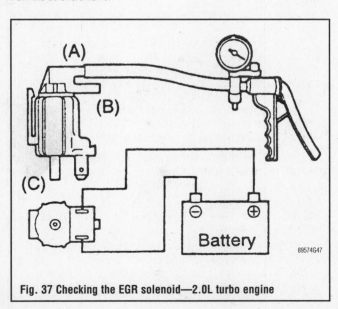

Fig. 37 Checking the EGR solenoid—2.0L turbo engine

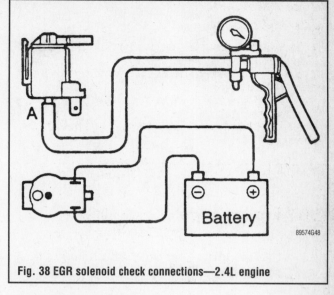

Fig. 38 EGR solenoid check connections—2.4L engine

2. Detach the harness connector.

3. Connect a hand-held vacuum pump to the nipple to which the white stripe vacuum hose was connected (2.0L turbo) or the A nipple (2.4L).

4. Check air tightness by applying a vacuum with voltage applied directly from the battery to the EGR control solenoid valve and without applying voltage.

5. For 2.0L turbo engines, compare with the following:

    a. With battery voltage not applied and the B nipple open, vacuum should be maintained.

    b. With battery voltage applied and the B nipple open, vacuum should leak.

    c. With battery voltage applied and the B nipple closed, vacuum should be maintained.

    d. For the 2.4L engines, compare with the following:

    e. With battery voltage not applied, vacuum should be maintained.

    f. With battery voltage applied, vacuum should leak.

6. Using an ohmmeter, measure the resistance between the solenoid valve terminals. The resistance should fall between 36–44 ohms when the engine temperature is 68°F (20°C).

REMOVAL & INSTALLATION

EGR Valve

◗ **See Figure 39**

1. Disconnect the negative battery cable.

2. Remove the air cleaner and intake hoses as required.

3. Tag and disconnect the vacuum hose from the EGR valve.

4. Remove the mounting bolts and the EGR valve from the engine.

5. Clean the mating surfaces on the valve and the engine. Make sure to remove all gasket material.

6. Inspect the valve for a sticking plunger, caused by excess carbon deposits. If such a condition exists, clean with appropriate solvent so valve seats correctly.

To install:

7. Install EGR valve with a new gasket in place.

8. Install the mounting bolts and tighten as follows:

- 1.8L engine—7–10 ft. lbs. (10—15 Nm).
- 1990–94 2.0L engine—10–15 ft. lbs. (15—22 Nm).
- 1995–98 engines—16 ft. lbs. (22 Nm).

9. Connect the vacuum hose to the EGR valve.

10. Install the air cleaner and air intake hoses as required.

11. Connect the negative battery cable.

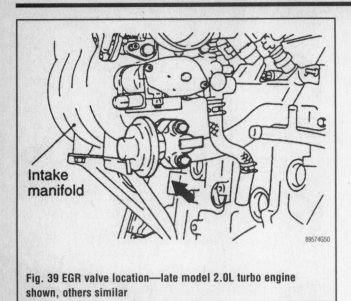

Fig. 39 EGR valve location—late model 2.0L turbo engine shown, others similar

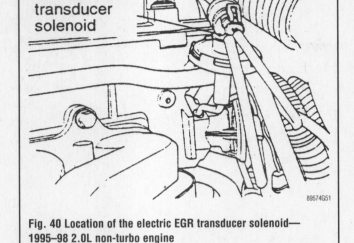

Fig. 40 Location of the electric EGR transducer solenoid—1995–98 2.0L non-turbo engine

EGR Temperature Sensor

1. Disconnect the negative battery cable.
2. Detach the electrical connector from the sensor.
3. Remove the sensor from the engine.

To install:

4. Install the sensor to the engine and tighten to 8 ft. lbs. (12 Nm).
5. Attach the electrical connector to the sensor.
6. Connect the negative battery cable.

Thermal Vacuum Valve

1. Disconnect the negative battery cable.
2. Detach the vacuum line from the thermo valve.
3. Using a wrench, remove the valve from the engine.

➡**When removing or installing the valve, do not allow wrenches or other tool to contact the resin part of the valve. Damage to the valve may occur.**

4. Inspect the vacuum hose for cracks and replace as required.

To install:

5. Apply sealant to the threads of the thermo valve and install into the engine.
6. Tighten the valve to 15–30 ft. lbs. (20–40 Nm). When installing the valve, do not allow the wrench to come in contact with the resin part of the valve.
7. Attach the vacuum hose to the valve.
8. Connect the negative battery cable.

EGR Solenoid

▶ **See Figures 40 and 41**

1. Disconnect the negative battery cable.
2. Label and disconnect the vacuum hoses from the EGR solenoid.
3. Disconnect the electrical harness from the solenoid.
4. Remove the solenoid from the mounting bracket and replace as required.

To install:

5. Install the solenoid to the mounting bracket and secure in position.
6. Attach the electrical connector.

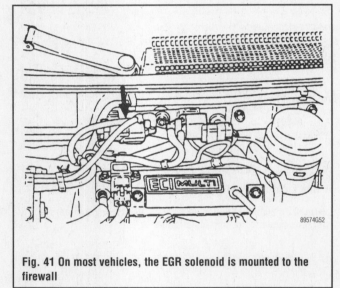

Fig. 41 On most vehicles, the EGR solenoid is mounted to the firewall

7. Connect the vacuum hoses to the solenoid making sure they are installed in their original location.
8. Connect the negative battery cable.

Thermal Vacuum Valve

1. Disconnect the negative battery cable.
2. Disconnect the vacuum line from the thermo valve.
3. Using a wrench, remove the valve from the engine.

➡**When removing or installing the valve, do not allow wrenches or other tool to contact the resin part of the valve. Damage to the valve may occur.**

4. Inspect the vacuum hose for cracks and replace as required.

To install:

5. Apply sealant to the threads of the thermo valve and install into the engine.

6. Tighten the valve to 15–30 ft. lbs. (20–40 Nm). When installing the valve, do not allow the wrench to come in contact with the resin part of the valve.

7. Reconnect the vacuum hose to the valve.

8. Reconnect the negative battery cable.

Manifold Differential Pressure Sensor

▶ See Figure 42

1. Disconnect the negative battery cable.
2. Unfasten the sensor electrical connector.
3. Unfasten the retaining bolts, then remove the sensor from the vehicle.
4. Installation is the reverse of the removal procedure.

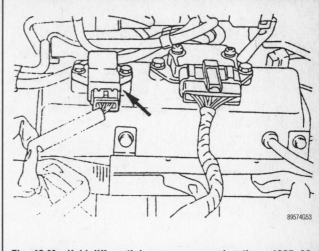

Fig. 42 Manifold differential pressure sensor location—1995–98 2.0L turbo engine

ELECTRONIC ENGINE CONTROLS

Engine Control Unit (ECU)

GENERAL INFORMATION

➡ When the term Electronic Control Unit (ECU) is used in this manual, it will refer to the engine control computer regardless that it may be a Electronic Control Unit (ECU), Powertrain Control Module (PCM) or Engine Control Module (ECM).

The heart of the electronic control system, which is found on the vehicles covered by this manual, is a computer control module. The module gathers information from various sensors, then controls fuel supply and engine emission systems. Most early model vehicles are equipped with an Engine Control Module (ECM) which, as its name implies, controls the engine and related emissions systems. Some ECMs may also control the Torque Converter Clutch (TCC) on automatic transaxle vehicles or the manual upshift light on manual transmission vehicles. Later model vehicles may be equipped with a Powertrain Control Module (PCM). This is similar to the original ECMs, but is designed to control additional systems as well. The PCM may control the manual transmission shift lamp or the shift functions of the electronically controlled automatic transmission.

Regardless of the name, all computer control modules are serviced in a similar manner. Care must be taken when handling these expensive components in order to protect them from damage. Carefully follow all instructions included with the replacement part. Avoid touching pins or connectors to prevent damage from static electricity.

❊❊ WARNING

To prevent the possibility of permanent control module damage, the ignition switch MUST always be OFF when disconnecting power from or reconnecting power to the module. This includes unplugging the module connector, disconnecting the negative battery cable, removing the module fuse or even attempting to jump your dead battery using jumper cables.

REMOVAL & INSTALLATION

▶ See Figures 43, 44 and 45

1. Turn the ignition switch to the OFF position.
2. If the ECU is mounted under the dash, remove the left and/or right side panel from the center console, or remove the under dash panel.
3. Remove the bolts holding the ECU to the mounting bracket.
4. Disconnect the wiring harness from the ECU and remove ECU from the vehicle.

To install:

5. Connect the electrical harness to the ECU. Make certain the multi-pin connector is firmly and squarely seated to the ECU.
6. Install the ECU in the mounting bracket and secure in position.

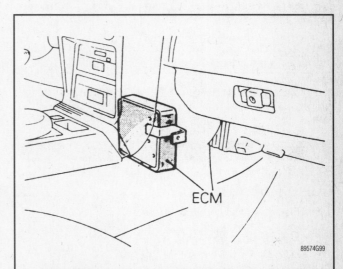

Fig. 43 On 1990–94 vehicles, the ECM is mounted behind the center console

Fig. 44 The ECM is located under the dash, on 1995–98 2.0L non-turbo engines

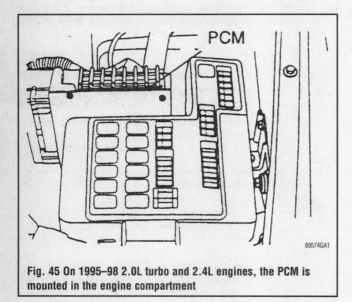

Fig. 45 On 1995–98 2.0L turbo and 2.4L engines, the PCM is mounted in the engine compartment

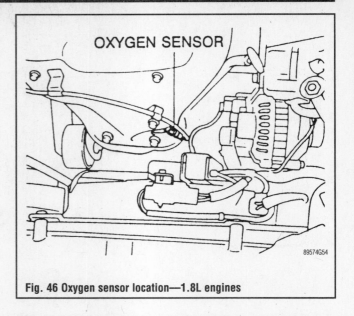

Fig. 46 Oxygen sensor location—1.8L engines

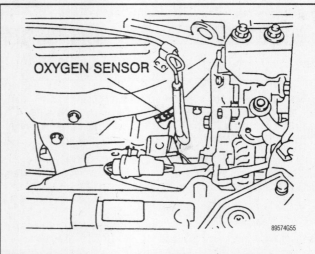

Fig. 47 Early 2.0L engines were equipped with a non-heated oxygen sensor. Later models utilized a heated one

7. If necessary, install the side panels to the center console or dash panel.

8. Connect the negative battery cable.

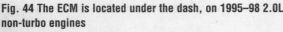

Non-Heated Oxygen Sensor

OPERATION

▶ See Figures 46 and 47

The oxygen sensor is usually located on the gathering area of the exhaust manifolds. All exhaust gas leaving the engine flows past the oxygen sensor. The oxygen sensor produces an electrical voltage when exposed to oxygen present in the exhaust gases. Where there is a large amount of oxygen present (lean mixture), the sensor produces a low voltage. When there is a lesser amount of oxygen present (rich mixture), the sensor produces a higher voltage. By monitoring the oxygen content and converting it to electrical voltage, the sensor acts as a rich/lean switch. The voltage from the sensor is transmitted to the Engine Control Unit (ECU), which changes the fuel injection ratio accordingly. On later models, the oxygen sensor may be electrically heated internally. This allows for faster switching during cold engine operation.

TESTING

➡If the oxygen sensor has failed, the driveability of the vehicle may not be influenced. Since the air fuel mixture ratio shifts toward the rich side, the driveability of the vehicle may become better. However, levels of hazardous components such as HC, CO, and NOx emitted out the tailpipe will be elevated. This is because the ECU is not controlling the air fuel mixture.

1.8L Engine

▶ See Figure 48

1. Before testing, make certain the engine is fully warm. Coolant temperature must be around 176–194°F (80–90°C).

2. Detach the oxygen sensor electrical connector.

3. Connect the positive probe of a digital ohmmeter to terminal 1 of the sensor connector. Attach the other meter probe to chassis ground.

4. Repeatedly race the engine; measure the voltage output of the sensor. As the mixture becomes richer from repeated racing of the engine, the sensor output voltage should register 0.6–1.0 volts.

5. If the voltage output is incorrect, the sensor will require replacement.

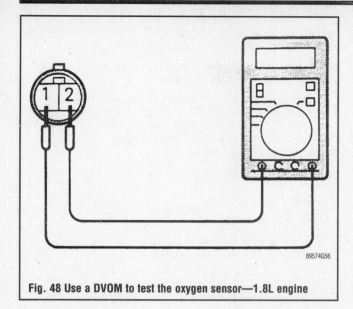

Fig. 48 Use a DVOM to test the oxygen sensor—1.8L engine

6. Shut the ignition OFF, disconnect the test equipment and reconnect the sensor to the wiring harness.

2.0L Engine

▶ **See Figures 49 and 50**

1. Detach the oxygen sensor electrical connector.
2. Measure the resistance between terminal Nos. 3 and 4. Correct resistance is approximately 12 ohms at 68°F.
3. If there is no continuity or if the resistance is not approximately correct, the sensor must be replaced.
4. Operate the engine until fully warmed up. Coolant temperature must be at least 176°F.
5. Using jumper wires, carefully connect terminal 3 to battery positive voltage and connect terminal No. 4 to a known good ground.

➡**Use extreme care when connecting the jumpers. Incorrect circuiting will destroy the sensor.**

6. Connect the probes of a digital voltmeter across to terminal No. 1 and terminal No. 2.
7. Repeatedly race the engine; measure the voltage output of the sensor. As the mixture becomes richer from repeated racing of the engine, the sensor output voltage should become 0.6–1.0 volt.

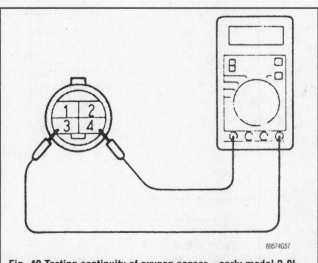

Fig. 49 Testing continuity of oxygen sensor—early model 2.0L engine

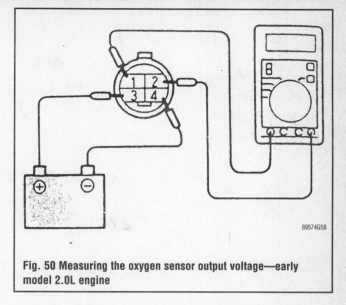

Fig. 50 Measuring the oxygen sensor output voltage—early model 2.0L engine

8. If the voltage output is incorrect, the sensor must be replaced.
9. Shut the ignition OFF, disconnect the test equipment and reconnect the sensor to the wiring harness.

REMOVAL & INSTALLATION

> ❉❉ **CAUTION**

The temperature of the exhaust system is extremely high after the engine has been run. To prevent personal injury, allow the exhaust system to cool completely before removing sensor from the exhaust system.

1. Detach the negative battery cable.
2. Raise and safely support the vehicle.
3. Detach the electrical connector from the oxygen sensor.
4. Using socket MD998770, or equivalent oxygen sensor socket, remove the oxygen sensor.

To install:

5. If installing old oxygen sensor, coat the threads with anti-seize compound. New sensors are already coated. Take care not to contaminate the oxygen sensor probe with the anti-seize compound.
6. Install the oxygen sensor into the exhaust manifold. Tighten the sensor, using the correct tool, to 33 ft. lbs. (45 Nm)
7. Attach the wiring to the sensor.
8. Carefully lower the vehicle.
9. Connect the negative battery cable.

Heated Oxygen Sensor

OPERATION

➡**Some late model vehicles utilize two heated oxygen sensors. One mounted in the exhaust manifold, and one threaded into the exhaust pipe.**

The heated oxygen sensor, mounted in the exhaust gas flow, is a device which produces an electrical voltage when exposed to oxygen present in the engine exhaust gases. The electrical voltage produced by the oxygen sensor is proportional to the amount of oxygen present in the exhaust and therefore, representative of the air/fuel ratio. The voltage produced by the sensor is sent to the ECM. The ECM will check whether the actual air/fuel mixture ratio is richer or leaner than the optimal (theoretical) ratio, and adjust accordingly. The heated oxygen sensor is electrically heated internally for faster switching during cold engine operation.

If the oxygen sensor has malfunctioned, the driveability of the vehicle may not be influenced. However, hazardous components (HC, CO, NOx) in the exhaust gas will increase.

TESTING

1990–94 2.0L Engine

▶ See Figures 51 and 52

1. Disconnect the oxygen sensor connector. Connect test harness MD998464 or equivalent, to the sensor harness. If the test harness is not available, perform the test procedure using the sensor harness terminals listed below. The color codes may not be the same on the sensor harness as they are for the test harness.

2. Measure the resistance across terminals **4** (blue connector of test harness) and **3** (red connector of test harness) of the oxygen sensor test connector or sensor harness. If no continuity, replace the sensor.

3. Start and run the engine until normal operating temperature is reached.

4. Using jumper wires, connect terminals **3** (red connector of test harness) and **4** (blue connector of test harness) of the oxygen sensor harness connector to the battery positive and negative terminals respectively.

➡ **Be sure to connect the voltmeter to the terminals carefully. Any short circuits could damage the sensor.**

5. Connect a digital voltmeter across terminals **1** (yellow connector of test harness) and **2** (black connector of test harness).While repeatedly racing the engine, measure the output voltage of the sensor.

6. The desired reading is 0.6–1.0 volts. If the reading differs from the desired voltage, replace the sensor.

1995–98 Vehicles

2.0L NON-TURBO ENGINE

▶ See Figures 53 and 54

1. To test the front heated oxygen sensor, perform the following:
   a. Disconnect the heated oxygen sensor connector.
   b. Using an digital voltmeter (DVOM), check for continuity (about 12

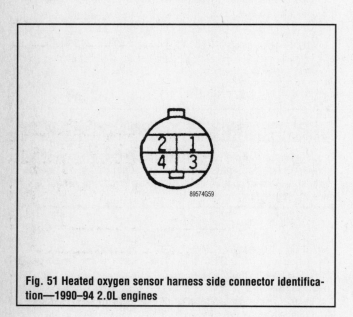

Fig. 51 Heated oxygen sensor harness side connector identification—1990–94 2.0L engines

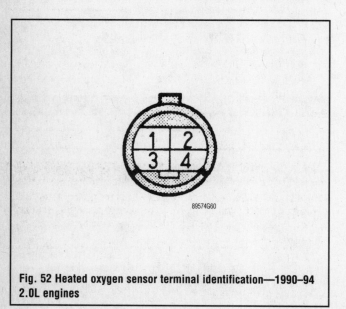

Fig. 52 Heated oxygen sensor terminal identification—1990–94 2.0L engines

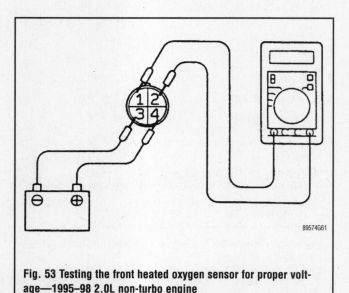

Fig. 53 Testing the front heated oxygen sensor for proper voltage—1995–98 2.0L non-turbo engine

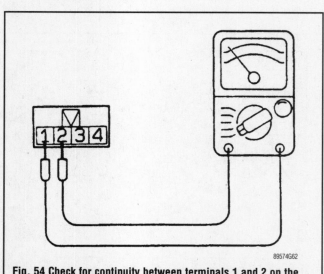

Fig. 54 Check for continuity between terminals 1 and 2 on the rear oxygen sensor—1995–98 2.0L non-turbo engine

volts at 68°F) between terminals 3 and 4 on the connector. If there is no continuity, replace the sensor.

    c. Start the engine and let run until normal operating temperatures are reached.

❋❋ WARNING

When connecting the jumper wires, be very careful, as the sensor can be damaged!

    d. Use jumper wires to connect terminal 3 of the sensor connector to the positive battery terminal and terminal 4 to the negative battery terminal.

    e. Connect a digital voltmemter between terminals 1 and 2.

    f. While repeatedly racing the engine, measure the voltage. It should be 0.6–1.0 volts. If not, replace the sensor.

2. To test the rear heated oxygen sensor, perform the following:

    a. Disconect the heated oxygen sensor connector.

    b. Using an digital voltmeter (DVOM), check for continuity (about 12 volts at 68°F) between terminals 1 and 2 on the connector. If there is no continuity, replace the sensor.

2.0L TURBO AND 2.4L ENGINES

▶ **See Figures 55, 56 and 57**

1. To test the front heated oxygen sensor, perform the following:

    a. Disconect the heated oxygen sensor connector and attach the special test harness (MD998464 or equivalent) to the connector on the heated oxygen sensor side.

    b. Make sure there is continuity (about 12 volts at 68°F) between terminal 1 (red clip) and terminal 3 (blue clip) on the heated oxygen sensor connector. If there is no continuity, replace the sensor.

    c. Start the engine and let run until normal operating temperatures are reached.

❋❋ WARNING

When connecting the jumper wires, be very careful, as the sensor can be damaged!

    d. Use jumper wires to connect terminal 1 (red clip) on the sensor connector to the positive battery cable and terminal 3 (blue clip) to the negative battery terminal.

    e. Connect a DVOM between terminal 2 (black clip) and 4 (white clip).

    f. While repeatedly racing the engine, measure the voltage. It should be 0.6–1.0 volts. If not, replace the sensor.

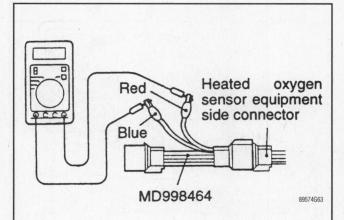

Fig. 55 Testing front heated oxygen sensor connector—1995–98 2.0L turbo and 2.4L engines

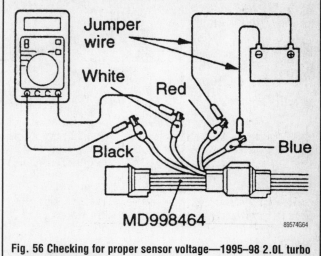

Fig. 56 Checking for proper sensor voltage—1995–98 2.0L turbo and 2.4L engines

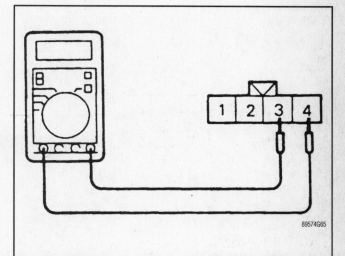

Fig. 57 Testing the rear oxygen sensor continuity—1995–98 2.0L turbo and 2.4L engines

2. To test the rear heated oxygen sensor, perform the following:

    a. Disconect the heated oxygen sensor connector.

    b. Using an digital voltmeter (DVOM), check for continuity (about 12 volts at 68°F) between terminals 3 and 4 on the connector. If there is no continuity, replace the sensor.

REMOVAL & INSTALLATION

▶ **See Figures 58, 59 and 60**

❋❋ CAUTION

The oxygen sensor, exhaust system and surrounding components become very hot during engine operation. Avoid personal injury by waiting for a cooled motor or wearing protective clothing and gloves.

1. Disconnect negative battery cable.
2. Raise and safely support the vehicle.
3. Remove the oxygen sensor from the exhaust manifold, or exhaust pipe, as applicable.

Fig. 58 Use a wrench or an oxygen sensor socket to loosen the sensor

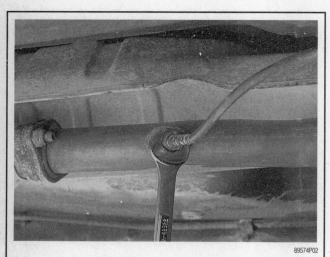

Fig. 59 Some models also use a second oxygen sensor threaded into the exhaust pipe near the catalytic converter

Fig. 60 Once loosened, remove the sensor from the exhaust pipe

To install:

4. If not already done, coat the threads of the replacement sensor with anti-seize compound. New sensors are already coated with the substance. Take great care not to contaminate the oxygen sensor probe with the anti-seize compound.

5. Install the oxygen sensor into the exhaust manifold or pipe, as applicable. Tighten the sensor to 33 ft. lbs. (45 Nm).

6. Reconnect the wiring harness to the sensor. Connect the negative battery cable.

Engine Coolant Temperature (ECT) Sensor

OPERATION

The engine coolant temperature sensor is located on the thermostat housing. It is a resistor type sensor which detects the engine coolant temperature. The warm-up state of the engine is judged from the sensor output voltage. When a cold signal is sent to the ECU, the fuel injection amount, idle revolution speed and the injection timing are suitably controlled.

When the coolant temperature sensor is faulty, the engine coolant temperature is regarded as being 176°F (80°C). Because of this, engine starting may be difficult, driveability may become poor and the idle quality may suffer during cold operating conditions. The trouble may not be noticed when the engine is at normal operating temperature.

TESTING

Except 1995–98 2.0L Non-Turbo Engine

▶ **See Figure 61**

1. Drain the engine coolant to a level below the intake manifold.

2. Disconnect the sensor wiring harness and remove the coolant temperature sensor from the engine.

3. Place the temperature sensing portion of the sensor into a pan of hot water. Use a thermometer to monitor the water temperature.

4. Measure the resistance across the sensor terminals while the sensor is in the water. Compare obtained reading to specifications:

    a. Water temperature of 32°F (0°C)—5.1–6.5 kilo-ohms present

    b. Water temperature of 68°F (20°C)—2.1–2.7 kilo-ohms present

    c. Water temperature of 104°F (40°C)—0.9–1.3 kilo-ohms present

    d. Water temperature of 176°F (80°C)—0.26–0.36 kilo-ohms present

5. If the resistance differs greatly from standard value, replace the sensor.

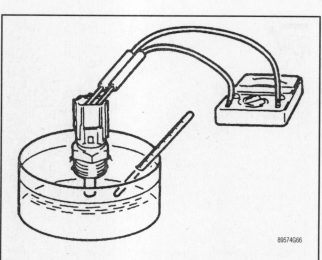

Fig. 61 Measure resistance with the ECT sensor in a pan of water—except 1995–98 2.0L turbo engines

1995–98 2.0L Non-Turbo Engine

▶ **See Figure 62**

1. Detach the engine coolant temperature sensor connector.
2. Measure the resistance between the sensor terminals, and compare with the following specifications:
    a. At 77°F (25°C) the resistance should be 9–11 kilo-ohms.
    b. At 212°F (100°C) the resistance should be 0.6–0.8 kilo-ohms.
3. If resistance falls outside of specifications, replace the sensor.

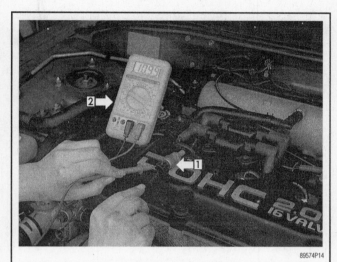

Fig. 62 Measure the resistance of the engine coolant temperature sensor (1) with an ohmmeter (2)—1996 2.0L engine shown

REMOVAL & INSTALLATION

▶ **See Figures 63, 64, 65 and 66**

1. Disconnect the negative battery cable.
2. Drain the engine coolant to a level below the intake manifold.
3. Unplug the sensor wiring harness.
4. Unthread and remove the sensor from the engine.

To install:

5. Coat the threads of the sensor with a suitable sealant and thread into the housing.

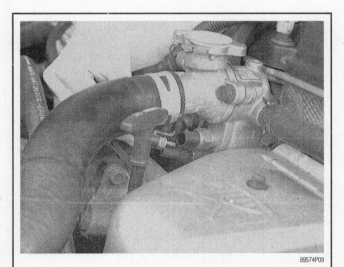

Fig. 63 Unplug the ECT sensor electrical connector

Fig. 64 Use a deep socket and an extension to reach the ECT sensor . . .

Fig. 65 . . . then remove the ECT sensor from the thermostat housing

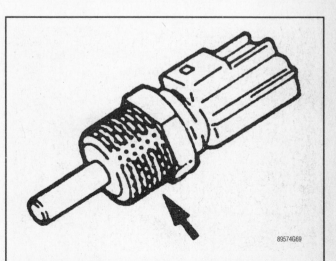

Fig. 66 Before installation, coat the threads of the sensor with a suitable sealant

6. Tighten the sensor to 22 ft. lbs. (30 Nm) for all except 1995–98 2.0L non-turbo engines. For 1995–98 2.0L non-turbo engines, tighten the sensor to 5 ft. lbs. (7 Nm).
7. Refill the cooling system to the proper level.
8. Attach the electrical connector to the sensor securely.
9. Connect the negative battery cable.

Intake Air Temperature (IAT) Sensor

OPERATION

▶ **See Figures 67 and 68**

The intake air temperature sensor (provided on the air flow sensor on all engines, except the 1995–98 2.0L non-turbo) is a resistor which measures the intake air temperature. The ECU will determine the intake air temperature according to the output voltage from the sensor, and compensates the fuel injection amount according to the intake air temperature.

When the intake air temperature sensor is faulty, it controls the fuel injection amount based on an intake air temperature default of 77°F (25°C).

The driveability of the vehicle may become poor during cold temperature operation. The trouble may not be noticeable when the ambient temperature is around 77°F (25°C).

TESTING

Except 1995–98 2.0L Non-Turbo Engine

▶ **See Figures 69, 70 and 71**

1. Detach the air flow sensor electrical connector.
2. If equipped with non-turbo engines, measure the resistance between terminals No. 4 and No. 6 of the electrical connector.
3. If equipped with turbo engine, measure the resistance between terminals No. 6 and No. 8 of the sensor electric connector.
4. Compare test readings to specifications:
    a. Sensor temperature of 32°F (0°C)—5.3–6.7 kilo-ohms
    b. Sensor temperature of 68°F (20°C)—2.3–3.0 kilo-ohms
    c. Sensor temperature of 176°F (80°C)—0.30–0.42 kilo-ohms
5. Measure the sensor resistance while heating the sensor area with a

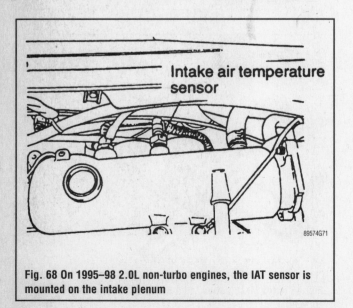

Fig. 67 Location of the intake air temperature sensor (integral with the volume air flow sensor)—1990–94 vehicles

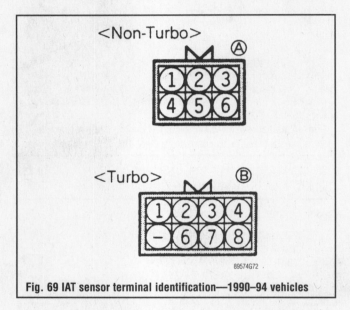

Fig. 69 IAT sensor terminal identification—1990–94 vehicles

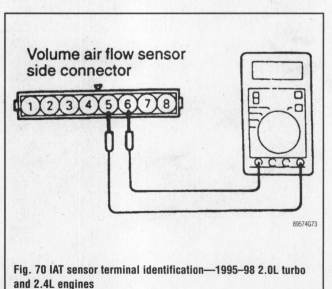

Fig. 70 IAT sensor terminal identification—1995–98 2.0L turbo and 2.4L engines

Fig. 68 On 1995–98 2.0L non-turbo engines, the IAT sensor is mounted on the intake plenum

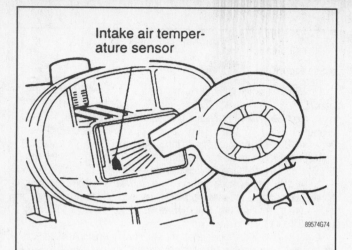

Fig. 71 Measure the intake air temperature sensor resistance while heating it with a hair drier

hair dryer. As the temperature of the sensor increases, sensor resistance should become smaller.

6. If the measured resistance deviates from the standard value or the resistance remains unchanged, replace the air flow sensor assembly.

1995–98 2.0L Non-Turbo Engine

▶ See Figure 72

1. Detach the IAT sensor connector.
2. If necessary, you can remove the sensor to test it.
3. Use a DVOM to measure the resistance between the sensor terminals and compare with the following specifications:
   a. At 77°F (25°C), the resistance should be 9–11 kilo-ohms.
   b. At 212°F (100°C), the resistance should be 0.6–0.8 ohms.
4. If the resistance is not within the specified range, replace the sensor.
5. If removed, install the sensor. Attach the connector.

Fig. 72 Use an ohmmeter (1) to measure the resistance of the IAT sensor (2). Note that this sensor is within specifications

REMOVAL & INSTALLATION

Except 1995–98 2.0L Non-Turbo Engines

▶ See Figure 67

1. Disconnect the negative battery cable.
2. Unplug the sensor electrical connector from the sensor.
3. If necessary, carefully remove the lid of the air filter housing.
4. Unfasten the retainers, then remove the sensor from the air cleaner housing.
5. Installation is the reverse of the removal procedure.

1995–98 2.0L Non-Turbo Engines

▶ See Figures 73, 74 and 75

1. Disconnect the negative battery cable.
2. Detach the IAT sensor harness connector.
3. Unthread the IAT sensor and remove from the intake plenum.

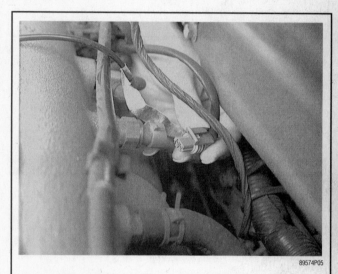

Fig. 73 Unplug the IAT sensor electrical connector

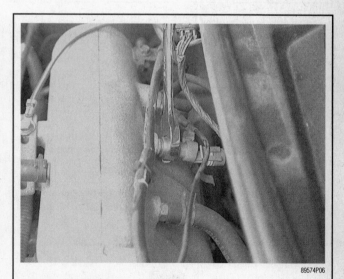

Fig. 74 Use a open-end wrench to loosen . . .

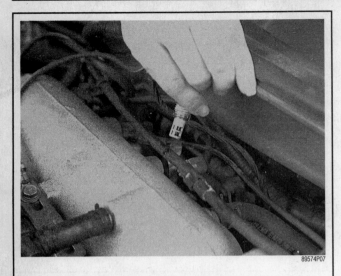

89574P07

Fig. 75 . . . then remove the IAT sensor from the vehicle

To install:

4. Apply Loctite® 24200 or equivalent sealant to the threads of the sensor and install in the intake plenum. Tighten the sensor to 5 ft. lbs. (7 Nm.

5. Attach the sensor electrical connector. Make sure it is connected securely.

6. Connect the negative battery cable.

Air Flow Sensor

OPERATION

The air flow sensor, including the air temperature sensor and barometric pressure sensor, is located inside the air filter housing. Care must be used when removing the air filter housing cover to avoid damaging the sensor assembly.

TESTING

Please refer to the intake air temperature sensor testing procedure in this section.

REMOVAL & INSTALLATION

1. Disconnect the negative battery cable.

2. Replacing the sensor requires disconnecting the electrical connector, then carefully removing the lid of the air filter housing.

➡**Handle the sensor assembly carefully, protecting it from impact, extremes of temperature and/or exposure to shop chemicals.**

3. Installation is the reverse of the removal procedure.

Throttle Position Sensor (TPS)

OPERATION

The Throttle Position Sensor (TPS) is an electrical resistor which is activated by the movement of the throttle shaft. It is mounted on the throttle body and senses the angle of the throttle blade opening. The voltage that the sensor produces increases or decreases according to the throttle blade opening. This voltage is transmitted to the ECU where it is used along with data from other sensors to adjust the air/fuel ratio to varying conditions and during acceleration, deceleration, idle, with wide open throttle operations.

TESTING

1990 Vehicles

▶ **See Figure 76**

1. With the ignition **OFF**, disconnect the sensor connector from the harness.

2. If equipped with 1.8L engine, connect test harness MD998474 or equivalent, to the TPS harness. If equipped with 2.0L engine, connect test harness MD998464 or equivalent, to the TPS harness. The test harness will prevent damage to the female connector. If the test is done without the test harness, do not insert the test probe into the female connector of the sensor.

3. On 1.8L engine, using an analog (needle type) ohmmeter, measure the resistance across the sensor power supply terminal (black clip) and the sensor ground terminal (red clip). Normal resistance is 3500–6500 ohms (3.5–6.5 Kohm;).

4. If equipped with 2.0L engine, using an analog (needle type) ohmmeter, measure the resistance across the sensor power supply terminal (white clip) and the sensor ground terminal (red clip). Normal resistance is 3500–6500 ohms (3.5–6.5 Kohm;).

5. If the measured value differs from the desired readings, the sensor must be replaced.

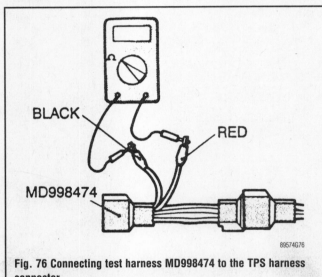

89574G76

Fig. 76 Connecting test harness MD998474 to the TPS harness connector

1991–98 Vehicles

▶ **See Figures 77, 78, 79, 80 and 81**

1. With the ignition **OFF**, detach the TP sensor connector.

2. For all vehicles, except 1995–98 2.0L non turbo engines, proceed as follows:

   a. Using an ohmmeter, measure the resistance across terminal No. **1** (sensor power supply) and terminal No. **4** (sensor ground terminal). Normal resistance is 3500–6500 ohms (3.5–6.5 Kohm;).

   b. Move the ohmmeter probes to test across terminal **2** and terminal **4**. Slowly operate the throttle from idle to wide open; the resistance shown on the meter must change evenly and in proportion to throttle movement.

3. For 1995–98 2.0L non-turbo engines, proceed as follows:

   a. Attach an ohmmeter, then measure the resistance across terminals 1 and 3. The resistance should be 3.5–6.5 kilo-ohms.

   b. Attach an ohmmeter, then measure the resistance across terminals 2 and 3.

   c. Open the throttle valve slowly until it is fully open from the idle position. The resistance should change smoothly to the opening angle of the throttle valve.

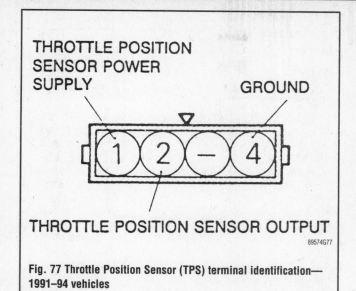

THROTTLE POSITION SENSOR POWER SUPPLY

GROUND

1 2 — 4

THROTTLE POSITION SENSOR OUTPUT

89574G77

Fig. 77 Throttle Position Sensor (TPS) terminal identification—1991–94 vehicles

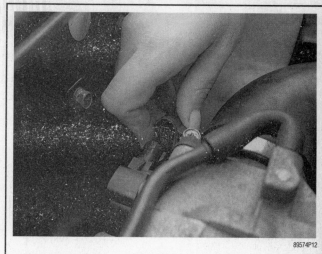

89574P12

Fig. 80 To measure the resistance, unplug the TPS electrical connector . . .

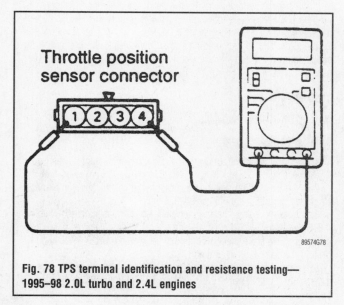

Throttle position sensor connector

1 2 3 4

89574G78

Fig. 78 TPS terminal identification and resistance testing—1995–98 2.0L turbo and 2.4L engines

89574P13

Fig. 81 . . . then use an ohmmeter to see if it is within specifications

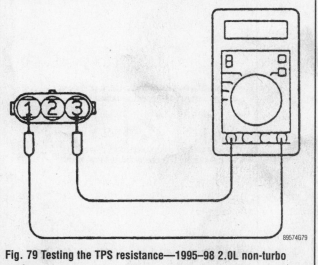

1 2 3

89574G79

Fig. 79 Testing the TPS resistance—1995–98 2.0L non-turbo engine

4. If resistance is out of specification or fails to change smoothly, the sensor must be replaced.

REMOVAL & INSTALLATION

▶ **See Figure 82**

1. Disconnect negative battery cable.
2. Detach the electrical connector from the throttle position sensor.
3. Remove the mounting screws from the sensor, being careful not to round the Phillips screw head.
4. Remove the sensor from the throttle body.
To install:
5. Install the throttle position sensor onto the throttle body and rotate the sensor counterclockwise on the throttle shaft and temporarily tighten the screws.
6. Connect the electrical harness to the sensor.
7. Tighten the retainer screws to 1.8 ft. lbs. (2.5 Nm).
8. Connect the negative battery cable.

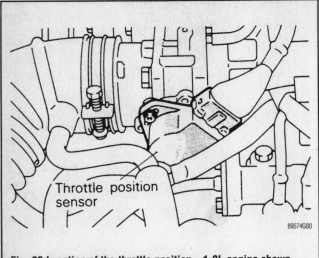

Fig. 82 Location of the throttle position—1.8L engine shown, others similar

Camshaft Position (CMP) Sensor

OPERATION

The computer control module uses the CMP sensor to determine the position of the No. 1 piston during its power stroke. This signal is used by the computer control module to calculate fuel injection mode of operation.

If the cam signal is lost while the engine is running, the fuel injection system will shift to a calculated fuel injected mode based on the last fuel injection pulse, and the engine will continue to run.

TESTING

1990–94 Vehicles

▶ See Figures 83 and 84

1. Detach the camshaft position sensor connector.
2. Attach an ohmmeter to connector harness terminal No. 3 on the 1.8L engine or terminal 4 on the 2.0L engine and ground and check for continuity. If there is no continuity, replace the sensor.

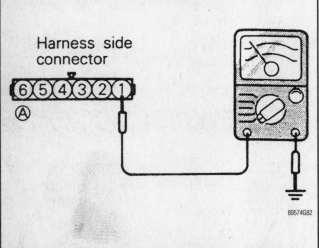

Fig. 83 Testing the camshaft position sensor harness for continuity—1.8L engine

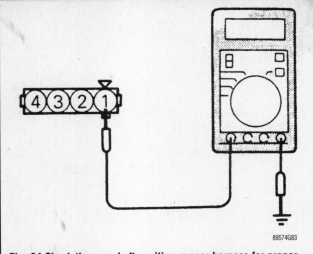

Fig. 84 Check the camshaft position sensor harness for proper voltage—2.0L engine

3. Check the voltage at the harness with the connector detached, ignition **ON** and the ohmmeter connected to ground and the No. 4 harness terminal for the 1.8L engine or the No. 1 harness terminal for the 2.0L engine. The voltage reading should be 4.8–5.2 ohms. If not within specifications, replace the harness. If within specifications replace the sensor.

1995–98 Vehicles

2.0L NON-TURBO ENGINES

▶ See Figure 85

1. Detach the sensor connector, then use an ohmmeter to measure at the harness side.
2. With the ignition switch **ON**, measure the voltage between harness No. 1 and ground. It should be 8.5–9.5 volts.
3. Check the voltage between terminal No. 3 and ground. It should be 4.8–5.2 volts.
4. Check to see if there is continuity between the No. 2 terminal and ground. There should be continuity.
5. If the voltage readings are correct, and there is continuity, replace the sensor. If not, repair or replace the harness, or the PCM may be faulty.

Fig. 85 Camshaft sensor terminal identification—1995–98 2.0L non-turbo engine

2.0L TURBO AND 2.4L ENGINES

♦ See Figure 86

1. Attach the connector, use test harness MD998478 or equivalent.
2. With the engine cranking, check the voltage between the No. 2 terminal and ground. It should be 0.4–3.0 volts.
3. With the engine idling, check the voltage between the No 2 terminal and ground. It should be 0.5–2.0 volts.
4. If these specifications are met, the PCM may be faulty.
5. Detach the sensor connector and measure at the harness side. Attach an ohmmeter.
6. With engine cranking, measure the voltage between terminal No. 2 and ground. It should be 0.4–3.0 volts.
7. With the engine idling, measure the voltage between terminal No. 2 and ground. It should be 4.8–5.2 volts.
8. Check to see if there is continuity between terminal No. 1 and ground, there should be continuity.
9. If the voltage readings are correct, and there is continuity, replace the sensor. If not, repair or replace the harness, or the PCM may be faulty.

Fig. 86 Camshaft position sensor terminal identification—2.0L turbo and 2.4L engines

REMOVAL & INSTALLATION

1995–98 Vehicles

2.0L NON-TURBO ENGINES

1. Disconnect the negative battery cable.
2. Detach the air intake hose.
3. Detach the camshaft position sensor connector.
4. Unfasten the retaining bolts, then remove the camshaft position sensor.
5. If necessary, remove the retaining bolts, then remove the target magnet.
To install:
6. If removed, install the target magnet by aligning the off-set tabs of the magnet with the off-set holes of the camshaft. Tighten the retaining bolts to 2 ft. lbs. (3 Nm).
7. Position the sensor, and secure with the retaining bolts. Tighten to 7 ft. lbs. (9 Nm).
8. Attach the sensor electrical connector.
9. Install the air intake hose, then connect the negative battery cable.

2.0L TURBO AND 2.4L ENGINES

♦ See Figures 87 and 88

1. Disconnect the negative battery cable.
2. Detach the sensor connector.
3. Unfasten the retaining bolt, then remove the sensor and the O-ring.
4. Installation is the reverse of the removal procedure.

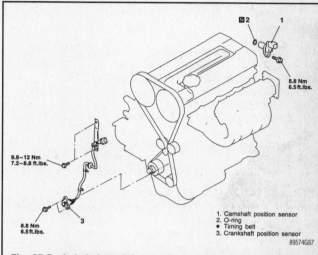

Fig. 87 Exploded view of the camshaft and crankshaft position sensors—2.0L turbo engines

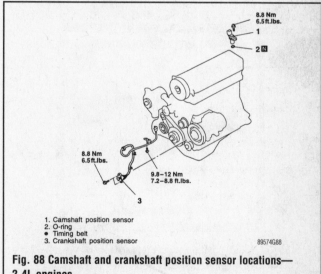

Fig. 88 Camshaft and crankshaft position sensor locations—2.4L engines

Crank Angle Sensor (Crankshaft Position Sensor)

TESTING

1995–98 Vehicles

2.0L NON-TURBO ENGINES

1. Detach the sensor connector, then use an ohmmeter to measure at the harness side.

2. With the ignition switch **ON**, measure the voltage between harness No. 1 and ground. It should be 8.5–9.5 volts.

3. Check the voltage between terminal No. 2 and ground. It should be 4.8–5.2 volts.

4. Check to see if there is continuity between the No. 3 terminal and ground. There should be continuity.

5. If the voltage readings are correct, and there is continuity, replace the sensor. If not, repair or replace the harness, or the PCM may be faulty.

2.0L TURBO AND 2.4L ENGINES

▶ **See Figure 89**

1. Attach the connector, use test harness MD998478 or equivalent.

2. With the engine cranking, check the voltage between the No. 2 terminal (black clip) and ground. It should be 0.4–4.0 volts.

3. With the engine idling, check the voltage between the No 2 terminal (black clip) and ground. It should be 1.5–2.5 volts.

4. If these specifications are met, the sensor and wiring is fine and the PCM may be faulty.

5. Detach the sensor connector and measure at the harness side. Attach an ohmmeter.

6. With the ignition switch **ON**, measure the voltage between terminal No. 3 and ground.

There should be positive battery voltage.

7. With the ignition switch **ON**, measure the voltage between terminal No. 2 and ground. It should be 4.8–5.2 volts.

8. Check to see if there is continuity between terminal No. 1 and ground, there should be continuity.

9. If the voltage readings are correct, and there is continuity, replace the sensor. If not, repair or replace the harness, or the PCM may be faulty.

Fig. 89 Crankshaft position sensor terminal identification—2.0L turbo and 2.4L engines

REMOVAL & INSTALLATION

1.8L Engines

▶ **See Figure 90**

1. Disconnect the negative battery cable.
2. Disconnect the sensor harness connector.
3. Unscrew the cap hold-down screws and lift off the cap.
4. Matchmark the coupling to the sensor housing and the housing to the engine.

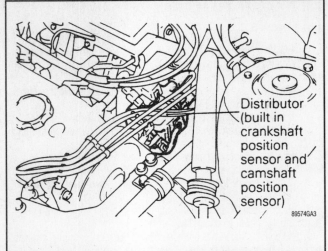

Fig. 90 On 1.8L the crankshaft and camshaft position sensors are built into the distributor

➡ **Do not crank the engine during this procedure. If the engine is cranked, the matchmark must be disregarded.**

5. Remove the hold-down nut.
6. Carefully remove the crank angle sensor assembly from the engine.

To install:

7. If the timing is not disturbed, perform the following procedures:

   a. Install a new housing O-ring and lubricate with clean oil.

   b. Install the assembly in the engine so the coupling is aligned with the matchmark on the housing and the housing is aligned with the matchmark on the engine. Make sure the sensor assembly is fully seated and the shaft is fully engaged.

   c. Install the hold-down nut.

   d. Connect the harness connector.

   e. Make sure the sealing O-ring is in place, install the cap and tighten the screws.

   f. Connect the negative battery cable.

   g. Adjust the ignition timing, if applicable, and tighten the hold-down nut.

8. If the timing is disturbed, perform the following procedures:

   a. Install a new housing O-ring and lubricate with clean oil.

   b. Position the engine so the No. 1 piston is at TDC of its compression stroke and the mark on the vibration damper is aligned with **0** on the timing indicator.

   c. Install the sensor in the engine so the factory matchmark on the coupling (notch) is aligned with the matchmark on the housing (punch mark) and the housing is aligned with the matchmark on the engine. Make sure the sensor assembly is fully seated and the shaft is fully engaged.

   d. Install the hold-down nut.

   e. Connect the harness connector.

   f. Make sure the sealing O-ring is in place, install the cap and tighten the screws.

   g. Connect the negative battery cable.

   h. Adjust the ignition timing, if applicable, and tighten the hold-down nut.

2.0L Non-Turbo Engines

▶ **See Figure 91**

1. Disconnect the negative battery cable.
2. Detach the crankshaft position sensor electrical connector.
3. Unfasten the retaining bolt, then remove the sensor.

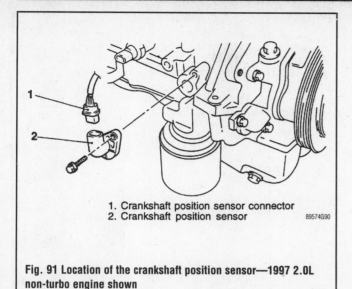

1. Crankshaft position sensor connector
2. Crankshaft position sensor

89574G90

Fig. 91 Location of the crankshaft position sensor—1997 2.0L non-turbo engine shown

To install:
4. Position the sensor and install the retaining bolt.
5. Attach the crankshaft position sensor electrical connector.
6. Connect the negative battery cable.

2.0L Turbo and 2.4L Engines

▶ See Figures 87 and 88

1. Disconnect the negative battery cable.
2. Remove the timing belt, as outlined in Section 3 of this manual.
3. Unplug the sensor connector.
4. Unfasten the retaining bolts, then remove the sensor from the vehicle.
5. Installation is the reverse of the removal procedure.

Knock Sensor

OPERATION

The knock sensor is normally mounted to the rear side of the engine block. It reacts to the ping or knock caused during detonation by sending a signal to the ECU. The ECU retards the timing to eliminate the detonation.

If the knock sensor is experiencing functional problems, a slight reduction in engine power may be felt. This is because the ignition timing will be forcibly retarded.

TESTING

▶ See Figures 92 and 93

➡The knock sensor test requires the use of an oscilloscope.

1. Position test probe of oscilloscope lead to the oscilloscope pick-up point as shown in the illustration.
2. Start the engine and allow to idle. Accelerate the engine to a maximum speed of 5,000 rpm and check the waveform on the scope.
3. If the test pattern obtained differentiates from the desired pattern shown in the illustration, replace the knock sensor.

REMOVAL & INSTALLATION

▶ See Figures 94 and 95

1. Disconnect the negative battery cable.
2. For 2.0L non-turbo engines, remove the engine under cover.

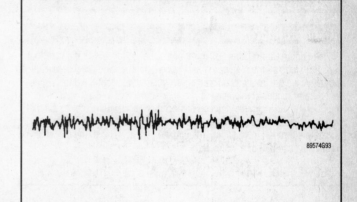

89574G92

Fig. 92 Knock sensor circuit. Note positioning of oscilloscope during testing.

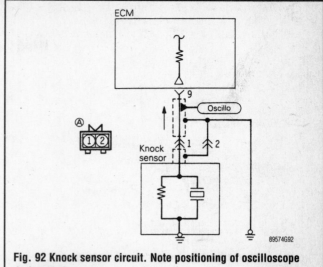

89574G93

Fig. 93 Ideal test pattern of knock sensor as seen on an oscilloscope

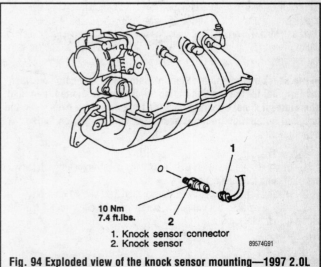

10 Nm
7.4 ft.lbs.

1. Knock sensor connector
2. Knock sensor

89574G91

Fig. 94 Exploded view of the knock sensor mounting—1997 2.0L non-turbo engine shown

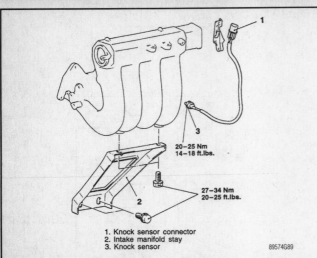

1. Knock sensor connector
2. Intake manifold stay
3. Knock sensor

20–25 Nm
14–18 ft.lbs.

27–34 Nm
20–25 ft.lbs.

89574G89

Fig. 95 Exploded view of the knock sensor—1995–98 2.0L turbo engines

3. Detach the electrical connector at the sensor.
4. For 2.0L turbo engines, remove the intake manifold stay.
5. Remove the sensor from the engine block.

To install:

6. Install the knock sensor in the opening in the engine block and tighten the sensor retainer.
7. Attach the electrical connector to the sensor.
8. Connect the negative battery cable.

TROUBLE CODES

General Information

The Engine Control Unit (ECU) monitors the signals of input and output sensors, some all the time and others at certain times and processes each signal. When the ECU has noticed an irregularity has continued for a specified time or longer from when the irregular signal was initially monitored, the ECU judges that a malfunction has occurred and will memorize the malfunction code. The code is then stored in the memory of the ECU and is accessible through the data link (diagnostic connector) with the use of an electronic scan tool or a voltmeter.

CHECK ENGINE/MALFUNCTION INDICATOR LIGHT

Among the on-board diagnostic items, a check engine/malfunction indicator light comes on to notify the driver of a emission control component irregularity. If the irregularity detected returns to normal or the engine control module judges that the component has returned to normal, the check engine/malfunction indicator light will be turned off. Moreover, if the ignition is turned **OFF** and then the engine is restarted, the check engine/malfunction indicator light will not be turned on until a malfunction is detected.

The check engine/malfunction indicator light will come on immediately after the ignition switch is turned **ON**. The light should stay lit for 5 seconds and then will go off. This indicates that the check engine/malfunction indicator lamp is operating normally. This does not signify a problem with the system.

➡The check engine/malfunction indicator lamp will come on when the terminal for the ignition timing adjustment is shorted to ground. Therefore, it is not abnormal that the light comes on even when the terminal for ignition timing is shorted at time of ignition timing adjustment.

To test the light:

1. Turn the ignition switch **ON**. Inspect the check engine/malfunction indicator lamp for illumination.
2. The light should be lit for 5 seconds and then should go out.
3. If the lamp does not illuminate, check for open circuit in the harness, blown fuse or blown bulb.

Reading Codes

Remember that the diagnostic trouble code identification refers only to the circuit, not necessarily to a specific component. For example, fault code 14 may indicate an error in the throttle position sensor circuit; it does not necessarily mean the TPS sensor has failed. Testing of all related wiring, connectors and the sensor itself may be required to locate the problem.

The ECU memory is capable of storing multiple codes. During diagnosis the codes will be transmitted in numerical order from lowest to highest, regardless of the order of occurrence. If multiple codes are stored, always begin diagnostic work with the lowest numbered code.

Make a note of the following:

1. When battery voltage is low, no detection of failure is possible. Be sure to check the battery voltage and other conditions before starting the test.
2. Diagnostic items are erased if the battery or the engine controller connection is disconnected. Do not disconnect either of these components until the diagnostic material present in the engine control module has been read completely.
3. Be sure to connect and disconnect the scan tool to the data link connector with the ignition key **OFF**. If the scan tool in connected or disconnected with the ignition key **ON**, ABS diagnostic trouble codes may be falsely stored and the ABS warning light may be illuminated.

With Scan Tool

◆ See Figures 96, 97 and 98

The procedure listed below is to be used only as a guide, when using Chrysler's DRB III, Mitsubishi's MUT-II, or equivalent scan tool. For specific operating instructions, follow the directions supplied with the particular scan tool being used.

1. Remove the under dash cover, if equipped. Connect the scan tool to the data link connector, located on the left underside of the instrument panel.
2. Using the scan tool, read and record the on-board diagnostic output.
3. Diagnose and repair the faulty components as required.
4. Turn the ignition switch **OFF** and then turn it **ON**.
5. Erase the diagnostic trouble code.
6. Recheck the diagnostic trouble code and make sure that the normal code is output.

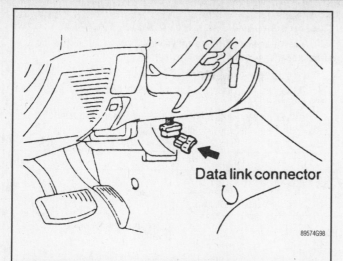

Fig. 96 The data link connector is located on the left under side of the instrument panel

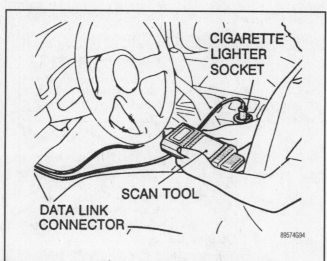

Fig. 97 Proper connection of the scan tool to read codes on 1990–94 vehicles

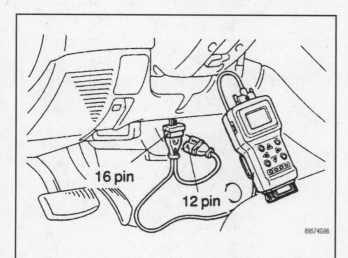

Fig. 98 Connections for the scan tool and data link connector to retrieve trouble codes on 1995–98 vehicles

Without Scan Tool

1990–94 VEHICLES

◗ See Figure 99

  1. Remove the under dash cover, if equipped.
  2. Connect an analog voltmeter between the on-board diagnostic output terminal of the data link connector and the ground terminal.
  3. Turn the ignition switch **ON**.
  4. Read the on-board diagnostic output pattern from the voltmeter and record.
  5. Diagnose and repair the faulty components as required.
  6. Erase the trouble code.
  7. Turn the ignition switch **ON**, and read the diagnostic trouble codes, checking that a normal code is output.

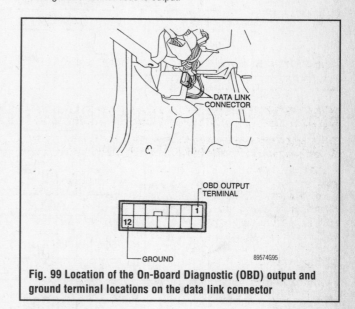

Fig. 99 Location of the On-Board Diagnostic (OBD) output and ground terminal locations on the data link connector

1995–98 VEHICLES

◗ See Figure 100

  1. Cycle the ignition key **ON-OFF-ON-OFF-ON**, within 5 seconds.
  2. Count the number of times the check engine lamp on the instrument panel flashes on and off. The number of flashes represents the trouble

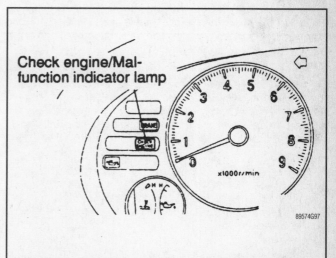

Fig. 100 Count the check engine light flashes to get the trouble codes

code. There is a slight pause between the flashes representing the first and second digits of the code. Longer pauses (about 4 seconds) separate individual trouble codes.

3. Diagnose and repair the faulty components as required.

4. Disconnect the negative battery cable for 10 or more seconds, then reconnect the cable to the battery.

5. Start the engine and let it run at idle for about 15 minutes after the engine has reached normal operating temperatures.

Clearing Codes

→**To erase diagnostic trouble codes with a scan tool, follow the directions given by the tools manufacturer.**

1. Turn the ignition switch **OFF**.

2. Disconnect the negative battery cable from the battery for 10 seconds or more, then reattach it.

3. Turn **ON** the ignition switch and read the diagnostic trouble codes checking that a normal code is output.

Output preference order	Diagnosis item	Diagnosis code			Check item (Remedy)
		Output signal pattern	No.	Memory	
1	Engine control unit		–	–	(Replace engine control unit)
2	Oxygen sensor	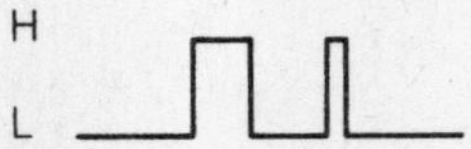	11	Retained	• Harness and connector • Fuel pressure • Injectors (Replace if defective) • Intake air leaks • Oxygen sensor
3	Air flow sensor	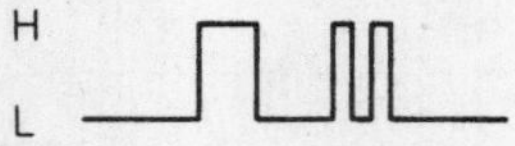	12	Retained	• Harness and connector (If harness and connector are normal, replace air flow sensor assembly.)
4	Intake air temperature sensor		13	Retained	• Harness and connector • Intake air temperature sensor
5	Throttle position sensor		14	Retained	• Harness and connector • Throttle position sensor • Idle position switch
6	Motor position sensor		15	Retained	• Harness and connector • Motor position sensor • Throttle position sensor

Fig. 101 Diagnostic trouble code chart (1 of 2)—1990–92 1.8L engines

89574C01

Output preference order	Diagnosis item	Diagnosis code			Check item (Remedy)
		Output signal pattern	No.	Memory	
7	Engine coolant temperature sensor	 H / L pattern	21	Retained	• Harness and connector • Engine coolant temperature sensor
8	Crank angle sensor	 H / L pattern	22	Retained	• Harness and connector (If harness and connector are normal, replace distributor assembly.)
9	No. 1 cylinder top dead center sensor	 H / L pattern	23	Retained	• Harness and connector (If harness and connector are normal, replace distributor assembly.)
10	Vehicle speed sensor (reed switch)	 H / L pattern	24	Retained	• Harness and connector • Vehicle speed sensor (reed switch)
11	Barometric pressure sensor	 H / L pattern	25	Retained	• Harness and connector (If harness and connector are normal, replace barometric pressure sensor assembly.)
12	Ignition timing adjustment signal	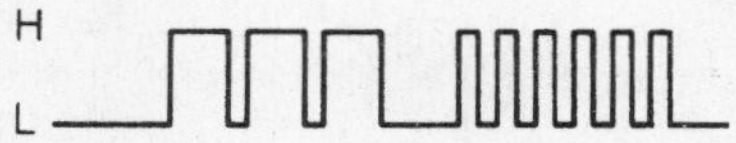 H / L pattern	36	–	• Harness and connector
13	Injector	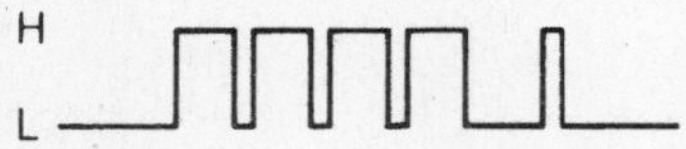 H / L pattern	41	Retained	• Harness and connector • Injector coil resistance
14	Fuel pump	 H / L pattern	42	Retained	• Harness and connector • Control relay
15	EGR <California>	 H / L pattern	43	Retained	• Harness and connector • EGR temperature sensor • EGR valve • EGR valve control solenoid valve • EGR valve control vacuum
16	Normal state	 H / L pattern	–	–	–

NOTE
Replace the engine control unit if a malfunction code is output although the inspection reveals that there is no problem with the check items.

89574C02

Fig. 102 Diagnostic trouble code chart (2 of 2)—1990–92 1.8L engines

Diagnostic trouble code		Diagnostic item	Check item (Remedy)	Memory
No.	Output signal pattern			
–	 H ⎍ (single step pattern) L	Engine control module	(Replace engine control module)	–
11	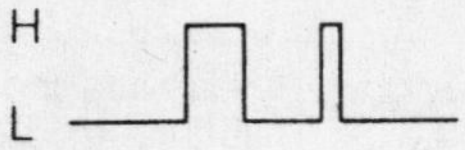 H (pattern) L	Oxygen sensor	• Harness and connector • Oxygen sensor • Fuel pressure • Injectors (Replace if defective.) • Intake air leaks	Retained
12	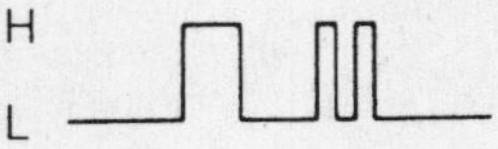 H (pattern) L	Volume air flow sensor	• Harness and connector (If harness and connector are normal, replace volume air flow sensor assembly.)	Retained
13	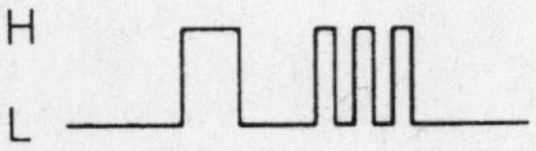 H (pattern) L	Intake air temperature sensor	• Harness and connector • Intake air temperature sensor	Retained
14	 H (pattern) L	Throttle position sensor	• Harness and connector • Throttle position sensor • Closed throttle position switch	Retained
15	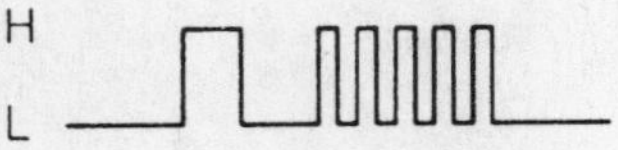 H (pattern) L	Idle speed control motor position sensor	• Harness and connector • Idle speed control motor position sensor • Throttle position sensor	Retained
21	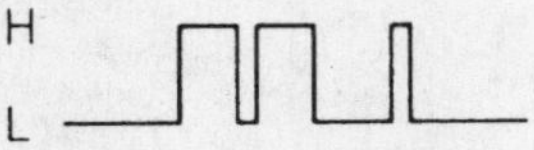 H (pattern) L	Engine coolant temperature sensor	• Harness and connector • Engine coolant temperature sensor	Retained
22	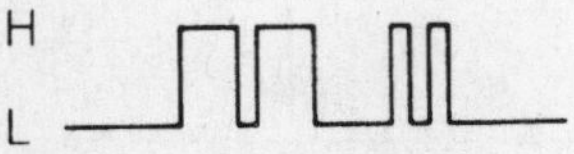 H (pattern) L	Crankshaft position sensor	• Harness and connector (If harness and connector are normal, replace distributor assembly.)	Retained

89574C03

Fig. 103 Diagnostic trouble code chart (1 of 2)—1993–94 1.8L engines

Diagnostic trouble code		Diagnostic item	Check item (Remedy)	Memory
No.	Output signal pattern			
23	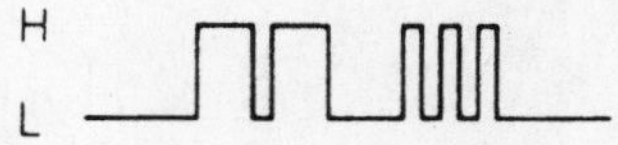 H ⎍⎍⎍ L	Camshaft position sensor	• Harness and connector (If harness and connector are normal, replace distributor assembly.)	Retained
24	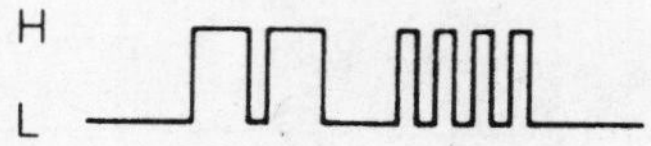 H L	Vehicle speed sensor (reed switch)	• Harness and connector • Vehicle speed sensor (reed switch)	Retained
25	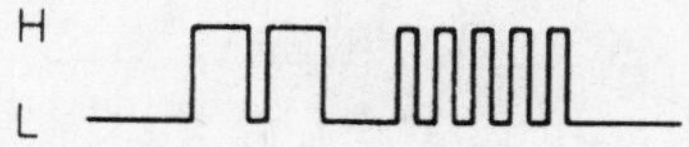 H L	Barometric pressure sensor	• Harness and connector (If harness and connector are normal, replace barometric pressure sensor assembly.)	Retained
36	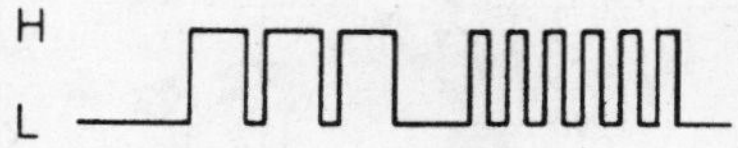 H L	Ignition timing adjustment signal	• Harness and connector	–
41	 H L	Injector	• Harness and connector • Injector coil resistance	Retained
42	 H L	Fuel pump	• Harness and connector • MFI relay	Retained
43	 H L	EGR <Califor- nia>	• Harness and connector • EGR temperature sensor • EGR valve • EGR solenoid • EGR valve control vacuum	Retained
–	 H L	Normal state	–	–

NOTE
1. Replace the engine control module if a diagnostic trouble code is output although the inspection reveals that there is no problem with the check items.

89574C04

Fig. 104 Diagnostic trouble code chart (2 of 2)—1993–94 1.8L engines

Output preference order	Diagnosis item	Diagnosis code			Check item (Remedy)
		Output signal pattern	No.	Memory	
1	Engine control unit	 H L ⎍	–	–	(Replace engine control unit)
2	Oxygen sensor	 H L ⎍⎍	11	Retained	• Harness and connector • Oxygen sensor • Fuel pressure • Injectors (Replace if defective) • Intake air leaks
3	Air flow sensor	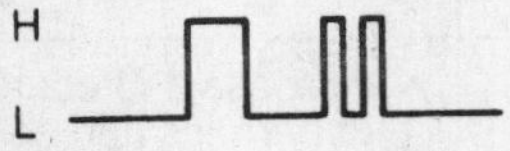 H L ⎍⎍⎍	12	Retained	• Harness and connector (If harness and connector are normal, replace air flow sensor assembly.)
4	Intake air temperature sensor	 H L ⎍⎍⎍⎍	13	Retained	• Harness and connector • Intake air temperature sensor
5	Throttle position sensor	 H L ⎍⎍⎍⎍⎍	14	Retained	• Harness and connector • Throttle position sensor • Idle position switch
6	Engine coolant temperature sensor	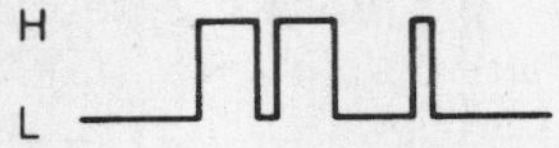 H L ⎍⎍⎍⎍	21	Retained	• Harness and connector • Engine coolant temperature sensor

89574C05

Fig. 105 Diagnostic trouble code chart (1 of 2)—1990–92 2.0L engines

Output preference order	Diagnosis item	Diagnosis code: Output signal pattern	Diagnosis code: No.	Diagnosis code: Memory	Check item (Remedy)
7	Crank angle sensor	H 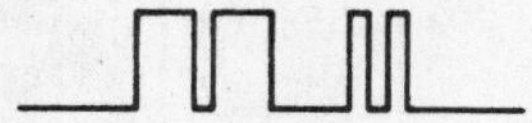 L	22	Retained	• Harness and connector (If harness and connector are normal, replace crank angle sensor assembly.)
8	Top dead center sensor (No. 1 and No. 4 cylinder)	H 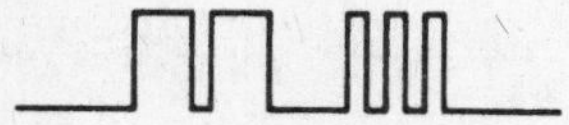 L	23	Retained	• Harness and connector (If harness and connector are normal, replace crank angle sensor assembly.)
9	Vehicle speed sensor (reed switch)	H 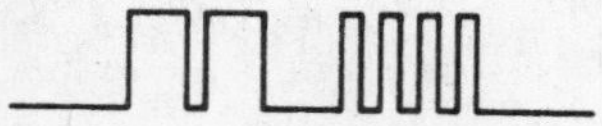 L	24	Retained	• Harness and connector • Vehicle speed sensor (reed switch)
10	Barometric pressure sensor	H 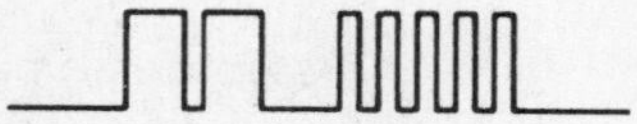 L	25	Retained	• Harness and connector (If harness and connector are normal, replace barometric pressure sensor assembly.)
11	Detonation sensor <Turbo>	H 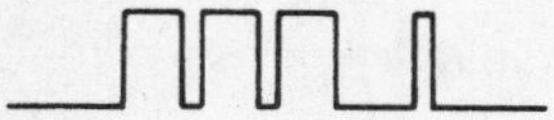 L	31	Retained	• Harness and connector • Detonation sensor
12	Injector	H 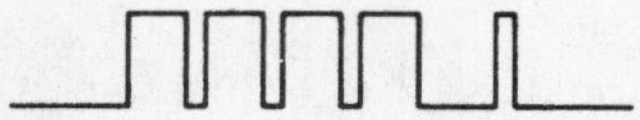 L	41	Retained	• Harness and connector • Injector coil resistance
13	Fuel pump	H 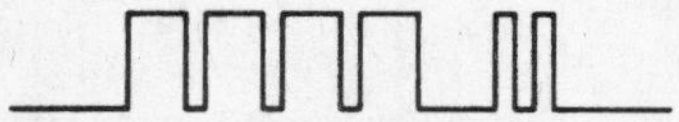 L	42	Retained	• Harness and connector • Control relay
14	EGR <California>	H 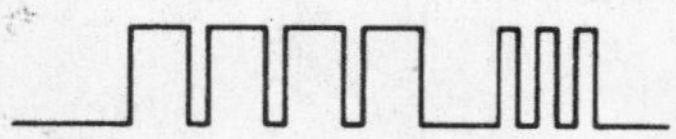 L	43	Retained	• Harness and connector • EGR temperature sensor • EGR valve • EGR valve control solenoid valve • EGR valve control vacuum
15	Ignition coil	H 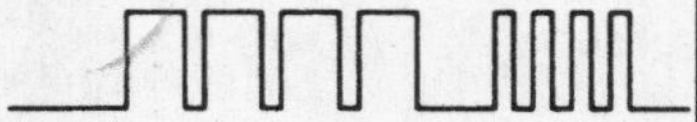 L	44	Retained	• Harness and connector • Ignition coil • Power transistor
16	Normal state	H 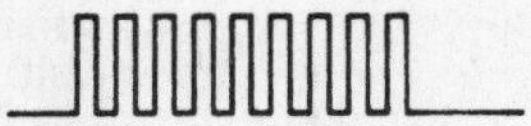 L	–	–	–

NOTE
Replace the engine control unit if a malfunction code is output although the inspection reveals that there is no problem with the check items.

89574C06

Fig. 106 Diagnostic trouble code chart (2 of 2)—1990–92 2.0L engines

Diagnostic trouble code		Diagnostic item	Check item (Remedy)	Memory
No.	Output signal pattern			
—	H ⎍‾‾‾‾ L	Engine control module	(Replace engine control module)	—
11	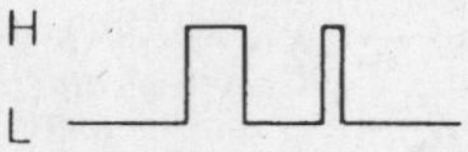 H ⎍⎍ L	Heated oxygen sensor	• Harness and connector • Heated oxygen sensor • Fuel pressure • Injectors (Replace if defective.) • Intake air leaks	Retained
12	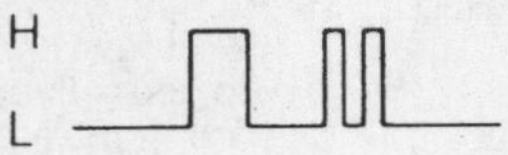 H ⎍⎍⎍ L	Volume air flow sensor	• Harness and connector (If harness and connector are normal, replace volume air flow sensor assembly.)	Retained
13	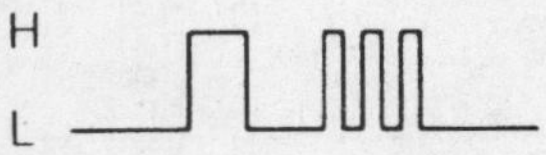 H ⎍⎍⎍⎍ L	Intake air temperature sensor	• Harness and connector • Intake air temperature sensor	Retained
14	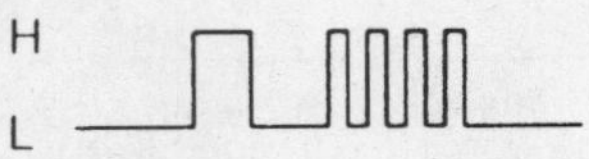 H ⎍⎍⎍⎍⎍ L	Throttle position sensor	• Harness and connector • Throttle position sensor • Closed throttle position switch	Retained
21	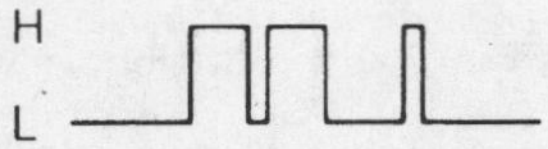 H ⎍⎍⎍⎍ L	Engine coolant temperature sensor	• Harness and connector • Engine coolant temperature sensor	Retained
22	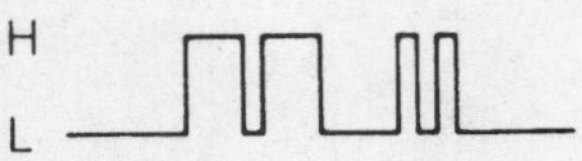 H ⎍⎍⎍⎍⎍ L	Crankshaft position sensor	• Harness and connector (If harness and connector are normal, replace crankshaft position assembly.)	Retained
23	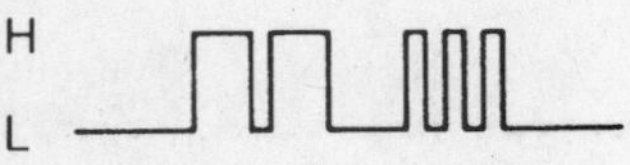 H ⎍⎍⎍⎍⎍⎍ L	Camshaft position sensor	• Harness and connector (If harness and connector are normal, replace crankshaft position assembly.)	Retained

89574C07

Fig. 107 Diagnostic trouble code chart (1 of 2)—1993–94 2.0L engines

Diagnostic trouble code		Diagnostic item	Check item (Remedy)	Memory
No.	Output signal pattern			
24	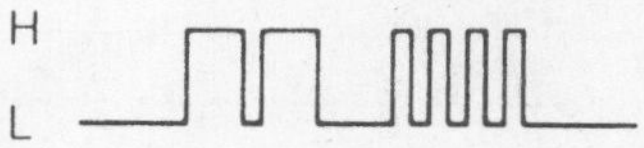	Vehicle speed sensor (reed switch)	• Harness and connector • Vehicle speed sensor (reed switch)	Retained
25	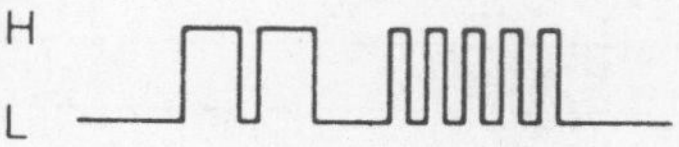	Barometric pressure sensor	• Harness and connector (If harness and connector are normal, replace barometric pressure sensor assembly.)	Retained
31		Knock sensor <Turbo>	• Harness and connector (If harness and connector are normal, replace knock sensor.)	Retained
41		Injector	• Harness and connector • Injector coil resistance	Retained
42	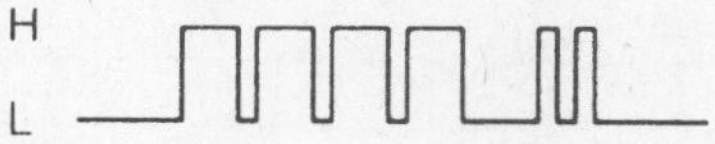	Fuel pump	• Harness and connector • MFI relay	Retained
43		EGR <California>	• Harness and connector • EGR temperature sensor • EGR valve • EGR solenoid • EGR valve control vacuum	Retained
44		Ignition coil, Ignition power transistor unit	• Harness and connector • Ignition coil • Ignition power transistor	Retained
–		Normal state	–	–

NOTE
1. Replace the engine control module if a diagnostic trouble code is output although the inspection reveals that there is no problem with the check items.

89574C08

Fig. 108 Diagnostic trouble code chart (2 of 2)—1993–94 2.0L engines

OBD-II DIAGNOSTIC TROUBLE CODE (DTC) APPLICATIONS

DTC	Applicable System or Component
Constant Memory Trouble Codes	
P0100	Volume air flow circuit malfunction
P0105	Barometric pressure circuit malfunction
P0107	MAP sensor voltage too low
P0108	MAP sensor voltage too high
P0110	IAT circuit malfunction
P0112	IAT sensor voltage low
P0113	IAT sensor voltage high
P0115	ECT circuit malfunction
P0117	ECT sensor voltage too low
P0118	ECT sensor voltage too high
P0120	TP sensor malfunction
P0121	TP sensor fault
P0121	TP sensor voltage does not agree with MAP (M/T)
P0122	TP sensor reference signal voltage too low
P0123	TP sensor reference signal voltage too high
P0125	Closed loop temperature not reached (M/T)
P0125	Excessive time to enter closed loop fuel control
P0130	O2 sensor circuit malfunction (bank 1 sensor 1)
P0131	Upstream HO2S voltage grounded
P0132	Upstream HO2S shorted to voltage
P0133	Upstream HO2S response (M/T)
P0134	Upstream HO2S stays at center
P0135	O2 sensor heater circuit malfunction (bank 1 sensor 1)
P0136	O2 sensor circuit malfunction (bank 1 sensor 2)
P0137	Downstream Ho2s voltage grounded
P0138	Downstream HO2S shorted to voltage (M/T)
P0139	Downstream HO2S stays at center (M/T)
P0141	Downstream HO2S heater failure (M/T)
P0141	O2 sensor heater circuit malfunction (bank 1 sensor 2)
P0170	Fuel trim malfunction
P0171	Fuel system lean
P0172	Fuel system rich
P0201	Injector #1 control circuit
P0202	Injector #2 control circuit
P0203	Injector #3 control circuit
P0204	Injector #4 control circuit
P0220	Fuel pump relay control circuit
P0300	Multiple cylinder misfire (M/T)
P0300	Random misfire detected
P0301	Cylinder #1 misfire
P0302	Cylinder #2 misfire
P0303	Cylinder #3 misfire
P0304	Cylinder #4 misfire
P0325	Knock sensor #1 circuit
P0335	No crankshaft reference signal at PCM
P0335	CKP sensor circuit malfunction

89574C09

Fig. 109 Diagnostic trouble code chart (1 of 3)—1995–98 engines

OBD-II DIAGNOSTIC TROUBLE CODE (DTC) APPLICATIONS

DTC	Applicable System or Component
Constant Memory Trouble Codes (continued)	
P0351	Ignition coil #1 primary circuit
P0352	Ignition coil #2 primary circuit
P0340	No cam signal at PCM
P0340	CMP sensor circuit malfunction
P0400	EGR flow malfunction
P0401	EGR system failure
P0403	EGR solenoid circuit
P0411	Too little or too much secondary air (M/T)
P0412	Pulsed secondary air injection solenoid circuit (M/T)
P0420	Catalyst efficiency below threshold (bank 1)
P0422	Catalytic converter efficiency failure (M/T)
P0440	Evaporative emission control system malfunction
P0441	Evaporative purge flow monitor failure
P0442	EVAP leak monitor small leak detected
P0443	EVAP solenoid circuit
P0443	EVAP control system purge control valve circuit malfunction
P0455	EVAP leak monitor large leak detected
P0500	No vehicle speed sensor signal/sensor malfunction
P0505	Idle air control motor circuit malfunction
P0510	Closed throttle position switch malfunction
P0551	Power steering pressure switch failure (M/T)
P0605	Internal controller failure
P0605	PCM failure - SPI communications
P0700	Transmission malfunction
P0700	EATX controller DTC center
P0705	Transaxle range sensor circuit malfunction
P0710	Transaxle fluid temperature sensor circuit malfunction
P1103	Turbocharger wastegate actuator malfunction
P1104	Turbocharger wastegate solenoid malfunction
P1105	Fuel pressure solenoid malfunction (turbo)
P1294	Target idle not reached within 200 rpm (M/T)
P1295	No 5 volts to TP sensor
P1296	No 5 volts to MAP sensor
P1297	No change in MAP from start to run
P1300	Ignition timing adjustment circuit malfunction
P1390	Timing belt skipped 1 tooth or more
P1391	Intermittent loss of CMP or CKP
P1400	Manifold differential pressure sensor circuit malfunction
P1486	EVAP leak monitor pinched hose found
P1487	High speed radiator fan control relay
P1489	High speed fan control relay circuit
P1490	Low speed fan control relay circuit
P1492	Battery temperature sensor voltage too high
P1493	Battery temperature sensor voltage too low
P1494	Evaporative emission ventilation solenoid switch or mechanical fault
P1495	Evaporative emission ventilation solenoid circuit

89574C10

Fig. 110 Diagnostic trouble code chart (2 of 3)—1995–98 engines

OBD-II DIAGNOSTIC TROUBLE CODE (DTC) APPLICATIONS

DTC	Applicable System or Component
Constant Memory Trouble Codes (continued)	
P1496	5 volts supply too low
P1500	Generator FR terminal circuit malfunction
P1600	Serial communication link malfunction
P1698	No CCD messages from TCM (A/T)
P1715	PG assembly malfunction
P1750	Solenoid assembly malfunction
P1791	Engine coolant temperature level input circuit (to TCM) malfunction
P1899	Park/neutral position switch failure

89574C11

Fig. 111 Diagnostic trouble code chart (3 of 3)—1995–98 engines

VACUUM DIAGRAMS

Following are vacuum diagrams for most of the engine and emissions package combinations covered by this manual. Because vacuum circuits will vary based on various engine and vehicle options, always refer first to the vehicle emission control information label, if present. Should the label be missing, or should vehicle be equipped with a different engine from the vehicle's original equipment, refer to the diagrams below for the same or similar configuration.

If you wish to obtain a replacement emissions label, most manufacturers make the labels available for purchase. The labels can usually be ordered from a local dealer.

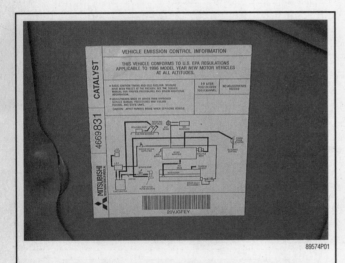

Fig. 112 The VECI label contains important information regarding your vehicle

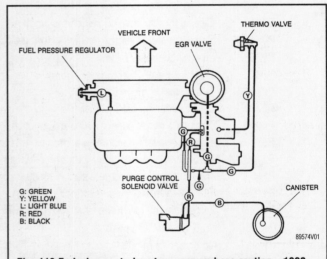

Fig. 113 Emission control system vacuum hose routing—1990 1.8L engine, Federal

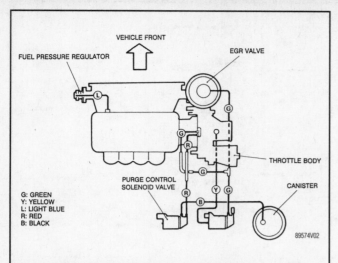

Fig. 114 Emission control system vacuum hose routing—1990 1.8L engine, California

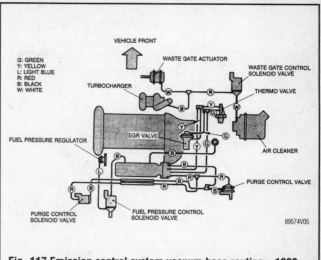

Fig. 117 Emission control system vacuum hose routing—1990 2.0L turbo engine, Federal

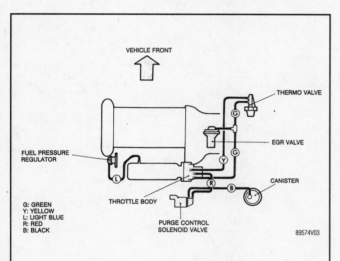

Fig. 115 Emission control system vacuum hose routing—1990 2.0L non-turbo engine, Federal

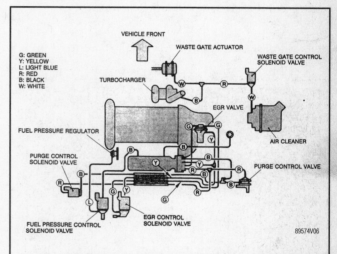

Fig. 118 Emission control system vacuum hose routing—1990 2.0L turbo engine, California

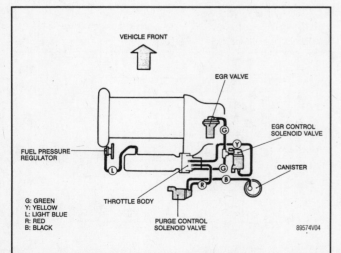

Fig. 116 Emission control system vacuum hose routing—1990 2.0L non-turbo engine, California

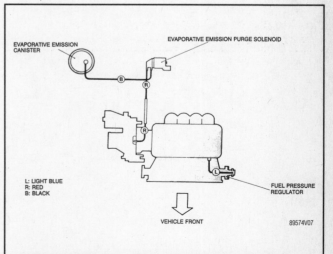

Fig. 119 Emission control system vacuum hose routing—1991–94 1.8L engine, Federal

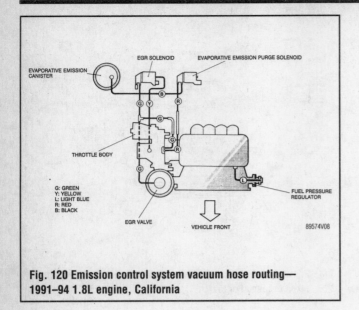

Fig. 120 Emission control system vacuum hose routing—1991–94 1.8L engine, California

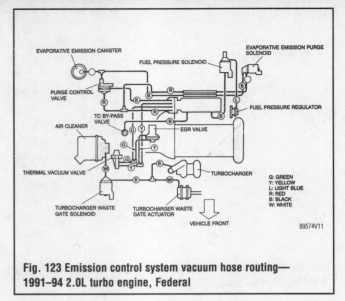

Fig. 123 Emission control system vacuum hose routing—1991–94 2.0L turbo engine, Federal

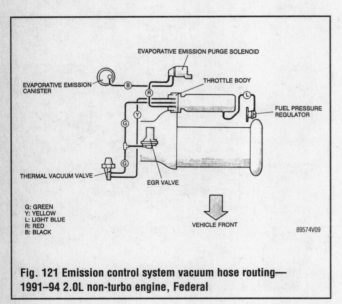

Fig. 121 Emission control system vacuum hose routing—1991–94 2.0L non-turbo engine, Federal

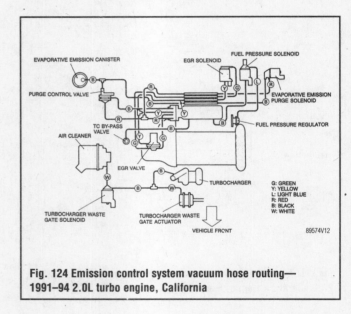

Fig. 124 Emission control system vacuum hose routing—1991–94 2.0L turbo engine, California

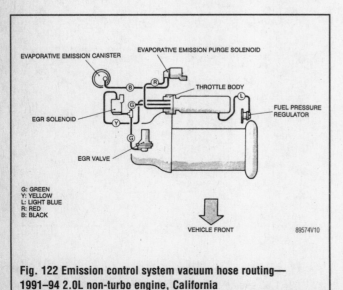

Fig. 122 Emission control system vacuum hose routing—1991–94 2.0L non-turbo engine, California

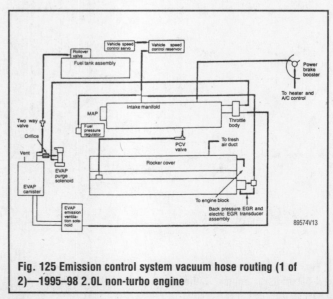

Fig. 125 Emission control system vacuum hose routing (1 of 2)—1995–98 2.0L non-turbo engine

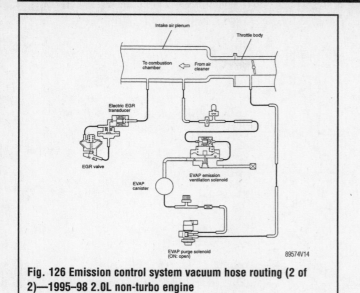

Fig. 126 Emission control system vacuum hose routing (2 of 2)—1995–98 2.0L non-turbo engine

Fig. 127 Emission control system vacuum hose routing (1 of 2)—1995–98 2.0L turbo engine

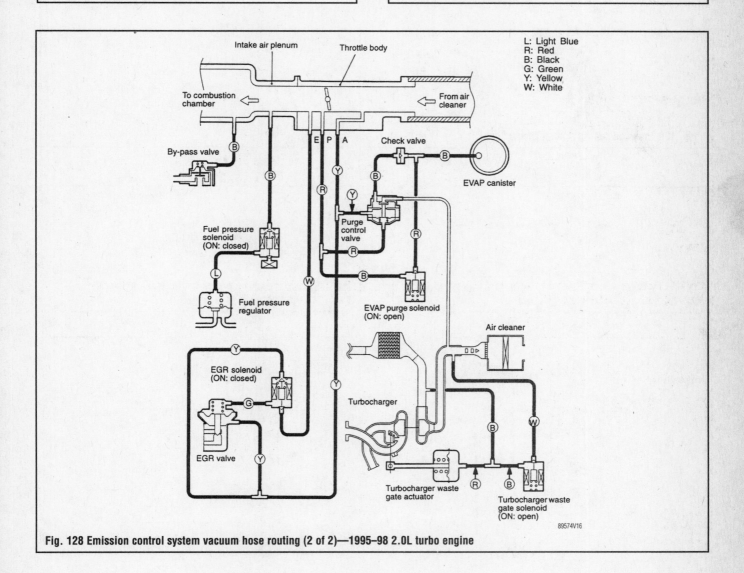

Fig. 128 Emission control system vacuum hose routing (2 of 2)—1995–98 2.0L turbo engine

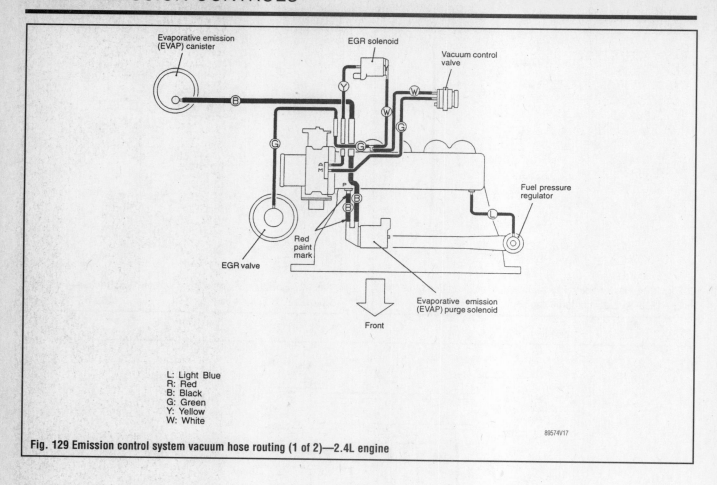

L: Light Blue
R: Red
B: Black
G: Green
Y: Yellow
W: White

89574V17

Fig. 129 Emission control system vacuum hose routing (1 of 2)—2.4L engine

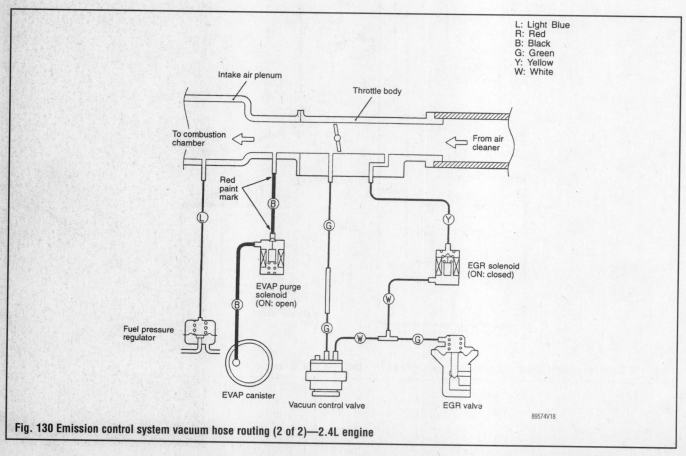

L: Light Blue
R: Red
B: Black
G: Green
Y: Yellow
W: White

89574V18

Fig. 130 Emission control system vacuum hose routing (2 of 2)—2.4L engine

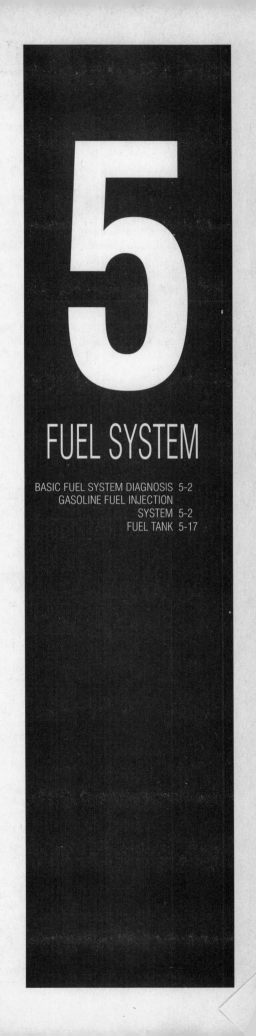

5

FUEL SYSTEM

BASIC FUEL SYSTEM DIAGNOSIS

When there is a problem starting or driving a vehicle, two of the most important checks involve the ignition and the fuel systems. The questions most mechanics attempt to answer first, "is there spark?" and "is there fuel?" will often lead to solving most basic problems. For ignition system diagnosis and testing, please refer to the information on engine electrical components and ignition systems found earlier in this manual. If the ignition system checks out (there is spark), then you must determine if the fuel system is operating properly (is there fuel?).

GASOLINE FUEL INJECTION SYSTEM

General Information

The Multi-Point Injection (MPI) system is electronically controlled by the Engine Control Module (ECM), based on data from various sensors. The ECM controls the fuel flow, idle speed and ignition timing.

Fuel is supplied to the injectors by an electric in-tank fuel pump and is distributed to the respective injectors via the main fuel pipe. The fuel pressure applied to the injector is constant and higher than the pressure in the intake manifold. The pressure is controlled by the fuel pressure regulator. The excess fuel is returned to the fuel tank through the fuel return pipe.

When an electric current flows in the injector, the injector valve is fully opened to supply fuel. Since the fuel pressure is constant, the amount of the fuel injected from the injector into the manifold is increased or decreased in proportion to the time the electric current flows. Based on ECU signals, the injectors inject fuel to the cylinder manifold ports in firing order.

The flow rate of the air drawn through the air cleaner is measured by the air flow sensor. The air enters the air intake plenum or manifold through the throttle body. In the intake manifold, the air is mixed with the fuel from the injectors and is drawn into the cylinder. The air flow rate is controlled according to the degree of the throttle valve and the servo motor openings. The system is monitored through a number of sensors which feed information on engine conditions and requirements to the ECM. The ECM calculates the injection time and rate according to the signals from the sensors.

Fuel System Service Precautions

Safety is an important factor when servicing the fuel system. Failure to conduct maintenance and repairs in a safe manner may result in serious personal injury. Maintenance and testing of the vehicle's fuel system components can be accomplished safely and effectively by adhering to the following rules and guidelines.

• To avoid the possibility of fire and personal injury, always disconnect the negative battery cable unless the repair or test procedure requires that battery voltage be applied.

• Always relieve the fuel system pressure prior to disconnecting any fuel system component (injector, fuel rail, pressure regulator, etc.), fitting or fuel line connection. Exercise extreme caution whenever relieving fuel system pressure to avoid exposing skin, face and eyes to fuel spray. Please be advised that fuel under pressure may penetrate the skin or any part of the body that it contacts.

• Always place a shop towel or cloth around the fitting or connection prior to loosening to absorb any excess fuel due to spillage. Ensure that all fuel spillage is quickly removed from engine surfaces. Ensure that all fuel soaked cloths or towels are deposited into a suitable waste container.

• Always keep a dry chemical (Class B) fire extinguisher near the work area.

• Do not allow fuel spray or fuel vapors to come into contact with a spark or open flame.

• Always use a backup wrench when loosening and tightening fuel line connection fittings. This will prevent unnecessary stress and torsion to fuel line piping. Always follow the proper torque specifications.

• Always replace worn fuel fitting O-rings. Do not substitute fuel hose where fuel pipe is installed.

Relieving Fuel System Pressure

In fuel injection systems, fuel under high pressure is supplied to the fuel rail and injectors. Because of the high pressure present, it is essential that the pressure be released prior to loosening any connections where fuel flows. If the pressure is not released and a line or fitting is loosened, fuel will leak out the line under pressure, possibly causing serious personal as well as property damage.

PROCEDURE

1990–94 Vehicles

▶ See Figure 1

1. Loosen the fuel filler cap to release fuel tank pressure.
2. Detach the fuel pump harness connector located at the rear of the fuel tank.
3. Start the vehicle and allow it to run until it stalls from lack of fuel. Turn the key to the **OFF** position.
4. Disconnect the negative battery cable, then reattach the fuel pump connector and reinstall the fuel filler cap. The fuel system can now be safely serviced, but make sure to always wrap shop towels around a fitting that is being disconnected to absorb residual fuel in the lines.

1995–98 Vehicles

▶ See Figures 2, 3, 4 and 5

1. Remove the rear seat cushion.
2. Remove the access plate, then detach the fuel pump connector.
3. Start the engine and allow it to run until it stops, due to lack of fuel. Turn the ignition switch to the **OFF** position.

89575G01

Fig. 1 On 1990–94 vehicles, the fuel pump harness connector is located at the rear of the fuel tank

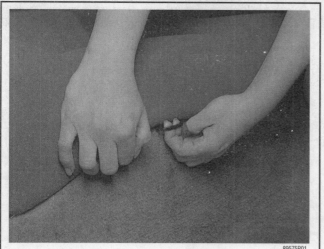

Fig. 2 Remove the rear seat cushion by pulling on the rings at the bottom of the seat

Fig. 3 Unfasten the access plate retaining screws . . .

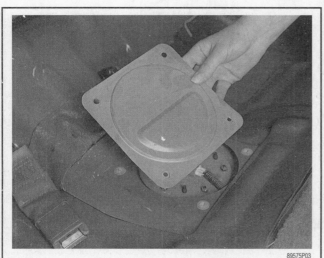

Fig. 4 . . . then remove the plate to reach the fuel pump connector

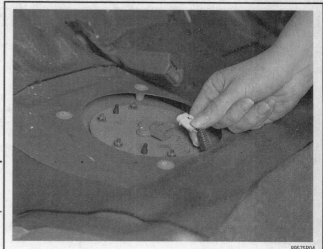

Fig. 5 Unplug the fuel pump connector to relieve the fuel system pressure

4. Disconnect the negative battery cable.
5. Attach the fuel pump connector and install the access plate.
6. Install the rear seat cushion.

Fuel Pump

REMOVAL & INSTALLATION

1990–94 Vehicles

EXCEPT AWD MODELS

▶ See Figures 6, 7, 8 and 9

1. Properly relieve the fuel system pressure as outlined earlier in this section.
2. Raise and safely support the vehicle.
3. Drain the fuel from the fuel tank into an approved gasoline container.
4. Remove the electrical connectors at the fuel pump. Make sure there is enough slack in the electrical harness of the fuel gauge unit to allow for the fuel tank to be lowered slightly. If not, label and disconnect the electrical harness at the fuel gauge unit.

✳✳ CAUTION

Cover the high pressure fuel hose with rags to prevent splash of fuel caused by residual pressure in the fuel pipe line.

5. Disconnect the high pressure fuel line connector at the pump.
6. Loosen self-locking nuts on tank support straps to the end of the stud bolts.
7. Remove the right side lateral rod attaching bolt and disconnect the arm from the right body coupling. Lower the lateral rod and suspend from the axle beam using wire.
8. Remove the holding bolt and gasket from the base of the tank.
9. Remove the fuel pump assembly.
To install:
10. Align the 3 projections on packing with the holes on the fuel pump and the nipples on the pump facing the same direction as before removal.
11. Install the holding bolt through the bottom of the tank. Make sure the gasket on the bolt is replaced and is not pinched during installation. Tighten to 10 ft. lbs. (14 Nm).
12. Install the right side lateral rod and attaching bolt into the right body coupling. Tighten loosely only, at this time.

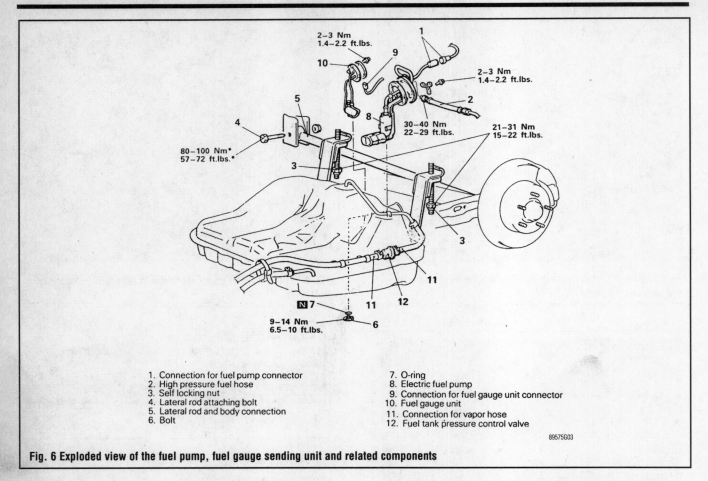

1. Connection for fuel pump connector
2. High pressure fuel hose
3. Self locking nut
4. Lateral rod attaching bolt
5. Lateral rod and body connection
6. Bolt
7. O-ring
8. Electric fuel pump
9. Connection for fuel gauge unit connector
10. Fuel gauge unit
11. Connection for vapor hose
12. Fuel tank pressure control valve

Fig. 6 Exploded view of the fuel pump, fuel gauge sending unit and related components

13. Tighten self-locking nuts on tank support straps until tank is seated fully. Tighten nuts to 22 ft. lbs. (31 Nm).

14. Install the high pressure fuel hose connector and tighten to 29 ft. lbs. (40 Nm).

15. Install the electrical connectors onto the fuel pump and gauge unit assemblies.

16. Lower the vehicle so the suspension supports the weight of the vehicle. Tighten the lateral rod attaching bolt to 58–72 ft. lbs. (80-100 Nm).

17. Refill the fuel tank with fuel drained during this procedure.

18. Connect the negative battery cable and check the entire system for proper operation and leaks.

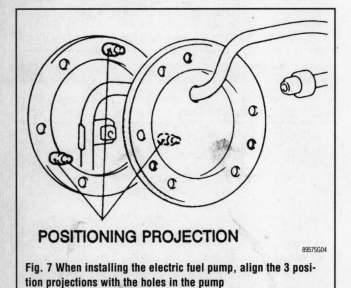

POSITIONING PROJECTION

Fig. 7 When installing the electric fuel pump, align the 3 position projections with the holes in the pump

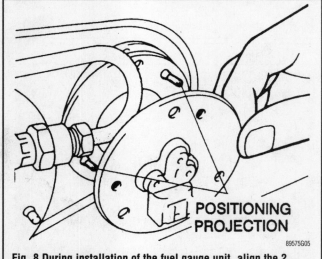

POSITIONING PROJECTION

Fig. 8 During installation of the fuel gauge unit, align the 2 position projections with the holes in the fuel gauge unit.

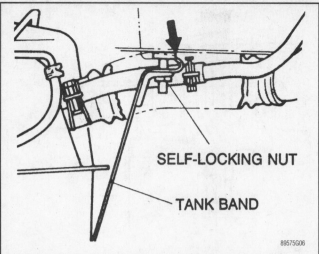

Fig. 9 Tighten the self-locking nuts until the rear end of the tank band contacts the body of the vehicle

AWD MODELS

▶ See Figures 10 and 11

1. Properly relieve the fuel system pressure as outlined earlier in this section.

2. The fuel pump is located in the fuel tank. Remove the hole cover located in the rear floor pan.

3. Partially drain the fuel tank into an approved gasoline container.

4. Remove the electrical connector from the fuel pump.

5. Remove the overfill limiter (two-way valve), as required.

6. Cover the hose connection with a shop towel to prevent any splash of fuel due to residual pressure in the fuel pipe. Remove the high pressure fuel hose connector.

7. Remove the fuel pump and gauge assembly from the tank. Note positioning of pump prior to removal from tank.

To install:

8. Align the 3 projections on the packing with the holes on the fuel pump and the nipples on the pump facing the same direction as before removal. Install the retainers and tighten to 2 ft. lbs. (3 Nm).

9. Install the high pressure hose connection and tighten to 29 ft. lbs. (40 Nm).

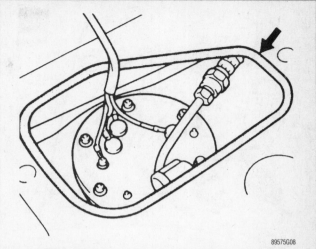

Fig. 11 Before installing the hole cover, apply a suitable sealant to the rear floor pan

10. Install the overfill limiter (two-way valve) and the electrical connector to the fuel pump.

11. Fill the fuel tank with the gasoline removed during this procedure.

12. Reconnect the negative battery cable and check the entire system for leaks.

13. Install MOPAR Rope Caulk Sealer part 4026044 or equivalent, to the rear floor pan and install the cover into place.

1995–98 Vehicles

▶ See Figures 12, 13, 14 and 15

➡On these vehicles, is possible to remove the fuel pump and/or gauge assembly by working through the access panel under the rear seat cushion instead of having to lower or remove the fuel tank.

1. Properly relieve the fuel system pressure, as outlined earlier in this section, but keep the rear seat cushion off and the connector(s) detached.

2. If not already done, remove the protector.

3. Disconnect the fuel pump hoses and connectors, then remove the fuel pump from the vehicle.

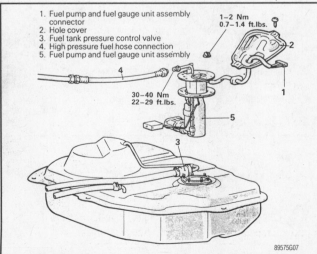

1. Fuel pump and fuel gauge unit assembly connector
2. Hole cover
3. Fuel tank pressure control valve
4. High pressure fuel hose connection
5. Fuel pump and fuel gauge unit assembly

1–2 Nm
0.7–1.4 ft.lbs.

30–40 Nm
22–29 ft.lbs.

Fig. 10 Exploded view of the fuel pump, gauge sending unit and related components

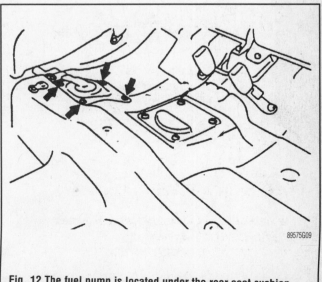

Fig. 12 The fuel pump is located under the rear seat cushion

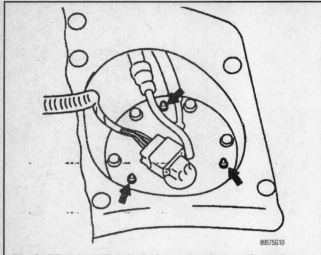

Fig. 13 When installing the fuel pump, make sure the projections are properly aligned with the holes in the pump assembly

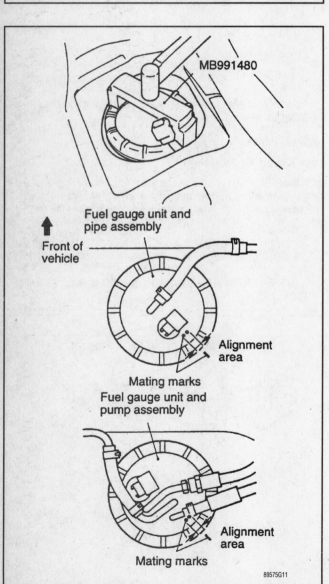

Fig. 14 On AWD vehicles, you need a spanner wrench to tighten the fuel pump assembly cap

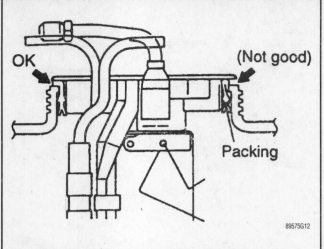

Fig. 15 The fuel pump packing must be properly installed for sealing purposes

To install:

4. For FWD vehicles, place the fuel pump in the vehicle, aligning the packing positioning projections with the holes in the fuel pump.

5. For AWD vehicles, perform the following:

   a. Check to be sure the fuel tank packing is not damaged. If it is, it must be replaced.

   b. Place soapy water on the inside of the packing, then install the fuel pump assembly. Do NOT tilt the assembly during installation.

   c. Apply soapy water to the outside thread of the fuel tank. Use special tool MB994180 or an equivalent spanner wrench to tighten the cap to the specified torque. Make sure that the marks on the fuel tank and pump assembly are aligned.

✳✳ WARNING

Make sure the pump assembly does not turn together with the cap when tightening the cap. If the mating marks are not aligned, the position of the flat will not be correct and the fuel gauge indicator light and gauge will not work properly.

6. For AWD vehicles, make sure the packing is installed properly, as shown in the accompanying figure.

7. For AWD vehicles, check for leaks as follows:

   a. Apply soapy water to the circumference of the cap.

   b. Choke the vapor hose and main hose, apply and internal pressure of 1.5 psi (10 kPa) or less from the return hose and make sure no bubbles form in the soapy water.

8. Install the protector and attach the fuel pump electrical connector.

9. Install the rear seat cushion.

10. Connect the negative battery cable.

TESTING

Fuel Pump Operation Check

▶ See Figures 16 and 17

1. Set the ignition switch to the **OFF** position.

2. Check that when battery voltage is directly applied to the fuel pump check terminal located in the engine compartment, the operating sound of the fuel pump can be heard.

➡Since the fuel pump is located in the fuel tank, its operating sound cannot be readily heard. Remove the fuel tank cap and listen to the operating sound through the filler port.

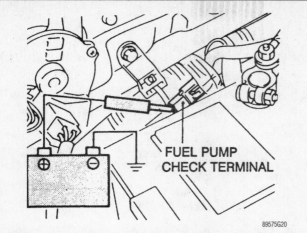

Fig. 16 Checking fuel pump operation with battery voltage applied to the fuel pump check terminal—1990–94 2.0L engine shown

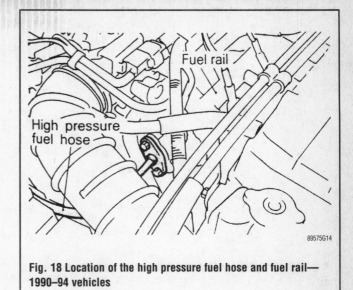

Fig. 18 Location of the high pressure fuel hose and fuel rail—1990–94 vehicles

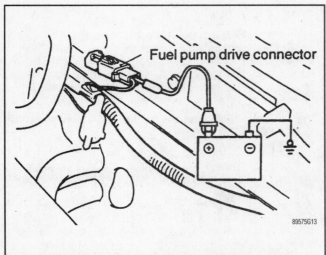

Fig. 17 Location of the fuel pump drive connector—1995–98 2.0L turbo and 2.4L engines shown

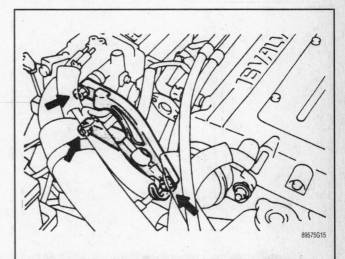

Fig. 19 High pressure fuel hose location—1995–98 2.0L turbo and 2.4L engine

3. Hold the high pressure fuel hose between your fingers and check that the fuel pressure in the lines can be felt.

Pressure Testing

EXCEPT 1995–98 2.0L NON-TURBO ENGINES

♦ **See Figures 18 thru 23**

1. Relieve the fuel system pressure as outlined earlier.

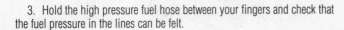

❊❊ CAUTION

Cover the hose connection with a shop towel to prevent the splash of fuel that can be caused by residual pressure in the fuel pipe line.

2. Disconnect the high pressure fuel line from the fuel rail.
3. On 1990–94 2.0L engine, remove the throttle body stay.
4. Connect a fuel pressure gauge to tools MD998709 and MD998742 or exact equivalent, with appropriate adapters, seals and/or gaskets to prevent leaks during the test. Install the gauge and adapter between the delivery pipe and high pressure hose.
5. Connect the negative battery cable.

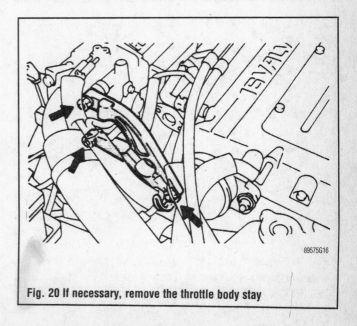

Fig. 20 If necessary, remove the throttle body stay

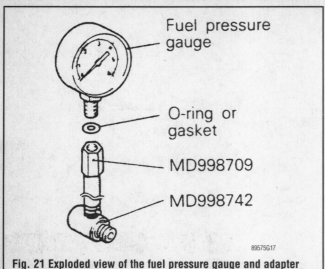

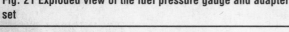

Fig. 21 Exploded view of the fuel pressure gauge and adapter set

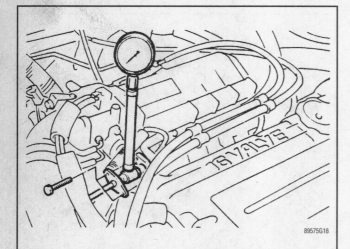

Fig. 22 Install of the fuel pressure gauge on the fuel rail—2.0L engine shown, others similar

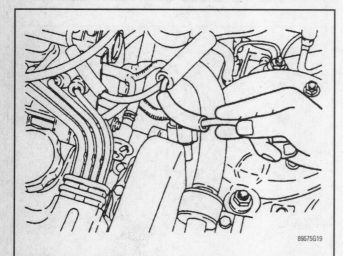

Fig. 23 Disconnect and plug the regulator vacuum hose, then measure the fuel pressure

6. For 1990–94 vehicles, apply battery voltage to the terminal for fuel pump check terminal located in the engine compartment. Run the fuel pump and check for leaks at the pressure gauge connection.

7. For 1995–98 vehicles, connect the fuel pump drive terminal to the positive battery terminal using a jumper wire to drive the fuel pump. Check the fuel pressure gauge and tool connections for leaks. Disconnect the jumper wire from the fuel pump drive terminal to stop the fuel pump.

8. Start the engine and run at curb idle speed.

9. For 1995–98 vehicles, measure the fuel pressure. For 2.0L turbo engines, the pressure should be 33 psi (230 kPa). For 2.4L engines, the fuel pressure should be 38 psi (270 kPa).

10. Locate and disconnect the vacuum hose from the fuel pressure regulator. Plug the end of the hose. Measure the fuel pressure and compare with the following specifications:
   a. 1990–94 non turbo engines:47–50 psi (330–350 kPa).
   b. 1990–94 turbo engines with manual transaxle:36–38 psi (250–270 kPa).
   c. 1990–94 turbo engines with automatic transaxle: 41–46 psi (290–320 kPa).
   d. 1995–98 2.0L turbo engines: 42–45 psi (289–309 kPa).
   e. 2.4L engines: 47–50 psi (330–350 kPa).

11. For 1990–94 vehicles, reconnect the pressure regulator vacuum hose, then measure the fuel pressure (engine idling) and compare with the following specifications:
   a. 1990–94 non turbo engines:38 psi (270 kPa).
   b. 1990–94 turbo engines with manual transaxle:27 psi (190 kPa).
   c. 1990–94 turbo engines with automatic transaxle: 33 psi (230 kPa).

12. After the fuel pressure stabilizes, race the engine 2–3 times and check that the fuel pressure does not fall when the engine is running at idle.

13. Check to be sure there is fuel pressure in the return hose by gently pressing the fuel return hose with fingers while racing the engine.

➡There will be no fuel pressure in the return hose when the volume of fuel flow is low.

14. If the results fall outside of specification, refer to the following:
   • If fuel pressure is too low, check for a clogged fuel filter, a defective fuel pressure regulator or a defective fuel pump, any of which will require replacement.
   • If fuel pressure is too high, the fuel pressure regulator is defective and will have to be replaced or the fuel return is bent or clogged.
   • If the fuel pressure reading does not change when the vacuum hose is disconnected, the hose is clogged or the valve is stuck in the fuel pressure regulator and it will have to be replaced.

15. Stop the engine and check for changes in the fuel pressure gauge. It should not drop. If the gauge reading does drop, watch the rate of drop. If fuel pressure drops slowly, the likely cause is a leaking injector which will require replacement. If the fuel pressure drops immediately after the engine is stopped, the check valve in the fuel pump isn't closing and the fuel pump will have to be replaced.

16. Relieve fuel system pressure.

17. Disconnect the high pressure hose and remove the fuel pressure gauge from the delivery pipe.

18. Install a new O-ring in the groove of the high pressure hose. Connect the hose to the delivery pipe and tighten the screws. After installation, apply battery voltage to the terminal for fuel pump activation to run the fuel pump. Check for leaks.

19. Reinstall the throttle body stay, if removed.

1995–98 2.0L NON-TURBO ENGINES

▶ See Figure 24

➡Testing the fuel pressure on these vehicles requires the use of a scan tool.

1. Properly relieve the fuel system pressure.
2. Remove the protective cover from the service valve on the fuel rail.
3. Connect Fuel Pressure Gauge MB995051 to the service valve.

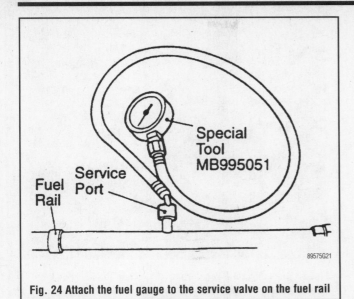

Fig. 24 Attach the fuel gauge to the service valve on the fuel rail

➡ **When using the scan tool fuel system test, the fuel pump relay stays energized for 7 minutes, until the test is stopped or until the ignition switch is turned of the OFF position.**

4. Turn the ignition key to the **ON** position. Use a suitable scan tool to access the "Fuel System Test". This test will activate the fuel pump and pressurize the system. The fuel pressure should be around 47–50 psi (330–350 kPa).

5. Use the scan tool to pressurize the fuel system, then make sure there is no fuel leakage from the service valve.

6. If the results fall outside of specification, refer to the following:

• If fuel pressure is too low, check for a clogged fuel filter, a defective fuel pressure regulator or a defective fuel pump, any of which will require replacement.

• If fuel pressure is too high, the fuel pressure regulator is defective and will have to be replaced or the fuel return is bent or clogged.

7. Using the scan tool, with the ignition key **ON**, repeat the fuel system test.

8. Turn the ignition switch **OFF**, then check the gauge reading. It's normal if the reading does not drop in about 2 minutes. If it does, check the rate of the drop and compare with the following:

• If the fuel pressure drops gradually, you have either a leaky injector or fuel regulator valve seat and the defective component should be replaced.

   a. If the fuel pressure drops sharply, check that the valve in the fuel pump is held open. If not, replace the fuel pump.

9. After testing has been completed, remove the fuel pressure gauge and install the protective cover onto the fuel rail service valve.

Throttle Body

REMOVAL & INSTALLATION

◆ **See Figures 25 thru 34**

1. Properly relieve the fuel system pressure as outlined earlier in this section.

2. Drain the engine cooling system into a suitable container.

3. For 1995–98 2.0L turbo and 2.4L engines, disconnect the negative and positive battery cables, then remove the battery from the vehicle.

4. Matchmark the location of the adjuster bolt on the accelerator cable mounting flange. This will assure that the cable is installed in its original location. Remove the throttle cable adjusting bolt and disconnect the cable from the lever on the throttle body. Position cable aside.

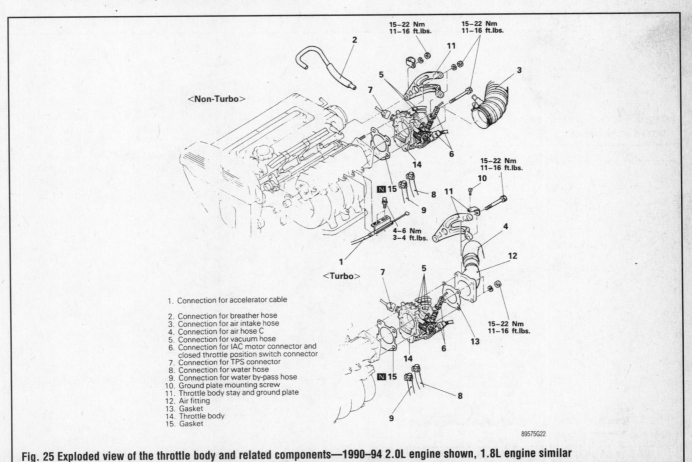

1. Connection for accelerator cable
2. Connection for breather hose
3. Connection for air intake hose
4. Connection for air hose C
5. Connection for vacuum hose
6. Connection for IAC motor connector and closed throttle position switch connector
7. Connection for TPS connector
8. Connection for water hose
9. Connection for water by-pass hose
10. Ground plate mounting screw
11. Throttle body stay and ground plate
12. Air fitting
13. Gasket
14. Throttle body
15. Gasket

Fig. 25 Exploded view of the throttle body and related components—1990–94 2.0L engine shown, 1.8L engine similar

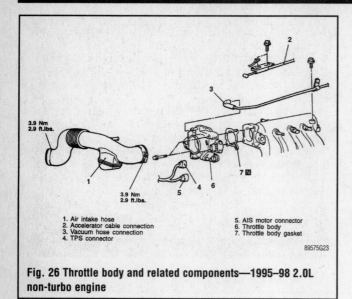

Fig. 26 Throttle body and related components—1995–98 2.0L non-turbo engine

1. Air intake hose
2. Accelerator cable connection
3. Vacuum hose connection
4. TPS connector
5. AIS motor connector
6. Throttle body
7. Throttle body gasket

89575G23

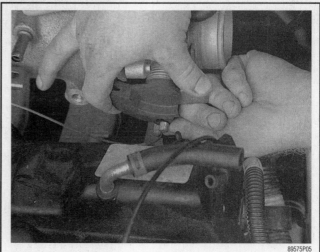

Fig. 28 Disconnect the accelerator cable from the lever on the throttle body

89575P05

5. Remove the connection for the breather hose and the air intake hose from the throttle body and position aside.

6. Tag and disconnect the necessary vacuum hoses.

7. Label and detach the electrical connectors at the throttle body, as necessary.

8. Disconnect the water and water by-pass hoses at the base of the throttle body.

9. If equipped, unfasten the ground plate mounting screws, then remove the throttle body stay and ground plate from the engine.

10. Remove the air fitting and gasket.

11. Unfasten the throttle body mounting bolts, then remove the throttle body from the engine. Remove and discard the gasket.

To install:

12. Clean all old gasket material from the both throttle body mounting surfaces. Install new gasket onto the intake manifold plenum mounting surface so the projection on the gasket is as illustrated.

➡**Poor idling quality and poor performance may be experienced if the gasket is installed incorrectly.**

13. Install the throttle body to the intake manifold plenum and tighten the mounting bolts to the specifications shown in the accompanying figures.

14. Install the air fitting, if equipped, making sure new gasket is in place.

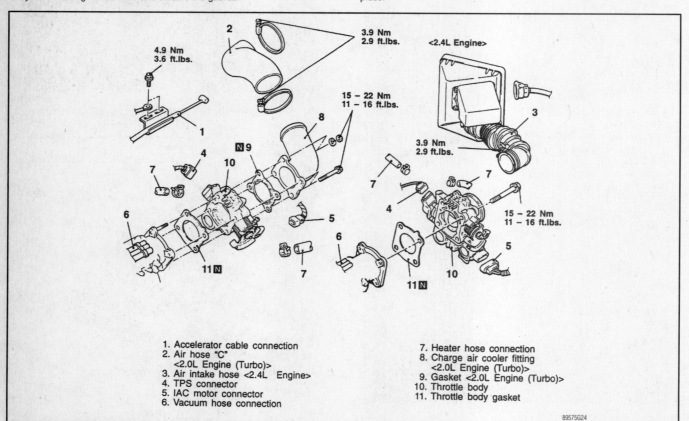

1. Accelerator cable connection
2. Air hose "C"
   <2.0L Engine (Turbo)>
3. Air intake hose <2.4L Engine>
4. TPS connector
5. IAC motor connector
6. Vacuum hose connection
7. Heater hose connection
8. Charge air cooler fitting
   <2.0L Engine (Turbo)>
9. Gasket <2.0L Engine (Turbo)>
10. Throttle body
11. Throttle body gasket

89575G24

Fig. 27 Throttle body mounting—1995–98 2.0L turbo and 2.4L engines

Fig. 29 Disconnect the vacuum hose from the throttle body

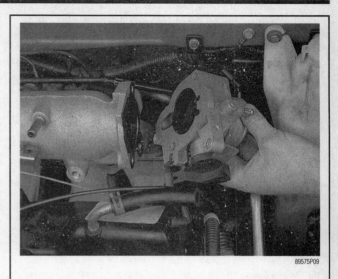

Fig. 32 . . . then remove the throttle body from the vehicle

Fig. 30 Tag and detach the TPS connector (1) and the IAC motor connector (2)

Fig. 33 Remove and discard the throttle body gasket, then thoroughly clean the mating surfaces

Fig. 31 Unfasten the throttle body-to-intake manifold retaining bolts . . .

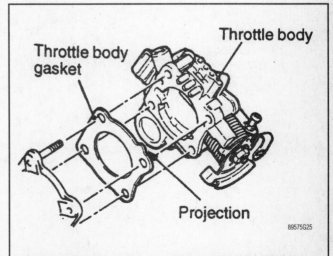

Fig. 34 During installation, make sure the throttle body base gasket is positioned properly

15. If equipped, install the throttle body stay and ground plate. Secure with retainers tightened to 11–16 ft. lbs. (15-22 Nm). Install the ground plate mounting screw.

16. Connect the water hoses to the throttle body. Install new hose clamps if required.

17. Attach the electrical and vacuum connectors to the throttle body, as tagged during removal.

18. Connect the accelerator cable to the throttle body and install the adjusting bolt in original position. Check adjustment of cable.

19. Install the air intake and breather hoses.

20. If removed, install the battery and connect the positive cable.

21. Connect the negative battery cable. Refill the cooling system.

CLEANING

1. Warm the engine to operating temperature and then turn the ignition **OFF**.

2. Remove the air intake hose from the throttle body.

3. Plug the by-pass inlet in the throttle body.

4. Spray cleaning solvent into the valve through the throttle body intake port and let is stand for approximately 5 minutes.

5. Start the engine and race it several times. Allow the engine to idle for about 1 minute. If the idling speed becomes unstable or if the engine stalls, slightly open the throttle valve to keep the engine running.

6. If the deposits on the throttle valve are not removed, repeat Steps 4 and 5.

7. Unplug the bypass passage inlet. Attach the air intake hose.

8. Disconnect the negative battery terminal for 10 seconds or more and then reconnect it.

9. Adjust the basic idle speed, if required.

➡**If the engine hunts (surges) at idle after the basic idle speed has been adjusted, disconnect the negative battery cable from the battery for at least 10 seconds and then, restart the engine and allow to idle.**

Fuel Rail and Injectors

REMOVAL & INSTALLATION

Except 1995–98 2.0L Non-Turbo Engines

▶ **See Figures 35, 36, 37, 38 and 39**

1. Properly relieve the fuel system pressure as outlined earlier in this section.

2. For 1990–94 vehicles, disconnect the PCV hose from the valve cover. On 1.8L engines, also disconnect the breather hose at the opposite end of the valve cover.

3. For 1995–98 vehicles, tag and disconnect the spark plug wires.

4. Remove the bolts holding the high pressure fuel line to the fuel rail and disconnect the line. Be prepared to contain fuel spillage; plug the line to keep out dirt and debris.

5. Remove the vacuum hose from the fuel pressure regulator.

6. Disconnect the fuel return hose from the pressure regulator. Remove the fuel pressure regulator mounting bolts and remove from the fuel rail.

7. On 1990–94 2.0L engines, remove the clamps holding the accelerator cable and remove the center engine cover from between the cam cover.

8. Label and detach the injector electrical connectors.

9. Remove the bolt(s) holding the fuel rail to the manifold. Carefully lift the rail up and remove it with the injectors attached. Be very careful not

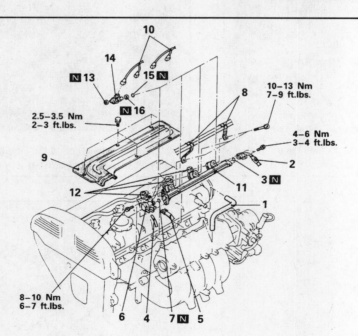

1. Connection for PCV hose
2. Connection for high pressure fuel hose
3. O-ring
4. Connection for vacuum hose
5. Connection for fuel return hose
6. Fuel pressure regulator
7. O-ring
8. Accelerator cable clamp
9. Center cover
10. Connection for control harness
11. Fuel rail
12. Insulator
13. Insulator
14. Injector
15. O-ring
16. Grommet

89575G27

Fig. 35 On 1990–94 2.0L engines, there is a center cover which must be removed for access to the fuel rail

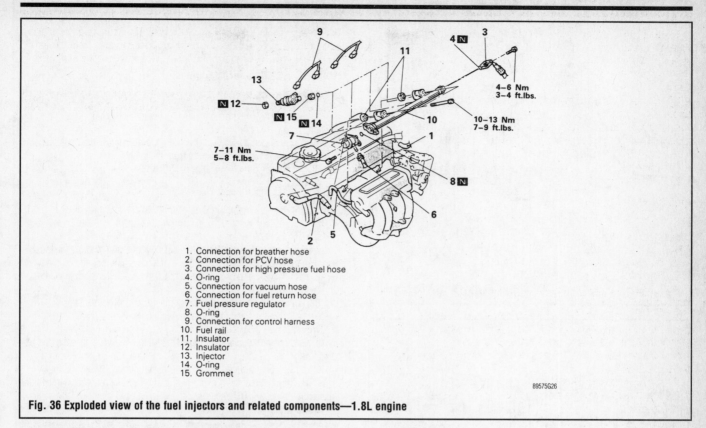

1. Connection for breather hose
2. Connection for PCV hose
3. Connection for high pressure fuel hose
4. O-ring
5. Connection for vacuum hose
6. Connection for fuel return hose
7. Fuel pressure regulator
8. O-ring
9. Connection for control harness
10. Fuel rail
11. Insulator
12. Insulator
13. Injector
14. O-ring
15. Grommet

Fig. 36 Exploded view of the fuel injectors and related components—1.8L engine

to drop any of the injectors. Place the rail and injectors in a safe location on a clean workbench; protect the tips of the injectors from dirt and/or impact.

10. Remove and discard the injector insulators from the intake manifold. The insulators are not reusable.

11. Remove the injectors from the fuel rail by pulling gently in a straight outward motion. Make certain the grommet and O-ring come off with the injector.

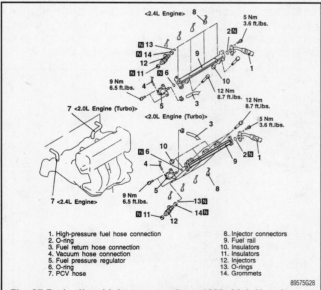

1. High-pressure fuel hose connection
2. O-ring
3. Fuel return hose connection
4. Vacuum hose connection
5. Fuel pressure regulator
6. O-ring
7. PCV hose
8. Injector connectors
9. Fuel rail
10. Insulators
11. Insulators
12. Injectors
13. O-rings
14. Grommets

Fig. 37 Fuel rail and injector mounting—1995–98 2.0L turbo and 2.4L engine

To install:

12. Install a new insulator in each injector port in the manifold.

13. Remove and discard the old grommet and O-ring from each injector. Install a new grommet and O-ring; coat the O-ring lightly with clean engine oil.

14. If the fuel pressure regulator was removed, replace the O-ring with a new one and coat it lightly with clean, thin oil. Insert the regulator straight into the rail, then check that it can be rotated freely. If it does not rotate smoothly, remove it and inspect the O-ring for deformation or jamming. When properly installed, align the mounting holes and tighten the retaining bolts to 8 ft. lbs. (11 Nm). This procedure must be followed even if the fuel rail was not removed.

15. Install the injector into the fuel rail, constantly turning the injector left and right during installation. When fully installed, the injector should still turn freely in the rail. If it does not, remove the injector and inspect the O-ring for deformation or damage.

16. Install the delivery pipe and injectors to the engine. Make certain that each injector fits correctly into its port and that the rubber insulators for the fuel rail mounts are in position.

17. Install the fuel rail retaining bolts and tighten them to 8 ft. lbs. (11 Nm). On 2.0L engines, install the accelerator cable retaining clips before the rail retaining bolts.

18. Connect the wiring harnesses to the appropriate injector.

19. On 1990–94 2.0L engines, reinstall the center cover. Tighten the retaining bolts to 3 ft. lbs. (4 Nm).

20. Connect the fuel return hose to the pressure regulator, then connect the vacuum hose.

21. Replace the O-ring on the high pressure fuel line, coat the O-ring lightly with clean, thin oil and install the line to the fuel rail. Tighten the mounting bolts to 4 ft. lbs. (6 Nm).

22. If disconnected, attach the spark plug wires as tagged during removal.

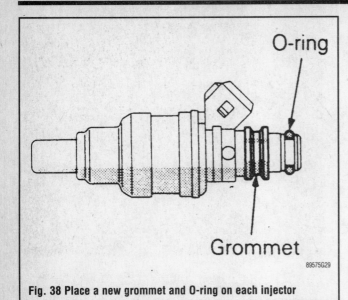

Fig. 38 Place a new grommet and O-ring on each injector

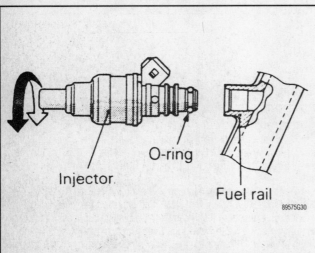

Fig. 39 The fuel injector must be properly installed in the fuel rail

23. If removed, connect the PCV hose and the breather hose.

24. Connect the negative battery cable. Pressurize the fuel system by turning the ignition **ON** and inspect all connections for leaks.

1995–98 2.0L Non-Turbo Engines

▶ **See Figures 40 thru 46**

1. Properly relieve the fuel system pressure as outlined earlier in this section.

2. Disconnect the negative (if not already done), and the positive battery cables, then remove the battery from the vehicle.

3. Disconnect the air intake hose.

4. Place a shop rag around the fitting, then detach the high-pressure fuel hose connection. Remove and discard the line O-ring.

5. Unfasten the fuel return hose connection.

6. If necessary, disconnect the pressure regulator vacuum hose and the injector harness connector.

7. Remove the fuel rail from the vehicle with the injectors attached. Be very careful not to drop the assembly. Place the rail and injectors in a safe location on a clean workbench; protect the tips of the injectors from dirt and/or impact.

8. Tag and detach the fuel injector electrical connectors.

9. Unfasten the injector-to-fuel rail retainers, then separate the injectors from the rail.

10. Remove and discard the injector O-rings. There is 1 at each end of the O-ring.

11. If necessary to remove the fuel pressure regulator, unfasten the snapring, then remove the pressure regulator from the fuel rail. Remove and discard the regulator O-rings.

To install:

❊❊ WARNING

When lubricating O-rings, do NOT allow any engine oil to get into the fuel rail!

12. If the regulator was removed, lightly lubricate new O-rings with clean engine oil, then install on he regulator. Position the regulator on the rail, then secure with the snapring.

13. Lightly coat new O-rings with clean engine oil, then install on the injector.

14. Install the injector into the fuel rail, constantly turning the injector left and right during installation. When fully installed, the injector should still turn freely in the rail. If it does not, remove the injector and inspect the O-ring for deformation or damage. Secure with the injector retainers.

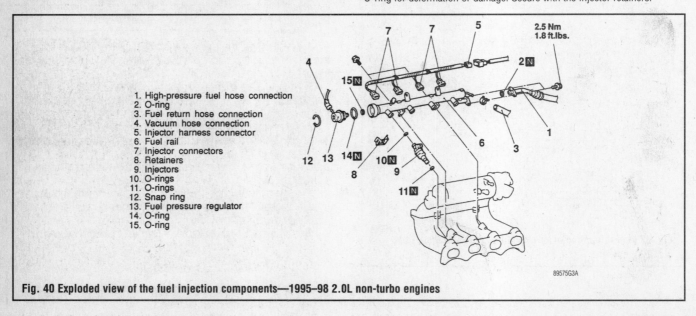

1. High-pressure fuel hose connection
2. O-ring
3. Fuel return hose connection
4. Vacuum hose connection
5. Injector harness connector
6. Fuel rail
7. Injector connectors
8. Retainers
9. Injectors
10. O-rings
11. O-rings
12. Snap ring
13. Fuel pressure regulator
14. O-ring
15. O-ring

Fig. 40 Exploded view of the fuel injection components—1995–98 2.0L non-turbo engines

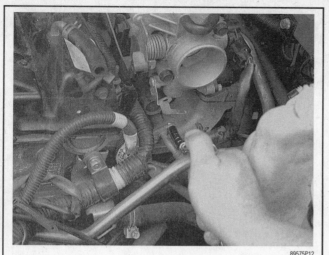

Fig. 41 After relieving system pressure, loosen the high pressure fuel line

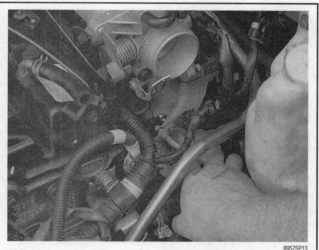

Fig. 42 Make sure to place a shop rag under the line to catch any fuel that may seep out after disconnection

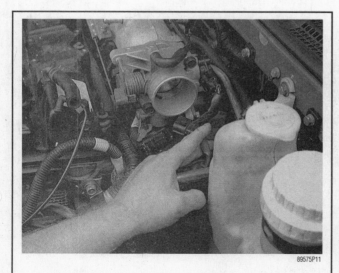

Fig. 43 Unplug the fuel injector harness connector

Fig. 44 After the fuel rail is removed, spread the retainer and remove the fuel injector

Fig. 45 As shown with arrows, there is an O-ring at the end of each injector

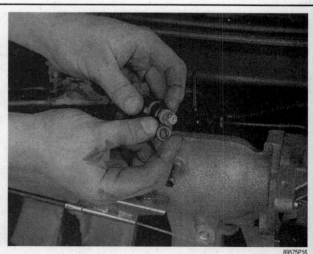

Fig. 46 The injector O-rings must be discarded and replaced with new ones before installation

15. Attach the injector electrical connectors, as tagged during removal.
16. Install the fuel rail into the vehicle and install the mounting bolts (if equipped).
17. Attach the injector harness connector and the pressure regulator vacuum hose.
18. Install the fuel return hose connection.
19. Install a new O-ring, then connect the high pressure fuel line. To ease connection, place a small amount of clean engine oil into the hose union before inserting.
20. Connect the air intake hose.
21. Install the battery, then connect the positive and negative battery cables.
22. Pressurize the fuel system by turning the ignition **ON** and inspect all connections for leaks.

TESTING

◆ See Figure 47

With the engine running at idle, use a stethoscope or similar tool to listen to the individual injectors. With the stethoscope, each injector should exhibit a distinct clicking as it functions. The speed of the clicking should increase with engine speed. Note that other injectors may be heard through a non-functioning injector.

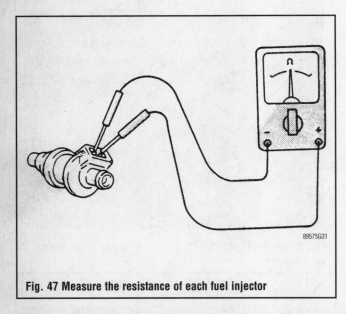

Fig. 47 Measure the resistance of each fuel injector

To check the resistance of each injector, perform the following:
1. Turn the ignition to the **OFF** position.
2. Disconnect the injector harness from the injector to be tested.
3. Measure the resistance across the injector terminals. Reference resistances are:
   a. All non-turbo engines, except 1995–98 2.0L engines: 13–16 ohms at 68°F (20°C).
   b. Turbocharged engines: 2–3 ohms at 68 degrees F.
   c. 1995–98 2.0L non-turbo engines:11–15 ohms at 68°F (20°C).
4. Reconnect the injector wiring harness.

Fuel Pressure Regulator

REMOVAL & INSTALLATION

◆ See Figure 48

1. Properly relieve the fuel system pressure as outlined earlier in this section.
2. If necessary for access to the regulator, disconnect the PCV hose from the valve cover. On 1.8L engines, also disconnect the breather hose at the opposite end of the valve cover.
3. Remove the vacuum hose from the fuel pressure regulator.
4. Disconnect the fuel return hose from the pressure regulator.
5. Remove the fuel regulator retainer bolts or remove the retaining snapring, then remove the fuel regulator from the fuel rail.
  To install:
6. Replace the O-ring on fuel pressure regulator with a new one and coat it lightly with clean, thin oil.
7. Insert the regulator straight into the rail, then check that it can be rotated freely.

➡**If it does not rotate smoothly, remove it and inspect the O-ring for deformation or damage.**

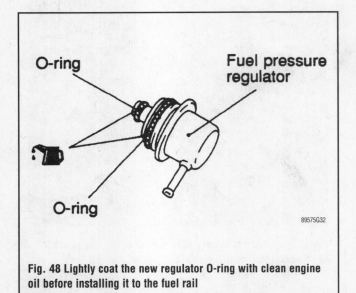

Fig. 48 Lightly coat the new regulator O-ring with clean engine oil before installing it to the fuel rail

8. When properly installed, align the mounting holes. If equipped, install and tighten the retaining bolts to 8 ft. lbs. (11 Nm). If equipped, install the regulator retaining snapring.
9. Connect the fuel return hose to the pressure regulator.
10. Install the vacuum hose to the fuel pressure regulator.
11. If removed, connect the PCV hose to the valve cover. On 1.8L engines, also connect the breather hose at the opposite end of the valve cover.
12. Connect the negative battery cable and pressurize the fuel system. Inspect for leaks.

FUEL TANK

Tank Assembly

REMOVAL & INSTALLATION

▶ **See Figures 49, 50, 51 and 52**

1. Properly relieve the fuel system pressure as outlined earlier in this section.
2. Drain the fuel from the fuel tank into an approved container.
3. Raise the vehicle and support safely.
4. For 1995–98 AWD vehicles, perform the following:
   a. Remove the driveshaft.
   b. Detach the heated oxygen sensor electrical connector.
   c. Remove the center exhaust pipe.
   d. Unfasten the retainers, then remove the fuel tank protector.
5. Disconnect the return hose, high pressure hose and vapor hoses from the fuel pump.
6. Disconnect the electrical connectors at the pump/sending unit.

✳✳ CAUTION

Cover all fuel hose connections with a shop towel, prior to disconnecting, to prevent splash of fuel that could be caused by residual pressure remaining in the fuel line.

7. Disconnect the filler and vent hoses.
8. Place a transmission jack under the center of the fuel tank and apply a slight upward pressure. Remove the fuel tank strap retaining nut or tank retaining nuts, as applicable.
9. Lower the tank slightly and disconnect any remaining electrical or hose connectors at the fuel tank.
10. Remove the fuel tank from the vehicle.

To install:

11. Install the fuel tank onto the transmission jack. Raise the tank in position under the vehicle. Leave enough clearance to attach the electrical and hose connections to the top of the fuel pump.
12. Attach all connections to the top of the tank.
13. Raise the tank completely and position the retainer straps around the fuel tank, if equipped. Install new fuel tank self-locking nuts and tighten.
14. Connect the return hose and high pressure hoses.
15. Install the vapor hose and the filler hose. Install the filler hose retainer screws to the fender, if removed.
16. For 1995–98 AWD vehicles, perform the following:
   a. Install the fuel tank protector and install the retainers.
   b. Install the center exhaust pipe.
   c. Attach the heated oxygen sensor electrical connector.
   d. Install the driveshaft.
17. Carefully lower the vehicle and pour the drained fuel back into the gas tank.
18. Connect the negative battery cable. Check the fuel pump for proper pressure and inspect the entire system for leaks.

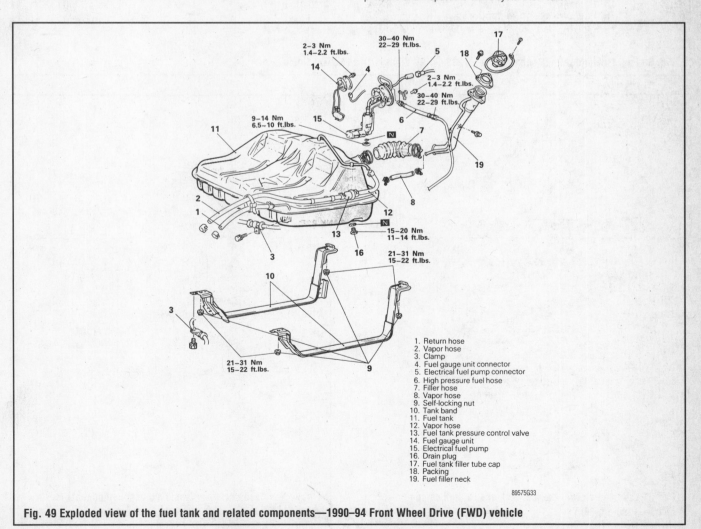

1. Return hose
2. Vapor hose
3. Clamp
4. Fuel gauge unit connector
5. Electrical fuel pump connector
6. High pressure fuel hose
7. Filler hose
8. Vapor hose
9. Self-locking nut
10. Tank band
11. Fuel tank
12. Vapor hose
13. Fuel tank pressure control valve
14. Fuel gauge unit
15. Electrical fuel pump
16. Drain plug
17. Fuel tank filler tube cap
18. Packing
19. Fuel filler neck

89575G33

Fig. 49 Exploded view of the fuel tank and related components—1990–94 Front Wheel Drive (FWD) vehicle

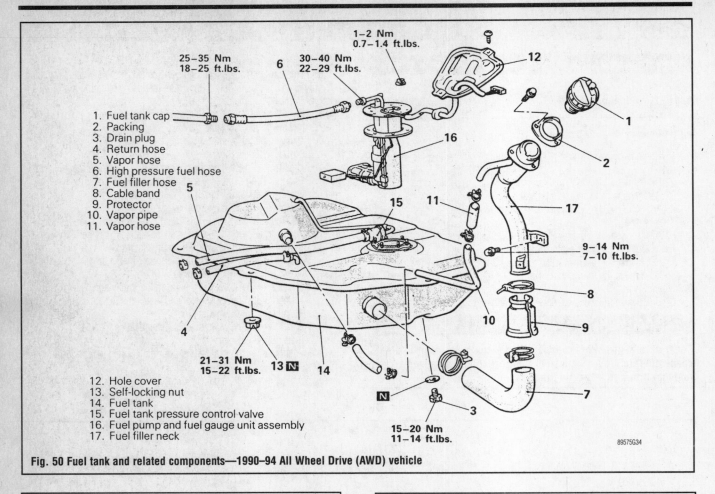

1. Fuel tank cap
2. Packing
3. Drain plug
4. Return hose
5. Vapor hose
6. High pressure fuel hose
7. Fuel filler hose
8. Cable band
9. Protector
10. Vapor pipe
11. Vapor hose

12. Hole cover
13. Self-locking nut
14. Fuel tank
15. Fuel tank pressure control valve
16. Fuel pump and fuel gauge unit assembly
17. Fuel filler neck

25–35 Nm
18–25 ft.lbs.

30–40 Nm
22–29 ft.lbs.

1–2 Nm
0.7–1.4 ft.lbs.

9–14 Nm
7–10 ft.lbs.

21–31 Nm
15–22 ft.lbs.

15–20 Nm
11–14 ft.lbs.

Fig. 50 Fuel tank and related components—1990–94 All Wheel Drive (AWD) vehicle

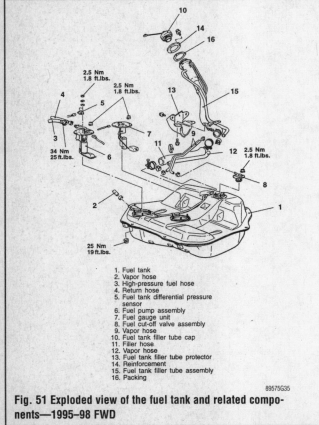

1. Fuel tank
2. Vapor hose
3. High-pressure fuel hose
4. Return hose
5. Fuel tank differential pressure sensor
6. Fuel pump assembly
7. Fuel gauge unit
8. Fuel cut-off valve assembly
9. Vapor hose
10. Fuel tank filler tube cap
11. Filler hose
12. Vapor hose
13. Fuel tank filler tube protector
14. Reinforcement
15. Fuel tank filler tube assembly
16. Packing

2.5 Nm
1.8 ft.lbs.

2.5 Nm
1.8 ft.lbs.

34 Nm
25 ft.lbs.

2.5 Nm
1.8 ft.lbs.

25 Nm
19 ft.lbs.

Fig. 51 Exploded view of the fuel tank and related components—1995–98 FWD

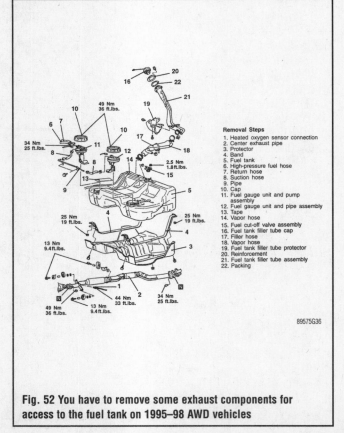

Removal Steps
1. Heated oxygen sensor connection
2. Center exhaust pipe
3. Protector
4. Band
5. Fuel tank
6. High-pressure fuel hose
7. Return hose
8. Suction hose
9. Pipe
10. Cap
11. Fuel gauge unit and pump assembly
12. Fuel gauge unit and pipe assembly
13. Tape
14. Vapor hose
15. Fuel cut-off valve assembly
16. Fuel tank filler tube cap
17. Filler hose
18. Vapor hose
19. Fuel tank filler tube protector
20. Reinforcement
21. Fuel tank filler tube assembly
22. Packing

49 Nm
36 ft.lbs.

34 Nm
25 ft.lbs.

2.5 Nm
1.8 ft.lbs.

25 Nm
19 ft.lbs.

25 Nm
19 ft.lbs.

13 Nm
9.4 ft.lbs.

49 Nm
36 ft.lbs.

13 Nm
9.4 ft.lbs.

44 Nm
33 ft.lbs.

34 Nm
25 ft.lbs.

Fig. 52 You have to remove some exhaust components for access to the fuel tank on 1995–98 AWD vehicles

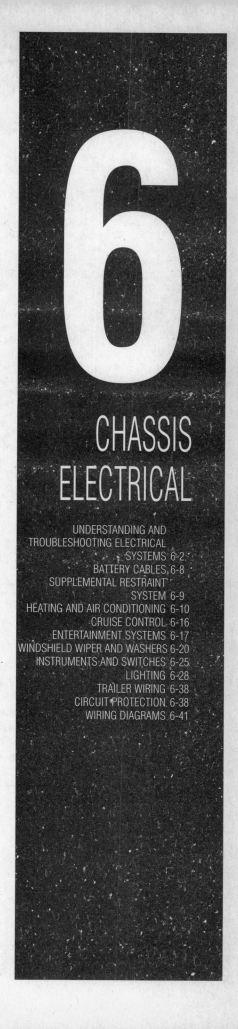

6

CHASSIS ELECTRICAL

UNDERSTANDING AND TROUBLESHOOTING ELECTRICAL SYSTEMS

Basic Electrical Theory

▶ **See Figure 1**

For any 12 volt, negative ground, electrical system to operate, the electricity must travel in a complete circuit. This simply means that current (power) from the positive terminal (+) of the battery must eventually return to the negative terminal (-) of the battery. Along the way, this current will travel through wires, fuses, switches and components. If, for any reason, the flow of current through the circuit is interrupted, the component fed by that circuit will cease to function properly.

Perhaps the easiest way to visualize a circuit is to think of connecting a light bulb (with two wires attached to it) to the battery—one wire attached to the negative (-) terminal of the battery and the other wire to the positive (+) terminal. With the two wires touching the battery terminals, the circuit would be complete and the light bulb would illuminate. Electricity would follow a path from the battery to the bulb and back to the battery. It's easy to see that with longer wires on our light bulb, it could be mounted anywhere. Further, one wire could be fitted with a switch so that the light could be turned on and off.

The normal automotive circuit differs from this simple example in two ways. First, instead of having a return wire from the bulb to the battery, the current travels through the chassis of the vehicle. Since the negative (-) battery cable is attached to the chassis and the chassis is made of electrically conductive metal, the chassis of the vehicle can serve as a ground wire to complete the circuit. Secondly, most automotive circuits contain multiple components which receive power from a single circuit. This lessens the amount of wire needed to power components on the vehicle.

Fig. 1 This example illustrates a simple circuit. When the switch is closed, power from the positive (+) battery terminal flows through the fuse and the switch, and then to the light bulb. The light illuminates and the circuit is completed through the ground wire back to the negative (-) battery terminal. In reality, the two ground points shown in the illustration are attached to the metal chassis of the vehicle, which completes the circuit back to the battery.

THE WATER ANALOGY

Electricity is the flow of electrons—hypothetical particles thought to constitute the basic "stuff" of electricity. Many people have been taught electrical theory using an analogy with water. In a comparison with water flowing through a pipe, the electrons would be the water.

The flow of electricity can be measured much like the flow of water through a pipe. The unit of measurement used is amperes, frequently abbreviated as amps (a). When connected to a circuit, an ammeter will measure the actual amount of current flowing through the circuit. When relatively few electrons flow through a circuit, the amperage is low. When many electrons flow, the amperage is high.

Just as water pressure is measured in units such as pounds per square inch (psi), electrical pressure is measured in units called volts (v). When a voltmeter is connected to a circuit, it is measuring the electrical pressure. The higher the voltage, the more current will flow through the circuit. The lower the voltage, the less current will flow.

While increasing the voltage in a circuit will increase the flow of current, the actual flow depends not only on voltage, but also on the resistance of the circuit. Resistance is the amount of force necessary to push the current through the circuit. The standard unit for measuring resistance is an ohm (W or omega). Resistance in a circuit varies depending on the amount and type of components used in the circuit. The main factors which determine resistance are:

• Material—some materials have more resistance than others. Those with high resistance are said to be insulators. Rubber is one of the best insulators available, as it allows little current to pass. Low resistance materials are said to be conductors. Copper wire is among the best conductors. Most vehicle wiring is made of copper.

• Size—the larger the wire size being used, the less resistance the wire will have. This is why components which use large amounts of electricity usually have large wires supplying current to them.

• Length—for a given thickness of wire, the longer the wire, the greater the resistance. The shorter the wire, the less the resistance. When determining the proper wire for a circuit, both size and length must be considered to design a circuit that can handle the current needs of the component.

• Temperature—with many materials, the higher the temperature, the greater the resistance. This principle is used in many of the sensors on the engine.

OHM'S LAW

The preceding definitions may lead the reader into believing that there is no relationship between current, voltage and resistance. Nothing can be further from the truth. The relationship between current, voltage and resistance can be summed up by a statement known as Ohm's law.

Voltage (E) is equal to amperage (I) times resistance (R): $E = I \times R$

Other forms of the formula are $R = E/I$ and $I = E/R$

In each of these formulas, E is the voltage in volts, I is the current in amps and R is the resistance in ohms. The basic point to remember is that as the resistance of a circuit goes up, the amount of current that flows in the circuit will go down, if voltage remains the same.

Electrical Components

POWER SOURCE

The power source for 12 volt automotive electrical systems is the battery. In most modern vehicles, the battery is a lead/acid electrochemical device consisting of six 2 volt subsections (cells) connected in series, so that the unit is capable of producing approximately 12 volts of electrical pressure. Each subsection consists of a series of positive and negative plates held a short distance apart in a solution of sulfuric acid and water.

The two types of plates are of dissimilar metals. This sets up a chemical reaction, and it is this reaction which produces current flow from the battery when its positive and negative terminals are connected to an electrical load. The power removed from the battery is replaced by the alternator, which forces electrons back through the battery, reversing the normal flow, and restoring the battery to its original chemical state.

GROUND

Two types of grounds are used in automotive electric circuits. Direct ground components are grounded through their mounting points. All other components use some sort of ground wire which is attached to the body or chassis of the vehicle. The electrical current runs through the chassis of the vehicle and returns to the battery through the ground (-) cable; if you look, you'll see that the battery ground cable connects between the battery and the body or chassis of the vehicle.

➡It should be noted that a good percentage of electrical problems can be traced to bad grounds.

PROTECTIVE DEVICES

◆ See Figure 2

It is possible for large surges of current to pass through the electrical system of your vehicle. If this surge of current were to reach the load in the circuit, it could burn it out or severely damage it. To prevent this, fuses, circuit breakers and/or fusible links are connected into the supply wires of the electrical system. These items are nothing more than a built-in weak spot in the system. When an abnormal amount of current flows through the system, these protective devices work as follows to protect the circuit:

• Fuse—when an excessive electrical current passes through a fuse, the fuse "blows" (the conductor melts) and opens the circuit, preventing the passage of current.

• Circuit Breaker—a circuit breaker is basically a self-repairing fuse. It will open the circuit in the same fashion as a fuse, but when the surge subsides, the circuit breaker can be reset and does not need replacement.

• Fusible Link—a fusible link (fuse link or main link) is a short length of special, Hypalon high temperature insulated wire that acts as a fuse. When an excessive electrical current passes through a fusible link, the thin gauge wire inside the link melts, creating an intentional open to protect the circuit. To repair the circuit, the link must be replaced. Some newer type fusible links are housed in plug-in modules, which are simply replaced like a fuse, while older type fusible links must be cut and spliced if they melt. Since this link is very early in the electrical path, it's the first place to look if nothing on the vehicle works, but the battery seems to be charged and is properly connected.

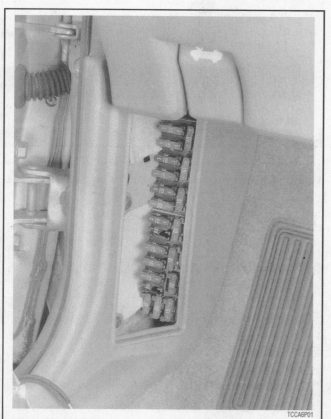

Fig. 2 Most vehicles use one or more fuse panels. This one is located in the driver's side kick panel

Always replace fuses, circuit breakers and fusible links with identically rated components. Under no circumstances should a component of higher or lower amperage rating be substituted.

SWITCHES & RELAYS

◆ See Figures 3 and 4

Switches are used in electrical circuits to control the passage of current. The most common use is to open and close circuits between the battery and the various electric devices in the system. Switches are rated according to the amount of amperage they can handle. If a sufficient amperage rated switch is not used in a circuit, the switch could overload and cause damage.

Some electrical components which require a large amount of current to operate use a special switch called a relay. Since these circuits carry a large amount of current, the thickness of the wire in the circuit is also greater. If this large wire were connected from the load to the control switch on the dashboard, the switch would have to carry the high amperage load and the dash would be twice as large to accommodate the increased size of the wiring harness. To prevent these problems, a relay is used.

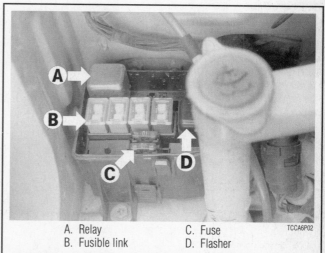

A. Relay   C. Fuse
B. Fusible link   D. Flasher

Fig. 3 The underhood fuse and relay panel usually contains fuses, relays, flashers and fusible links

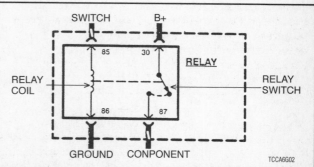

Fig. 4 Relays are composed of a coil and a switch. These two components are linked together so that when one operates, the other operates at the same time. The large wires in the circuit are connected from the battery to one side of the relay switch (B+) and from the opposite side of the relay switch to the load (component). Smaller wires are connected from the relay coil to the control switch for the circuit and from the opposite side of the relay coil to ground.

Relays are composed of a coil and a switch. These two components are linked together so that when one operates, the other operates at the same time. The large wires in the circuit are connected from the battery to one side of the relay switch and from the opposite side of the relay switch to the load. Most relays are normally open, preventing current from passing through the circuit. Additional, smaller wires are connected from the relay coil to the control switch for the circuit and from the opposite side of the relay coil to ground. When the control switch is turned on, it grounds the smaller wire to the relay coil, causing the coil to operate. The coil pulls the relay switch closed, sending power to the component without routing it through the inside of the vehicle. Some common circuits which may use relays are the horn, headlights, starter, electric fuel pump and rear window defogger systems.

LOAD

Every complete circuit must include a "load" (something to use the electricity coming from the source). Without this load, the battery would attempt to deliver its entire power supply from one pole to another. The electricity would take a short cut to ground and cause a great amount of damage to other components in the circuit by developing a tremendous amount of heat. This condition could develop sufficient heat to melt the insulation on all the surrounding wires and reduce a multiple wire cable to a lump of plastic and copper.

WIRING & HARNESSES

The average automobile contains about 1/2 mile of wiring, with hundreds of individual connections. To protect the many wires from damage and to keep them from becoming a confusing tangle, they are organized into bundles, enclosed in plastic or taped together and called wiring harnesses. Different harnesses serve different parts of the vehicle. Individual wires are color coded to help trace them through a harness where sections are hidden from view.

Automotive wiring or circuit conductors can be either single strand wire, multi-strand wire or printed circuitry. Single strand wire has a solid metal core and is usually used inside such components as alternators, motors, relays and other devices. Multi-strand wire has a core made of many small strands of wire twisted together into a single conductor. Most of the wiring in an automotive electrical system is made up of multi-strand wire, either as a single conductor or grouped together in a harness. All wiring is color coded on the insulator, either as a solid color or as a colored wire with an identification stripe. A printed circuit is a thin film of copper or other conductor that is printed on an insulator backing. Occasionally, a printed circuit is sandwiched between two sheets of plastic for more protection and flexibility. A complete printed circuit, consisting of conductors, insulating material and connectors for lamps or other components is called a printed circuit board. Printed circuitry is used in place of individual wires or harnesses in places where space is limited, such as behind instrument panels.

Since automotive electrical systems are very sensitive to changes in resistance, the selection of properly sized wires is critical when systems are repaired. A loose or corroded connection or a replacement wire that is too small for the circuit will add extra resistance and an additional voltage drop to the circuit.

The wire gauge number is an expression of the cross-section area of the conductor. The most common system for expressing wire size is the American Wire Gauge (AWG) system. As gauge number increases, area decreases and the wire becomes smaller. An 18 gauge wire is smaller than a 4 gauge wire. A wire with a higher gauge number will carry less current than a wire with a lower gauge number. Gauge wire size refers to the size of the strands of the conductor, not the size of the complete wire. It is possible, therefore, to have two wires of the same gauge with different diameters because one may have thicker insulation than the other.

12 volt automotive electrical systems generally use 10, 12, 14, 16 and 18 gauge wire. Main power distribution circuits and larger accessories usually use 10 and 12 gauge wire. Battery cables are usually 4 or 6 gauge, although 1 and 2 gauge wires are occasionally used.

It is essential to understand how a circuit works before trying to figure out why it doesn't. An electrical schematic shows the electrical current paths when a circuit is operating properly. Schematics break the entire electrical system down into individual circuits. In a schematic, no attempt is made to represent wiring and components as they physically appear on the vehicle; switches and other components are shown as simply as possible. Face views of harness connectors show the cavity or terminal locations in all multi-pin connectors to help locate test points.

CONNECTORS

▶ **See Figures 5 and 6**

Three types of connectors are commonly used in automotive applications-weatherproof, molded and hard shell.

• Weatherproof—these connectors are most commonly used in the engine compartment or where the connector is exposed to the elements. Terminals are protected against moisture and dirt by sealing rings which provide a weathertight seal. All repairs require the use of a special terminal and the tool required to service it. Unlike standard blade type terminals, these weatherproof terminals cannot be straightened once they are bent. Make certain that the connectors are properly seated and all of the sealing rings are in place when connecting leads.

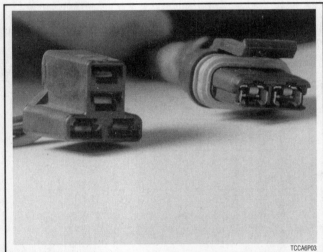

TCCA6P03

Fig. 5 Hard shell (left) and weatherproof (right) connectors have replaceable terminals

TCCA6P04

Fig. 6 Weatherproof connectors are most commonly used in the engine compartment or where the connector is exposed to the elements

• Molded—these connectors require complete replacement of the connector if found to be defective. This means splicing a new connector assembly into the harness. All splices should be soldered to insure proper contact. Use care when probing the connections or replacing terminals in them, as it is possible to create a short circuit between opposite terminals. If this happens to the wrong terminal pair, it is possible to damage certain components. Always use jumper wires between connectors for circuit checking and NEVER probe through weatherproof seals.

• Hard Shell—unlike molded connectors, the terminal contacts in hard-shell connectors can be replaced. Replacement usually involves the use of a special terminal removal tool that depresses the locking tangs (barbs) on the connector terminal and allows the connector to be removed from the rear of the shell. The connector shell should be replaced if it shows any evidence of burning, melting, cracks, or breaks. Replace individual terminals that are burnt, corroded, distorted or loose.

Test Equipment

Pinpointing the exact cause of trouble in an electrical circuit is most times accomplished by the use of special test equipment. The following describes different types of commonly used test equipment and briefly explains how to use them in diagnosis. In addition to the information covered below, the tool manufacturer's instructions booklet (provided with the tester) should be read and clearly understood before attempting any test procedures.

JUMPER WIRES

✳✳ CAUTION

Never use jumper wires made from a thinner gauge wire than the circuit being tested. If the jumper wire is of too small a gauge, it may overheat and possibly melt. Never use jumpers to bypass high resistance loads in a circuit. Bypassing resistances, in effect, creates a short circuit. This may, in turn, cause damage and fire. Jumper wires should only be used to bypass lengths of wire.

Jumper wires are simple, yet extremely valuable, pieces of test equipment. They are basically test wires which are used to bypass sections of a circuit. Although jumper wires can be purchased, they are usually fabricated from lengths of standard automotive wire and whatever type of connector (alligator clip, spade connector or pin connector) that is required for the particular application being tested. In cramped, hard-to-reach areas, it is advisable to have insulated boots over the jumper wire terminals in order to prevent accidental grounding. It is also advisable to include a standard automotive fuse in any jumper wire. This is commonly referred to as a "fused jumper". By inserting an in-line fuse holder between a set of test leads, a fused jumper wire can be used for bypassing open circuits. Use a 5 amp fuse to provide protection against voltage spikes.

Jumper wires are used primarily to locate open electrical circuits, on either the ground (-) side of the circuit or on the power (+) side. If an electrical component fails to operate, connect the jumper wire between the component and a good ground. If the component operates only with the jumper installed, the ground circuit is open. If the ground circuit is good, but the component does not operate, the circuit between the power feed and component may be open. By moving the jumper wire successively back from the component toward the power source, you can isolate the area of the circuit where the open is located. When the component stops functioning, or the power is cut off, the open is in the segment of wire between the jumper and the point previously tested.

You can sometimes connect the jumper wire directly from the battery to the "hot" terminal of the component, but first make sure the component uses 12 volts in operation. Some electrical components, such as fuel injectors, are designed to operate on about 4 volts, and running 12 volts directly to these components will cause damage.

TEST LIGHTS

▶ See Figure 7

The test light is used to check circuits and components while electrical current is flowing through them. It is used for voltage and ground tests. To use a 12 volt test light, connect the ground clip to a good ground and probe wherever necessary with the pick. The test light will illuminate when voltage is detected. This does not necessarily mean that 12 volts (or any particular amount of voltage) is present; it only means that some voltage is present. It is advisable before using the test light to touch its ground clip and probe across the battery posts or terminals to make sure the light is operating properly.

✳✳ WARNING

Do not use a test light to probe electronic ignition spark plug or coil wires. Never use a pick-type test light to probe wiring on computer controlled systems unless specifically instructed to do so. Any wire insulation that is pierced by the test light probe should be taped and sealed with silicone after testing.

Like the jumper wire, the 12 volt test light is used to isolate opens in circuits. But, whereas the jumper wire is used to bypass the open to operate the load, the 12 volt test light is used to locate the presence of voltage in a circuit. If the test light illuminates, there is power up to that point in the circuit; if the test light does not illuminate, there is an open circuit (no power). Move the test light in successive steps back toward the power source until the light in the handle illuminates. The open is between the probe and a point which was previously probed.

The self-powered test light is similar in design to the 12 volt test light, but contains a 1.5 volt penlight battery in the handle. It is most often used in place of a multimeter to check for open or short circuits when power is isolated from the circuit (continuity test).

The battery in a self-powered test light does not provide much current. A weak battery may not provide enough power to illuminate the test light even when a complete circuit is made (especially if there is high resistance in the circuit). Always make sure that the test battery is strong. To check the battery, briefly touch the ground clip to the probe; if the light glows brightly, the battery is strong enough for testing.

➡**A self-powered test light should not be used on any computer controlled system or component. The small amount of electricity transmitted by the test light is enough to damage many electronic automotive components.**

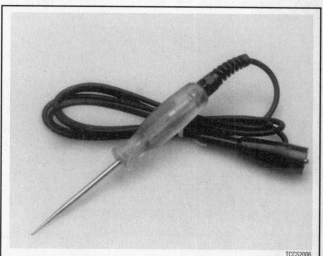

TCCS2006

Fig. 7 A 12 volt test light is used to detect the presence of voltage in a circuit

MULTIMETERS

Multimeters are an extremely useful tool for troubleshooting electrical problems. They can be purchased in either analog or digital form and have a price range to suit any budget. A multimeter is a voltmeter, ammeter and ohmmeter (along with other features) combined into one instrument. It is often used when testing solid state circuits because of its high input impedance (usually 10 megaohms or more). A brief description of the multimeter main test functions follows:

• Voltmeter—the voltmeter is used to measure voltage at any point in a circuit, or to measure the voltage drop across any part of a circuit. Voltmeters usually have various scales and a selector switch to allow the reading of different voltage ranges. The voltmeter has a positive and a negative lead. To avoid damage to the meter, always connect the negative lead to the negative (-) side of the circuit (to ground or nearest the ground side of the circuit) and connect the positive lead to the positive (+) side of the circuit (to the power source or the nearest power source). Note that the negative voltmeter lead will always be black and that the positive voltmeter will always be some color other than black (usually red).

• Ohmmeter—the ohmmeter is designed to read resistance (measured in ohms) in a circuit or component. All ohmmeters will have a selector switch which permits the measurement of different ranges of resistance (usually the selector switch allows the multiplication of the meter reading by 10, 100, 1,000 and 10,000). Since the meters are powered by an internal battery, the ohmmeter can be used as a self-powered test light. When the ohmmeter is connected, current from the ohmmeter flows through the circuit or component being tested. Since the ohmmeter's internal resistance and voltage are known values, the amount of current flow through the meter depends on the resistance of the circuit or component being tested. The ohmmeter can also be used to perform a continuity test for suspected open circuits. In using the meter for making continuity checks, do not be concerned with the actual resistance readings. Zero resistance, or any ohm reading, indicates continuity in the circuit. Infinite resistance indicates an opening in the circuit. A high resistance reading where there should be none indicates a problem in the circuit. Checks for short circuits are made in the same manner as checks for open circuits, except that the circuit must be isolated from both power and normal ground. Infinite resistance indicates no continuity to ground, while zero resistance indicates a dead short to ground.

✳✳ WARNING

Never use an ohmmeter to check the resistance of a component or wire while there is voltage applied to the circuit.

• Ammeter—an ammeter measures the amount of current flowing through a circuit in units called amperes or amps. At normal operating voltage, most circuits have a characteristic amount of amperes, called "current draw" which can be measured using an ammeter. By referring to a specified current draw rating, then measuring the amperes and comparing the two values, one can determine what is happening within the circuit to aid in diagnosis. An open circuit, for example, will not allow any current to flow, so the ammeter reading will be zero. A damaged component or circuit will have an increased current draw, so the reading will be high. The ammeter is always connected in series with the circuit being tested. All of the current that normally flows through the circuit must also flow through the ammeter; if there is any other path for the current to follow, the ammeter reading will not be accurate. The ammeter itself has very little resistance to current flow and, therefore, will not affect the circuit, but it will measure current draw only when the circuit is closed and electricity is flowing. Excessive current draw can blow fuses and drain the battery, while a reduced current draw can cause motors to run slowly, lights to dim and other components to not operate properly.

Troubleshooting Electrical Systems

When diagnosing a specific problem, organized troubleshooting is a must. The complexity of a modern automotive vehicle demands that you approach any problem in a logical, organized manner. There are certain troubleshooting techniques which are standard:

• Establish when the problem occurs. Does the problem appear only under certain conditions? Were there any noises, odors or other unusual symptoms?

• Isolate the problem area. To do this, make some simple tests and observations, then eliminate the systems that are working properly. Check for obvious problems, such as broken wires and loose or dirty connections. Always check the obvious before assuming something complicated is the cause.

• Test for problems systematically to determine the cause once the problem area is isolated. Are all the components functioning properly? Is there power going to electrical switches and motors? Performing careful, systematic checks will often turn up most causes on the first inspection, without wasting time checking components that have little or no relationship to the problem.

• Test all repairs after the work is done to make sure that the problem is fixed. Some causes can be traced to more than one component, so a careful verification of repair work is important in order to pick up additional malfunctions that may cause a problem to reappear or a different problem to arise. A blown fuse, for example, is a simple problem that may require more than another fuse to repair. If you don't look for a problem that caused a fuse to blow, a shorted wire (for example) may go undetected.

Experience has shown that most problems tend to be the result of a fairly simple and obvious cause, such as loose or corroded connectors, bad grounds or damaged wire insulation which causes a short. This makes careful visual inspection of components during testing essential to quick and accurate troubleshooting.

Testing

OPEN CIRCUITS

▶ See Figure 8

1. Isolate the circuit from power and ground.
2. Connect the self-powered test light or ohmmeter ground clip to a good ground and probe sections of the circuit sequentially.
3. If the light is out or there is infinite resistance, the open is between the probe and the circuit ground.
4. If the light is on or the meter shows continuity, the open is between the probe and end of the circuit toward the power source.

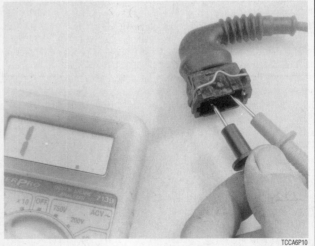

Fig. 8 The infinite reading on this multimeter (1 .) indicates that the circuit is open

SHORT CIRCUITS

➡**Never use a self-powered test light to perform checks for opens or shorts when power is applied to the electrical system under test. The 12 volt vehicle power will quickly burn out the light bulb in the test light.**

1. Isolate the circuit from power and ground.

2. Connect the self-powered test light or ohmmeter ground clip to a good ground and probe any easy-to-reach test point in the circuit.

3. If the light comes on or there is continuity, there is a short somewhere in the circuit.

4. To isolate the short, probe a test point at either end of the isolated circuit (the light should be on or the meter should indicate continuity).

5. Leave the test light probe engaged and sequentially open connectors or switches, remove parts, etc. until the light goes out or continuity is broken.

6. When the light goes out, the short is between the last two circuit components which were opened.

VOLTAGE

◆ See Figures 9 and 10

This test determines voltage available from the battery and should be the first step in any electrical troubleshooting procedure. Many electrical problems, especially on computer controlled systems, can be caused by a low state of charge in the battery. Excessive corrosion at the battery cable terminals can cause poor contact that will prevent proper charging and full battery current flow.

1. Set the voltmeter selector switch to the 20V position.

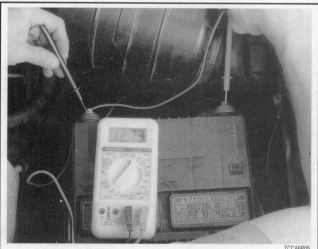
Fig. 9 Using a multimeter to check battery voltage. This battery is fully charged
TCCA6P05

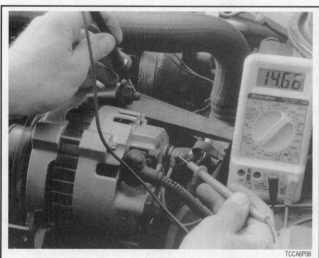
Fig. 10 Testing voltage output between the alternator's BAT terminal and ground. This voltage reading is normal
TCCA6P06

2. Connect the multimeter negative lead to the battery's negative (-) post or terminal and the positive lead to the battery's positive (+) post or terminal.

3. Turn the ignition switch ON to provide a load.

4. A well charged battery should register over 12 volts. If the meter reads below 11.5 volts, the battery power may be insufficient to operate the electrical system properly.

VOLTAGE DROP

◆ See Figure 11

When current flows through a load, the voltage beyond the load drops. This voltage drop is due to the resistance created by the load and also by small resistances created by corrosion at the connectors and damaged insulation on the wires. The maximum allowable voltage drop under load is critical, especially if there is more than one load in the circuit, since all voltage drops are cumulative.

1. Set the voltmeter selector switch to the 20 volt position.

2. Connect the multimeter negative lead to a good ground.

3. Operate the circuit and check the voltage prior to the first component (load).

4. There should be little or no voltage drop in the circuit prior to the first component. If a voltage drop exists, the wire or connectors in the circuit are suspect.

5. While operating the first component in the circuit, probe the ground side of the component with the positive meter lead and observe the voltage readings. A small voltage drop should be noticed. This voltage drop is caused by the resistance of the component.

6. Repeat the test for each component (load) down the circuit.

7. If a large voltage drop is noticed, the preceding component, wire or connector is suspect.

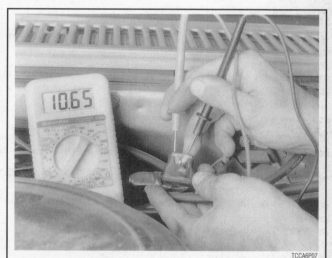
Fig. 11 This voltage drop test revealed high resistance (low voltage) in the circuit
TCCA6P07

RESISTANCE

◆ See Figures 12 and 13

✳✳ WARNING

Never use an ohmmeter with power applied to the circuit. The ohmmeter is designed to operate on its own power supply. The normal 12 volt automotive electrical system current could damage the meter!

1. Isolate the circuit from the vehicle's power source.

2. Ensure that the ignition key is OFF when disconnecting any components or the battery.

Fig. 12 Checking the resistance of a coolant temperature sensor with an ohmmeter. Reading is 1.04 kilohms

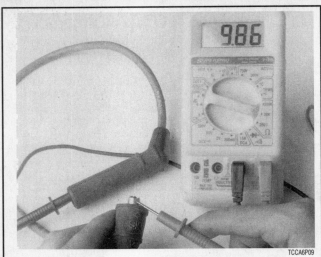

Fig. 13 Spark plug wires can be checked for excessive resistance using an ohmmeter

3. Where necessary, also isolate at least one side of the circuit to be checked, in order to avoid reading parallel resistances. Parallel circuit resistances will always give a lower reading than the actual resistance of either of the branches.

4. Connect the meter leads to both sides of the circuit (wire or component) and read the actual measured ohms on the meter scale. Make sure the selector switch is set to the proper ohm scale for the circuit being tested, to avoid misreading the ohmmeter test value.

Wire and Connector Repair

Almost anyone can replace damaged wires, as long as the proper tools and parts are available. Automotive wire and terminals are available to fit almost any need. Even the specialized weatherproof, molded and hard shell connectors are now available from aftermarket suppliers.

Be sure the ends of all the wires are fitted with the proper terminal hardware and connectors. Wrapping a wire around a stud is never a permanent solution and will only cause trouble later. Replace wires one at a time to avoid confusion. Always route wires exactly the same as the factory.

➡**If connector repair is necessary, only attempt it if you have the proper tools. Weatherproof and hard shell connectors require special tools to release the pins inside the connector. Attempting to repair these connectors with conventional hand tools will damage them.**

BATTERY CABLES

Disconnecting the Cables

When working on any electrical component on the vehicle, it is always a good idea to disconnect the negative (-) battery cable. This will prevent potential damage to many sensitive electrical components such as the Engine Control Module (ECM), radio, alternator, etc.

➡**Any time you disengage the battery cables, it is recommended that you disconnect the negative (-) battery cable first. This will prevent your accidentally grounding the positive (+) terminal to the body of the vehicle when disconnecting it, thereby preventing damage to the above mentioned components.**

Before you disconnect the cable(s), first turn the ignition to the **OFF** position. This will prevent a draw on the battery which could cause arcing (electricity trying to ground itself to the body of a vehicle, just like a spark plug jumping the gap) and, of course, damaging some components such as the alternator diodes.

When the battery cable(s) are reconnected (negative cable last), be sure to check that your lights, windshield wipers and other electrically operated safety components are all working correctly. If your vehicle contains an Electronically Tuned Radio (ETR), don't forget to also reset your radio stations. Ditto for the clock.

SUPPLEMENTAL RESTRAINT SYSTEM

General Information

▶ See Figures 14 and 15

The Supplemental Restraint System (SRS), found on 1995–98 vehicles, is designed to be used along with the front seat belts to reduce the risk or amount of injury by deploying one or both air bags during certain frontal collisions.

The air bag system is made up of left and right front impact sensors, air bag modules for the driver (in the steering wheel) and front passenger (right side instrument panel above the glove compartment), SRS diagnosis unit (with a safing sensor) and a SRS warning lamp in the instrument cluster.

The SRS system is designed to deploy when the safing sensor, along with either or both of the impact sensors simultaneously activate while the ignition is **ON**. The sensors will activate during front or near-frontal impacts of moderate to severe force.

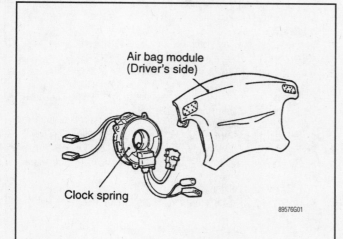

Fig. 14 The driver's side air bag inflator module is mounted to the steering wheel

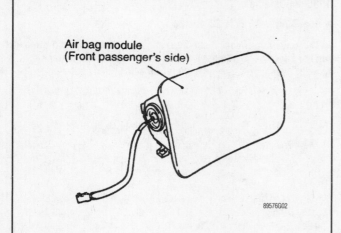

Fig. 15 There is also a passenger side air bag module located above the glove compartment

DISARMING THE SYSTEM

▶ See Figure 16

To disarm the SRS system, disconnect the negative battery cable and wrap the cable end with insulating tape to avoid accidental contact with the terminal. Wait at least 60 seconds after disconnecting the cable to proceed with the necessary service.

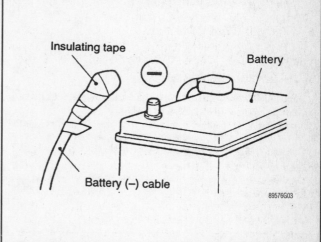

Fig. 16 For extra assurance, wrap the battery cable with tape to avoid contact with the terminal and possible air bag deployment

ARMING THE SYSTEM

▶ See Figure 17

After finishing the service procedures, remove the tape, then reconnect the negative battery cable. Turn the ignition to the **ON** position and check to make sure the SRS warning light illuminates for 7 seconds and then turns off. If so, the system is operating properly. If not, you should take your vehicle to a reputable repair shop for diagnosis.

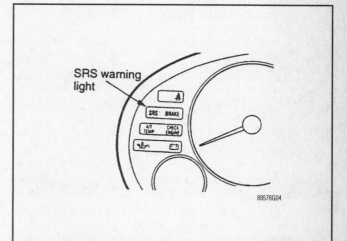

Fig. 17 After arming the system, if the SRS light stays illuminated for 7 seconds and then goes off, the air bag system is functioning properly

HEATING & AIR CONDITIONING

Blower Motor

REMOVAL & INSTALLATION

1990–94 Vehicles

▶ See Figure 18

1. Disconnect battery negative cable.
2. If equipped, remove the right side duct.
3. Disconnect the molded hose from the blower assembly.
4. Remove the blower motor assembly.
5. Remove the packing seal.
6. If replacing the motor assembly, remove the fan retaining nut and fan.

To install:

7. Check that the blower motor shaft is not bent and that the packing is in good condition. Clean all parts of dust, etc.
8. Assemble the motor and fan. Install the blower motor then connect the motor terminals to battery voltage. Check that the blower motor operates smoothly. Then, reverse the polarity and check that the blower motor operates smoothly in the reverse direction.
9. Install the molded hose and duct, if removed.
10. Connect the negative battery cable and check the climate control system for proper operation.

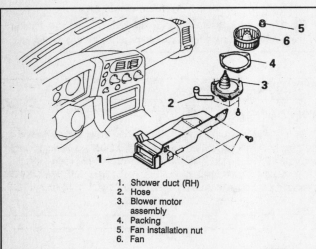

1. Shower duct (RH)
2. Hose
3. Blower motor assembly
4. Packing
5. Fan installation nut
6. Fan

89576G05

Fig. 18 Exploded view of the blower motor and related components—1990–94 vehicles

1995–98 Vehicles

▶ See Figure 19

1. Disconnect the negative battery cable.
2. Remove the stopper, then lower the glove compartment assembly.

✳✳ CAUTION

Some models covered by this manual may be equipped with a Supplemental Restraint System (SRS), which uses an air bag. Whenever working near any of the SRS components, such as the impact sensors, the air bag module, steering column and instrument panel, disable the SRS, as described in Section 6.

3. If necessary, remove the blower resistor.
4. For non-turbo vehicles equipped with A/C, unfasten the retainers, then remove the automatic compressor ECM from the vehicle.
5. Unfasten the retaining bolts, then remove the blower motor and fan from the vehicle.
6. If necessary to remove the entire blower unit, perform the following:

   a. Remove the instrument panel, as outlined in Section 10 of this manual.

   b. Remove the retaining clip by using a Philips-head screwdriver to push the pin (in the center of the clip) inward about 0.08 in. (2mm), then pull the clip out to remove it.

✳✳ WARNING

Do not push the pin in more than necessary because the grommet may be damaged, or the pin may fall in.

7. For vehicles without A/C, remove the joint duct.
8. If equipped with A/C, unfasten the cooling until bolts and nuts.
9. Remove the blower unit assembly from the vehicle.

To install:

10. If removed, position the blower unit in the vehicle and perform the following:

   a. If equipped with A/C, install the cooling unit bolts and nuts.

   b. For vehicles not equipped with A/C, install the joint duct.

   c. Install the retaining clip by inserting with the pin pulled out, then pushing the pin inward until the head is flush with the grommet.

   d. Install the instrument panel.

11. Position the blower fan and motor in the vehicle, and secure with the retainer(s).
12. For non-turbo vehicles with A/C, install the automatic compressor ECM.
13. If removed, install the resistor.
14. Place the glove compartment in the proper closed position, then install the stopper.
15. Connect the negative battery cable.

Heater Core

REMOVAL & INSTALLATION

1990–94 Vehicles

▶ See Figures 20, 21, 22 and 23

➡The evaporator housing can be removed by itself, without removing the console, instrument panel or heater core. The heater core, though, cannot be removed without removing the evaporator.

1. If equipped with A/C, have the system properly discharged at a reputable repair shop.
2. Disconnect the negative battery cable.
3. Drain the cooling system into a suitable container.
4. If equipped with A/C, disconnect the refrigerant lines from the evaporator. Cover the exposed ends of the lines to minimize contamination.
5. Remove the instrument panel, as outlined in Section 10 of this manual.
6. Remove the floor console by first removing the plugs, then the screws retaining the side covers and the small cover piece in front of the shifter. Remove the shifter knob, manual transmission, and the cup holder. Remove both small pieces of upholstery to gain access to retainer screws. Disconnect both electrical connectors from the front of the console. Remove the shoulder harness guide plates and the console assembly.
7. Remove both stamped steel reinforcement pieces.

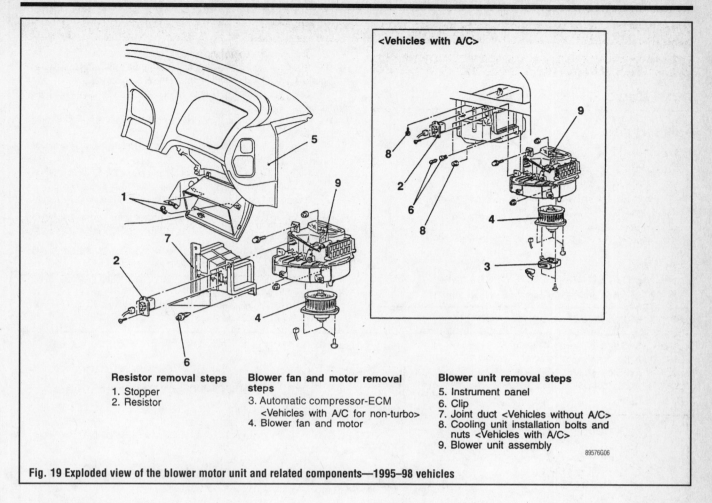

Resistor removal steps
1. Stopper
2. Resistor

Blower fan and motor removal steps
3. Automatic compressor-ECM
   <Vehicles with A/C for non-turbo>
4. Blower fan and motor

Blower unit removal steps
5. Instrument panel
6. Clip
7. Joint duct <Vehicles without A/C>
8. Cooling unit installation bolts and nuts <Vehicles with A/C>
9. Blower unit assembly

Fig. 19 Exploded view of the blower motor unit and related components—1995–98 vehicles

8. Remove the lower ductwork from the heater box.
9. Remove the upper center duct.
10. Vehicles without air conditioning will have a square duct in place of the evaporator. Remove this duct if present. If the vehicle is equipped with air conditioning, remove the evaporator assembly:
    a. Remove the wiring harness connectors and the electronic control unit.
    b. Remove the drain hose and lift out the evaporator unit.

c. If servicing the assembly, disassemble the housing and remove the expansion valve and evaporator.
11. With the evaporator removed, remove the heater unit. To prevent bolts from falling inside the blower assembly, set the inside/outside air-selection damper to the position that permits outside air introduction.
12. Remove the cover plate around the heater tubes and remove the core fastener clips. Pull the heater core from the heater box, being careful not to damage the fins or tank ends.

Fig. 20 To prevent bolts from falling inside the blower, set the air selector damper to the position that allows outside air into the vehicle

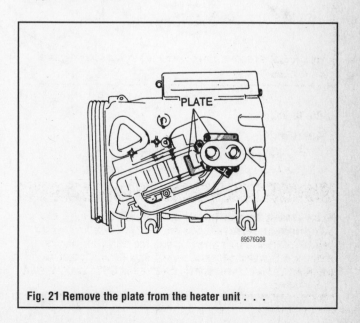

Fig. 21 Remove the plate from the heater unit . . .

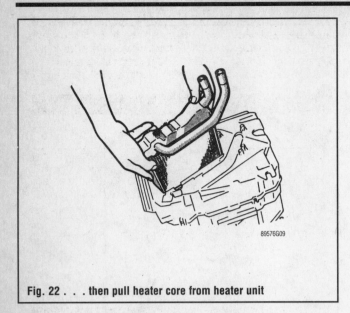

Fig. 22 . . . then pull heater core from heater unit

To install:

13. Install the heater core to the heater box. Install the clips and cover.

14. Install the heater box and connect the duct work.

15. Assemble the housing, evaporator and expansion valve, making sure the gaskets are in good condition. Install the evaporator housing.

16. Using new lubricated O-rings, connect the refrigerant lines to the evaporator.

17. Install the electronic transmission ELC box. Connect all wires and control cables.

18. Install the instrument panel assembly and the console by reversing their removal procedures.

19. Connect the negative battery cable and check the entire climate control system for proper operation. Check the system for leaks.

20. If equipped with A/C, take the vehicle to a reputable repair shop to have the A/C system evacuated and recharged.

1995–98 Vehicles

◆ **See Figure 24**

1. Properly disarm the SRS system by disconnecting the negative battery cable and waiting 60 seconds.

2. Drain the engine coolant into a suitable container.

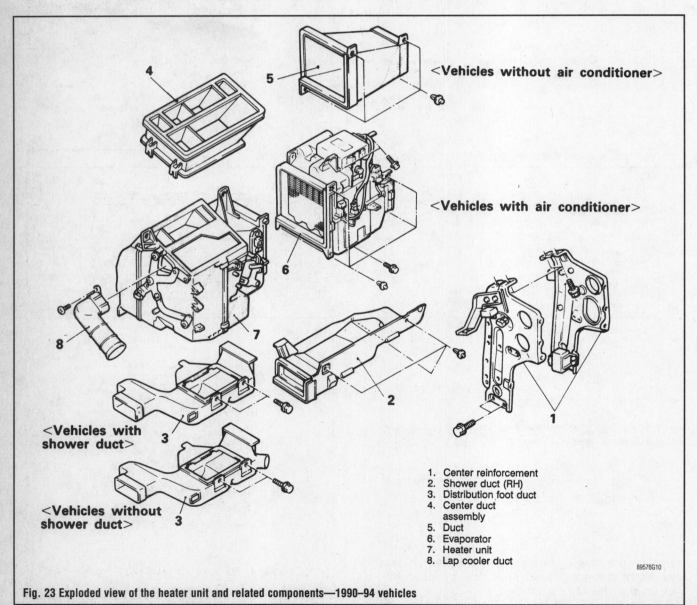

<Vehicles without air conditioner>

<Vehicles with air conditioner>

<Vehicles with shower duct>

<Vehicles without shower duct>

1. Center reinforcement
2. Shower duct (RH)
3. Distribution foot duct
4. Center duct assembly
5. Duct
6. Evaporator
7. Heater unit
8. Lap cooler duct

Fig. 23 Exploded view of the heater unit and related components—1990–94 vehicles

3. Remove the instrument panel, as outlined in Section 10 of this manual.

4. Disconnect the heater hose connections.

5. Remove the center stay and duct.

6. Remove the semi rear heater duct.

7. Remove the foot distribution duct.

8. If equipped with A/C, remove the cooling unit bolt and nut.

9. Remove the retaining clip by using a Philips-head screwdriver to push the pin (in the center of the clip) in about 0.08 in. (2mm), then pull the clip out to remove it.

❄❄ WARNING

Do not push the pin in more than necessary because the grommet may be damaged or the pin may fall in.

10. Remove the heater unit after sliding the cooling unit toward you slightly.

11. Remove the heater core from the vehicle.

To install:

12. Position the heater core in the vehicle.

13. Install the heater unit.

14. Install the retaining clip by inserting with the pin pulled out, then pushing the pin inward until the head is flush with the grommet.

15. If equipped with A/C, install the cooling unit bolt and nut.

16. Connect the foot distribution duct.

17. Install the semi rear heater duct.

18. Install the center duct and stay.

19. Attach the heater hose connection(s).

20. Install the instrument panel, as outlined in Section 10 of this manual.

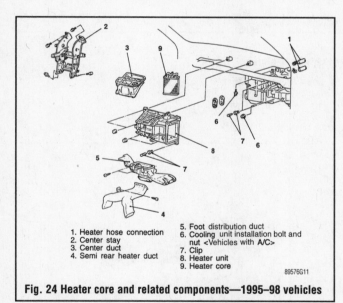

1. Heater hose connection
2. Center stay
3. Center duct
4. Semi rear heater duct
5. Foot distribution duct
6. Cooling unit installation bolt and nut <Vehicles with A/C>
7. Clip
8. Heater unit
9. Heater core

89576G11

Fig. 24 Heater core and related components—1995–98 vehicles

Air Conditioning Components

REMOVAL & INSTALLATION

Repair or service of air conditioning components is not covered by this manual, because of the risk of personal injury or death, and because of the legal ramifications of servicing these components without the proper EPA certification and experience. Cost, personal injury or death, environmental damage, and legal considerations (such as the fact that it is a federal crime to vent refrigerant into the atmosphere), dictate that the A/C components on your vehicle should be serviced only by a Motor Vehicle Air Conditioning (MVAC) trained, and EPA certified automotive technician.

➡ If your vehicle's A/C system uses R-12 refrigerant and is in need of recharging, the A/C system can be converted over to R-134a refrigerant (less environmentally harmful and expensive). Refer to Section 1 for additional information on R-12 to R-134a conversions, and for additional considerations dealing with your vehicle's A/C system.

Control Cables

ADJUSTMENT

1. Disconnect the negative battery cable. Remove the glove box, if necessary.

2. Move the mode selection lever to the **DEFROST** position. Move the mode selection damper lever FULLY INWARD and connect the cable to the lever. Adjust as required.

3. Move the temperature control lever to its HOTTEST position. Move the blend air damper lever FULLY DOWNWARD and connect the cable to the lever. Adjust as required.

4. Move the air selection control lever to the **RECIRC** position. Move the air selection damper FULLY INWARD and connect the cable to the lever. Adjust as required.

Control Panel

REMOVAL & INSTALLATION

▶ **See Figures 25 and 26**

1990–94 Vehicles

1. Disconnect the negative battery cable.

2. Remove the radio and tape player assembly.

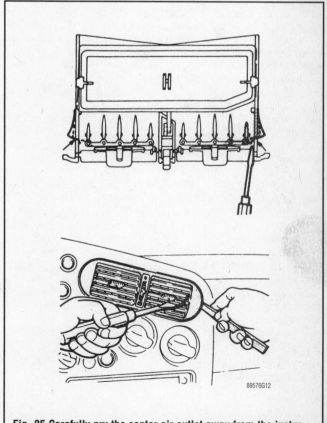

89576G12

Fig. 25 Carefully pry the center air outlet away from the instrument cluster bezel

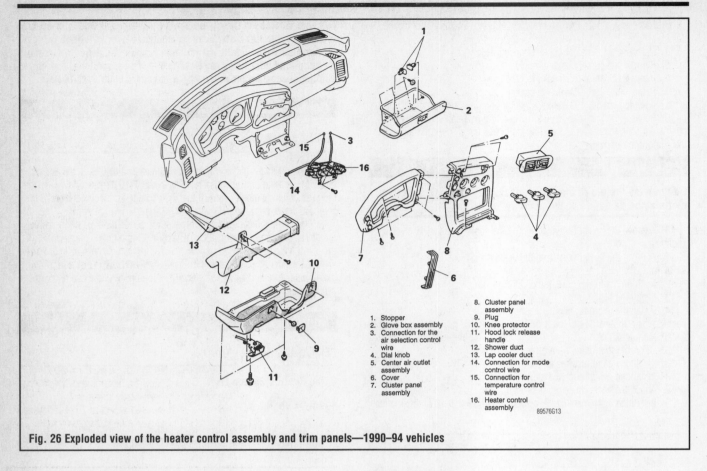

1. Stopper	8. Cluster panel assembly
2. Glove box assembly	9. Plug
3. Connection for the air selection control wire	10. Knee protector
	11. Hood lock release handle
4. Dial knob	12. Shower duct
5. Center air outlet assembly	13. Lap cooler duct
6. Cover	14. Connection for mode control wire
7. Cluster panel assembly	15. Connection for temperature control wire
	16. Heater control assembly

89576G13

Fig. 26 Exploded view of the heater control assembly and trim panels—1990–94 vehicles

3. Remove the stopper, then remove the glove box assembly.

4. Detach the connector for the air-selection wire.

5. Remove the dial control knob(s) from the control head.

6. Remove the center air outlet by disengaging the tabs with a flat blade tool and carefully prying out.

7. Remove the instrument cluster bezel and radio bezel.

8. Remove the knee protector and lower the hood lock release handle.

9. Remove the left side lower duct work.

10. Disconnect the air, temperature and mode selection control cables from the heater housing.

11. Remove the mounting screws and the control head from the instrument panel.

To install:

12. Feed the control cable through the instrument panel, attach the connectors, then install the control head assembly and secure with the screws.

13. Move the mode selection lever to the **DEFROST** position. Move the mode selection damper lever FULLY INWARD and connect the cable to the lever. Install the clip.

14. Move the temperature control lever to its HOTTEST position. Move the blend air damper lever FULLY DOWNWARD and connect the cable to the lever. Install the clip.

15. Move the air selection control lever to the **RECIRC** position. Move the air selection damper FULLY INWARD and connect the cable to the lever. Install the clip.

16. Connect the negative battery cable and check the entire climate control system for proper operation.

17. If everything is satisfactory, install the remaining interior pieces in the reverse order of removal.

1995–98 Vehicles

▶ See Figures 27, 28 and 29

1. Disconnect the negative battery cable.

2. Unfasten the retaining clips and remove the center trim panel.

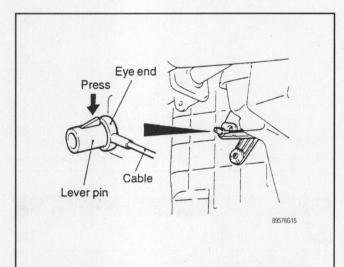

89576G15

Fig. 27 Press the lever pin in, then disconnect the cable from the control

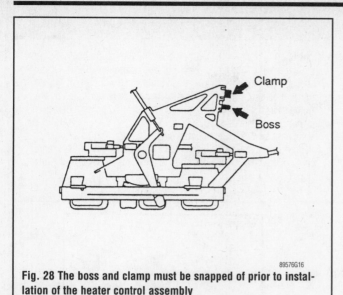

89576G16

Fig. 28 The boss and clamp must be snapped of prior to installation of the heater control assembly

3. Remove the center floor console, as outlined in Section 10 of this manual.

4. Remove the radio/tape and/or CD player assembly.

5. Remove the retaining stopper.

6. Remove the control assembly as follows:

    a. Remove the retaining screw(s).

    b. Press the lever pin to disconnect the air outlet changeover damper cable.

➡**The boss and clamp are needed for the assembly line during factory installation, however they are not necessary for service procedures.**

c. Snap the boss and clamp with a pair of nippers, to remove the heater control assembly from the vehicle.

To install:

7. Install the control panel, as follows:

    a. Set the temperature control knob on the panel to **MAX HOT**.

    b. Set the air mix damper lever at the upper part of the heater unit to the **MAX HOT** position, then attach the cable to the lever pin.

    c. Push the outer cable in the direction of the arrow so that there is no looseness, then secure with the clip.

    d. Set the knob for the air outlet changeover on the control to the **DEF** position.

    e. Set the air outlet changeover damper lever of the heater unit to the **DEF** position, then attach the cable to the lever pin.

    f. Push the outer cable in the direction of the arrow so there is no looseness, then secure it with the clip.

    g. Set the lever for the inside/outside air changeover on the heater control assembly to the air recirculation position.

    h. Set the inside/outside air changeover damper lever of the blower unit to the air recirculation position (with the inside/outside air changeover damper lever touched to the stopper of the blower case), then attach the cable to the lever pin.

    i. Push the outer cable in the direction of the arrow so that there is no looseness, then secure it with the clip.

    j. Properly position the control assembly and secure with the retaining screw(s).

8. Install the stopper.

9. Connect the negative battery cable and check the climate control system for proper operation before installing the remaining components.

10. Install the radio/tape and/or CD player assembly.

11. Install the center floor console, as outlined in Section 10 of this manual.

12. Install the center trim panel, making sure the clips are engaged properly.

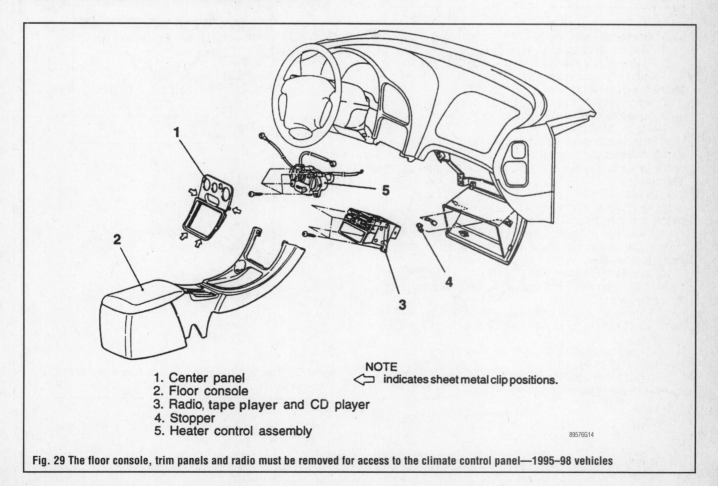

1. Center panel
2. Floor console
3. Radio, tape player and CD player
4. Stopper
5. Heater control assembly

NOTE
◁ indicates sheet metal clip positions.

89576G14

Fig. 29 The floor console, trim panels and radio must be removed for access to the climate control panel—1995–98 vehicles

CRUISE CONTROL

▶ **See Figure 30**

Cruise control is a speed control system that maintains a desired vehicle speed under normal driving conditions. However, steep grades up or down may cause variations in the selected speeds. The electronic cruise control system has the capability to cruise, coast, resume speed, accelerate, "tap-up" and "tap-down".

The main parts of the cruise control system are the functional control switches, speed control assembly, actuator, intermediate link, auto-cruise control module assembly, speed sensor, and the release switches.

Depending upon the year and/or model of your vehicle, the cruise control system is either vacuum or electronically controlled. The cruise control module assembly contains a low speed limit which will prevent system engagement below 25 mph (40 km/h). The module is controlled by the functional switches located on a lever on the steering column or steering wheel and on the instrument panel.

The release switches are mounted on the brake/clutch/accelerator pedal bracket. When the brake or clutch pedal is depressed, the cruise control system is electrically disengaged and the throttle is returned to the idle position.

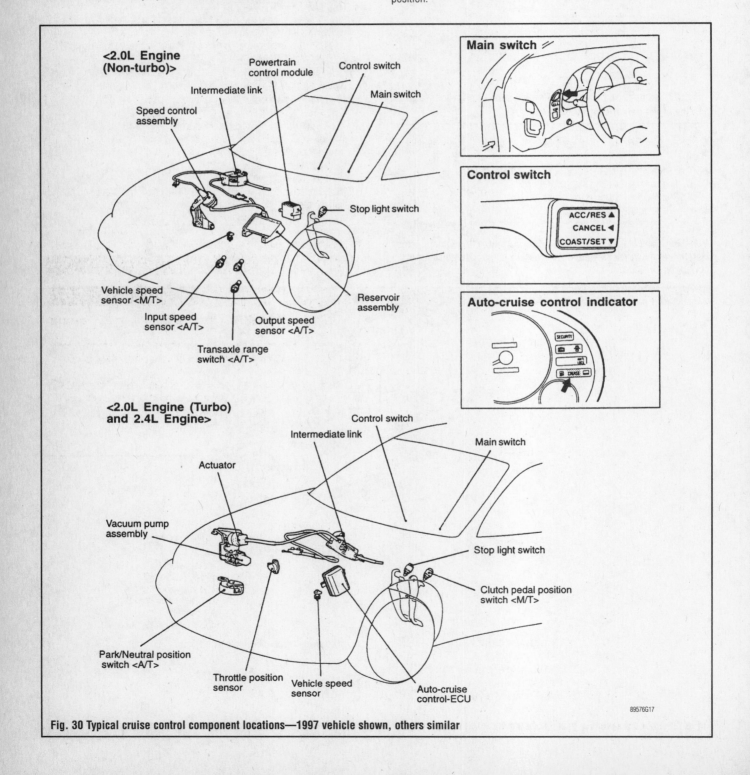

Fig. 30 Typical cruise control component locations—1997 vehicle shown, others similar

89576G17

CRUISE CONTROL TROUBLESHOOTING

Problem	Possible Cause
Will not hold proper speed	Incorrect cable adjustment
	Binding throttle linkage
	Leaking vacuum servo diaphragm
	Leaking vacuum tank
	Faulty vacuum or vent valve
	Faulty stepper motor
	Faulty transducer
	Faulty speed sensor
	Faulty cruise control module
Cruise intermittently cuts out	Clutch or brake switch adjustment too tight
	Short or open in the cruise control circuit
	Faulty transducer
	Faulty cruise control module
Vehicle surges	Kinked speedometer cable or casing
	Binding throttle linkage
	Faulty speed sensor
	Faulty cruise control module
Cruise control inoperative	Blown fuse
	Short or open in the cruise control circuit
	Faulty brake or clutch switch
	Leaking vacuum circuit
	Faulty cruise control switch
	Faulty stepper motor
	Faulty transducer
	Faulty speed sensor
	Faulty cruise control module

Note: Use this chart as a guide. Not all systems will use the components listed.

TCCA6C01

ENTERTAINMENT SYSTEMS

Radio/Tape Player/CD Player

REMOVAL & INSTALLATION

♦ **See Figures 31 thru 38**

1. Disconnect the negative battery cable. Wait at least 60 seconds before beginning the remainder of the procedure, in order to disarm the Supplemental Restraint System (SRS).
2. Using a plastic trim tool, remove the radio panel. Pry the lower part of the radio panel away first, then separate and remove the panel.

✳✳ WARNING

When removing and installing the floor console, do NOT allow it to bump against the SRS-ECU!

3. For 1995–98 vehicles, remove the floor console assembly, as outlined in Section 10 of this manual.
4. Remove the mounting bolts and pull the radio receiver, tape player or CD player out slightly. Detach all harness connectors and remove the unit from the vehicle.
5. Installation is the reverse of the removal procedure.

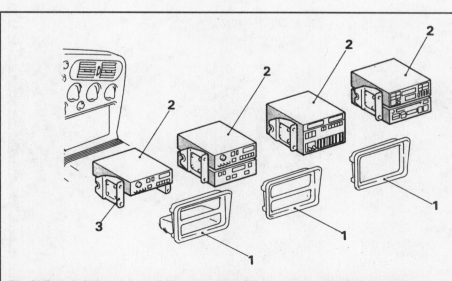

1. Radio panel
2. Radio, Radio with tape player, Radio and tape player with CD player
3. Radio bracket

89576G19

Fig. 31 Exploded view of the radio, tape player or CD player removal—1990–94 vehicles

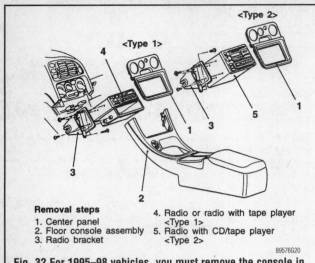

Removal steps
1. Center panel
2. Floor console assembly
3. Radio bracket
4. Radio or radio with tape player <Type 1>
5. Radio with CD/tape player <Type 2>

Fig. 32 For 1995–98 vehicles, you must remove the console in order to access the radio

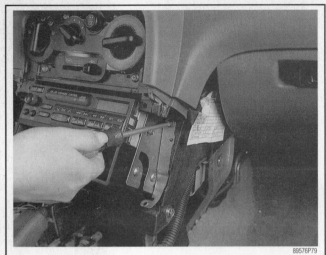

Fig. 35 After removing the console, unfasten the radio mounting screws

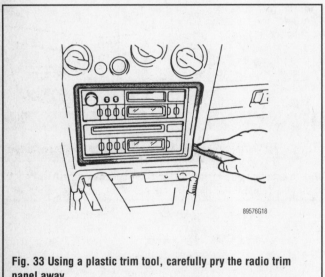

Fig. 33 Using a plastic trim tool, carefully pry the radio trim panel away

Fig. 36 Pull the radio out enough to access the connectors

Fig. 34 Remove the center trim panel for access to the radio retainers

Fig. 37 Unplug the electrical connector from the rear of the radio . . .

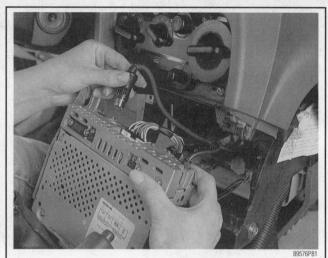

Fig. 38 . . . then disconnect the antenna lead and remove the radio from the vehicle

Speakers

REMOVAL & INSTALLATION

Front Speaker

▶ See Figure 39

1. Disconnect the negative battery cable.
2. Remove the front speaker garnish.
3. Remove the retainers, detach the harness connector and remove the front speaker.

✳✳ WARNING

Handle the speaker carefully to avoid damaging the cone during removal and installation.

4. Installation is the reverse of the removal procedure

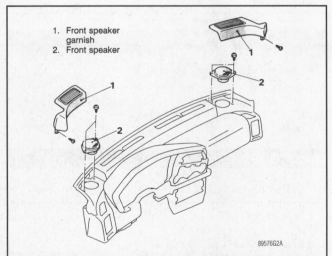

1. Front speaker garnish
2. Front speaker

Fig. 39 Front speaker mounting—early model shown, later models similar

Door Speaker

▶ See Figure 40

1. Disconnect the negative battery cable.
2. Remove the door trim panel. Refer to the procedure in Section 10.
3. Remove the mounting screws, detach the harness connector and remove the front speaker.

✳✳ WARNING

Handle the speaker carefully to avoid damaging the cone during removal and installation.

4. Installation is the reverse of the removal procedure

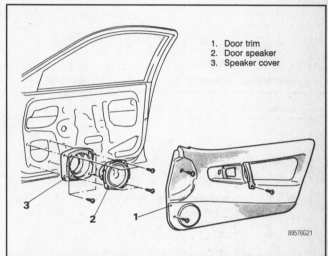

1. Door trim
2. Door speaker
3. Speaker cover

Fig. 40 You must remove the door trim panel for access to the door speakers

Rear Speaker

EXCEPT ECLIPSE SPYDER

▶ See Figures 41 and 42

1. Disconnect the negative battery cable.
2. Remove the luggage compartment side tray.
3. Remove the speaker retainers and lift the speaker from the speaker cover. Detach the harness connector.

✳✳ WARNING

Handle the speaker carefully to avoid damaging the cone during removal and installation.

4. Installation is the reverse of the removal procedure.
5. Connect the negative battery cable.

ECLIPSE SPYDER

▶ See Figure 43

1. Disconnect the negative battery cable.
2. Remove the speaker garnish cover.
3. Unfasten the retaining screws.
4. Partially lift the speaker up, detach the connectors, then remove the speaker from the vehicle.
5. If necessary, remove the speaker brackets.
6. Installation is the reverse of the removal procedure.

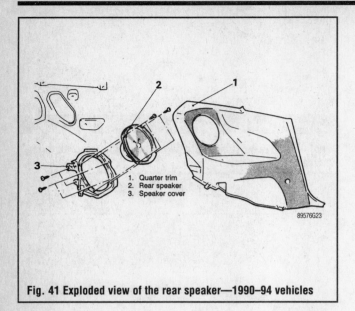

Fig. 41 Exploded view of the rear speaker—1990–94 vehicles

1. Quarter trim
2. Rear speaker
3. Speaker cover

89576G23

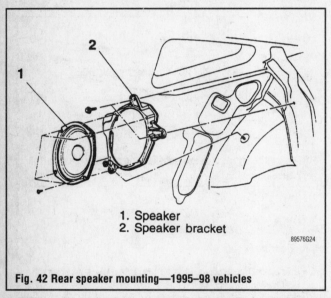

1. Speaker
2. Speaker bracket

89576G24

Fig. 42 Rear speaker mounting—1995–98 vehicles

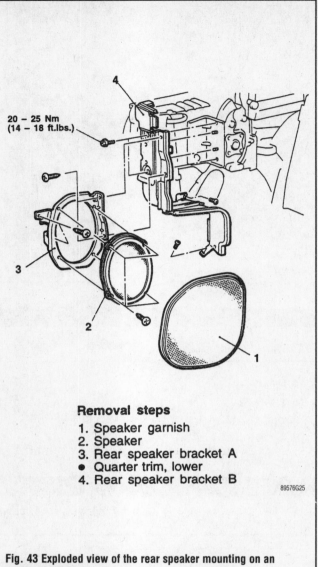

20 – 25 Nm
(14 – 18 ft.lbs.)

Removal steps

1. Speaker garnish
2. Speaker
3. Rear speaker bracket A
• Quarter trim, lower
4. Rear speaker bracket B

89576G25

Fig. 43 Exploded view of the rear speaker mounting on an Eclipse Spyder

WINDSHIELD WIPER AND WASHERS

Windshield Wiper Blade and Arm

REMOVAL & INSTALLATION

Front

▶ **See Figures 44 thru 49**

1. Disconnect the negative battery cable.
2. Remove the windshield wiper arms by removing the cap, unscrewing the cap nuts then lifting the arms from the linkage posts.

To install:

3. Install the wiper blade and arm assemblies. Tighten the retaining nuts to 7–12 ft. lbs. (10–16 Nm).
4. Note that the driver's side wiper arm should be marked **D** or **Dr** and the passenger's side wiper arm should be marked **A** or **As**. The identification marks should be located at the base of the arm, near the pivot. Install the arms so the blades are 1 inch from the garnish molding when parked.
5. Connect the negative battery cable and check the wiper system for proper operation.

Rear

1. Disconnect the negative battery cable.
2. Remove the rear wiper arm by removing the cover, unscrewing the nut and lifting the arm from the linkage post.
3. Installation is the reverse of the removal procedure.

Wiper Motor

REMOVAL & INSTALLATION

Front

▶ **See Figures 50, 51, 52, 53 and 54**

1. Disconnect the negative battery cable.
2. Remove the windshield wiper arms by unscrewing the cap nuts and lifting the arms from the linkage post.
3. Remove the front deck garnish panel.

Fig. 44 Remove the wiper arm retaining nut cap

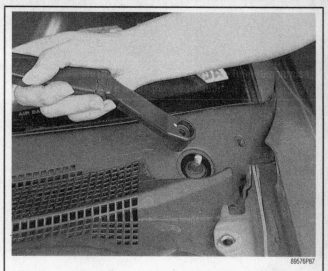

Fig. 47 . . . then remove the wiper arm from the linkage post

Fig. 45 Use a socket to loosen the windshield wiper arm retaining nut

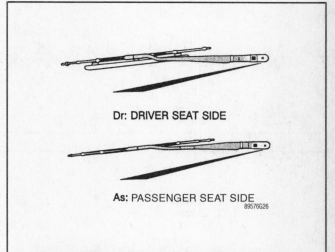

Dr: DRIVER SEAT SIDE

As: PASSENGER SEAT SIDE

Fig. 48 The wiper arms should have identification marks for installation purposes

Fig. 46 Once the nut is removed, matchmark the position of the arm for proper alignment during installation . . .

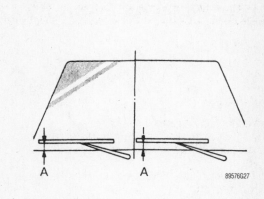

Fig. 49 Install the arms so the blades are 1 in. from the garnish molding when they are in the parked position

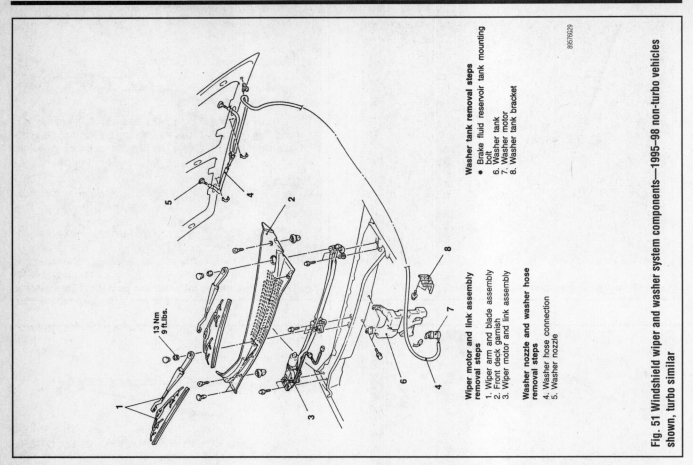

13 Nm
9 ft.lbs.

Wiper motor and link assembly removal steps
1. Wiper arm and blade assembly
2. Front deck garnish
3. Wiper motor and link assembly

Washer nozzle and washer hose removal steps
4. Washer hose connection
5. Washer nozzle

Washer tank removal steps
● Brake fluid reservoir tank mounting bolt
6. Washer tank
7. Washer motor
8. Washer tank bracket

Fig. 51 Windshield wiper and washer system components—1995–98 non-turbo vehicles shown, turbo similar

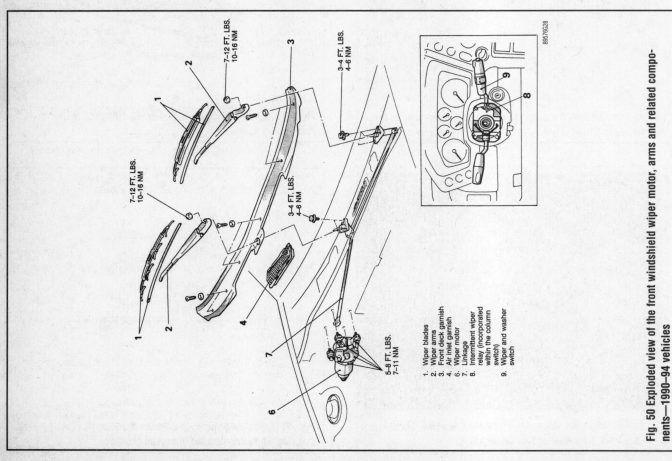

7-12 FT. LBS.
10–16 NM

3-4 FT. LBS.
4-6 NM

7-12 FT. LBS.
10–16 NM

3-4 FT. LBS.
4-6 NM

5-8 FT. LBS.
7-11 NM

1. Wiper blades
2. Wiper arms
3. Front deck garnish
4. Air inlet garnish
6. Wiper motor
7. Linkage
8. Intermittent wiper relay (incorporated within the column switch)
9. Wiper and washer switch

Fig. 50 Exploded view of the front windshield wiper motor, arms and related components—1990–94 vehicles

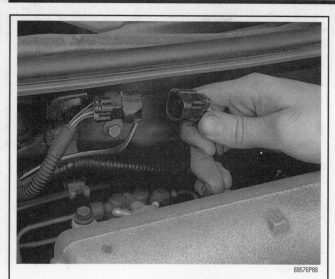

Fig. 52 Unplug the wiper motor electrical connector

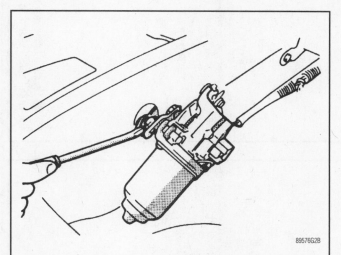

Fig. 53 On 1990–94 vehicles, disconnect the linkage from the motor after removing the mounting bolts

Fig. 54 Unfasten the motor and link mounting bolts, then remove from the vehicle as an assembly

4. For 1990–94 vehicles, remove the air inlet trim pieces and remove the hole cover.

5. Detach the wiper motor electrical connector.

6. For 1990–94 vehicles, remove the wiper motor by loosening the mounting bolts, removing the motor assembly, then disconnecting the linkage.

7. For 1995–98 vehicles, unfasten the retaining bolts, then remove the wiper motor and link as an assembly.

➡The installation angle of the crank arm and motor has been factory set; do not remove them unless it is necessary to do so. If they must be removed, remove them only after marking their mounting positions.

To install:

8. For 1990–94 vehicles, install the windshield wiper motor and connect the linkage. Tighten the motor retaining bolts to 5–8 ft. lbs. (7–11 Nm).

9. For 1995–98 vehicles, install the wiper motor and link assembly.

10. Install all trim pieces taken off during removal.

11. Reinstall the wiper blades. Note that the driver's side wiper arm should be marked **D** or **Dr** and the passenger's side wiper arm should be marked **A** or **As**. The identification marks should be located at the base of the arm, near the pivot. Install the arms so the blades are 1 inch from the garnish molding when parked.

12. Connect the negative battery cable and check the wiper system for proper operation.

Rear

1990–94 VEHICLES

◀ **See Figure 55**

1. Disconnect the negative battery cable.

2. Remove the rear wiper arm by removing the cover, unscrewing the nut and lifting the arm from the linkage post.

3. Remove the large interior trim panel. Use a plastic trim removal tool to unhook the trim clips of the liftgate trim.

4. If equipped with rear air spoiler, remove the wiper grommet.

5. Remove the rear wiper assembly motor. Do not loosen the grommet for the wiper post.

To install:

6. Install the wiper motor and secure with the retaining bolts. Tighten to 5–7 ft. lbs. (7–10 Nm).

7. Install the grommet. Mount the grommet so the arrow on the grommet is pointing upward.

8. Install the wiper blade and arm assembly.

9. Connect the negative battery cable and check the rear wiper for proper operation.

10. If operation is satisfactory, fit the tabs on the upper part of the liftgate trim into the liftgate clips and secure the liftgate trim.

1995–98 VEHICLES

◀ **See Figure 56**

1. Disconnect the negative battery cable.

2. Remove the rear wiper arm by removing the cover, unscrewing the nut and lifting the arm from the linkage post.

3. Remove the spacer assembly.

4. Remove the liftgate lower trim.

5. Unfasten the retaining bolt(s), then remove the rear wiper motor from the vehicle.

To install:

6. Position the rear wiper motor in the vehicle and secure with the retaining bolt(s). Tighten to 5.4 ft. lbs. (7.4 Nm).

7. Install the spacer.

8. Install the rear wiper blade and arm assembly.

9. Connect the negative battery cable, then check the wiper for proper operation, before installing the trim panel.

10. Install the liftgate lower trim panel.

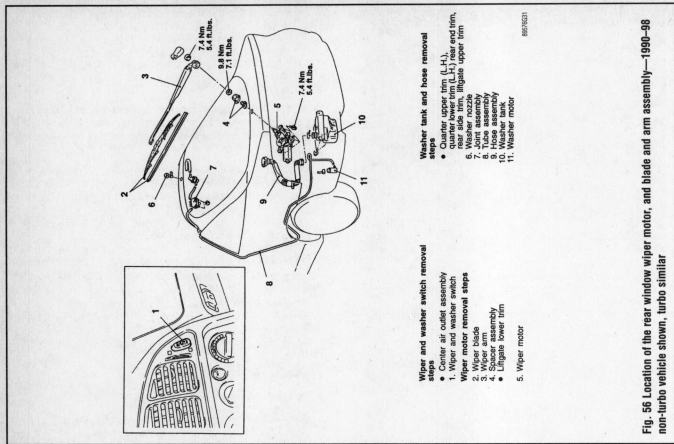

89576G31

Wiper and washer switch removal steps
- Center air outlet assembly
1. Wiper and washer switch

Wiper motor removal steps
2. Wiper blade
3. Wiper arm
- Spacer assembly
- Liftgate lower trim

5. Wiper motor

Washer tank and hose removal steps
- Quarter upper trim (L.H.), quarter lower trim (L.H.) rear end trim, rear side trim, liftgate upper trim
6. Washer nozzle
7. Joint assembly
8. Tube assembly
9. Hose assembly
10. Washer tank
11. Washer motor

Fig. 56 Location of the rear window wiper motor, and blade and arm assembly—1990-98 non-turbo vehicle shown, turbo similar

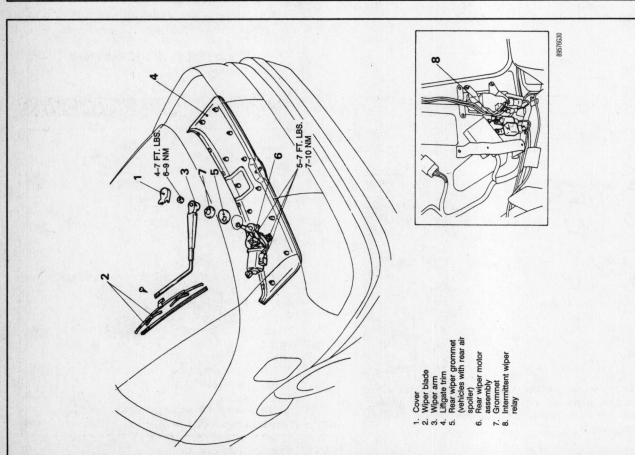

89576G30

1. Cover
2. Wiper blade
3. Wiper arm
4. Liftgate trim
5. Rear wiper grommet (vehicles with rear air spoiler)
6. Rear wiper motor assembly
7. Grommet
8. Intermittent wiper relay

Fig. 55 Rear wiper blade and arm, and motor mounting—1990-94 vehicles

Windshield Washer Motor

REMOVAL & INSTALLATION

Front

1990–94 VEHICLES

◆ See Figure 57

1. Disconnect the negative battery cable.
2. Remove the washer nozzle and detach the harness connector from the pump motor, if accessible.
3. Disconnect the washer tube.
4. Partially raise and support the vehicle, then remove the driver's side wheel and tire assembly.

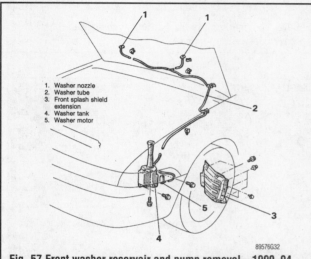

1. Washer nozzle
2. Washer tube
3. Front splash shield extension
4. Washer tank
5. Washer motor

89576G32

Fig. 57 Front washer reservoir and pump removal—1990–94 vehicles

5. Remove the front splash shield extension from the left front wheel well area. Unplug the pump motor harness, if still connected.
6. Remove the tank retainers and the tank from the vehicle. Remove the washer motor assembly from the tank and replace as required.
7. Installation is the reverse of the removal procedure.

1995–98 VEHICLES

◆ See Figure 51

1. Disconnect the negative battery cable.
2. For non-turbo vehicles, remove the brake master cylinder reservoir mounting bolt.
3. Remove the retaining bolt, then remove the washer tank from the vehicle.
4. Remove the washer motor from the vehicle.
5. If necessary, remove the washer tank bracket.
6. Installation is the reverse of the removal procedure.

Rear

1990–94 VEHICLES

1. Disconnect the negative battery cable.
2. Remove the rear side trim panel.
3. Disconnect the electrical harness from the reservoir.
4. Remove the reservoir retainers. Disconnect the fluid feed tubes at the tank and remove.
5. Installation is the reverse of the removal procedure.

1995–98 VEHICLES

◆ See Figure 56

1. Disconnect the negative battery cable.
2. Remove the left side quarter upper and lower trim panels, then remove the rear end trim, rear side trim and liftgate upper trim.
3. Remove the washer nozzle.
4. Remove the joint assembly and tube assembly.
5. For turbo vehicles, remove the tube assembly and remove the spare tire.
6. Unfasten the retainers, then remove the rear washer tank and motor.
7. Installation is the reverse of the removal procedure.

INSTRUMENTS AND SWITCHES

Instrument Cluster

REMOVAL & INSTALLATION

◆ See Figures 58 thru 65

1. Disconnect the negative battery cable. Wait at least 60 seconds to continue, in order to disarm the SRS system, if equipped.
2. Remove the steering wheel, as outlined in section 8 of this manual.
3. If necessary, remove the retaining screws, then remove the upper and lower steering column covers.
4. For 1990–94 vehicles, remove the screw cover on the side of the cluster panel assembly.
5. Unfasten the necessary retainers or use a suitable prytool, as applicable, to remove the front instrument cluster bezel.
6. Unfasten the retaining screws, then remove the instrument cluster from the vehicle.
7. Disassemble and remove gauges or the speedometer as required.

➡If the speedometer cable adapter requires service, disconnect the cable at the transaxle end. Pull the cable slightly toward the vehicle interior, release the lock by turning the adapter to the right or left and remove the adapter.

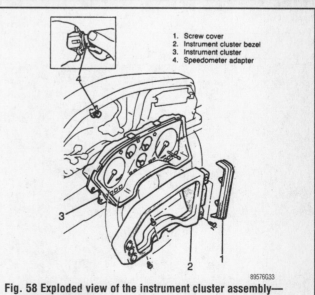

1. Screw cover
2. Instrument cluster bezel
3. Instrument cluster
4. Speedometer adapter

89576G33

Fig. 58 Exploded view of the instrument cluster assembly— 1990–94 vehicles shown

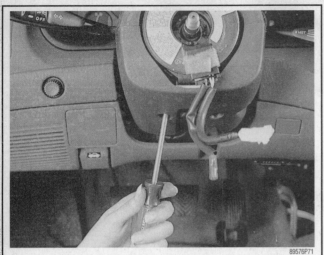

Fig. 59 After removing the steering wheel, unfasten the column cover screws . . .

Fig. 62 . . . then remove the instrument cluster bezel for access to the cluster retainers

Fig. 60 . . . then remove the upper and lower steering column covers

Fig. 63 Remove the instrument cluster assembly retaining screws

Fig. 61 Use a stubby screwdriver to remove the instrument cluster bezel screws . . .

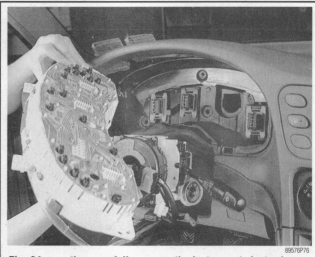

Fig. 64 . . . then carefully remove the instrument cluster from the vehicle

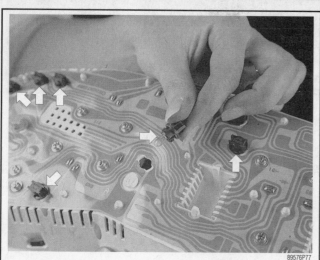

Fig. 65 If necessary, you can replace the gauge bulbs at the rear of the cluster while it is removed

To install:

8. Position the instrument cluster in the dash. Make sure the connectors are securely engaged. Be careful not to damage the printed circuit board or any gauge components.

9. Install the instrument cluster bezel. Secure the retainers.

10. Install the screw cover on the side of the cluster panel.

11. Install the steering wheel.

12. Connect the negative battery cable and check all cluster-related items for proper operation.

Gauges

REMOVAL & INSTALLATION

▶ See Figure 66

1. Remove the instrument cluster from the vehicle.

2. Remove the trip counter reset knob from the cluster assembly by carefully pulling it towards you.

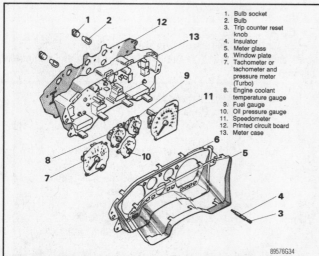

1. Bulb socket
2. Bulb
3. Trip counter reset knob
4. Insulator
5. Meter glass
6. Window plate
7. Tachometer or tachometer and pressure meter (Turbo)
8. Engine coolant temperature gauge
9. Fuel gauge
10. Oil pressure gauge
11. Speedometer
12. Printed circuit board
13. Meter case

Fig. 66 Exploded view of the combination meter (cluster) assembly

3. Carefully separate the meter glass and the window plate from the meter case by gently pulling apart.

4. Remove the retainers and the tachometer or tachometer and pressure gauge, engine coolant temperature gauge, fuel gauge, oil pressure gauge, speedometer or circuit board as required.

To install:

5. Install the removed gauge(s) into the cluster assembly and secure in position.

6. Install the meter glass and the window plate.

7. Install the trip knob to the cluster.

8. Install the instrument cluster into the vehicle.

9. Connect the negative battery cable.

10. Check all gauge and speedometer for proper operation.

Windshield Wiper Switch

The windshield wiper switch and the intermittent wiper relay is built into a multi-function combination switch that is mounted on the steering column. Refer to Section 8 for removal and installation procedures.

Rear Window Wiper Switch

REMOVAL & INSTALLATION

1990–94 Vehicles

▶ See Figure 67

1. Disconnect the negative battery cable.

2. Remove the cluster panel containing the hazard switch, rear window defogger switch and rear wiper switch.

3. Unfasten the retaining screw, then remove the switch holder from the back of the panel. Remove the rear wiper switch and replace as required.

4. Installation is the reverse of the removal procedure.

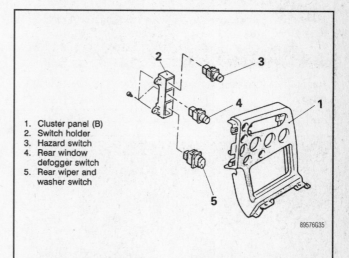

1. Cluster panel (B)
2. Switch holder
3. Hazard switch
4. Rear window defogger switch
5. Rear wiper and washer switch

Fig. 67 Exploded view of the rear wiper and washer switch and related switches—1990–94 vehicles

1995–98 Vehicles

▶ See Figure 68

1. Disconnect the negative battery cable.

2. Remove the center air outlet assembly by removing the retainers, or carefully prying it away from the instrument panel.

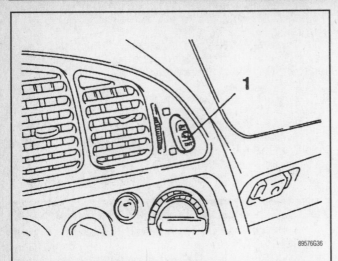

Fig. 68 The rear wiper switch is mounted in the center air outlet assembly—1995–98 vehicles

LIGHTING

Headlights

REMOVAL & INSTALLATION

Sealed Beam Headlights

▶ See Figure 69

1. Raise the headlights using the pop-up switch.
2. Disconnect the negative battery cable.
3. Unfasten the retaining screws, then remove the upper and the lower headlight bezels.
4. Remove the headlight retaining ring screws, and the headlight retaining ring.
5. Pull the headlight partially out, detach the connector, then remove headlight assembly from the vehicle.
   To install:
6. Attach the headlight electrical connector.

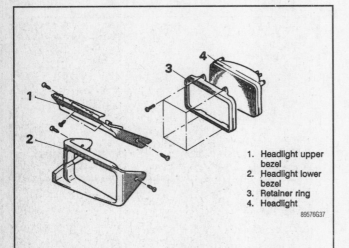

1. Headlight upper bezel
2. Headlight lower bezel
3. Retainer ring
4. Headlight

Fig. 69 Exploded view of the sealed beam headlight assembly and related components

3. Remove the rear wiper and washer switch from the outlet assembly.
4. Installation is the reverse of the removal procedure.
5. Connect the negative battery cable.

Headlight Switch

The headlight, turn signal and dimmer switches are built into a multi-function combination switch that is mounted on the steering column. Refer to Section 8 for removal and installation procedures.

Ignition Switch

The ignition switch is mounted in the steering column. For removal and installation procedures, please refer to Section 8 of this manual.

7. Properly position the headlight and the retaining ring, then install the retaining screws.
8. Install the headlight bezels and secure with the retaining screws.
9. Connect the negative battery cable.

Composite Headlights

▶ See Figures 70 thru 75

✷✷ CAUTION

Halogen bulbs contain gas under pressure. Handling the bulbs incorrectly could cause it to shatter into flying glass fragments. Do NOT leave the light switch ON. Always allow the bulb to cool before removal. Handle the bulb only by the base; avoid touching the glass itself. When-ever handling a halogen bulb, ALWAYS follow these precautions:
  • **Turn the headlight switch OFF and allow the bulb to cool before changing it. Leave the switch OFF until the change is complete.**
  • **ALWAYS wear eye protection when changing a halogen bulb.**
  • **Handle the bulb only by its base. Avoid touching the glass.**
  • **DO NOT drop or scratch the bulb.**
  • **Keep dirt and moisture away from the bulb.**
  • **Place the used bulb in the new bulb's carton and dispose of it properly.**

1. Open the vehicle's hood and secure it in an upright position.
2. Disconnect the negative battery cable.
3. If necessary, for 1995–98 vehicles, remove the air cleaner assembly and radiator reserve tank.
4. Remove the socket cover by pulling it straight off, or turning it clockwise then pulling it off.
5. For 1990–94 vehicles, remove the valve mounting spring and pull the valve out toward you, together with the connector.
6. For 1995–98 vehicles, carefully twist the bulb and socket counterclockwise, then pull the assembly from the headlight housing.
7. Holding the base of the bulb, detach it from the connector harness.
   To install:
8. Holding the base of the bulb, install it securely in the connector.
9. Install the connector and bulb assembly in the housing and either twist to lock into position, or install the valve mounting spring, as applicable.

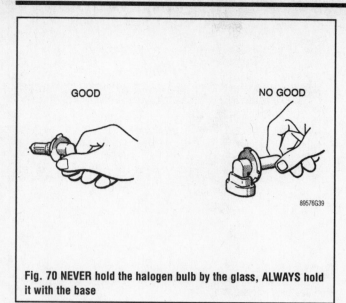

Fig. 70 NEVER hold the halogen bulb by the glass, ALWAYS hold it with the base

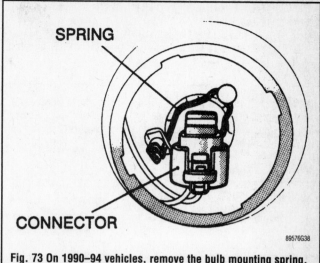

Fig. 73 On 1990–94 vehicles, remove the bulb mounting spring, then pull the bulb and connector out

Fig. 71 The headlight bulbs are accessed through weatherproof covers

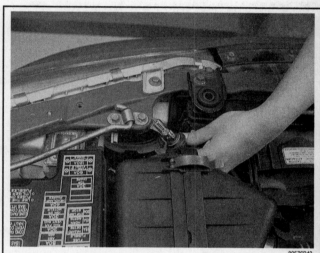

Fig. 74 Turn the inner head light bulb and socket, then pull it from the headlight housing assembly

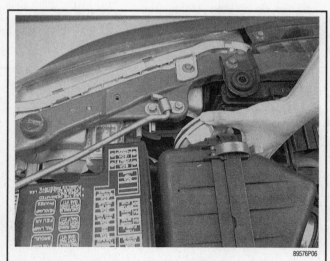

Fig. 72 Twist and pull on the cover to unlock it in order to access the headlight bulb and socket assembly

Fig. 75 Unplug the bulb from the socket, being careful not to touch the glass portion of the bulb

10. Install the sealing cover by pushing it on and/or turning it counter-clockwise. Make sure the cover is installed securely or the lens will be out of focus, or water may get into the light unit.

11. Disconnect the negative battery cable and check the headlight operation.

MANUAL OPERATION OF CONCEALED HEADLIGHTS

If the headlight covers will not raise electrically, remove the fusible link from the relay box, then remove the boot on the rear area of the pop-up motor and turn the manual knob clockwise until the cover is open. Perform this procedure on both the left and right sides.

AIMING THE HEADLIGHTS

▶ **See Figures 76, 77, 78 and 79**

The headlights must be properly aimed to provide the best, safest road illumination. The lights should be checked for proper aim and adjusted as necessary. Certain state and local authorities have requirements for head-light aiming; these should be checked before adjustment is made.

✸✸ CAUTION

About once a year, when the headlights are replaced or any time front end work is performed on your vehicle, the headlight should be accurately aimed by a reputable repair shop using the proper equipment. Headlights not properly aimed can make it virtually impossible to see and may blind other drivers on the road, possibly causing an accident. Note that the following procedure is a temporary fix, until you can take your vehicle to a repair shop for a proper adjustment.

Headlight adjustment may be temporarily made using a wall, as described below, or on the rear of another vehicle. When adjusted, the lights should not glare in oncoming car or truck windshields, nor should they illuminate the passenger compartment of vehicles driving in front of you. These adjustments are rough and should always be fine-tuned by a repair shop which is equipped with headlight aiming tools. Improper adjustments may be both dangerous and illegal.

For most of the vehicles covered by this manual, horizontal and vertical aiming of each sealed beam unit is provided by two adjusting screws which move the retaining ring and adjusting plate against the tension of a coil spring. There is no adjustment for focus; this is done during headlight manufacturing.

➡**Because the composite headlight assembly is bolted into position, no adjustment should be necessary or possible. Some applications,**

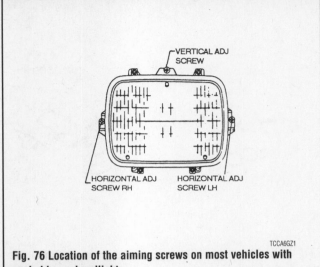

TCCA6GZ1

Fig. 76 Location of the aiming screws on most vehicles with sealed beam headlights

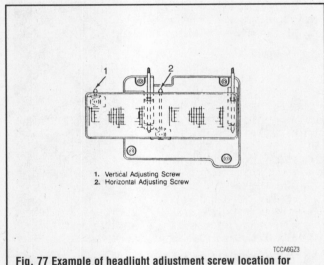

1. Vertical Adjusting Screw
2. Horizontal Adjusting Screw

TCCA6GZ3

Fig. 77 Example of headlight adjustment screw location for composite headlamps

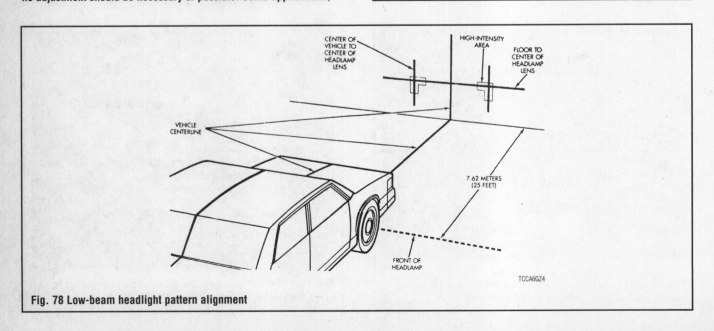

TCCA6GZ4

Fig. 78 Low-beam headlight pattern alignment

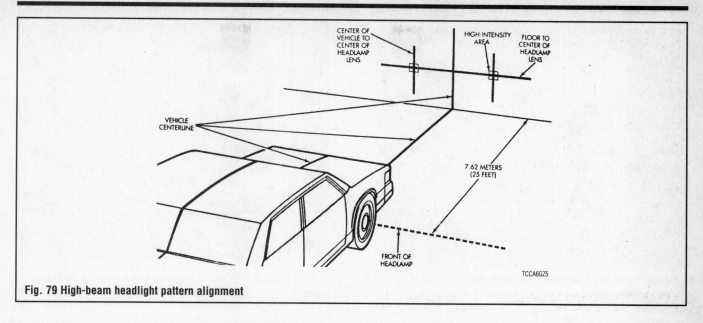

Fig. 79 High-beam headlight pattern alignment

however, may be bolted to an adjuster plate or may be retained by adjusting screws. If so, follow this procedure when adjusting the lights, BUT always have the adjustment checked by a reputable shop.

Before removing the headlight bulb or disturbing the headlamp in any way, note the current settings in order to ease headlight adjustment upon reassembly. If the high or low beam setting of the old lamp still works, this can be done using the wall of a garage or a building:

1. Park the vehicle on a level surface, with the fuel tank about ½ full and with the vehicle empty of all extra cargo (unless normally carried). The vehicle should be facing a wall which is no less than 6 feet (1.8m) high and 12 feet (3.7m) wide. The front of the vehicle should be about 25 feet from the wall.

2. If aiming is to be performed outdoors, it is advisable to wait until dusk in order to properly see the headlight beams on the wall. If done in a garage, darken the area around the wall as much as possible by closing shades or hanging cloth over the windows.

3. Turn the headlights **ON** and mark the wall at the center of each light's low beam, then switch on the brights and mark the center of each light's high beam. A short length of masking tape which is visible from the front of the vehicle may be used. Although marking all four positions is advisable, marking one position from each light should be sufficient.

4. If neither beam on one side is working, and if another like-sized vehicle is available, park the second one in the exact spot where the vehicle was and mark the beams using the same-side light. Then switch the vehicles so the one to be aimed is back in the original spot. It must be parked no closer to or farther away from the wall than the second vehicle.

5. Perform any necessary repairs, but make sure the vehicle is not moved, or is returned to the exact spot from which the lights were marked. Turn the headlights **ON** and adjust the beams to match the marks on the wall.

6. Have the headlight adjustment checked as soon as possible by a reputable repair shop.

Signal and Marker Lights

REMOVAL & INSTALLATION

Front Turn Signal and Parking Lights

1990–94 VEHICLES

◆ See Figure 80

1. Remove the front garnish.
2. If equipped, with pop-up headlights, raise the headlights using the switch.

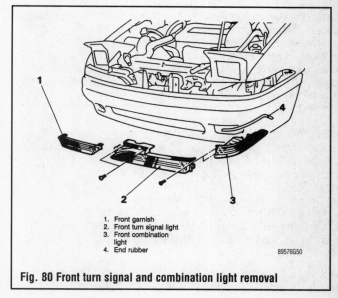

1. Front garnish
2. Front turn signal light
3. Front combination light
4. End rubber

Fig. 80 Front turn signal and combination light removal

3. Disconnect the negative battery cable.
4. Disconnect the front turn signal light. Remove the retainers and the turn signal light.
5. Remove the retainers and the front combination light.
6. Installation is the reverse of the removal procedure.

1995–98 VEHICLES

◆ See Figures 81 and 82

1. Disconnect the negative battery cable.
2. Remove the turn signal bulb and socket assembly from the housing.
3. Pull the parking light bulb from the socket.
4. Installation is the reverse of the removal procedure.

Front Side Marker Light

◆ See Figures 83, 84, 85 and 86

1. Disconnect the negative battery cable.
2. Either remove the mounting screws or use a small prytool to remove the front side marker lamp.
3. Pull the side marker lens and bulb from the vehicle.

Fig. 81 Remove the turn signal light bulb and socket from the housing assembly . . .

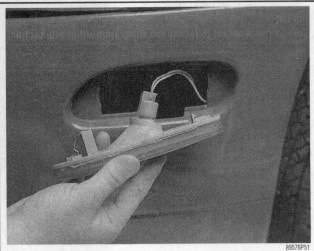

Fig. 84 Pull the side marker lens and bulb assembly from the vehicle

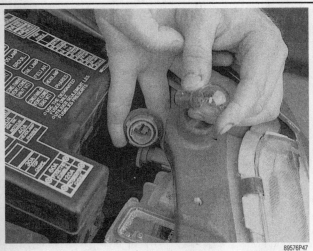

Fig. 82 . . . then twist and pull the parking light bulb out of the socket assembly

Fig. 85 Twist the bulb and socket 1/4 turn, then pull the socket from the housing

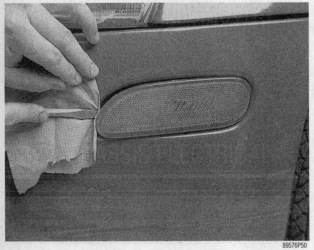

Fig. 83 On some vehicles you may have to remove the side marker lens by carefully prying it off

Fig. 86 Pull the side marker bulb from the socket and replace, if necessary

4. Twist the bulb and socket to remove it from the housing.

5. Pull the bulb from the socket and replace if necessary.

To install:

6. Insert the boss of the front side marker light into the clip areas of the front fender. Insert the ribs of the front side marker light into the mounting holes on the headlight side. Then, if equipped, secure the front side marker light with the mounting screws.

7. Connect the negative battery cable and check lamp operation.

Rear Turn Signal, Brake and Parking Light

1990–94 VEHICLES

▶ **See Figures 87, 88 and 89**

1. Disconnect the negative battery cable.

2. Remove the back-up lights and license plate light from the rear panel garnish, if equipped.

3. Remove the rear deck garnish panel.

4. Open the trunk, then remove the panel to access the rear light assembly retainers.

5. Unfasten the retainers, then pull the rear combination light assembly away from the rear of the vehicle.

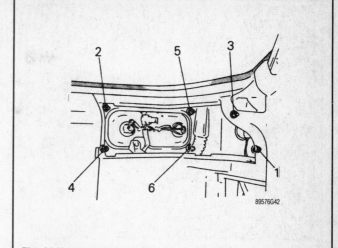

Fig. 89 You must tighten the rear combination light in the proper sequence to ensure proper sealing

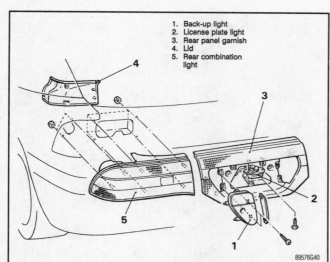

1. Back-up light
2. License plate light
3. Rear panel garnish
4. Lid
5. Rear combination light

Fig. 87 Exploded view of the rear combination light removal—1990–94 Talon

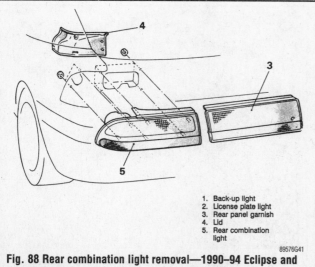

1. Back-up light
2. License plate light
3. Rear panel garnish
4. Lid
5. Rear combination light

Fig. 88 Rear combination light removal—1990–94 Eclipse and Laser shown

6. Remove the bulb and socket assembly from the light assembly by turning to unlock, then pulling it from the housing.

7. Replace the bulb as necessary.

To install:

8. Installation is the reverse of the removal procedure.

9. When installing the rear lighting assembly, make sure to follow the correct tightening sequence.

10. Connect the negative battery cable, then check for proper light operation.

1995–98 VEHICLES

▶ **See Figures 90 thru 101**

1. Disconnect the negative battery cable.

2. Open the rear compartment hatch, then remove the retainers, then remove the inner trim panel in order to get to the rear light retainers.

3. Turn the necessary bulb and socket assembly to unlock it from the housing, then pull it from the housing.

4. Pull the bulb from the socket and replace with a new one of the same type.

5. Installation is the reverse of the removal procedure.

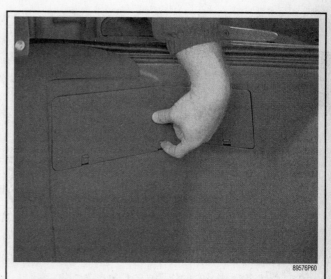

Fig. 90 From inside the trunk, unlatch the retaining clips . . .

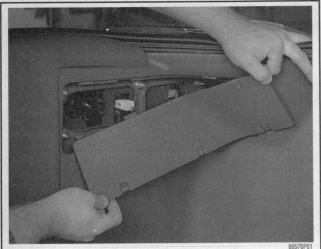

Fig. 91 . . . then remove the trim panel for access to the rear light assemblies

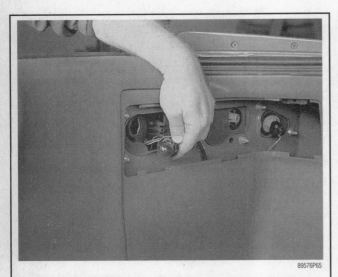

Fig. 92 Pull the garnish light bulb and socket from the housing

Fig. 93 . . . then twist and pull the bulb from the socket and replace if necessary

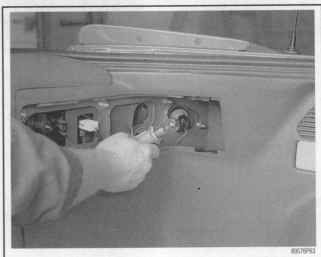

Fig. 94 Remove the brake/turn signal socket from the housing assembly . . .

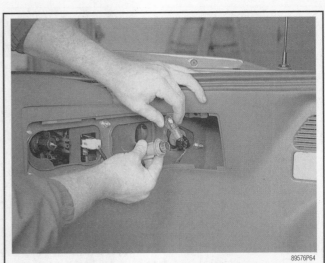

Fig. 95 . . . then twist and pull the bulb straight out of the socket

Fig. 96 If necessary, twist and remove the other (side) brake/turn signal socket from the housing . . .

Fig. 97 . . . then remove the bulb from the socket

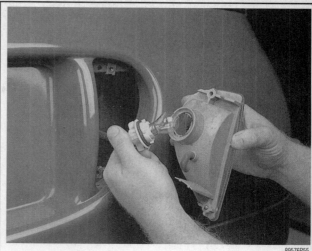

Fig. 100 Twist the bulb and socket to unlock it, then pull it from the reverse lamp housing

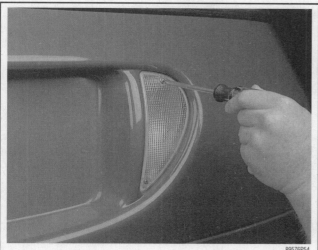

Fig. 98 If necessary to replace the reverse light bulb, unfasten the lens retaining screws

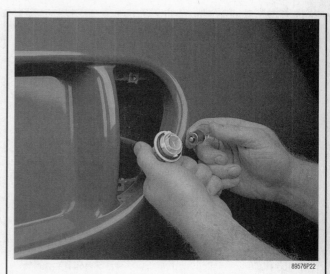

Fig. 101 Pull the bulb from the socket and replace, if necessary

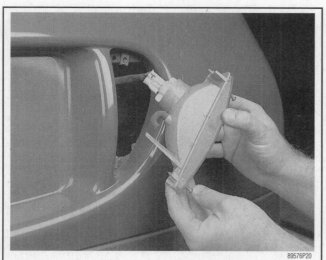

Fig. 99 Pull the lens and socket assembly away from the rear bumper fascia

High-Mount Brake Light

WITH REAR SPOILER

▶ See Figure 102

1. Disconnect the negative battery cable.
2. Remove the retainers and the high-mount brake light unit assembly.
3. Disconnect the socket harness and remove from the vehicle.
4. Installation is the reverse of the removal procedure.

WITHOUT REAR SPOILER

▶ See Figure 103

1. Disconnect the negative battery cable.
2. Remove the square retainer clips or bolts from the high-mount brake light cover and remove the cover.
3. Remove the fasteners and the lens and bracket. Remove the gasket.
4. Installation is the reverse of the removal procedure.

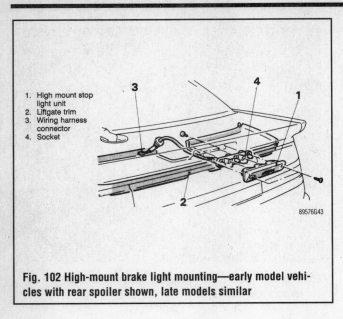

1. High mount stop light unit
2. Liftgate trim
3. Wiring harness connector
4. Socket

89576G43

Fig. 102 High-mount brake light mounting—early model vehicles with rear spoiler shown, late models similar

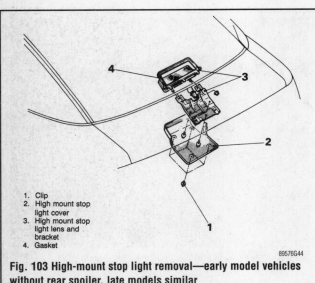

1. Clip
2. High mount stop light cover
3. High mount stop light lens and bracket
4. Gasket

89576G44

Fig. 103 High-mount stop light removal—early model vehicles without rear spoiler, late models similar

License Plate Light

▶ See Figures 104, 105, 106 and 107

1. Disconnect the negative battery cable.
2. Unfasten the license plate lens retaining screws, then lower the lamp from its installed position.
3. Turn the bulb and socket to unlock it, then pull the assembly from the housing. Remove the bulb and replace if burned out.
4. Installation is the reverse of the removal procedure.

Trunk Interior Lights

▶ See Figures 108, 109 and 110

To replace the interior cargo area light bulbs, disconnect the negative battery cable, then refer to the accompanying figures.

Rear View Mirror Lights

▶ See Figures 111 and 112

To remove the bulb(s) from the rear view mirror, disconnect the negative battery cable, then refer to the accompanying figures.

89576P56

Fig. 104 Remove the license plate lamp retaining screws . . .

89576P57

Fig. 105 . . . then lower the license plate lamp from its mounting position

89576P58

Fig. 106 Twist, then pull the bulb and socket from the housing . . .

Fig. 107 . . . then pull the license plate bulb from the socket and replace if necessary

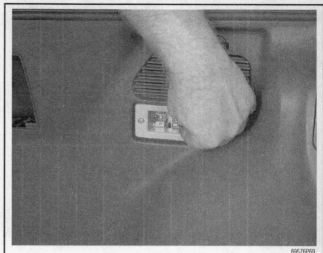

Fig. 110 . . . then pull the trunk light bulb out of the lamp housing

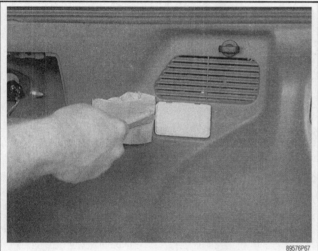

Fig. 108 Use a prytool with a rag behind it (to avoid scratching the trim) to remove the cargo area lens

Fig. 111 Remove the lens from the bottom of the rear view mirror

Fig. 109 Remove the cargo area light lens to access the bulb . . .

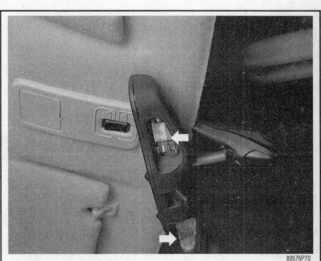

Fig. 112 After the lens is removed, you can access the map light bulb(s) at the bottom of the rear view mirror

Fog Lights

REMOVAL & INSTALLATION

▶ **See Figures 113 and 114**

1. Disconnect the negative battery cable.
2. Unfasten the retainer(s), then remove the fog light assembly.

3. Remove the bulb attaching spring, then pull the bulb from the assembly, holding it by the base, NOT by the glass.
4. Installation is the reverse of the removal procedure.

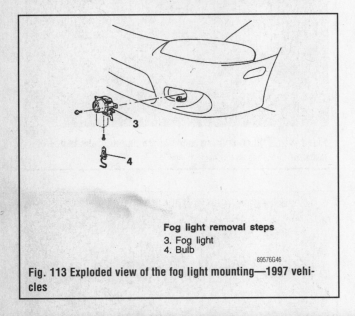

Fog light removal steps
3. Fog light
4. Bulb

89576G46

Fig. 113 Exploded view of the fog light mounting—1997 vehicles

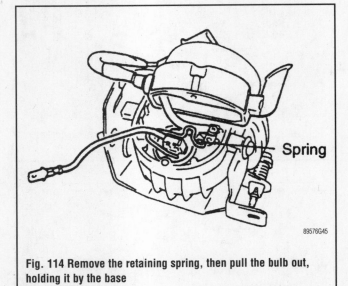

Spring

89576G45

Fig. 114 Remove the retaining spring, then pull the bulb out, holding it by the base

TRAILER WIRING

➡ **The vehicles covered by this manual were not designed with trailer towing in mind. Proper consideration should be given concerning the above normal load that will be placed on your vehicle during trailer towing. These vehicles may not be the best choice for such conditions.**

Wiring the vehicle for towing is fairly easy. There are a number of good wiring kits available and these should be used, rather than trying to design your own.

All trailers will need brake lights and turn signals as well as tail lights and side marker lights. Most areas require extra marker lights for overwide trailers. Also, most areas have recently required back-up lights for trailers, and most trailer manufacturers have been building trailers with back-up lights for several years.

Additionally, some Class I, most Class II and just about all Class III trailers will have electric brakes. Add to this number an accessories wire, to operate trailer internal equipment or to charge the trailer's battery, and you can have as many as seven wires in the harness.

Determine the equipment on your trailer and buy the wiring kit necessary. The kit will contain all the wires needed, plus a plug adapter set which includes the female plug, mounted on the bumper or hitch, and the male plug, wired into, or plugged into the trailer harness.

When installing the kit, follow the manufacturer's instructions. The color coding of the wires is usually standard throughout the industry. One point to note: some domestic vehicles, and most imported vehicles, have separate turn signals. On most domestic vehicles, the brake lights and rear turn signals operate with the same bulb. For those vehicles with separate turn signals, you can purchase an isolation unit so that the brake lights won't blink whenever the turn signals are operated, or, you can go to your local electronics supply house and buy four diodes to wire in series with the brake and turn signal bulbs. Diodes will isolate the brake and turn signals. The choice is yours. The isolation units are simple and quick to install, but far more expensive than the diodes. The diodes, however, require more work to install properly, since they require the cutting of each bulb's wire and soldering in place of the diode.

One, final point, the best kits are those with a spring loaded cover on the vehicle mounted socket. This cover prevents dirt and moisture from corroding the terminals. Never let the vehicle socket hang loosely; always mount it securely to the bumper or hitch.

CIRCUIT PROTECTION

Fuses

▶ **See Figures 115 thru 120**

There are a number of fuse blocks on these vehicles. The multi-purpose fuse block is located inside the passenger compartment of the vehicle, under the instrument panel, towards the left of the steering column. The dedicated fuses are located in the engine compartment at the left rear corner (if equipped with A/C) and also in front of the right strut tower. Blade type fuses are used.

A blade type fuse has test taps provided to allow checking of the fuse itself, without removing it from the fuse block. A test light can be used. The fuse is okay if the test light comes ON when its one test lead is connected to the test taps (one at a time) and the other lead is grounded. Change the position of the ignition switch so the fuse circuit being tested has voltage applied to it.

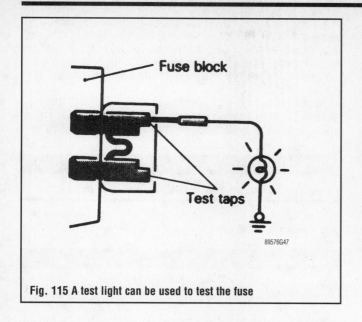

Fig. 115 A test light can be used to test the fuse

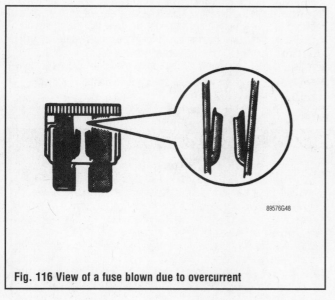

Fig. 116 View of a fuse blown due to overcurrent

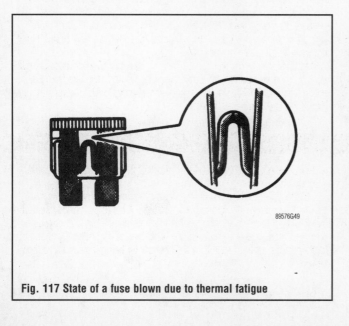

Fig. 117 State of a fuse blown due to thermal fatigue

Fig. 118 The lid on the fuse block in the engine compartment has the identification information

Fig. 119 Remove the fuse panel lid by unfastening the clips and pulling it up and off the panel

Fig. 120 Pull the suspect fuse up and out of its receptacle and check the element

When a fuse is blown, there are two probable causes as follows: One is that the fuse was blown due to a flow of current exceeding its rating. The other is that it is blown due to a repeated ON/OFF current flowing through it. Which of the two causes is responsible can be easily determined by a visual check as described below:

1. Fuse blown due to current exceeding rating:

As seen in the illustration, a fuse that is blown due to an exceeding current has a section missing. If the blown fuse looks like this, do not replace the fuse with a new one hastily since a current heavy enough to blow the fuse had flowed through it. First, check the circuit for shorting and check for abnormal electrical parts. Only after the correction of such a shorting condition, the fuse is to be replaced with one of the same capacity. Never use a fuse of a larger capacity than the one blown. If such a fuse is used, electrical components or wiring can be damaged before the fuse blows in the event that an overcurrent occurs again.

2. Fuse blown due to repeated current ON/OFF flow:

The figure shows a fuse blown due to repeated current ON/OFF. Normally, this type of problem occurs after fairly long period of use and hence is less frequent than the above type. In this case, you may simply replace the fuse with a new fuse of the same capacity.

Fusible Links

✳✳ CAUTION

Do not replace blown fusible links with standard wire. Only fusible type wire with Hypalon insulation can be used, or damage to the electrical system will occur!

A number of fusible links are used on these vehicles to protect wiring and electrical components. There is a collection of fusible links located near the battery. These are referred to as the main fuse links. A second group of links are located in the box with the dedicated fuses. If replacement of a fuse link is required, use the exact same link as removed.

When a fusible link blows it is very important to find out why. They are placed in the electrical system for protection against dead shorts to ground, which can be caused by electrical component failure or various wiring failures.

✳✳ CAUTION

Do not just replace the fusible link to correct a problem!

When replacing all fusible links, they are to be replaced with the same type of prefabricated link available from your vehicle manufacturer.

Flashers

REPLACEMENT

The turn signal and hazard flasher unit is located in the multi-purpose fuse panel located under the driver's left side knee protector. They are replaced by simply pulling them straight out. Note that the prongs are arranged in such a way that the flasher must be properly oriented before attempting to install it. Turn the flasher until the orientation of the prongs is correct and simply push it firmly in until the prongs are fully engaged.

INDEX OF WIRING DIAGRAMS

89576W01

SAMPLE DIAGRAM: HOW TO READ & INTERPRET WIRING DIAGRAMS

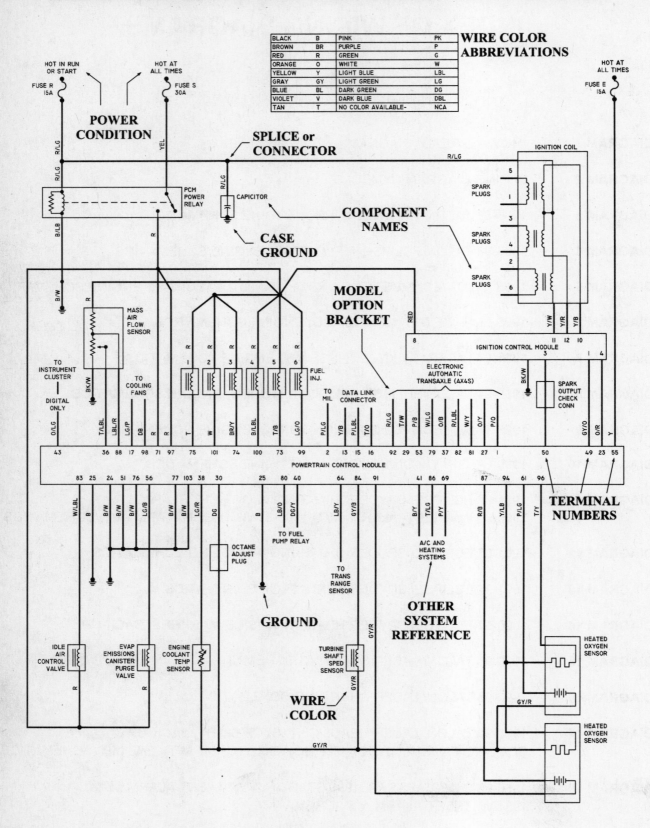

BLACK	B	PINK	PK
BROWN	BR	PURPLE	P
RED	R	GREEN	G
ORANGE	O	WHITE	W
YELLOW	Y	LIGHT BLUE	LBL
GRAY	GY	LIGHT GREEN	LG
BLUE	BL	DARK GREEN	DG
VIOLET	V	DARK BLUE	DBL
TAN	T	NO COLOR AVAILABLE-	NCA

WIRE COLOR ABBREVIATIONS

DIAGRAM 1

TCCA6W01

WIRING DIAGRAM SYMBOLS

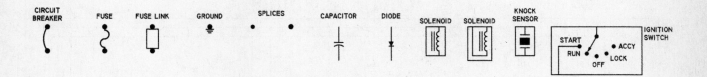

CIRCUIT BREAKER   FUSE   FUSE LINK   GROUND   SPLICES   CAPACITOR   DIODE   SOLENOID   SOLENOID   KNOCK SENSOR   IGNITION SWITCH

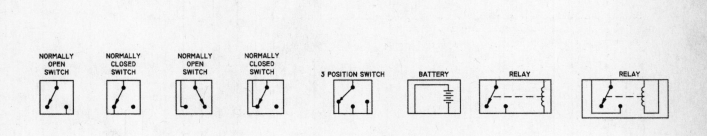

NORMALLY OPEN SWITCH   NORMALLY CLOSED SWITCH   NORMALLY OPEN SWITCH   NORMALLY CLOSED SWITCH   3 POSITION SWITCH   BATTERY   RELAY   RELAY

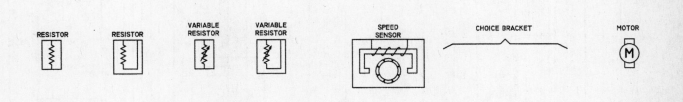

RESISTOR   RESISTOR   VARIABLE RESISTOR   VARIABLE RESISTOR   SPEED SENSOR   CHOICE BRACKET   MOTOR

    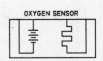

BULB   BULB   LED   OXYGEN SENSOR   OXYGEN SENSOR   HEATING ELEMENT   HEATING ELEMENT

DIAGRAM 2

TCCA6W02

1996-98 Talon MFI (Non-Turbo) Engine Schematics

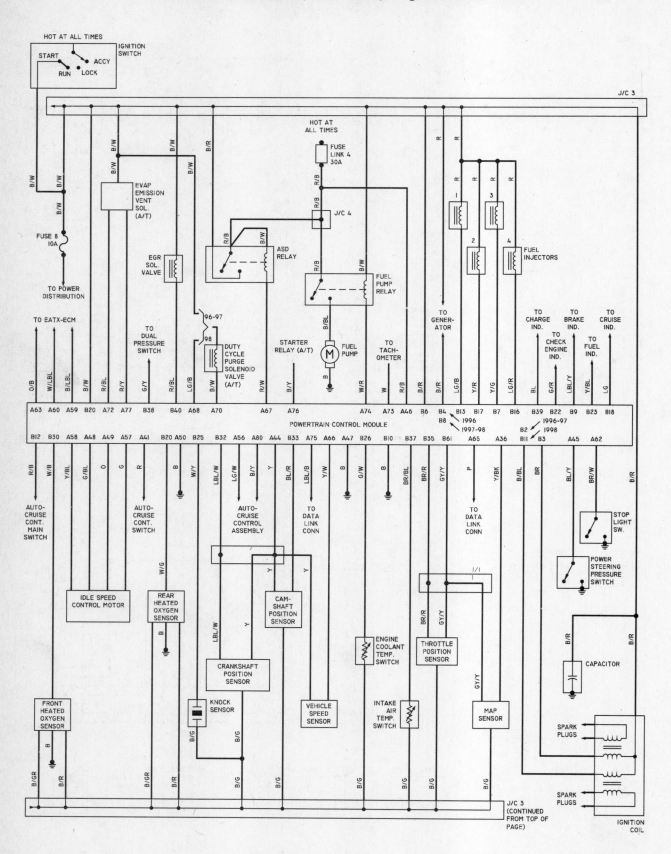

DIAGRAM 3

89576E01

1996-98 Talon & Eclipse MFI (Turbo) Engine Schematics
1996-98 Eclipse 2.4L MFI Engine Schematics

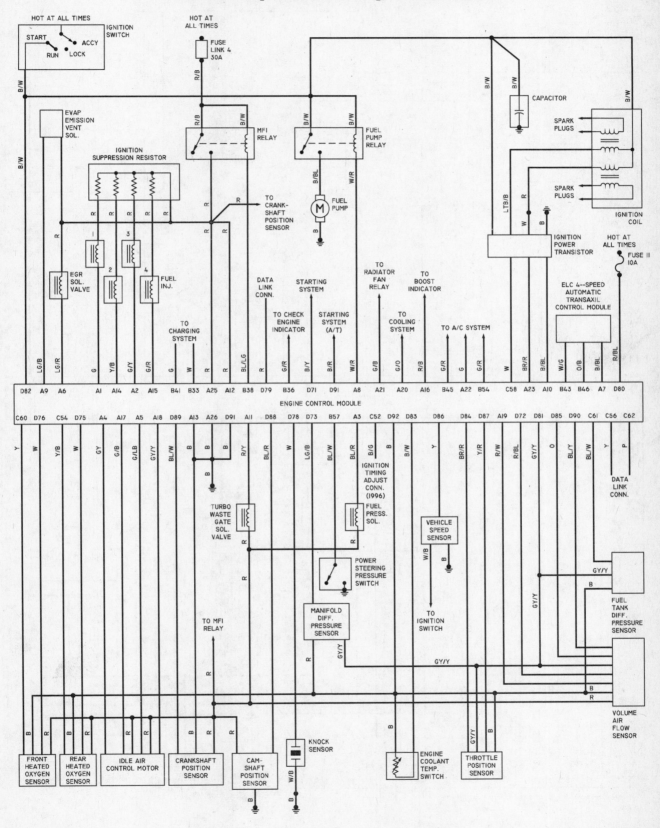

DIAGRAM 4

89576E02

1994-95 Talon & Eclipse MFI (Turbo) Engine Schematics

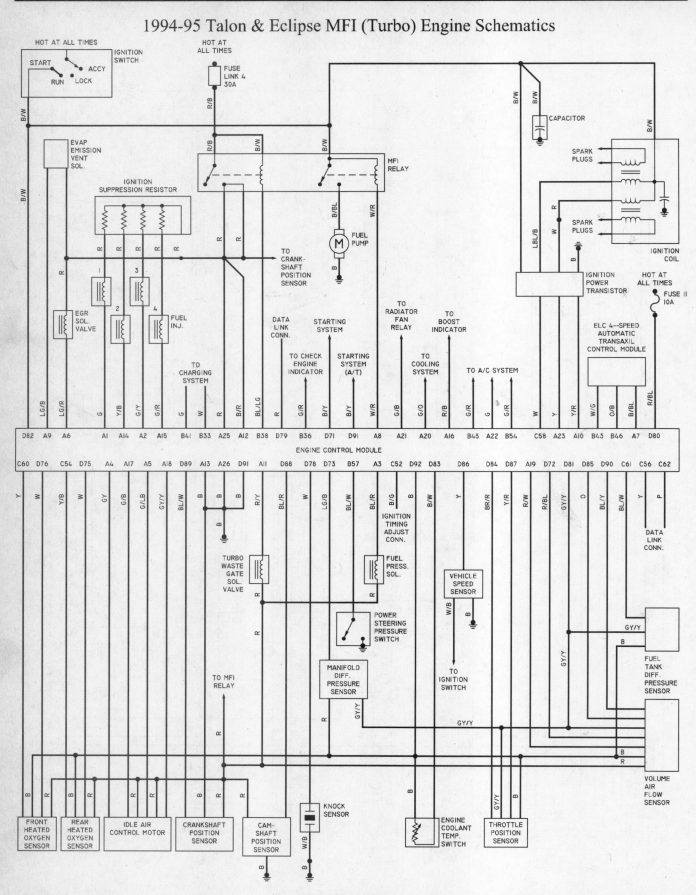

DIAGRAM 5

89576E03

1995 Eclipse MFI (Non-Turbo) Engine Schematics

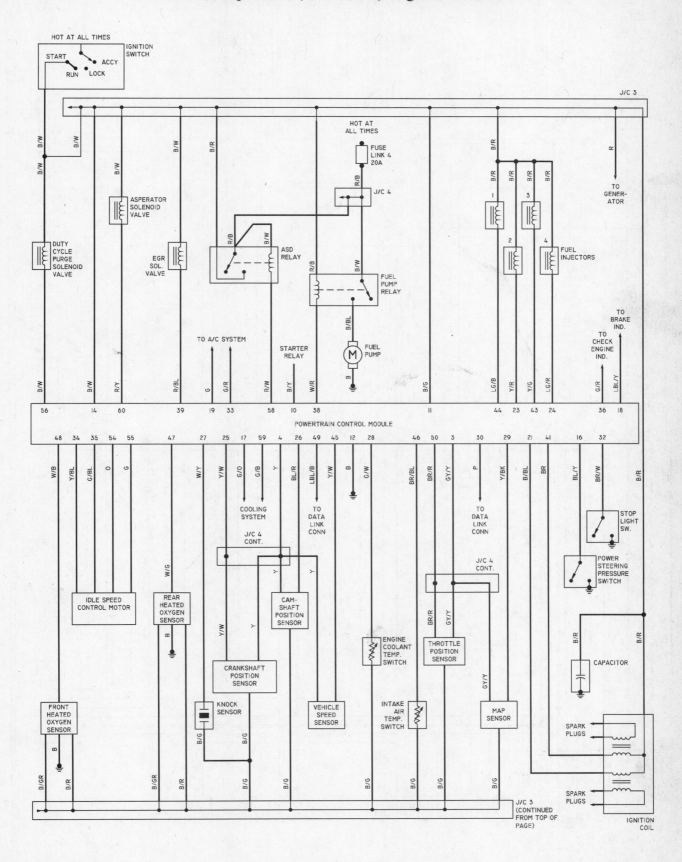

DIAGRAM 6

89576E08

1991-94 Laser/Talon/Eclipse 1.8L Engine Schematics

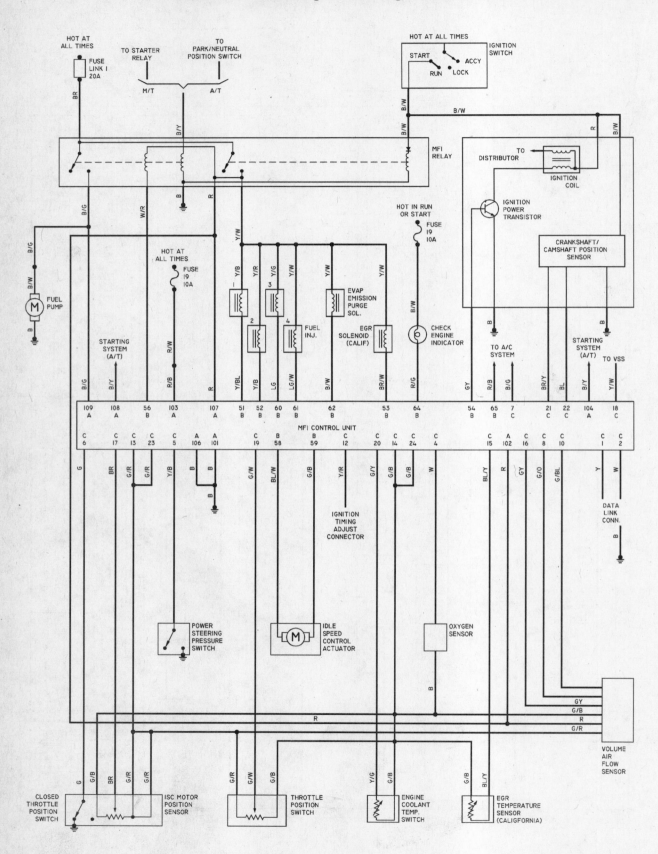

DIAGRAM 7

89576E06

1990-94 Talon/Eclipse 2.0L DOHC (Turbo) Engine Schematics

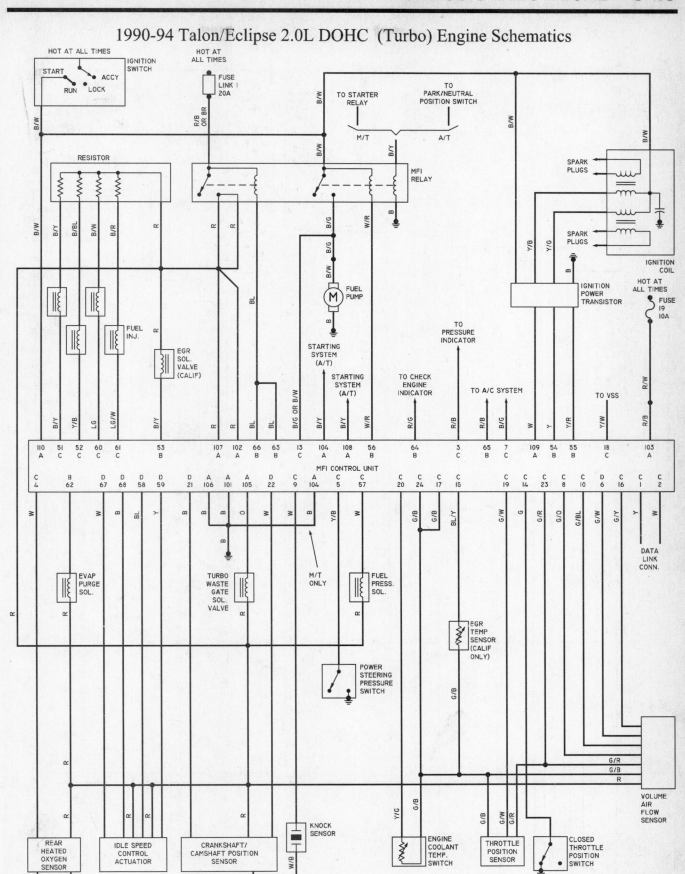

DIAGRAM 8

89576E04

1990-94 Laser/Talon/Eclipse 2.0L DOHC (Non-Turbo) Engine Schematics

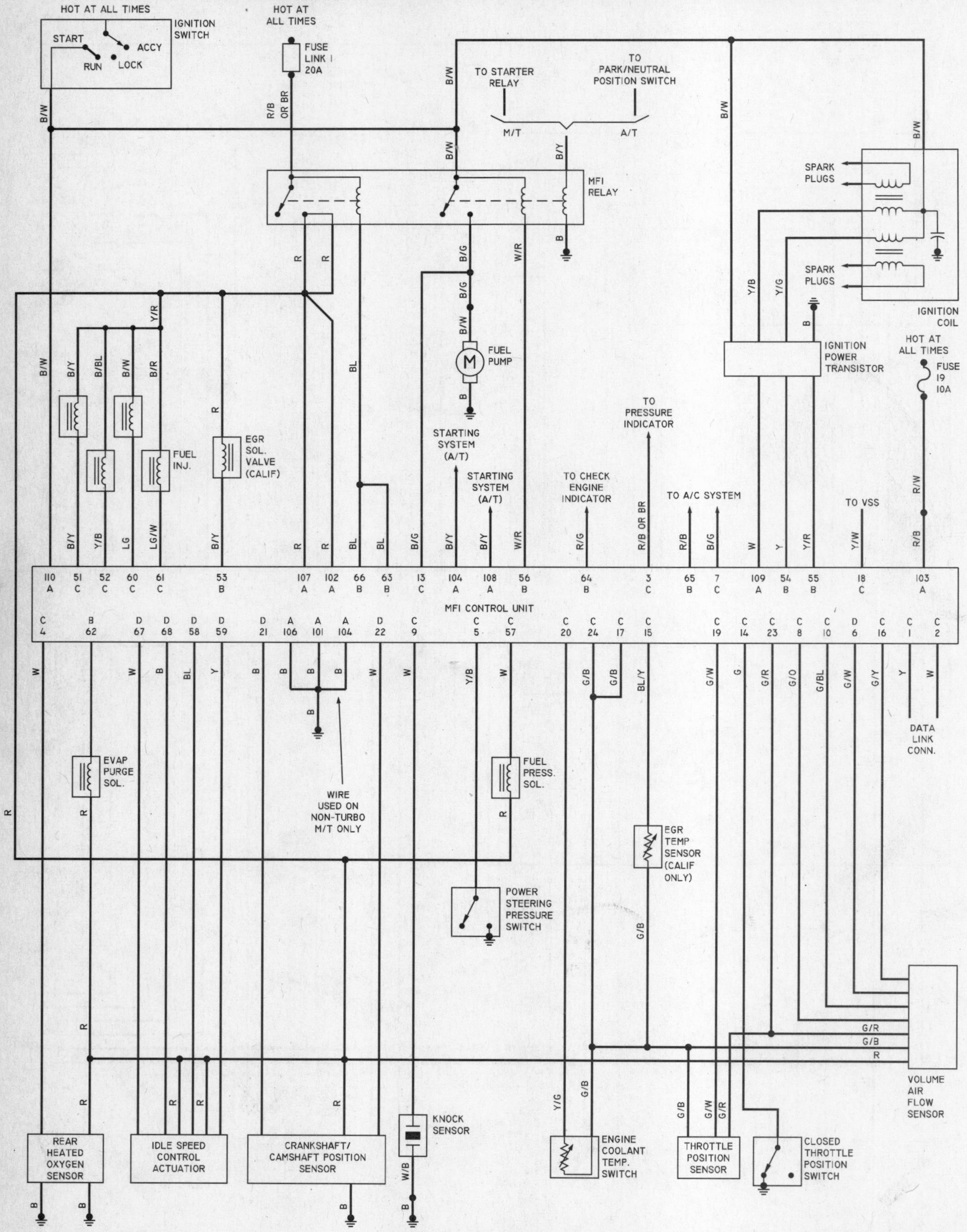

DIAGRAM 9

89576E05

1990 Laser/Talon/Eclipse 1.8L Engine Schematics

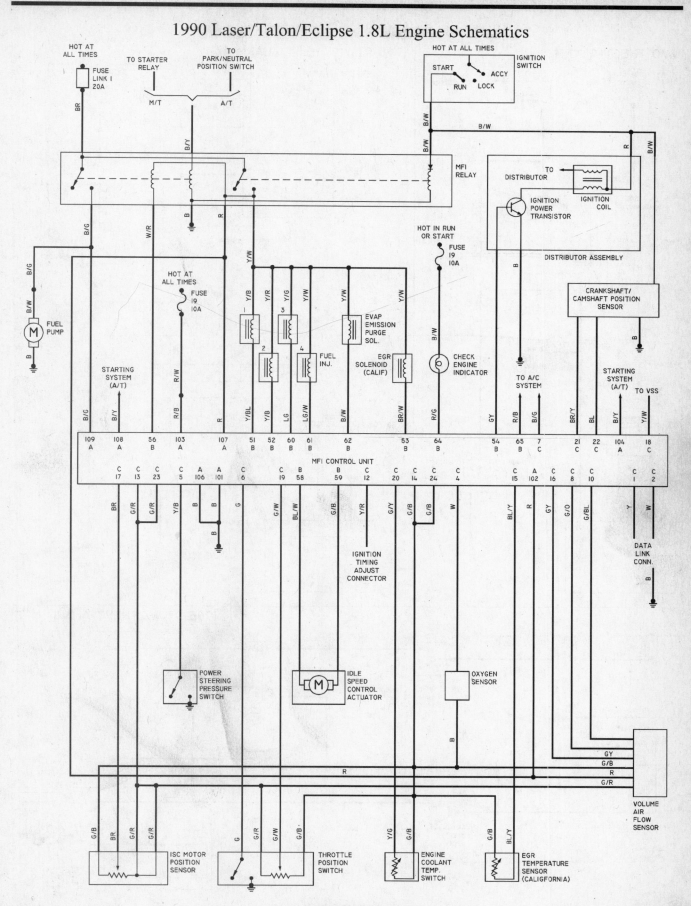

DIAGRAM 10

89576E07

1991-97 Eclipse/ Spyder Chassis Shematics

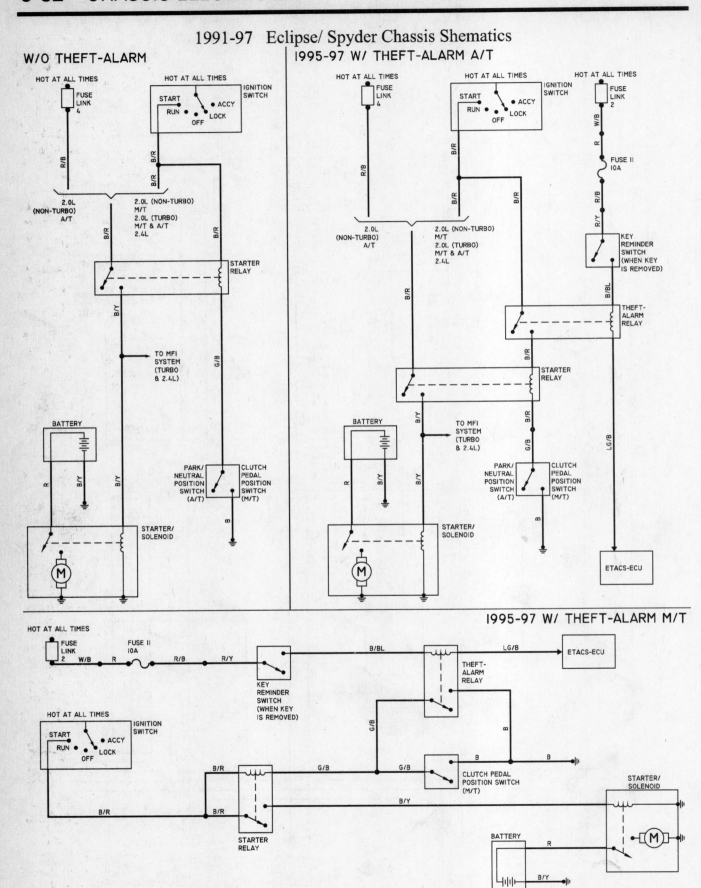

DIAGRAM 11

89576B01

1991-97 Eclipse/Spyder Chassis Schematics

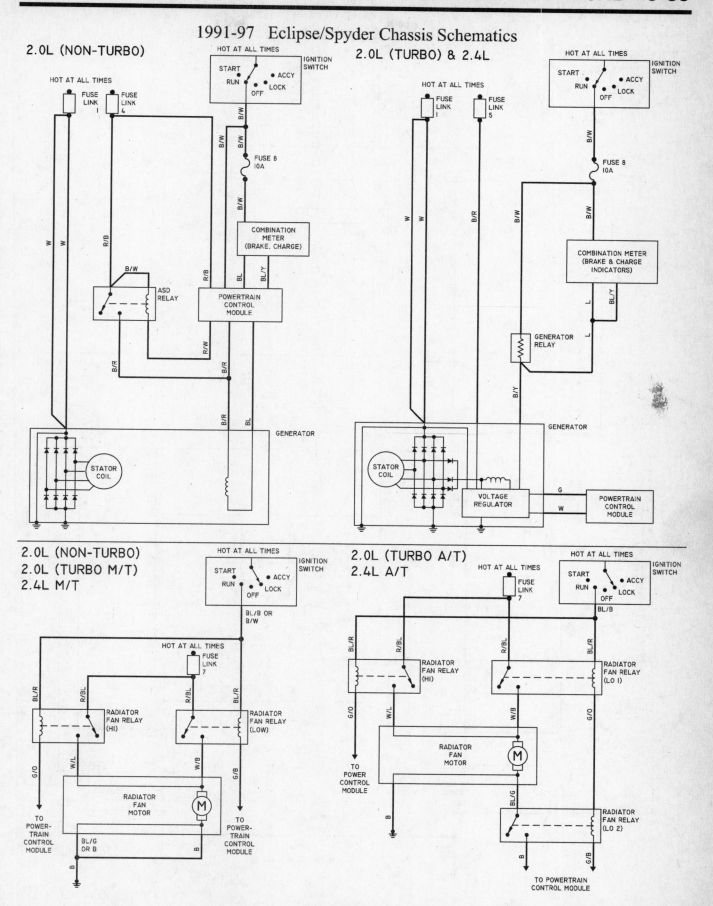

DIAGRAM 12

89576B02

1991-97 Eclipse/Spyder Chassis Schematics

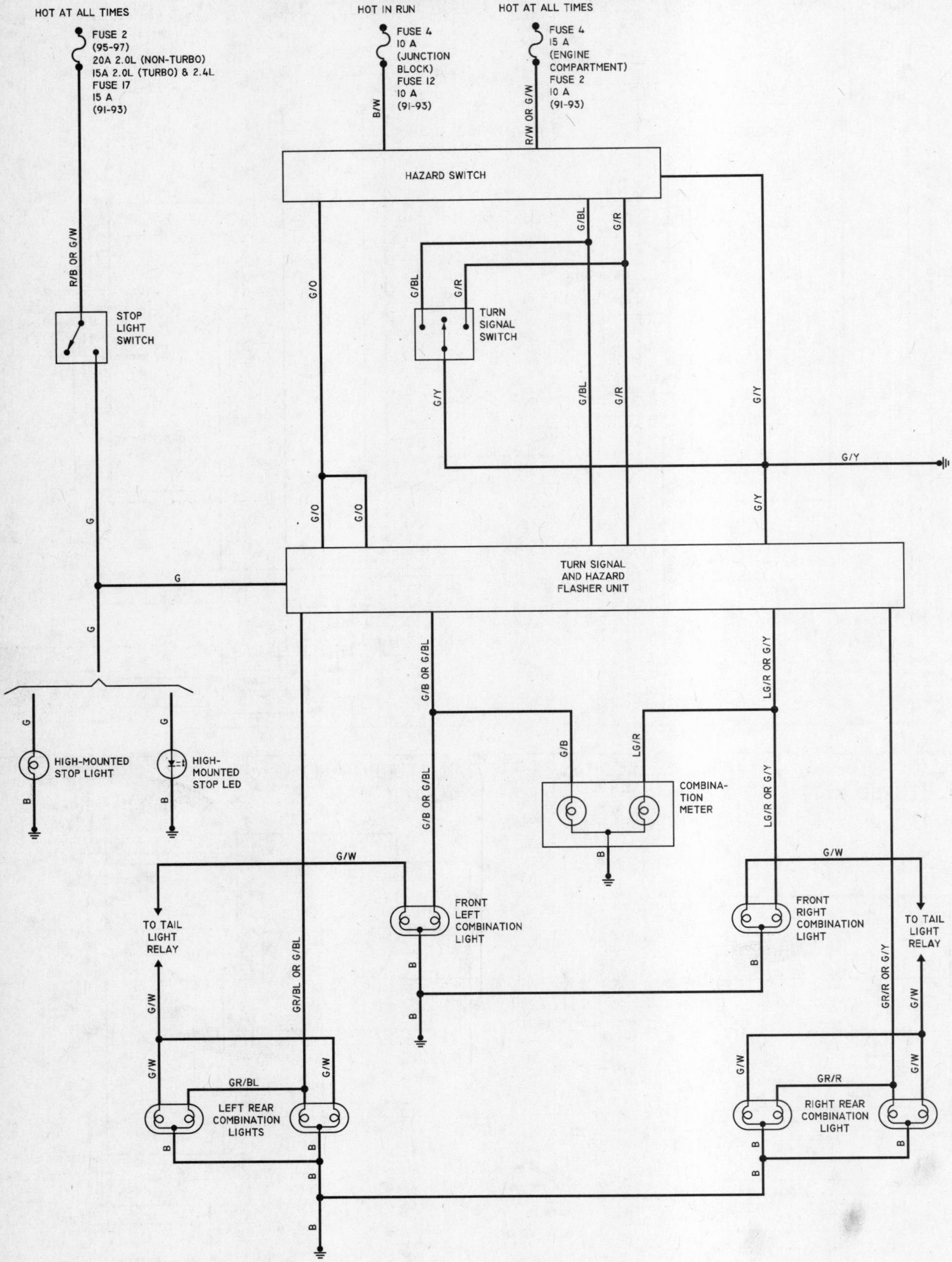

HOT AT ALL TIMES
FUSE 2
(95-97)
20A 2.0L (NON-TURBO)
15A 2.0L (TURBO) & 2.4L
FUSE 17
15 A
(91-93)

HOT IN RUN
FUSE 4
10 A
(JUNCTION BLOCK)
FUSE 12
10 A
(91-93)

HOT AT ALL TIMES
FUSE 4
15 A
(ENGINE COMPARTMENT)
FUSE 2
10 A
(91-93)

R/B OR G/W

B/W

R/W OR G/W

HAZARD SWITCH

STOP LIGHT SWITCH

TURN SIGNAL SWITCH

G/O

G/BL

G/R

G/BL

G/R

G/Y

G/BL

G/R

G/Y

G/Y

G/Y

G/O

G/O

G

TURN SIGNAL AND HAZARD FLASHER UNIT

G

HIGH-MOUNTED STOP LIGHT

HIGH-MOUNTED STOP LED

B

B

G/B OR G/BL

G/B

LG/R

LG/R OR G/Y

LG/R OR G/Y

COMBINATION METER

B

G/W

G/W

G/B OR G/BL

TO TAIL LIGHT RELAY

FRONT LEFT COMBINATION LIGHT

FRONT RIGHT COMBINATION LIGHT

TO TAIL LIGHT RELAY

B

GR/R OR G/Y

G/W

G/W

GR/BL OR G/BL

B

G/W

G/W

GR/BL

LEFT REAR COMBINATION LIGHTS

B

B

B

G/W

G/W

GR/R

RIGHT REAR COMBINATION LIGHT

B

B

B

DIAGRAM 13

89576B03

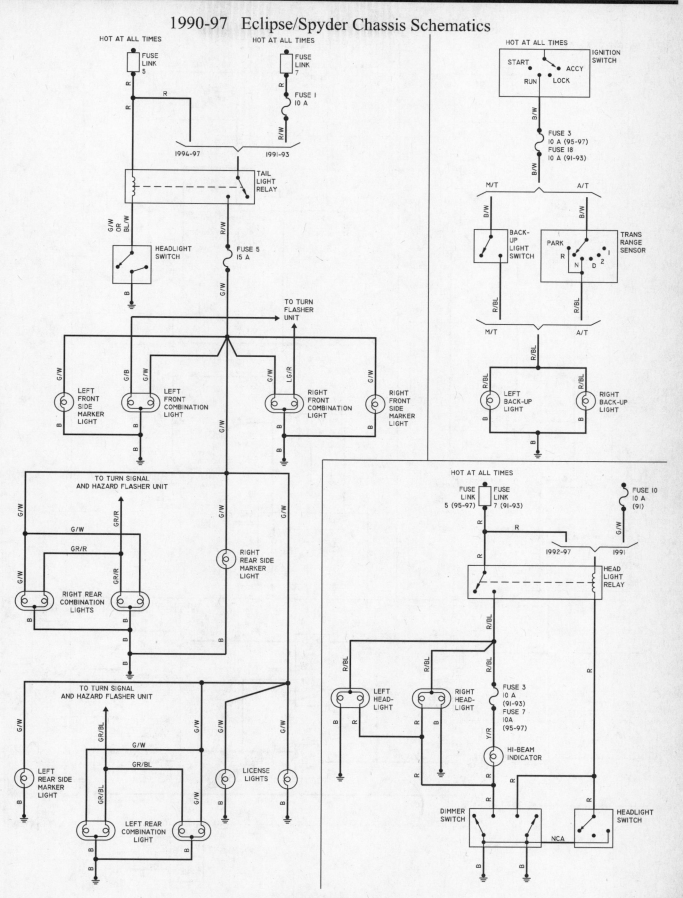

1990-97 Eclipse/Spyder Chassis Schematics

DIAGRAM 14

89576B04

1990-97 Eclipse/Spyder Chassis Schematics

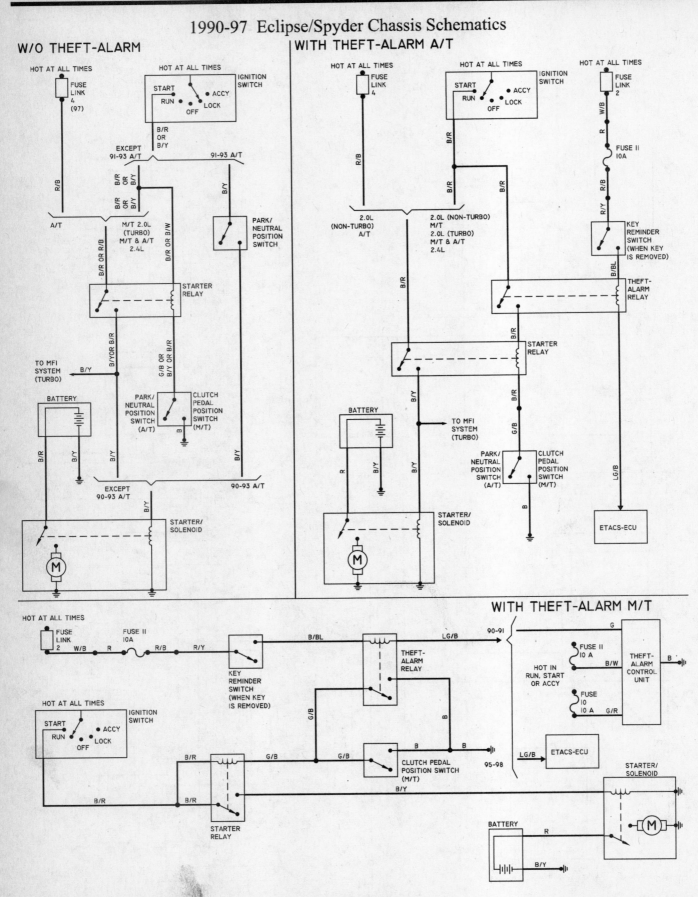

DIAGRAM 15

89576B05

1990-98 Talon/Laser Chassis Schematics

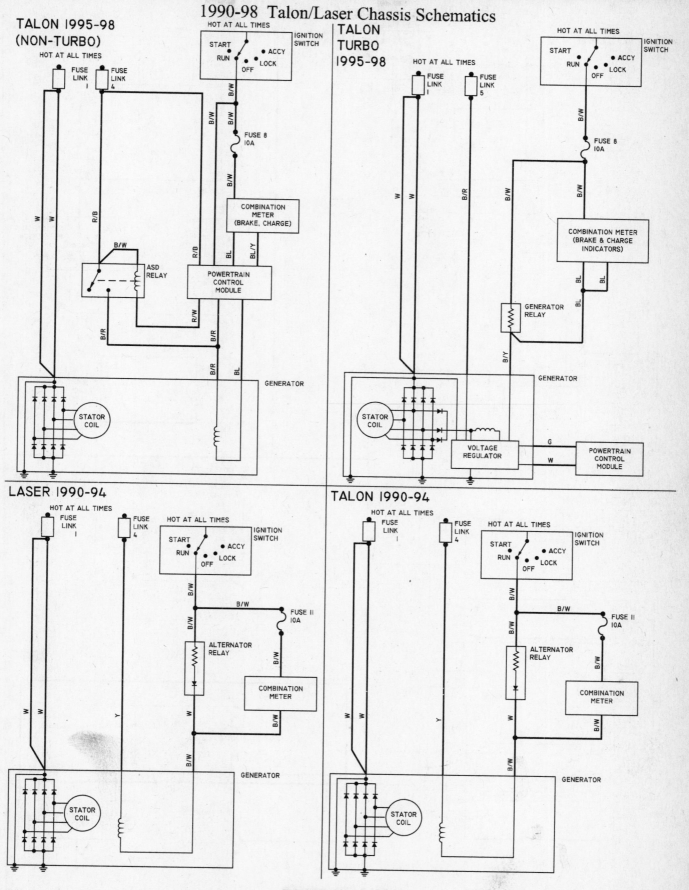

TALON 1995-98 (NON-TURBO)

TALON TURBO 1995-98

LASER 1990-94

TALON 1990-94

DIAGRAM 16

89576B06

1990-98 Talon/Laser Chassis Schematics

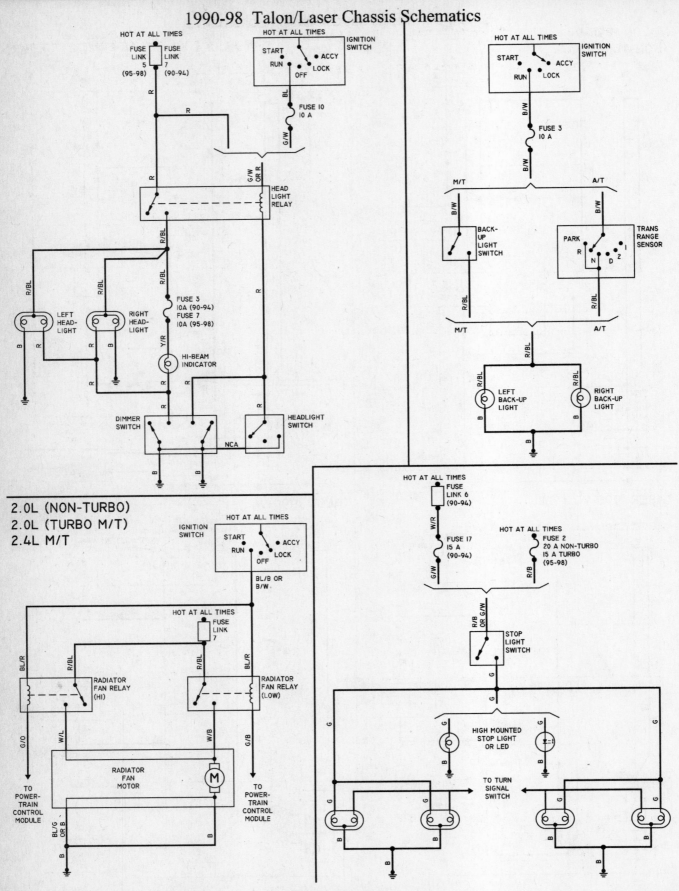

DIAGRAM 17

89576B07

1991-97 Eclipse/Spyder Chassis Schematics

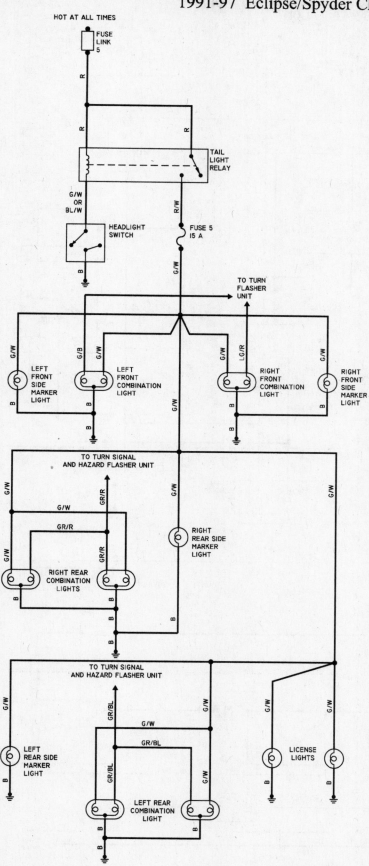

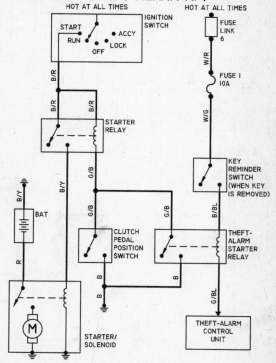

DIAGRAM 18

89576B08

1990-98 Talon/Laser Chassis Schematics

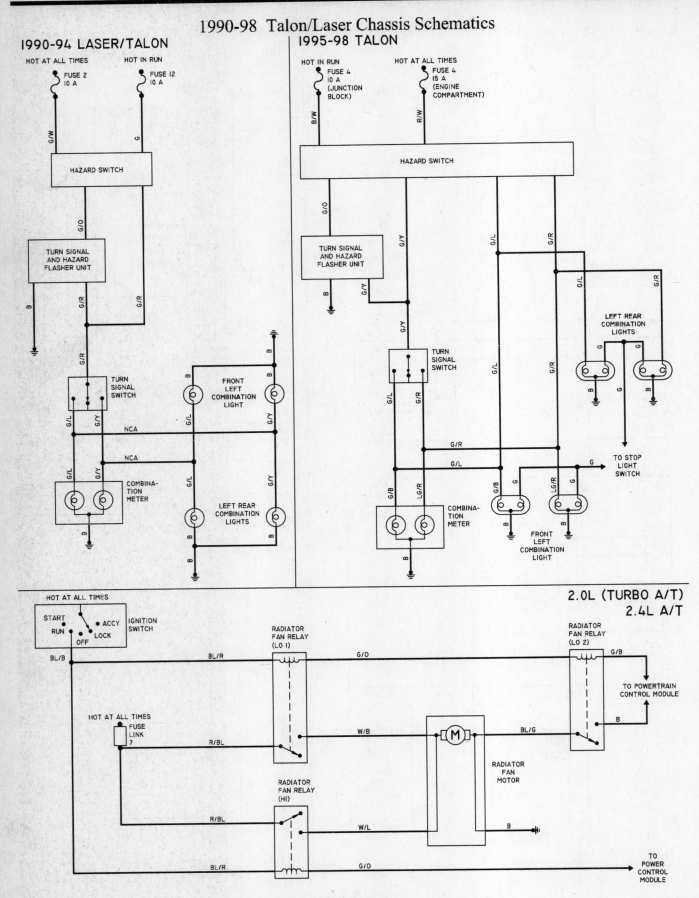

1990-94 LASER/TALON

1995-98 TALON

2.0L (TURBO A/T)
2.4L A/T

DIAGRAM 19

89576B09

7

DRIVE TRAIN

MANUAL TRANSAXLE

Understanding the Manual Transaxle

Because of the way an internal combustion engine breathes, it can produce torque, or twisting force, only within a narrow speed range. Most modern, overhead valve pushrod engines must turn at about 2500 rpm to produce their peak torque. By 4500 rpm they are producing so little torque that continued increases in engine speed produce no power increases. The torque peak on overhead camshaft engines is generally much higher, but much narrower.

The manual transaxle and clutch are employed to vary the relationship between engine speed and the speed of the wheels so that adequate engine power can be produced under all circumstances. The clutch allows engine torque to be applied to the transaxle input shaft gradually, due to mechanical slippage. Consequently, the vehicle may be started smoothly from a full stop. The transaxle changes the ratio between the rotating speeds of the engine and the wheels by the use of gears. The gear ratios allow full engine power to be applied to the wheels during acceleration at low speeds and at highway/passing speeds.

In a front wheel drive transaxle, power is usually transmitted from the input shaft to a mainshaft or output shaft located slightly beneath and to the side of the input shaft. The gears of the mainshaft mesh with gears on the input shaft, allowing power to be carried from one to the other. All forward gears are in constant mesh and are free from rotating with the shaft unless the synchronizer and clutch is engaged. Shifting from one gear to the next causes one of the gears to be freed from rotating with the shaft and locks another to it. Gears are locked and unlocked by internal dog clutches which slide between the center of the gear and the shaft. The forward gears employ synchronizers; friction members which smoothly bring gear and shaft to the same speed before the toothed dog clutches are engaged.

Adjustments

SHIFT LINKAGE

1. Disconnect the shift linkage from the transaxle.
2. On the transaxle, put select lever in **N** and move the shift lever in **4th** gear. Depress the clutch, if necessary, to shift.
3. Move the shift lever in the vehicle to the **4th** gear position until it contacts the stop.
4. Turn the adjuster turnbuckle so the shift cable eye aligns with the eye in the gear shift lever. When installing the cable eye, make sure the flange side of the plastic bushing at the shift cable end is on the cotter pin side.
5. The cables should be adjusted so the clearance between the shift lever and the 2 stoppers are equal when the shift lever is moved to 3rd and 4th gear. Move the shift lever to each position and check that the shifting is smooth.

Back-up Light Switch

REMOVAL & INSTALLATION

The switch is screwed into the right side of the transaxle case and is replaceable, but not adjustable.

1. Disconnect the wiring harness from the switch.
2. Unscrew the switch from the transaxle case. Do not remove the steel ball from the switch mounting bore. If it falls out, make sure that you retrieve it and put it back.
3. Install the switch using a new gasket. Tighten the switch to 22–25 ft. lbs. (29–33 Nm). Check for proper operation.

Manual Transaxle Assembly

REMOVAL & INSTALLATION

1990–94 Vehicles

⬧ See Figures 1, 2, 3 and 4

➥If the vehicle is going to be rolled while the halfshafts are out of the vehicle, obtain 2 outer CV-joints or proper equivalent tools and install to the hubs. If the vehicle is rolled without the proper torque applied to the front wheel bearings, the bearings will no longer be usable.

1. Disconnect the negative and positive battery cables, then remove the battery.
2. Disconnect the air intake hoses.
3. Drain the transaxle and transfer case fluid, if equipped, into a suitable waste container.
4. Remove the cotter pin securing the select and shift cables and remove the cable ends from the transaxle. Discard the cotter pin.
5. Remove the connection for the clutch release cylinder and without disconnecting the hydraulic line, secure aside.
6. Detach the backup light switch harness and position aside.
7. Unplug the starter electrical connections, if necessary, remove the starter motor and position aside.
8. Remove the transaxle upper part coupling bolt, then remove the transaxle mount bracket. Remove the upper transaxle mounting bolts.
9. Raise the vehicle and support safely on jackstands. Remove the undercover and the front wheels.
10. Remove the cotter pin and disconnect the tie rod end from the steering knuckle.
11. Remove the self-locking nut from the halfshafts. Disconnect the lower arm ball joint from the steering knuckle.
12. Remove the halfshafts from the transaxle.
13. On AWD vehicles, disconnect the front exhaust pipe.
14. On AWD vehicles, remove the transfer case by removing the attaching bolts, moving the transfer case to the left and lowering the front side. Remove it from the rear driveshaft. Be careful of the oil seal. Do not allow the driveshaft to hang; once the front is removed from the transfer, tie it up. Cover the transfer case openings to keep out dirt.
15. Remove the cover from the transaxle bellhousing. On AWD, also remove the crossmember and the triangular gusset.
16. Remove the transaxle lower coupling bolt. It is just above the halfshaft opening on 2WD or transfer case opening on AWD.
17. Support the weight of the engine from above (chain hoist). Support the transaxle using a transmission jack and remove the remaining lower mounting bolts.
18. On turbocharged vehicles, be careful not to damage the lower radiator hose with the transaxle housing during removal. Wrap tape on both the lower hose and the transaxle housing to prevent damage. Move the transaxle assembly to the right and carefully lower it from the vehicle.

To install:

19. Installation is the reverse of the procedure. Please note the following important steps.
20. Refer the accompanying figures for tightening specifications.
21. Always use new cotter pins during installation.
22. When installing the halfshafts, use new circlips on the axle ends. Try to keep the inboard joint straight in relation to the axle. Be careful not to damage the oil seal lip of the transaxle with the serrated part of the halfshaft.

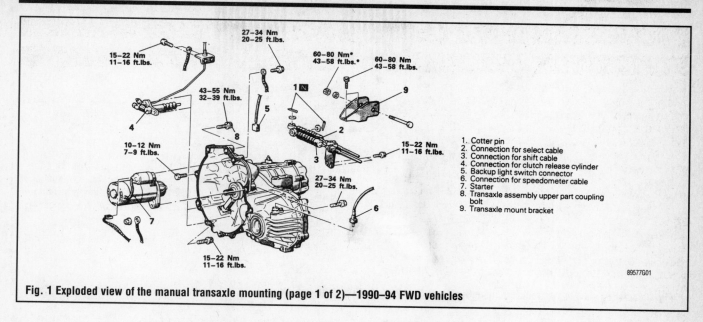

15–22 Nm
11–16 ft.lbs.

27–34 Nm
20–25 ft.lbs.

60–80 Nm*
43–58 ft.lbs.*

60–80 Nm
43–58 ft.lbs.

1 [N]

9

43–55 Nm
32–39 ft.lbs.

5

4

8

2

3

10–12 Nm
7–9 ft.lbs.

15–22 Nm
11–16 ft.lbs.

27–34 Nm
20–25 ft.lbs.

6

7

15–22 Nm
11–16 ft.lbs.

1. Cotter pin
2. Connection for select cable
3. Connection for shift cable
4. Connection for clutch release cylinder
5. Backup light switch connector
6. Connection for speedometer cable
7. Starter
8. Transaxle assembly upper part coupling bolt
9. Transaxle mount bracket

89577G01

Fig. 1 Exploded view of the manual transaxle mounting (page 1 of 2)—1990–94 FWD vehicles

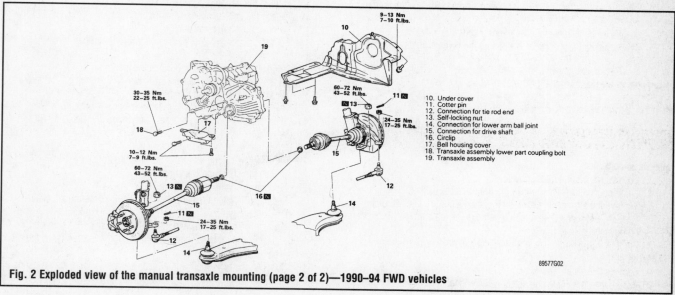

19

10

9–13 Nm
7–10 ft.lbs.

30–35 Nm
22–25 ft.lbs.

60–72 Nm
43–52 ft.lbs.

11 [N]

18

17

13 [N]

24–35 Nm
17–25 ft.lbs.

10–12 Nm
7–9 ft.lbs.

15

60–72 Nm
43–52 ft.lbs.

13 [N]

15

16 [N]

12

11 [N]

24–35 Nm
17–25 ft.lbs.

12

14

14

10. Under cover
11. Cotter pin
12. Connection for tie rod end
13. Self-locking nut
14. Connection for lower arm ball joint
15. Connection for drive shaft
16. Circlip
17. Bell housing cover
18. Transaxle assembly lower part coupling bolt
19. Transaxle assembly

89577G02

Fig. 2 Exploded view of the manual transaxle mounting (page 2 of 2)—1990–94 FWD vehicles

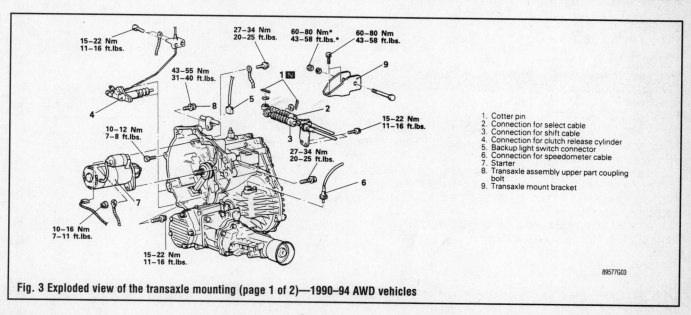

15–22 Nm
11–16 ft.lbs.

27–34 Nm
20–25 ft.lbs.

60–80 Nm*
43–58 ft.lbs.*

60–80 Nm
43–58 ft.lbs.

1 [N]

9

43–55 Nm
31–40 ft.lbs.

5

4

8

2

3

10–12 Nm
7–8 ft.lbs.

15–22 Nm
11–16 ft.lbs.

27–34 Nm
20–25 ft.lbs.

6

7

10–16 Nm
7–11 ft.lbs.

15–22 Nm
11–16 ft.lbs.

1. Cotter pin
2. Connection for select cable
3. Connection for shift cable
4. Connection for clutch release cylinder
5. Backup light switch connector
6. Connection for speedometer cable
7. Starter
8. Transaxle assembly upper part coupling bolt
9. Transaxle mount bracket

89577G03

Fig. 3 Exploded view of the transaxle mounting (page 1 of 2)—1990–94 AWD vehicles

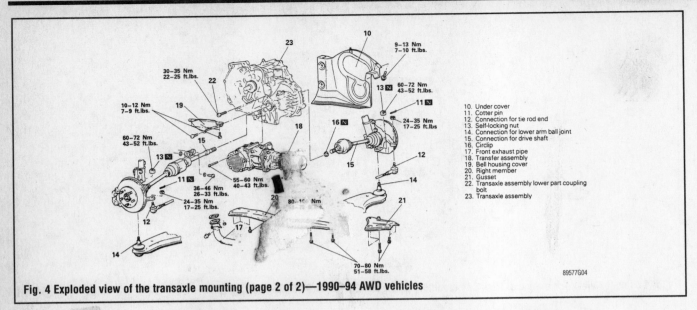

Fig. 4 Exploded view of the transaxle mounting (page 2 of 2)—1990–94 AWD vehicles

10. Under cover
11. Cotter pin
12. Connection for tie rod end
13. Self-locking nut
14. Connection for lower arm ball joint
15. Connection for drive shaft
16. Circlip
17. Front exhaust pipe
18. Transfer assembly
19. Bell housing cover
20. Right member
21. Gusset
22. Transaxle assembly lower part coupling bolt
23. Transaxle assembly

89577G04

23. When installing the battery, first connect the positive cable, then the negative.

24. Make sure the vehicle is level when refilling the transaxle.

25. Check for proper operation. Make sure the reverse lights come on when in reverse.

1995–98 Vehicles

▶ See Figures 5, 6, 7, 8 and 9

1. Disconnect the negative and positive battery cables, then remove the battery.

2. Drain the transaxle and transfer case fluid, if equipped, into a suitable waste container.

3. Remove the engine under cover.

4. If equipped with AWD, remove the transfer case assembly.

5. Remove the air cleaner cover, then disconnect the air intake hose.

6. For 2.0L turbo and 2.4L engines, remove the remaining 2 air hoses.

7. Remove the battery tray.

8. For 2.0L turbo engines and all AWD vehicles, remove the evaporative emission canister and holder.

9. Remove the battery tray stay.

10. Detach the shift cable and select cable connection.

11. Unplug the back-up light switch connector.

12. Detach the vehicle speed sensor connector.

13. Remove the starter motor.

14. For 2.0L turbo and 2.4L engines, remove the upper transaxle assembly mounting bolts.

15. Unfasten the rear roll stopper bracket mounting bolts.

16. Attach a suitable engine support fixture to the engine.

17. Unfasten the driveshaft retaining nut.

18. Use a floor jack to carefully raise the transaxle assembly, then remove the transaxle mounting bracket nuts. Be careful not to tilt the transaxle.

19. Raise and safely support the vehicle.

20. Separate the tie rod end from the steering knuckle.

21. Detach the stabilizer link connection.

22. Remove the damper fork.

23. Separate the lateral lower ball joint from the steering knuckle.

24. Disconnect the lower ball joint from the steering knuckle.

25. Use a large prybar between the transaxle case and driveshaft to carefully disconnect the driveshaft. Do not insert the bar too far or the oil seal may be damaged.

26. Suspend the driveshaft with a piece of wire so there are no bends in any of the joints.

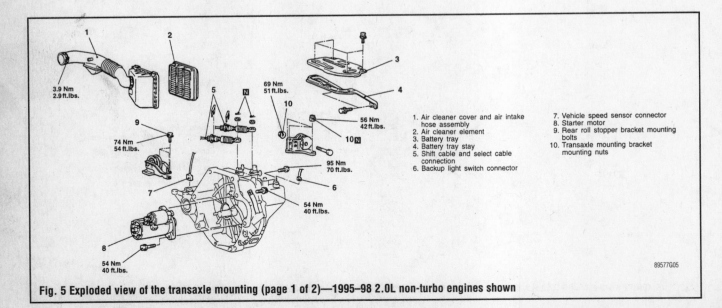

1. Air cleaner cover and air intake hose assembly
2. Air cleaner element
3. Battery tray
4. Battery tray stay
5. Shift cable and select cable connection
6. Backup light switch connector
7. Vehicle speed sensor connector
8. Starter motor
9. Rear roll stopper bracket mounting bolts
10. Transaxle mounting bracket mounting nuts

89577G05

Fig. 5 Exploded view of the transaxle mounting (page 1 of 2)—1995–98 2.0L non-turbo engines shown

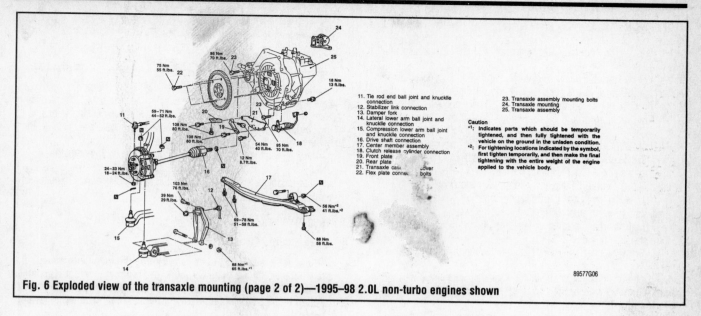

11. Tie rod end ball joint and knuckle connection
12. Stabilizer link connection
13. Damper fork
14. Lateral lower arm ball joint and knuckle connection
15. Compression lower arm ball joint and knuckle connection
16. Drive shaft connection
17. Center member assembly
18. Clutch release cylinder connection
19. Front plate
20. Rear plate
21. Transaxle cable cover
22. Flex plate connection bolts

23. Transaxle assembly mounting bolts
24. Transaxle mounting
25. Transaxle assembly

Caution
*1: Indicates parts which should be temporarily tightened, and then fully tightened with the vehicle on the ground in the unladen condition.
*2: For tightening locations indicated by the symbol, first tighten temporarily, and then make the final tightening with the entire weight of the engine applied to the vehicle body.

89577G06

Fig. 6 Exploded view of the transaxle mounting (page 2 of 2)—1995–98 2.0L non-turbo engines shown

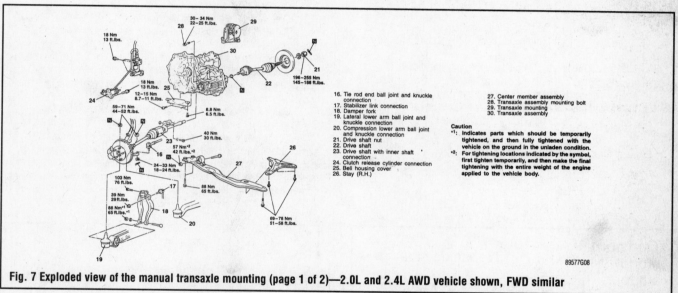

16. Tie rod end ball joint and knuckle connection
17. Stabilizer link connection
18. Damper fork
19. Lateral lower arm ball joint and knuckle connection
20. Compression lower arm ball joint and knuckle connection
21. Drive shaft nut
22. Drive shaft
23. Drive shaft with inner shaft connection
24. Clutch release cylinder connection
25. Bell housing cover
26. Stay (R.H.)

27. Center member assembly
28. Transaxle assembly mounting bolt
29. Transaxle mounting
30. Transaxle assembly

Caution
*1: Indicates parts which should be temporarily tightened, and then fully tightened with the vehicle on the ground in the unladen condition.
*2: For tightening locations indicated by the symbol, first tighten temporarily, and then make the final tightening with the entire weight of the engine applied to the vehicle body.

89577G08

Fig. 7 Exploded view of the manual transaxle mounting (page 1 of 2)—2.0L and 2.4L AWD vehicle shown, FWD similar

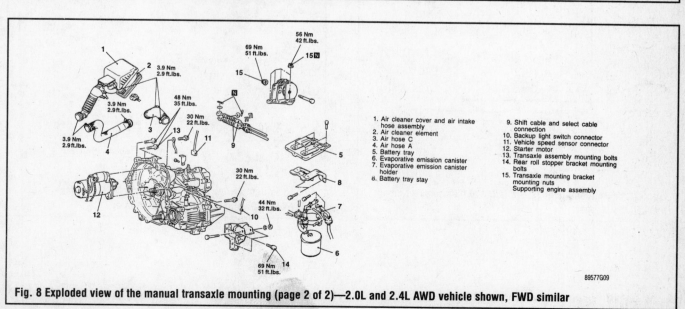

1. Air cleaner cover and air intake hose assembly
2. Air cleaner element
3. Air hose C
4. Air hose A
5. Battery tray
6. Evaporative emission canister
7. Evaporative emission canister holder
8. Battery tray stay

9. Shift cable and select cable connection
10. Backup light switch connector
11. Vehicle speed sensor connector
12. Starter motor
13. Transaxle assembly mounting bolts
14. Rear roll stopper bracket mounting bolts
15. Transaxle mounting bracket mounting nuts
Supporting engine assembly

89577G09

Fig. 8 Exploded view of the manual transaxle mounting (page 2 of 2)—2.0L and 2.4L AWD vehicle shown, FWD similar

27. Plug the hole in the transaxle case to prevent foreign materials from getting into the case.

28. For 2.0L non-turbo engines, remove the center member assembly at this time.

29. Remove the clutch release cylinder, but do not disconnect the fluid line and affix the cylinder to the body with the lines attached.

30. For 2.0L non-turbo engines, remove the front and rear plates.

31. For 2.0L non-turbo engines, remove the transaxle case lower cover.

32. For 2.0L turbo and 2.4L engines, remove the bell housing cover and right-hand side stay. Remove the center crossmember.

33. Use a suitable jack to support the transaxle.

34. For 2.0L non-turbo engines, perform the following:

a. Unfasten the flex plate connecting bolts. You will need to turn the crankshaft to get to all of the bolts.

b. Matchmark the position of the flex plate and clutch pressure plate for installation purposes.

c. Press the clutch pressure plate into the transaxle to make removal easier.

35. Unfasten the transaxle mounting bolts, then carefully lower the transaxle from the vehicle.

To install:

36. Installation is the reverse of the removal procedure. Please note the following important steps.

37. Align the notches on the stopper with the transaxle mount bracket with the arrow mark facing the direction shown in the accompanying figure. Then, install the stopper.

38. Refer the accompanying figures for tightening specifications.

39. Always use new cotter pins during installation.

40. When installing the halfshafts, use new circlips on the axle ends. Try to keep the inboard joint straight in relation to the axle. Be careful not to damage the oil seal lip of the transaxle with the serrated part of the half-shaft.

41. When installing the battery, first connect the positive cable, then the negative.

42. Make sure the vehicle is level when refilling the transaxle.

43. Check for proper operation. Make sure the reverse lights come on when in reverse.

Halfshafts

REMOVAL & INSTALLATION

Engine size, transaxle type, whether the joint is an inboard or outboard joint, even which side of the vehicle is being serviced could make a difference in joint type. Be sure to properly identify the joint before attempting joint or boot replacement. Look for identification numbers at the large end of the boots and/or on the end of the metal retainer bands.

The 2 types of joints used are the Birfield Joint, (B.J.) and the Tripod Joint (T.J.). Special grease and clamps are used with these joints and is normally supplied with the replacement joint and/or boot kit. Do not use regular chassis grease.

1990–94 Vehicles

◆ **See Figures 10 and 11**

➡**If the vehicle is going to be rolled while the halfshafts are out of the vehicle, obtain 2 outer CV-joints or proper equivalent tools and install to the hubs. If the vehicle is rolled without the proper torque applied to the front wheel bearings, the bearings will no longer be usable.**

1. Disconnect the negative battery cable.

2. Raise and safely support the vehicle. Remove the wheel and tire assemblies.

3. Remove the cotter pin, halfshaft nut and washer. Discard the cotter pin.

4. Raise the vehicle and support safely. If removing the right halfshaft, remove the retainer bolt and the speedometer drive from the right extension housing.

5. Remove the lower ball joint and the tie rod end from the steering knuckle.

6. On halfshafts with an inner shaft (AWD vehicles), remove the center support bearing bracket bolts and washers. Now remove the halfshaft by setting up a puller on the outside wheel hub and pushing the halfshaft from the front hub. Tap the shaft union at the joint case with a plastic hammer to remove the halfshaft and inner shaft from the transaxle.

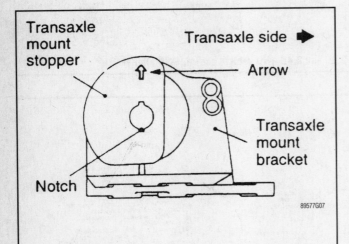

Fig. 9 Proper alignment and installation of the transaxle mount bracket and stopper

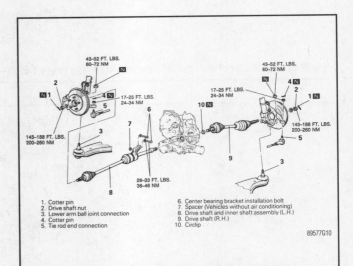

Fig. 10 Exploded view of the front halfshaft assemblies— 1990–94 AWD vehicles shown, FWD similar

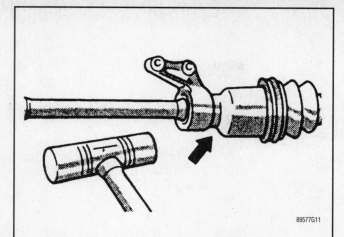

Fig. 11 Remove the halfshaft from the transaxle assembly by tapping the T.J. case with a plastic hammer—AWD vehicle shown

7. On one piece halfshafts (FWD vehicles), remove the halfshaft from the hub/knuckle by setting up a puller on the outside wheel hub and pushing the halfshaft from the front hub. After pressing the outer shaft, insert a prybar between the transaxle case and the halfshaft and pry the shaft from the transaxle.

❊❊ WARNING

Do not pull on the shaft; doing so damages the inboard joint. Do not insert the prybar too far or the oil seal in the case may be damaged.

To install:

8. Inspect the halfshaft boot for damage or deterioration. Check the ball joints and splines for wear.
9. Replace the circlips on the ends of the halfshafts.
10. Insert the halfshaft into the transaxle. Make sure it is fully seated.
11. Pull the strut assembly outward and install the other end of the halfshaft into the hub.
12. Install the center bearing bracket bolts and tighten to 33 ft. lbs. (45 Nm), if equipped.
13. Install the washer so the chamfered edge faces outward. Install the halfshaft nut and tighten temporarily.

14. Install the tie rod end and ball joint to the steering knuckle.
15. Install the wheel and lower the vehicle to the floor. Tighten the axle nut with the brakes applied. Tighten the nut to 145–188 ft. lbs. (200–260 Nm).
16. Install a new cotter pin and bend to secure.

1995–98 Vehicles

◗ **See Figures 12 and 13**

1. Raise and safely support the vehicle.
2. Remove the wheel and tire assemblies.
3. Remove and discard the cotter pin, then remove the driveshaft nut.
4. Separate the tie rod end from the steering knuckle.
5. Detach the stabilizer link ball joint and damper fork connection.
6. Remove the retainers, then remove the damper fork.
7. Separate the lateral lower control arm ball joint from the steering knuckle.
8. Disconnect the compression lower ball joint from the steering knuckle.
9. For FWD vehicles, remove the halfshaft from the vehicle.
10. For AWD vehicles, unfasten the halfshaft retaining bolt, then remove the halfshaft and inner shaft (left side) or halfshaft (right side).
11. Remove the circlip from the end of the halfshaft.

To install:

12. Install the circlip on the end of the halfshaft.
13. Position the halfshaft assembly in the vehicle.
14. For AWD vehicles, install the retaining bolt, and tighten to 30 ft. lbs. (40 Nm).
15. Install the compression lower ball joint and lateral lower ball joint into the steering knuckle.
16. Install the damper fork.
17. Install the remaining components in the reverse order of removal. Tighten the retainers to the specifications shown in the accompanying figures.

OVERHAUL

Engine size, transaxle type, whether the joint is an inboard or outboard joint, even which side of the vehicle is being serviced could make a difference in joint type. Be sure to properly identify the joint before attempting joint or boot replacement. Look for identification numbers at the large end of the boots and/or on the end of the metal retainer bands.

The 2 types of joints used are the Birfield Joint, (B.J.) and the Tripod Joint (T.J.). Special grease and clamps are used with these joints and is normally supplied with the replacement joint and/or boot kit. Do not use regular chassis grease.

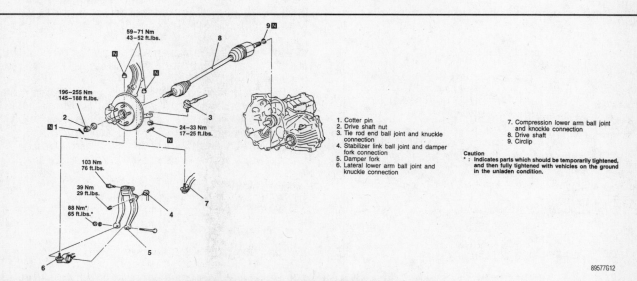

1. Cotter pin
2. Drive shaft nut
3. Tie rod end ball joint and knuckle connection
4. Stabilizer link ball joint and damper fork connection
5. Damper fork
6. Lateral lower arm ball joint and knuckle connection
7. Compression lower arm ball joint and knuckle connection
8. Drive shaft
9. Circlip

Caution
* : Indicates parts which should be temporarily tightened, and then fully tightened with vehicles on the ground in the unladen condition.

Fig. 12 Exploded view of the driveshaft (halfshaft) assembly—1995–98 FWD vehicles

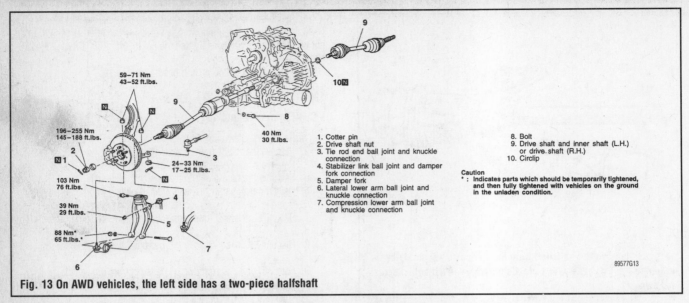

1. Cotter pin
2. Drive shaft nut
3. Tie rod end ball joint and knuckle connection
4. Stabilizer link ball joint and damper fork connection
5. Damper fork
6. Lateral lower arm ball joint and knuckle connection
7. Compression lower arm ball joint and knuckle connection
8. Bolt
9. Drive shaft and inner shaft (L.H.) or drive shaft (R.H.)
10. Circlip

Caution
* : Indicates parts which should be temporarily tightened, and then fully tightened with vehicles on the ground in the unladen condition.

59–71 Nm
43–52 ft.lbs.

196–255 Nm
145–188 ft.lbs.

40 Nm
30 ft.lbs.

24–33 Nm
17–25 ft.lbs.

103 Nm
76 ft.lbs.

39 Nm
29 ft.lbs.

88 Nm*
65 ft.lbs.*

Fig. 13 On AWD vehicles, the left side has a two-piece halfshaft

Correct installation of the CV-boot is essential for its longevity. A specification is given for the distance between the large and small boot bands. This is so the boot will not be installed either too loose or too tight, which could cause early wear and cracking, allowing the grease to get out and water and dirt in, leading to early joint failure.

FWD Vehicle

1990–94 VEHICLES

◆ See Figures 14 and 15

Both of the halfshaft boots are going to be removed from the T.J. case side of the halfshaft.

1. Disconnect the negative battery cable. Remove the halfshaft from the vehicle.

2. Remove the T.J. boot bands from the boot. Side cutter pliers can be used to cut off the metal retaining bands. Remove the T.J. case from the halfshaft.

3. Remove the snapring next to the tripod joint spider assembly from the halfshaft with snapring pliers. Remove the spider assembly from the shaft.

➡ Do not disassemble the spider and use care in handling.

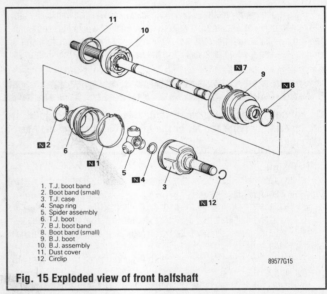

1. T.J. boot band
2. Boot band (small)
3. T.J. case
4. Snap ring
5. Spider assembly
6. T.J. boot
7. B.J. boot band
8. Boot band (small)
9. B.J. boot
10. B.J. assembly
11. Dust cover
12. Circlip

Fig. 15 Exploded view of front halfshaft

4. If the boot is be reused, wrap vinyl tape around the spline part of the shaft so the boot will not be damaged when removed. Remove the dynamic damper, if used, and boots from the shaft.

To install:

5. Double check that the correct replacement parts are being installed. Wrap vinyl tape around the splines to protect the boot and install the boots and damper, if used, in the correct order.

6. Fill the inside of the boot with the specified grease. Often the grease supplied in the replacement parts kit is meant to be divided in half, with half being used to lubricate the joint and half being used inside the boot. Keep grease off the rubber part of the dynamic damper (if used).

7. Secure the boot bands with the halfshaft in a horizontal position. Make sure the boot span on the halfshaft is 3.23–3.47 in. (82–88mm) in length.

8. Install halfshaft into vehicle.

1995–98 VEHICLES

◆ See Figures 16, 17, 18, 19 and 20

1. Disconnect the negative battery cable.
2. Remove the halfshaft from the vehicle.
3. Remove the large and small T.J. boot bands. You can use a pair of side cutters or a prytool to remove the bands.

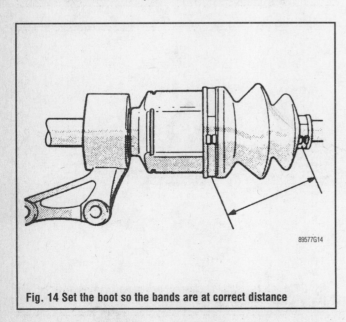

Fig. 14 Set the boot so the bands are at correct distance

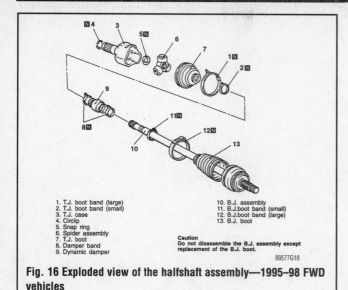

1. T.J. boot band (large)
2. T.J. boot band (small)
3. T.J. case
4. Circlip
5. Snap ring
6. Spider assembly
7. T.J. boot
8. Damper band
9. Dynamic damper
10. B.J. assembly
11. B.J. boot band (small)
12. B.J. boot band (large)
13. B.J. boot

Caution
Do not disassemble the B.J. assembly except replacement of the B.J. boot.

Fig. 16 Exploded view of the halfshaft assembly—1995–98 FWD vehicles

4. Remove the T.J. case from the B.J. assembly, then wipe the grease from inside of the T.J. case.

5. Remove the retaining circlip.

6. Use a pair of snapring pliers to remove the snapring from the driveshaft, then carefully take the spider assembly out of the driveshaft. Clean the spider but be careful not to damage it, and do not disassemble it.

7. Wipe the grease from the splines, then remove the T.J. boot. If the boot is going to be reused, wrap plastic tape around the driveshaft spline so the boot is not damaged when it is removed.

8. Unfasten the damper band, then remove the dynamic damper.

9. Remove the B.J. assembly.

10. Use a prytool to remove the small and large bands from the B.J. boots, then remove the B.J. boot.

➡**Do not disassemble the B.J. assembly, except the replacement of the B.J. boot.**

To install:

11. Install the B.J. boot large and small boot bands, as follows:

   a. Wrap plastic tape around the spline part on the driveshaft, then install small B.J. boot band and B.J. boot.

   b. Install the smaller side of the B.J. boot band so that one shaft groove can be seen.

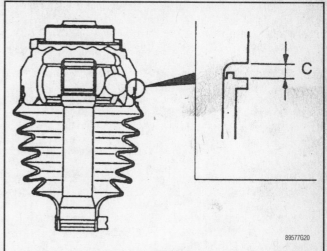

Fig. 18 Install the boot to adjust the clearance between the boot end and the stepped part of the housing

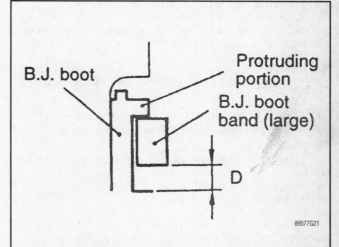

B.J. boot

Protruding portion
B.J. boot band (large)

Fig. 19 Once the large B.J. boot band is installed, there should be some clearance as shown

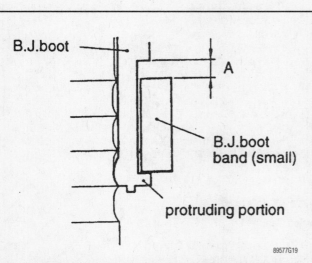

B.J.boot

A

B.J.boot band (small)

protruding portion

Fig. 17 Install the small boot so there is some clearance (A), as shown

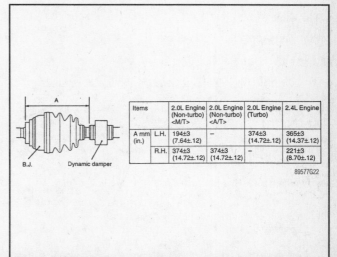

Items		2.0L Engine (Non-turbo) <M/T>	2.0L Engine (Non-turbo) <A/T>	2.0L Engine (Turbo)	2.4L Engine
A mm (in.)	L.H.	194±3 (7.64±.12)	–	374±3 (14.72±.12)	365±3 (14.37±.12)
	R.H.	374±3 (14.72±.12)	374±3 (14.72±.12)	–	221±3 (8.70±.12)

Fig. 20 Install the dynamic damper as shown, making sure the proper specifications are met

c. Turn the adjusting bolt of the boot band crimper tool to adjust the opening dimension to the standard value of 0.114 in. (2.9mm). When more than 0.114 in. (2.9mm) screw in the adjusting bolt, when less that 0.114 in. (2.9mm), loosen the adjusting bolt less that one full turn.

d. Place the small boot band along the protruding portion, and install it so that there is some clearance (A) along the other side. Hold the driveshaft perpendicularly, then use a suitable boot band crimping tool to crimp the small boot band until the tool touches the stopper.

e. Check that the crimped width is within 0.094–0.110 in. (2.4–2.8mm).

f. Check that the B.J. boot band is secured correctly. If not, repeat the last 3 steps.

g. Apply the proper amount of grease the boot. For 2.0L non-turbo engines, the proper amount is 3.88 oz. (110 g) and for 2.0K turbo and 2.4L engines, the proper amount is 4.59 ox. (130 g).

h. Install the B.J. boot to adjust the clearance (C) between the B.J. boot end and the stepped phase of the B.J. housing is within 0.004–0.061 in. (0.1–1.55mm).

i. Adjust the opening dimension (W) to the standard value, which is 0.126 in. (3.2mm).

j. Place the large B.J. boot band along the protruding part, then install it so there is some clearance along the other side. Use a boot band crimping tool to properly crimp the large band.

k. Check that the crimped width is between 0.094–0.110 in. (2.4–2.8mm). Make sure the boot band is secured properly. If not, repeat the last 3 steps.

12. Install the B.J. assembly.

13. Install the dynamic damper assembly, and compare with the specifications shown in the accompanying figure. Install the damper band.

14. Install the T.J. boot.

➡**The grease supplied in the repair kit should be equally divided in half for use at the joint and inside the boot.**

15. Install the spider assembly to the shaft from the direction of the spline beveled section. After applying the proper amount of grease to the T.J. case , insert the driveshaft, then apply grease once again. The grease specifications are:

a. 2.0L non-turbo engines: 3.70 oz. (105 g).

b. 2.0L turbo and 2.4L engines: 4.23 oz. (120 g).

16. Install the retaining snapring and circlip.

17. Install the T.J. boot bands by setting the boot bands at the specified distance in order to adjust the amount of air inside the boot, then tighten the bands securely. The standard value is 3.03–3.27 in. (77–83 mm).

18. Install the halfshaft in the vehicle, as outlined earlier.

19. Connect the negative battery cable.

AWD Vehicle

1990–94 VEHICLES

▶ **See Figures 21 and 22**

1. Disconnect the negative battery cable. Remove the halfshaft from the vehicle.

2. Remove the T.J. large and small boot bands. Remove the T.J. case from inner shaft assembly.

3. Remove the snapring next to the tripod joint spider assembly from the halfshaft with snapring pliers. Remove the spider assembly from the shaft.

➡**Do not disassemble the spider and use care in handling.**

4. If the boot is be reused, wrap vinyl tape around the spline part of the shaft so the boot will not be damaged when removed.

5. Remove the inner and the outer dust seals from the center support bearing assembly. Remove the center bearing from the shaft.

6. Remove the inner shaft assembly, together with the seal plate, from the T.J. case. Using puller tool, remove the inner shaft from the center bearing bracket.

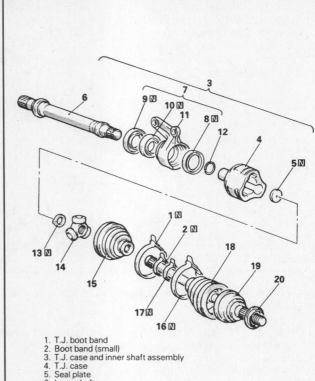

1. T.J. boot band
2. Boot band (small)
3. T.J. case and inner shaft assembly
4. T.J. case
5. Seal plate
6. Inner shaft
7. Bracket assembly
8. Outer dust seal
9. Inner dust seal
10. Center bearing
11. Center bearing bracket
12. Circlip
13. Snap ring
14. Spider assembly
15. T.J. boot
16. B.J. boot band
17. Boot band (small)
18. B.J. boot
19. B.J. assembly
20. Dust cover

Fig. 21 Exploded view of the front halfshaft and related components—1990–94 FWD vehicle

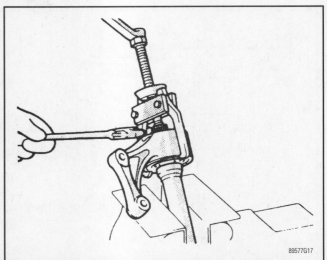

Fig. 22 Use a suitable jawed puller tool to remove the inner shaft from the center bearing bracket

To install:

7. Apply multi-purpose grease to the center bearing and inside the center bearing bracket. Using proper size driver, press fit the center bearing into the center bearing bracket.

8. Apply multi-purpose grease to the rear surfaces of both dust seals and install. Use a pipe to hold the inner race of the center bearing and force the inner shaft into place.

9. Install the boots in place. Apply grease to the inner shaft splines, then press fit it into the T.J. case. Press the seal plate into the T.J. case.

10. Fill the join and the boot with the specified grease, enclosed in the repair kit. Divide the grease in half between the joint and the boot. Keep grease off the rubber part of the dynamic damper (if used).

11. Secure the boot bands with the halfshaft in a horizontal position. Make sure the boot span on the halfshaft is 3.23–3.47 in. (82–88mm) in length.

12. Install halfshaft into vehicle.

1995–98 VEHICLES

▶ **See Figures 23, 24, 25, 26 and 27**

1. Disconnect the negative battery cable.
2. Remove the halfshaft from the vehicle.

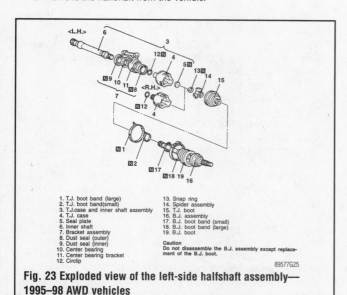

1. T.J. boot band (large)
2. T.J. boot band(small)
3. T.J.case and inner shaft assembly
4. T.J. case
5. Seal plate
6. Inner shaft
7. Bracket assembly
8. Dust seal (outer)
9. Dust seal (inner)
10. Center bearing
11. Center bearing bracket
12. Circlip
13. Snap ring
14. Spider assembly
15. T.J. boot
16. B.J. assembly
17. B.J. boot band (small)
18. B.J. boot band (large)
19. B.J. boot

Caution
Do not disassemble the B.J. assembly except replacement of the B.J. boot.

89577G25

Fig. 23 Exploded view of the left-side halfshaft assembly— 1995–98 AWD vehicles

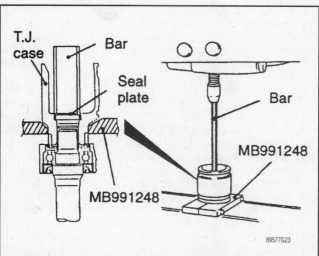

89577G23

Fig. 24 Use a inner shaft removal tool to remove the inner shaft and seal plate from the T.J. case

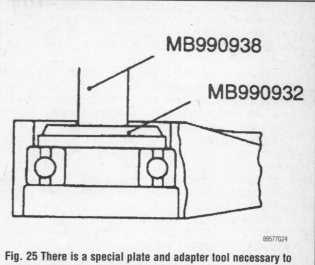

89577G24

Fig. 25 There is a special plate and adapter tool necessary to remove and install the center bearing

3. Remove the large and small T.J. boot bands. You can use a pair of side cutters or a prytool to remove the bands.

4. Remove the T.J. case and inner shaft assembly (if equipped).

5. Remove the T.J. case from the B.J. assembly, then wipe the grease from inside of the T.J. case.

6. Remove the seal plate.

7. With the inner shaft in a soft-jawed vise, use a suitable inner shaft removal tool, to remove the inner shaft, along with the seal plate, from the T.J. case. Remove the inner shaft from the bracket using a jawed puller.

8. Remove the bracket assembly.

9. Remove the outer and inner dust seals.

10. Remove the center bearing using the special tools shown in the accompanying figure.

11. Remove the center bearing bracket.

12. Remove the retaining circlip.

13. Use snapring pliers to remove the snapring from the driveshaft, then take the spider assembly from the driveshaft. Carefully clean the spider, being careful damage or disassemble the driveshaft.

14. Wipe the grease from the splines, then remove the T.J. boot. If the boot is going to be reused, wrap plastic tape around the driveshaft spline so the boot is not damaged when it is removed.

15. Remove the B.J. assembly.

16. Use a prytool to remove the small and large bands from the B.J. boots, then remove the B.J. boot.

➡**Do not disassemble the B.J. assembly, except the replacement of the B.J. boot.**

To install:

17. Install the B.J. boot, and large and small boot bands, as follows:

a. Wrap plastic tape around the spline part on the driveshaft, then install small B.J. boot band and B.J. boot.

b. Install the smaller side of the B.J. boot band so that one shaft groove can be seen.

c. Turn the adjusting bolt of the boot band crimper tool to adjust the opening dimension to the standard value of 0.114 in. (2.9mm). When more than 0.114 in. (2.9mm) screw in the adjusting bolt, when less that 0.114 in. (2.9mm), loosen the adjusting bolt less that one full turn.

d. Place the small boot band along the protruding portion, and install it so that there is some clearance (A) along the other side. Hold the driveshaft perpendicularly, then use a suitable boot band crimping tool to crimp the small boot band until the tool touches the stopper.

e. Check that the crimped width is within 0.094–0.110 in. (2.4–2.8mm).

f. Check that the B.J. boot band is secured correctly. If not, repeat the last 3 steps.

g. Install the repair kit grease, 3.35 oz. (95 g) to the boot. Install the B.J. boot to adjust the clearance between the boot end and the stepped phase of the housing within 0.004–0.061 in. (0.10–1.55mm).

h. Adjust the opening dimension (W) to 0.126 in. (3.2mm).

i. Place the large B.J. boot band along the protruding part, then install it so there is some clearance along the other side. Use a boot band crimping tool to properly crimp the large band.

j. Check that the crimped width is between 0.094–0.110 in. (2.4–2.8mm). Make sure the boot band is secured properly. If not, repeat the last 3 steps.

18. Install the B.J. assembly.

19. Install the T.J. boot.

20. Install the spider assembly to the shaft from the direction of the splined beveled section.

21. Use the special tools to install the center bearing. Install the center bearing bracket.

22. Install the dust seals as follows:

a. Apply a multi-purpose grease to the rear surfaces of the inner and outer dust seals. For the inner seal, apply 0.25–0.35 oz. (7–10 g) and for the outer seal, apply 0.14–0.21 oz. (4–6 g) or grease.

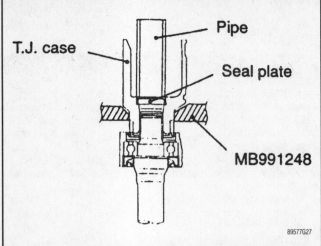

Fig. 27 Hold the case with the shaft removal tool, then use pipe to press the seal plate into the case

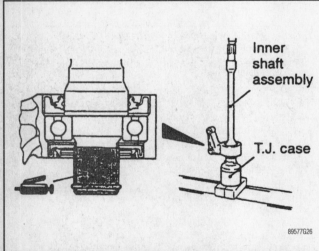

Fig. 26 After applying suitable grease, press fit the inner shaft into the T.J. case

b. Use a seal adapter and press assembly to install the dust seal so that its surface is even with the center bearing bracket.

c. Apply the grease to the lip of each dust seal, but when applying the grease, make sure it doesn't get on anything outside the lip.

23. Install the bracket assembly.

24. Use a proper sized adapter to install the inner shaft.

25. Install the seal plate and T.J. case.

26. Install the T.J. case and inner shaft, as follows:

a. Apply multi-purpose grease to the inner shaft spline then press fit the shaft into the T.J. case.

b. Use an inner shaft removal tool to support the T.J. case, then use a 1.18 in. (30mm) diameter pipe to press the seal plate into the T.J. case.

c. Fill the T.J. case with 3.70 oz. (105 g) or the grease supplied in the repair kit. The grease should be divided in half for use at the joint and inside the boot.

27. Install the small and large T.J. boots, as follows:

a. Set the boot bands at the proper distance to adjust the amount of air inside the boot, then tighten the boot band securely. The standard value is 3.03–3.27 in. (77–83mm).

28. Install the halfshaft in the vehicle.

CLUTCH

Understanding the Clutch

✳✳ CAUTION

The clutch driven disc may contain asbestos, which has been determined to be a cancer causing agent. Never clean clutch surfaces with compressed air! Avoid inhaling any dust from any clutch surface! When cleaning clutch surfaces, use a commercially available brake cleaning fluid.

The purpose of the clutch is to disconnect and connect engine power at the transaxle. A vehicle at rest requires a lot of engine torque to get all that weight moving. An internal combustion engine does not develop a high starting torque (unlike steam engines) so it must be allowed to operate without any load until it builds up enough torque to move the vehicle. Torque increases with engine rpm. The clutch allows the engine to build up torque by physically disconnecting the engine from the transaxle, relieving the engine of any load or resistance.

The transfer of engine power to the transaxle (the load) must be smooth and gradual; if it weren't, drive line components would wear out or break quickly. This gradual power transfer is made possible by gradually releasing the clutch pedal. The clutch disc and pressure plate are the connecting link between the engine and transaxle. When the clutch pedal is released, the disc and plate contact each other (the clutch is engaged) physically joining the engine and transaxle. When the pedal is pushed inward, the disc and plate separate (the clutch is disengaged) disconnecting the engine from the transaxle.

Most clutches utilize a single plate, dry friction disc with a diaphragm-style spring pressure plate. The clutch disc has a splined hub which attaches the disc to the input shaft. The disc has friction material where it contacts the flywheel and pressure plate. Torsion springs on the disc help absorb engine torque pulses. The pressure plate applies pressure to the clutch disc, holding it tight against the surface of the flywheel. The clutch operating mechanism consists of a release bearing, fork and cylinder assembly.

The release fork and actuating linkage transfer pedal motion to the release bearing. In the engaged position (pedal released) the diaphragm spring holds the pressure plate against the clutch disc, so engine torque is transmitted to the input shaft. When the clutch pedal is depressed, the release bearing pushes the diaphragm spring center toward the flywheel. The diaphragm spring pivots the fulcrum, relieving the load on the pressure plate. Steel spring straps riveted to the clutch cover lift the pressure plate from the clutch disc, disengaging the engine drive from the transaxle and enabling the gears to be changed.

The clutch is operating properly if:
1. It will stall the engine when released with the vehicle held stationary.
2. The shift lever can be moved freely between 1st and reverse gears when the vehicle is stationary and the clutch disengaged.

Clutch Disc and Pressure Plate

REMOVAL & INSTALLATION

1990—94 Vehicles

♦ See Figure 28

1. Disconnect the negative battery cable. Raise and safely support the vehicle.
2. Remove the transaxle assembly from the vehicle.
3. Remove the pressure plate attaching bolts, pressure plate and clutch disc. If the pressure plate is to be reused, loosen the bolts in a diagonal pattern, 1 or 2 turns at a time. This will prevent warping the clutch cover assembly.
4. Remove the return clip and the pressure plate release bearing. Do not use solvent to clean the bearing.

. . . then carefully remove the clutch and pressure plate assembly from the flywheel

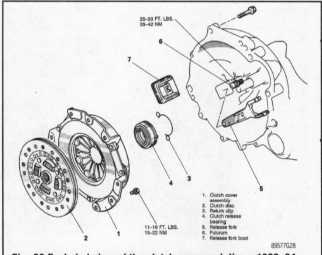

1. Clutch cover assembly
2. Clutch disc
3. Return clip
4. Clutch release bearing
5. Release fork
6. Fulcrum
7. Release fork boot

25–33 FT. LBS.
35–42 NM

11–16 FT. LBS.
15–22 NM

Fig. 28 Exploded view of the clutch cover and disc—1990–94 vehicles

Check across the flywheel surface, it should be flat

Loosen and remove the clutch and pressure plate bolts evenly, a little at a time . . .

If necessary, lock the flywheel in place and remove the retaining bolts . . .

. . . then remove the flywheel from the crankshaft in order to replace it or have it machined

Install a clutch alignment arbor, to align the clutch assembly during installation

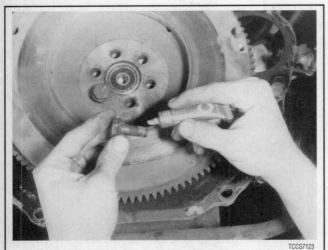

Upon installation, it is usually a good idea to apply a thread-locking compound to the flywheel bolts

You may want to use a threadlocking compound on the clutch assembly bolts

Be sure that the flywheel surface is clean, before installing the clutch

Be sure to use a torque wrench to tighten all bolts

5. Inspect the clutch release fork and fulcrum for damage or wear. If necessary, remove the release fork and unthread the fulcrum from the cable.

6. Carefully inspect the condition of the clutch components and replace any worn or damaged parts.

To install:

7. Inspect the flywheel for heat damage or cracks. Resurface or replace the flywheel as required. Install the flywheel using new bolts.

8. Install the fulcrum and tighten to 25 ft. lbs. (35 Nm). Install the release fork. Apply a coating of multi-purpose grease to the point of contact with the fulcrum and the point of contact with the release bearing. Apply a coating of multi-purpose grease to the end of the release cylinder's push rod and the push rod hole in the release fork.

➡ **When installing the clutch, apply grease to each part, but be careful not to apply excessive grease; excessive grease will cause clutch slippage and shudder.**

9. Apply multi-purpose grease to the clutch release bearing. Pack the bearing inner surface and the groove with grease. Do not apply grease to the resin portion of the bearing. Place the bearing in position and install return clip.

10. Apply a coating of grease to the clutch disc splines and then use a brush to rub it in the grooves. Using a universal clutch disc alignment tool, position the clutch disc on the flywheel. Install the retainer bolts and tighten a little at a time, in a diagonal sequence. Tighten them to a final torque of 16 ft. lbs. (22 Nm). Remove the aligning tool.

11. Install the transaxle assembly and check for proper clutch operation.

1995–98 Vehicles

2.0L NON-TURBO ENGINE

▶ **See Figures 29 and 30**

1. Remove the transaxle from the vehicle.
2. Unscrew the fittings, then remove the clutch oil tube. Plug or cap the ends to prevent contamination from entering the line.
3. Remove the release (slave) cylinder.
4. Unfasten the retaining bolts, then remove the clutch and flywheel assembly. Remove the driveplate.
5. Remove the clutch release bearing.
6. Remove the clutch release lever.
7. Remove the clutch control equip stud.
8. Remove the boot.

To install:

9. Install the boot assembly.
10. Install the clutch control equip stud.
11. Apply a suitable grease to the clutch release lever, as shown in the accompanying figure. Install the clutch release lever.
12. Install the clutch release bearing.
13. Apply a suitable grease to the clutch disc splines, squeezing it in place with a brush. Install the driven plate, and the clutch and flywheel assembly.
14. Install the clutch release (slave) cylinder.
15. Install the clutch oil tube.
16. Install the transaxle in the vehicle.

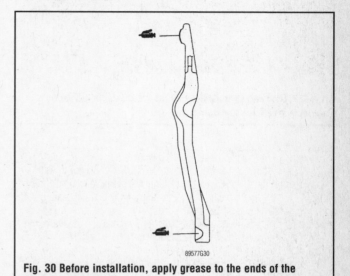

89577G30

Fig. 30 Before installation, apply grease to the ends of the clutch release lever

2.0L TURBO AND 2.4L ENGINES

▶ **See Figures 31, 32, 33 and 34**

1. Remove the transaxle from the vehicle.
2. Unscrew the fittings, then remove the clutch oil tubes.
3. Unfasten the retaining bolt, then remove the clutch oil fluid chamber.
4. Remove the clutch release (slave) cylinder union bolt, the gaskets and the union.

Fig. 29 Exploded view of the clutch system components— 1995–98 2.0L non-turbo engines

75 Nm
55 ft.lbs.

Drive plate

1. Oil tube
2. Clutch release cylinder
3. Clutch & flywheel assembly
4. Clutch release bearing
5. Clutch release lever
6. Clutch control equip stud
7. Boot

89577G29

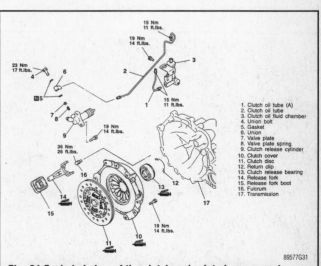

Fig. 31 Exploded view of the clutch and related components— 1995–98 2.0L turbo and 2.4L engines

15 Nm
11 ft.lbs.
19 Nm
14 ft.lbs.
23 Nm
17 ft.lbs.
15 Nm
11 ft.lbs.
19 Nm
14 ft.lbs.
36 Nm
26 ft.lbs.
19 Nm
14 ft.lbs.

1. Clutch oil tube (A)
2. Clutch oil tube
3. Clutch oil fluid chamber
4. Union bolt
5. Gasket
6. Union
7. Valve plate
8. Valve plate spring
9. Clutch release cylinder
10. Clutch cover
11. Clutch disc
12. Return clip
13. Clutch release bearing
14. Release fork
15. Release fork boot
16. Fulcrum
17. Transmission

89577G31

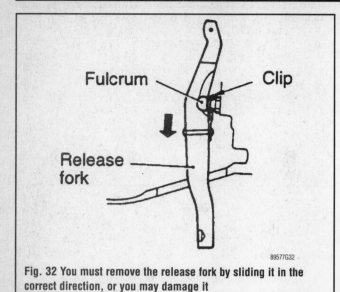

Fig. 32 You must remove the release fork by sliding it in the correct direction, or you may damage it

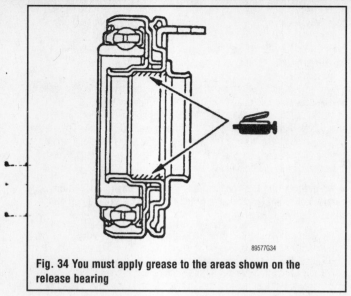

Fig. 34 You must apply grease to the areas shown on the release bearing

5. Remove the valve plate and valve plate spring.

6. Remove the clutch release (slave) cylinder.

7. Unfasten the clutch cover retaining bolts, slowly and evenly in a criss-cross pattern, then remove the clutch cover. Remove the clutch disc.

8. Unfasten the return clip, then remove the clutch release bearing.

9. Slide the release fork in the direction of the arrow shown in the accompanying figure, then detach the fulcrum from the clip to remove the release fork. Be careful not to cause damage to the clip by pushing the fork in any other direction or removing it with force.

10. Remove the release fork boot and fulcrum.

To install:

11. Install the fulcrum and the release fork boot.

12. Apply grease to the areas shown on the clutch release fork, then install the fork.

13. Before installation, apply a suitable grease to the areas shown on the clutch release bearing.

14. Install the return clip.

15. Apply a suitable grease to the clutch disc splines, squeezing it in plate with a brush. Install the clutch disc, using a suitable guide to position the disc on the flywheel.

16. Install the clutch cover.

17. Install the clutch release (slave) cylinder.

18. Install the valve plate spring and valve plate.

19. Install the gasket, union, gasket and union bolt on the release cylinder.

20. Install the clutch oil fluid chamber. Uncap or unplug the clutch oil tubes, then attach them and tighten the fittings to 11 ft. lbs. (15 Nm).

21. Install the transaxle assembly.

ADJUSTMENTS

Free-Play

1. Measure the clutch pedal height from the face of the pedal pad to the firewall.

2. Compare the measured value with the proper distance of 6.93–7.17 in. (176–182mm).

3. Measure the clutch pedal clevis pin play at the face of the pedal pad. Press the pedal lightly until resistance is met, and measure this distance. The clutch pedal clevis pin play should be within 0.04–0.12 in. (1–3mm).

4. If the clutch pedal height or clevis pin play are not within the standard values, adjust as follows:

    a. For vehicles without cruise control, turn and adjust the stop bolt so the pedal height is the standard value, then tighten the locknut.

    b. For vehicles with cruise control, detach the clutch switch connector and turn the switch to obtain the standard clutch pedal height. Then, lock by tightening the locknut.

    c. Turn the pushrod to adjust the clutch pedal clevis pin play to agree with the standard value and secure the pushrod with the locknut.

➠**When adjusting the clutch pedal height or the clutch pedal clevis pin play, be careful not to push the pushrod toward the master cylinder.**

    d. Check that when the clutch pedal is depressed all the way, the interlock switch switches over from ON to OFF.

Clutch Master Cylinder

REMOVAL & INSTALLATION

◆ **See Figures 35 thru 42**

1. Disconnect the negative battery cable.

2. Remove the air cleaner assembly.

3. Remove the master cylinder reservoir cap, then remove as much fluid as possible with a clean syringe.

4. You may want to unfasten the relay bracket for access to the master cylinder assembly.

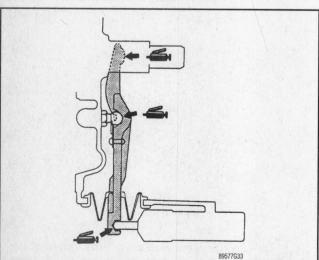

Fig. 33 Apply a suitable grease to the areas designated on the release fork

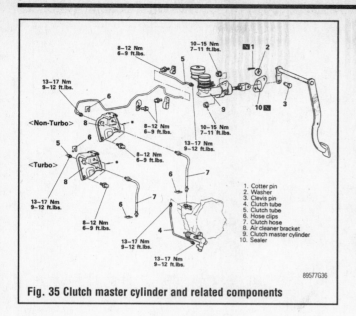

Fig. 35 Clutch master cylinder and related components

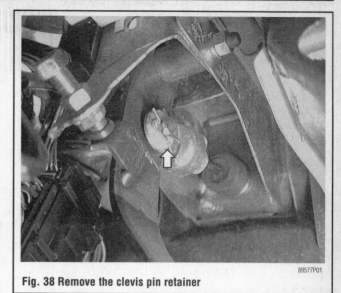

Fig. 38 Remove the clevis pin retainer

Fig. 36 On some vehicles, it may be necessary to unfasten the relay mounting bracket

Fig. 39 Unfasten the master cylinder reservoir-to-firewall retainers

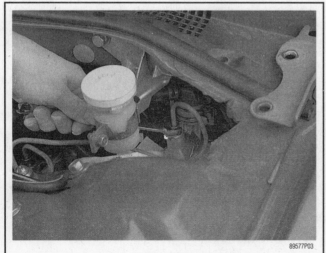

Fig. 37 Use a flare nut wrench to loosen the fluid lines from the master cylinder

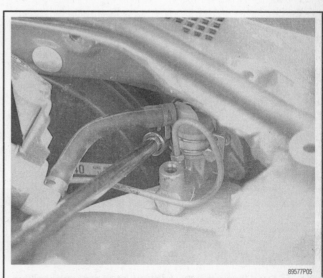

Fig. 40 Remove the master cylinder retaining nuts . . .

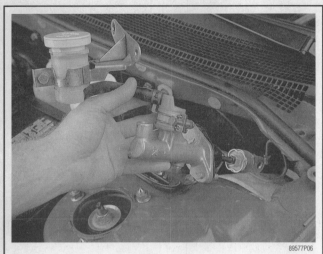

Fig. 41 . . . then remove the clutch master cylinder from the vehicle

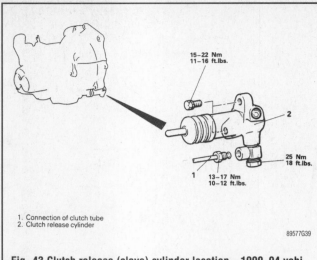

1. Connection of clutch tube
2. Clutch release cylinder

Fig. 43 Clutch release (slave) cylinder location—1990–94 vehicles shown

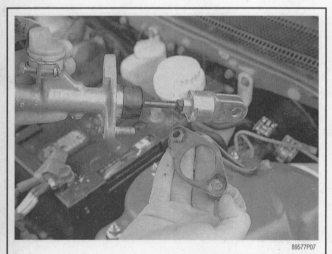

Fig. 42 The seal between the mounting flange and firewall should be replaced

Fig. 44 With the vehicle raised and supported, use a suitable wrench to loosen . . .

5. Loosen the clutch fluid line at the master cylinder and allow any remaining fluid to drain into a suitable container. Use care; brake fluid damages paint. Once the line is disconnected, plug it to avoid getting any contamination in the system.

6. Remove the clevis pin retainer from the clutch pedal and remove the washer and clevis pin.

7. Unfasten the retaining nuts, then pull the cylinder from the firewall. A seal should be between the mounting flange and firewall. This seal should be replaced.

8. The installation is the reverse of the removal procedure.

9. Lubricate all pivot points with grease.

10. Bleed the system at the slave cylinder using fresh DOT 3 brake fluid and check the adjustment of the clutch pedal.

Clutch Release (Slave) Cylinder

REMOVAL & INSTALLATION

▶ See Figures 43 thru 48

1. Disconnect the negative battery cable. Remove necessary underhood components in order to gain access to the clutch release cylinder.

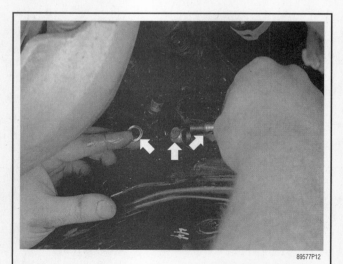

Fig. 45 . . . then remove the fluid line fitting from the slave cylinder

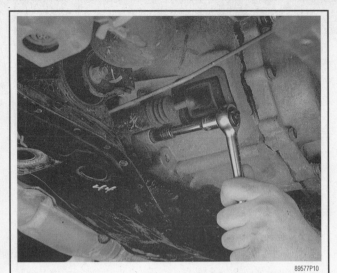

Fig. 46 Remove the release (slave) cylinder mounting bolts . . .

Fig. 47 . . . then remove the release (slave) cylinder from the transaxle housing

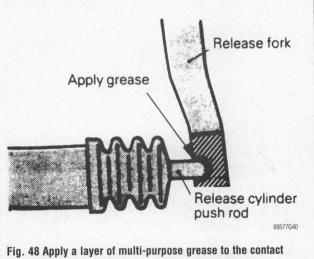

Fig. 48 Apply a layer of multi-purpose grease to the contact point of the release cylinder pushrod and release fork

2. Disconnect the hydraulic line from the slave cylinder and allow the system to drain into a suitable container.

3. Unfasten the retaining bolts and pull the cylinder from the transaxle housing.

4. The installation is the reverse of the removal procedure.

5. Lubricate all pivot points with grease.

6. Fill the system with clean brake fluid meeting DOT 3 specifications.

7. Bleed the system and adjust the clutch pedal height and the clevis pin play.

HYDRAULIC CLUTCH SYSTEM BLEEDING

▶ **See Figures 49 and 50**

➡ **Do not allow the reservoir to run out of fluid during bleeding.**

1. Fill the reservoir with clean brake fluid meeting DOT 3 specifications.

2. Attach a hose to the bleeder valve on the slave cylinder with the other end of the hose submerged in a container at least half fill of fresh DOT 3 brake fluid from a sealed container.

3. Press the clutch pedal to the floor, then loosen the bleed screw on the slave cylinder.

4. Tighten the bleed screw and release the clutch pedal.

5. Repeat the procedure until the fluid is free of air bubbles.

Fig. 49 Attach a hose, with the other end in a container of fresh brake fluid (1), to the bleeder valve (2) on the slave cylinder

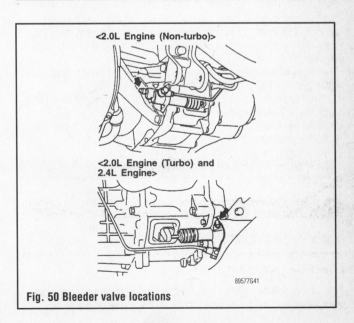

Fig. 50 Bleeder valve locations

AUTOMATIC TRANSAXLE

Understanding Automatic Transaxles

The automatic transaxle allows engine torque and power to be transmitted to the front wheels within a narrow range of engine operating speeds. It will allow the engine to turn fast enough to produce plenty of power and torque at very low speeds, while keeping it at a sensible rpm at high vehicle speeds (and it does this job without driver assistance). The transaxle uses a light fluid as the medium for the transmission of power. This fluid also works in the operation of various hydraulic control circuits and as a lubricant. Because the transaxle fluid performs all of these functions, trouble within the unit can easily travel from one part to another. For this reason, and because of the complexity and unusual operating principles of the transaxle, a very sound understanding of the basic principles of operation will simplify troubleshooting.

Neutral Safety Switch

REMOVAL & INSTALLATION

1. Disconnect the negative battery cable.
2. Disconnect the selector cable from the lever.
3. Remove the 2 retaining screws and lift off the switch.
4. The installation is the reverse of the removal procedure. Do not tighten the bolts until the switch is adjusted.
5. Make sure the engine only starts in **P** and **N**. Also make sure the reverse lights turn ON in **R**.

ADJUSTMENT

☀ WARNING

If the switch is faulty, the engine may start with the vehicle "in gear". If this happens the vehicle will accelerate when the engine starts. Keep the brakes on and be ready to switch the key off instantly.

1. Locate the neutral safety switch on the top of the transaxle.
2. Place the selector lever in **N**.
3. Loosen the 2 adjusting nuts to free up the cable and lever.
4. Place the safety switch manual control lever in **N**.
5. Note that 1 end of the safety switch manual control lever and the switch body have a hole in the ends. These holes, if properly adjusted, should be aligned.
6. If adjustment is required, loosen the mounting bolt and rotate the switch body until they are in alignment. Tighten the locknut to 9 ft. lbs. (12 Nm).
7. Loosen the adjuster nuts and gently pull the transaxle control cable to remove any slack. Tighten the nut to 10 ft. lbs. (14 Nm).
8. Verify that the switch lever moves to positions corresponding to each position of the selector lever.
9. Make sure the engine only starts in **P** and **N**. Also make sure the reverse lights turn ON in **R**.

Automatic Transaxle

REMOVAL & INSTALLATION

1990–94 Vehicles

▶ See Figures 51 and 52

1. Disconnect the negative, then the positive battery cables.
2. Remove the battery and battery tray.

3. On 1990–91 vehicles equipped with auto-cruise, remove the control actuator and bracket.
4. Drain the transaxle fluid.
5. Remove the air cleaner assembly, intercooler and air hose, as required.
6. Remove the adjusting nut and disconnect the shift cable.
7. Disconnect and tag the electrical connectors for the solenoid, neutral safety switch (inhibitor switch), the pulse generator kickdown servo switch and oil temperature sensor.
8. Disconnect the speedometer cable and oil cooler lines.
9. Disconnect the wires to the starter motor and remove the starter.
10. Remove the upper transaxle to engine bolts.
11. Support the transaxle and remove the transaxle mounting bracket.
12. Raise the vehicle and support safely. Remove the sheet metal under guard.
13. Remove the tie rod ends and the ball joints from the steering knuckle.
14. Remove the halfshafts by inserting a prybar between the transaxle case and the driveshaft and prying the shaft from the transaxle. Do not pull on the driveshaft. Doing so damages the inboard joint. Use the prybar. Do

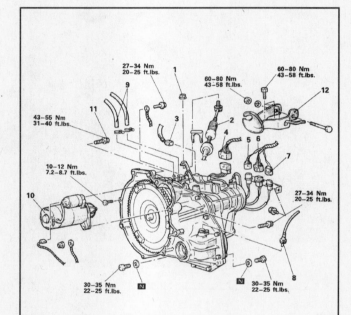

1. Adjusting nut
2. Connection for transaxle control cable
3. Connection for solenoid connector
4. Connection for park/neutral position switch connector
5. Connection for pulse generator connector
6. Connection for kickdown servo switch connector
7. Connection for oil temperature sensor connector
8. Connection for speedometer cable
9. Connection for oil cooler hose
10. Starter motor
11. Upper coupling bolt for transaxle assembly and engine assembly
12. Transaxle mount bracket

89577G42

Fig. 51 Exploded view of the automatic transaxle and related components (page 1 of 2)—1990–94 FWD vehicles shown

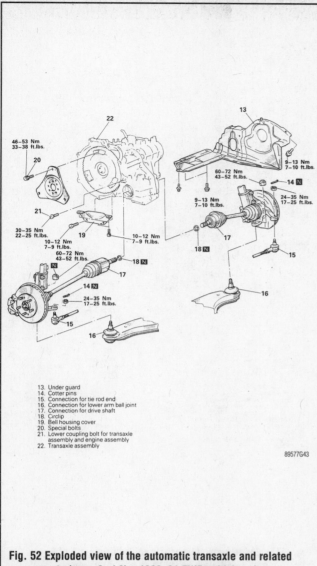

Fig. 52 Exploded view of the automatic transaxle and related components (page 2 of 2)—1990–94 FWD vehicles shown

13. Under guard
14. Cotter pins
15. Connection for tie rod end
16. Connection for lower arm ball joint
17. Connection for drive shaft
18. Circlip
19. Bell housing cover
20. Special bolts
21. Lower coupling bolt for transaxle assembly and engine assembly
22. Transaxle assembly

89577G43

not insert the prybar so far the oil seal in the case is damaged. Tie the half-shafts aside.

15. On AWD vehicles, disconnect the exhaust pipe and remove the transfer case.

16. Remove the lower bellhousing cover and remove the special bolts holding the flexplate to the torque converter. To remove, turn the engine crankshaft with a box wrench and bring the bolts into a position appropriate for removal, one at a time. After removing the bolts, push the torque converter toward the transaxle so it doesn't stay on the engine allowing oil to pour out the converter hub or cause damage to the converter.

17. Remove the lower transaxle to engine bolts and remove the transaxle assembly.

To install:

18. After the torque converter has been mounted on the transaxle, install the transaxle assembly on the engine. Tighten the driveplate bolts to 34–38 ft. lbs. (46–53 Nm). Install the bellhousing cover.

19. On AWD, install the transfer case and frame pieces. Connect the exhaust pipe using a new gasket.

20. The remainder of installation is the reverse of the removal procedure.

21. Make sure to tighten the retainers to the specifications shown in the accompanying figure.

22. Refill with the proper type and amount of fluid.

23. Start the engine and allow to idle for 2 minutes. Apply parking brake and move selector through each gear position, ending in **N**. Recheck fluid level and add if necessary. Fluid level should be between the marks in the **HOT** range.

1995–98 Vehicles

▶ See Figures 53 thru 58

1. Disconnect the negative, then the positive battery cables.
2. Drain the transaxle fluid into a suitable container.
3. Unfasten the retainers, then remove the engine undercover.
4. Remove the air cleaner cover and the air intake hose. Remove the air cleaner element.
5. For 2.0L turbo engines, remove the two air hoses.
6. Remove the battery tray and tray stay.
7. For the 2.0L turbo engine, remove the evaporative emission canister and holder.
8. Detach the transaxle control cable connection.
9. Remove the engine oil dipstick and guide assembly.
10. Remove the starter motor.

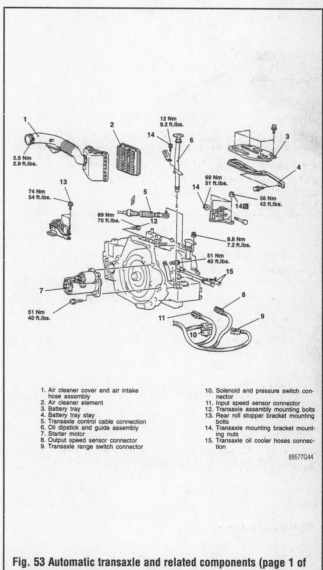

1. Air cleaner cover and air intake hose assembly
2. Air cleaner element
3. Battery tray
4. Battery tray stay
5. Transaxle control cable connection
6. Oil dipstick and guide assembly
7. Starter motor
8. Output speed sensor connector
9. Transaxle range switch connector
10. Solenoid and pressure switch connector
11. Input speed sensor connector
12. Transaxle assembly mounting bolts
13. Rear roll stopper bracket mounting bolts
14. Transaxle mounting bracket mounting nuts
15. Transaxle oil cooler hoses connection

89577G44

Fig. 53 Automatic transaxle and related components (page 1 of 2)—1995–98 2.0L non-turbo engines

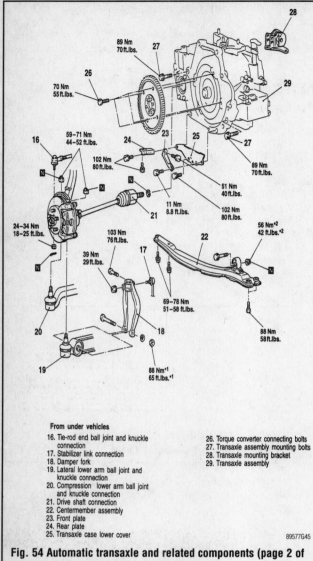

From under vehicles

16. Tie-rod end ball joint and knuckle connection.
17. Stabilizer link connection.
18. Damper fork.
19. Lateral lower arm ball joint and knuckle connection.
20. Compression lower arm ball joint and knuckle connection.
21. Drive shaft connection.
22. Centermember assembly.
23. Front plate.
24. Rear plate.
25. Transaxle case lower cover.

26. Torque converter connecting bolts.
27. Transaxle assembly mounting bolts.
28. Transaxle mounting bracket.
29. Transaxle assembly.

89577G45

Fig. 54 Automatic transaxle and related components (page 2 of 2)—1995–98 2.0L non-turbo engines

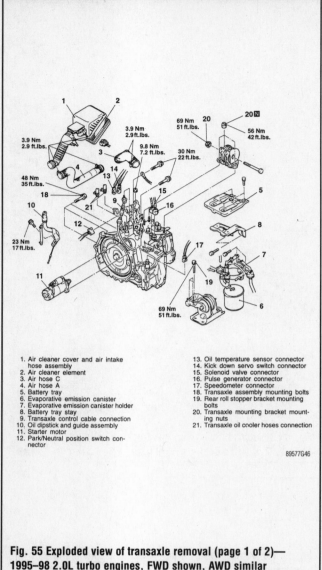

1. Air cleaner cover and air intake hose assembly
2. Air cleaner element
3. Air hose C
4. Air hose A
5. Battery tray
6. Evaporative emission canister
7. Evaporative emission canister holder
8. Battery tray stay
9. Transaxle control cable connection
10. Oil dipstick and guide assembly
11. Starter motor
12. Park/Neutral position switch connector

13. Oil temperature sensor connector
14. Kick down servo switch connector
15. Solenoid valve connector
16. Pulse generator connector
17. Speedometer connector
18. Transaxle assembly mounting bolts
19. Rear roll stopper bracket mounting bolts
20. Transaxle mounting bracket mounting nuts
21. Transaxle oil cooler hoses connection

89577G46

Fig. 55 Exploded view of transaxle removal (page 1 of 2)—1995–98 2.0L turbo engines, FWD shown, AWD similar

11. For the 2.0L non-turbo engines, detach the output speed sensor and the transaxle range switch connectors. Unplug the solenoid and pressure switch and the input speed sensor connectors.

12. For the 2.0L turbo and 2.4L engines, detach the connectors from the following components:

    a. Park/neutral position switch

    b. Oil temperature sensor

    c. Kick-down servo switch

    d. Solenoid valve

    e. Pulse generator

    f. Speedometer

13. Remove the transaxle mounting bolts.

14. Unfasten the rear roll stopper bracket mounting bolts.

15. Carefully raise the transaxle with a suitable jack, then remove the transaxle mounting bracket mounting nuts. Be sure not to tilt the transaxle.

16. Disconnect and plug the transaxle oil cooler lines.

17. Attach a suitable engine support fixture to the engine.

18. Raise and safely support the vehicle.

19. Separate the tie-rod end from the steering knuckle.

20. Detach the stabilizer link connection.

21. Remove the retainers, then remove the damper fork.

22. Separate the lateral and compression lower ball joints from the steering knuckle.

23. For FWD vehicles, detach the driveshaft connection.

24. For AWD vehicles, perform the following:

    a. Remove the driveshaft nut.

    b. Use a prytool to carefully separate the driveshaft from the transaxle case, then remove the drive shaft with the inner shaft connection.

25. For 2.0L turbo and 2.4L engines, remove the bell housing cover and the right hand stay.

26. Remove the centermember assembly.

27. For 2.0L non-turbo engines, unfasten the retainers, then remove the front and rear plates.

28. If equipped, remove the transaxle case lower cover.

29. Unfasten the torque converter/drive plate connecting bolts, as follows:

    a. Use a transaxle jack to support the transaxle assembly. Support the transaxle case side, not the oil pan.

    b. Matchmark the torque converter and drive plate.

    c. Unfasten the bolts while turning the crankshaft.

    d. To make removal easier, press the torque converter into the transaxle.

30. Remove the transaxle assembly mounting bolts, the mounting bracket, then lower and remove the transaxle assembly from the vehicle.

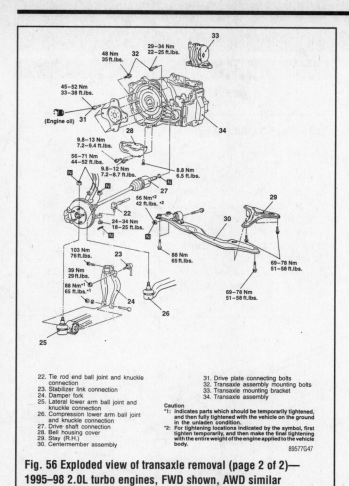

22. Tie rod end ball joint and knuckle connection
23. Stabilizer link connection
24. Damper fork
25. Lateral lower arm ball joint and knuckle connection
26. Compression lower arm ball joint and knuckle connection
27. Drive shaft connection
28. Bell housing cover
29. Stay (R.H.)
30. Centermember assembly
31. Drive plate connecting bolts
32. Transaxle assembly mounting bolts
33. Transaxle mounting bracket
34. Transaxle assembly

Caution
*1: indicates parts which should be temporarily tightened, and then fully tightened with the vehicle on the ground in the unladen condition.
*2: For tightening locations indicated by the symbol, first tighten temporarily, and then make the final tightening with the entire weight of the engine applied to the vehicle body.

89577G47

Fig. 56 Exploded view of transaxle removal (page 2 of 2)—1995–98 2.0L turbo engines, FWD shown, AWD similar

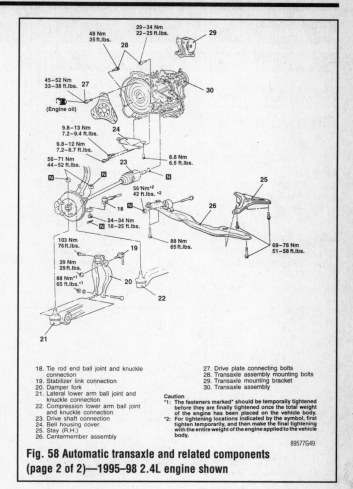

18. Tie rod end ball joint and knuckle connection
19. Stabilizer link connection
20. Damper fork
21. Lateral lower arm ball joint and knuckle connection
22. Compression lower arm ball joint and knuckle connection
23. Drive shaft connection
24. Bell housing cover
25. Stay (R.H.)
26. Centermember assembly
27. Drive plate connecting bolts
28. Transaxle assembly mounting bolts
29. Transaxle mounting bracket
30. Transaxle assembly

Caution
1: The fasteners marked should be temporarily tightened before they are finally tightened once the total weight of the engine has been placed on the vehicle body.
*2: For tightening locations indicated by the symbol, first tighten temporarily, and then make the final tightening with the entire weight of the engine applied to the vehicle body.

89577G49

Fig. 58 Automatic transaxle and related components (page 2 of 2)—1995–98 2.4L engine shown

31. Installation is the reverse of the removal procedure.
32. Make sure to note all fastener tightening specifications on the accompanying figures.

Halfshaft

REMOVAL & INSTALLATION

For halfshaft removal, installation and overhaul, refer to the Halfshaft procedures located under the manual transaxle portion of this section.

1. Air cleaner cover and air intake hose assembly
2. Air cleaner element
3. Battery tray
4. Battery tray stay
5. Transaxle control cable connection
6. Oil dipstick and guide assembly
7. Starter motor
8. Park/Neutral position switch connector
9. Oil temperature sensor connector
10. Kick down servo switch connector
11. Solenoid valve connector
12. Pulse generator connector
13. Speedometer connector
14. Transaxle assembly mounting bolts
15. Rear roll stopper bracket mounting bolts
16. Transaxle mounting bracket mounting nuts
17. Transaxle oil cooler hoses connection

89577G48

Fig. 57 Automatic transaxle and related components (page 1 of 2)—1995–98 2.4L engine shown

TRANSFER CASE

Rear Output Shaft Seal

REMOVAL & INSTALLATION

▶ **See Figures 59 and 60**

1. Raise and support the vehicle safely.
2. Remove the propeller shaft from the transfer assembly. Place a drain pan under the rear of the transfer assembly to catch any fluid that leaks out.
3. Using a flat-bladed prying tool, carefully remove the oil seal from the transfer dust seal guard.

To install:

4. Using proper size seal driver tool, install the seal into the dust seal guard and the transfer assembly.
5. Install the rear propeller shaft.
6. Carefully lower the vehicle and inspect the transfer assembly fluid level.

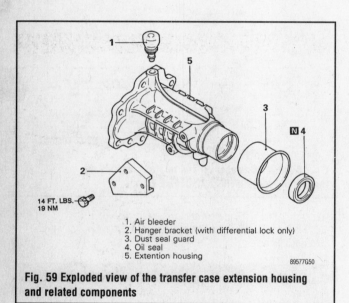

14 FT. LBS.
19 NM

1. Air bleeder
2. Hanger bracket (with differential lock only)
3. Dust seal guard
4. Oil seal
5. Extention housing

89577G50

Fig. 59 Exploded view of the transfer case extension housing and related components

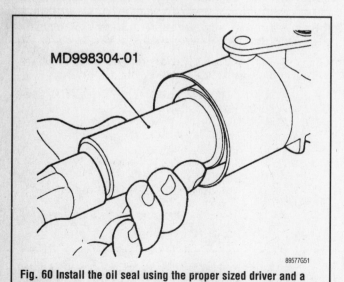

MD998304-01

89577G51

Fig. 60 Install the oil seal using the proper sized driver and a hammer

Transfer Case Assembly

REMOVAL & INSTALLATION

▶ **See Figures 61, 62 and 63**

1. Disconnect the battery negative cable.
2. Raise the vehicle and support safely. Drain the transfer oil.
3. Disconnect the front exhaust pipe.
4. Unbolt the transfer case assembly and remove by sliding it off the rear propeller shaft. Be careful not to damage the oil seal in the transfer case output housing. Do not let the rear propeller shaft hang; suspend it from a frame piece. Cover the opening in the transaxle and transfer case to keep oil from dripping and to keep dirt out.

To install:

5. Lubricate the driveshaft sleeve yoke and oil seal lip on the transfer extension housing. Install the transfer case assembly to the transaxle. Use

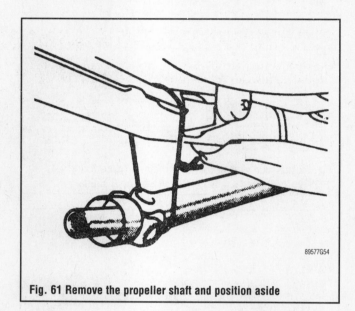

89577G54

Fig. 61 Remove the propeller shaft and position aside

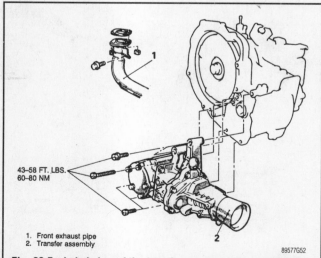

43–58 FT. LBS.
60–80 NM

1. Front exhaust pipe
2. Transfer assembly

89577G52

Fig. 62 Exploded view of the transfer case mounting—1990–94 vehicles

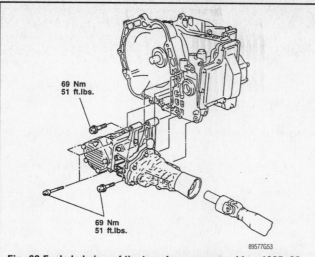

Fig. 63 Exploded view of the transfer case assembly—1995–98 vehicles with automatic transaxle shown

care when installing the rear propeller shaft to the transfer case output shaft.

6. Tighten the transfer case to transaxle bolts to 40–43 ft. lbs. (55–60 Nm) on manual transaxle vehicles or 43–58 ft. lbs. (60–80 Nm) on automatic transaxle vehicles.

7. Install the exhaust pipe using a new gasket.

8. Refill the transfer case with gear oil of classification GL-4 or higher, SAE 75W-85W or 75W-90. Check fluid level in transaxle and add as required.

DRIVELINE

Propeller Shaft

REMOVAL & INSTALLATION

▶ **See Figures 64 and 65**

1. Disconnect the negative battery cable. Raise the vehicle and support safely.

2. The rear driveshaft is a 3-piece unit, with a front, center and rear propeller shaft. Remove the nuts and insulators from the center support bearing. Work carefully. There will be a number of spacers which will differ from vehicle to vehicle. Check the number of spacers and write down their locations for reference during reassembly.

3. Matchmark the rear differential companion flange and the rear driveshaft flange yoke. Remove the companion shaft bolts and remove the driveshaft, keeping it as straight as possible so as to ensure that the boot is not damaged or pinched. Use care to keep from damaging the oil seal in the output housing of the transfer case.

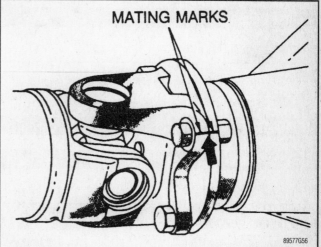

Fig. 65 Apply mating marks on the flange yoke and differential companion flange

➡**Damage to the boot can be avoided and work will be easier if a piece of cloth or similar material is inserted in the boot.**

4. Do not lower the rear of the vehicle or oil will flow from the transfer case. Cover the opening to keep dirt out.

To install:

5. Position the driveshaft in the vehicle, making sure to align the matchmarks at the rear yoke.

6. Install the bolts at the rear differential flange and tighten to 22–25 ft. lbs. (30–35 Nm).

7. Install the center support bearing with all spacers in place. Tighten the retaining nuts to 22–25 ft. lbs. (30–35 Nm).

8. Check the fluid levels in the transfer case and rear differential case.

U-JOINT REPLACEMENT

1. Make mating marks on the yoke and the universal joint that is to be disassembled. Remove the snaprings from the yoke with snapring pliers.

2. Force out the bearing journals from the yoke using a large C-clamp. Install a collar on the fixed side of the C-clamp. Press the journal bearing

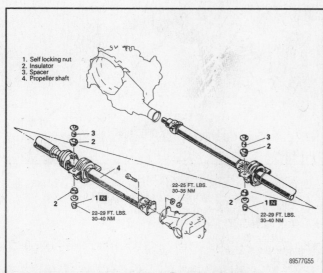

Fig. 64 Exploded view of the propeller shaft mounting

into the collar by applying pressure with the C-clamp, on the opposite side.

3. Pull the journal bearing from the yoke.

➡**If the journal bearing is hard to remove, strike the yoke with a plastic hammer.**

4. Press the journal shaft using C-clamp or similar tool, to remove the remaining bearings.

5. Once all bearings are removed, remove the journal.

To install:

6. Apply multi-purpose grease to the shafts, grease sumps, dust seal lips and needle roller bearings of the replacement U-joint. Do not apply excessive grease. Otherwise, faulty fitting of bearing caps and errors in selection of snaprings may result.

7. Press fit the journal bearings to the yoke using a C-clamp as follows:

 a. Install a solid base onto the bottom of the C-clamp.

 b. Insert both bearings into the yoke. Hold and press fit them by tightening the C-clamp.

 c. Install snaprings of the same thickness onto both sides of each yoke.

 d. Press the bearing and journal into 1 side by using a brass bar with diameter of 0.59 in. (15mm).

8. Measure the clearance between the snapring and the groove wall of the yoke with a feeler gauge. If the clearance exceeds 0.0008–0.0024 in. (0.02-0.06mm), the snap rings should be replaced.

Center Bearing

REMOVAL & INSTALLATION

1. Place mating marks on the companion flange and the Lobro joint assembly.

2. Remove the Lobro joint installation bolts. Separate the Lobro joint from the companion flange.

3. Place mating marks on the center yoke and center propeller shaft, and the companion flange and the rear propeller shaft.

4. Remove the self-locking nuts. Remove the center yoke and companion flange.

5. Place mating marks on the center bearing assembly front bracket and the center propeller shaft, and the center bearing assembly rear bracket and the rear propeller shaft. Remove the center bearing bracket.

➡**The mounting rubber can not be removed from the center bearing bracket.**

6. Pull out the front and rear center bearings with a commercially available puller.

To install:

7. Apply multi-purpose grease to the center bearing front and rear grease grooves and to the dust seal lip. Be sure to fit the bearing into the rubber mount groove on the center bearing bracket.

➡**Face the bearing dust seal to the side of the center bearing bracket mating mark.**

8. Assemble the center bearing to the center propeller shaft and rear propeller shaft. Face the side onto which the center bearing bracket mating marks is placed and the dust seal is installed toward the side of the center propeller shaft and rear propeller shaft.

9. Apply a thin and even coat of the grease, enclosed with the repair kit, to the rubber packing on the companion flange. Align the mating marks on the center propeller shaft and the companion flange, then press fit the center bearing with self-locking nuts.

10. Install the Lobro joint assembly installation bolts. Secure the companion flange and Lobro joint assembly with the installation bolts. Check for grease leakage from the Lobro joint boot and companion flange installation parts.

REAR AXLE

Rear Halfshaft and Seal

REMOVAL & INSTALLATION

◆ **See Figures 66 and 67**

1. Disconnect the negative battery cable. Raise the vehicle and support safely.

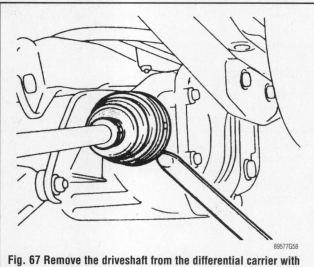

Fig. 67 Remove the driveshaft from the differential carrier with a prybar

2. Remove the bolts that attach the rear halfshaft to the companion flange.

3. Use a prybar to pry the inner shaft out of the differential case. Don't insert the prybar too far or the seal could be damaged.

4. Remove the rear driveshaft from the vehicle.

5. If necessary, carefully pry the oil seal from the rear differential using a flat tipped prying tool.

To install:

6. Install a new oil seal into the rear differential housing using proper size driver.

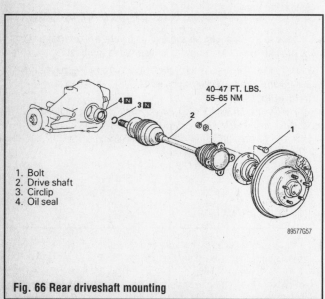

40–47 FT. LBS.
55–65 NM

1. Bolt
2. Drive shaft
3. Circlip
4. Oil seal

Fig. 66 Rear driveshaft mounting

7. Replace the circlip and install the rear driveshaft to the differential case. Make sure it snaps in place.

8. Install the companion flange bolts and tighten to 40–47 ft. lbs. (55–65 Nm).

9. Check the fluid level in the rear differential.

Differential Carrier

REMOVAL & INSTALLATION

1. Raise the vehicle and support safely.
2. Drain the differential gear oil and remove the center exhaust pipe.
3. Matchmark and remove the rear driveshaft.
4. Remove the rear halfshafts.
5. Remove the center exhaust pipe and muffler assembly, as required.
6. The large mounting bolts that hold the differential carrier support plate to the underbody may use self-locking nuts. Before removing them, support the rear axle assembly in the middle with a transaxle jack. Remove the nuts, then remove the support plate(s) and the square dynamic damper from the rear of the carrier.
7. Lower the differential carrier and remove from the vehicle.

To install:

8. Raise the rear differential carrier into position and install support member bolts. Install new locknuts on all support bolts.
9. Install new circlips on both rear driveshafts and install.
10. Install the propeller shaft.
11. Install the center exhaust pipe and muffler.
12. Lower the vehicle. With the vehicle level, fill the rear differential.

Stub Axle Shaft, Bearing and Seal

REMOVAL & INSTALLATION

1. Disconnect the negative battery cable.
2. Raise and support the vehicle safely.
3. Remove the tire and wheel assembly from the vehicle.
4. If equipped with ABS, remove the rear wheel speed sensor.

➡**Be cautious to ensure that the tip of the pole piece on the rear speed sensor does not come in contact with other parts during removal. Sensor damage could occur.**

5. Remove the rear caliper and support assembly out of the way. Remove the brake disc.
6. Remove the driveshaft and companion flange installation bolts, nuts and washers. Move the end of shaft slightly to access the self-locking nut.
7. Using axle holding tool MB990211-01 or equivalent, secure the rear axle shaft in position, then remove the self-locking nut.
8. Using puller and adapter MB990211-01 and MB990241-01 or equivalents, remove the rear axle shaft from the trailing arm.
9. If equipped with ABS, remove the rear rotor from the axle assembly using collar and press. The rotor is a press fit.
10. Remove the outer bearing and dust cover concurrently from the axle shaft using a press.
11. Using puller, remove the oil seal and inner bearing from the trailing arm.

12. Inspect the companion flange and axle shaft for wear or damage. Inspect the dust cover for deformation or damage. Inspect the bearings for burning or declaration. Replace components as required.

To install:

13. Using the proper driver, press fit the inner bearing onto the trailing arm. Press fit the oil seal onto the trailing arm with the depression in the oil seal facing upward, and until it contacts the shoulder on the inner arm.

➡**When tapping the oil seal in, use a plastic hammer to lightly tap the top and circumference of the seal installation tool, press fitting gradually and evenly.**

14. Press fit the dust covers onto the axle until it contacts the axle shaft shoulder. Install the innermost cover so the depression is facing upward.

➡**When tapping the oil seal in, use a plastic hammer to lightly tap the top and circumference of the seal installation tool, press fitting gradually and evenly.**

15. Apply multi-purpose grease around the entire circumference of the inner side of the outer bearing seal lip. Press fit the outer bearing to the axle shaft so that the bearing seal lip surface is facing towards the axle shaft flange.

16. Press fit the rear rotor to the axle shaft with the rear rotor groove surface towards the axle shaft flange.

17. Install the rear axle shaft to the trailing arm temporarily. Install the companion flange to the rear axle shaft, then install a new self-locking nut.

18. While holding the rear axle shaft in position using holding fixture tool MB990767-01 or equivalent, tighten a new self-locking nut to 159 ft. lbs. (220 Nm).

19. Install the drive shaft nuts, washers and bolts. Tighten to 47 ft. lbs. (65 Nm).

20. Install the rear brake disc, caliper assembly and parking brake.

21. Install the tire and wheel assembly and lower the vehicle. Check the parking brake stroke and adjust as required.

22. Before moving the vehicle, pump the brakes until a firm pedal is achieved.

Rear Pinion Seal

REMOVAL & INSTALLATION

1. Raise the vehicle and support safely.
2. Matchmark the rear propeller shaft and companion flange and remove the shaft. Don't let it hang from the transaxle. Tie it up to the underbody.
3. Hold the companion flange stationary and remove the large self-locking nut in the center of the companion flange.
4. Using a puller, remove the flange. Pry the old seal out.

To install:

5. Apply a thin coat of multi-purpose grease to the seal lip and the companion flange seal contacting surface. Install the new seal with an appropriate driver.

6. Install the companion flange. Install a new locknut and torque to 116–159 ft. lbs. (157–220). The rotation torque of the drive pinion should be about 4 inch lbs. for new or reused, oiled bearings.

7. Install the propeller shaft.

TORQUE SPECIFICATIONS

Component	ft. lbs.	inch lbs.	Nm
Automatic Transaxle			
Bell housing cover-to-engine bolts			
1990-94 vehicles	7-9		10-12
1995-98 vehicles	7.2-9.4		9.8-13
Transaxle-to-engine bolts			
1990-94 vehicles			
8mm bolts	22-25		30-35
10mm bolts	7.2-8.7		10-12
1995-98 vehicles	see illustrations		
Back-up light switch	22-25		30-35
Clutch			
Clutch cover bolts			
1990-94 vehicles	11-16		15-22
1995-98 vehicles			
2.0L turbo and 2.4L engines	14		19
Drive plate to clutch and flywheel bolt			
1995-98 2.0L non-turbo engines	55		75
Fluid line flare nut			
1990-94 vehicles	9-12		13-17
1995-98 vehicles	11		15
Master cylinder-to-firewall bolts			
1990-94 vehicles	7-11		10-15
1995-98 vehicles	9		12
Release cylinder bleeder plug			
1990-94 vehicles	7-9		9-13
1995-98 vehicles	8		11
Release cylinder mounting bolt			
1990-94 vehicles	14		19
1995-98 vehicles	11-16		15-22
Release cylinder union bolt			
1990-94 vehicles	18		25
1995-98 vehicles	17		23
Release fork fulcrum			
1990-94 vehicles	25-30		35-42
1995-98 vehicles	24		36
Manual transaxle			
Transaxle-to-engine bolts			
1990-94 vehicles			
8mm bolt	7-9		10-12
10mm bolt	22-25		30-35
12mm bolt	32-39		43-55
1995-98 vehicles			
Non-turbo engines	70		95
Turbo Engines	35		48
Transfer Case			
Extension housing bolts			
1990-94 vehicles	11-15		15-22
1995-98 vehicles	14		19
Transfer case bolts			
1990-94 vehicles	40-43		55-60
1995-98 vehicles	40-44		54-59
Transfer case cover bolts			
1990-94 vehicles	26-30		35-42
1995-98 vehicles	29		39

89577C01

8

STEERING

WHEELS

Wheel Assembly

REMOVAL & INSTALLATION

▶ **See Figure 1**

1. Park the vehicle on a level surface.
2. Remove the jack, tire iron and, if necessary, the spare tire from their storage compartments.
3. Check the owner's manual or refer to Section 1 of this manual for the jacking points on your vehicle. Then, place the jack in the proper position.
4. If equipped with lug nut trim caps, remove them by either unscrewing or pulling them off the lug nuts, as appropriate. Consult the owner's manual, if necessary.
5. If equipped with a wheel cover or hub cap, insert the tapered end of the tire iron in the groove and pry off the cover.
6. Apply the parking brake and block the diagonally opposite wheel with a wheel chock or two.

➡**Wheel chocks may be purchased at your local auto parts store, or a block of wood cut into wedges may be used. If possible, keep one or two of the chocks in your tire storage compartment, in case any of the tires has to be removed on the side of the road.**

7. If equipped with an automatic transmission/transaxle, place the selector lever in **P** or Park; with a manual transmission/transaxle, place the shifter in Reverse.
8. With the tires still on the ground, use the tire iron/wrench to break the lug nuts loose.

➡**If a nut is stuck, never use heat to loosen it or damage to the wheel and bearings may occur. If the nuts are seized, one or two heavy hammer blows directly on the end of the bolt usually loosens the rust. Be careful, as continued pounding will likely damage the brake drum or rotor.**

9. Using the jack, raise the vehicle until the tire is clear of the ground. Support the vehicle safely using jackstands.
10. Remove the lug nuts, then remove the tire and wheel assembly.

To install:

11. Make sure the wheel and hub mating surfaces, as well as the wheel lug studs, are clean and free of all foreign material. Always remove rust from the wheel mounting surface and the brake rotor or drum. Failure to do so may cause the lug nuts to loosen in service.

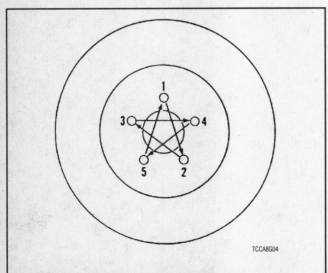

Fig. 1 Typical wheel lug tightening sequence

TCCA8G04

12. Install the tire and wheel assembly and hand-tighten the lug nuts.
13. Using the tire wrench, tighten all the lug nuts, in a crisscross pattern, until they are snug.
14. Raise the vehicle and withdraw the jackstand, then lower the vehicle.
15. Using a torque wrench, tighten the lug nuts in a crisscross pattern to 87–101 ft. lbs. (120–140 Nm). Check your owner's manual or refer to Section 1 of this manual for the proper tightening sequence.

✳✳ WARNING

Do not overtighten the lug nuts, as this may cause the wheel studs to stretch or the brake disc (rotor) to warp.

16. If so equipped, install the wheel cover or hub cap. Make sure the valve stem protrudes through the proper opening before tapping the wheel cover into position.
17. If equipped, install the lug nut trim caps by pushing them or screwing them on, as applicable.
18. Remove the jack from under the vehicle, and place the jack and tire iron/wrench in their storage compartments. Remove the wheel chock(s).
19. If you have removed a flat or damaged tire, place it in the storage compartment of the vehicle and take it to your local repair station to have it fixed or replaced as soon as possible.

INSPECTION

Inspect the tires for lacerations, puncture marks, nails and other sharp objects. Repair or replace as necessary. Also check the tires for tread wear and air pressure as outlined in Section 1 of this manual.
Check the wheel assemblies for dents, cracks, rust and metal fatigue. Repair or replace as necessary.

Wheel Lug Studs

REPLACEMENT

Front Wheel

➡**If the vehicle is equipped with ABS, removal and disassembly of the front hub is required. Refer to the appropriate procedure in this Section for the removal and installation procedure.**

1. Raise and support the vehicle safely. Remove the front wheel.
2. Remove the caliper and support assembly and position out of the way. It is not necessary to disconnect the brake hose from the caliper. Do not allow the brake hose to stretch or twist or damage to the hose may occur.
3. Remove the brake disc.
4. Position the wheel stud to be replaced towards the cut out area of the dust shield.
5. Carefully press the stud out of the front hub and remove from the vehicle.

To install:

6. Install the new stud into the hub. Draw the into place using the nut and a stack of washers. Make sure the stud is fully seated.

➡**If there is not enough clearance between the hub and the dust shield to install the new stud, removal of the front hub from the steering knuckle will be required. Refer to the appropriate procedure in this Section for the procedure.**

7. Install the brake disc.
8. Install the caliper support and caliper assembly onto the vehicle.
9. Install the tire and wheel assembly. Lower the vehicle.
10. Before moving the vehicle, pump the brakes until a firm pedal is achieved.

Rear Wheel

2WD VEHICLE

1. Disconnect the negative battery cable.
2. Raise and support the vehicle safely.
3. Remove the tire and wheel assembly from the vehicle.
4. Remove the rear caliper. Remove the brake disc.
5. Remove the hub cap and the wheel bearing nut. Remove the tongued washer from the rear axle hub.
6. Remove the rear hub bearing unit.
7. Using the appropriate equipment, drive the lug nut stud from the hub bearing unit.

To install:

8. Install the new stud into the hub. Draw the into place using the nut and a stack of washers. Make sure the stud is fully seated.
9. Install the rear bearing hub assembly onto the vehicle and install the tongued washer. Install a new wheel bearing nut. Tighten new bearing nut to 188 ft. lbs. (260 Nm) torque.
10. Once the bearing nut is tightened, align with the indentation in the spindle and crimp. This will lock the nut in place.
11. Install the hub (bearing nut) cap.
12. Install the brake disc, caliper and parking brake cable.
13. Install the tire and wheel assembly.
14. Lower the vehicle. Before moving the vehicle, pump the brakes until a firm pedal is achieved.

AWD VEHICLE

1. Disconnect the negative battery cable.
2. Raise and support the vehicle safely.
3. Remove the tire and wheel assembly from the vehicle.
4. Remove the rear caliper and support assembly out of the way. Remove the brake disc.
5. Remove the driveshaft and companion flange installation bolts, nuts and washers. Move end of shaft slightly to access the self-locking nut.
6. Using axle holding tool MB990211-01 or equivalent, secure the rear axle shaft in position, then remove the self-locking nut.
7. Using puller and adapter MB990211-01 and MB990241-01 or equivalents, remove the rear axle shaft.
8. Press the broken lug nut stud from the axle shaft.

To install:

9. Install the rear axle shaft to the trailing arm temporarily. Install the companion flange to the rear axle shaft, then install the self-locking nut.
10. While holding the rear axle shaft in position using tool MB990767-01 or equivalent, tighten a new self-locking nut to 159 ft. lbs. (220 Nm).
11. Install the driveshaft nuts, washers and bolts. Tighten to 47 ft. lbs. (65 Nm).
12. Install the rear brake disc, caliper assembly and parking brake.
13. Install the tire and wheel assembly and lower the vehicle. Check the parking brake stroke and adjust as required.
14. Before moving the vehicle, pump the brakes until a firm pedal is achieved.

FRONT SUSPENSION

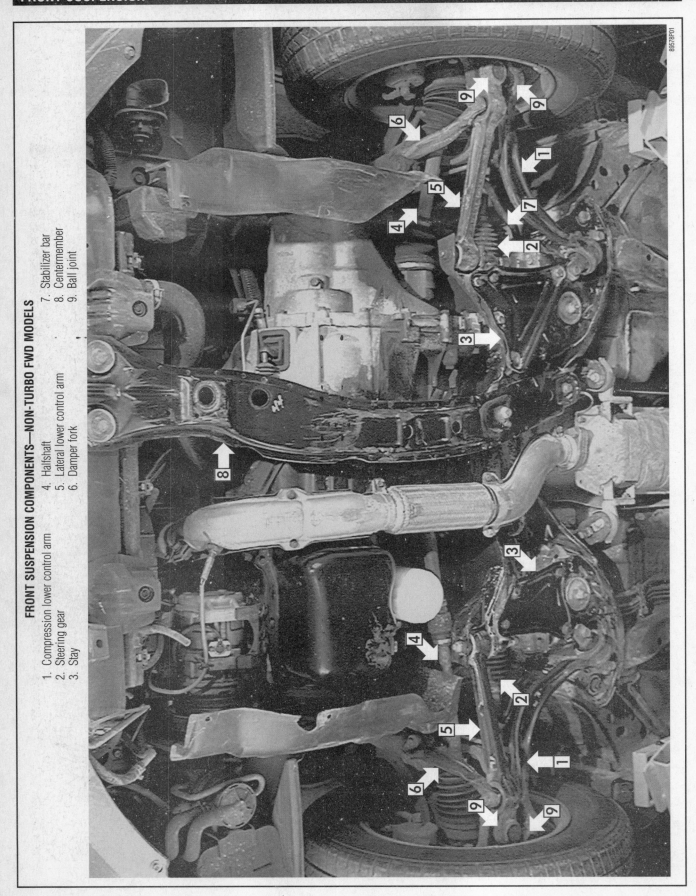

FRONT SUSPENSION COMPONENTS—NON-TURBO FWD MODELS

1. Compression lower control arm
2. Steering gear
3. Stay
4. Halfshaft
5. Lateral lower control arm
6. Damper fork
7. Stabilizer bar
8. Centermember
9. Ball joint

FRONT SUSPENSION COMPONENTS—AWD MODELS

1. Shock absorber
2. Damper fork
3. Ball joints
4. Compression lower control arm
5. Stabilizer bar
6. Lateral lower control arm
7. Stay
8. Centermember
9. Steering gear

89078P65

MacPherson Strut

REMOVAL & INSTALLATION

1990–94 Vehicles

▶ **See Figures 2 and 3**

1. Disconnect the negative battery cable.
2. Raise and safely support vehicle.
3. Remove the wheel and tire assembly.
4. Remove the brake hose and tube bracket retainer bolt and bracket from the front strut. Do not pry the brake hose and tube clamp away when removing.
5. If equipped with ABS, disconnect the front speed sensor mounting clamp from the strut.
6. Support the lower arm using floor jack or equivalent. Remove the lower strut to knuckle bolts. Once the mounting bolts have been removed, jack up the lower arm. Use a piece of wire to attach the brake hose, tube and driveshaft to the knuckle and to help keep the weight off. These components are not to be pulled.
7. Before removing the top bolts, make matchmarks on the body and the strut insulator for proper reassembly. If this plate is installed improperly, the wheel alignment will be wrong. Remove the strut upper mounting bolts. Remove the strut assembly from the vehicle.

To install:

8. Install the strut to the vehicle and install the top mounting bolts. Make sure the insulator is installed so the matchmarks made during disassembly are in alignment. Tighten the mounting bolts to 36 ft. lbs. (50 Nm).
9. Position the strut on the knuckle and install the mounting bolts. While holding the head of the lower mounting bolt, tighten the nuts to 80–101 ft. lbs. (110–140 Nm).
Install the brake hose bracket and the ABS clamp.
10. Install the wheel and tire assembly.
11. Carefully lower the vehicle.
12. Take the vehicle to a reputable repair shop to have the alignment checked and adjusted, if necessary.

1995–98 Vehicles

▶ **See Figures 4 thru 12**

1. Remove the top shock absorber assembly mounting nuts from inside the engine compartment.
2. Raise and safely support the vehicle. Remove the wheel and tire assembly.

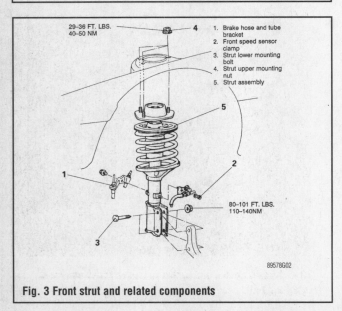

89578G01

Fig. 2 Removal of front strut lower mounting bolts

Fig. 3 Front strut and related components

1. Brake hose and tube bracket
2. Front speed sensor clamp
3. Strut lower mounting bolt
4. Strut upper mounting nut
5. Strut assembly

29–36 FT. LBS. 40–50 NM

80–101 FT. LBS. 110–140NM

89578G02

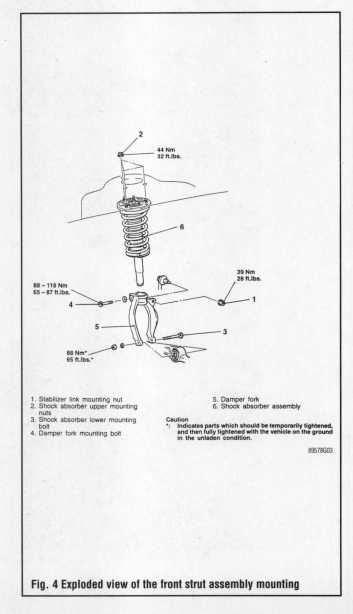

44 Nm
32 ft.lbs.

88 – 118 Nm
65 – 87 ft.lbs.

39 Nm
28 ft.lbs.

88 Nm*
65 ft.lbs.*

1. Stabilizer link mounting nut
2. Shock absorber upper mounting nuts
3. Shock absorber lower mounting bolt
4. Damper fork mounting bolt
5. Damper fork
6. Shock absorber assembly

Caution
*: Indicates parts which should be temporarily tightened, and then fully tightened with the vehicle on the ground in the unladen condition.

89578G03

Fig. 4 Exploded view of the front strut assembly mounting

Fig. 5 From inside the engine compartment, unfasten the upper shock assembly retaining bolts

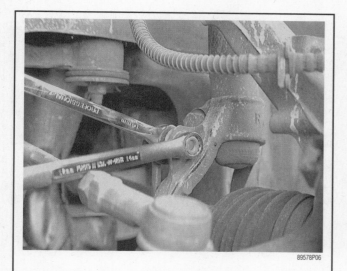

Fig. 6 Unfasten the stabilizer link mounting nut . . .

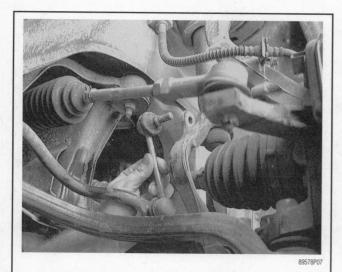

Fig. 7 . . . then separate the link from the damper fork

Fig. 8 Use 2 wrenches to loosen the lower shock absorber retaining bolt . . .

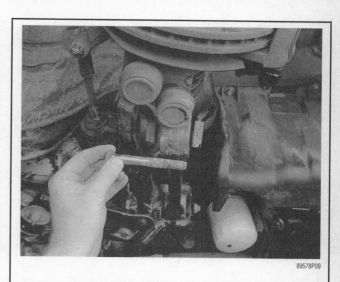

Fig. 9 . . . then remove the lower mounting bolt

Fig. 10 Use a ratchet and socket to loosen the damper fork retaining bolt . . .

Fig. 11 . . . then remove the bolt and the damper fork assembly

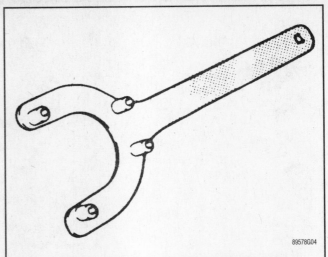

Fig. 13 Spring seat holder tool used to disassemble 1990–94 strut assemblies

Fig. 12 Maneuver the shock absorber assembly from the vehicle

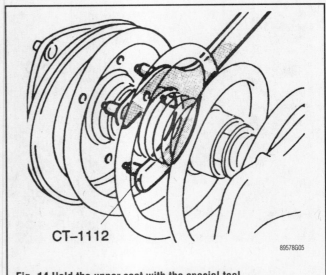

Fig. 14 Hold the upper seat with the special tool . . .

3. Remove the stabilizer link mounting nut.
4. Unfasten the shock absorber assembly lower mounting bolts.
5. Remove the damper fork mounting bolt, then remove the damper fork from the vehicle.
6. Remove the shock absorber assembly by maneuvering it out of the vehicle.
7. Installation is the reverse of the removal procedure. Be sure to tighten the retainers to the specifications shown in the accompanying figure.

OVERHAUL

1990–94 Vehicles

♦ See Figures 13 thru 19

1. Remove the strut from the vehicle.
2. Remove the dust cover from the top of the strut.

➥The self-locking nut should only be loosened. Do not remove the nut.

3. While holding the spring upper seat with retainer tool CT–1112 or equivalent, loosen the self-locking nut.

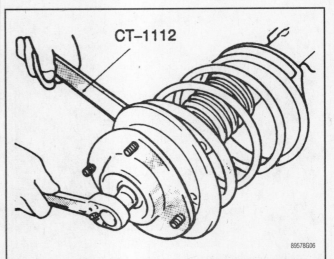

Fig. 15 . . . then loosen, but do not remove, the self-locking nut

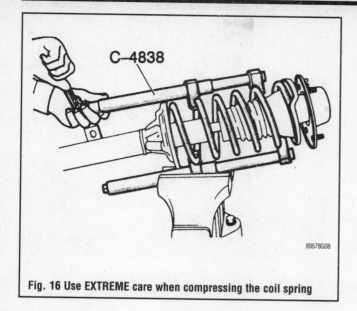

Fig. 16 Use EXTREME care when compressing the coil spring

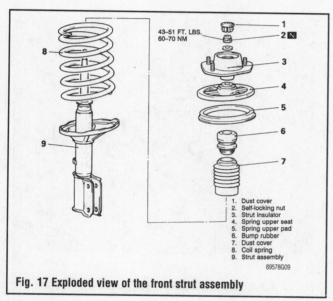

43–51 FT. LBS.
60–70 NM

1. Dust cover
2. Self-locking nut
3. Strut insulator
4. Spring upper seat
5. Spring upper pad
6. Bump rubber
7. Dust cover
8. Coil spring
9. Strut assembly

Fig. 17 Exploded view of the front strut assembly

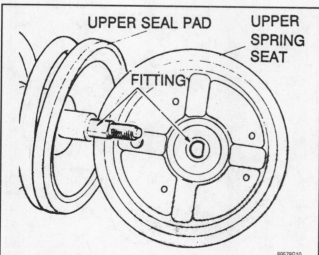

UPPER SEAL PAD

UPPER SPRING SEAT

FITTING

Fig. 18 Fit notch in the strut rod to the shaped hole in the spring seat

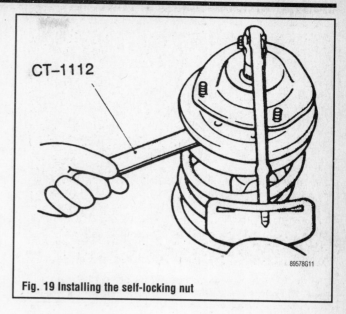

Fig. 19 Installing the self-locking nut

4. Place the strut assembly in a soft-jawed vise, then carefully compress the coil spring using spring compressor tool C–4838 or equivalent. Install the compressor tools so they are of equal distance apart. Tighten the compressor tools slowly and evenly. Do not use air tools on the spring compressors.

5. Once the spring is compressed, remove the locknut.

6. Remove the strut insulator, spring seat spring pad, bumper rubber and dust cover. Remove the coil spring.

7. Inspect all parts for rust, damage or corrosion and replace as required.

To assemble:

8. Install the spring onto the strut assembly.

9. Join the dust cover and the bump rubber and install onto the strut.

10. Assembly the spring upper seat tot he piston rod, fitting the notch in the rod to the shaped hole in the spring seat. Line up the holes in the strut assembly spring lower seat with the hole in the spring upper seat. This is made easier using a long piece of stock to act as a guide.

11. Install the strut insulator.

12. Install the self-locking nut. With the coil spring held compressed, provisionally tighten the self-locking nut. Correctly align both ends of the coil spring with the grooves in the spring seat, and loosen the spring compressor tool.

13. While holding the spring upper seat with tool CT–1112 or equivalent, tighten the new locknut to 43–51 ft. lbs. (60–70 Nm).

14. Apply multi-purpose grease to the bearing part of the strut and insulator.

➡When applying grease to the strut and insulator, make sure the grease does not adhere to the rubber portion of the insulator.

15. Install the dust cover onto the strut. Install the strut onto the vehicle.

1995–98 Vehicles

♦ See Figures 20 thru 29

1. Remove the shock and strut assembly from the vehicle.

❄❄❄ **CAUTION**

Do not use air tools to tighten the compressor tool bolt.

2. Use the proper spring compressing tools (MB991237 and MB991239) to compress the coil spring. Make sure to install the tools evenly so the maximum length will be attained within the installation range.

3. While holding the piston rod, remove the self-locking nut.

4. Remove the washer.

5. Remove the upper bushing A, the upper bracket assembly and the upper spring pad.

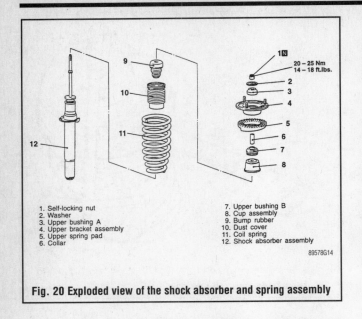

1. Self-locking nut
2. Washer
3. Upper bushing A
4. Upper bracket assembly
5. Upper spring pad
6. Collar
7. Upper bushing B
8. Cup assembly
9. Bump rubber
10. Dust cover
11. Coil spring
12. Shock absorber assembly

Fig. 20 Exploded view of the shock absorber and spring assembly

Fig. 23 Remove the self-locking nut and washer

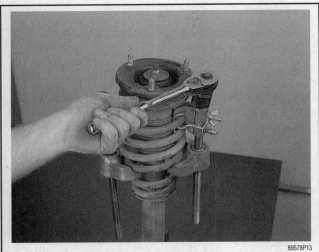

Fig. 21 Assemble the proper compressor tools on the spring, then compress with a ratchet or wrench. Do not use air tools!

Fig. 24 Remove the upper bushing and bracket assemblies

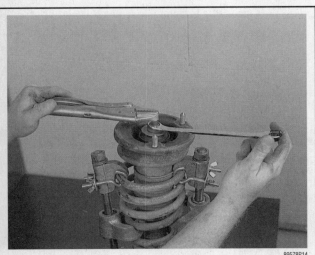

Fig. 22 Hold the piston rod with a pair of locking pliers, then remove the self-locking nut

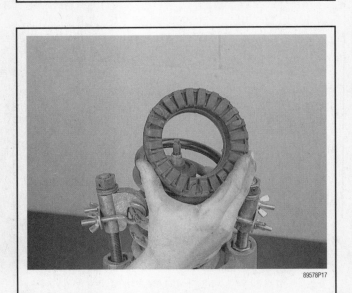

Fig. 25 Lift off the upper spring pad

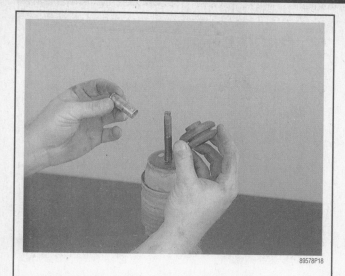

Fig. 26 Remove the collar and the other bushing

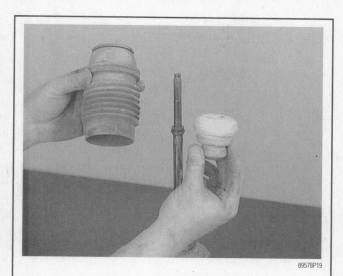

Fig. 27 Remove the rubber bumper and dust cover

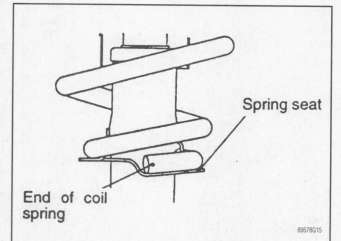

Fig. 28 Make sure to align the coil spring with the stepped part of the shock spring seat

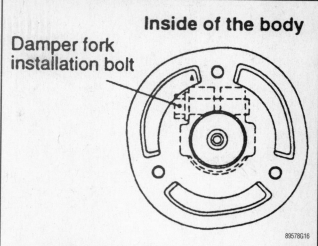

Fig. 29 Make sure the upper bracket bolts are in proper position with the damper fork

6. Remove the collar, upper bushing B, cup assembly, rubber bumper and dust cover.

7. Separate the coil spring and shock absorber assemblies.

To assemble:

8. Use the compressor tools to compress the coil spring, then install it to the shock absorber. Align the edge of the coil spring to the stepped portion of the shock absorber spring seat.

9. Install the dust cover, rubber bumper, cup, upper bushing B, collar and upper spring pad.

10. Install the upper bracket assembly, installing it so the position of the three bolts are in the proper orientation with the damper fork, as shown in the accompanying figure.

11. Install the other upper bushing.

12. Install the washer and the self-locking nut. Temporarily tighten the self-locking nut, then remove the spring compressor tools and tighten the nut to 14–18 ft. lbs. (20–25 Nm) using a torque wrench. Do not use air tools to tighten the self-locking nut!

13. Install the shock absorber assembly in the vehicle.

Upper Ball Joint

INSPECTION

♦ **See Figure 30**

1. Shake the ball joint stud a few times, then install the nut to the stud and use a preload socket (MB990326 or equivalent) and an inch lb. torque wrench to measure the breakaway torque of the ball joint. The reading should be 3–22 inch lbs. (0.3–2.5 Nm).

2. If the measured value is higher than the standard, the upper control arm must be replaced.

3. If the value is lower than the standard, check that the ball joint turns smoothly without excessive plate. If so, the ball joint is OK.

4. Also, check the ball joint dust cover for cracks or other damage, if found, the upper control arm must be replaced.

REMOVAL & INSTALLATION

If the upper ball joint exceeds specifications, replacement is required. However, upper ball joints can not be replaced individually, but must be replaced with the whole upper control arm assembly, as a unit. Refer to the upper control arm removal and installation procedure in this section.

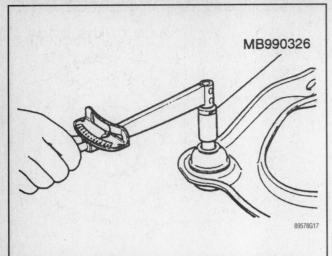

Fig. 30 Measure the torque of the ball joint to see if it needs to be replaced

Lower Ball Joint

INSPECTION

◆ **See Figure 30**

1990–94 Vehicles

If the lower ball joint is found to be defective, replacement of the lower control arm is required.

1. Remove the lower control arm from the vehicle.

2. Shake the ball joint stud several times. If movement is noticed, replace the lower arm assembly.

3. Mount 2 nuts on the ball joint stud. Using torque wrench, turn the nuts and the stud of the ball joint while watching the torque measured on the wrench. This value is the ball joint starting torque.

4. Compare obtained torque to the standard value of 26–87 in. lbs. (10 Nm).

5. If the starting torque exceeds the upper limit of the standard value, replace the lower arm assembly.

6. If the starting torque is within specifications, the ball joint can be reused, unless it has excessive play.

7. A new grease boot can be installed using a large socket for a driver.

1995–98 Vehicles

1. Shake the ball joint stud a few times, then install the nut to the stud and use a preload socket (MB990326 or equivalent) and an inch lb. torque wrench to measure the breakaway torque of the ball joint. The readings should be as follows:

    a. Compression lower control arm ball joint: 4–22 inch lbs. (0.5–2.5 Nm).

    b. Lateral lower control arm ball joint: 13 inch lbs. (1.5 Nm) or less.

2. If the measured value is higher than the standard, the lateral or compression lower control arm must be replaced, as applicable.

3. If the value is lower than the standard, check that the ball joint turns smoothly without excessive plate. If so, the ball joint is OK.

4. Also, check the ball joint dust cover for cracks or other damage, if found, the control arm must be replaced.

REMOVAL & INSTALLATION

If the lower ball joint exceeds specifications, replacement is required. However, lower ball joints can not be replaced separately, but must be replaced with the lower arm, as a unit. Refer to lower arm removal and installation procedure in this section.

Stabilizer Bar

REMOVAL & INSTALLATION

1990–94 Vehicles

FWD VEHICLES

◆ **See Figures 31, 32, 33, 34 and 35**

1. Disconnect the negative battery cable.

2. Raise and safely support vehicle. Remove the front exhaust pipe and gasket from the manifold and using wire, tie it down and out of the way.

➡**When relocating the front exhaust pipe, make sure the flexible joint is not bent more than a few degrees of damage to the pipe joint may occur.**

3. Remove the center crossmember rear installation bolts.

4. Remove the stabilizer link bolts. On the pillow-ball type, hold ball stud with a hex wrench and remove the self-locking nut with a box wrench.

5. Remove the stabilizer bar bolts and mounts.

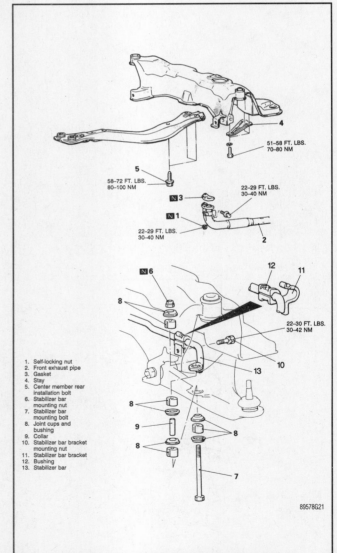

1. Self-locking nut
2. Front exhaust pipe
3. Gasket
4. Stay
5. Center member rear installation bolt
6. Stabilizer bar mounting nut
7. Stabilizer bar mounting bolt
8. Joint cups and bushing
9. Collar
10. Stabilizer bar bracket mounting nut
11. Stabilizer bar bracket
12. Bushing
13. Stabilizer bar

Fig. 31 Exploded view of the rubber bushing type stabilizer bar—FWD vehicle

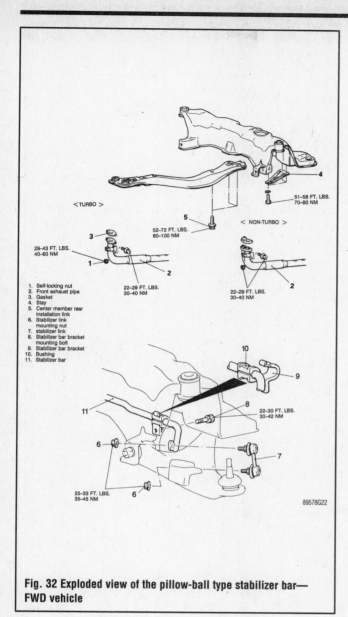

1. Self-locking nut
2. Front exhaust pipe
3. Gasket
4. Stay
5. Center member rear installation link
6. Stabilizer link mounting nut
7. stabilizer link
8. Stabilizer bar bracket mounting bolt
9. Stabilizer bar bracket
10. Bushing
11. Stabilizer bar

Fig. 32 Exploded view of the pillow-ball type stabilizer bar—FWD vehicle

Fig. 33 Use wrench to secure the ball stud of the stabilizer link while removing the mounting nuts

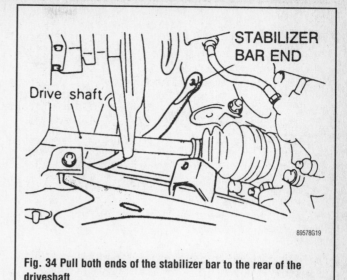

Fig. 34 Pull both ends of the stabilizer bar to the rear of the driveshaft

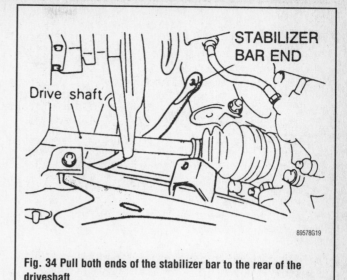

Fig. 35 Pull the stabilizer bar out of the vehicle diagonally

6. Remove the bar from the vehicle.
   a. Pull both ends of the stabilizer bar toward the rear of the vehicle.
   b. Move the right stabilizer bar end until the end clears the lower arm.
   c. Remove the stabilizer bar out the right side of the vehicle.
7. Inspect all bushings for wear and deterioration and replace as required. Check the stabilizer bar for damage, and replace as required.
   To install:
8. Install the stabilizer bar into the vehicle.
9. Install the stabilizer bar brackets on the vehicle, following any side locational markings on the brackets. Temporarily tighten the stabilizer bar bracket. Align the bushing end with the marked part of the stabilizer bar and then fully tighten the stabilizer bar bracket.
10. If equipped with the pillow-ball type mounting, install the stabilizer bar links and link mounting nuts. Using a wrench, secure the ball studs at both ends of the stabilizer link while tightening the mounting nuts. Tighten the nuts on the stabilizer bar bolt so that the distance of bolt protrusion above the top of the nut is 0.63–0.70 in. (16–18mm).
11. Install the front exhaust pipe with new gasket in place. Tighten new self-locking nuts to 29 ft. lbs. (40 Nm).
12. Connect the negative battery cable.

AWD VEHICLES

♦ See Figure 36

1. Disconnect the negative battery cable.
2. Remove the front exhaust pipe.
3. Remove the center gusset and transfer assembly.
4. Using a wrench to secure the ball studs at both ends of the stabilizer link, remove the stabilizer link mounting nuts. Remove the stabilizer link.
5. Remove the stabilizer bar bracket installation bolt and the stabilizer bar bracket and bushing.
6. Disconnect the stabilizer bar coupling at the right lower control arm. Pull out the left side stabilizer edge, pulling it out between the driveshaft and the lower arm. Pull out the right side bar below the lower arm.

To install:

7. Install the bar into the vehicle in the same manner as removal.
8. Temporarily tighten the stabilizer bar bracket. Align the bushing end with the marked part of the stabilizer bar and then fully tighten the stabilizer bar bracket.
9. Install and tighten the stabilizer bar bracket bolt.
10. Install the stabilizer bar links and link mounting nuts. Using a wrench, secure the ball studs at both ends of the stabilizer link while tightening the mounting nuts. Tighten the nuts on the stabilizer bar bolt so that the distance of bolt protrusion above the top of the nut is 0.63–0.70 in. (16–18mm).
11. Install the transfer assembly and gusset.
12. Install the left crossmember. Tighten the rear mounting bolts to 58 ft. lbs. (80 Nm) and the front mounting bolts to 72 ft. lbs. (100 Nm).

1995–98 Vehicles

♦ See Figures 37, 38 and 39

1. Disconnect the negative battery cable.
2. Raise and safely support vehicle.
3. Unfasten the stabilizer link mounting nuts.
4. Remove the stabilizer link.
5. Remove the stabilizer bar bracket.
6. Remove the bushing, then remove the stabilizer bar from the vehicle.
7. Inspect the stabilizer bar, bushings and bolts for wear, damage and/or deterioration and replace as necessary.
8. If the stabilizer link ball joint dust cover was damaged during removal, it can be replaced, as follows:
   a. Remove the clip ring with a small prytool, then remove the dust cover.

To install:

9. To install the dust cover, perform the following:
   a. Apply multipurpose grease to the inside the dust cover.
   b. Use plastic tape on the stabilizer threads, then install the dust cover on the stabilizer link.
   c. Secure the cover using the clip ring. When installing the clip ring, align the ends at a 90° angle from the axis from the axis of the stabilizer link.
10. Installation is the reverse of the removal procedure.
11. When installing the stabilizer bar, position it so the marking on the bar and the edge of the bracket becomes the reference value, then tighten the stabilizer bar bracket mounting bolt.

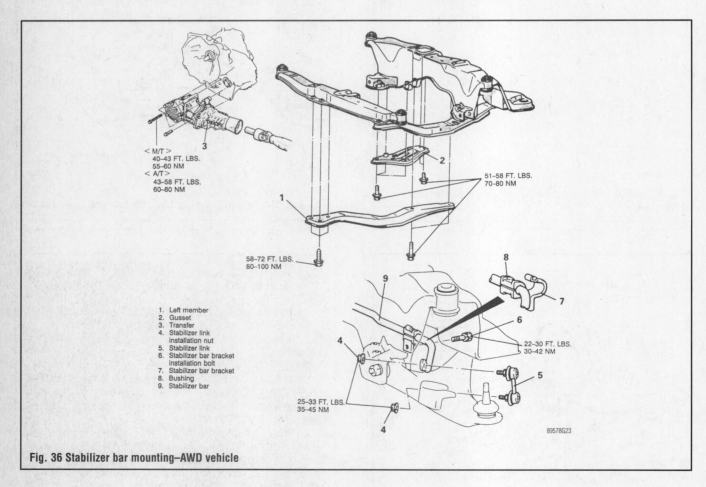

< M/T >
40–43 FT. LBS.
55–60 NM
< A/T >
43–58 FT. LBS.
60–80 NM

51–58 FT. LBS.
70–80 NM

58–72 FT. LBS.
80–100 NM

22–30 FT. LBS.
30–42 NM

25–33 FT. LBS.
35–45 NM

1. Left member
2. Gusset
3. Transfer
4. Stabilizer link installation nut
5. Stabilizer link
6. Stabilizer bar bracket installation bolt
7. Stabilizer bar bracket
8. Bushing
9. Stabilizer bar

89578G23

Fig. 36 Stabilizer bar mounting—AWD vehicle

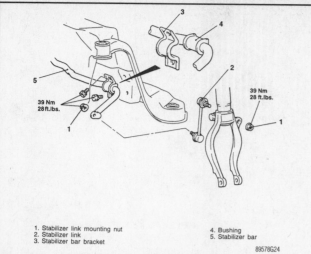

1. Stabilizer link mounting nut
2. Stabilizer link
3. Stabilizer bar bracket

4. Bushing
5. Stabilizer bar

89578G24

Fig. 37 Exploded view of the stabilizer bar and related components—1995–98 vehicles

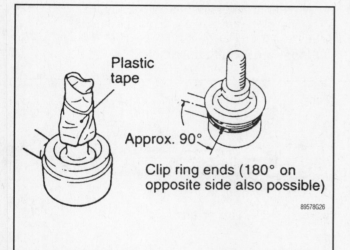

Plastic tape

Approx. 90°

Clip ring ends (180° on opposite side also possible)

89578G26

Fig. 38 Wrap the stabilizer threads with plastic tape, then install the dust cover

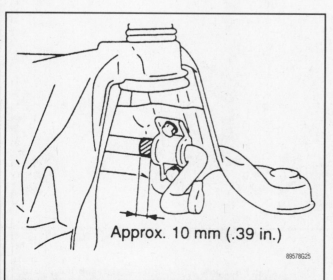

Approx. 10 mm (.39 in.)

89578G25

Fig. 39 Proper installation of the stabilizer bar and bracket

Upper Control Arm

REMOVAL & INSTALLATION

▶ **See Figures 40 thru 47**

1. Disconnect the negative battery cable.
2. Unfasten the self-locking nut from inside the engine compartment.
3. Raise and safely support the front of the vehicle securely on jackstands.
4. Separate the upper ball joint and steering knuckle connection, using a suitable puller (MB991113 or equivalent) to loosen the tie rod end mounting nut. Only loosen the nut, do NOT remove it. Its also a good idea to support the puller with a piece of cord to prevent it from flying off.
5. If not already done, remove the upper control arm self-locking nut, then remove the upper control arm from the vehicle.
6. If necessary, remove the retainers, then remove the upper arm shaft assemblies.

To install:

7. Install the upper control arm shaft at the angle shown in the accompanying figure. If the shaft is installed at the proper angle, then reference dimension is determined as shown in the accompanying figure.

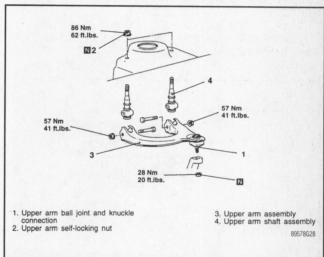

1. Upper arm ball joint and knuckle connection
2. Upper arm self-locking nut

3. Upper arm assembly
4. Upper arm shaft assembly

89578G28

Fig. 40 Exploded view of the upper control arm and related components

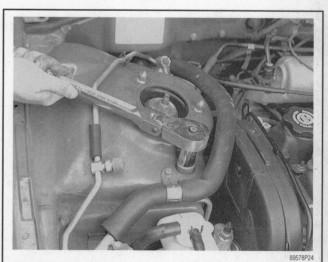

89578P24

Fig. 41 From inside the engine compartment, unfasten the control arm self-locking nuts

Fig. 42 Unfasten the mounting nut

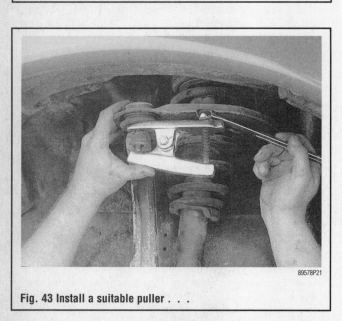

Fig. 43 Install a suitable puller . . .

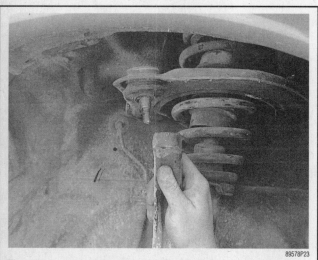

Fig. 44 . . . then separate the upper control arm ball joint from the steering knuckle

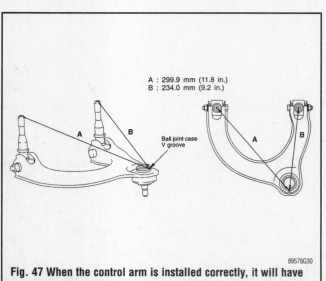

Fig. 45 Remove the upper control arm from the vehicle

Fig. 46 The upper control arm must be installed at the proper angle

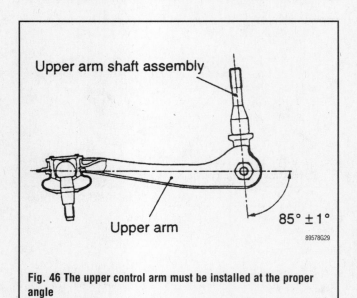

Fig. 47 When the control arm is installed correctly, it will have the proper dimensions

8. The remainder of installation is the reverse of the removal procedure.

9. Tighten the retainers to the specification shown in the accompanying figure.

Lower Control Arm

REMOVAL & INSTALLATION

1990–94 Vehicles

◗ **See Figures 48, 49 and 50**

1. Disconnect the negative battery cable.
2. Raise the vehicle and support safely.

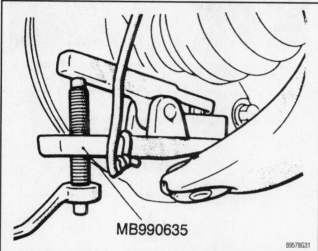

Fig. 48 Use a suitable puller (MB990635 or equivalent) to separate the lower control arm ball joint from the knuckle using

3. Remove sway bar links or mounting nuts and bolts from lower control arm. Remove the joint cups and bushings, if equipped.

4. Disconnect the ball joint stud from the steering knuckle.

5. Remove the inner lower arm mounting bolts and nut.

6. Remove the rear mount bolts. Remove the rear retainer clamp if equipped.

7. Remove the arm from the vehicle.

8. Remove the rear rod bushing, if service is required.

To install:

9. Assemble the control arm and bushing. Install the control arm to the vehicle and install the inner mounting bolts. Install new nut and snug temporarily.

10. Install the rear mount clamp, bolts and replacement nuts. Tighten the clamp mounting nuts to 34 ft. lbs. (47 Nm). Temporarily tighten the

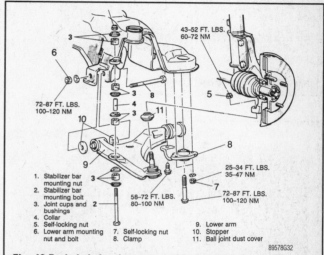

1. Stabilizer bar mounting nut
2. Stabilizer bar mounting bolt
3. Joint cups and bushings
4. Collar
5. Self-locking nut
6. Lower arm mounting nut and bolt
7. Self-locking nut
8. Clamp
9. Lower arm
10. Stopper
11. Ball joint dust cover

Fig. 49 Exploded view lower control arm—1990–94 models equipped with rubber bushing type stabilizer

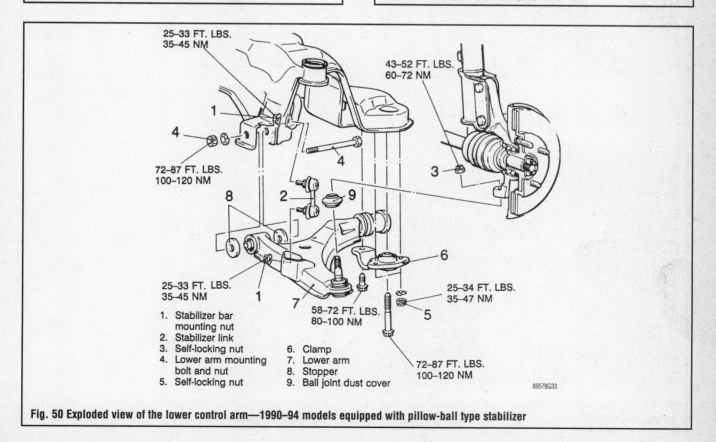

1. Stabilizer bar mounting nut
2. Stabilizer link
3. Self-locking nut
4. Lower arm mounting bolt and nut
5. Self-locking nut
6. Clamp
7. Lower arm
8. Stopper
9. Ball joint dust cover

Fig. 50 Exploded view of the lower control arm—1990–94 models equipped with pillow-ball type stabilizer

clamp mounting bolt. Once the weight of the vehicle is on the suspension, the bolt will be tightened to 72 ft. lbs. (100 Nm).

11. Connect the ball joint stud to the knuckle. Install a new nut and torque to 43–52 ft. lbs. (60–72 Nm).

12. Install the sway bar and links.

13. Lower the vehicle to the floor for the final tightening of the inner frame mount bolt.

14. Once the full weight of the vehicle is on the suspension, tighten the inner lower arm mounting bolt nuts to 87 ft. lbs. (120 Nm). Tighten the inner clamp mounting bolt to 72 ft. lbs. (100 Nm).

15. Inspect all suspension bolts, making sure they all have been fully tightened.

16. Connect the negative battery cable.

1995–98 Vehicles

▶ See Figure 51

COMPRESSION LOWER CONTROL ARM

▶ See Figures 52, 53, 54 and 55

1. Raise and safely support the vehicle.
2. Remove the front wheel and tire assembly.
3. Use the proper tool and disconnect the compression lower arm ball joint from the steering knuckle.
4. Remove the two mounting bolts and remove the compression lower arm.

To install:

5. Install the compression lower arm. Tighten the two mounting bolts to 60 ft. lbs. (81 Nm).

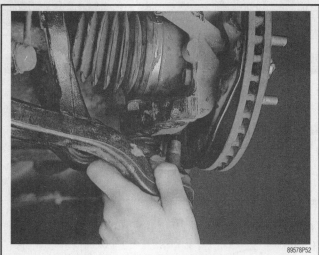

Fig. 52 Separate the compression lower ball joint from the knuckle

6. Using a new self-locking nut, connect the ball joint to the knuckle assembly. Tighten the nut to 43–51 ft. lbs. (59–71 Nm).

7. Install the wheel assembly and safely lower the vehicle to the floor.

8. Check and adjust the front wheel alignment if necessary.

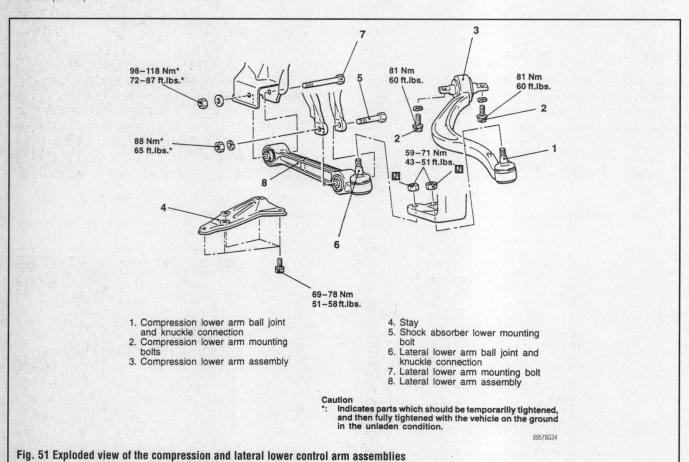

1. Compression lower arm ball joint and knuckle connection
2. Compression lower arm mounting bolts
3. Compression lower arm assembly
4. Stay
5. Shock absorber lower mounting bolt
6. Lateral lower arm ball joint and knuckle connection
7. Lateral lower arm mounting bolt
8. Lateral lower arm assembly

Caution
*: Indicates parts which should be temporarily tightened, and then fully tightened with the vehicle on the ground in the unladen condition.

Fig. 51 Exploded view of the compression and lateral lower control arm assemblies

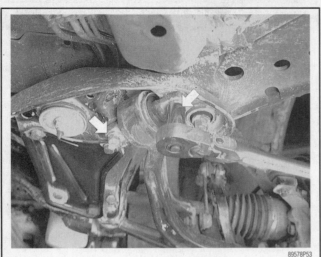

Fig. 53 Unfasten the two compression lower control arm (see arrows)

LATERAL LOWER ARM

▶ **See Figures 56, 57 and 58**

1. Raise and safely support the vehicle.
2. Remove the wheel assembly.
3. Remove the stay (bracket).
4. Remove the shock absorber lower mounting bolt.
5. Use the proper puller tool and disconnect the lateral lower arm from the knuckle assembly.
6. Remove the lateral lower arm mounting bolt and the lateral arm.

To install:

7. Install the lateral lower arm and temporarily install the mounting bolt. Do not tighten the bolt until the vehicle is on the floor at normal riding height.
8. Use a new self-locking nut and connect the ball joint to the knuckle assembly. Tighten the self-locking nut to 43–51 ft. lbs. (59–71 Nm).
9. Install the shock absorber lower mounting bolt, secure with the nut and torque to 64 ft. lbs. (88 Nm).
10. Install the stay with the bolts and tighten them to 51–58 ft. lbs. (69–78 Nm).
11. Install the wheel assembly and lower the vehicle to the floor.

Fig. 54 Remove the remaining mounting bolt . . .

Fig. 56 After separating the later lower ball joint from the knuckle, unfasten the mounting bolt . . .

Fig. 55 . . . then remove the compression lower control arm from the vehicle

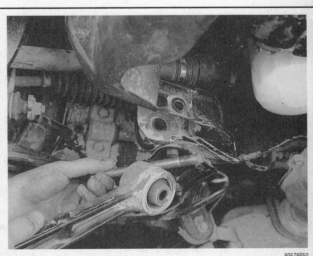

Fig. 57 . . . then remove the mounting bolt and pull the lateral lower control arm from the vehicle

Fig. 58 To install, position the lateral lower arm in the vehicle, then install the mounting bolt hand-tight

89578P51

12. Tighten the lateral lower arm through-bolt and nut to 71–85 ft. lbs. (98–118 Nm).

13. Check and adjust the front wheel alignment if necessary.

Front Wheel Hub, Knuckle and Bearing

REMOVAL & INSTALLATION

1990–94 Vehicles

♦ **See Figures 59 thru 65**

1. Disconnect the negative battery cable.
2. Remove the cotter pin from the driveshaft nut. With the brakes applied, loosen the halfshaft nut.
3. Raise the vehicle and support safely. Remove the halfshaft nut. If equipped with ABS, remove the front wheel speed sensor.
4. Remove the caliper assembly and brake pads. Suspend the caliper with a wire.
5. Remove the ball joint and tie rod end from the steering knuckle.
6. Remove the halfshaft by setting up a puller on the outside wheel hub and pushing the halfshaft from the front hub. After pressing the outer shaft, insert a prybar between the transaxle case and the halfshaft and pry the shaft from the transaxle.
7. Unbolt the lower end of the strut and remove the hub and steering knuckle assembly from the vehicle.
8. To disassemble, proceed as follows:

   a. Install the hub/knuckle assembly in a vise. Using a puller, remove the hub from the knuckle.

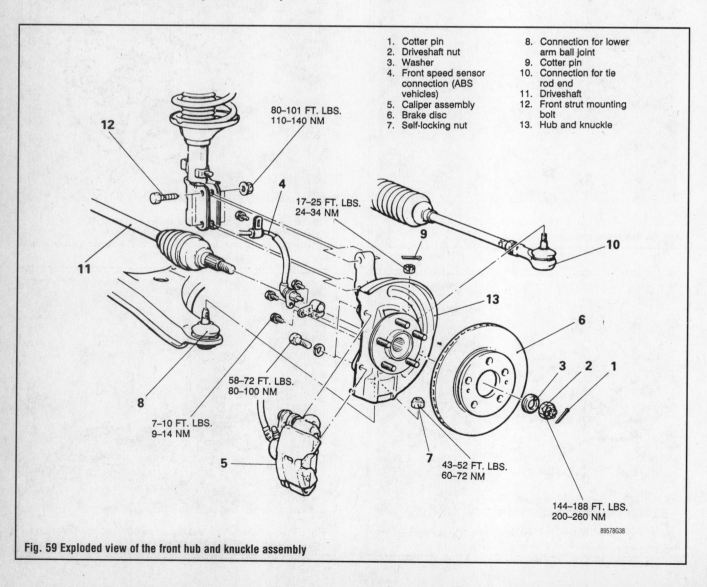

1. Cotter pin
2. Driveshaft nut
3. Washer
4. Front speed sensor connection (ABS vehicles)
5. Caliper assembly
6. Brake disc
7. Self-locking nut
8. Connection for lower arm ball joint
9. Cotter pin
10. Connection for tie rod end
11. Driveshaft
12. Front strut mounting bolt
13. Hub and knuckle

80–101 FT. LBS.
110–140 NM

17–25 FT. LBS.
24–34 NM

58–72 FT. LBS.
80–100 NM

7–10 FT. LBS.
9–14 NM

43–52 FT. LBS.
60–72 NM

144–188 FT. LBS.
200–260 NM

89578G38

Fig. 59 Exploded view of the front hub and knuckle assembly

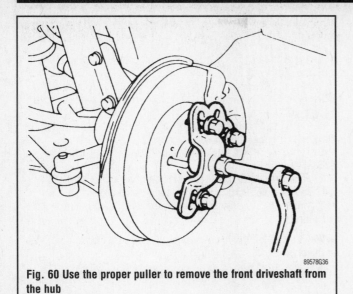

Fig. 60 Use the proper puller to remove the front driveshaft from the hub

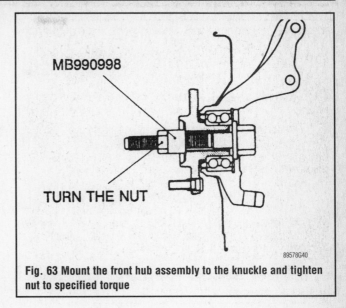

Fig. 63 Mount the front hub assembly to the knuckle and tighten nut to specified torque

MB990998

TURN THE NUT

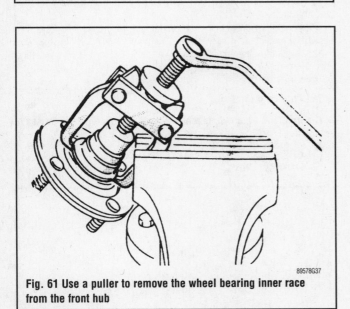

Fig. 61 Use a puller to remove the wheel bearing inner race from the front hub

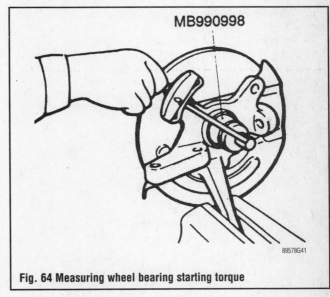

MB990998

Fig. 64 Measuring wheel bearing starting torque

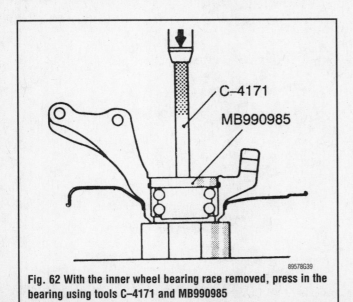

C–4171
MB990985

Fig. 62 With the inner wheel bearing race removed, press in the bearing using tools C–4171 and MB990985

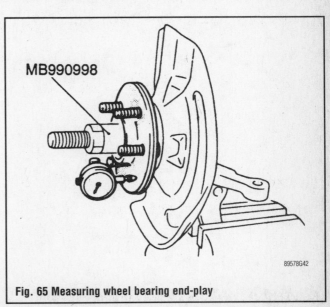

MB990998

Fig. 65 Measuring wheel bearing end-play

➥**Do not use a hammer to accomplish this or the bearing will be damaged.**

b. Carefully remove the oil seal from the axle side of the knuckle using a small prying tool.

c. Remove the wheel bearing inner race from the front hub using a puller.

➥**Be careful that the front hub does not fall when the inner race is removed.**

d. Remove the snapring from the axle side of the knuckle. Remove the bearing from the knuckle using a puller.

e. Once the bearing is removed, the bearing outer race can be removed by tapping out with a brass drift pin and a hammer.

To install:

f. To assembly, proceed as follows:

g. Fill the wheel bearing with multipurpose grease. Apply a thin coating of multipurpose grease to the knuckle and bearing contact surfaces.

h. Press the wheel bearing into the knuckle using the appropriate pressing tool. Once the bearing is installed, install the inner race using the proper driving tool.

i. Drive the oil seal into the knuckle by using the proper size driver. Drive seal into knuckle until it is flush with the knuckle end surface.

j. Using pressing tool MB990998-01 or equivalent, mount the front hub assembly into the knuckle. Tighten the nut of the pressing tool to 144–188 ft. lbs. (200–260 Nm). Rotate the hub to seat the bearing.

k. Mount the knuckle assembly in a vise. Check the hub assembly turning torque and end-play as follows:

l. Using a torque wrench and socket MB990998-01 or equivalent, turn the hub in the knuckle assembly. Note the reading on the torque wrench and compare to the desired reading of 16 inch lbs. (1.8 Nm) or less.

m. Check for roughness when turning the bearing.

n. Mount a dial indicator on the hub so the pointer contacts the machined surface on the hub.

o. Rotate the hub and read the movement of the needle.

p. Compare the reading to the limit of 0.008 in. (0.2mm).

q. If the starting torque or the hub end-play are not within specifications while the nut is tightened to 144–188 ft. lbs. (200–260 Nm), the bearing, hub or knuckle have probably not been installed correctly. Repeat the disassembly and assembly procedure and recheck starting torque and end-play.

9. Install the hub and knuckle assembly onto the vehicle. Install the lower ball joint stud into the steering knuckle and install new nut. Tighten to 52 ft. lbs. (72 Nm).

10. Install the halfshaft into the transaxle extension housing and guide the outer end through the hub/knuckle assembly.

11. Install the 2 front strut lower mounting bolts and tighten to 80–101 ft. lbs. (110–140 Nm).

12. Install the connection for the tie rod end and tighten nut to 25 ft. lbs. (34 Nm). Install new cotter pin and bend to lock nut in position.

13. Install the brake disc and caliper assembly.

14. Install the front speed sensor, if removed.

➥**When installing front speed sensor, make sure harness is routed in the original position and that it is not twisted.**

15. Install the washer and new locknut to the end of the halfshaft. Tighten the locknut snugly.

16. Install the tire and wheel assembly onto the vehicle. Lower the vehicle to the ground.

17. With the weight of the vehicle on the ground and the brakes applied, tighten the locknut to 144–188 ft. lbs. (260 Nm).

18. Install the cotter pin in the first matching holes and bend it securely.

1995–98 Vehicles

▶ **See Figures 66 and 67**

➥**The front hub assembly is a sealed unit and should not be disassembled.**

1. Raise and safely support the vehicle.

2. Remove the wheel and tire assembly.

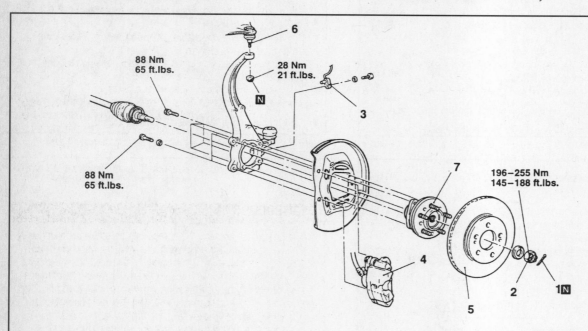

1. Cotter pin
2. Drive shaft nut
3. Front wheel speed sensor <Vehicles with ABS>
4. Caliper assembly
5. Brake disc
6. Upper arm ball joint and knuckle connection
7. Front hub assembly

88 Nm 65 ft.lbs.
28 Nm 21 ft.lbs.
88 Nm 65 ft.lbs.
196–255 Nm 145–188 ft.lbs.

Caution
The front hub assembly should not be disassembled.

89578G43

Fig. 66 Exploded view of the front hub bearing assembly and related components—1995–98 vehicles

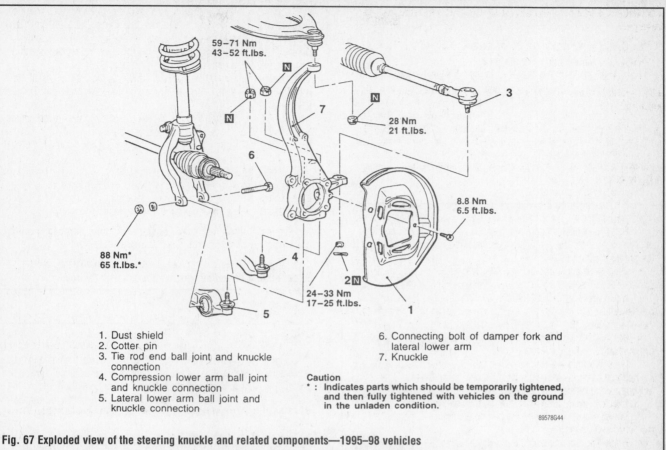

1. Dust shield
2. Cotter pin
3. Tie rod end ball joint and knuckle connection
4. Compression lower arm ball joint and knuckle connection
5. Lateral lower arm ball joint and knuckle connection
6. Connecting bolt of damper fork and lateral lower arm
7. Knuckle

Caution
* : Indicates parts which should be temporarily tightened, and then fully tightened with vehicles on the ground in the unladen condition.

89578G44

Fig. 67 Exploded view of the steering knuckle and related components—1995–98 vehicles

3. Remove and discard the driveshaft nut cotter pin.
4. Remove the driveshaft nut, holding the rotor in place with a suitable tool.
5. If equipped with ABS, remove the front wheel speed sensor.
6. Unbolt the caliper assembly and suspend out of the way with a piece of wire. Do not disconnect the fluid line.
7. Use a suitable puller to separate the upper control arm ball joint from the steering knuckle.
8. Unfasten the retaining bolts, then remove the front hub assembly. Shift the knuckle to the outside in order to keep the clearance between the front hub mounting bolts and driveshaft. Be careful not to damage the ball joint boot. If equipped with ABS, be careful not to damage the rotor.

➡ **If steering knuckle removal is necessary proceed with the following steps.**

9. Unfasten the retaining bolts, then remove the dust shield.
10. Remove and discard the cotter pin, then separate the tie rod end from the steering knuckle using a puller.
11. Use a suitable puller to separate the compression and lateral lower control arm ball joints from the steering knuckle.
12. Unfasten the connecting nut and bolt of the damper fork and lateral lower control arm.
13. Remove the steering knuckle from the vehicle.

To install:
14. Position the steering knuckle in the vehicle. Install the connecting bolt and nut and secure hand-tight.
15. Attach the lateral and compression lower control arm ball joints into the steering knuckle.
16. Fasten the tie rod end ball joint to the steering knuckle, then install the retaining nut and tighten to 17–25 ft. lbs. (24–33 Nm). Install a new cotter pin and bend over securely.

17. Install the dust shield and secure with the retaining bolt. 6.5 ft. lbs. (8.5 Nm).
18. Position the front hub assembly, then secure with the retaining bolts. Tighten to 65 ft. lbs. (88 Nm).
19. Fasten the upper control arm ball joint to the steering knuckle.
20. Install the brake disc (rotor) and caliper.
21. If equipped, install the front wheel speed sensor.
22. Install the driveshaft nut. Hold the rotor in position while tightening the driveshaft nut to 145–188 ft. lbs. (196–255 Nm). If the cotter pin holes does not match, tighten the nut up to 188 ft. lbs. (225 Nm) maximum. Install a new cotter pin in the first matching holes, then bend it over securely.
23. Install the wheel and tire assembly, then carefully lower the vehicle.

Wheel Alignment

If the tires are worn unevenly, if the vehicle is not stable on the highway or if the handling seems uneven in spirited driving, the wheel alignment should be checked. If an alignment problem is suspected, first check for improper tire inflation and other possible causes. These can be worn suspension or steering components, accident damage or even unmatched tires. If any worn or damaged components are found, they must be replaced before the wheels can be properly aligned. Wheel alignment requires very expensive equipment and involves minute adjustments which must be accurate; it should only be performed by a trained technician. Take your vehicle to a properly equipped shop.

Following is a description of the alignment angles which are adjustable on most vehicles and how they affect vehicle handling. Although these angles can apply to both the front and rear wheels, usually only the front suspension is adjustable.

CASTER

▶ **See Figure 68**

Looking at a vehicle from the side, caster angle describes the steering axis rather than a wheel angle. The steering knuckle is attached to a control arm or strut at the top and a control arm at the bottom. The wheel pivots around the line between these points to steer the vehicle. When the upper point is tilted back, this is described as positive caster. Having a positive caster tends to make the wheels self-centering, increasing directional stability. Excessive positive caster makes the wheels hard to steer, while an uneven caster will cause a pull to one side. Overloading the vehicle or sagging rear springs will affect caster, as will raising the rear of the vehicle. If the rear of the vehicle is lower than normal, the caster becomes more positive.

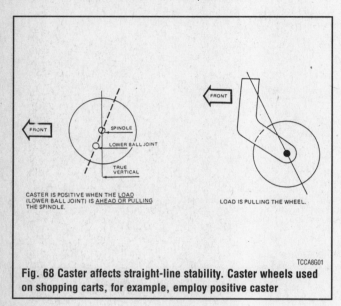

Fig. 68 Caster affects straight-line stability. Caster wheels used on shopping carts, for example, employ positive caster

CAMBER

▶ **See Figure 69**

Looking from the front of the vehicle, camber is the inward or outward tilt of the top of wheels. When the tops of the wheels are tilted in, this is negative camber; if they are tilted out, it is positive. In a turn, a slight amount of negative camber helps maximize contact of the tire with the road. However, too much negative camber compromises straight-line stability, increases bump steer and torque steer.

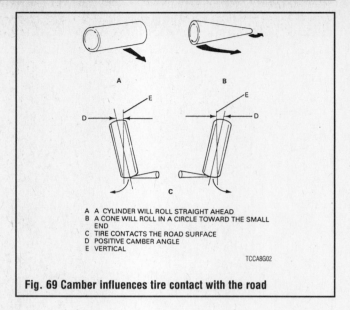

Fig. 69 Camber influences tire contact with the road

TOE

▶ **See Figure 70**

Looking down at the wheels from above the vehicle, toe angle is the distance between the front of the wheels, relative to the distance between the back of the wheels. If the wheels are closer at the front, they are said to be toed-in or to have negative toe. A small amount of negative toe enhances directional stability and provides a smoother ride on the highway.

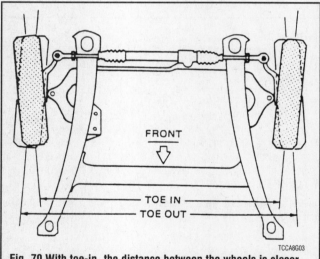

Fig. 70 With toe-in, the distance between the wheels is closer at the front than at the rear

REAR SUSPENSION

REAR SUSPENSION COMPONENT LOCATION—NON-TURBO FWD VEHICLE

1. Shock absorber assembly
2. Toe lower control arm
3. Lower control arm
4. Trailing arm
5. Crossmember

89578P03

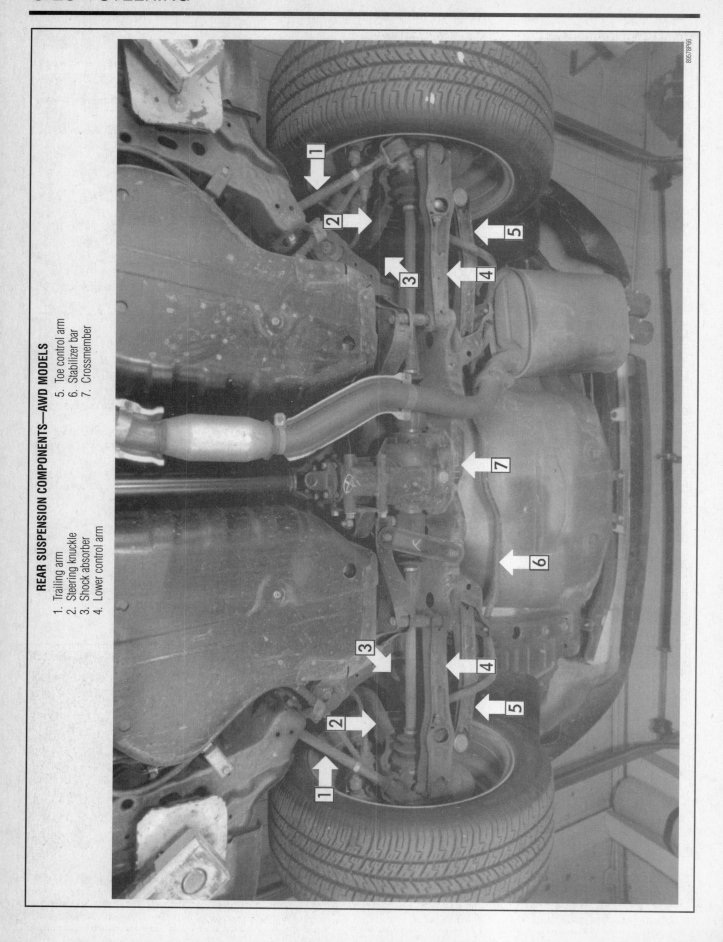

REAR SUSPENSION COMPONENTS—AWD MODELS

1. Trailing arm
2. Steering knuckle
3. Shock absorber
4. Lower control arm
5. Toe control arm
6. Stabilizer bar
7. Crossmember

Strut Assembly

REMOVAL & INSTALLATION

1990–94 Vehicles

▶ **See Figures 71, 72 and 73**

1. Disconnect the negative battery cable. Remove the trunk interior trim to gain access to the top mounting nuts.
2. Remove the top cap and upper shock mounting nuts.
3. Remove the brake tube bracket bolt.
4. mc>Raise and safely support torsion axle and arm assembly slightly. Make sure the jack does not contact the lateral rod.

➡ **Always use a wooden block between the jack receptacle and the axle beam. Place the jack at the center of the axle beam.**

5. Remove the shock lower mounting bolt and remove the assembly from the vehicle.
6. Installation is the reverse of the removal procedure. Tighten the upper shock mounting nuts to 29 ft. lbs. (40 Nm) and the lower mounting bolt to 72 ft. lbs. (100 Nm).

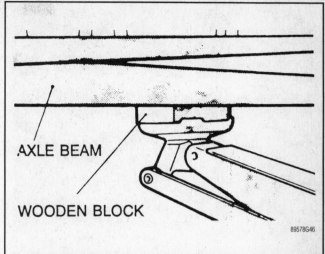

AXLE BEAM

WOODEN BLOCK

89578G46

Fig. 73 Support axle beam with wooden block between jack and center of axle beam

1995–98 Vehicles

▶ **See Figures 74 thru 81**

1. For all vehicles, except the Eclipse Spyder, remove the service lid in the luggage compartment.
2. For the Eclipse Spyder, remove the luggage compartment side trim.
3. Remove the cap and flange nuts securing the upper mounting bracket to the body of the vehicle. Do not remove the larger nut in the center of the shock absorber.
4. Raise and safely support the vehicle.
5. Remove the bolt attaching the lower end of the shock to the knuckle and remove the shock absorber from the vehicle.

To install:

6. Install the upper bracket of the shock to the vehicle. Tighten the mounting nuts to 32 ft. lbs. (44 Nm).
7. Raise the suspension up with a jack or adjustable stand to align the shock absorber lower mounting holes.
8. Install the lower mounting bolt. Tighten the bolt to 71 ft. lbs.
9. Remove the jack or stand and safely lower the vehicle to the floor.
10. Install the cap and service lid.

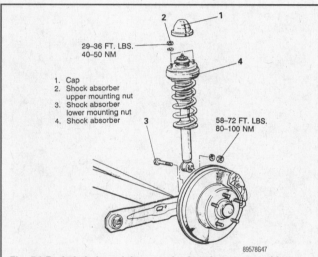

2   1

29–36 FT. LBS.
40–50 NM

1. Cap
2. Shock absorber upper mounting nut
3. Shock absorber lower mounting nut
4. Shock absorber

4

58–72 FT. LBS.
80–100 NM

3

89578G47

Fig. 71 Exploded view of the rear shock and strut assembly— 1990–94 FWD vehicles

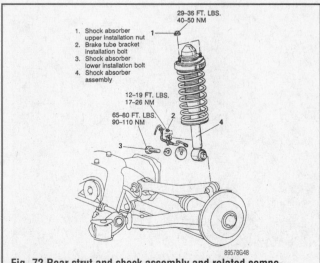

29–36 FT. LBS.
40–50 NM

1. Shock absorber upper installation nut
2. Brake tube bracket installation bolt
3. Shock absorber lower installation bolt
4. Shock absorber assembly

1

12–19 FT. LBS.
17–26 NM

2

65–80 FT. LBS.
90–110 NM

4

3

89578G48

Fig. 72 Rear strut and shock assembly and related components—1990–94 AWD vehicles

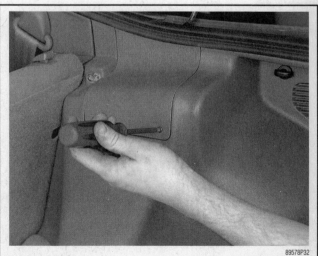

89578P32

Fig. 74 Open the luggage compartment, then unfasten the service lid retaining screws . . .

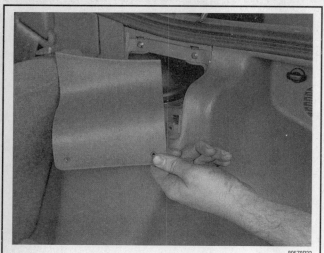

Fig. 75 . . . then remove the cover for access to the upper mounting nuts

Fig. 76 Remove the cap, exposing the upper mounting nuts

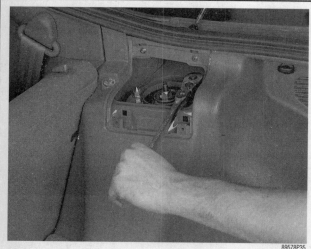

Fig. 77 Unfasten the three outer retaining nuts. Do NOT remove larger center nut

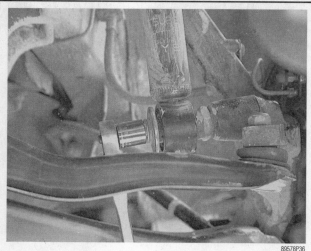

Fig. 78 Once the vehicle is raised, loosen the lower shock-to-knuckle attaching bolt

Fig. 79 Remove the lower mounting bolt and washer . . .

Fig. 80 . . . then carefully remove the shock and spring assembly from the vehicle

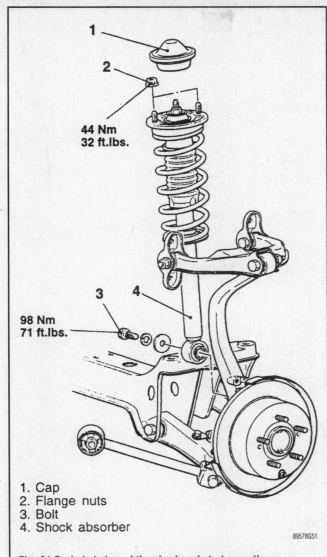

1. Cap
2. Flange nuts
3. Bolt
4. Shock absorber

Fig. 81 Exploded view of the shock and strut mounting—1995–98 vehicles

44 Nm
32 ft.lbs.

98 Nm
71 ft.lbs.

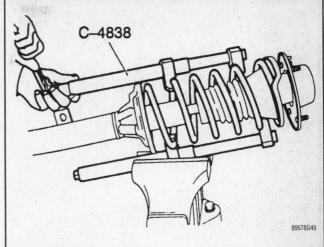

Fig. 82 Compress coil springs before removing piston rod tightening nut

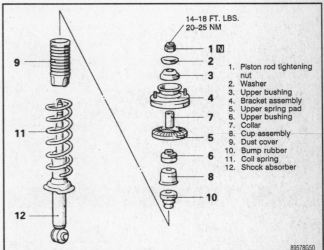

14–18 FT. LBS.
20–25 NM

1. Piston rod tightening nut
2. Washer
3. Upper bushing
4. Bracket assembly
5. Upper spring pad
6. Upper bushing
7. Collar
8. Cup assembly
9. Dust cover
10. Bump rubber
11. Coil spring
12. Shock absorber

Fig. 83 Exploded view of the rear strut disassembly—1990–94 FWD vehicles shown, AWD similar

OVERHAUL

1990–94 Vehicles

▶ **See Figures 82 and 83**

1. Compress the spring on the shock absorber.

➡**Do not use an air tool to tighten the bolt on the spring compressor tool.**

2. Once the spring is compressed, remove the piston rod tightening nut.
3. Remove the upper bushings, washer, bracket, collar and spring pad from the shock taking note of their exact position and orientation.
4. Remove the compressed spring from the shock absorber.
To assemble:
5. Install the compressed spring onto the shock absorber, making sure the edge of the coil spring is aligned against the edge of the shock absorber spring seat.

6. Install the dust cover, cup assembly, spring pad, bracket assembly and washer to the shock piston in their original locations.
7. Align the top bracket assembly with the end of the spring and install a new piston rod tightening nut. While holding the piston rod, tighten the nut to 18 ft. lbs. (25 Nm).
8. Align the spring so the lower edge fits into the indent in the spring seat and the upper edge fits into the spring pad groove, then slowly release the spring compressor tool.
9. Fill the shock cap with grease and install onto the shock absorber assembly.

1995–98 Vehicles

▶ **See Figure 84**

1. Use a suitable coil spring compressor and compress the coil spring. An air tool should not be used to tighten the spring compressor.
2. While holding the piston rod, remove the self-locking nut.
3. Remove the upper bracket assembly and spring pad.

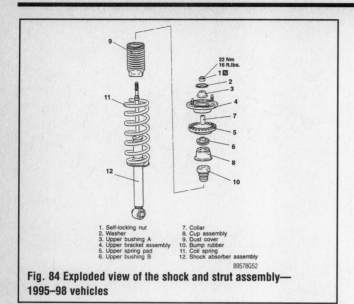

Fig. 84 Exploded view of the shock and strut assembly—1995–98 vehicles

4. Remove the collar, upper bushing, cup assembly, bump rubber and dust cover.

5. Remove the coil spring from the strut.

To install:

6. Align the end of the coil spring with the stepped part of the spring seat and install the compressed coil spring on the strut.

7. Install the dust cover, bump rubber, cup assembly, upper bushing, collar, upper spring pad and bracket assembly on the strut.

8. Install the upper bushing and washer on the piston rod.

9. Install a new self-locking nut on the piston rod. Temporarily tighten the nut.

10. Carefully remove the spring compressor from the spring. Tighten the self-locking nut to 16 ft. lbs. (25 Nm).

Upper Control Arm

REMOVAL & INSTALLATION

1990–94 Vehicles

▶ See Figure 85

1. Disconnect the negative battery cable. Raise and safely support vehicle. Remove the tire and wheel assembly.

2. Support the rear lower control arm. Remove the brake line clamp bolt.

3. Remove the nut and separate the upper ball joint from the rear trailing arm/steering knuckle.

4. Matchmark the eccentric on the upper installation bolt and remove from the control arm.

5. Remove the upper arm from the vehicle.

To install:

6. Install the arm to the vehicle and install the upper arm installation bolt. Align the matchmarks and tighten the nut snugly only.

7. Install the upper arm ball joint to the rear spindle assembly and install new nut. Tighten to 52 ft. lbs. (72 Nm) torque.

8. Install the tire and wheel assembly.

9. Lower the vehicle until the suspension supports its weight. Tighten the upper arm installation bolt to 116 ft. lbs. (160 Nm).

10. Check the rear wheel alignment.

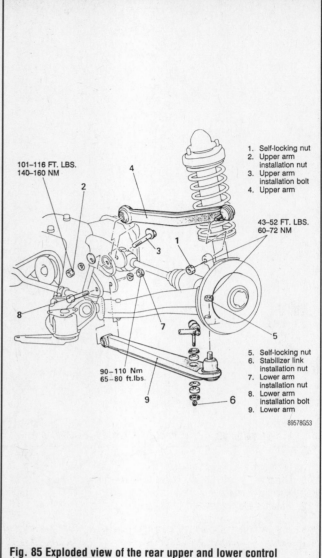

Fig. 85 Exploded view of the rear upper and lower control arms—1990–94 vehicles

1995–98 Vehicles

▶ See Figure 86

1. Raise and safely support the vehicle, then remove the wheel and tire assembly.

2. Remove the through-bolt securing the upper arm to the knuckle.

3. Unfasten the four bolts securing the upper arm to the vehicle.

4. Remove the upper control arm assembly.

5. Remove the through-bolts and nuts and remove the upper arm to body brackets.

To install:

6. Install the upper arm to body brackets to the upper arm. Tighten the bolts and nuts to 41 ft. lbs. (57 Nm).

7. Install the upper arm to the vehicle and tighten the four bolts to 28 ft. lbs. (39 Nm).

8. Install the through-bolt securing the upper arm to the knuckle and secure hand-tight. Do not final tighten the nut until the vehicle is on the floor at normal riding height.

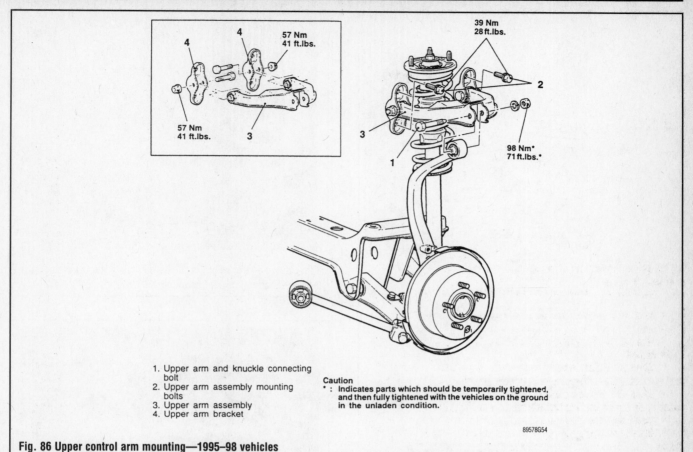

1. Upper arm and knuckle connecting bolt
2. Upper arm assembly mounting bolts
3. Upper arm assembly
4. Upper arm bracket

Caution
* : Indicates parts which should be temporarily tightened, and then fully tightened with the vehicles on the ground in the unladen condition.

89578G54

Fig. 86 Upper control arm mounting—1995–98 vehicles

9. Install the wheel and tire assembly.

10. Carefully lower the vehicle to the floor, then tighten the nut for the through-bolt to 71 ft. lbs. (98 Nm).

11. Have the wheel alignment checked and adjusted if necessary.

Lower Control Arm

REMOVAL & INSTALLATION

1990–94 Vehicles

▶ See Figure 85

1. Disconnect the negative battery cable. Raise and safely support vehicle. Remove the tire and wheel assembly.

2. Remove the stabilizer link installation nut. Remove the spacers, bushings and washers.

3. Loosen the lower arm ball joint nut and separate the ball joint using the appropriate tool. Once the ball joint stud is broken loose, remove the nut and the stud from the lower arm.

4. Unfasten the lower arm installation bolt, then remove the arm from the vehicle.

To install:

5. Install the lower arm onto the vehicle. Install the lower arm installation bolt and tighten snugly only.

6. Install the lower ball joint into the hole in the lower control arm and secure with new nut. Tighten nut to 52 ft. lbs. (72 Nm) torque.

7. Install the stabilizer link spacers, bushings and washers. Secure in place using new nut.

8. Lower the vehicle until the suspension supports its weight. Tighten the lower arm installation bolt to 80 ft. lbs. (110 Nm).

9. Have the rear wheel alignment checked and adjusted if necessary.

1995–98 Vehicles

▶ See Figures 87 thru 92

1. Raise and safely support the vehicle.

2. Remove the wheel and tire assembly.

3. If equipped with a lower arm cover, remove the cover.

4. Disconnect the stabilizer link from the lower arm.

5. If equipped with ABS, remove the wheel speed sensor clamp bolts.

6. Remove the through-bolt securing the lower arm to the knuckle.

7. Remove the through-bolt securing the lower arm to the suspension crossmember.

8. Remove the lower control arm.

9. If necessary, remove the toe control arm from the vehicle as follows:

 a. Use a suitable puller to separate the toe control arm ball joint and steering knuckle connection.

 b. Matchmark the toe control arm and eccentric cam bolt for installation purposes.

 c. Unfasten the toe control arm mounting bolt, then remove the toe control arm from the vehicle.

To install:

10. If removed, install the toe control arm and secure with the retaining bolt, as aligned during removal

11. Install the lower arm to the suspension crossmember and the knuckle but do not tighten the through-bolts until the vehicle is on the floor at normal riding height.

12. Install the ABS wheel speed sensor clamp bolts to the lower arm, if removed.

13. Connect the stabilizer link to the lower arm.

14. Install the lower arm cover if removed.

15. Install the wheel and tire assembly.

16. Carefully lower the vehicle to the floor and tighten the through-bolts to 71 ft. lbs. (98

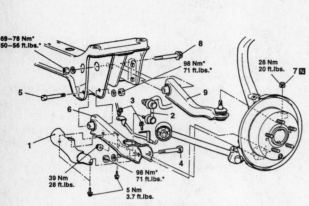

69–78 Nm*
50–56 ft.lbs.*

98 Nm*
71 ft.lbs.*

28 Nm
20 ft.lbs. 7 N

8

9

5

6

3

1

2

4

39 Nm
28 ft.lbs.

98 Nm*
71 ft.lbs.*

5 Nm
3.7 ft.lbs.

Lower arm assembly removal steps

1. Lower arm cover
   <Vehicles with aero parts>
2. Stabilizer link ball joint and lower
   arm connection
3. ABS wheel-speed sensor clamp
   bolts <Vehicles with ABS>
4. Lower arm assembly and knuckle
   connecting bolt
5. Lower arm assembly mounting bolt
6. Lower arm assembly

**Toe control arm assembly removal
steps**

7. Toe control arm ball joint and
   knuckle connection
8. Toe control arm assembly mounting
   bolt
9. Toe control arm assembly

Caution
* : Indicates parts which should be temporarily tightened,
    and then fully tightened with the vehicles on the ground
    in the unladen condition.

89578G56

Fig. 87 Exploded view of the lower control arm and related components—1995–98 vehicles

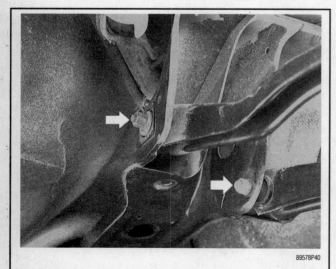

89578P40

Fig. 88 Location of the control arm mounting bolts (see arrows)

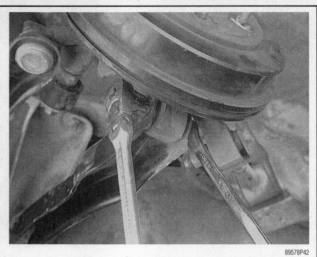

89578P42

Fig. 89 Use a wrench and a ratchet to loosen the lower control arm-to-steering knuckle mounting bolt . . .

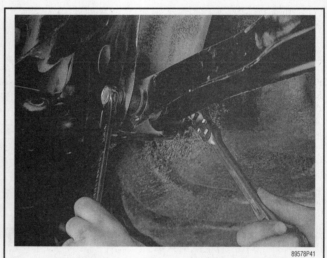

89578P41

Fig. 90 Unfasten the lower control arm-to-crossmember through bolt . . .

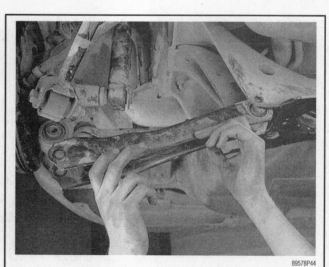

89578P44

Fig. 91 . . . then remove the lower control arm from the vehicle

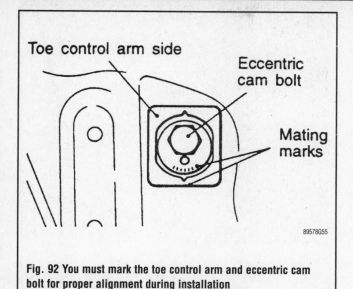

Fig. 92 You must mark the toe control arm and eccentric cam bolt for proper alignment during installation

Trailing Arm

REMOVAL & INSTALLATION

1990–94 Vehicles

♦ **See Figures 93, 94 and 95**

1. Disconnect the negative battery cable. Raise and safely support the vehicle.

2. Disconnect the parking brake cable from the caliper and trailing arm. Remove the rear caliper from the brake disc and suspend with a wire. Remove the brake disc.

3. Remove the bolt(s) holding the speed sensor bracket to the knuckle and remove the assembly from the vehicle.

➡**The speed sensor has a pole piece projecting from it. This exposed tip must be protected from impact or scratches. Do not allow the pole piece to contact the toothed wheel during removal or installation.**

4. Remove the driveshaft to companion flange bolts and nuts and separate the axle from the companion flange.

5. While holding the axle stationary using tool MB990767–01 or equivalent, remove the self-locking nut and remove the axle hub companion flange. Remove the dust shield.

6. Remove the upper arm and lower arm mounting bolts, and using a special splitter tool, separate the ball joints from the arms.

7. Remove the rear shock absorber lower mounting bolt.

8. Remove the trailing arm front mounting nuts and bolts and remove the trailing arm from the vehicle.

9. Remove the connecting rod from the front of the trailing arm using puller tool MB991254 or equivalent.

To install:

10. Assemble the trailing arm and connecting rod. Install the trailing arm to the vehicle and secure in place with the front mounting nuts and bolts. Tighten the nuts snugly at this time. Complete the final tightening of the trailing arm installation bolt when the full weight of the vehicle is on the suspension.

11. Install both control arms to the trailing arm, using new self-locking nuts. Tighten the stud nuts to 52 ft. lbs. (72 Nm).

12. Install the lower shock bolt and tighten to 80 ft. lbs. (110 Nm).

13. On FWD, install the sway bar link. Install the parking brake parts and axle hub unit.

14. On AWD, install the dust shield, axle hub and companion flange with a new self-locking nut. Connect the rear axle to the companion flange.

15. Temporarily install the speed sensor to the knuckle; tighten the bolts only finger-tight.

16. Route the cable correctly and loosely install the clips and retainers. All clips must be in their original position and the sensor cable must not be twisted. Improper installation may cause cable damage and possibly system failure.

➡**The wiring in the harness is easily damaged by twisting and flexing. Use the white stripe on the outer insulation to keep the sensor harness properly placed.**

17. Use a brass or other non-magnetic feeler gauge to check the air gap between the tip of the pole piece and the toothed wheel. Correct gap is 0.012–0.035 inch (0.3–0.9mm). Tighten the 2 sensor bracket bolts to 10 ft. lbs. (14 Nm) with the sensor located so the gap is the same at several points on the toothed wheel. If the gap is incorrect, it is likely that the toothed wheel is worn or improperly installed.

18. Install the brake disc, caliper and connect the parking brake cable, if not already done. Install the mounting clamps bolts.

19. Double check everything for correct routing and installation. Lower the vehicle so its full weight is on the floor.

20. Tighten the front trailing arm/spindle assembly mount nuts to 101–116 ft. lbs. (140–160 Nm).

21. Take your vehicle to a suitable repair shop, then have then perform a rear wheel alignment.

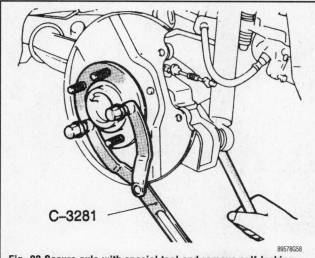

Fig. 93 Secure axle with special tool and remove self-locking nut

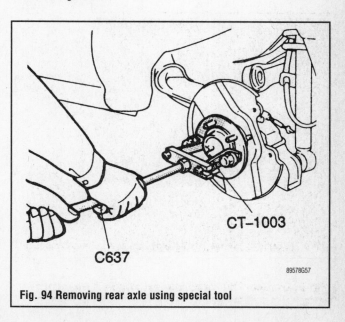

Fig. 94 Removing rear axle using special tool

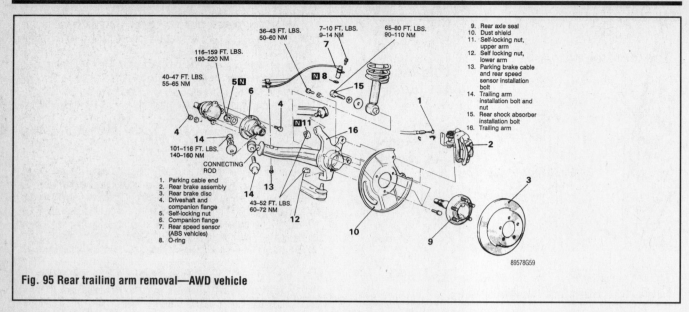

Fig. 95 Rear trailing arm removal—AWD vehicle

1995–98 Vehicles

▶ **See Figures 96, 97, 98, 99 and 100**

1. Disconnect the negative battery cable. Raise and safely support the vehicle.

2. Unfasten the knuckle and trailing arm connecting bolt.

3. Remove the grommet.

4. Remove the trailing arm mounting bolt and the stopper. Remove the trailing arm from the vehicle.

5. Installation is the reverse of the removal procedure.

6. When tightening the retainers, hand-tighten them until the vehicle is safely lowered, then final tighten them to the specifications shown in the accompanying figure.

7. Have the wheel alignment checked and adjusted if necessary.

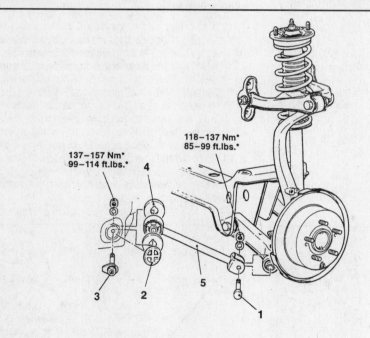

Removal steps

1. Knuckle and trailing arm assembly connecting bolt
2. Grommet
3. Trailing arm assembly mounting bolt
4. Stopper
5. Trailing arm assembly

Caution
* : **Indicates parts which should be temporarily tightened, and then fully tightened with the vehicles on the ground in the unladen condition.**

Fig. 96 Exploded view of the trailing arm and related components—1995–98 vehicles

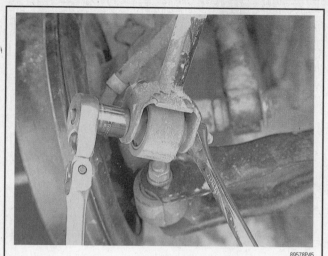

Fig. 97 With a wrench holding the nut, use a ratchet to loosen the knuckle-to-trailing arm connecting bolt

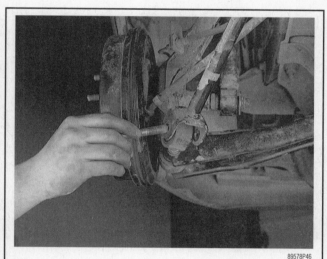

Fig. 98 . . . then remove the through bolt

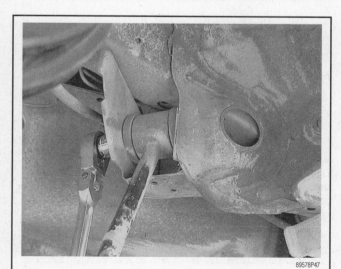

Fig. 99 Unfasten the trailing arm mounting bolt

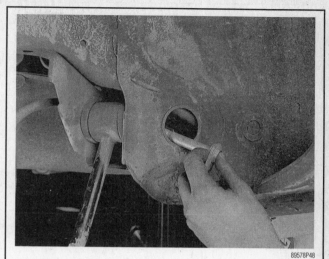

Fig. 100 Pull the bolt out through the access hole in the cross-member

Stabilizer Bar

REMOVAL & INSTALLATION

1990–94 Vehicles

◢ See Figure 101

1. Raise and support the vehicle safely.
2. Place a jack under the rear axle and suspension assembly.
3. Remove the self-locking nuts and crossmember bracket.
4. Remove the retainer bolts and the stabilizer bar brackets. Remove the bushing.
5. Hold the stabilizer bar with a wrench. Remove the self-locking nut.
6. Once the stabilizer bar nut is removed, remove the joint cups and stabilizer rubber bushing.
7. Hold the stabilizer link with a wrench and remove the self-locking nuts. Remove the stabilizer link.
8. Lower the jack supporting the rear axle slightly. Maintain a slight gap between the rear suspension and the body of the vehicle.
9. Remove the stabilizer bar.
10. Inspect the bar for damage, wear and deterioration and replace as required.

To install:

11. Install the stabilizer bar into the vehicle. Raise the rear axle and suspension into place.
12. Install the stabilizer link into the stabilizer bar and install a new self-locking nut. Tighten the nut to 33 ft. lbs. (45 Nm).
13. Install the joint cups and stabilizer rubber to the link. Install a new self-locking nut onto the link. While holding the stabilizer link ball studs with a wrench, tighten the self-locking nut so the protrusion of the stabilizer link is within 0.354–0.433 in. (9–11mm).
14. Install the center stabilizer bar bushings, brackets and bolts. Tighten the bolts to 10 ft. lbs. (14 Nm).
15. Install the parking brake cable and rear speed sensor installation bolt.
16. Install the crossmember bracket and tighten the bolt to 61 ft. lbs. (85 Nm). Tighten the crossmember bracket mounting nut to 94 ft. lbs. (130 Nm).
17. Install the rubber insulators and new self-locking nuts onto the crossmember brackets. Tighten the nuts to 80–94 ft. lbs. (110–130 Nm).
18. Lower the vehicle.

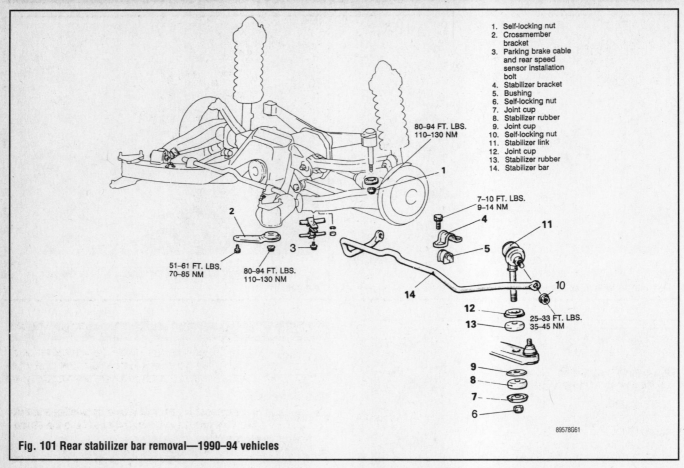

1. Self-locking nut
2. Crossmember bracket
3. Parking brake cable and rear speed sensor installation bolt
4. Stabilizer bracket
5. Bushing
6. Self-locking nut
7. Joint cup
8. Stabilizer rubber
9. Joint cup
10. Self-locking nut
11. Stabilizer link
12. Joint cup
13. Stabilizer rubber
14. Stabilizer bar

80–94 FT. LBS. 110–130 NM

7–10 FT. LBS. 9–14 NM

51–61 FT. LBS. 70–85 NM

80–94 FT. LBS. 110–130 NM

25–33 FT. LBS. 35–45 NM

Fig. 101 Rear stabilizer bar removal—1990–94 vehicles

1995–98 Vehicles

▶ See Figure 102

1. Raise and safely support the vehicle.
2. Remove the rear wheels.
3. If equipped with lower control arm covers, remove them.
4. Remove the stabilizer link mounting nuts and remove the link.
5. Remove the bolts securing the stabilizer bar brackets.
6. Remove the stabilizer bar from the vehicle.

To install:

7. Install the stabilizer bar so the identification mark is on the left and install the bushing and brackets. Tighten the mounting bolts to 7–10 ft. lbs. (9–14 Nm).
8. Install the stabilizer links and torque the nuts to 28 ft. lbs. (39 Nm).
9. Install the lower control arm cover if removed.
10. Install the wheels and lower the vehicle to the floor.

Rear Wheel Hub, Knuckle and Bearing

REMOVAL & INSTALLATION

1990–94 Vehicles

▶ See Figures 103 and 104

1. Raise the vehicle and support safely.
2. Remove the tire and wheel assembly.
3. Remove the bolt(s) holding the speed sensor bracket to the knuckle and remove the assembly from the vehicle.

➡**The speed sensor has a pole piece projecting from it. This exposed tip must be protected from impact or scratches. Do not allow the pole piece to contact the toothed wheel during removal or installation.**

4. Remove the caliper from the brake disc and suspend with a wire. Do not disconnect the brake hose from the caliper.
5. Remove the brake disc.
6. Remove the grease cap, self-locking nut and tongued washer.
7. Remove the rear hub assembly.

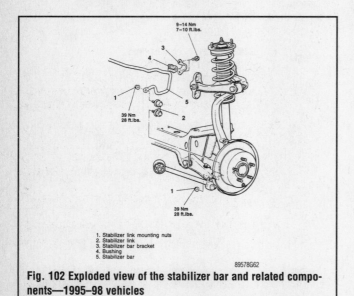

9–14 Nm 7–10 ft.lbs.

39 Nm 28 ft.lbs.

39 Nm 28 ft.lbs.

1. Stabilizer link mounting nuts
2. Stabilizer link
3. Stabilizer bar bracket
4. Bushing
5. Stabilizer bar

Fig. 102 Exploded view of the stabilizer bar and related components—1995–98 vehicles

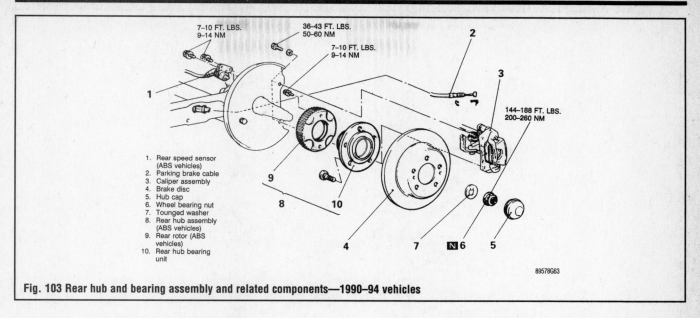

7–10 FT. LBS.
9–14 NM

36–43 FT. LBS.
50–60 NM

7–10 FT. LBS.
9–14 NM

144–188 FT. LBS.
200–260 NM

1. Rear speed sensor (ABS vehicles)
2. Parking brake cable
3. Caliper assembly
4. Brake disc
5. Hub cap
6. Wheel bearing nut
7. Tounged washer
8. Rear hub assembly (ABS vehicles)
9. Rear rotor (ABS vehicles)
10. Rear hub bearing unit

Fig. 103 Rear hub and bearing assembly and related components—1990–94 vehicles

8. If equipped with ABS, remove the retainer bolts and the rear rotor assembly from the back side of the bearing assembly. Replace the rear hub bearing assembly as required.

➡**The rear hub assembly can not be disassembled. If bearing replacement is required, replace the assembly as a unit.**

To install:

9. Install the rear rotor to the back side of the bearing assembly and secure with the retainer bolts. Install the hub assembly.

10. Install the tongued washer and a new self-locking nut. Tighten the nut to 144–188 ft. lbs. (200–260 Nm), align with the indentation in the spindle, and crimp the wall of the nut. This will lock the nut in position.

11. Set up a dial indicator and measure the end-play while moving the hub in and out. If the end-play exceeds 0.004 in. (0.01mm), retighten the nut. If still beyond the limit, replace the hub unit.

12. Install the grease cap and brake components removed during this procedure.

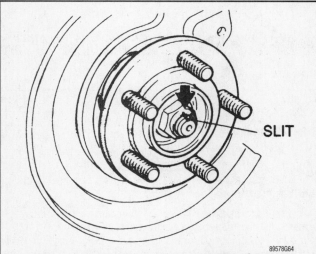

SLIT

Fig. 104 Crimp the wheel bearing nut at the spindle indentation–1990–94 vehicles

13. Temporarily install the speed sensor to the knuckle; tighten the bolts only finger-tight.

14. Route the cable correctly and loosely install the clips and retainers. All clips must be in their original position and the sensor cable must not be twisted. Improper installation may cause cable damage and possibly system failure.

➡**The wiring in the harness is easily damaged by twisting and flexing. Use the white stripe on the outer insulation to keep the sensor harness properly placed.**

15. Use a brass or other non-magnetic feeler gauge to check the air gap between the tip of the pole piece and the toothed wheel. Correct gap is 0.012–0.035 in. (0.3–0.9mm). Tighten the 2 sensor bracket bolts to 10 ft. lbs. (14 Nm) with the sensor located so the gap is the same at several points on the toothed wheel. If the gap is incorrect, it is likely that the toothed wheel is worn or improperly installed.

16. Install the tire and wheel assembly.

17. Prior to moving the vehicle, pump the brakes unit a firm pedal is obtained.

1995–98 Vehicles

▶ **See Figures 105 and 106**

1. Raise and safely support the vehicle.
2. Remove the front wheel and tire assembly.
3. For AWD vehicles, remove the driveshaft.
4. If equipped with ABS, remove the rear wheel speed sensor.
5. If equipped with rear disc brakes, unbolt the caliper and suspend from the body with a suitable piece of wire. Do not disconnect the fluid line. Remove the rotor.
6. If equipped with drum brakes, remove the brake drum.
7. For FWD vehicles, remove the clip mounting bolt.
8. For AWD vehicles, remove the shoe and lining assembly.
9. For vehicles with disc brakes, remove the parking brake shoe and lining assembly.
10. For AWD vehicles, remove the parking brake cable clip, then detach the cable.
11. Remove the retaining bolts, then remove the rear hub and bearing assembly.

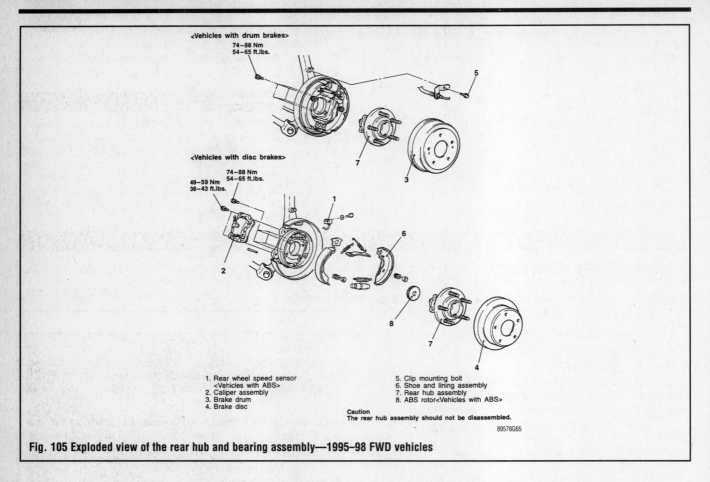

Fig. 105 Exploded view of the rear hub and bearing assembly—1995–98 FWD vehicles

1. Rear wheel speed sensor
   <Vehicles with ABS>
2. Caliper assembly
3. Brake drum
4. Brake disc
5. Clip mounting bolt
6. Shoe and lining assembly
7. Rear hub assembly
8. ABS rotor<Vehicles with ABS>

Caution
The rear hub assembly should not be disassembled.

89578G65

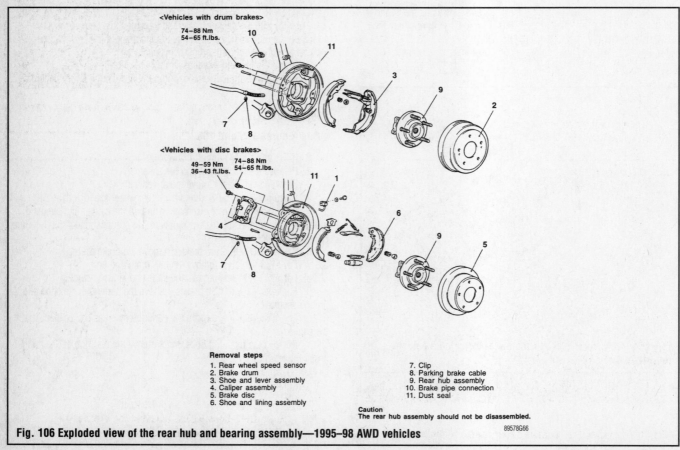

Fig. 106 Exploded view of the rear hub and bearing assembly—1995–98 AWD vehicles

Removal steps
1. Rear wheel speed sensor
2. Brake drum
3. Shoe and lever assembly
4. Caliper assembly
5. Brake disc
6. Shoe and lining assembly
7. Clip
8. Parking brake cable
9. Rear hub assembly
10. Brake pipe connection
11. Dust seal

Caution
The rear hub assembly should not be disassembled.

89578G66

12. For FWD vehicles, if equipped with ABS, use a suitable inner shaft remover to press off the ABS rotor.

To install:

13. If removed, install the ABS rotor.
14. Install the rear hub and bearing and secure with the mounting bolts.
15. For AWD vehicles, attach the parking brake cable, then install the retaining clip.
16. If equipped with disc brakes, install the parking brake shoe and lining assembly.
17. For AWD vehicles, install the shoe and lining assembly.
18. For FWD vehicles, install the clip mounting bolt.
19. If equipped with drum brakes, install the brake drum.
20. If equipped with disc brakes, install the rotor then position the caliper and secure with the retaining bolts.

21. If equipped, install the rear wheel speed sensor.
22. For AWD vehicles, install the driveshaft.
23. Install the front wheel and tire assembly, then carefully lower the vehicle.

Rear End Alignment

On FWD vehicles, camber and toe-in are pre-set at the factory. These settings cannot be adjusted. If not within specifications, replace the bent or damaged components. On AWD vehicles, camber and toe-in can be adjusted. However, proper measurement and adjustment required special tool and equipment. Rear alignment inspection and adjustments should be left to those who have the proper equipment and experience. Refer to the front suspension section for information on alignment angles.

STEERING

Steering Wheel

REMOVAL & INSTALLATION

▶ **See Figures 107 thru 117**

1. Position the wheels in the straight ahead position, then turn the ignition to the **LOCK** position.
2. Disconnect the negative battery cable. If equipped with SRS, wrap the negative cable with insulated tape and wait at least 60 seconds before continuing the procedure, in order to allow the air bag system time to disarm.
3. For 1990–94 vehicles, remove the horn pad from the steering wheel by unfastening the retaining screws from the rear of the pad, then push the pad upward to remove. Detach horn button connector.
4. For 1995—98 vehicles, unfasten the retaining screws, the carefully pull the SRS inflate module away from the steering wheel. Detach the connector(s), then remove the module from the vehicle, then place the module, top side facing up, on a suitable workbench.
5. Remove steering wheel retaining nut.
6. Matchmark the steering wheel to the shaft.
7. Use a steering wheel puller to remove the steering wheel. Do not hammer on steering wheel to remove it. The collapsible column mechanism may be damaged.

To install:

8. Line up the matchmarks and install the steering wheel to the shaft.
9. Tighten the steering wheel attaching nut to 33 ft. lbs. (45 Nm) for 1990–94 vehicles or to 30 ft. lbs. (41 Nm) for 1995–98 vehicles.

10. For 1990–94 vehicles, reconnect the horn connector and install the horn pad, securing it with the retaining screws.
11. For 1995–98 vehicles, attach the connector(s), then install the SRS inflate module and secure with the retainers.

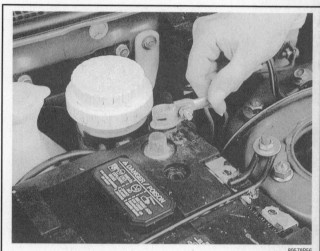

Fig. 108 . . . then remove the negative cable from the terminal and wrap with insulated tape

Fig. 107 Unfasten the negative battery cable retaining nut . . .

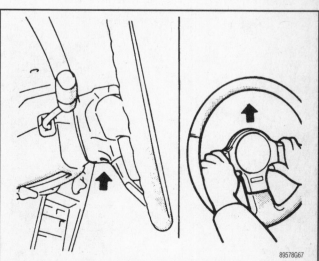

Fig. 109 On 1990–94 vehicles, unfasten the screws, then remove the horn pad by pushing it upward

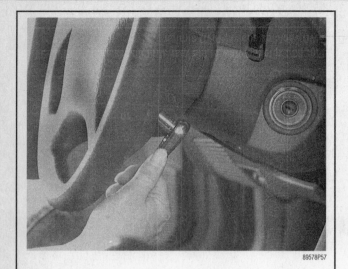

Fig. 110 Unfasten the inflator module retaining screws

Fig. 111 Carefully pull the inflator module away from the steering wheel . . .

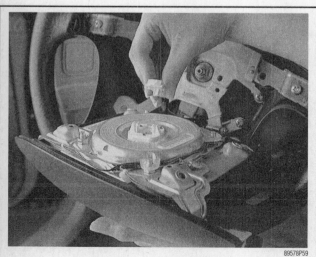

Fig. 112 . . . then detach the connector from the SRS inflator module

Fig. 113 Loosen the retaining nut at the center of the steering wheel . . .

Fig. 114 . . . then remove the steering wheel shaft nut

Fig. 115 Use a pen to matchmark the steering wheel-to-shaft position

12. For FWD vehicles, if equipped with ABS, use a suitable inner shaft remover to press off the ABS rotor.

To install:

13. If removed, install the ABS rotor.

14. Install the rear hub and bearing and secure with the mounting bolts.

15. For AWD vehicles, attach the parking brake cable, then install the retaining clip.

16. If equipped with disc brakes, install the parking brake shoe and lining assembly.

17. For AWD vehicles, install the shoe and lining assembly.

18. For FWD vehicles, install the clip mounting bolt.

19. If equipped with drum brakes, install the brake drum.

20. If equipped with disc brakes, install the rotor then position the caliper and secure with the retaining bolts.

21. If equipped, install the rear wheel speed sensor.

22. For AWD vehicles, install the driveshaft.

23. Install the front wheel and tire assembly, then carefully lower the vehicle.

Rear End Alignment

On FWD vehicles, camber and toe-in are pre-set at the factory. These settings cannot be adjusted. If not within specifications, replace the bent or damaged components. On AWD vehicles, camber and toe-in can be adjusted. However, proper measurement and adjustment required special tool and equipment. Rear alignment inspection and adjustments should be left to those who have the proper equipment and experience. Refer to the front suspension section for information on alignment angles.

STEERING

Steering Wheel

REMOVAL & INSTALLATION

▶ **See Figures 107 thru 117**

1. Position the wheels in the straight ahead position, then turn the ignition to the **LOCK** position.

2. Disconnect the negative battery cable. If equipped with SRS, wrap the negative cable with insulated tape and wait at least 60 seconds before continuing the procedure, in order to allow the air bag system time to disarm.

3. For 1990–94 vehicles, remove the horn pad from the steering wheel by unfastening the retaining screws from the rear of the pad, then push the pad upward to remove. Detach horn button connector.

4. For 1995—98 vehicles, unfasten the retaining screws, the carefully pull the SRS inflate module away from the steering wheel. Detach the connector(s), then remove the module from the vehicle, then place the module, top side facing up, on a suitable workbench.

5. Remove steering wheel retaining nut.

6. Matchmark the steering wheel to the shaft.

7. Use a steering wheel puller to remove the steering wheel. Do not hammer on steering wheel to remove it. The collapsible column mechanism may be damaged.

To install:

8. Line up the matchmarks and install the steering wheel to the shaft.

9. Tighten the steering wheel attaching nut to 33 ft. lbs. (45 Nm) for 1990–94 vehicles or to 30 ft. lbs. (41 Nm) for 1995–98 vehicles.

10. For 1990–94 vehicles, reconnect the horn connector and install the horn pad, securing it with the retaining screws.

11. For 1995–98 vehicles, attach the connector(s), then install the SRS inflate module and secure with the retainers.

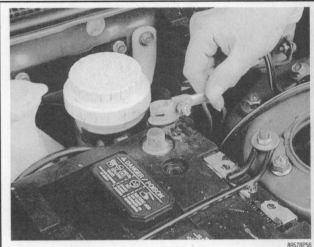

Fig. 108 . . . then remove the negative cable from the terminal and wrap with insulated tape

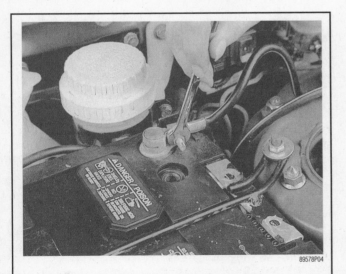

Fig. 107 Unfasten the negative battery cable retaining nut . . .

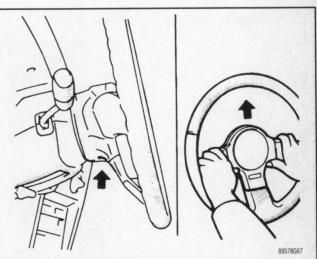

Fig. 109 On 1990–94 vehicles, unfasten the screws, then remove the horn pad by pushing it upward

Fig. 110 Unfasten the inflator module retaining screws

Fig. 111 Carefully pull the inflator module away from the steering wheel . . .

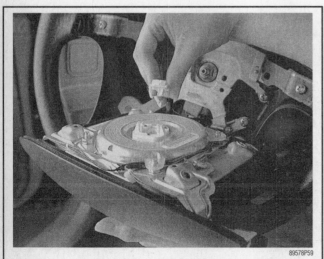

Fig. 112 . . . then detach the connector from the SRS inflator module

Fig. 113 Loosen the retaining nut at the center of the steering wheel . . .

Fig. 114 . . . then remove the steering wheel shaft nut

Fig. 115 Use a pen to matchmark the steering wheel-to-shaft position

Fig. 116 Assemble a suitable puller on the steering wheel, tighten the center screw . . .

Fig. 117 . . . then remove the steering wheel from the shaft

12. If equipped with SRS, remove the tape from the battery cable.

13. Connect the negative battery cable.

14. If equipped with SRS, turn the ignition **ON** and check the SRS warning light for proper operation.

Turn Signal (Combination) Switch

REMOVAL & INSTALLATION

1990–94 Vehicles

▶ See Figure 118

➡ The headlights, turn signals, dimmer switch, windshield/washer and, on some models, the cruise control function are all built into 1 multi-function combination switch that is mounted on the steering column.

1. Disconnect the negative battery cable.

2. Remove the knee protector panel under the steering column, then the upper and lower column cover.

3. Remove the horn pad attaching screw on the under side of the steering wheel and remove the horn pad by pushing the pad upward.

4. Matchmark and remove the steering wheel with a steering wheel puller. Do not hammer on the steering wheel to remove it or the collapsible mechanism may be damaged.

5. Locate the rectangular plugs in the knee protector on either side of the steering column. Pry these plugs out and remove the screws. Remove the screws from the hood lock release lever and position lever aside. Remove the knee protector.

6. Remove the upper and lower column cover.

7. Remove the lap cooler duct.

8. Remove the band retaining the switch wiring.

9. Detach all connectors, remove the wiring clip. Remove the retainers and the column switch assembly.

To install:

10. Install the switch assembly and secure the clip. Make sure no wires are pinched or out of place.

11. Install the lap cooler ducts.

12. Install the column covers and knee protector.

13. Install the steering wheel. Tighten the steering wheel-to-column nut to 33 ft. lbs. (45 Nm).

14. Connect the negative battery cable and check all functions of the combination switch for proper operation.

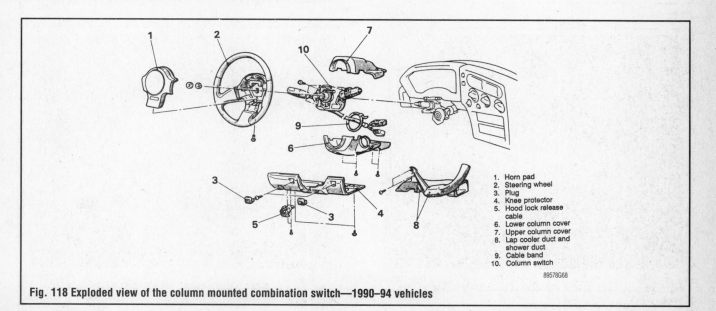

1. Horn pad
2. Steering wheel
3. Plug
4. Knee protector
5. Hood lock release cable
6. Lower column cover
7. Upper column cover
8. Lap cooler duct and shower duct
9. Cable band
10. Column switch

Fig. 118 Exploded view of the column mounted combination switch—1990–94 vehicles

1995–98 Vehicles

♦ **See Figure 119**

1. Position the wheels in the straight ahead position, then turn the ignition to the **LOCK** position.

2. Disconnect the negative battery cable. Wrap the negative cable with insulated tape and wait at least 60 seconds before continuing the procedure, in order to allow the air bag system time to disarm.

3. Remove the steering wheel.

4. Unfasten the retainers, then remove lower column cover.

5. Remove the screw, then remove the column pad.

6. Unfasten the retainers, then remove the upper column cover.

7. Remove the retainers, then remove the clock spring and combination switch assembly.

To install:

8. Install the combination switch assembly and clock spring and secure with the retainers.

9. Install the column covers and pad.

10. Install the steering wheel.

11. Remove the tape from the negative battery cable, then connect the cable.

12. Turn the ignition **ON** and check the SRS warning light for proper operation.

Ignition Lock/Switch

REMOVAL & INSTALLATION

♦ **See Figures 120, 121, 122 and 123**

1. Position the wheels in the straight ahead position, then turn the ignition to the **LOCK** position.

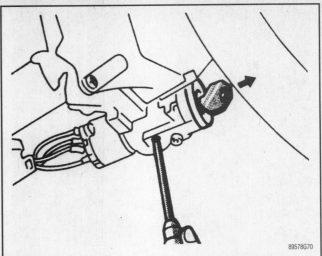

Fig. 120 Use a suitable screwdriver to remove the ignition lock cylinder

2. Disconnect the negative battery cable. If equipped with SRS, wrap the negative cable with insulated tape and wait at least 60 seconds before continuing the procedure, in order to allow the air bag system time to disarm.

3. Remove the steering wheel.

4. Remove the hood lock release lever from the lower panel.

5. Remove the lower instrument panel knee protector.

6. Remove the upper and lower steering column cover.

7. Remove the clip that holds the wiring against the steering column.

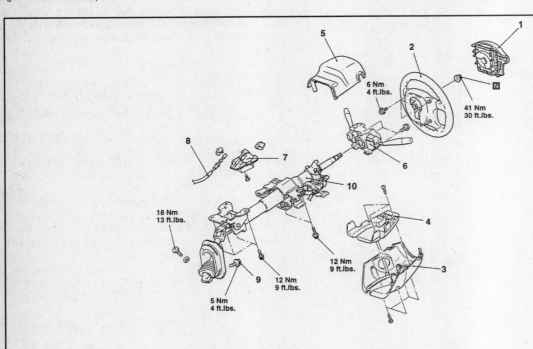

1. Air bag module
2. Steering wheel
3. Lower column cover
4. Column pad
5. Upper column cover
6. Clock spring and column switch assembly
7. Cover <A/T>
8. Key interlock cable <A/T>
9. Retainer attachment bolt
10. Steering column assembly

Fig. 119 Exploded view of the combination switch and related components—1995–98 vehicles

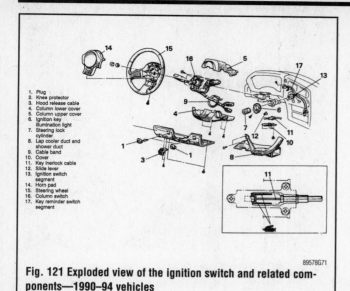

Fig. 121 Exploded view of the ignition switch and related components—1990–94 vehicles

1. Plug
2. Knee protector
3. Hood release cable
4. Column lower cover
5. Column upper cover
6. Ignition key illumination light
7. Steering lock cylinder
8. Lap cooler duct and shower duct
9. Cable band
10. Cover
11. Key inerlock cable
12. Slide lever
13. Ignition switch segment
14. Horn pad
15. Steering wheel
16. Column switch
17. Key reminder switch segment

89578G71

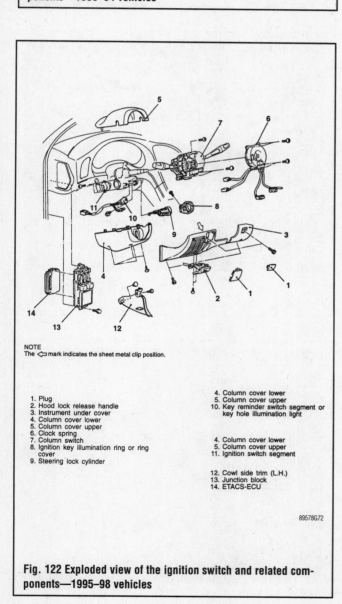

Fig. 122 Exploded view of the ignition switch and related components—1995–98 vehicles

NOTE
The ⟨= mark indicates the sheet metal clip position.

1. Plug
2. Hood lock release handle
3. Instrument under cover
4. Column cover lower
5. Column cover upper
6. Clock spring
7. Column switch
8. Ignition key illumination ring or ring cover
9. Steering lock cylinder

4. Column cover lower
5. Column cover upper
10. Key reminder switch segment or key hole illumination light

4. Column cover lower
5. Column cover upper
11. Ignition switch segment

12. Cowl side trim (L.H.)
13. Junction block
14. ETACS-ECU

89578G72

SLIDE LEVER   STEERING LOCK CYLINDER

KEY INTERLOCK CABLE

APPLY GREASE

89578G73

Fig. 123 Installation of the slide lever to the steering lock cylinder—1990–94 vehicles

8. Remove the key reminder switch, if equipped. Unplug the ignition switch from the steering lock cylinder and remove.

9. Insert the key into the steering lock cylinder and turn to the **ACC** position.

10. With a small cross-tip screwdriver, push the lock pin of the steering lock cylinder inward and then pull the lock cylinder out towards you.

➡ **When equipped with automatic transaxle, the vehicles have safety-lock systems and will have a key interlock cable installed in a slide lever on the side of the key cylinder. Carefully unhook the interlock cable from the lock cylinder while withdrawing cylinder from lock housing.**

To install:

11. With the ignition key removed, install the slide lever to the steering lock cylinder. Connect the interlock cable to the slide lever and the steering lock cylinder. Apply grease to the interlock cable and install cylinder into the lock housing.

12. If equipped with key interlock system, place the gearshift selector in **P** with the engine **OFF**. Check the system operation as follows:

a. Check that the gear select lever can not be moved and the button on the lever can not be pushed under with the ignition key in the **LOCK** or **OFF** position, and the brake pedal not depressed.

b. Turn the ignition key to the **ACC** position. Depress the brake pedal. Press the button on the select lever. Check to be sure that under this conditions, the select lever can be moved from the from the **P** position to any other position. Press the button a few times to be sure that the select lever moves smoothly.

c. Check to be sure that at all other positions of the select lever other than **P**, the ignition key can not be turned to the **OFF** position. Check to be sure the ignition key turns smoothly to the **OFF** position when the selector lever is in the **P** position.

13. If a malfunction is discovered with the shift lock mechanism, adjust or check the key interlock system.

14. Install the ignition switch plug carefully and make sure no wires in the harness are pinched.

15. Install the wiring clip. Align the matchmarks and install the steering wheel to the steering shaft. Install the steering wheel retainer nut and tighten to 33 ft. lbs. (45 Nm).

16. Install the steering column covers.

17. Install the knee protector.

18. Connect the negative battery cable and check the ignition switch and lock for proper operation.

Tie Rod Ends

REMOVAL & INSTALLATION

▶ **See Figures 124 thru 129**

1. Disconnect the battery negative cable. Raise the vehicle and support safely.

2. Wire brush the threads on the tie rod shaft and lubricate with penetrating oil. Loosen the locknut.

3. Remove the cotter pin and nut and press the tie rod end from the steering knuckle.

4. Hold the tie rod shaft with locking pliers and turn the tie rod end off, counting the number of turns for installation.

To install:

5. Install the tie rod end the same number of turns that it took to remove the old one. Tighten the locknut to secure tie rod in place.

6. Install the tie rod stud into the steering knuckle and install nut. Tighten the nut to 25 ft. lbs. (34 Nm) and install new cotter pin.

7. Perform front end alignment.

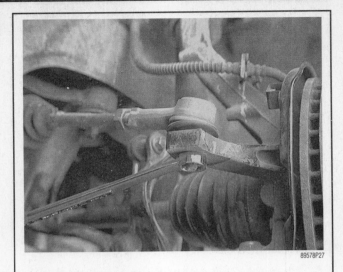

Fig. 126 Unfasten the tie rod end nut . . .

Fig. 124 Matchmark the installed position of the tie rod end

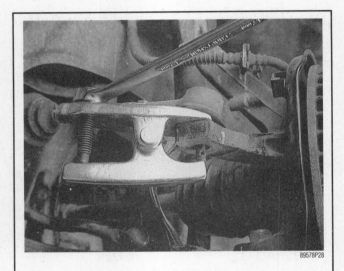

Fig. 127 . . . then install a suitable puller

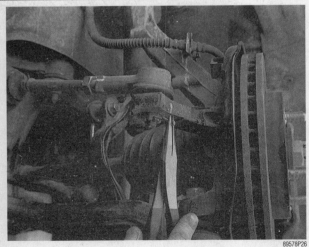

Fig. 125 Use a pair of needle-nose pliers to remove the cotter pin from the tie rod end

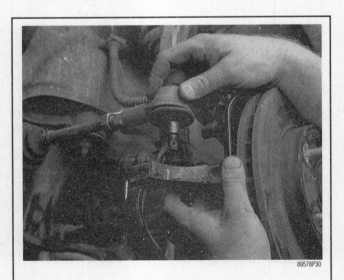

Fig. 128 Separate the tie rod end from the steering knuckle

Fig. 129 Unscrew the tie rod end, counting the number of turns for installation purposes

Manual Steering Gear

REMOVAL & INSTALLATION

♦ See Figure 130

1. Position the wheels in a straight ahead position. Disconnect the negative battery cable. Raise the vehicle and support safely.
2. Remove the bolt holding lower steering column joint to the rack and pinion input shaft.
3. Remove the cotter pins and, using the proper separating tools, disconnect the tie rod ends from the knuckle.
4. Locate the triangular brace near the stabilizer bar brackets on the crossmember and remove both the brace and the stabilizer bar bracket.
5. Place a jack under the center member. Remove the through bolt from the round roll stopper. Remove the rear bolts from the center crossmember.
6. Disconnect the front exhaust pipe and tie out of the way. Lower the center member slightly.
7. Remove the rack and pinion steering assembly and its rubber mounts. Move the rack to the right to remove from the crossmember. While tilting downward, remove the rack assembly from the left side of the vehicle. Use caution to avoid damaging the boots.

To install:

8. Install the rack and mounting bolts, tightening bolts to 43–58 ft. lbs. (60–80 Nm). When installing the rubber rack mounts, align the projection of the mounting rubber with the indentation in the crossmember.
9. Raise the center member using the jack and install the center support rear bolts. Tighten to 72 ft. lbs. (100 Nm).
10. Install the roll stopper bolt and new nut. Tighten nut to 47 ft. lbs. (65 Nm). Remove the jack supporting the center member.
11. Install the joint assembly and gear box connecting bolt and tighten to 14 ft. lbs. (20 Nm).
12. Reposition the exhaust pipe and connect to the manifold.
13. Install the stabilizer bar brackets and brace.
14. Connect the tie rod ends to the steering knuckles. Install the retaining nuts.
15. Perform a front end alignment.

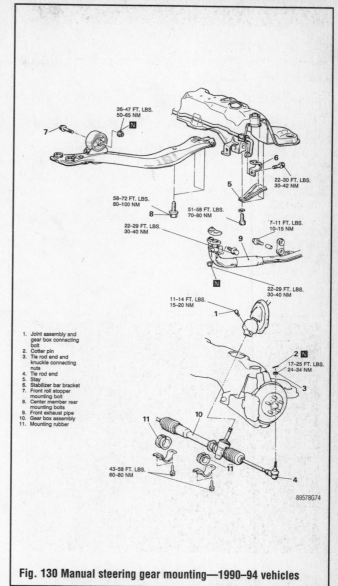

36–47 FT. LBS. 50–65 NM

58–72 FT. LBS. 80–100 NM

51–58 FT. LBS. 70–80 NM

22–30 FT. LBS. 30–42 NM

7–11 FT. LBS. 10–15 NM

22–29 FT. LBS. 30–40 NM

22–29 FT. LBS. 30–40 NM

11–14 FT. LBS. 15–20 NM

17–25 FT. LBS. 24–34 NM

43–58 FT. LBS. 60–80 NM

1. Joint assembly and gear box connecting bolt
2. Cotter pin
3. Tie rod end and knuckle connecting nuts
4. Tie rod end
5. Stay
6. Stabilizer bar bracket
7. Front roll stopper mounting bolt
8. Center member rear mounting bolts
9. Front exhaust pipe
10. Gear box assembly
11. Mounting rubber

Fig. 130 Manual steering gear mounting—1990–94 vehicles

Power Steering Gear

REMOVAL & INSTALLATION

1990–94 Vehicles

♦ See Figure 131

1. Disconnect the negative battery cable. Drain the power steering fluid. Raise the vehicle and support safely.
2. Remove the bolt holding lower steering column joint to the rack and pinion input shaft.
3. Remove the transfer case, if equipped.
4. Remove the cotter pins and using the proper tools, separate the tie rod ends from the steering knuckle.

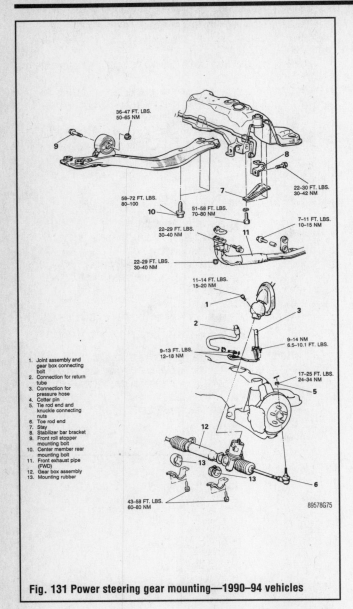

1. Joint assembly and gear box connecting bolt
2. Connection for return tube
3. Connection for pressure hose
4. Cotter pin
5. Tie rod end and knuckle connecting nuts
6. Toe rod end
7. Stay
8. Stabilizer bar bracket
9. Front roll stopper mounting bolt
10. Center member rear mounting bolt
11. Front exhaust pipe (FWD)
12. Gear box assembly
13. Mounting rubber

Fig. 131 Power steering gear mounting—1990–94 vehicles

5. Locate the triangular brace near the stabilizer bar brackets on the crossmember and remove both the brace and the stabilizer bar bracket.

6. Support the center crossmember. Remove the through bolt from the round roll stopper and remove the rear bolts from the center crossmember.

7. Disconnect the front exhaust pipe, if equipped with FWD.

8. Disconnect the power steering fluid pressure pipe and return hose from the rack fittings. Plug the fittings to prevent excess fluid leakage.

9. Lower the crossmember slightly. Remove the rack and pinion steering assembly and its rubber mounts. Move the rack to the right to remove from the crossmember. Tilt the assembly downward and remove from the left side of the vehicle. Use caution to avoid damaging the boots.

To install:

10. Install the rack and install the mounting bolts. Tighten the mounting bolts to 43–58 ft. lbs. (60–80 Nm). When installing the rubber rack mounts, align the projection of the mounting rubber with the indentation in the crossmember.

11. Connect the power steering fluid lines to the rack.

12. Connect the exhaust pipe, if removed.

13. Raise the crossmember into position. Install the center member mounting bolts and tighten to 72 ft. lbs. (100 Nm). Install the roll stopper bolt and new nut. Tighten nut to 47 ft. lbs. (65 Nm).

14. Install the stabilizer bar brackets and brace.

15. Connect the tie rod ends and tighten nuts to 25 ft. lbs. (34 Nm).

16. Install the transfer case, if removed.

17. Refill the reservoir with power steering fluid and bleed the system.

18. Have a repair shop check the front end alignment, and adjust if necessary.

1995–98 Vehicles

▶ **See Figure 132**

1. Disconnect the negative battery cable.

2. Drain the power steering fluid into a suitable container.

3. Raise and safely support the vehicle.

4. Remove the stabilizer bar.

5. For 2.0L non-turbo engines, remove the windshield washer fluid reservoir.

6. For 2.0L turbo and 2.4L engines, perform the following:

   a. Remove the brake fluid reservoir.

   b. Unbolt the A/C compressor and position aside. Do NOT disconnect the refrigerant lines.

7. Remove the joint assembly and gear body connecting bolt.

8. Disconnect the power steering pipe connection.

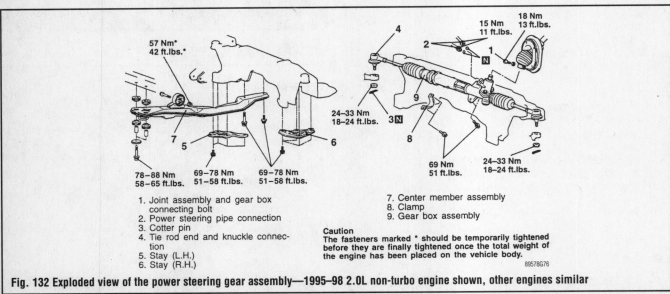

1. Joint assembly and gear box connecting bolt
2. Power steering pipe connection
3. Cotter pin
4. Tie rod end and knuckle connection
5. Stay (L.H.)
6. Stay (R.H.)
7. Center member assembly
8. Clamp
9. Gear box assembly

Caution
The fasteners marked * should be temporarily tightened before they are finally tightened once the total weight of the engine has been placed on the vehicle body.

Fig. 132 Exploded view of the power steering gear assembly—1995–98 2.0L non-turbo engine shown, other engines similar

9. Use a suitable puller to separate the tie rod end and knuckle connection.

10. Unfasten the retaining bolts, then remove the left and right side stays.

11. Remove the retainers, then remove the center member assembly.

12. Unfasten the retaining clamp, then remove the power steering gear assembly.

13. Installation is the reverse of the removal procedure.

14. Refill the reservoir with power steering fluid and bleed the system.

15. Have a repair shop check the front end alignment, and adjust if necessary.

Power Steering Pump

REMOVAL & INSTALLATION

1990–94 Vehicles

▶ See Figure 133

1. Disconnect the battery negative cable.

2. Remove the pressure switch connector from the side of the pump.

3. If the alternator is located under the oil pump, cover it with a shop towel to protect it from oil.

4. Disconnect the return fluid line. Remove the reservoir cap and allow the return line to drain the fluid from the reservoir. If the fluid is contaminated, disconnect the ignition high tension cable and crank the engine several times to drain the fluid from the gearbox.

5. Disconnect the pressure line.

6. Remove the pump drive belt and unbolt the pump from its bracket.

To install:

7. Install the pump, wrap the belt around the pulley and tighten the mounting bolts.

8. Replace the O-rings and connect the pressure line. Connect the pressure line so the notch in the fitting aligns and contacts the pump's guide bracket.

9. Connect the return line. Connect the pressure switch connector.

10. Adjust the belt tension and tighten the adjusting bolts.

11. Refill the reservoir and bleed the system.

1995–98 Vehicles

▶ See Figures 134 and 135

1. Disconnect the battery negative cable.

2. Drain the power steering fluid into a suitable container.

3. Remove the power steering drive belt.

4. Cover the A/C compressor or alternator, as applicable, with a shop towel, then disconnect the suction and pressure hoses from the power steering pump. Remove the gaskets.

5. Detach the pressure switch connector.

6. Unfasten the retaining bolts, then remove the pump assembly.

7. If necessary, remove the retainers, then remove the pump bracket.

8. Installation is the reverse of the removal procedure.

9. For vehicles with A/C, when installing the power steering pump, install it to the bracket so that it faces toward the front of the vehicle. Then use the A/C pulley to adjust the belt tension.

10. Refill the reservoir and bleed the system.

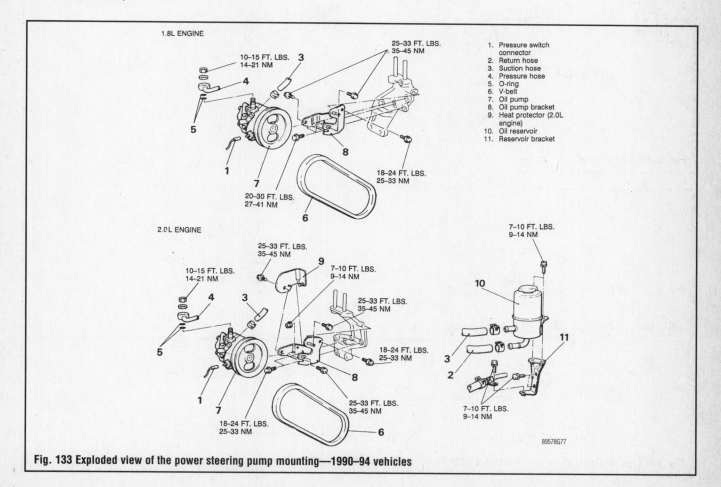

1. Pressure switch connector
2. Return hose
3. Suction hose
4. Pressure hose
5. O-ring
6. V-belt
7. Oil pump
8. Oil pump bracket
9. Heat protector (2.0L engine)
10. Oil reservoir
11. Reservoir bracket

Fig. 133 Exploded view of the power steering pump mounting—1990–94 vehicles

89578G77

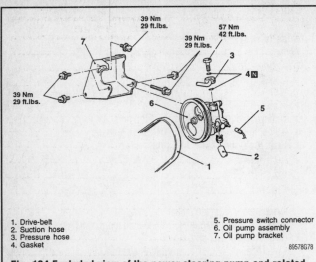

1. Drive-belt
2. Suction hose
3. Pressure hose
4. Gasket

5. Pressure switch connector
6. Oil pump assembly
7. Oil pump bracket

89578G78

Fig. 134 Exploded view of the power steering pump and related components—1995–98 2.0L non-turbo engines

BLEEDING

1. Raise the vehicle and support safely.
2. Manually turn the oil pump pulley a few times.
3. Turn the steering wheel all the way to the left and to the right 5 or 6 times.
4. Disconnect the ignition high tension cable and, while operating the starter motor intermittently, turn the steering wheel all the way to the left and right 5–6 times for 15–20 seconds. During bleeding, make sure the fluid in the reservoir never falls below the lower position of the filter. If bleeding is attempted with the engine running, the air will be absorbed in the fluid. Bleed only while cranking.
5. Connect ignition high tension cable, start engine and allow to idle.
6. Turn the steering wheel left and right until there are no air bubbles in the reservoir. Confirm that the fluid is not milky and the level is up to the specified position on the gauge. Confirm that there is very little change in the fluid level when the steering wheel is turned. If the fluid level changes more than 0.2 in., the air has not been completely bled. Repeat the process.

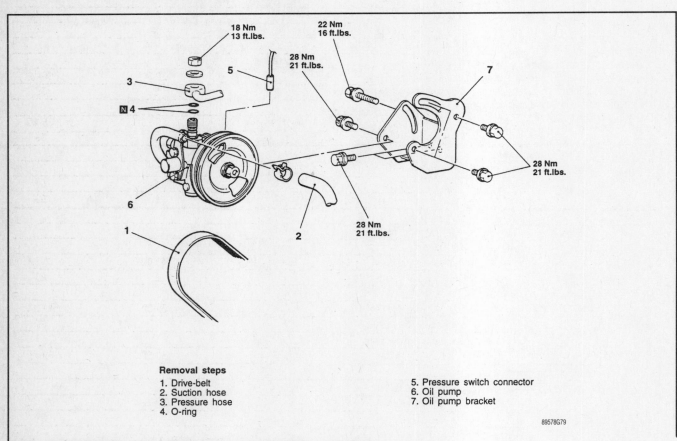

Removal steps
1. Drive-belt
2. Suction hose
3. Pressure hose
4. O-ring

5. Pressure switch connector
6. Oil pump
7. Oil pump bracket

89578G79

Fig. 135 Power steering pump mounting—1995–98 2.0L turbo and 2.4L engines

TORQUE SPECIFICATIONS

Component	ft. lbs.	inch lbs.	Nm
Front Suspension			
Lower control arm			
1990-94 vehicles	72-87		100-120
1995-98 vehicles			
Compression lower arm nuts	60		81
Lateral lower arm nuts			
Front	65		88
Rear	72-87		98-118
Ball joint-to-control arm nuts and bolts (lower)	43-52		59-72
MacPherson strut			
Damper fork lower mounting bolt			
1995-98 vehicles	65		88
Strut-to-damper fork bolts			
1995-98 vehicles	65-87		88-116
Strut-to-knuckle bolts			
1990-94 vehicles	80-101		110-140
Upper strut-to-body nuts			
1990-94 vehicles	29-36		40-50
1995-98 vehicles	32		44
Stabilizer bar			
Stabilizer bar retainers			
1990-94 vehicles	22-30		30-42
1995-98 vehicles	28		39
Stabilizer link retainers			
1990-94 vehicles	25-33		35-45
1995-98 vehicles	28		39
Upper Control Arm			
Ball joint-to-control arm nut	20		28
Mounting nuts	41		57
Upper self-locking nut (in engine compartment)	62		86
Rear Suspension			
Lower control arm			
Ball joint-to-control arm nut			
1990-94 vehicles	43-52		60-72
1995-98 vehicles	20		28
Mounting bolt/nut			
1990-94 vehicles	65-80		90-110
1995-98 vehicles	71		98
Toe control arm mounting bolt/nut			
1995-98 vehicles	50-56		69-78
Shock absorbers			
Lower shock mounting nut/bolt			
1990-94 vehicles	58-72		80-100
1995-98 vehicles	71		98
Upper shock-to-body nuts			
1990-94 vehicles	29-36		40-50
1995-98 vehicles	32		44

89578C01

TORQUE SPECIFICATIONS

Component	ft. lbs.	inch lbs.	Nm
Stabilizer bar			
Bar mounting bolts/nuts			
1990-94 vehicles	7-10		9-14
1995-98 vehicles	7-10		9-14
Link mounting bolts/nuts			
1990-94 vehicles	25-33		35-45
1995-98 vehicles	28		39
Trailing Arm			
Mounting bolts/nuts			
1990-94 vehicles	43-52		60-72
1995-98 vehicles			
Front	85-99		118-137
Rear	99-114		137-157
Upper Control Arm			
Mounting nuts/bolts			
1990-94 vehicles	101-116		140-160
1995-98 vehicles	28		39
Self-locking nuts/bolts			
1990-94 vehicles	43-52		60-72
Upper arm-to-knuckle bolt/nut			
1995-98 vehicles	71		98
Steering			
Outer tie rod end			
Ball joint-to-knuckle nut			
1990-94 vehicles	17-25		24-34
1995-98 vehicles	18-24		24-33
Tie rod end locking nut	36-40		50-55
SRS driver's side inflator module screws			
1995-98 vehicles	4		6
Steering gear mounting nuts/bolts			
1990-94 vehicles	43-58		60-80
1995-98 vehicles	51		69
Steering wheel retaining nut			
1990-94 vehicles	25-33		35-45
1995-98 vehicles	30		41

89578C02

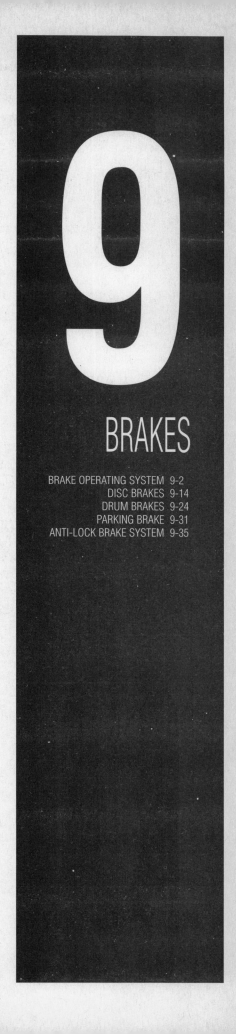

9

BRAKES

BRAKE OPERATING SYSTEM

Basic Operating Principles

Hydraulic systems are used to actuate the brakes of all modern automobiles. The system transports the

power required to force the frictional surfaces of the braking system together from the pedal to the individual brake units at each wheel. A hydraulic system is used for two reasons.

First, fluid under pressure can be carried to all parts of an automobile by small pipes and flexible hoses without taking up a significant amount of room or posing routing problems.

Second, a great mechanical advantage can be given to the brake pedal end of the system, and the foot pressure required to actuate the brakes can be reduced by making the surface area of the master cylinder pistons smaller than that of any of the pistons in the wheel cylinders or calipers.

The master cylinder consists of a fluid reservoir along with a double cylinder and piston assembly. Double type master cylinders are designed to separate the front and rear braking systems hydraulically in case of a leak. The master cylinder coverts mechanical motion from the pedal into hydraulic pressure within the lines. This pressure is translated back into mechanical motion at the wheels by either the wheel cylinder (drum brakes) or the caliper (disc brakes).

Steel lines carry the brake fluid to a point on the vehicle's frame near each of the vehicle's wheels. The fluid is then carried to the calipers and wheel cylinders by flexible tubes in order to allow for suspension and steering movements.

In drum brake systems, each wheel cylinder contains two pistons, one at either end, which push outward in opposite directions and force the brake shoe into contact with the drum.

In disc brake systems, the cylinders are part of the calipers. At least one cylinder in each caliper is used to force the brake pads against the disc.

All pistons employ some type of seal, usually made of rubber, to minimize fluid leakage. A rubber dust boot seals the outer end of the cylinder against dust and dirt. The boot fits around the outer end of the piston on disc brake calipers, and around the brake actuating rod on wheel cylinders.

The hydraulic system operates as follows: When at rest, the entire system, from the piston(s) in the master cylinder to those in the wheel cylinders or calipers, is full of brake fluid. Upon application of the brake pedal, fluid trapped in front of the master cylinder piston(s) is forced through the lines to the wheel cylinders. Here, it forces the pistons outward, in the case of drum brakes, and inward toward the disc, in the case of disc brakes. The motion of the pistons is opposed by return springs mounted outside the cylinders in drum brakes, and by spring seals, in disc brakes.

Upon release of the brake pedal, a spring located inside the master cylinder immediately returns the master cylinder pistons to the normal position. The pistons contain check valves and the master cylinder has compensating ports drilled in it. These are uncovered as the pistons reach their normal position. The piston check valves allow fluid to flow toward the wheel cylinders or calipers as the pistons withdraw. Then, as the return springs force the brake pads or shoes into the released position, the excess fluid reservoir through the compensating ports. It is during the time the pedal is in the released position that any fluid that has leaked out of the system will be replaced through the compensating ports.

Dual circuit master cylinders employ two pistons, located one behind the other, in the same cylinder. The primary piston is actuated directly by mechanical linkage from the brake pedal through the power booster. The secondary piston is actuated by fluid trapped between the two pistons. If a leak develops in front of the secondary piston, it moves forward until it bottoms against the front of the master cylinder, and the fluid trapped between the pistons will operate the rear brakes. If the rear brakes develop a leak, the primary piston will move forward until direct contact with the secondary piston takes place, and it will force the secondary piston to actuate the front brakes. In either case, the brake pedal moves farther when the brakes are applied, and less braking power is available.

All dual circuit systems use a switch to warn the driver when only half of the brake system is operational. This switch is usually located in a valve body which is mounted on the firewall or the frame below the master cylinder. A hydraulic piston receives pressure from both circuits, each circuit's pressure being applied to one end of the piston. When the pressures are in balance, the piston remains stationary. When one circuit has a leak, however, the greater pressure in that circuit during application of the brakes will push the piston to one side, closing the switch and activating the brake warning light.

In disc brake systems, this valve body also contains a metering valve and, in some cases, a proportioning valve. The metering valve keeps pressure from traveling to the disc brakes on the front wheels until the brake shoes on the rear wheels have contacted the drums, ensuring that the front brakes will never be used alone. The proportioning valve controls the pressure to the rear brakes to lessen the chance of rear wheel lock-up during very hard braking.

Warning lights may be tested by depressing the brake pedal and holding it while opening one of the wheel cylinder bleeder screws. If this does not cause the light to go on, substitute a new lamp, make continuity checks, and, finally, replace the switch as necessary.

The hydraulic system may be checked for leaks by applying pressure to the pedal gradually and steadily. If the pedal sinks very slowly to the floor, the system has a leak. This is not to be confused with a springy or spongy feel due to the compression of air within the lines. If the system leaks, there will be a gradual change in the position of the pedal with a constant pressure.

Check for leaks along all lines and at wheel cylinders. If no external leaks are apparent, the problem is inside the master cylinder.

DISC BRAKES

Instead of the traditional expanding brakes that press outward against a circular drum, disc brake systems utilize a disc (rotor) with brake pads positioned on either side of it. An easily-seen analogy is the hand brake arrangement on a bicycle. The pads squeeze onto the rim of the bike wheel, slowing its motion. Automobile disc brakes use the identical principle but apply the braking effort to a separate disc instead of the wheel.

The disc (rotor) is a casting, usually equipped with cooling fins between the two braking surfaces. This enables air to circulate between the braking surfaces making them less sensitive to heat buildup and more resistant to fade. Dirt and water do not drastically affect braking action since contaminants are thrown off by the centrifugal action of the rotor or scraped off the by the pads. Also, the equal clamping action of the two brake pads tends to ensure uniform, straight line stops. Disc brakes are inherently self-adjusting. There are three general types of disc brake:

1. A fixed caliper.
2. A floating caliper.
3. A sliding caliper.

The fixed caliper design uses two pistons mounted on either side of the rotor (in each side of the caliper). The caliper is mounted rigidly and does not move.

The sliding and floating designs are quite similar. In fact, these two types are often lumped together. In both designs, the pad on the inside of the rotor is moved into contact with the rotor by hydraulic force. The caliper, which is not held in a fixed position, moves slightly, bringing the outside pad into contact with the rotor. There are various methods of attaching floating calipers. Some pivot at the bottom or top, and some slide on mounting bolts. In any event, the end result is the same.

DRUM BRAKES

Drum brakes employ two brake shoes mounted on a stationary backing plate. These shoes are positioned inside a circular drum which rotates with the wheel assembly. The shoes are held in place by springs. This allows them to slide toward the drums (when they are applied) while keeping the linings and drums in alignment. The shoes are actuated by a wheel cylinder which is mounted at the top of the backing plate. When the brakes are applied, hydraulic pressure forces the wheel cylinder's actuating links outward. Since these links bear directly against the top of the brake shoes, the tops of the shoes are then forced against the inner side of the drum. This action forces the bottoms of the two shoes to contact the brake drum by rotating the entire assembly slightly (known as servo action). When pressure within the wheel cylinder is relaxed, return springs pull the shoes back away from the drum.

Most modern drum brakes are designed to self-adjust themselves during application when the vehicle is moving in reverse. This motion causes both shoes to rotate very slightly with the drum, rocking an adjusting lever, thereby causing rotation of the adjusting screw. Some drum brake systems are designed to self-adjust during application whenever the brakes are applied. This on-board adjustment system reduces the need for maintenance adjustments and keeps both the brake function and pedal feel satisfactory.

Brake Light Switch

REMOVAL & INSTALLATION

▶ See Figure 1

1. Disconnect the negative battery cable.
2. Detach the stop lamp switch electrical harness connector.
3. Loosen the locknut holding the switch to the bracket. Remove the locknut and the switch.

To install:

4. Install the new switch and install the locknut, tightening it just snug.
5. Reposition the brake light switch so that the distance between the outer case of the switch and the pedal is 0.02–0.04 in. (0.5–1.0mm). Note that the switch plunger must press against the pedal to keep the brake lights off. As the pedal moves away from the switch, the plunger extends and closes the switch, which turns on the stop lights.
6. Hold the switch in the correct position and tighten the locknut.
7. Connect the wiring to the switch.
8. Check the operation of the switch. Turn the ignition key to the **ON** position but do not start the engine. Have an assistant observe the brake lights at the rear of the vehicle while you push on the brake pedal. The lights should come on just as the brake pedal passes the point of free play.
9. Adjust the brake light switch as necessary. The small amount of free play in the pedal should not trigger the brake lights; if the switch is set incorrectly, the brake lights will flicker due to pedal vibration on road bumps.

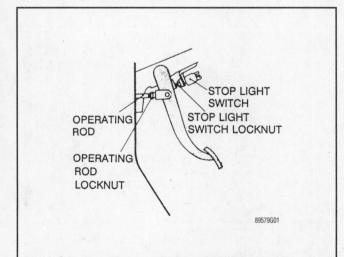

Fig. 1 The brake light switch is retained to the bracket with a locknut

Master Cylinder

REMOVAL & INSTALLATION

1990–94 Vehicles

▶ See Figure 2

1. Disconnect the negative battery cable.
2. Remove the master cylinder reservoir cap, then use a clean turkey baster or equivalent to siphon out as much fluid as possible and place in a suitable container. Install the cap.
3. If equipped, detach the fluid level sensor connector.
4. Disconnect the brake lines from the master cylinder. A separate fluid reservoir is used. Plug the lines to prevent drainage.
5. Unfasten the 2 nuts securing the master cylinder to the brake booster, then remove the master cylinder.

To install:

6. Install master cylinder to the mounting studs and install the retaining nuts. Tighten the mounting nuts to 9 ft. lbs. (12 Nm).
7. Unplug and install the brake lines to the master cylinder.
8. Fill the reservoir to the proper level with clean DOT 3 brake fluid. Bleed the master cylinder.
9. If equipped, attach the fluid level sensor.
10. Apply the brake pedal and check for firmness. If the pedal is spongy, air is present in the system. If air remains in the system, bleeding the entire system is required.
11. Adjust the brake pedal, as outlined later in this section.
12. Check the brakes for proper operation and leaks.

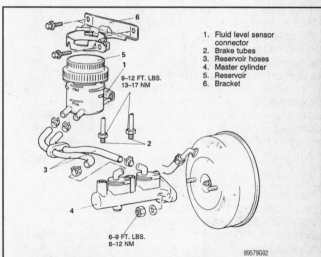

1. Fluid level sensor connector
2. Brake tubes
3. Reservoir hoses
4. Master cylinder
5. Reservoir
6. Bracket

Fig. 2 Exploded view of the master cylinder-to-power booster mounting

1995–98 Vehicles

▶ See Figures 3 thru 13

1. Disconnect the negative battery cable.
2. Remove the master cylinder reservoir cap, then use a clean turkey baster or equivalent to siphon out as much fluid as possible and place in a suitable container. Install the cap.
3. Disconnect and plug the lines from the brake master cylinder reservoir.
4. Detach the fluid level sensor connector, unfasten the retainers, then remove the master cylinder reservoir.
5. For vehicles equipped with manual transaxle, remove the clutch master cylinder reservoir bracket.

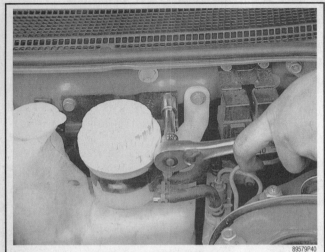

Fig. 3 Unfasten the master cylinder reservoir mounting bracket bolts

Fig. 4 Unfasten the brake hose retaining clamps and disconnect the hose from the master cylinder

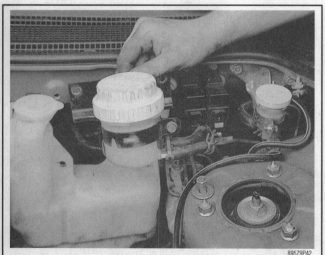

Fig. 5 Detach the fluid level sensor connector, then remove the master cylinder reservoir

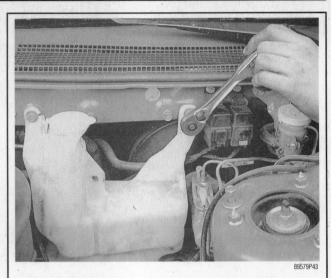

Fig. 6 Unfasten the washer fluid reservoir tank mounting bolts. . .

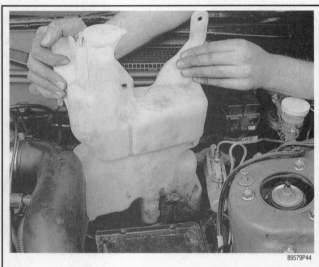

Fig. 7 . . . then remove the tank and position it out of the way

Fig. 8 Use a flare nut wrench to disconnect and plug the brake lines from the master cylinder

Fig. 9 Unfasten the master cylinder-to-power booster retaining nuts . . .

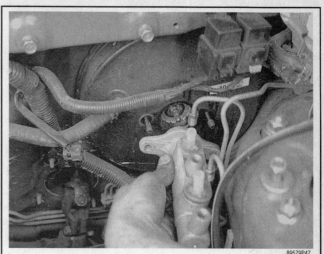

Fig. 10 . . . then remove the master cylinder assembly from the vehicle

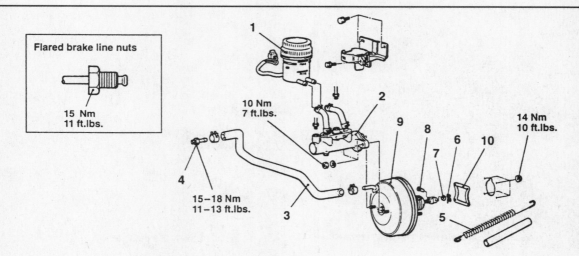

Flared brake line nuts

15 Nm
11 ft.lbs.

10 Nm
7 ft.lbs.

14 Nm
10 ft.lbs.

15–18 Nm
11–13 ft.lbs.

Master cylinder removal steps

1. Reservoir
2. Master cylinder
● Adjustment of clearance between brake booster push rod and primary piston

Caution
The check valve should not be removed from the vacuum hose. If the check valve is defective, replace it together with the vacuum hose.

Brake booster removal steps

2. Master cylinder
● Adjustment of clearance between brake booster push rod and primary piston
3. Vacuum hose (With built-in check valve)
4. Fitting
5. Brake pedal return spring
6. Snap pin
7. Washer
8. Clevis pin
9. Brake booster
10. Sealer

Fig. 11 Exploded view of the master cylinder and power brake booster—1995–98 vehicles

6. For 2.0L non-turbo engines, perform the following:
a. Disconnect the positive battery cable, then remove the battery.
b. Remove the relay mounting bolts.
c. Remove the washer tank mounting bolts and move the tank aside.
7. For 2.0L turbo and 2.4L engines, perform the following:
a. Remove the centermember mounting bolts.
b. Remove the engine mount bracket.

c. Unfasten the A/C compressor mounting bolts and position the compressor aside, but do NOT disconnect the refrigerant lines.
d. Remove the A/C high pressure hose clamp, but do NOT disconnect the line.
e. Disconnect the power steering pressure hose, pipe and return pipe clamp mounting bolts. Do NOT disconnect the fluid lines.
8. Disconnect and plug the brake lines from the master cylinder.
9. Unfasten the master cylinder-to-power booster retaining nuts, then remove the master cylinder from the vehicle.

To install:

10. Adjust the clearance (A) between the brake booster pushrod and the primary piston as follows:

a. Calculate the clearance A from the B, C and D measurements, as shown in the accompanying figure.

A equals B minus C minus D.

b. The clearance should be 0.256–0.335 in. (0.65–0.858mm). When brake booster negative pressure 9.7 psi (67 kPa) is applied, then clearance value will become 0.004–0.012 in. (0.1–0.3mm).

11. Install the master cylinder to the brake booster, then install the retaining nuts. Tighten the nuts to 7 ft. lbs. (10 Nm).

12. Install the master cylinder reservoir, securing the retainers.

13. Attach the fluid level sensor connector, then unplug and connect the fluid lines to the reservoir.

14. The remainder of installation is the reverse of the removal procedure. Fill the reservoir with the proper type and amount of DOT 3 brake fluid from a fresh, sealed container.

15. Bleed the brake system, as outlined later in this section.

16. Adjust the brake pedal, as outlined later in this section.

BRAKE PEDAL ADJUSTMENTS

Brake Pedal Height

▶ See Figures 14, 15 and 16

Measure the brake pedal height from the floor of the vehicle to the upper surface of the brake pedal. The distance should be 6.9–7.1 in (176–181mm). If the brake pedal height is incorrect, adjust as follows:

1. Disconnect the stop lamp switch connector.

2. Loosen the locknut on the base of the stop light switch and move the switch to a position where it does not contact the brake pedal.

3. Loosen the operating rod locknut. Adjust the height of the brake pedal by turning the operating rod using pliers. Once the desired pedal height is obtained, tighten the locknut on the operating rod.

4. Screw the stop light switch until the it contacts the brake pedal stopper. Turn switch in until the brake pedal just starts to move. At this point, return (loosen) the stoplight switch ½–1 turn and secure in this position by tightening the locknut. In this position, the distance between the lower stop light switch case and the brake pedal stop should be 0.02–0.04 in. (0.5–1.0mm).

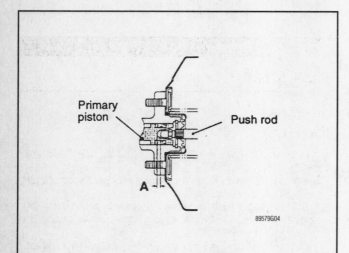

Fig. 12 The brake booster pushrod and primary piston clearance (A) must be adjusted

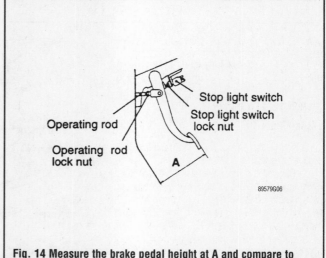

Fig. 14 Measure the brake pedal height at A and compare to specifications

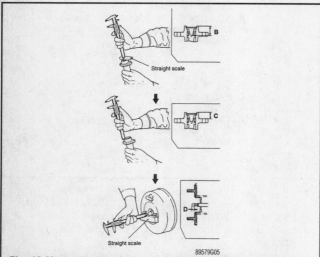

Fig. 13 Measuring the clearance of the pushrod-to-primary piston

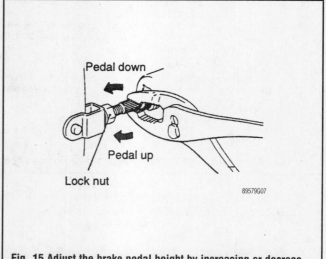

Fig. 15 Adjust the brake pedal height by increasing or decreasing the length of the operating rod

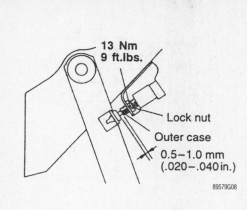

Fig. 16 Inspect the clearance between the stop light switch and the brake pedal stop and compare to specifications

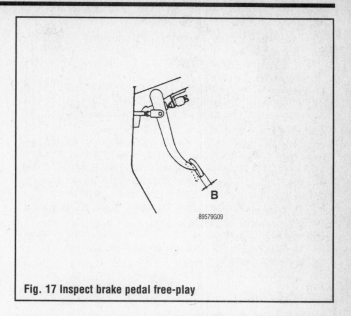

Fig. 17 Inspect brake pedal free-play

5. Connect the electrical connector to the stop light switch.

6. Check to be sure that the stop lights are not illuminated with no pressure on the brake pedal.

7. Without starting the vehicle, depress the brake pedal. If the brake light switch is properly connected, the brake lights will illuminate.

Brake Pedal Free-Play

♦ See Figure 17

1. With the engine off, depress the brake pedal fully several times to evacuate the vacuum in the booster.

2. Once all the vacuum assist has been eliminated, press the brake pedal down by hand and confirm that the amount of movement before resistance is felt is within 0.1–0.3 in. (3–8mm).

3. If the free-play is less than desired, confirm that the brake light switch is in proper adjustment.

4. If there is excessive free-play, look for wear or play in the clevis pin and brake pedal arm. Replace worn parts as required and recheck brake pedal free-play.

Power Brake Booster

REMOVAL & INSTALLATION

1990–94 Vehicles

♦ See Figure 18

1. Disconnect the negative battery cable. Siphon the brake fluid from the master cylinder reservoir.

2. Remove and relocate the air conditioning relay box and the solenoid valve located at the power brake unit.

3. Disconnect the vacuum hose from the booster by pulling it straight off. Prying off the vacuum hose could damage the check valve installed in the brake booster vacuum hose.

4. Detach the electrical harness connector from the brake level sensor.

5. Remove the nuts attaching the master cylinder to the booster and remove the master cylinder and position aside. If necessary, disconnect and plug the brake fluid lines at the master cylinder.

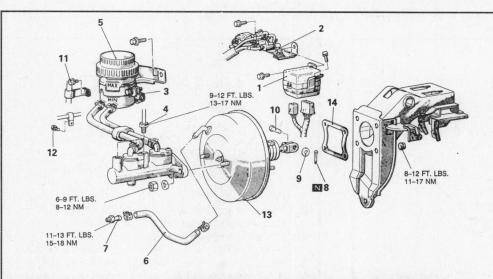

1. Relay box for air conditioner
2. Solenoid valve
3. Brake fluid level sensor connector
4. Brake tube
5. Master cylinder, hose and reservoir assembly
6. Vacuum hoses with check valve
7. Fitting
8. Cotter pin
9. Washer
10. Clevis pin
11. Fuel return tube installation bolt
12. Brake tube installation bolt
13. Brake booster
14. Sealer

Fig. 18 Exploded view of the power brake booster and related components—1990–94 vehicles

6. From inside the passenger compartment, remove the cotter pin and clevis pin that secures the booster pushrod to the brake pedal.

7. From inside the vehicle, remove the nuts that attach the booster to the dash panel. Remove the brake booster from the engine compartment.

To install:

8. Install the brake booster to the dash panel. From inside the vehicle, install the attaching nuts and tighten to 12 ft. lbs. (17 Nm).

9. Apply grease to the clevis pin and install with washers in place. Install new cotter pin and bend to secure in place.

10. Attach the vacuum hose to the booster fitting.

11. Install the master cylinder assembly to the mounting studs on the brake booster. Install the master cylinder mounting nuts and tighten to 9 ft. lbs. (12 Nm).

12. Reconnect the brake fluid reservoir to the master cylinder, if disconnected. Attach the electrical connector to the brake fluid level sensor.

13. Install the solenoid valve assembly and the relay box, if removed. Connect the negative battery cable.

14. Add fluid to the brake fluid reservoir as required. Bleed the master cylinder. If after bleeding the master cylinder the brake pedal feels soft, bleed the brake system at all wheels.

15. Check the brake system for proper operation.

1995–98 Vehicles

▶ **See Figures 11, 12, 13, 19 and 20**

1. Disconnect the negative battery cable. Siphon the brake fluid from the master cylinder reservoir.

2. Remove the master cylinder, as outlined earlier in this section.

3. Disconnect the vacuum hose (with the built-in check valve).

4. Unfasten the brake line fitting.

5. From inside the vehicle, perform the following:
   a. Remove the brake pedal return spring.
   b. Remove the snap pin.
   c. Remove the washer.
   d. Unfasten the clevis pin.

➡ **On 2.0L turbo and 2.4l engines, you must slide the engine forward to remove the brake booster from the body.**

6. Unfasten the retaining bolts, then remove the brake booster. Once the booster is removed, remove the sealer.

To install:

7. Installation is the reverse of the removal procedure. Make sure the lubricate the components shown in the accompanying figure.

8. When attaching the vacuum hose, connect the hose to the nipple as shown in the accompanying figure. Secure the hose with the clip. Make sure the check valve and the pipe part of the brake booster do not contact

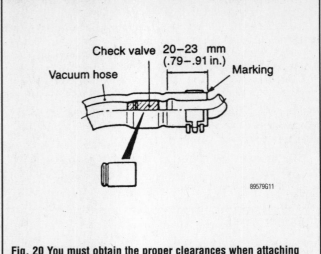

Fig. 20 You must obtain the proper clearances when attaching the vacuum hose

each other. When connecting, make sure the markings face upwards. Install the other end of the vacuum hose fully onto its port on the engine. Use the retaining clamp to secure the hose.

9. Make sure to adjust the clearance adjustment between the brake booster pushrod and the primary piston, as follows:
   a. Calculate the clearance A from the B, C and D measurements, as shown in the accompanying figure.
   A equals B minus C minus D.
   b. The clearance should be 0.256–0.335 in. (0.65–0.858mm). When brake booster negative pressure 9.7 psi (67 kPa) is applied, then clearance value will become 0.004–0.012 in. (0.1–0.3mm).

10. Install the master cylinder, as outlined earlier in this section.

Proportioning Valve

REMOVAL & INSTALLATION

▶ **See Figures 21 and 22**

1. Disconnect the negative battery cable. Siphon the brake fluid from the master cylinder reservoir and place in a suitable container.

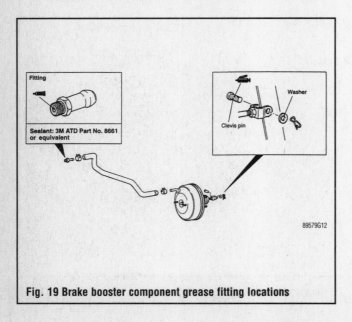

Fig. 19 Brake booster component grease fitting locations

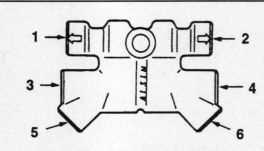

1. Proportioning valve – Rear brake (L.H.)
2. Proportioning valve – Rear brake (R.H.)
3. Proportioning valve – Front brake (R.H.)
4. Proportioning valve – Front brake (L.H.)
5. Proportioning valve – Master cylinder (secondary)
6. Proportioning valve – Master cylinder (primary)

Fig. 21 Proportioning valve brake line locations and identification—1995–98 vehicles

2. For 1995–98 2.0L turbo and 2.4L engines, remove the cruise control link assembly mounting bolts.

3. For 1995–98 2.0L non-turbo engines, remove the intake manifold, as outlined in Section 3 of this manual.

4. Label and disconnect the brake lines from the proportioning valve. Cap the lines to avoid getting any contaminants in the system.

5. Remove the proportioning valve mounting bolt, then remove the valve from the engine compartment.

➡Do not disassemble the proportioning valve because its performance depends on the set load of the spring inside the valve. If defective, replace the proportioning valve.

6. Installation is the reverse of the removal procedure. Tighten the flared brake line nuts to 11 ft. lbs. (15 Nm).

7. Once the valve is installed, bleed the brake system.

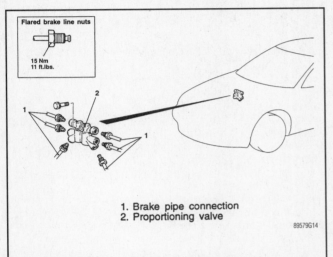

Fig. 22 The proportioning valve is mounted in the engine compartment—1995–98 vehicles shown

Brake Hoses and Lines

Metal lines and rubber brake hoses should be checked frequently for leaks and external damage. Metal lines are particularly prone to crushing and kinking under the vehicle. Any such deformation can restrict the proper flow of fluid and therefore impair braking at the wheels. Rubber hoses should be checked for cracking or scraping; such damage can create a weak spot in the hose and it could fail under pressure.

Any time the lines are removed or disconnected, extreme cleanliness must be observed. Clean all joints and connections before disassembly (use a stiff bristle brush and clean brake fluid); be sure to plug the lines and ports as soon as they are opened. New lines and hoses should be flushed clean with brake fluid before installation to remove any contamination.

REMOVAL & INSTALLATION

▶ See Figures 23 thru 32

1. Disconnect the negative battery cable.
2. Raise and safely support the vehicle on jackstands.
3. Remove any wheel and tire assemblies necessary for access to the particular line you are removing.
4. Thoroughly clean the surrounding area at the joints to be disconnected.
5. Place a suitable catch pan under the joint to be disconnected.
6. Using two wrenches (one to hold the joint and one to turn the fitting), disconnect the hose or line to be replaced.
7. Disconnect the other end of the line or hose, moving the drain pan if necessary. Always use a back-up wrench to avoid damaging the fitting.

8. Disconnect any retaining clips or brackets holding the line and remove the line from the vehicle.

➡If the brake system is to remain open for more time than it takes to swap lines, tape or plug each remaining clip and port to keep contaminants out and fluid in.

To install:

9. Install the new line or hose, starting with the end farthest from the master cylinder. Connect the other end, then confirm that both fittings are correctly threaded and turn smoothly using finger pressure. Make sure the new line will not rub against any other part. Brake lines must be at least ½ in. (13mm) from the steering column and other moving parts. Any protective shielding or insulators must be reinstalled in the original location.

❄❄ WARNING

Make sure the hose is NOT kinked or touching any part of the frame or suspension after installation. These conditions may cause the hose to fail prematurely.

10. Using two wrenches as before, tighten each fitting.
11. Install any retaining clips or brackets on the lines.

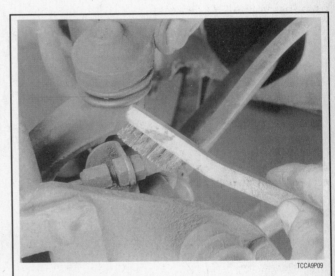

Fig. 23 Use a brush to clean the fittings of any debris

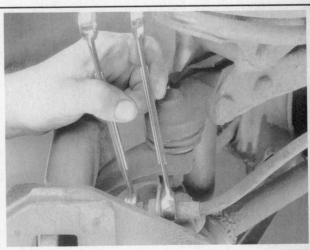

Fig. 24 Use two wrenches to loosen the fitting. If available, use flare nut type wrenches

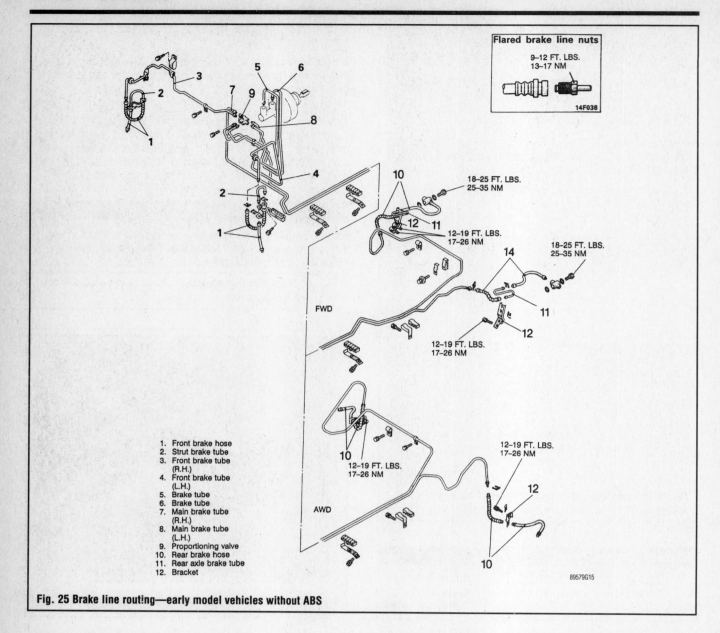

Flared brake line nuts

9–12 FT. LBS.
13–17 NM

14F038

18–25 FT. LBS.
25–35 NM

12–19 FT. LBS.
17–26 NM

18–25 FT. LBS.
25–35 NM

12–19 FT. LBS.
17–26 NM

FWD

12–19 FT. LBS.
17–26 NM

12–19 FT. LBS.
17–26 NM

AWD

1. Front brake hose
2. Strut brake tube
3. Front brake tube (R.H.)
4. Front brake tube (L.H.)
5. Brake tube
6. Brake tube
7. Main brake tube (R.H.)
8. Main brake tube (L.H.)
9. Proportioning valve
10. Rear brake hose
11. Rear axle brake tube
12. Bracket

89579G15

Fig. 25 Brake line routing—early model vehicles without ABS

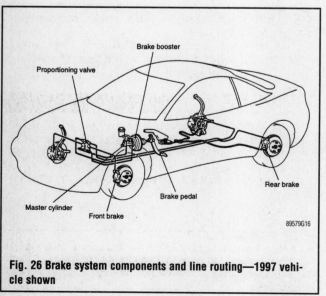

Brake booster

Proportioning valve

Rear brake

Master cylinder

Front brake

Brake pedal

89579G16

Fig. 26 Brake system components and line routing—1997 vehicle shown

89579P48

Fig. 27 Remove all of the clips securing the brake hose

Fig. 28 Unroute the brake hose from the retaining brackets

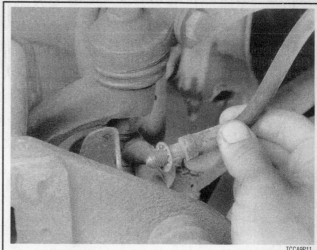

Fig. 31 Any gaskets/crush washers should be replaced with new ones during installation

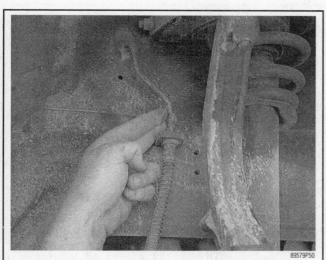

Fig. 29 If necessary, unfasten the metal brake line from the hose

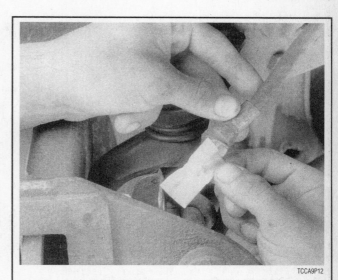

Fig. 32 Tape or plug the line to prevent contamination

12. If removed, install the wheel and tire assemblies, then carefully lower the vehicle to the ground.

13. Refill the brake master cylinder reservoir with clean, fresh brake fluid, meeting DOT 3 specifications. Properly bleed the brake system.

14. Connect the negative battery cable.

Brake System Bleeding

Bleeding the brake system is required anytime the normally closed system has been opened to the atmosphere. When bleeding the system, keep the brake fluid level in the master cylinder reservoir above ½ full. If the reservoir is empty, air will be pushed through the system. If equipped with ABS, refer to the ABS portion of Section 9 for bleeding procedure.

PROCEDURE

➡️If using a pressure bleeder, follow the instructions furnished with the unit and choose the correct adapter for the application. Do not substitute an adapter that "almost fits" as it will not work and could be dangerous.

Fig. 30 After all the retainers are unfastened, remove the brake hose from the vehicle

Master Cylinder

▶ **See Figures 33 and 34**

Due to the location of the fluid reservoir, bench bleeding of the master cylinder is not recommended. The master cylinder is to be bled while mounted on the brake booster. If the fluid reservoir runs dry, bleeding of the entire system will be necessary. Two people will be required to bleed the brake system.

1. Fill the brake fluid reservoir with clean brake fluid.

2. For 1990–94 vehicles, disconnect the brake tube from the master cylinder.

3. Have a helper slowly depress the brake pedal. Once depressed, hold it in that position. Brake fluid will be expelled from the master cylinder.

✱✱ CAUTION

When bleeding the brakes, keep your face away from area. Spewing fluid may cause facial and/or visual damage. Do not allow brake fluid to spill on the car's finish; it will remove the paint.

4. While the pedal is held down, use a finger to close the outlet port of the master cylinder. While the port is closed, have the helper release the brake pedal.

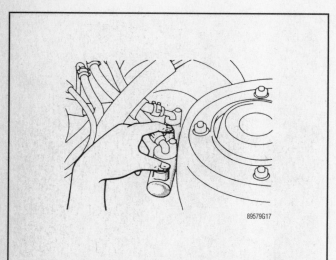

89579G17

Fig. 33 Close the outlet ports on the master cylinder using fingers–1990–94 vehicles shown

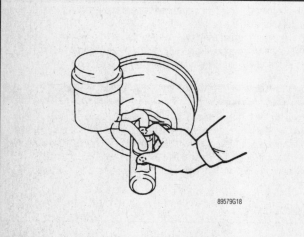

89579G18

Fig. 34 Location of the master cylinder outlet ports on 1995–98 vehicles

5. Repeat this procedure 3 or 4 times, until all air is bled from the master cylinder. Check the brake fluid in the reservoir every 4–5 times, making sure the reservoir does not run dry. Add clean DOT 3 brake fluid to the reservoir as needed. All air is bled from the master cylinder when the fluid expelled from the port is free of bubbles.

6. Connect the brake tube to the port on the master cylinder. Add clean fluid to fill the reservoir to the appropriate level.

Calipers/Wheel Cylinders

▶ **See Figures 35 thru 41**

1. Fill the master cylinder with fresh brake fluid. Check the level often during this procedure. Raise and safely support the vehicle.

2. Starting with the wheel farthest from the master cylinder (passenger side rear wheel), remove the protective cap from the bleeder and place where it will not be lost. Clean the bleeder screw.

3. Have an assistant start the engine and run at idle.

✱✱ CAUTION

When bleeding the brakes, keep face away from the brake area. Spewing fluid may cause physical and/or visual damage. Do not allow brake fluid to spill on the car's finish; it will remove the paint.

4. If the system is empty, the most efficient way to get fluid down to the wheel is to loosen the bleeder about ½–¾ turn, place a finger firmly over the bleeder and have a helper pump the brakes slowly until fluid comes out the bleeder. Once fluid is at the bleeder, close it before the pedal is released inside the vehicle.

➡ **If the pedal is pumped rapidly, the fluid will churn and create small air bubbles, which are almost impossible to remove from the system. These air bubbles will accumulate and a spongy pedal will result.**

5. Once fluid has been pumped to the caliper, open the bleed screw again, have the helper press the brake pedal to the floor, lock the bleeder and have the helper slowly release the pedal. Wait 15 seconds and repeat the procedure (including the 15 second wait) until no more air comes out of the bleeder upon application of the brake pedal. Remember to close the bleeder before the pedal is released inside the vehicle each time the bleeder is opened. If not, air will be introduced into the system.

6. If a helper is not available, connect a small hose to the bleeder, place the end in a container of brake fluid and proceed to pump the pedal from inside the vehicle until no more air comes out the bleeder. The hose will prevent air from entering the system.

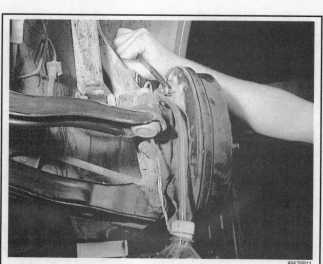

89579P11

Fig. 35 Attach a piece of hose submerged in clear brake fluid, then loosen the bleeder valve

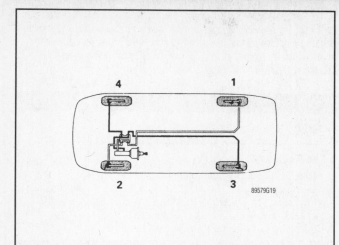

Fig. 36 Bleed the air from the brake system in the sequence shown

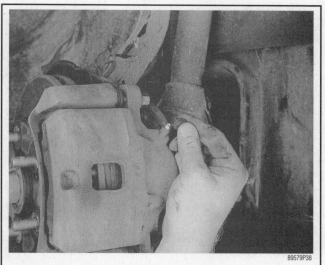

Fig. 37 Remove the bleeder valve cap . . .

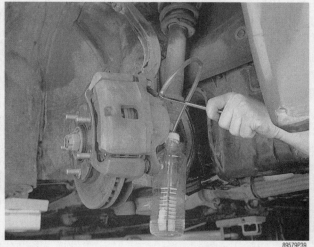

Fig. 38 . . . then attach a hose with the other end submerged in brake fluid and loosen the valve

Fig. 39 Remove the brake line from the back of the brake backing plate

Fig. 40 View of the brake line after disconnection

Fig. 41 Remove the bleeder valve from the brake backing plate

7. Repeat the procedure on the remaining calipers/wheel cylinders in the following order:
   a. Left front caliper
   b. Left rear caliper/wheel cylinder
   c. Right front caliper

8. Hydraulic brake systems must be totally flushed if the fluid becomes contaminated with water, dirt or other corrosive chemicals. To flush, bleed the entire system until all fluid has been replaced with the correct type of new fluid.

9. Install the bleeder cap on the bleeder to keep dirt out. Always road test the vehicle after brake work of any kind is done.

DISC BRAKES

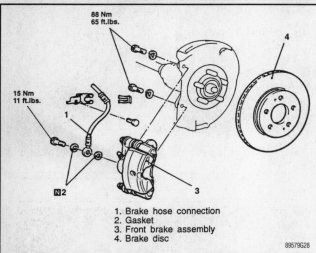

Fig. 42 Exploded view of the front disc brake components—1995–98 vehicles shown

1. Brake hose connection
2. Gasket
3. Front brake assembly
4. Brake disc

88 Nm
65 ft.lbs.

15 Nm
11 ft.lbs.

89579G28

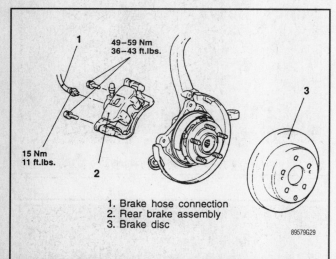

Fig. 43 Exploded view of the rear disc brake components—1995–98 vehicles shown

1. Brake hose connection
2. Rear brake assembly
3. Brake disc

49–59 Nm
36–43 ft.lbs.

15 Nm
11 ft.lbs.

89579G29

Brake Pads

☀ CAUTION

Older brake pads or shoes contain asbestos, which has been determined to be a cancer causing agent. Never clean the brake surfaces with compressed air! Avoid inhaling any dust from brake surfaces! When cleaning brakes, use commercially available brake cleaning fluids.

REMOVAL & INSTALLATION

◆ See Figures 44 thru 58

1. Disconnect the negative battery cable.
2. Remove some of the brake fluid from the master cylinder reservoir. The reservoir should be no more than ½ full. When the pistons are depressed into the calipers, excess fluid will flow up into the reservoir.
3. Raise the vehicle and support safely.
4. Remove the appropriate tire and wheel assemblies. For rear disc brakes, loosen the parking brake cable adjustment from inside the vehicle.
5. Remove the caliper lock and guide pins and lift the caliper assembly from the caliper support. Tie the caliper out of the way using wire. Do not allow the caliper to hang by the brake line.
6. Remove the outer shim, brake pads and spring clips from the caliper support. Take note of positioning of each to aid in installation.
7. Install the wheel lug nuts onto the studs and tighten. This is done to hold the disc on the hub.
8. Using a spring scale, turn the disc in a forward direction and measure the rotation sliding resistance of the hub.
9. Clean the caliper piston. For front disc brakes, use a C-clamp or equivalent tool to press the piston back into the caliper bore. For rear disc brakes, use driver tool MB990652 or equivalent, to thread the piston into the caliper bore. Be sure at this point, that the stopper groove of the piston correctly fits into the projection on the replacement brake pads rear surface.

To install:

10. Install the brake pads, shims and spring clip to the caliper support. Install the caliper over the brake pads.

➡ **Be careful that the piston boot does not become caught when lowering the caliper onto the support. Do not twist the brake hose during caliper installation.**

11. Lubricate and install the caliper guide and lock pins in their original positions. For front disc brakes, tighten guide and locking pins to 23 ft. lbs. (32 Nm) on vehicles built up to May, 1989. On vehicles built during

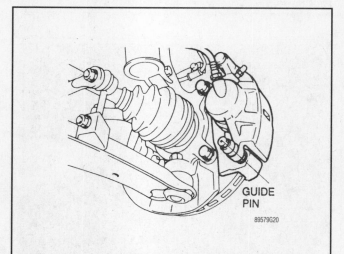

Fig. 44 Location of the front caliper guide pin (bottom) and lock pin (top)

GUIDE PIN

89579G20

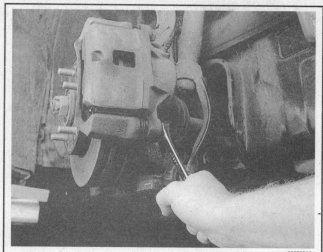

Fig. 45 Use a suitable wrench to loosen the caliper mounting bolts

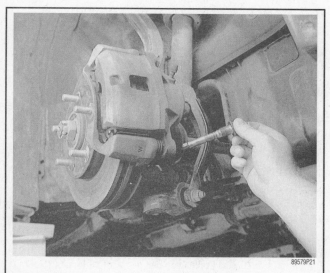

Fig. 46 Withdraw the caliper guide pin from the assembly

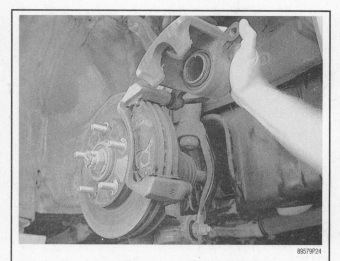

Fig. 47 View of the brake pad assemblies with the caliper lifted from the support

Fig. 48 With the caliper lifted up away from the support, remove the outer pad . . .

Fig. 49 . . . then remove the inner pad from the assembly

Fig. 50 Remove the upper clip (see arrow) and inspect it for damage . . .

Fig. 51 . . . there is also a bottom clip which should be removed, inspected and replaced if necessary

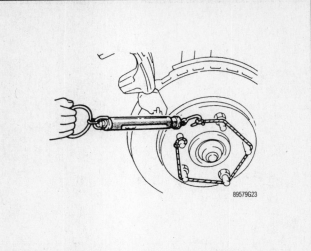

Fig. 54 Use a spring scale to measure the hub turning torque—front shown, rear similar

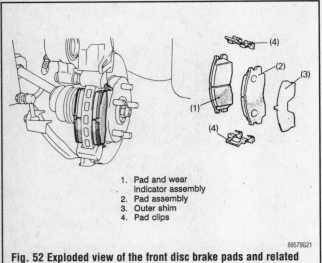

1. Pad and wear indicator assembly
2. Pad assembly
3. Outer shim
4. Pad clips

Fig. 52 Exploded view of the front disc brake pads and related components—1990–94 vehicles

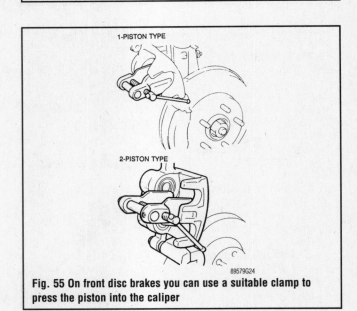

1-PISTON TYPE

2-PISTON TYPE

Fig. 55 On front disc brakes you can use a suitable clamp to press the piston into the caliper

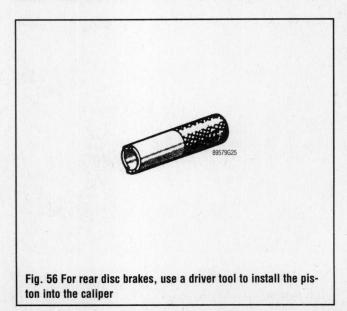

1. Outer shim
2. Pad assembly
3. Pad clips
4. Pad clips

Fig. 53 Removing rear disc brake pads, shims and spring clips from the caliper assembly

Fig. 56 For rear disc brakes, use a driver tool to install the piston into the caliper

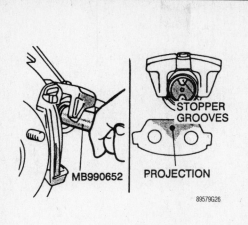

Fig. 57 Use the driver tool to thread the piston into the rear caliper bore

and after May, 1989 to 1990 vehicles, tighten caliper guide and locking pins to 58–72 ft. lbs. (80–80 Nm). For 1995–98 vehicles tighten the front caliper guide and locking pines to 65 ft. lbs. (88 Nm). For rear disc brakes, tighten the caliper guide and lock pins to 36–43 ft. lbs. (50–60 Nm).

12. For rear disc brakes, start the engine and forcefully depress the brake pedal 5–6 times. Apply the parking brake, then make sure the adjustment is within specifications. Adjust the parking brake cable, as required.

13. Check the disc brake drag force as follows:

a. Start the engine and press the brake pedal firmly a few times to seat the pads.

b. Once the pads are seated, shut the engine OFF.

c. Turn the brake disc forward 10 times.

d. Using a spring scale, measure the rotation sliding resistance of the hub in the forward direction.

e. Calculate the drag torque of the disc brake by subtracting the value obtained in Step 8 (force required to turn hub alone) from the value obtained in Step D (force required to turn hub with caliper and pads installed). Compare calculated force with desired force of 15 lbs. (70 N) or less.

14. If the calculated disc brake drag force is greater than specifications,

disassemble and clean the piston. Check for corrosion or worn piston seal and check the sliding condition of the lock pin and guide pin.

15. Install the tire and wheel assemblies. Connect the negative battery cable.

16. Lower the vehicle. Test the brakes for proper operation.

INSPECTION

◆ **See Figures 59, 60 and 61**

The disc brake pads have wear indicators that contact the brake disc when the brake pad thickness becomes 0.08 in. (2.0mm) and emit a squealing sound to worn the driver.

Inspect the thickness of the brake linings by looking through the brake caliper body check port. The standard value of the brake pad is 0.39 in. (10mm). The thickness limit of the lining is 0.08 in. (2.0mm).

When the limit is exceeded, replace the pads on both sides of the brake disc and also the brake pads on the wheel on the opposite side of the vehicle. Do not replace 1 pad on a caliper because the wear indicator is hitting, without replacing the other pad on the same wheel as well as the brake pads on the other front or rear wheel, as applicable.

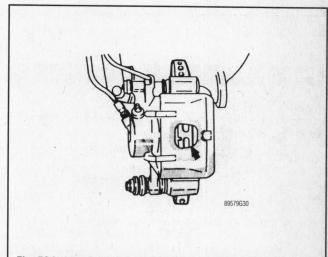

Fig. 59 Inspect front disc pad thickness through caliper body check port

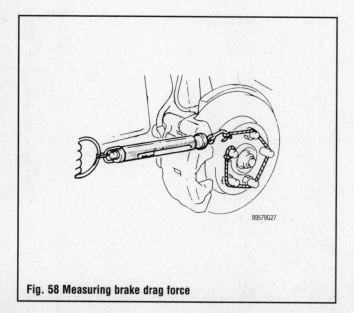

Fig. 58 Measuring brake drag force

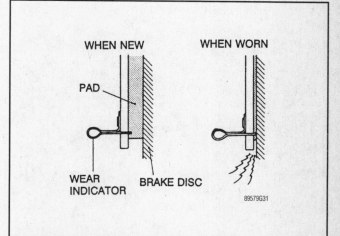

Fig. 60 The disc brake pads have wear indicators which will make a squeaking noise when the pads become worn and need to be replaced

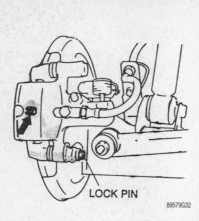

Fig. 61 Location of the brake pad inspection hole for rear disc brakes

If there is a significant difference in the thickness of the pads on the left and right sides, check the sliding condition of the piston, lock pin sleeve and guide pin sleeve.

Brake Caliper

REMOVAL & INSTALLATION

▶ See Figures 44, 52, 55 and 62 thru 71

1. Disconnect the negative battery cable.
2. Remove some of the brake fluid from the master cylinder reservoir. The reservoir should be no more than ½ full. When the pistons are depressed into the calipers, excess fluid will flow up into the reservoir.
3. Raise the vehicle and support safely.
4. Remove the appropriate tire and wheel assembly. For rear disc brakes, loosen the parking brake cable adjustment from inside the vehicle.
5. If replacement or overhaul of the caliper is necessary, disconnect the brake hose from the caliper as follows:
   a. Hold the nut on the brake hose side and loosen the flared brake line nut.

Fig. 62 If replacing or overhauling the caliper, loosen the flared brake line bolt . . .

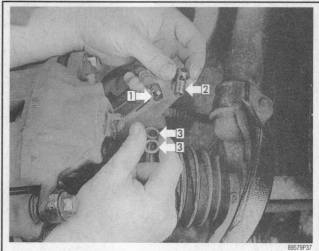

Fig. 63 . . . then remove the brake hose (1), fitting (2) and gaskets (3)

Fig. 64 Unfasten the caliper guide pin . . .

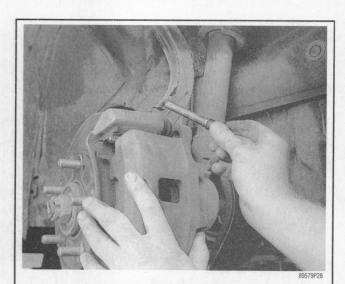

Fig. 65 . . . then withdraw the pin from the caliper bore

Fig. 66 Lift the caliper away from the support

Fig. 69 Unfasten the support mounting bolts . . .

Fig. 67 If you're just replacing the pads, you can suspend the caliper from the strut with a piece wire

Fig. 70 . . . then remove the support from the rotor

Fig. 68 To remove the caliper support, unfasten the retaining bolts

b. Remove the brake hose from the caliper.

6. Remove the caliper guide and lock pins. Lift the caliper and slide the assembly toward the inside of the wheel well until it separates from the lock pin.

7. If replacing the brake pads, suspend the caliper from the body with a suitable piece of wire. It is not necessary to disconnect the brake hose.

To install:

8. Position the caliper on the caliper support. Install the guide pin and lock pin. On some vehicles, there are markings to distinguish the guide and locking pins. Identification marks may also appear on the bolt heads. They should be installed in their original locations.

9. For front disc brakes, tighten the caliper retainers as follows:

a. For 1990–94 vehicles, tighten the guide and locking pins to 23 ft. lbs. (32 Nm) on vehicles built up to May, 1989, and on vehicles built during and after May, 1989, tighten caliper guide and locking pins to 58–72 ft. lbs. (80–100 Nm).

b. On 1995–98 vehicles, tighten the guide and locking pins to 65 ft. lbs. (88 Nm).

10. For rear disc brakes, tighten the caliper retainers to 36–43 ft. lbs. (50–60 Nm).

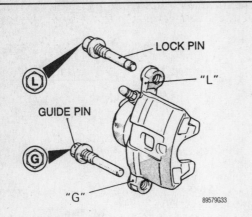

LOCK PIN

"L"

GUIDE PIN

"G"

89579G33

Fig. 71 If equipped, install the guide and lock pins so the identification mark on the caliper body and head mark on the pins are aligned

TCCA9P01

Fig. 72 For some types of calipers, use compressed air to drive the piston out of the caliper, but make sure to keep your fingers clear

11. Install the brake hose onto the caliper with new washers in place. If equipped with brake hose retainer bolt, tighten bolt to 25 ft. lbs. (35 Nm) torque. If no bolt is used, tighten the brake hose fitting to 9–12 ft. lbs. (13–17 Nm) for 1990–94 vehicles. For 1995–98 vehicles, tighten the brake hose fitting to 11 ft. lbs. (15 Nm).

➡**Do not twist the brake hose during installation.**

12. Install the wheel and tire assembly. Carefully lower the vehicle and connect the negative battery cable.

13. If the brake line was disconnected, properly bleed the brake system.

OVERHAUL

▶ **See Figures 72 thru 79**

➡**Some vehicles may be equipped dual piston calipers. The procedure to overhaul the caliper is essentially the same with the exception of multiple pistons, O-rings and dust boots.**

1. Remove the caliper from the vehicle and place on a clean workbench.

✳✳ CAUTION

NEVER place your fingers in front of the pistons in an attempt to catch or protect the pistons when applying compressed air. This could result in personal injury!

➡**Depending upon the vehicle, there are two different ways to remove the piston from the caliper. Refer to the brake pad replacement procedure to make sure you have the correct procedure for your vehicle.**

2. The first method is as follows:

a. Stuff a shop towel or a block of wood into the caliper to catch the piston.

b. Remove the caliper piston using compressed air applied into the caliper inlet hole. Inspect the piston for scoring, nicks, corrosion and/or worn or damaged chrome plating. The piston must be replaced if any of these conditions are found.

3. For the second method, you must rotate the piston to retract it from the caliper.

4. If equipped, remove the anti-rattle clip.

5. Use a prytool to remove the caliper boot, being careful not to scratch the housing bore.

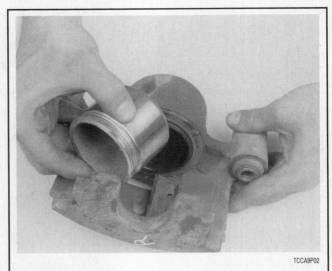

TCCA9P02

Fig. 73 Withdraw the piston from the caliper bore

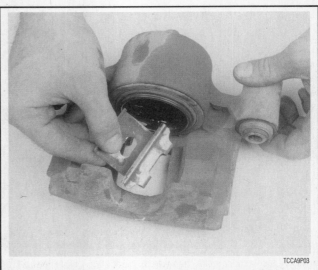

TCCA9P03

Fig. 74 On some vehicles, you must remove the anti-rattle clip

Fig. 75 Use a prytool to carefully pry around the edge of the boot . . .

TCCA9P04

6. Remove the piston seals from the groove in the caliper bore.

7. Carefully loosen the brake bleeder valve cap and valve from the caliper housing.

8. Inspect the caliper bores, pistons and mounting threads for scoring or excessive wear.

9. Use crocus cloth to polish out light corrosion from the piston and bore.

10. Clean all parts with denatured alcohol and dry with compressed air.

To assemble:

11. Lubricate and install the bleeder valve and cap.

12. Install the new seals into the caliper bore grooves, making sure they are not twisted.

13. Lubricate the piston bore.

14. Install the pistons and boots into the bores of the calipers and push to the bottom of the bores.

15. Use a suitable driving tool to seat the boots in the housing.

16. Install the caliper in the vehicle.

17. Install the wheel and tire assembly, then carefully lower the vehicle.

18. Properly bleed the brake system.

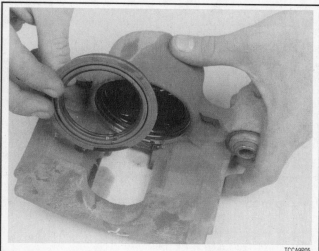

Fig. 76 . . . then remove the boot from the caliper housing, taking care not to score or damage the bore

TCCA9P05

Fig. 78 Use the proper size driving tool and a mallet to properly seal the boots in the caliper housing

TCCA9P07

Fig. 77 Use extreme caution when removing the piston seal; DO NOT scratch the caliper bore

TCCA9P06

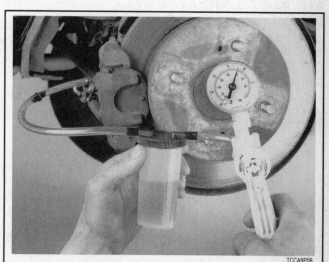

Fig. 79 There are tools, such as this Mighty-Vac, available to assist in proper brake system bleeding

TCCA9P08

Brake Disc (Rotor)

REMOVAL & INSTALLATION

▶ **See Figures 80, 81, 82, 83 and 84**

1. Raise the vehicle and support safely. Remove appropriate wheel assembly.

2. Remove the caliper and brake pads. Support the caliper out of the way using wire, it is not necessary to disconnect the brake line from the caliper.

3. For rear disc brake rotor, disconnect the parking brake connection at the rear caliper assembly.

4. The rotor on some models is held to the hub by 2 small threaded screws. Remove screws, if equipped, and pull the rotor from the hub assembly.

5. Installation is the reverse of the removal process.

INSPECTION

Using a micrometer, measure the disc thickness at eight positions, approximately 45 degrees apart and 0.39 in. (10mm) in from the outer edge of the disc. The minimum thickness is 0.882 in. (22.4mm) for front rotors or 0.331 in. (8.4mm), with a maximum thickness variation of 0.0006 in. (0.015mm).

If the disc is beyond limits for thickness, remove it and install a new one. If the thickness variation exceeds the specifications, replace the disc or turn rotor with on the car type brake lathe.

89579P34

Fig. 80 On some vehicles you may have to thread in 2 bolts . . .

89579P35

Fig. 81 . . . in order to pull the rotor away from the hub

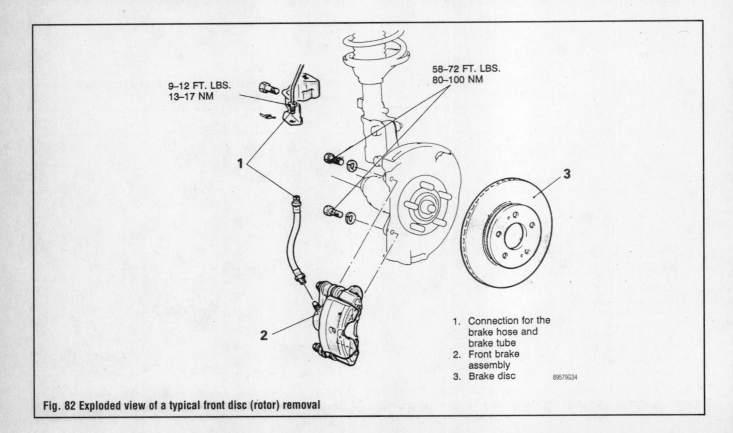

9–12 FT. LBS.
13–17 NM

58–72 FT. LBS.
80–100 NM

1

3

2

1. Connection for the brake hose and brake tube
2. Front brake assembly
3. Brake disc

89579G34

Fig. 82 Exploded view of a typical front disc (rotor) removal

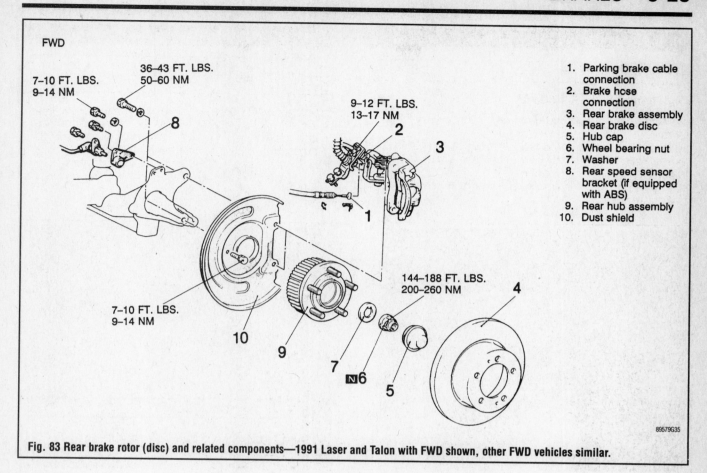

FWD

7–10 FT. LBS.
9–14 NM

36–43 FT. LBS.
50–60 NM

9–12 FT. LBS.
13–17 NM

7–10 FT. LBS.
9–14 NM

144–188 FT. LBS.
200–260 NM

1. Parking brake cable connection
2. Brake hose connection
3. Rear brake assembly
4. Rear brake disc
5. Hub cap
6. Wheel bearing nut
7. Washer
8. Rear speed sensor bracket (if equipped with ABS)
9. Rear hub assembly
10. Dust shield

89579G35

Fig. 83 Rear brake rotor (disc) and related components—1991 Laser and Talon with FWD shown, other FWD vehicles similar.

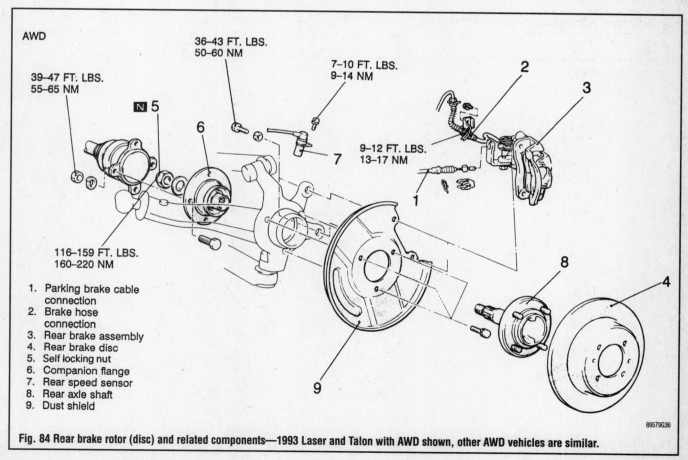

AWD

39–47 FT. LBS.
55–65 NM

36–43 FT. LBS.
50–60 NM

7–10 FT. LBS.
9–14 NM

9–12 FT. LBS.
13–17 NM

116–159 FT. LBS.
160–220 NM

1. Parking brake cable connection
2. Brake hose connection
3. Rear brake assembly
4. Rear brake disc
5. Self locking nut
6. Companion flange
7. Rear speed sensor
8. Rear axle shaft
9. Dust shield

89579G36

Fig. 84 Rear brake rotor (disc) and related components—1993 Laser and Talon with AWD shown, other AWD vehicles are similar.

DRUM BRAKES

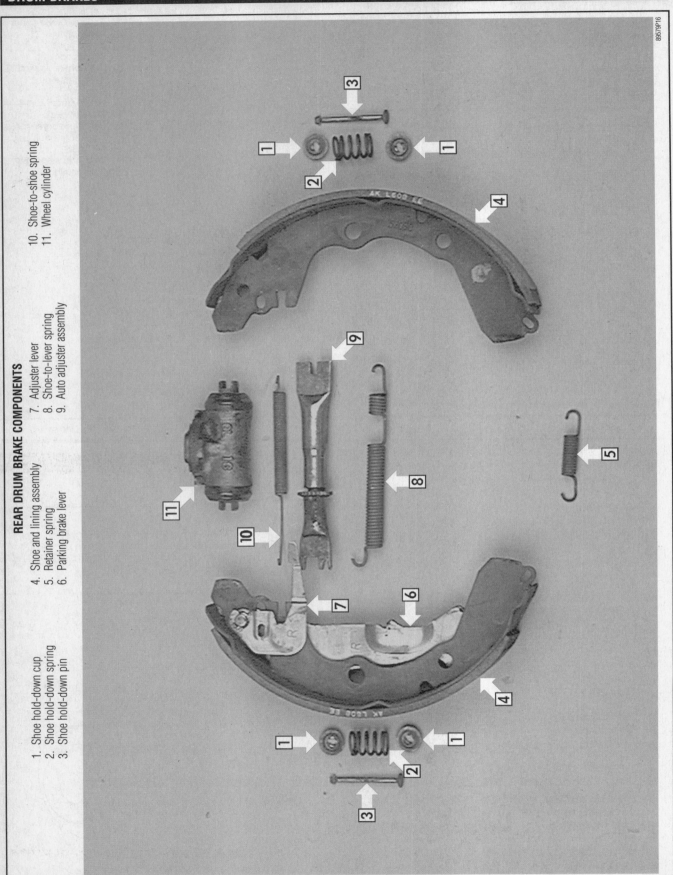

REAR DRUM BRAKE COMPONENTS

1. Shoe hold-down cup
2. Shoe hold-down spring
3. Shoe hold-down pin
4. Shoe and lining assembly
5. Retainer spring
6. Parking brake lever
7. Adjuster lever
8. Shoe-to-lever spring
9. Auto adjuster assembly
10. Shoe-to-shoe spring
11. Wheel cylinder

89579P16

Brake Drums

✳✳ CAUTION

Older brake pads or shoes may contain asbestos, which has been determined to be a cancer causing agent. Never clean the brake surfaces with compressed air! Avoid inhaling any dust from any brake surface! When cleaning brake surfaces, use a commercially available brake cleaning fluid.

REMOVAL & INSTALLATION

▶ See Figures 85 and 86

1. Raise and safely support the vehicle.
2. Remove the wheel and tire assembly.
3. Pull the drum from the hub and bearing assembly.
4. If the drum is difficult to remove, thread bolts into the drum to remove it from the hub and bearing.
5. Once the drum is removed, inspect for damage and/or wear and replace or refinish as necessary.

Fig. 85 You may have to thread bolts into the drum assembly . . .

Fig. 86 . . . in order to pull the brake drum from the hub and bearing assembly

To install:

6. Position the brake drum over the hub and bearing assembly.
7. Install the wheel and tire assembly, then carefully lower the vehicle.

INSPECTION

▶ See Figure 87

1. With the brake drum removed from the vehicle, measure the inside diameter of the hub and drum at two or more locations.
2. The service limit specification is 9.1 in. (231mm).
3. Replace the brake drums and shoe and lining assemblies when the wear exceeds the limit or is badly out of balance.

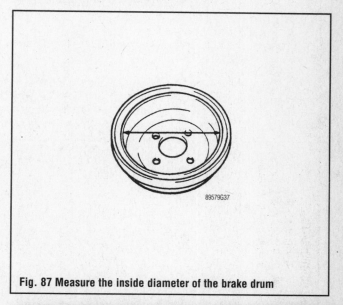

Fig. 87 Measure the inside diameter of the brake drum

Brake Shoes

INSPECTION

▶ See Figure 88

1. Remove the brake drum.
2. Measure the wear of the brake lining at the place worn the most. The service limit for replacement is 0.039 in. (1.0mm).

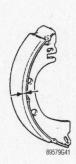

Fig. 88 Measure the thickness of the lining where it is worn the most

3. Replace the shoe and lining assembly is any located is less than the limit. Whenever the shoe and lining assembly is replaced, be sure to replace the left and right side assemblies as a set to prevent the car from pulling to one side when braking.

4. If there is a big difference between the thicknesses of the shoe and lining assembly on the left and right sides, check the sliding condition of the wheel cylinder piston.

REMOVAL & INSTALLATION

▶ **See Figures 89 thru 99**

1. Disconnect the negative battery cable.
2. Remove some of the brake fluid from the master cylinder reservoir. The reservoir should be no more than ½ full.
3. Raise the vehicle and support safely.
4. Remove the appropriate tire and wheel assembly. Loosen the parking brake cable adjusting nut.
5. Remove the brake drum.
6. If removing all of the brake drum components, remove the shoe-to-shoe spring.
7. Remove the shoe-to-lever spring. Although there are special tools to remove this, a pair of pliers usually works just as well.

Fig. 91 Remove the adjuster lever assembly

Fig. 89 Overall view of the brake drum components (installed)

Fig. 92 Remove the auto adjuster assembly

Fig. 90 Use a pair of pliers or a special brake tool to remove the shoe-to-lever spring

Fig. 93 Remove the lower brake shoe retaining spring

Fig. 94 Remove the hold-down spring and cup assembly

Fig. 95 With the shoes attached by the spring, pull them apart to clear the hub and bearing . . .

Fig. 96 . . . then detach the parking brake cable and remove the shoe and linings from the vehicle

18. If necessary, unfasten the rear brake pipe connection.

19. Remove the snap ring.

20. Remove the brake backing plate assembly, if necessary.

21. Installation is the reverse of the removal procedure. Grease the points shown in the accompanying figure.

22. Make sure to install the wave washer as shown in the accompanying figure.

23. Use a suitable pair of pliers to install the retainer on the pin securely.

Wheel Cylinder

REMOVAL & INSTALLATION

▶ **See Figures 100, 101, 102 and 103**

1. Disconnect the negative battery cable.

2. Remove some of the brake fluid from the master cylinder reservoir. The reservoir should be no more than ½ full.

3. Raise the vehicle and support safely.

4. Remove the appropriate tire and wheel assembly. Loosen the parking brake cable adjusting nut.

5. Remove the brake drum.

6. Remove the shoe-to-lever spring and the shoe-to-shoe spring.

7. Remove the auto adjuster assembly.

8. Disconnect the brake line connection from the rear of the brake backing plate. Plug or cap the line to avoid contaminating the system.

9. Unfasten the retainers, then remove the wheel cylinder from the brake backing plate.

10. If necessary, remove the bleeder screw.

To install:

11. If removed, install the bleeder screw and tighten to 6 ft. lbs. (8 Nm).

12. Position the wheel cylinder to the backing plate and secure with the retainers. Tighten to 7 ft. lbs. (10 Nm).

13. Unplug the brake pipe, then connect and tighten to 11 ft. lbs. (15 Nm).

14. Install the auto adjuster, shoe-to-shoe spring and shoe-to-lever spring.

15. Install the brake drum.

16. Install the wheel and tire assembly, then carefully lower the vehicle.

17. Properly bleed the brake system, as outlined earlier in this section.

8. Remove the adjuster lever, then remove the auto adjuster assembly.

9. Remove the lower brake hose retainer spring.

10. Remove the front hold-down cup and spring, then remove the rear hold-down cup.

11. If just replacing the shoe and linings, not other components such as the brake backing plate, perform the following:

   a. With the shoes still attached by the spring, pull them apart to clear the hub, then disconnect the parking brake cable and remove the shoe and lining assembly from the vehicle.

   b. Unfasten the spring and separate the shoe and linings.

12. If its necessary to remove all of the drum brake components, perform the remainder of the procedure.

13. Remove the shoe-to-shoe spring, then remove the rear shoe and lining assembly.

14. Remove the shoe and lever assembly.

15. Use a prytool to open the retainer joint, then remove the retainer.

16. Remove the wave washer, then remove the parking brake lever.

17. Remove the other shoe and lining assembly and the shoe hold-down pin.

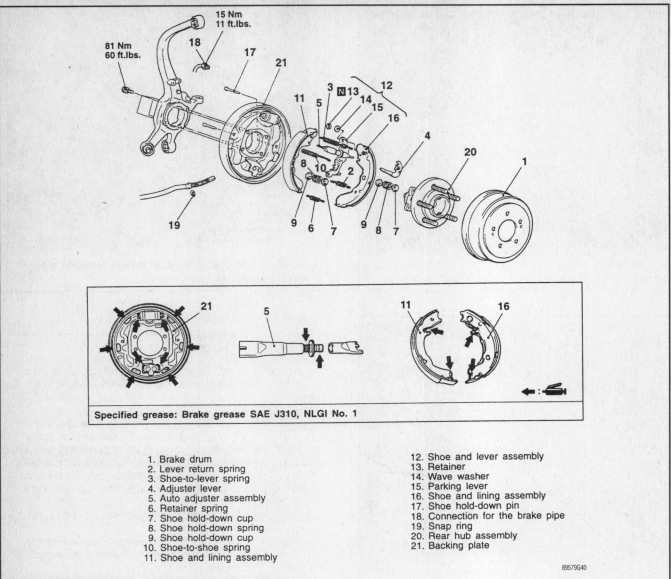

Specified grease: Brake grease SAE J310, NLGI No. 1

1. Brake drum
2. Lever return spring
3. Shoe-to-lever spring
4. Adjuster lever
5. Auto adjuster assembly
6. Retainer spring
7. Shoe hold-down cup
8. Shoe hold-down spring
9. Shoe hold-down cup
10. Shoe-to-shoe spring
11. Shoe and lining assembly

12. Shoe and lever assembly
13. Retainer
14. Wave washer
15. Parking lever
16. Shoe and lining assembly
17. Shoe hold-down pin
18. Connection for the brake pipe
19. Snap ring
20. Rear hub assembly
21. Backing plate

89579G40

Fig. 97 Exploded view of the rear drum brake components

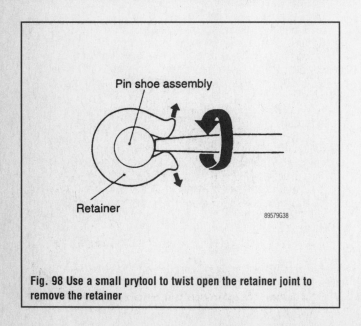

Fig. 98 Use a small prytool to twist open the retainer joint to remove the retainer

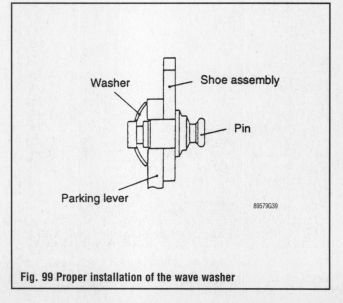

Fig. 99 Proper installation of the wave washer

Fig. 100 Remove the brake line from the rear of the brake backing plate

Fig. 101 Unfasten the wheel cylinder mounting nuts . . .

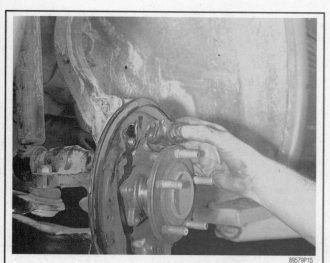

Fig. 102 . . . then remove the wheel cylinder from the brake backing plate

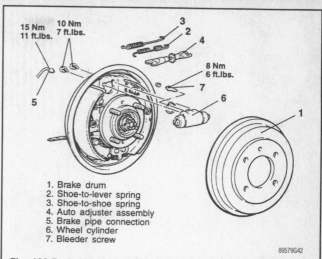

15 Nm
11 ft.lbs.
10 Nm
7 ft.lbs.
8 Nm
6 ft.lbs.

1. Brake drum
2. Shoe-to-lever spring
3. Shoe-to-shoe spring
4. Auto adjuster assembly
5. Brake pipe connection
6. Wheel cylinder
7. Bleeder screw

Fig. 103 Exploded view of the wheel cylinder mounting and related components

OVERHAUL

▶ See Figures 104 thru 113

Wheel cylinder overhaul kits may be available, but often at little or no savings over a reconditioned wheel cylinder. It often makes sense with these components to substitute a new or reconditioned part instead of attempting an overhaul.

If no replacement is available, or you would prefer to overhaul your wheel cylinders, the following procedure may be used. When rebuilding and installing wheel cylinders, avoid getting any contaminants into the system. Always use clean, new, high quality brake fluid. If dirty or improper fluid has been used, it will be necessary to drain the entire system, flush the system with proper brake fluid, replace all rubber components, then refill and bleed the system.

1. Remove the wheel cylinder from the vehicle and place on a clean workbench.

2. First remove and discard the old rubber boots, then withdraw the pistons. Piston cylinders are equipped with seals and a spring assembly, all located behind the pistons in the cylinder bore.

3. Remove the remaining inner components, seals and spring assembly. Compressed air may be useful in removing these components. If no

Fig. 104 Remove the outer boots from the wheel cylinder

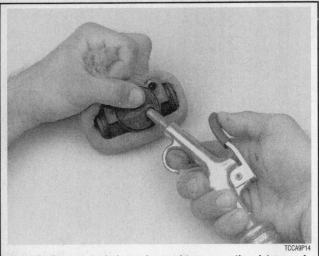

Fig. 105 Compressed air can be used to remove the pistons and seals

Fig. 106 Remove the pistons, cup seals and spring from the cylinder

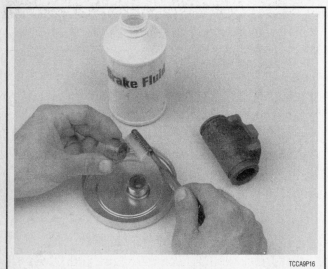

Fig. 107 Use brake fluid and a soft brush to clean the pistons . . .

compressed air is available, be VERY careful not to score the wheel cylinder bore when removing parts from it. Discard all components for which replacements were supplied in the rebuild kit.

4. Wash the cylinder and metal parts in denatured alcohol or clean brake fluid.

✳✳ WARNING

Never use a mineral-based solvent such as gasoline, kerosene or paint thinner for cleaning purposes. These solvents will swell rubber components and quickly deteriorate them.

5. Allow the parts to air dry or use compressed air. Do not use rags for cleaning, since lint will remain in the cylinder bore.
6. Inspect the piston and replace it if it shows scratches.
7. Lubricate the cylinder bore and seals using clean brake fluid.
8. Position the spring assembly.
9. Install the inner seals, then the pistons.
10. Insert the new boots into the counterbores by hand. Do not lubricate the boots.
11. Install the wheel cylinder.

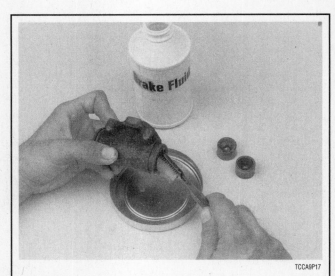

Fig. 108 . . . and the bore of the wheel cylinder

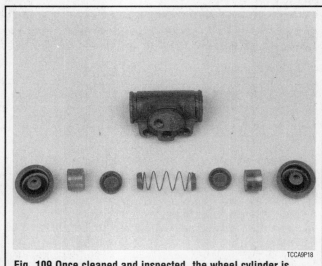

Fig. 109 Once cleaned and inspected, the wheel cylinder is ready for assembly

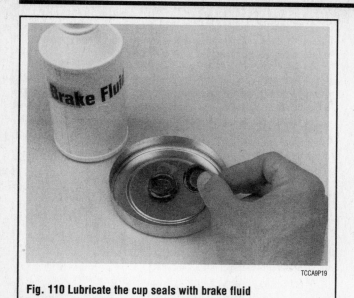

Fig. 110 Lubricate the cup seals with brake fluid

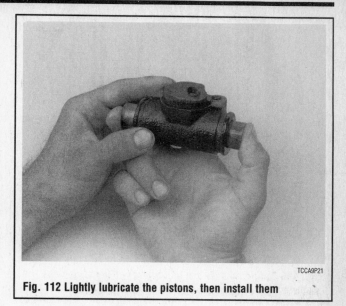

Fig. 112 Lightly lubricate the pistons, then install them

Fig. 111 Install the spring, then the cup seals in the bore

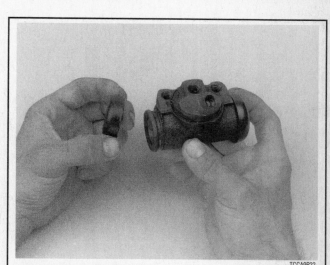

Fig. 113 The boots can now be installed over the wheel cylinder ends

PARKING BRAKE

Cables

REMOVAL & INSTALLATION

1990–94 Vehicles

▶ See Figures 114, 115 and 116

1. Disconnect the negative battery cable.
2. Remove the floor console from the vehicle as follows:
   a. Remove the screw plugs in the side covers. Remove the retainer screws and the side covers from the vehicle.
   b. Remove the front mounting screw cover from the floor console. Remove the manual transaxle shift lever knob.
   c. Remove the cup holder and the carpet inserts from the floor console assembly.
   d. Label and disconnect the electrical wire harness connections for the floor console.
   e. Remove the mounting bolts and the floor console from the vehicle.

3. Loosen the cable adjusting nut and disconnect the rear brake cables from the actuator. Remove the center cable clamp and grommet.
4. Raise the vehicle and support safely. Remove the parking brake cable clip and retainer spring. Disconnect the cable end from the parking brake assembly.
5. Unfasten any remaining frame retainers and remove the cables from the vehicle.

To install:

6. The parking brake cables may be color coded to indicate side. Check the parking brake cables for an identification mark. If present, position the cables as follows:
   a. AWD vehicle—yellow cable goes on left side
   b. AWD vehicle—orange cable goes on right side
   c. FWD vehicle—white cable goes on right side
   d. FWD vehicle—no color marking goes on left side
7. Install the cable to the rear actuator. Secure in place with the parking brake cable clip and retainer spring.
8. Position the cable in the under the vehicle and install retainers loose.

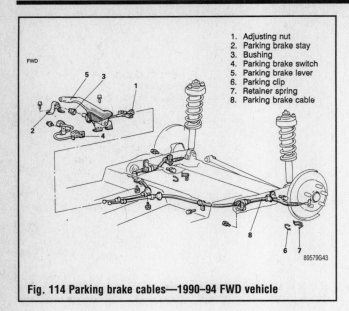

Fig. 114 Parking brake cables—1990–94 FWD vehicle

1. Adjusting nut
2. Parking brake stay
3. Bushing
4. Parking brake switch
5. Parking brake lever
6. Parking clip
7. Retainer spring
8. Parking brake cable

FWD

89579G43

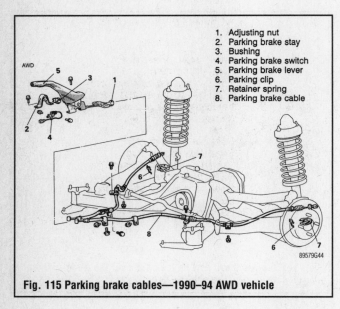

Fig. 115 Parking brake cables—1990–94 AWD vehicle

1. Adjusting nut
2. Parking brake stay
3. Bushing
4. Parking brake switch
5. Parking brake lever
6. Parking clip
7. Retainer spring
8. Parking brake cable

AWD

89579G44

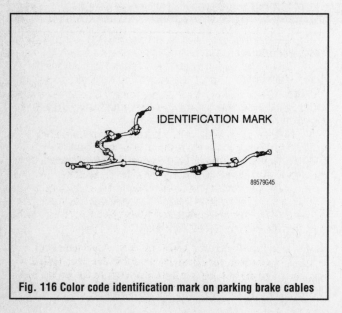

Fig. 116 Color code identification mark on parking brake cables

IDENTIFICATION MARK

89579G45

9. Reattach the parking brake cables to the actuator inside the vehicle. Tighten the adjusting nut until the proper tension is placed on the cable. Adjust the parking brake stroke.

10. Secure all cable retainers. Apply and release the parking brake a number of times once all adjustments have been made. With the rear wheels raised, make sure the parking brake is not causing excess drag on the rear wheels.

11. Install the floor console assembly as follows:

   a. Install the floor console in position in the vehicle. Position the seat belts as required. Install the console retainer bolts.

   b. Reconnect the electrical harness connectors to the vehicle body harness.

   c. Install the carpet and the cup holder to the console assembly. Install the manual shift knob.

   d. Install the side covers and retainers. Cover retainer screws with plugs.

   e. Connect the negative battery cable and check console electrical components for proper operation.

12. Road test the vehicle and check for proper brake operation. Check that the parking brake holds the vehicle on an incline. Road test the vehicle and check for proper brake operation. Check that the parking brake holds the vehicle on an incline.

1995–98 Vehicles

DRUM BRAKES

▶ See Figure 117

1. Disconnect the negative battery cable.
2. Remove the front floor console, as outlined in Section 10 of this manual. Detach the parking brake cables from the retainers.
3. Raise and safely support the vehicle, then remove the wheel and tire assembly.
4. Remove the brake drum.
5. Remove the following components:

   a. Shoe-to-lever spring.
   b. Auto adjuster assembly.
   c. Shoe-to-shoe spring.
   d. Retainer spring.
   e. Lever return spring.
   f. Shoe hold-down cup, spring and pin.

6. Remove the shoe and lining assembly.
7. Unfasten the retaining clip and bolts, then remove the parking brake cable assembly.
8. Installation is the reverse of the removal procedure.
9. Adjust the parking brake lever stroke.

DISC BRAKES

▶ See Figures 118 and 119

1. Disconnect the negative battery cable.
2. Remove the front floor console, as outlined in Section 10 of this manual. Detach the parking brake cables from the retainers.
3. Remove the rear brake assembly (caliper and pads) and position it aside, supported with wire or equivalent.
4. Remove the front and rear shoe-to-anchor springs.
5. Remove the adjusting wheel spring and the adjuster.
6. Remove the strut and the strut return spring.
7. Remove the shoe hold-down cup, spring and pin.
8. Remove the shoe and lining assembly.
9. Unfasten the clips and the retaining bolts, then remove the parking brake cable(s).
10. Installation is the reverse of the removal procedure.
11. Install the adjuster to the shoe adjusting bolt of the left hand wheel is attached toward the front of the vehicle and the shoe adjusting bolt of the right hand wheel is toward the rear of the vehicle.
12. The load on the respective shoe-to-anchor springs is different, so the spring in the figure has been painted, as shown in the accompanying figure.
13. Before installing the console, adjust the parking brake lever stroke.

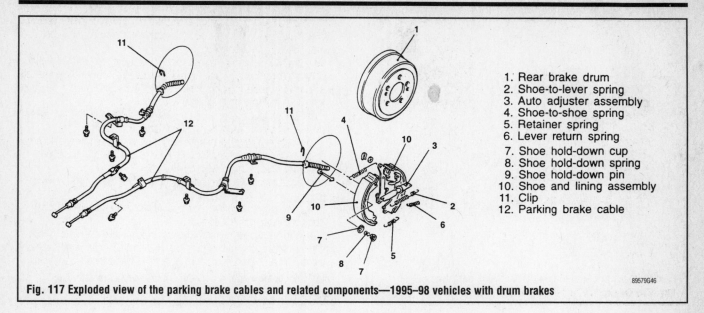

1. Rear brake drum
2. Shoe-to-lever spring
3. Auto adjuster assembly
4. Shoe-to-shoe spring
5. Retainer spring
6. Lever return spring
7. Shoe hold-down cup
8. Shoe hold-down spring
9. Shoe hold-down pin
10. Shoe and lining assembly
11. Clip
12. Parking brake cable

Fig. 117 Exploded view of the parking brake cables and related components—1995–98 vehicles with drum brakes

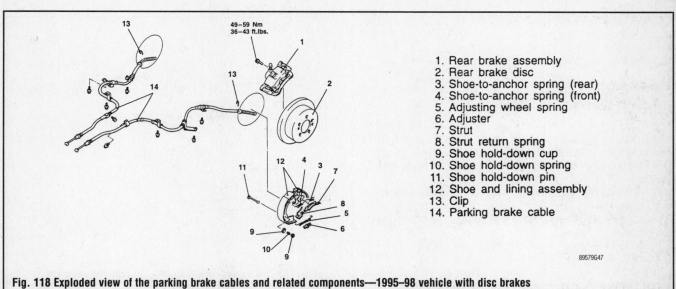

1. Rear brake assembly
2. Rear brake disc
3. Shoe-to-anchor spring (rear)
4. Shoe-to-anchor spring (front)
5. Adjusting wheel spring
6. Adjuster
7. Strut
8. Strut return spring
9. Shoe hold-down cup
10. Shoe hold-down spring
11. Shoe hold-down pin
12. Shoe and lining assembly
13. Clip
14. Parking brake cable

Fig. 118 Exploded view of the parking brake cables and related components—1995–98 vehicle with disc brakes

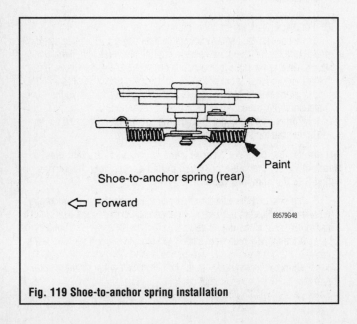

Fig. 119 Shoe-to-anchor spring installation

ADJUSTMENT

1990–94 Vehicles

▶ See Figure 120

1. Make sure the parking brake cable is free and is not frozen or sticking. With the engine running, forcefully depress the brake pedal 5–6 times.

2. Apply the parking brake while counting the number of notches. Check desired parking brake stroke should be 5–7 notches.

3. If adjustment is required, remove the carpeting from inside the floor console. This will expose the adjusting nut within the console.

4. Loosen the locknut on the cable rod. Rotate the adjusting nut to adjust the parking brake stroke to the 5–7 notch setting. After making the adjustment, check there is no looseness between the adjusting nut and the parking brake lever, then tighten the locknut.

➡**Do not adjust the parking brake too tight. If the number of notches is less than specification, the cable has been pulled too much and the automatic adjuster will fail or the brakes will drag.**

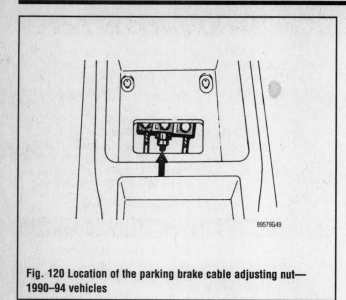

Fig. 120 Location of the parking brake cable adjusting nut—1990–94 vehicles

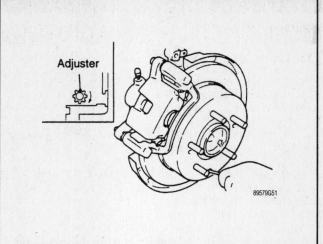

Fig. 122 Location of the adjuster wheel—vehicles with disc brakes

5. After adjusting the lever stroke, raise the rear of the vehicle and safely support. With the parking brake lever in the released position, turn the rear wheels to confirm that the rear brakes are not dragging.

6. Check that the parking brake holds the vehicle on an incline.

1995–98 Vehicles

♦ **See Figures 121, 122 and 123**

1. Pull the parking brake lever with a force of about 45 lbs. (196 N) and count the number of notches. On vehicles with disc brakes, the value should be 3–5 notches. On vehicles with drum brakes, the value should be 5–7 notches.

2. If the parking brake stroke is not within the standard value, adjust is necessary.

3. Remove the carpeting from inside the floor console. This will expose the adjusting nut within the console.

4. Loosen the adjusting nut to the end of the cable rod, freeing the parking brake cable.

5. For drum brakes, perform the following:

a. With the engine idling, forcefully depress the brake pedal 5 or 6 times and make sure the pedal stroke stops changing. If the pedal stroke stops changing, the automatic-adjustment mechanism is functioning normally, and the clearance between the shoe and drum is correct.

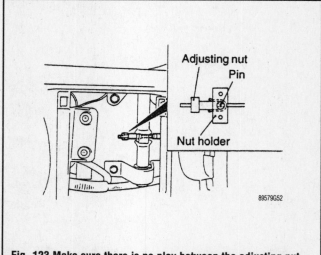

Fig. 123 Make sure there is no play between the adjusting nut and the pin

6. For disc brakes, perform the following:

a. Remove the adjustment hole plug, then using a flat tipped screwdriver, turn the adjuster in the direction of the arrow (shown in the accompanying figure), which expands the shoe) so that the disc will not rotate.

b. Return the adjuster 5 notches in the direction opposite to the direction of the arrow.

c. Turn the adjusting nut to adjust the parking brake lever stroke to within the standard value range.

➡**If the number of brake lever notches engages is less that the standard value, the cable has been pulled excessively. Be sure to adjust it to the standard value.**

d. After making the adjustment, check to be sure that there is no play between the adjusting nut and the pin. Also check that the adjusting nut is securely held at the nut holder.

e. After adjusting the lever stroke, jack up and support the rear of the vehicle.

f. With the parking brake lever released, turn the rear wheel to confirm that the rear brakes are not dragging.

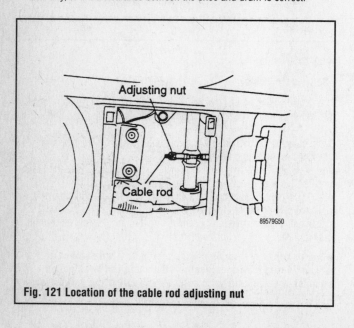

Fig. 121 Location of the cable rod adjusting nut

ANTI-LOCK BRAKE SYSTEM

General Description

▶ **See Figures 124 and 125**

Anti-lock braking systems are designed to prevent locked-wheel skidding during hard braking or during braking on slippery surfaces. The front wheels of a vehicle cannot apply steering force if they are locked and sliding; the vehicle will continue in its previous direction of travel. The four wheel anti-lock brake systems found on these vehicles holds the individual wheels just below the point of locking, thereby allowing some steering response and preventing the rear of the vehicle from sliding sideways.

Electrical signals are sent from the wheel speed sensors to the ABS control unit; when the system detects impending lock-up at any wheel, solenoid valves within the hydraulic unit cycle to control the line pressure as needed. The systems employ normal master cylinder and vacuum booster arrangements; no hydraulic accumulator is used, nor is any high pressure fluid stored within the system. The system employs a conventional master cylinder and vacuum booster arrangements; no hydraulic accumulator is used, nor is any high pressure fluid stored within the system.

The Front Wheel Drive (FWD) vehicle family uses a 3-channel anti-lock system. The 3-channel system uses 3 solenoids in the hydraulic unit to control brake pressure in the left front, right front and rear circuits. A proportioning valve within the rear circuit equalizes pressure to each rear wheel.

The All Wheel Drive (AWD) vehicle family use a 2 channel system. The left front and right rear wheels share a control solenoid as do the right front and left rear wheels. The system contains a select–low valve which reacts to reduced pressure in one circuit and balances the pressure to the opposite rear wheel. In this fashion, the anti-lock function is provided at 3 wheels, rather than just the one originating the lock-up signal.

General Information

Both FWD and AWD systems monitor and compare wheel speed based on the inputs from the wheel speed sensors. The brake pressure is controlled according to the impending lock-up computations of the ABS control unit.

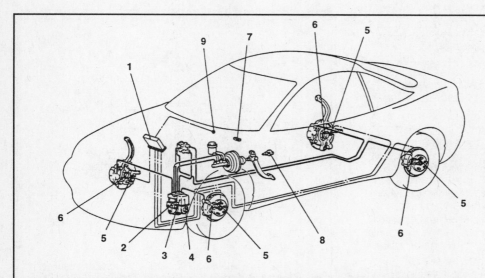

1. ABS-ECU
2. Hydraulic unit
3. ABS valve relay
4. ABS motor relay
5. Wheel speed sensor
6. ABS rotor
7. Data link connector
8. Stop light switch
9. ABS warning light

89579G57

Fig. 124 Anti-lock Brake System (ABS) components—1997 FWD vehicle shown, others similar

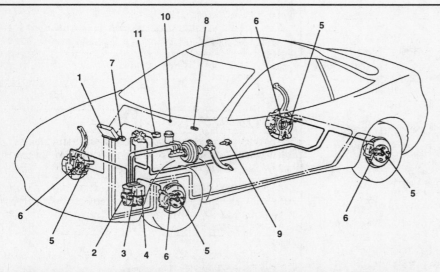

1. ABS-ECU
2. Hydraulic unit
3. ABS valve relay
4. ABS motor relay
5. Wheel speed sensor
6. ABS rotor
7. ABS power relay
8. Data link connector
9. Stop light switch
10. ABS warning light
11. G-sensor

89579G58

Fig. 125 Location of the ABS system components—1997 AWD vehicle shown, others similar

On the FWD vehicles using a 3-channel system, if either front wheel approaches lock-up, the controller actuates the individual solenoid for that wheel, reducing pressure in the line. Impending lock-up at either rear wheel will engage the rear control solenoid; hydraulic pressure is reduced equally to both rear wheels, reducing the tendency of the rear to skid sideways under braking.

The AWD vehicles incorporate a G–sensor into the system to give the ABS control unit an acceleration signal; this is used in conjunction with engine rpm and wheel speed signals to determine high or low friction road conditions. If the system detects impending wheel lock at, for example, the left front wheel, the solenoid controlling the left front/right rear circuit is activated to reduce line pressures. The select–low valve (common to both channels) reacts to the pressure change and reduces the pressure to the other rear wheel. This system overcomes some of the inherent problems of applying ABS to all wheel drive vehicles.

The system incorporates an idle-up control which raises engine speed to 1800 rpm during braking. This eliminates engine braking during ABS–engaged stops and allows the control system to apply maximum stopping effort.

Also found on the AWD is a delay valve which prevents simultaneous front and rear wheel slip by momentarily delaying rear wheel cylinder pressure when ever front wheel line pressure increases sharply. This insures more even application of braking force to the ground and better vehicle control for the operator.

Three separate relays aid the operation of the ABS system. The ABS motor relay (for the pump motor) and the ABS valve relay are located together immediately adjacent to the hydraulic unit under the hood.

The ABS power relay is mounted on a separate bracket next to the anti-lock control unit in the right rear quarter panel. Each of the relays may be replaced in the usual fashion, although care must be taken to release wiring connector clips before removing the relay.

FLAT BATTERY REMEDY

When booster cables are used to start the engine when the battery is completely flat and the vehicle is immediately driven without waiting for the battery to recharge itself, the engine may misfire, and driving may not be possible. This is due to the fact that the ABS consumes a great amount of current for it self-check functions; the remedy is to either allow the battery to recharge sufficiently, or to disconnect the electrical harness connector for the ABS circuit, thus disabling the ABS system. The ABS warning light will illuminate when the connector is disconnected.

After the battery has been sufficiently charged, engage the ABS electrical connector and restart the engine. Check to be sure the ABS warning lamp is not illuminated.

SYSTEM PRECAUTIONS

• Certain components within the ABS system are not intended to be serviced or repaired individually. Only those components with removal and installation procedures should be serviced.

• Do not use rubber hoses or other parts not specifically specified for the ABS system. When using repair kits, replace all parts included in the kit. Partial or incorrect repair may lead to functional problems and require the replacement of components.

• Lubricate rubber parts with clean, fresh brake fluid to ease assembly. Do not use lubricated shop air to clean parts; damage to rubber components may result.

• Use only DOT 3 brake fluid from an unopened container.

• If any hydraulic component or line is removed or replaced, it may be necessary to bleed the entire system.

• A clean repair area is essential. Always clean the reservoir and cap thoroughly before removing the cap. The slightest amount of dirt in the fluid may plug an orifice and impair the system function. Perform repairs after components have been thoroughly cleaned; use only denatured alcohol to clean components. Do not allow ABS components to come into contact with any substance containing mineral oil; this includes used shop rags.

• The Anti-Lock control unit is a microprocessor similar to other computer units in the vehicle. Ensure that the ignition switch is **OFF** before removing or installing controller harnesses. Avoid static electricity discharge at or near the controller.

• If any arc welding is to be done on the vehicle, the ALCU connectors should be disconnected before welding operations begin.

DEPRESSURIZING THE SYSTEM

The ABS system requires no special system depressurization prior to the opening of hydraulic lines or bleeding of the system.

System Diagnosis

▶ **See Figures 126, 127, 128 and 129**

Diagnosis of the ABS system consists of 3 general steps, performed in order:

1. The visual or preliminary inspection, including inspection of the basic brake system, is always required before any other steps are taken.

89579G56

Fig. 126 You can connect a scan tool to the data link connector to retrieve ABS trouble codes

Diagnostic trouble code		Diagnostic trouble code	
No.	Scan tool (DRB-II) display letters	No.	Scan tool (DRB-II) display letters
11	FL SPD SENSOR	41	SOL V FRONT L
12	FR SPD SENSOR	42	SOL V FRONT R
13	RL SPD SENSOR	43	SOL V REAR
14	RR SPD SENSOR	51	VALVE RLY
15	SENSOR FAULT	52	MOTOR RLY
22	STOP SW	55	ECU

89579G53

Fig. 127 ABS diagnostic trouble code list—1991–94 vehicles

89579G55

Diagnostic trouble code No.	Inspection item	Diagnostic content	Detection conditions
11	Right front wheel speed sensor	Open circuit	A,B
12	Left front wheel speed sensor		
13	Right rear wheel speed sensor		
14	Left rear wheel speed sensor		
15	Wheel speed sensor system	Abnormal output signal	B
21	G sensor	Broken wire in G sensor or OFF malfunction	B
22	Stop light switch system	Open circuit or ON malfunction	B
41	Left front solenoid valve system	No response to solenoid valve drive signal	B
42	Right front solenoid valve system		B
43	Rear solenoid valve system	The currents flowing through right and left valves are different under the same condition.	B
51	Valve relay system	Valve relay OFF failure	A,B
52	Motor relay or motor system	Motor relay OFF failure and motor drive failure	B
55	ABS-ECU	ABS-ECU internal failure (program maze, etc.)	A,B

Detection conditions
A: During system check immediately after starting
B: While driving

Fig. 129 ABS diagnostic trouble code list—1995–98 FWD vehicles

89579G54

Diagnostic trouble code No.	Inspection item	Diagnostic content	Detection conditions
11	Right front wheel speed sensor	Open circuit	A, B
12	Left front wheel speed sensor		
13	Right rear wheel speed sensor		
14	Left rear wheel speed sensor		
15	Wheel speed sensor system	Abnormal output signal	B
16	Power supply system	Abnormal battery positive voltage	A, B
21	Right front wheel speed sensor	Excessive gap or short circuit	B
22	Left front wheel speed sensor		
23	Right rear wheel speed sensor		
24	Left rear wheel speed sensor		
38	Stop light switch system	Open circuit or ON malfunction	A, B
41	Right front solenoid valve system	No response to solenoid valve drive signal	A, B
42	Left front solenoid valve system		
43	Rear solenoid valve system		
51	Valve relay system	Valve relay OFF failure	A, B
53	Motor relay or motor system	Motor relay OFF failure and motor drive failure	B
63	ABS-ECU	Malfunction in ABS-ECU (program maze, etc.)	A, B

Detection conditions
A: During system check immediately after starting
B: When driving

Fig. 128 ABS diagnostic trouble code list—1995–98 FWD vehicles

2. Initial diagnosis is then made by a careful analysis of the ANTI-LOCK Warning Lamp display during start-up and operation. The warning lamp troubleshooting chart will direct the use of further charts and detailed testing based on initial findings.

✳✳ WARNING

Make sure the ignition is turned OFF before the scan tool is installed!

3. The ABS system may be further checked with the DRB-III, MUT-II or equivalent diagnostic scan tool, provided the correct cartridges are used. The scan tool, will allow various components of the system to be operated for testing purposes. Connect the scan tool according to instructions furnished with the tool. The system will enter diagnostic mode and prompt the operator through the assorted system checks and tests.

VISUAL INSPECTION

Remember to first determine if the problem is related to the anti-lock system or not. The anti-lock system is made up of 2 basic sub-systems:

1. The hydraulic system, which may be diagnosed and serviced using normal brake system procedures, however, there is a need to determine whether the problem is related to the ABS components or not.
2. The electrical system which may be diagnosed using the charts and diagnostic tools.

Before diagnosing an apparent ABS problem, make absolutely certain that the normal braking system is in correct working order. Many common brake problems (dragging lining, seepage, etc.) will affect the ABS system. A visual check of specific system components may reveal problems creating an apparent ABS malfunction. Performing this inspection may reveal a simple failure, thus eliminating extended diagnostic time.

3. Inspect the brake fluid level in the reservoir.
4. Inspect brake lines, hoses, master cylinder assembly, and brake calipers for leakage.
5. Visually check brake lines and hoses for excessive wear, heat damage, punctures, contact with other parts, missing clips or holders, blockage or crimping.
6. Check the calipers for rust or corrosion. Check for proper sliding action if applicable.
7. Check the caliper pistons for freedom of motion during application and release.
8. Inspect the wheel speed sensors for proper mounting and connections.
9. Inspect the toothed wheels for broken teeth or poor mounting.
10. Inspect the wheels and tires on the vehicle. They must be of the same size and type to generate accurate speed signals. Check also for approximately equal tire pressures.
11. Confirm the fault occurrence with the operator. Certain driver induced faults may cause dash warning lamps to light. Excessive wheel spin on low-traction surfaces or high speed acceleration may also set fault codes and trigger a warning lamp. These induced faults are not system failures but examples of vehicle performance outside the parameters of the controller.
12. The most common cause of intermittent faults is not a failed sensor but a loose, corroded or dirty connector. Incorrect installation of the wheel speed sensor will cause a loss of wheel speed signal. Check harness and component connectors carefully.

➡ If the battery on the vehicle has been completely drained, always recharge the battery before driving. If the vehicle is driven immediately after jump starting, the ABS self-check may draw enough current to make the engine run improperly. An alternate solution is to disconnect the ABS connector at the hydraulic unit. This will disable the ABS and illuminate the dash warning lamp. Reconnect the ABS when the battery is sufficiently charged.

GENERAL INFORMATION

▶ See Figure 130

Both the amber ANTI-LOCK light and red BRAKE light are located on the instrument cluster. Each lamp warns the operator of a possible fault in the respective system. A fault in one system may cause the other lamp to illuminate depending on the nature and severity of the problem. The operation or behavior of the amber warning lamp is one of the prime diagnostic tools for the system.

When the system is operating correctly, the ANTI-LOCK warning lamp will flash either twice (FWD) or 4 times (AWD) vehicles, in about 1 second with the ignition switch **ON**, then the lamp will turn **OFF**. During the lamp illumination the control unit checks the valve relays for proper function. When the ignition is turned to **START**, power to the ABS controller is interrupted and the warning lamp stays **ON**. Once the ignition returns to the **ON** position, power is restored and the system re-checks itself. This self test again yields either the two or four blinks. The warning lamp goes out and should stay off during operation of the vehicle.

Perform the following procedure to determine if the warning lamp and the ABS system is functioning properly:

FWD Vehicles

1. Turn the ignition switch **ON** and verify the ABS light flashes twice in about 1 second; then goes **OFF**. During this time the valve relay is being tested.
2. Turn the ignition switch to the **START** position. The light should remain **ON**.
3. When the ignition switch is returned from the **START** position to the **ON** position the light should flash twice again and then go **OFF**. Once again the valve relay is tested.
4. If the light does not illuminate as specified, inspection of the ABS system is required.

AWD Vehicles

1. Turn the ignition switch **ON** and verify the ABS light flashes 4 times in about 1 second; then goes **OFF**. During this time the valve relay is being tested.
2. Turn the ignition switch to the **START** position. The light should remain **ON**.

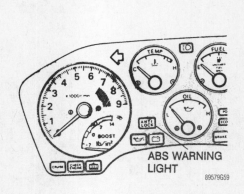

Fig. 130 ABS warning lamp location—1991–94 FWD and AWD vehicles shown

3. When the ignition switch is returned from the **START** position to the **ON** position the light should flash 4 times again and then go **OFF**. Once again the valve relay is tested.

4. If the light does not illuminate as specified, inspection of the ABS system is required.

Hydraulic Unit

The hydraulic unit is located in the engine compartment. It contains the solenoid valves and the pump/motor assembly which provides pressurized fluid for the anti-lock system when necessary. Hydraulic units are not interchangeable on any vehicles. Neither unit is serviceable; if any fault occurs within the hydraulic unit, the entire unit must be replaced.

REMOVAL & INSTALLATION

1991–94 Vehicles

▶ See Figures 131 and 132

1. Disconnect the negative battery cable. Use a syringe or similar device to remove as much fluid as possible from the reservoir. Some fluid will be spilled from lines during removal of the hydraulic unit so make sure to protect adjacent painted surfaces.

2. On turbocharged engine, remove the center intercooler duct. Loosen the clamps and remove the bolts holding the duct to the air cleaner.

3. Disconnect the brake lines from the hydraulic unit. Correct reassembly is critical. Label or identify the lines before removal. Plug each line immediately after removal.

4. Remove the cover from the relay box. Disconnect the electrical harness to the hydraulic unit.

5. Disconnect the hydraulic unit ground strap from the chassis.

6. Remove the 3 nuts holding the hydraulic unit. Remove the unit upwards.

➡ The hydraulic unit is heavy; use care when removing it. The unit must remain in the upright position at all times and be protected from impact and shock.

7. Set the unit upright supported by blocks on the workbench. The hydraulic unit must not be tilted or turned upside down. No component of the hydraulic unit should be loosened or disassembled.

8. The bracket assemblies and relays may be removed if desired.

To install:

9. Install the relays and brackets if removed.

10. Install the hydraulic unit into the vehicle, keeping it upright at all times.

11. Install the retaining nuts and tighten.

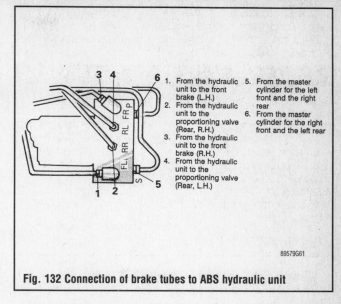

1. From the hydraulic unit to the front brake (L.H.)
2. From the hydraulic unit to the proportioning valve (Rear, R.H.)
3. From the hydraulic unit to the front brake (R.H.)
4. From the hydraulic unit to the proportioning valve (Rear, L.H.)
5. From the master cylinder for the left front and the right rear
6. From the master cylinder for the right front and the left rear

Fig. 132 Connection of brake tubes to ABS hydraulic unit

12. Connect the ground strap to the chassis bracket. Connect the hydraulic unit wiring harness.

13. Install the cover on the relay box.

14. Connect each brake line loosely to the correct port and double check the placement. Tighten each line to 10 ft. lbs. (13.5 Nm).

15. Fill the reservoir to the MAX line with brake fluid.

16. Bleed the master cylinder, then bleed the brake lines.

17. If equipped, install the intercooler air duct.

1995–98 Vehicles

▶ See Figures 133 and 134

1. Disconnect the negative battery cable. Use a syringe or similar device to remove as much fluid as possible from the reservoir. Some fluid will be spilled from lines during removal of the hydraulic unit so make sure to protect adjacent painted surfaces.

2. Remove the left side splash shield.

3. Remove the left side headlight assembly.

4. For the 2.0L non-turbo engine, remove the following components:
   a. Air cleaner assembly
   b. Engine Control Module (ECM)
   c. Relay box bracket

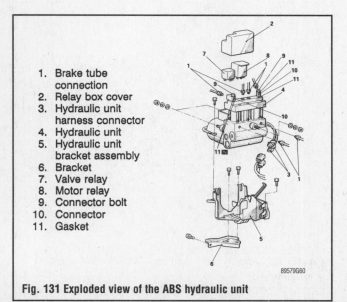

1. Brake tube connection
2. Relay box cover
3. Hydraulic unit harness connector
4. Hydraulic unit
5. Hydraulic unit bracket assembly
6. Bracket
7. Valve relay
8. Motor relay
9. Connector bolt
10. Connector
11. Gasket

Fig. 131 Exploded view of the ABS hydraulic unit

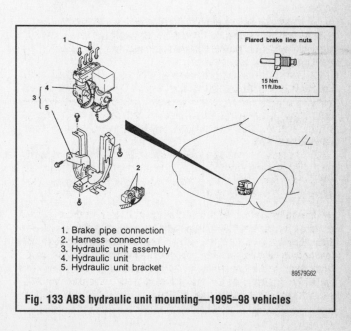

Flared brake line nuts

15 Nm
11 ft.lbs.

1. Brake pipe connection
2. Harness connector
3. Hydraulic unit assembly
4. Hydraulic unit
5. Hydraulic unit bracket

Fig. 133 ABS hydraulic unit mounting—1995–98 vehicles

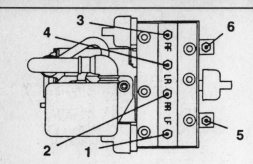

1. Hydraulic unit – Front brake (L.H.)
2. Hydraulic unit – Rear brake (R.H.)
3. Hydraulic unit – Front brake (R.H.)
4. Hydraulic unit – Rear braker (L.H.)
5. Hydraulic unit – Master cylinder (Secondary)
6. Hydraulic unit – Master cylinder (Primary)

89579G63

Fig. 134 Hydraulic unit brake line connection identification

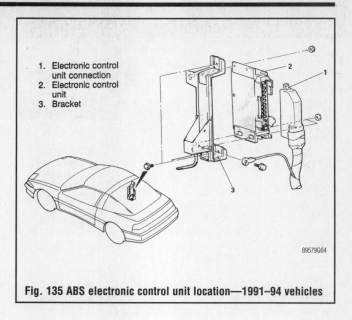

1. Electronic control unit connection
2. Electronic control unit
3. Bracket

89579G64

Fig. 135 ABS electronic control unit location—1991–94 vehicles

5. For 2.0L turbo and 2.4L engines, unfasten the power steering fluid reservoir mounting bolts. Remove the power steering pressure pipe and return pipe clamp mounting bolts.
6. Disconnect the brake lines from the hydraulic unit.
7. Detach the electrical harness connector.
8. Unfasten the bolts, then remove the hydraulic unit assembly.

✳✳ WARNING

Be careful when removing the hydraulic unit, as it is heavier than is looks. Do not disassemble, drop or turn the unit upside down.

9. If necessary, you can remove the retainers then separate the hydraulic unit from the bracket.
10. Installation is the reverse of the removal, but make sure to connect the brake lines to the unit as shown in the accompanying figure.
11. Properly bleed the brake system, as outlined in this section.

Anti-Lock Control Unit (ALCU)/Engine Control Unit (ECU)

The anti-lock control unit is located behind the right rear quarter trim panel on 1991–94 vehicles or under the passenger side of the dash on 1995–98 vehicles. It is a micro-processor capable of dealing with many inputs simultaneously and controls the function of the solenoid valves within the hydraulic unit.

REMOVAL & INSTALLATION

1991–94 Vehicles

▶ See Figure 135

1. Turn the key to the **OFF** position. Ensure that the ignition switch remains **OFF** throughout the procedure.
2. Disconnect the negative battery cable.
3. Remove the interior right rear quarter trim panel and rear seat back and/or cushion.
4. Release the lock on the bottom of the connector; disconnect the multi-pin connector from the control unit. Access may be easier if the external ground is disconnected from the bracket.
5. Remove the retaining nuts and remove the control unit from its bracket. The bracket may be removed, if desired.

To install:

6. Place the bracket in position. Install the controller and tighten the retaining nuts.
7. Connect the ground wire to the bracket if removed. Ensure a proper, tight connection. The ground must be connected before the multi-pin harness is connected.
8. Connect the multi-pin connector and secure the lock.
9. Install the rear quarter trim panel and seat.
10. Connect the negative battery cable.

1995–98 Vehicles

▶ See Figure 136

1. Disconnect the negative battery cable.
2. Remove the right side cowl side trim panel and front scuff plate.
3. Unfasten the retainers, then remove the control unit cover.
4. Detach the electrical connector.
5. Remove the retaining nuts, then remove the ABS control unit.
6. Installation is the reverse of the removal procedure.

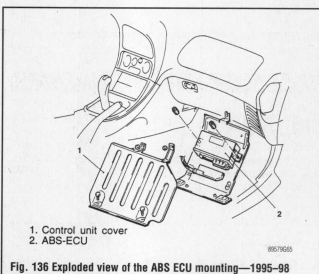

1. Control unit cover
2. ABS-ECU

89579G65

Fig. 136 Exploded view of the ABS ECU mounting—1995–98 vehicles

ABS Power Relay

TESTING

▶ See Figure 137

1. Disconnect the system relay.
2. Connect the positive lead of a voltmeter to terminal **3** of the relay connector and the other lead to ground.
3. Verify that there is approximately 12 volts with the ignition switch **ON**. If not as specified, inspect the ABS system fuse and wiring to the relay.
4. Turn the ignition switch **OFF**. Disconnect the system relay and remove from the ABS control unit bracket.
5. Connect a jumper wire from the positive battery terminal to terminal **2** of the relay. Connect terminal **4** of the relay to ground. Using and ohmmeter, measure the resistance present at terminals **1** and **3**, while power is supplied. The meter should read continuity.
6. Disconnect the power supply and ground from the relay.
7. Connect an ohmmeter between terminals **2** and **4** on the relay and check the resistance. Continuity should be present.
8. Connect the ohmmeter leads between terminals **1** and **3** and check the resistance. No continuity should be present.
9. If the readings are not as specified, replace the relay.
10. If the relay test good, inspect the control unit and wiring.

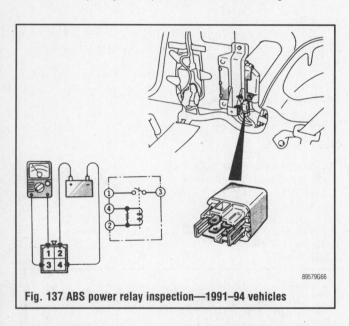

Fig. 137 ABS power relay inspection—1991–94 vehicles

G–Sensor

The G-sensor is used only on the AWD vehicles. It is mounted under the rear seat cushion, directly between the seat belt heads on 1991–94 vehicles. On 1995–98 vehicles, the sensor is mounted behind the front floor console. The sensor transmits acceleration and deceleration information to the Anti-lock control unit. This data is used in conjunction with individual wheel speed and engine data, allowing the controller to determine the approximate road friction. This friction factor is then used to compute the proper control of the solenoid valves.

TESTING

1991–94 Vehicles

▶ See Figures 138 and 139

1. Remove the sensor and position on a level surface.
2. Connect an ohmmeter between the terminal of the sensor and verify there is continuity.

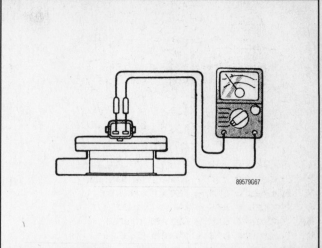

Fig. 138 G–sensor inspection—checking for continuity of sensor while on flat surface

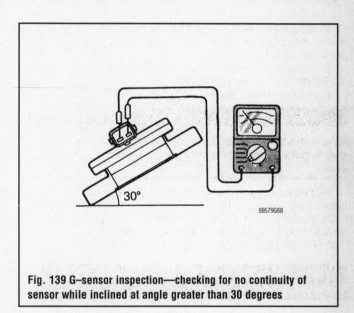

Fig. 139 G–sensor inspection—checking for no continuity of sensor while inclined at angle greater than 30 degrees

3. Tilt the sensor slowly 30 degrees in the direction of vehicle travel and verify the ohmmeter reads infinity.
4. Tilt the sensor slowly 30 degrees toward the rear of the vehicle and verify the ohmmeter reads infinity.
5. If not as specified, replace the G sensor.

1995–98 Vehicles

▶ See Figures 140 and 141

1. Detach the G-sensor connector, then connect the test harness set MB991348, or equivalent, between the terminals of the detached connector.
2. Turn the ignition switch **ON** and take a reading of the output voltage between terminals 2 and 3. The reading should be 2.4–2.6 volts.
3. With the special tool still connected, secure the G-sensor so that the front mark on the sensor mounting surface is facing straight down, then take a reading of the output voltage between terminals 2 and 3. The reading should be 3.3–3.7 volts.
4. If the voltage is outside the standard value, after checking to be sure the wiring is operating properly, replace the G-sensor.

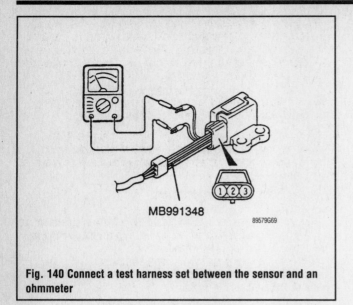

Fig. 140 Connect a test harness set between the sensor and an ohmmeter

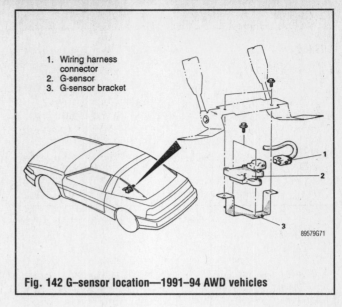

1. Wiring harness connector
2. G-sensor
3. G-sensor bracket

Fig. 142 G–sensor location—1991–94 AWD vehicles

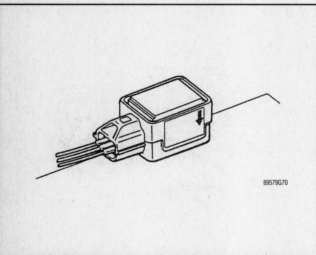

Fig. 141 Position the G-sensor with the front mark on the mounting surface facing straight down, then take a voltage reading

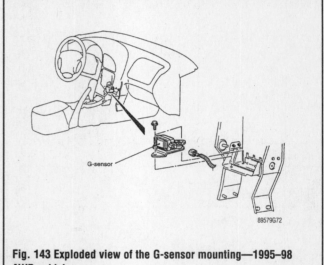

Fig. 143 Exploded view of the G-sensor mounting—1995–98 AWD vehicles

REMOVAL & INSTALLATION

▶ **See Figures 142 and 143**

1. Insure that the ignition switch is **OFF** throughout the procedure.
2. Disconnect the negative battery cable.
3. For 1991–94 vehicles, remove the rear seat cushion.
4. For 1995–98 vehicles, remove the radio/tape/CD player assembly, as outlined in Section 6 of this manual.
5. Disconnect the wiring harness from the G–sensor.
6. Remove the retaining bolts and remove the sensor.

To install:

7. Position the sensor on the mounting bracket. Tighten the retaining bolts.
8. Connect the electrical harness.

9. Install the rear seat cushion or radio, as applicable.
10. Connect the negative battery cable.

Wheel Speed Sensors

Each wheel is equipped with a magnetic sensor mounted a fixed distance from a toothed ring which rotates with the wheel. The sensors are replaceable but not interchangeable; each must be fitted to its correct location. The toothed rings are replaceable although disassembly of the hub or axle shaft is required.

The wheel speed sensor is designed to produce a voltage directly proportional to the speed of the wheel. In other words as the speed of the wheel increases, so does the voltage. The voltage should not fluctuate when the wheel speed (speedometer) reading is steady.

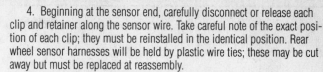

TESTING

1991–94 Vehicles

♦ **See Figure 144**

1. Raise and safely support the vehicle.
2. Detach the suspected malfunctioning sensor wire connector.
3. Connect an ohmmeter to the sensor connector 2 terminals.
4. The resistances should be 0.8–1.2 kilo-ohms for 1991–94 vehicles, or 1.0–1.2 kilo-ohms for 1995–98 vehicles.
5. If the resistance is not within specifications, replace the speed sensor.

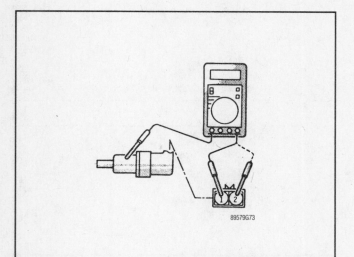

Fig. 144 Measure the resistance between the speed sensor terminals

REMOVAL & INSTALLATION

♦ **See Figures 145 thru 152**

1. Elevate and safely support the vehicle.
2. Remove the wheel and tire assembly and the disc brake rotor.
3. Remove the inner fender or splash shield.

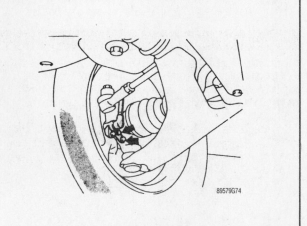

Fig. 145 Front speed sensor and mounting bolt—1991–94 vehicles

4. Beginning at the sensor end, carefully disconnect or release each clip and retainer along the sensor wire. Take careful note of the exact position of each clip; they must be reinstalled in the identical position. Rear wheel sensor harnesses will be held by plastic wire ties; these may be cut away but must be replaced at reassembly.
5. Detach the sensor connector at the end of the harness.
6. Remove the two bolts holding the speed sensor bracket to the knuckle and remove the assembly from the vehicle.

➡**The speed sensor has a pole piece projecting from it. This exposed tip must be protected from impact or scratches. Do not allow the pole piece to contact the toothed wheel during removal or installation.**

7. Remove the sensor from the bracket.
To install:
8. Assemble the sensor onto the bracket. Note that the brackets are different for the left and right front wheels, as well as both side rear wheels. Each bracket has identifying letters stamped on it.
9. Identify the front speed sensor brackets as follows:
   a. FR: Indicates that the bracket is for the front speed sensor.
   b. R: Indicates that the bracket is for the right wheel.
   c. L: Indicates that the bracket is for the left wheel.

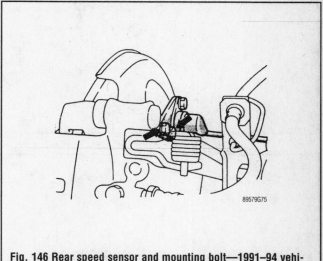

Fig. 146 Rear speed sensor and mounting bolt—1991–94 vehicles

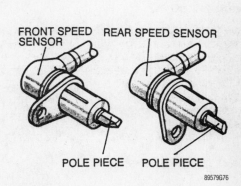

Fig. 147 Inspect removed speed sensor for damaged pole piece. Also check pole piece for foreign material or metal adhesion

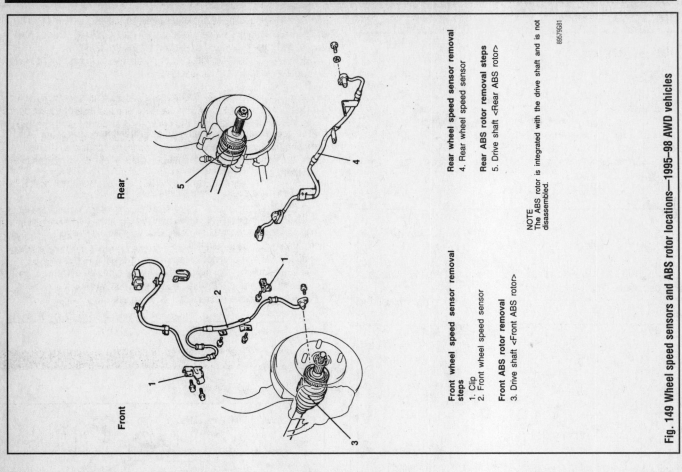

Front wheel speed sensor removal
steps
1. Clip
2. Front wheel speed sensor

Front ABS rotor removal
3. Drive shaft <Front ABS rotor>

Rear wheel speed sensor removal
4. Rear wheel speed sensor

Rear ABS rotor removal steps
5. Drive shaft <Rear ABS rotor>

NOTE
The ABS rotor is integrated with the drive shaft and is not disassembled.

89579G81

Fig. 149 Wheel speed sensors and ABS rotor locations—1995–98 AWD vehicles

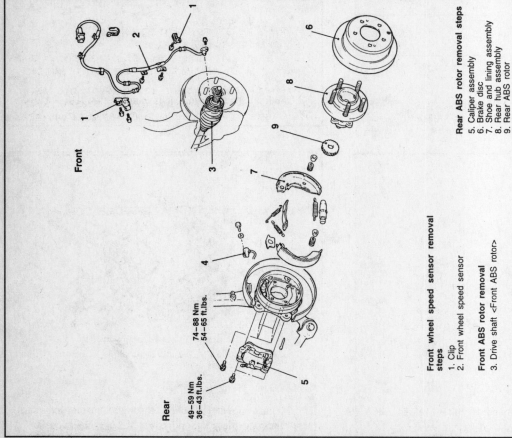

Front wheel speed sensor removal
steps
1. Clip
2. Front wheel speed sensor

Front ABS rotor removal
3. Drive shaft <Front ABS rotor>

Rear wheel speed sensor removal
4. Rear wheel speed sensor

Rear ABS rotor removal steps
5. Caliper assembly
6. Brake disc
7. Shoe and lining assembly
8. Rear hub assembly
9. Rear ABS rotor

Rear

49–59 Nm
36–43 ft.lbs.

74–88 Nm
54–65 ft.lbs.

NOTE
The front ABS rotor, integrated with the drive shaft, can not be disassembled.

89579G80

Fig. 148 Exploded view of the wheel speed sensors and ABS rotor—1995–98 FWD vehicles

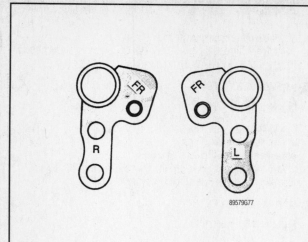

Fig. 150 Left and right speed sensor brackets with identification markings—1991–94 vehicles

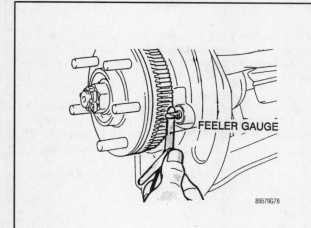

Fig. 151 Checking the clearance between the pole piece of the speed sensor and the rotor's toothed surface—1991–94 vehicles

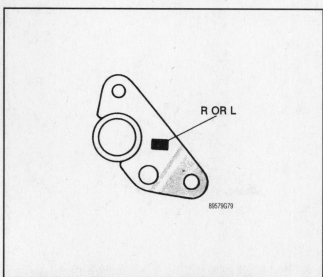

Fig. 152 Rear speed sensor bracket identification marking

10. Identify the rear speed sensor brackets as follows:
  a. R: Indicates that the bracket is for the right wheel.
  b. L: Indicates that the bracket is for the left wheel.
11. Temporarily install the speed sensor to the spindle or knuckle; tighten the bolts only finger tight.

➡**During speed sensor installation to the mounting bracket, make sure the letters FR are visible. Be careful when installing the speed sensor on the vehicle, that the pole piece at the tip of the sensor does not strike the toothed edge of the rotor, and damage them.**

12. Route the cable correctly and loosely install the clips and retainers. All clips must be in their original position and the sensor cable must not be twisted. Improper installation may cause cable damage and system failure.
13. Use a brass or other non-magnetic feeler gauge to check the air gap between the tip of the pole piece and the toothed wheel. The correct gap is 0.012–0.035 inch (0.3–0.9mm). Tighten the 2 sensor bracket bolts to 10 ft. lbs. (14 Nm) with the sensor located so that the gap is the same at several points on the toothed wheel. If the gap is incorrect, it is likely that the toothed wheel is worn or improperly installed.
14. Tighten the screws and bolts for the cable retaining clips.
15. Install the disc brake rotor, inner fender or splash shield.
16. Install the wheel and tire assembly. Lower the vehicle to the ground.
17. Inspect the brake system for proper operation.

Toothed Wheels/ABS Rotor

REMOVAL & INSTALLATION

▶ **See Figures 148 and 149**

Front Wheel Ring

1991–94 VEHICLES

▶ **See Figure 153**

1. Elevate and safely support the vehicle.
2. Remove the wheel and tire assembly.
3. Remove the wheel speed sensor and disconnect sufficient harness clips to allow the sensor and wiring to be moved out of the work area.

➡**The speed sensor has a pole piece projecting from it. This exposed tip must be protected from impact or scratches. Do not allow the pole piece to contact the toothed wheel during removal or installation.**

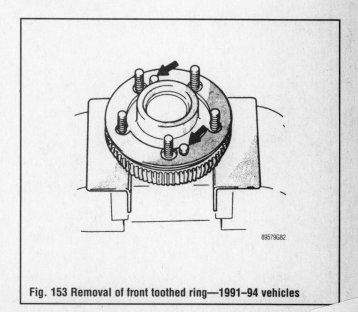

Fig. 153 Removal of front toothed ring—1991–94 vehicles

4. Remove the front hub and knuckle assembly.

5. Remove the hub from the knuckle.

6. Support the hub in a vise with protected jaws. Remove the retaining bolts from the toothed wheel and remove the toothed wheel.

To install:

7. Fit the new toothed wheel onto the hub and tighten the retaining bolts to 7 ft. lbs. (10 Nm).

8. Assemble the hub to the knuckle

9. Install the hub and knuckle assembly onto the vehicle.

10. Install the wheel speed sensor following procedures given in this section.

11. Install the wheel and tire assembly.

12. Lower the vehicle to the ground. Inspect the brake system for proper operation.

1995–98 VEHICLES

▶ **See Figures 148 and 149**

The front ABS rotor is integral with the driveshaft. If the rotor required replacement, you must replace the driveshaft assembly.

Rear Wheel Ring

1990–94 FWD VEHICLES

▶ **See Figure 154**

1. Raise and safely support the vehicle.

2. Remove the wheel and tire assembly. Remove the rear brake rotor.

3. Remove the wheel speed sensor and disconnect sufficient harness clips to allow the sensor and wiring to be moved out of the work area.

➡**The speed sensor has a pole piece projecting from it. This exposed tip must be protected from impact or scratches. Do not allow the pole piece to contact the toothed wheel during removal or installation.**

4. Remove the rear hub assembly.

5. Support the hub in a vise with protected jaws. Remove the retaining bolts from the toothed wheel and remove the toothed wheel.

To install:

6. Fit the new toothed wheel onto the hub and tighten the retaining bolts to 7 ft. lbs. (10 Nm).

7. Install the hub assembly to the vehicle. The center hub nut is not reusable. The new nut must be tightened to 144–188 ft. lbs. (200–260 Nm). After the nut is tightened, align the nut with the spindle indentation and crimp the nut in place.

8. Install the wheel speed sensor following procedures given in this section.

9. Install the brake rotor, caliper and tire assembly.

10. Lower the vehicle to the ground. Check the brakes for proper operation.

1995–98 FWD VEHICLES

▶ **See Figure 148**

1. Remove the brake caliper assembly.

2. Remove the brake disc (rotor).

3. Reove the shoe and lining assembly.

4. Remove the rear hub assembly, then remove the rear ABS rotor.

5. Installation is the reverse of the removal procedure.

1990–94 AWD VEHICLES

▶ **See Figures 155 and 156**

1. Disconnect the negative battery cable. Raise and safely support the vehicle.

2. Remove the wheel and tire assembly.

3. Disconnect the parking brake cable at the caliper.

4. Remove the speed sensor and its O-ring. Disconnect sufficient clamps and wire ties to allow the sensor to be moved well out of the work area.

➡**The speed sensor has a pole piece projecting from it. This exposed tip must be protected from impact or scratches. Do not allow the pole piece to contact the toothed wheel during removal or installation.**

5. Remove the brake caliper and brake disc.

6. Matchmark the drive shaft to the companion flange. Remove the 3 retaining nuts and bolts holding the outer end of the driveshaft to the companion flange. Swing the axle shaft away and support it with stiff wire. Do not overextend the joint in the axle; do not allow it to hang of its own weight.

7. Remove the retaining nut and washer on the back of the driveshaft. Use special tool MB990767 or equivalent, to counterhold the hub.

8. Remove the companion flange from the knuckle.

9. Using an axle puller which bolts to the wheel lugs, remove the axle shaft assembly.

10. Fit the shaft assembly in a press with the toothed wheel completely supported by a bearing plate such as special tool MB990560 or equivalent.

11. Press the toothed wheel off the axle shaft.

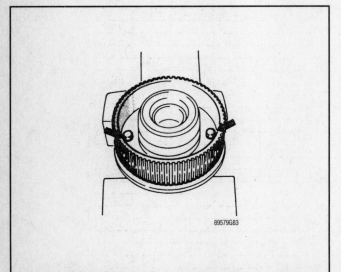

Fig. 154 Removal of rear toothed ring—1990–94 FWD vehicles

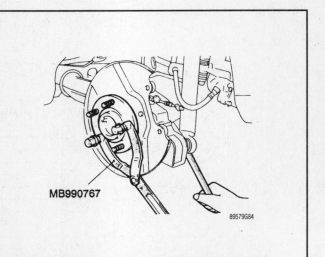

Fig. 155 Holding the rear axle shaft stationary using tool MB990767

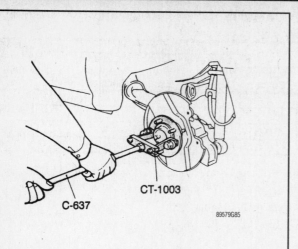

Fig. 156 Removing the rear axle shaft using tool CT–1003 and tool C–637

C-637

CT-1003

89579G85

To install:

12. Press the new toothed wheel onto the shaft with the groove facing the axle shaft flange.

13. Install the axle shaft to the knuckle and fit the companion flange in place.

14. Install the lock washer and a new self–locking nut on the axle shaft. Hold the axle shaft stationary and torque nut to 116–159 ft. lbs. (160–220 Nm).

15. Swing the axle assembly into place and install the nuts and bolts. Tighten each to 45 ft. lbs. (61 Nm).

16. Install the brake disc and caliper.

17. Install the wheel speed sensor. Always use a new O-ring.

18. Connect the parking brake cable to the caliper.

19. Install the wheel and tire.

20. Lower the vehicle to the ground and check for proper brake operation.

1995–98 AWD VEHICLES

▶ See Figure 149

The rear ABS rotor is integral with the driveshaft. If the rotor required replacement, you must replace the driveshaft assembly.

BRAKE SPECIFICATIONS
All measurements in inches unless noted

Year	Model		Master Cylinder Bore	Original Thickness	Minimum Thickness	Maximum Runout	Original Inside Diameter	Max. Wear Limit	Maximum Machine Diameter	Front	Rear
				Brake Disc			Brake Drum Diameter			Wheel Cylinder or Caliper Bore	
1990	Eclipse	F	①	0.940	0.882	0.003	—	—	—	0.080	—
		R	—	0.390	0.331	0.003	—	—	—	—	0.080
	Laser	F	①	0.940	0.882	0.003	—	—	—	0.080	—
		R	—	0.390	0.331	0.003	—	—	—	—	0.080
	Talon	F	①	0.940	0.882	0.003	—	—	—	0.080	—
		R	—	0.390	0.331	0.003	—	—	—	—	0.080
1991	Eclipse	F	②	0.940	0.882	0.003	—	—	—	0.080	—
		R	—	0.390	0.331	0.003	—	—	—	—	0.080
	Laser	F	②	0.940	0.882	0.003	—	—	—	0.080	—
		R	—	0.390	0.331	0.003	—	—	—	—	0.080
	Talon	F	②	0.940	0.882	0.003	—	—	—	0.080	—
		R	—	0.390	0.331	0.003	—	—	—	—	0.080
1992	Eclipse	F	②	0.940	0.882	0.003	—	—	—	0.080	—
		R	—	0.390	0.331	0.003	—	—	—	—	0.080
	Laser	F	②	0.940	0.882	0.003	—	—	—	0.080	—
		R	—	0.390	0.331	0.003	—	—	—	—	0.080
	Talon	F	②	0.940	0.882	0.003	—	—	—	0.080	—
		R	—	0.390	0.331	0.003	—	—	—	—	0.080
1993	Eclipse	F	③	0.940	0.882	0.003	—	—	—	0.080	—
		R	—	0.390	0.331	0.003	—	—	—	—	0.080
	Laser	F	③	0.940	0.882	0.003	—	—	—	0.080	—
		R	—	0.390	0.331	0.003	—	—	—	—	0.080
	Talon	F	③	0.940	0.882	0.003	—	—	—	0.080	—
		R	—	0.390	0.331	0.003	—	—	—	—	0.080
1994	Eclipse	F	③	0.940	0.880	0.003	—	—	—	0.079	—
		R	—	0.390	0.330	0.003	—	—	—	—	0.079
	Laser	F	③	0.940	0.880	0.003	—	—	—	0.079	—
		R	—	0.390	0.330	0.003	—	—	—	—	0.079
	Talon	F	③	0.940	0.880	0.003	—	—	—	0.079	—
		R	—	0.390	0.330	0.003	—	—	—	—	0.079
1995	Eclipse	F	④	0.940	0.880	0.003	—	—	—	0.079	⑦
		R	—	⑤	⑥	0.003	8.00	—	8.10	—	0.079
	Talon	F	④	0.940	0.880	0.003	—	—	—	0.080	0.080
		R	—	⑤	⑥	0.003	—	—	—	0.080	0.080
1996	Eclipse	F	④	0.940	0.880	0.003	—	—	—	0.079	⑦
		R	—	⑤	⑥	0.003	9.00	—	9.10	—	0.079
	Talon	F	④	0.940	0.880	0.003	—	—	—	0.080	0.080
		R	—	⑤	⑥	0.003	—	—	—	0.080	0.080
1997	Eclipse	F	④	0.940	0.880	0.003	—	—	—	0.079	⑦
		R	—	⑤	⑥	0.003	9.00	—	9.10	—	0.079
	Talon	F	④	0.940	0.880	0.003	—	—	—	0.080	0.080
		R	—	⑤	⑥	0.003	—	—	—	0.080	0.080

89579C01

BRAKE SPECIFICATIONS
All measurements in inches unless noted

Year	Model		Master Cylinder Bore	Brake Disc Original Thickness	Brake Disc Minimum Thickness	Maximum Runout	Brake Drum Diameter Original Inside Diameter	Brake Drum Diameter Max. Wear Limit	Brake Drum Diameter Maximum Machine Diameter	Wheel Cylinder or Caliper Bore Front	Wheel Cylinder or Caliper Bore Rear
1998	Eclipse	F	④	0.940	0.880	0.003	—	—	—	0.079	⑦
		R	—	⑤	⑥	0.003	9.00	—	9.10	—	0.079
	Talon	F	④	0.940	0.880	0.003	—	—	—	0.080	0.080
		R	—	⑤	⑥	0.003	—	—	—	0.080	0.080

① Non-turbo engines: 0.875
  Turbo engines: 0.938
② Non-turbo without ABS: 0.875
  Non-turbo with ABS: 0.938
  Turbo with FWD: 0.875
  Turbo with AWD: 1.0
③ Non-turbo without ABS: 0.875
  Non-turbo with ABS: 0.938
  Turbo with FWD: 1.0
  Turbo with AWD: 1.0
④ Without ABS or AWD: 0.938
  With ABS or AWD: 1.0
⑤ FWD Vehicles: 0.390
  AWD Vehicles: 0.790
⑥ FWD Vehicles: 0.330
  AWD Vehicles: 0.720
⑦ Drum shoe: 0.040

89579C02

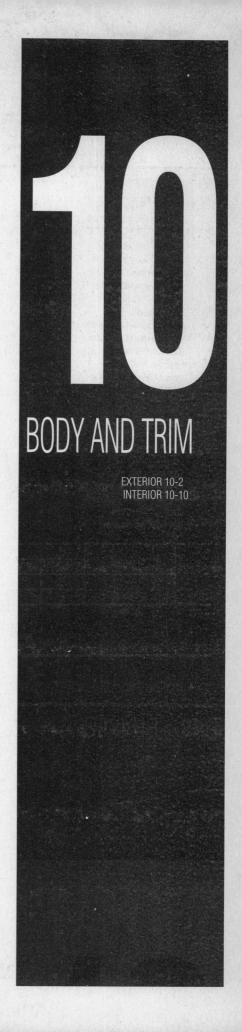

10

BODY AND TRIM

EXTERIOR

Doors

REMOVAL & INSTALLATION

▶ **See Figures 1, 2 and 3**

1. Disconnect the negative battery terminal.
2. If equipped with power door locks, windows or any other power option located on the door, detach the necessary electrical connector(s). On some vehicles, it may be necessary to remove the inner door panel and waterproof film from the door to access the connector(s).
3. Remove the wire harness retainers and extract the harness from the door.
4. Remove the spring pin and disconnect the door check strap. To prevent the strap from falling inside the door, install the retainer into the hole in the end of the check rod.
5. Matchmark the position of both the upper and lower door hinge to aid in alignment during installation. While supporting the door, remove the door-to-hinge bolts and lift the door from the vehicle.

To install:

6. Position the door on the vehicle and loosely install the hinge bolts.

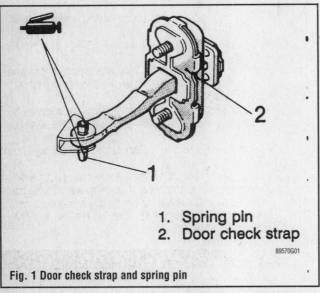

1. Spring pin
2. Door check strap

Fig. 1 Door check strap and spring pin

89570G01

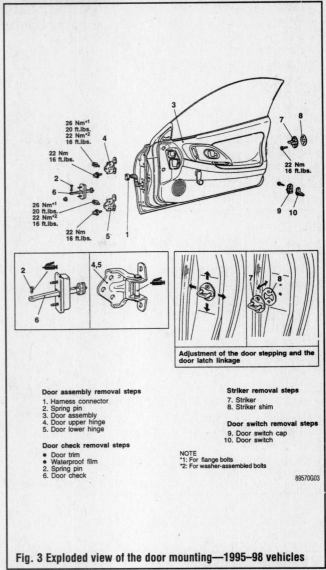

Adjustment of the door stepping and the door latch linkage

Door assembly removal steps
1. Harness connector
2. Spring pin
3. Door assembly
4. Door upper hinge
5. Door lower hinge

Door check removal steps
● Door trim
● Waterproof film
2. Spring pin
6. Door check

Striker removal steps
7. Striker
8. Striker shim

Door switch removal steps
9. Door switch cap
10. Door switch

NOTE
*1: For flange bolts
*2: For washer-assembled bolts

89570G03

Fig. 3 Exploded view of the door mounting—1995–98 vehicles

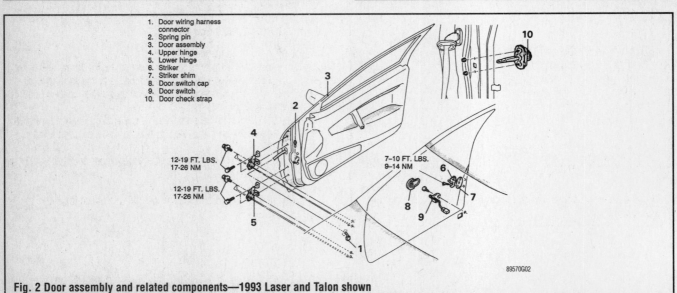

1. Door wiring harness connector
2. Spring pin
3. Door assembly
4. Upper hinge
5. Lower hinge
6. Striker
7. Striker shim
8. Door switch cap
9. Door switch
10. Door check strap

12-19 FT. LBS.
17-26 NM

12-19 FT. LBS.
17-26 NM

7-10 FT. LBS.
9-14 NM

89570G02

Fig. 2 Door assembly and related components—1993 Laser and Talon shown

7. Align each hinge to the matchmarks and secure the hinge mounting bolts. Tighten to the specifications shown in the accompanying figures.

8. Install and connect the electrical wire harness. Secure harness to the door using retainers.

9. Install the door check so that the identification mark faces upwards. Reinstall the interior door trim panel, if removed.

10. Close the door slowly and check for proper alignment. Adjust the door as required and reconnect the negative battery cable.

ADJUSTMENT

▶ See Figures 4, 5 and 6

Adjustment of the door hinge is made easier with hinge bolt loosening wrench MB990834-01 or equivalent.

1. Apply appropriate tape to the fender and door edges to protect painted surfaces from damage.

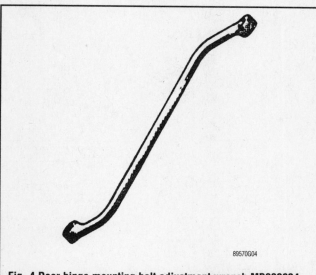

Fig. 4 Door hinge mounting bolt adjustment wrench MB990834

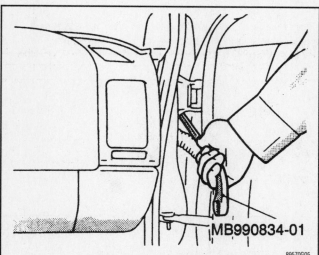

Fig. 5 Using the special wrench to loosen the door upper hinge mounting bolts

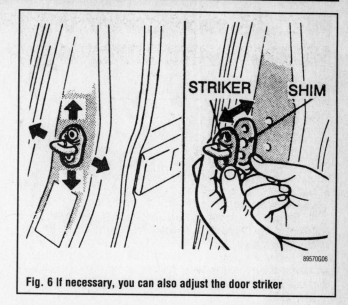

Fig. 6 If necessary, you can also adjust the door striker

2. Use the special wrench to loosen the hinge mounting bolts on the body side of the door slightly.

3. Adjust the door so the clearance around the door is uniform on all sides.

4. Tighten the hinge bolts to 12–19 ft. lbs. (17–26 Nm), once the door is in the desired position.

5. When the hinge has been replaced, adjust the alignment as follows:

   a. Install the hinge in position on the vehicle aligning the matchmarks made during removal.

   b. Loosen the hinge mounting bolts on the door side of the hinge.

   c. Adjust the alignment of the fender panel with the front of the door panel.

   d. Once the desired positioning is obtained, tighten the hinge mounting bolts in place.

6. To adjust the door striker, loosen the striker mounting bolts and adjust positioning as required. Increase or decease the number of shims behind the striker to adjust the engagement of the striker with the door.

7. Tighten the striker mounting bolts to 10 ft. lbs. (14 Nm) once the adjustment has been made.

Hood

REMOVAL & INSTALLATION

▶ See Figures 7, 8, 9 and 10

1. Open the hood completely.

2. Protect the cowl panel and hood from scratches during this operation. Apply protection tape or cover body surfaces before starting work.

3. Scribe a mark showing the location of each hinge on the hood to aid in alignment during installation.

4. Have an assistant help hold the hood while you remove the hood-to-hinge bolts. Use care not to damage hood or vehicle during hood removal.

5. Disconnect the connection for the washer tubes and nozzles. Lift the hood off of the vehicle.

To install:

6. Position the hood on hinges and align with the scribe marks made during removal.

Fig. 7 Use a paint marker to matchmark the installed position of the hood hinges

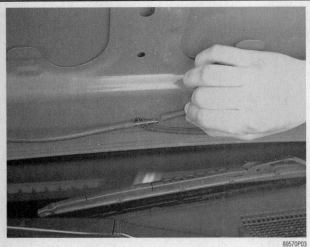

Fig. 8 Unplug the windshield washer fluid connection from the center of the hood

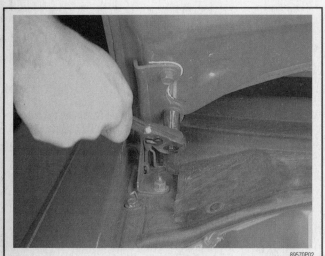

Fig. 9 With an assistant supporting the hood, unfasten the retaining bolts

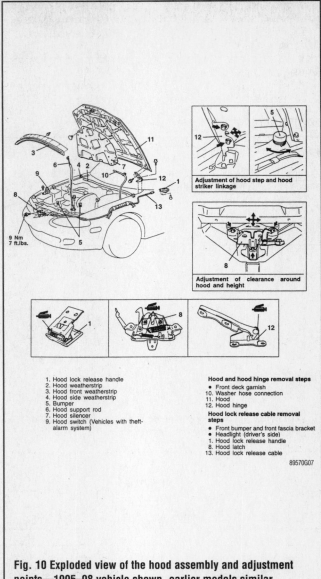

1. Hood lock release handle
2. Hood weatherstrip
3. Hood front weatherstrip
4. Hood side weatherstrip
5. Bumper
6. Hood support rod
7. Hood silencer
9. Hood switch (Vehicles with theft-alarm system)

Adjustment of hood step and hood striker linkage

Adjustment of clearance around hood and height

9 Nm
7 ft.lbs.

Hood and hood hinge removal steps
• Front deck garnish
10. Washer hose connection
11. Hood
12. Hood hinge

Hood lock release cable removal steps
• Front bumper and front fascia bracket
• Headlight (driver's side)
1. Hood lock release handle
8. Hood latch
13. Hood lock release cable

Fig. 10 Exploded view of the hood assembly and adjustment points—1995–98 vehicle shown, earlier models similar

7. Install and tighten the mounting bolts with enough torque to hold hood in place.

8. Close the hood slowly to check for proper alignment. Do not slam the hood closed, alignment is normally required.

9. Open the hood and adjust so that all clearances are the same and the hood panel is flush with the body.

10. After all adjustments are complete, torque hood-to-hinge bolts to 10 ft. lbs. (14 Nm) torque.

ALIGNMENT

▶ **See Figure 10**

1. To adjust the hood in a forward or rearward and left or right directions, loosen the hood mounting bolts and position so the clearance is uniform on all sides.

2. To adjust the front edges of the hood in a vertical direction, turn the hood bumper cushions as required.

3. To adjust the hood lock, remove the retainer clips and the front fascia bracket. Loosen the hood latch attaching bolts slightly. Move the hood latch assembly to adjust the attachment between the hood and latch assembly.

Liftgate

REMOVAL & INSTALLATION

▶ **See Figures 11 and 12**

1. Open the tailgate completely.
2. Remove the inner liftgate trim panels and water deflector.
3. If equipped, remove the liftgate gas spring.

4. On models equipped with electrical options in the tailgate, disconnect the wiring harness connectors and pull the wiring from the liftgate.
5. Disconnect the rear washer tube at the liftgate.
6. Scribe hinge location marks on the liftgate to aid in installation.
7. Safely support the liftgate. Disconnect the liftgate stopper from the tailgate and position out of the way. Disconnect the rear defroster connector, if equipped.
8. Remove the liftgate-to-hinge bolts and remove the tailgate from the vehicle.

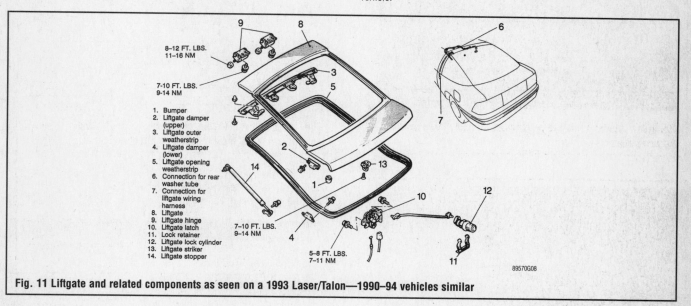

8–12 FT. LBS.
11–16 NM

7–10 FT. LBS.
9–14 NM

1. Bumper
2. Liftgate damper (upper)
3. Liftgate outer weatherstrip
4. Liftgate damper (lower)
5. Liftgate opening weatherstrip
6. Connection for rear washer tube
7. Connection for liftgate wiring harness
8. Liftgate
9. Liftgate hinge
10. Liftgate latch
11. Lock retainer
12. Liftgate lock cylinder
13. Liftgate striker
14. Liftgate stopper

7–10 FT. LBS.
9–14 NM

5–8 FT. LBS.
7–11 NM

89570G08

Fig. 11 Liftgate and related components as seen on a 1993 Laser/Talon—1990–94 vehicles similar

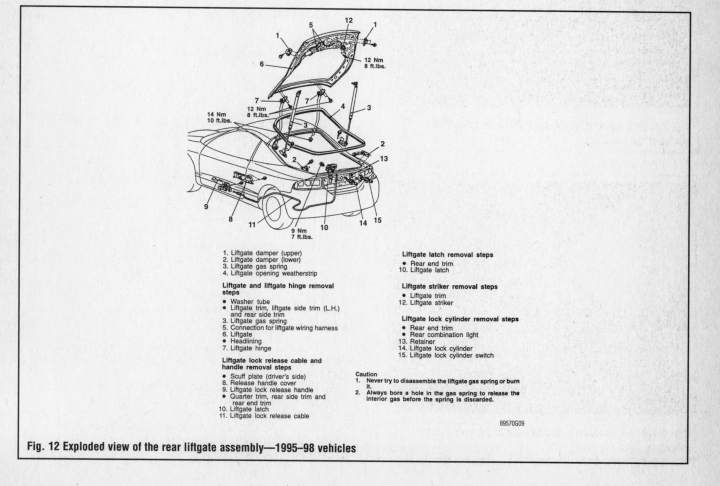

12 Nm
8 ft.lbs.

12 Nm
8 ft.lbs.

14 Nm
10 ft.lbs.

9 Nm
7 ft.lbs.

1. Liftgate damper (upper)
2. Liftgate damper (lower)
3. Liftgate gas spring
4. Liftgate opening weatherstrip

Liftgate and liftgate hinge removal steps
• Washer tube
• Liftgate trim, liftgate side trim (L.H.) and rear side trim
3. Liftgate gas spring
5. Connection for liftgate wiring harness
6. Liftgate
• Headlining
7. Liftgate hinge

Liftgate lock release cable and handle removal steps
• Scuff plate (driver's side)
8. Release handle cover
9. Liftgate lock release handle
• Quarter trim, rear side trim and rear end trim
10. Liftgate latch
11. Liftgate lock release cable

Liftgate latch removal steps
• Rear end trim
10. Liftgate latch

Liftgate striker removal steps
• Liftgate trim
12. Liftgate striker

Liftgate lock cylinder removal steps
• Rear end trim
• Rear combination light
13. Retainer
14. Liftgate lock cylinder
15. Liftgate lock cylinder switch

Caution
1. Never try to disassemble the liftgate gas spring or burn it.
2. Always bore a hole in the gas spring to release the interior gas before the spring is discarded.

89570G09

Fig. 12 Exploded view of the rear liftgate assembly—1995–98 vehicles

To install:

9. Position the liftgate on the vehicle and align the hinge scribe marks.

10. Install the liftgate-to-hinge bolts and tighten to 8–10 ft. lbs. (12–14 Nm).

11. Install the liftgate stopper and tighten mounting bolt, if removed.

12. Install and reconnect the electrical harness to all connectors at the liftgate.

13. Install all interior trim panels removed.

14. Close the liftgate slowly to check for proper alignment. Adjust liftgate positioning, if necessary.

ALIGNMENT

▶ **See Figures 13 and 14**

To adjust the door in forward/rearward and left/right directions, loosen the hinge bolts and position the tailgate as required.

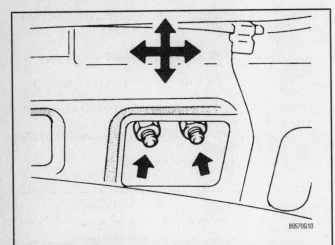

Fig. 13 Vertical and horizontal movement of the liftgate can be obtained by loosening the liftgate hinge mounting bolts and adjusting liftgate

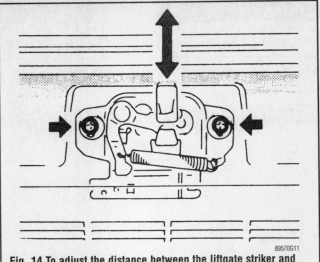

Fig. 14 To adjust the distance between the liftgate striker and the liftgate latch, loosen the latch mounting bolts

To adjust the tailgate lock striker, loosen the mounting bolts and using a plastic hammer, tap the striker to the desired position. Removing of the lower trim panel is normally required to access the striker.

Trunk Lid

REMOVAL & INSTALLATION

▶ **See Figure 15**

1. Disconnect the negative battery cable. Open the trunk lid fully.

2. Detach the electrical connector.

3. Support the trunk lid in the open position.

4. Insert a small prytool into the lock cover slit, remove the lock covers, then remove the trunk lid gas springs.

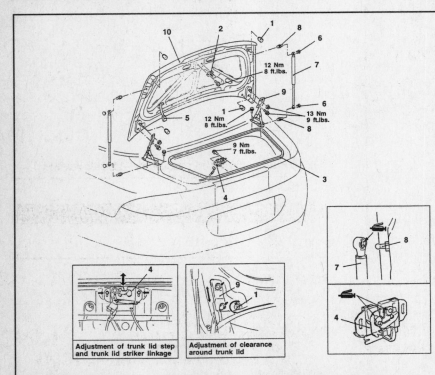

1. Bumper
2. Trunk lid striker
3. Trunk lid opening weatherstrip

Trunk lid latch removal steps

- Rear end trim
4. Trunk lid latch

Trunk lid gas spring removal steps

6. Lock cover
7. Trunk lid gas spring
8. Ball joint

Trunk lid removal steps

5. Harness connector
6. Lock cover
7. Trunk lid gas spring
9. Trunk lid hinge
10. Trunk lid

Fig. 15 Exploded view of the trunk lid assembly and related components

5. Unfasten the retaining bolts, then remove the trunk lid hinges.
6. Remove the trunk lid from the vehicle
7. Installation is the reverse of the removal procedure.
8. Make sure to tighten the retainers to the specifications shown in the accompanying figure.
9. If necessary, you can align the trunk lid, as shown in the accompanying figure.

Outside Mirror

REMOVAL & INSTALLATION

♦ See Figure 16

1. Disconnect the negative battery cable. Remove the door interior trim panel and water proof film.
2. On directly controlled mirror (manual mirror), remove the set screw and the adjustment knob.
3. Remove the inner mirror cover.
4. If the mirror is electric, disconnect the wire harness.
5. Remove the mounting nuts and the door trim bracket. Lift the mirror from the vehicle.
To install:
6. Position the mirror on the vehicle. Install the door trim bracket and the mounting nuts.
7. If the mirror is electric, reconnect the wire harness.
8. Install the inner cover.
9. On manual mirrors, install the knob and set screw.
10. Install the water proof film and the door interior trim panel.
11. Connect the negative battery cable.
12. If electric, cycle the mirror several times to make sure that it works properly.

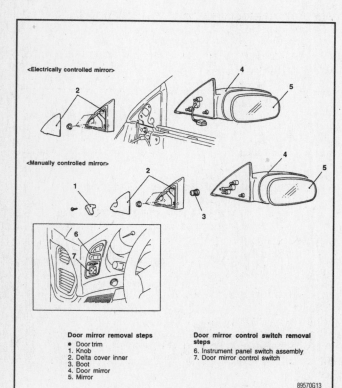

Fig. 16 Door mirror and related components—1995–98 vehicles shown, earlier models similar

Antenna

REPLACEMENT

♦ See Figures 17 and 18

1. Disconnect the negative battery cable.
2. Remove the luggage compartment side trim.
3. Remove the ring nut from the base of the antenna mast. If equipped with a whip antenna, remove the mast.
4. Remove any necessary luggage compartment trim panels to access the antenna.
5. If the antenna is electric, disconnect the electrical harness connector.
6. Disconnect the radio feeder wire connection at the antenna assembly base.
7. Disconnect the ground wire. Remove the antenna assembly mounting screws and nuts and the antenna from the vehicle.
To install:
8. Install the antenna assembly onto the vehicle and secure in place using the mounting nuts and screws.
9. Attach the ground wire, feeder wire and the electrical harness connector.
10. Install the ring nut and the antenna mast. Tighten the antenna mast to 4 ft. lbs. (5 Nm).
11. If equipped with electric antenna, connect the negative battery cable and check antenna operation.
12. Reinstall the luggage compartment side trim.

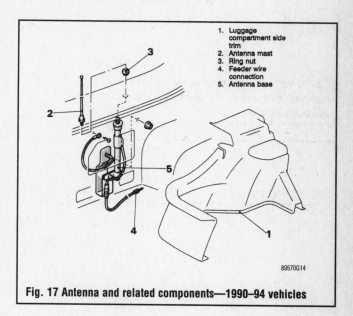

Fig. 17 Antenna and related components—1990–94 vehicles

Fenders

REMOVAL & INSTALLATION

1990–94 Vehicles

♦ See Figures 19 and 20

1. Disconnect the negative battery cable.
2. Remove the front deck garnish as follows:
   a. Remove the windshield wiper arms.
   b. Remove the mounting bolts and the front deck garnish from the vehicle.

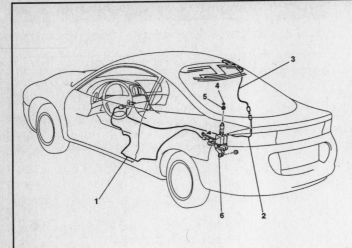

Antenna feeder cable (for motor antenna side) removal steps
- Front seat (driver's side)
- Rear seat cushion and seatback (L.H.)
- Radio, tape player and CD player
- Rear speaker (L.H.)
- Rear side trim (L.H.) and cowl side trim (L.H.)
1. Antenna feeder cable

Antenna feeder cable A (for glass antenna side) removal steps
- Front seat (passenger's side)
- Rear seat cushion and seatback (R.H.)
- Quarter trim lower (R.H.) and cowl side trim (R.H.)
2. Antenna feeder cable A

Antenna feeder cable B (for glass antenna side) removal steps
- Rear seat cushion and seatback (R.H.)
- Quarter trim (R.H.), liftgate side trim (R.H.) and upper trim
3. Antenna feeder cable B

Whip antenna removal steps
- Rear side trim (L.H.)
4. Ring nut
5. Base
6. Motor antenna

89570G15

Fig. 18 Exploded view of the power antenna assembly and related components—1995–98 vehicles, except Spyder

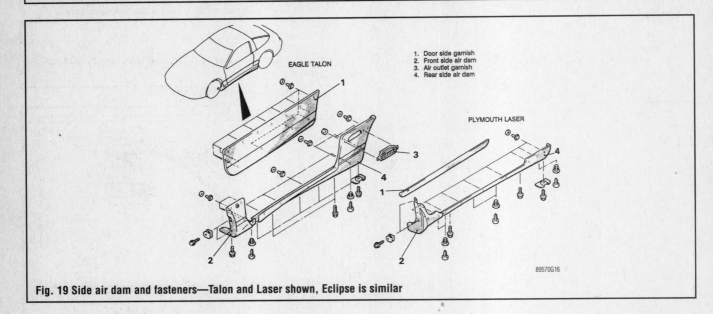

EAGLE TALON

PLYMOUTH LASER

1. Door side garnish
2. Front side air dam
3. Air outlet garnish
4. Rear side air dam

89570G16

Fig. 19 Side air dam and fasteners—Talon and Laser shown, Eclipse is similar

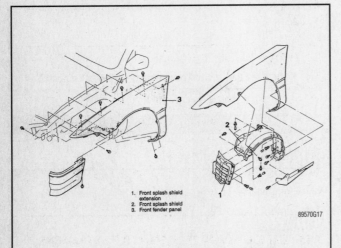

1. Front splash shield extension
2. Front splash shield
3. Front fender panel

89570G17

Fig. 20 Fender and related components—Laser and Talon shown, Eclipse is similar

3. Remove the turn signal lamp and the combination lamp.

4. Remove the headlamp lower bezel.

5. Remove the side air dam and air outlet garnish.

6. Remove the retainer bolts and the front splash shield extension, if equipped.

7. Remove the retainers and the front splash shield.

8. Remove the retainer bolts along the upper, lower and rear side of the fender.

9. Remove the fender from the vehicle.

To install:

10. Apply sealant between the fender and the body panels. This will assure that there are no gaps when the fender is mounted. Install the fender to the vehicle and tighten all retainer bolts to 4 ft. lbs. (6 Nm).

11. Install the fender splash shield and secure in place using retainers.

12. Install front splash shield extension, if removed.

13. Install the side air dam, headlamp bezel, front turn signal lamp and the combination lamp.

14. Install the front deck garnish and wiper arms.

15. Connect the negative battery cable.

1995–98 Vehicles

▶ **See Figure 21**

1. From under the vehicle, unfasten the retainers, then remove the undercover splash shield.

2. Remove the bumper as follows:

   a. Remove the front side marker light.

   b. Remove the retaining bolts, then remove the front bumper center plate.

   c. Unfasten the retainers, then remove the front bumper.

   d. If necessary remove the front bumper corner plate, pad and front fascia bracket.

3. Remove the retainers, then remove the wheel well splash shield.

4. Remove the side air dam.

5. Unfasten the retainers, then remove the front fender panel.

6. Installation is the reverse of the removal procedure.

Convertible Top

MOTOR REPLACEMENT

▶ **See Figure 22**

1. Disconnect the negative battery cable.
2. Remove the lower quarter trim panel.
3. Remove the rear speaker brackets.
4. Remove the spacers.

5. Unfasten the retaining bolts, removing the lower bolts with the spacers first, then remove the upper bolts.

6. Detach the motor electrical connector, then remove the topstack drive motor.

7. Installation is the reverse of the removal procedure.

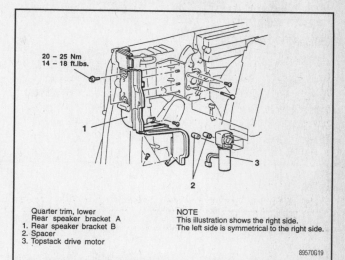

20 – 25 Nm
14 – 18 ft.lbs.

Quarter trim, lower
Rear speaker bracket A
1. Rear speaker bracket B
2. Spacer
3. Topstack drive motor

NOTE
This illustration shows the right side.
The left side is symmetrical to the right side.

89570G19

Fig. 22 Convertible top motor (topstack drive motor) location and mounting

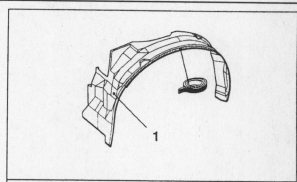

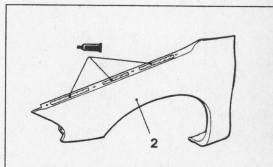

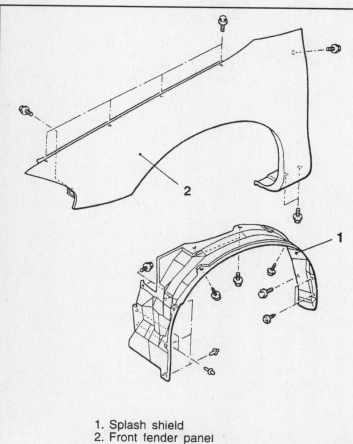

1. Splash shield
2. Front fender panel

Sealant:
3M ATD Part No. 8625 or equivalent

Sealant:
3M ATD Part No. 8531 or 3M ATD Part No. 8646, or equivalent

89570G18

Fig. 21 Exploded view of the front fender assembly and related components—1995–98 vehicles

INTERIOR

Instrument Panel and Pad

REMOVAL & INSTALLATION

1990–94 Vehicles

▶ See Figures 23, 24, 25 and 26

For installation of the instrument panel, different types of fasteners were used. During installation, it is important that these fasteners are installed in their original locations. To aid in this, the specific fasteners and their positions are referenced by letters in the exploded views of the instrument panel which follow.

1. Disconnect the negative battery cable.
2. Remove the floor console.
3. The fasteners for the knee protectors are covered by plugs. Remove the plugs and the screws from the knee protector assembly. Remove the assembly from the vehicle.
4. Remove the retainer and the hood lock release handle from the vehicle.
5. Remove the steering column upper and lower covers.
6. Remove the retainers from the cluster panel assembly and remove from the vehicle.
7. Remove the radio trim plate. Using a plastic trim tool, carefully pry the lower part of the radio panel outward and remove it from the console.
8. Remove the radio retainers and the radio from the console. Disconnect the electrical harness and the antenna lead from the radio and remove it from the vehicle.

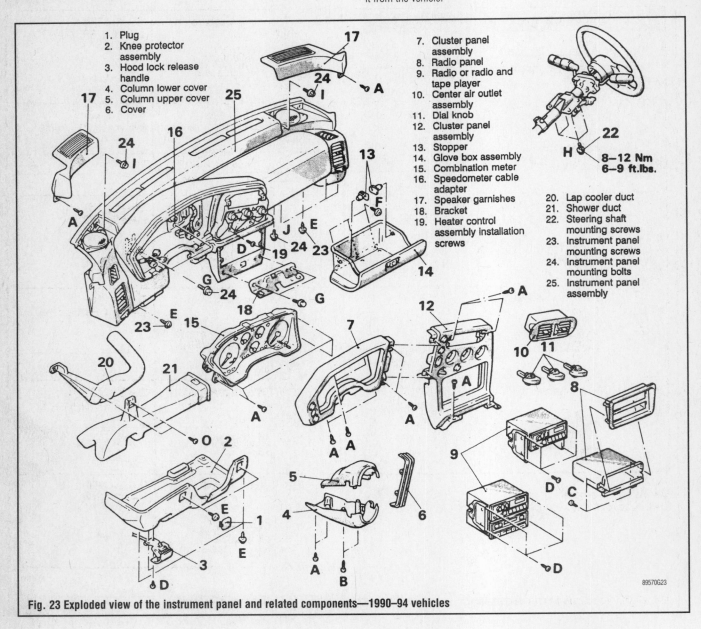

1. Plug
2. Knee protector assembly
3. Hood lock release handle
4. Column lower cover
5. Column upper cover
6. Cover
7. Cluster panel assembly
8. Radio panel
9. Radio or radio and tape player
10. Center air outlet assembly
11. Dial knob
12. Cluster panel assembly
13. Stopper
14. Glove box assembly
15. Combination meter
16. Speedometer cable adapter
17. Speaker garnishes
18. Bracket
19. Heater control assembly installation screws
20. Lap cooler duct
21. Shower duct
22. Steering shaft mounting screws
23. Instrument panel mounting screws
24. Instrument panel mounting bolts
25. Instrument panel assembly

8–12 Nm
6–9 ft.lbs.

89570G23

Fig. 23 Exploded view of the instrument panel and related components—1990–94 vehicles

Symbol	Part name and shape	Size mm (in.)	Symbol	Part name and shape	Size mm (in.)
A	Tapping screw (Black) 	D = 5 (.20) L = 20 (.79)	H	Washer assembled bolt 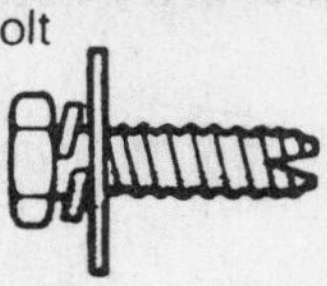	D = 8 (.31) L = 25 (.98)
B	Tapping screw 	D = 5 (.20) L = 25 (.98)	I	Washer assembled bolt 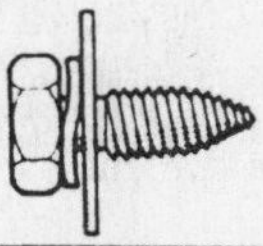	D = 6 (.24) L = 16 (.63)
C	Tapping screw 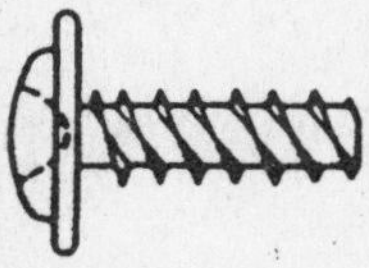	D = 4 (.16) L = 10 (.39)	J	Washer assembled bolt 	D = 6 (.24) L = 16 (.63)
D	Tapping screw 	D = 5 (.20) L = 16 (.63)	K	Tapping screw 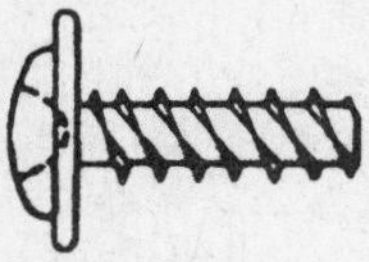	D = 5 (.20) L = 16 (.63)
E	Washer assembled screw (Black) 	D = 6 (.24) L = 20 (.79)	L	Machine screw (Black) 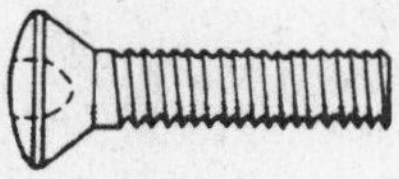	D = 4 (.16) L = 10 (.39)
F	Washer assembled screw (Black) 	D = 5 (.20) L = 20 (.79)	M	Machine screw (Black) 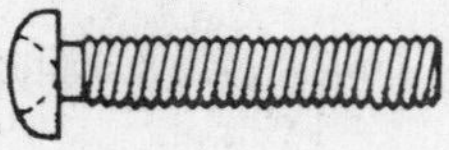	D = 4 (.16) L = 10 (.39)
G	Washer assembled bolt 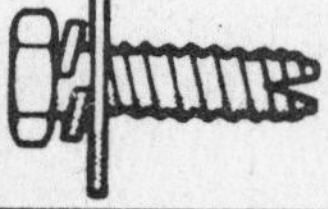	D = 6 (.24) L = 16 (.63)	N	Washer assembled screw 	D = 5 (.20) L = 16 (.63)
			O	Tapping screw 	D = 5 (.20) L = 12 (.47)

D — Thread diameter
L — Effective thread length

89570G20

Fig. 24 The instrument panel retainers should be installed in the positions from which they were removed

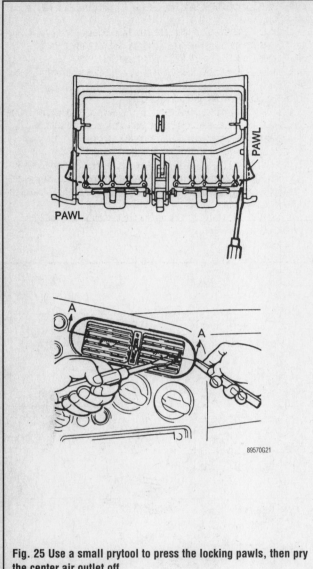

Fig. 25 Use a small prytool to press the locking pawls, then pry the center air outlet off

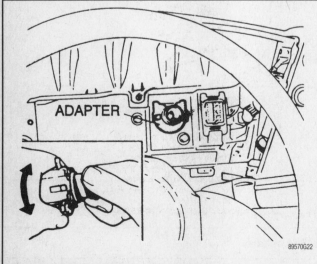

Fig. 26 Removing the speedometer cable adapter

9. Remove the center air outlet assembly. While depressing the locking pawls of the center air outlet assembly with a small flat-bladed prytool, remove the center air outlet assembly by prying outward with plastic trim tool.

10. Remove the screw retainers from each dial knob on the center cluster. Gently pull the dial knobs from the center cluster panel assembly.

11. Remove the fasteners and the cluster panel assembly from the vehicle. Disconnect the harness connectors as required.

12. Remove the stoppers from inside the glove box assembly. Remove the retainers and the glove box from the vehicle.

13. Remove the retainers from the combination meter. Pull the meter out slightly. Disconnect the electrical connections from the combination meter.

14. Disconnect the speedometer cable from the combination meter as follows:

    a. Detach the speedometer cable from the transaxle assembly.

    b. Pull the speedometer cable slightly toward the vehicle interior.

    c. Release the cable lock by turning the adapter to the left or right, and then remove the adapter.

15. Remove the right and left speaker covers. Disconnect and remove the speakers from the instrument panel assembly.

16. Remove the heater control assembly retaining screws and disconnect the harness connectors. Remove the heater control assembly from the vehicle.

17. Remove the lap cooler duct and the shower duct taking note of their orientation.

18. Remove the steering shaft mounting bolts and allow the steering wheel to rest on the front seat cushion. Make sure no harness wires or connections are being pulled or stretched.

19. Remove the instrument panel retaining bolts, label and disconnect all electrical harness connectors. Remove the instrument panel from the vehicle. Disassemble components as required.

To install:

20. Install the instrument panel into the vehicle, reconnect all harness connections and install retaining bolts. Before installing bolts, make sure the electrical harness wires were not pinched during instrument panel installation.

21. Raise the steering shaft into position and install the mounting bolts. Tighten the bolts to 9 ft. lbs. (12 Nm).

22. Install the lap cooler duct and the shower duct in the same position as removed. Install the mounting screw to hold in position.

23. Install the heater control assembly, making sure to reconnect all connections prior to installation.

24. Reconnect both front speakers to the radio harness and install into instrument panel. Install the speaker garnishes.

25. Reconnect the speedometer cable to the combination meter. Make sure the cable locks in position on the back of the meter assembly.

26. Install the combination meter into the instrument panel and secure in place. Reattach the speedometer cable to the transaxle assembly.

27. Install the glove box assembly and door stops.

28. Install the center panel assembly. Connect the radio equipment harness connections and install into cluster panel. Secure components in position.

29. Install the center air outlet assembly, radio trim panel and dial knobs.

30. Install the upper and the lower steering column covers.

31. Install the hood lock release handle and the knee protector. Install the mounting screws and the plugs.

32. Install the floor console.

33. Connect the negative battery cable and check operation of all gauges and meters.

1995–98 Vehicles

♦ See Figures 27 and 28

1. Disconnect the negative battery cable, then wrap the cable in insulated tape. Wait at least 60 seconds before continuing to allow the SRS system time to disable.

2. Remove the floor console assembly.

3. Remove the steering wheel and column cover(s), as outlined in Section 8.

4. Unfasten the retaining screws, then remove the meter (instrument cluster) bezel.

5. Remove the mounting screws, then remove the combination meter (instrument cluster).

6. Remove the radio/tape player and/or CD player and the mounting box.

7. Unplug the console side cover screw covers, then unfasten the retainers and remove the side covers.

8. Remove the sunglasses holder.

9. Remove the glove compartment by pushing the stoppers toward the rear of the vehicle to unlock them, then remove the glove compartment assembly.

10. Remove the passenger side air bag module by unfastening the retaining screws, accessible through the glove compartment opening, detach the connector and remove the module.

11. Remove the hood lock release handle. The handle is secured with a screw.

12. Remove the retainers, then remove the left side instrument panel under cover.

13. Remove the center air outlet assembly by carefully prying it out.

14. Remove the heater control assembly as outlined in Section 6.

15. Remove the instrument panel switch assembly.

16. Unfasten the retainers, then remove the right side instrument panel under cover.

17. Remove the front speaker assemblies.

18. Unfasten the remaining retainers, tag and detach the necessary connectors, then remove the instrument panel assembly from the vehicle.

19. Installation is the reverse of the removal procedure.

20. Make sure to install all retainers in their original positions.

21. When installing the center air outlet assembly, perform the following:

a. Turn the cool air bypass lever of the center air outlet fully downward.

b. Pull the cool air bypass damper lever fully toward you to install the cable to the lever pin.

c. Push the outer cable to take up the slack, then secure with the retaining clip.

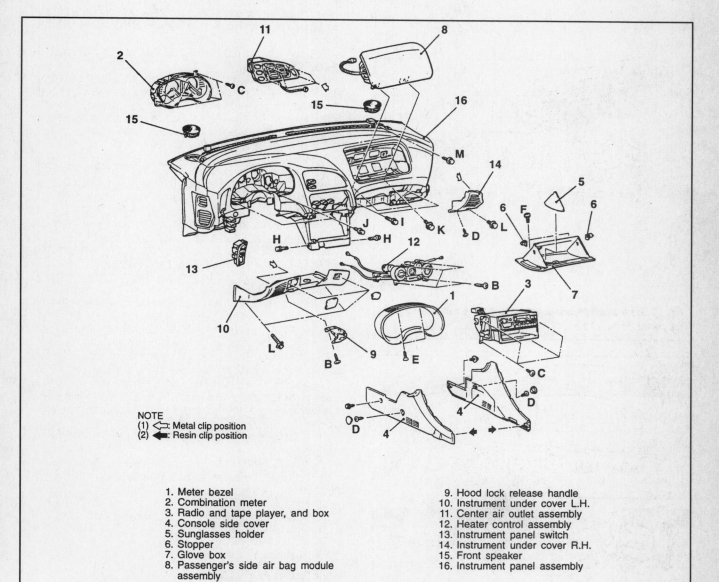

NOTE
(1) ⟵□: Metal clip position
(2) ◀: Resin clip position

1. Meter bezel
2. Combination meter
3. Radio and tape player, and box
4. Console side cover
5. Sunglasses holder
6. Stopper
7. Glove box
8. Passenger's side air bag module assembly
9. Hood lock release handle
10. Instrument under cover L.H.
11. Center air outlet assembly
12. Heater control assembly
13. Instrument panel switch
14. Instrument under cover R.H.
15. Front speaker
16. Instrument panel assembly

89570G24

Fig. 27 Exploded view of the instrument panel and related components—1995–98 vehicles

Name	Symbol	Size mm (in.) (D × L)	Color	Shape
Tapping screw	A	5 × 16 (.20 × .62)	–	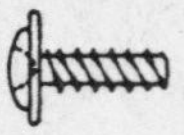
	B	5 × 12 (.20 × .47)	–	
	C	5 × 16 (.20 × .62)	–	
	D	5 × 16 (.20 × .62)	Black	
	E	5 × 20 (.20 × .79)	Black	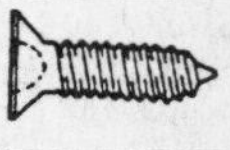
Washer assembled screw	F	5 × 16 (.20 × .62)	–	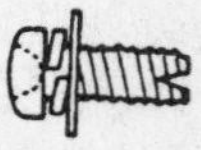
	G	5 × 16 (.20 × .62)	Black	
Washer assembled bolt	H	6 × 16 (.24 × .62)	–	
	I	6 × 16 (.24 × .62)	Black	
	J	6 × 20 (.24 × .79)	–	
	K	6 × 20 (.24 × .79)	–	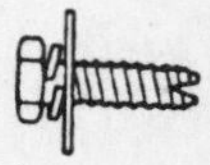
	L	6 × 25 (.24 × .79)	Black	
	M	6 × 16 (.24 × .62)	–	

D = Thread diameter
L = Effective thread length

89570G25

Fig. 28 Use care to install the instrument panel retainers in their original locations

Console

REMOVAL & INSTALLATION

▶ **See Figures 29 thru 38**

1. Disconnect the negative battery cable. If equipped with SRS, wrap the cable in insulated tape, then wait at least 60 seconds before continuing to allow the SRS system time to disable.

❄❄ CAUTION

If equipped with SRS, be careful not to let the console bump against the SRS-ECU during removal and installation.

2. If necessary, remove the center console trim panel.
3. Remove the screw plugs in the side covers. Remove the retainer screws and the side covers from the vehicle.

4. Remove the front mounting screw cover from the floor console.
5. Remove the ashtray and cup holder assemblies. If equipped, remove the carpet inserts from the floor console assembly.
6. If equipped, remove the manual transaxle shift lever knob.
7. Label and detach the electrical wire harness connections for the floor console.
8. Remove the mounting bolts/screws and the floor console from the vehicle. Disassemble components as required.
   To install:
9. Install the floor console in position in the vehicle and secure with the retaining bolts/screws.
10. Attach the electrical harness connectors to the vehicle body harness, as tagged during removal.
11. Install the carpet and the cup holder/ashtray assembly to the console assembly.
12. Install the side covers and retainers. Cover retainer screws with plugs.
13. Connect the negative battery cable and check console electrical components for proper operation.

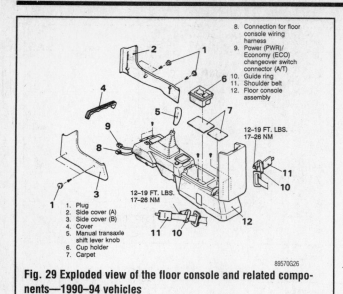

Fig. 29 Exploded view of the floor console and related components—1990–94 vehicles

8. Connection for floor console wiring harness
9. Power (PWR)/ Economy (ECO) changeover switch connector (A/T)
10. Guide ring
11. Shoulder belt
12. Floor console assembly

12–19 FT. LBS. 17–26 NM

1. Plug
2. Side cover (A)
3. Side cover (B)
4. Cover
5. Manual transaxle shift lever knob
6. Cup holder
7. Carpet

89570G26

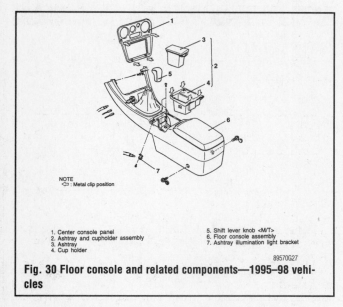

Fig. 30 Floor console and related components—1995–98 vehicles

NOTE
⇦ : Metal clip position

1. Center console panel
2. Ashtray and cupholder assembly
3. Ashtray
4. Cup holder
5. Shift lever knob <M/T>
6. Floor console assembly
7. Ashtray illumination light bracket

89570G27

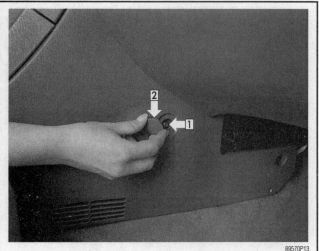

Fig. 31 The console side cover retaining screws (1) are hidden by plugs (2)

89570P13

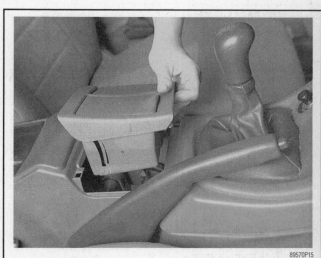

Fig. 32 After unfastening the screws, remove the console side panels

89570P20

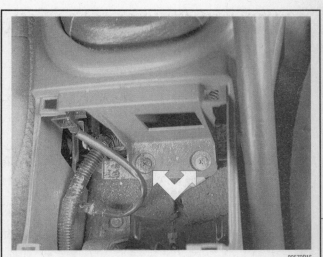

Fig. 33 Lift the ashtray and cup holder assembly up and out of the console

89570P15

Fig. 34 There are two retaining screws (see arrows) under the cup holder and ashtray assembly

89570P16

Fig. 35 For vehicles equipped with a manual transaxle, remove the shift lever knob

Fig. 36 Unfasten the remaining console mounting screws . . .

Fig. 37 . . . pull the console partially up and detach the connectors . . .

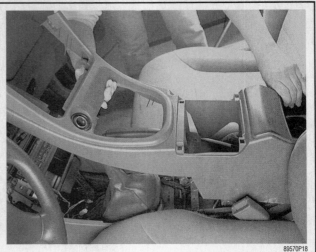

Fig. 38 . . . then remove the console from the vehicle. Be careful not to bump it against the SRS-ECU, if equipped

Door Panels

REMOVAL & INSTALLATION

▶ **See Figures 39 thru 49**

1. Disconnect the negative battery cable.
2. Insert a shop towel behind the window regulator handle and push the retainer clip outward. Once the clip is removed, remove the window glass regulator handle and escutcheon.
3. Remove the door grip/pull handle mounting screws and the grip from the door panel.
4. Remove the door pull handle cover. Remove the pull handle, if equipped.
5. For 1990–94 vehicles, if equipped with door mounted speakers, remove the speaker covers and the speakers from the door assembly.
6. If equipped, unfasten the door trim panel retaining screws.
7. Pull the door panel gently from the door. The panel is retained by spring clips. To separate the clips from the door, slide a small prying tool behind the clip and carefully pull the clip, with the door panel, outward. Try not to bend the door panel or damage may occur.
8. Once all retainer clips are removed from the door, remove the door panel assembly. If equipped with power windows or mirrors, remember to detach the electrical connector from the switch prior to removal.
9. Carefully remove any retainer clips that remained in the door during panel removal. If damaged, replace the retainer clips.
10. If necessary, on 1995–98 vehicles, remove the door speaker and speaker cover.
11. At this time, you can remove the waterproof film from the door.
To install:
12. If removed, install the waterproof film from the door.
13. On 1995–98 vehicles, if removed, install the speaker assemblies. Don't forget to connect the wiring.
14. Install and missing or damaged retainer clips into the door panel. Attach the electrical harness connector to the electric switches on the door panel and install the door panel onto the vehicle. Push retainers into the holes in the door until they lock into position. If any clips do not lock, replace with new ones.
15. Install the door grip onto the door panel.
16. On 1990–94 vehicles, install the door speakers to the door panel making sure to attach harness connectors prior to installation. Install the speaker covers.
17. Install the escutcheon and clip to the regulator handle, close the window glass fully, then install the handle so it is in the position shown in the accompanying figure.
18. Connect the negative battery cable.

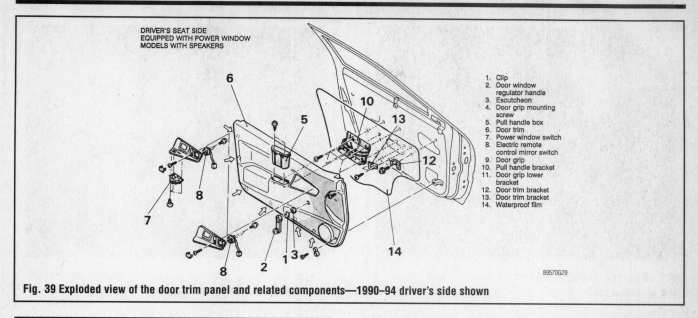

DRIVER'S SEAT SIDE
EQUIPPED WITH POWER WINDOW
MODELS WITH SPEAKERS

1. Clip
2. Door window regulator handle
3. Escutcheon
4. Door grip mounting screw
5. Pull handle box
6. Door trim
7. Power window switch
8. Electric remote control mirror switch
9. Door grip
10. Pull handle bracket
11. Door grip lower bracket
12. Door trim bracket
13. Door trim bracket
14. Waterproof film

89570G29

Fig. 39 Exploded view of the door trim panel and related components—1990–94 driver's side shown

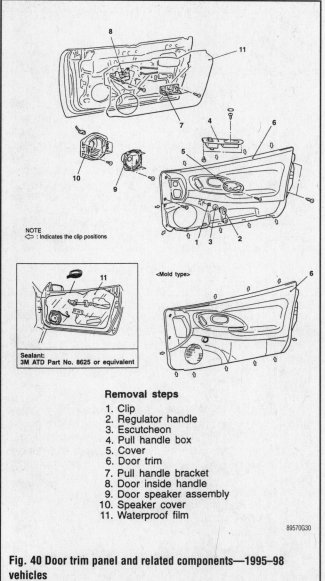

NOTE
◁ : Indicates the clip positions

Sealant:
3M ATD Part No. 8625 or equivalent

<Mold type>

Removal steps
1. Clip
2. Regulator handle
3. Escutcheon
4. Pull handle box
5. Cover
6. Door trim
7. Pull handle bracket
8. Door inside handle
9. Door speaker assembly
10. Speaker cover
11. Waterproof film

89570G30

Fig. 40 Door trim panel and related components—1995–98 vehicles

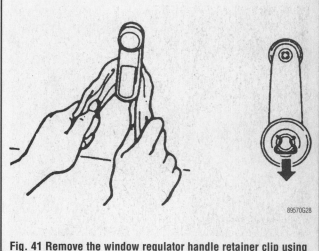

89570G28

Fig. 41 Remove the window regulator handle retainer clip using a shop towel

89570P06

Fig. 42 When removing the regulator handle (1), be careful not to lose the retaining clip (2)

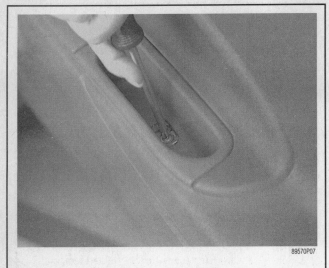

Fig. 43 Remove the door pull handle retaining screw . . .

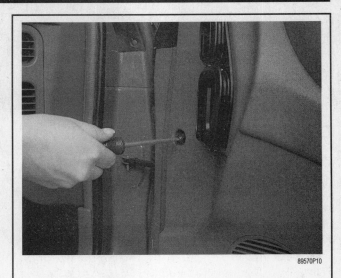

Fig. 46 If necessary, remove any door panel retaining screws . . .

Fig. 44 . . . then remove the pull handle from the door panel

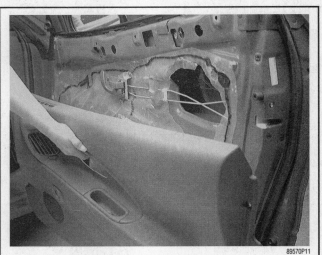

Fig. 47 . . . then carefully pull the door trim panel away from the door. Be careful not to lose any of the retaining clips

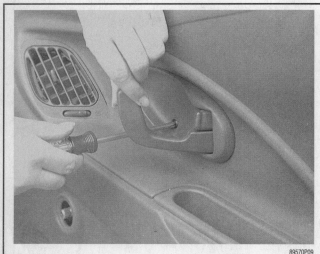

Fig. 45 Pull out on the door handle, then unfasten the screw and remove the handle cover

Fig. 48 If necessary, you can unfasten the retainers and remove the door speakers

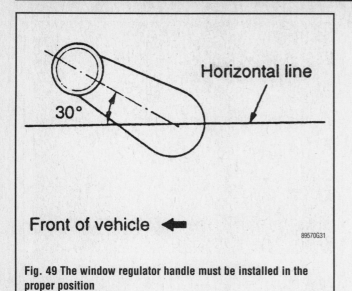

Fig. 49 The window regulator handle must be installed in the proper position

Door Locks

REMOVAL & INSTALLATION

Manual Locks

▶ **See Figures 50 and 51**

1. Disconnect the negative battery cable.
2. Remove the door interior trim panel and weatherproof film. Position the door glass so the key cylinder and related components are accessible.
3. Disconnect the actuator rod(s) from the lock cylinder. If equipped with a theft alarm system, detach the electrical connector at the door key cylinder unlock switch.

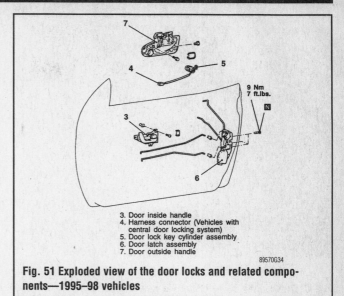

3. Door inside handle
4. Harness connector (Vehicles with central door locking system)
5. Door lock key cylinder assembly
6. Door latch assembly
7. Door outside handle

Fig. 51 Exploded view of the door locks and related components—1995–98 vehicles

4. Remove the retainer ring from the base of the door lock cylinder.
5. Remove the door lock key cylinder from the vehicle.
6. Installation is the reverse of the removal procedure.

Power Locks

▶ **See Figures 51 and 52**

1. Disconnect the negative battery cable.
2. Remove the door trim panel and waterproof film.
3. Disconnect the door lock actuator from the door latch assembly.
4. Remove the retainer bolt and nut. Detach the electrical connector, then remove the door latch assembly from the door.
5. Remove the retainer ring from the base of the door lock cylinder.
6. Remove the door lock key cylinder from the vehicle.
7. Installation is the reverse of the removal procedure.

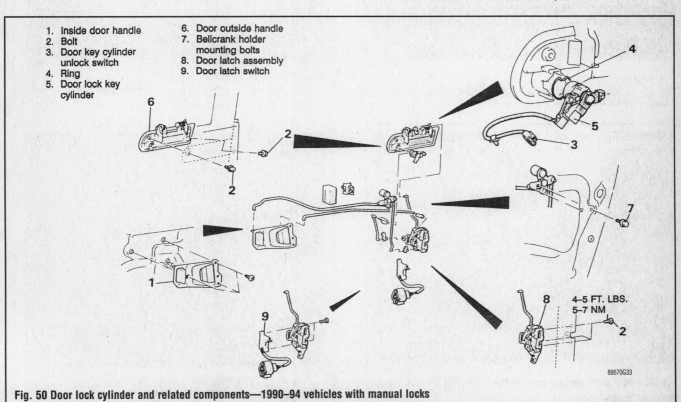

1. Inside door handle
2. Bolt
3. Door key cylinder unlock switch
4. Ring
5. Door lock key cylinder
6. Door outside handle
7. Bellcrank holder mounting bolts
8. Door latch assembly
9. Door latch switch

Fig. 50 Door lock cylinder and related components—1990–94 vehicles with manual locks

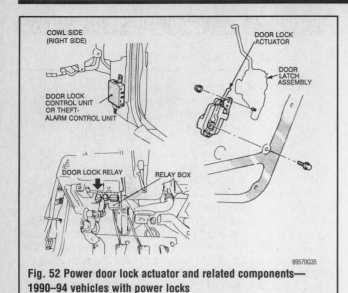

Fig. 52 Power door lock actuator and related components—1990–94 vehicles with power locks

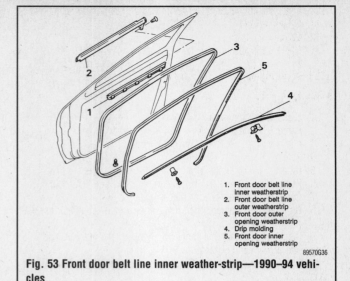

1. Front door belt line inner weatherstrip
2. Front door belt line outer weatherstrip
3. Front door outer opening weatherstrip
4. Drip molding
5. Front door inner opening weatherstrip

Fig. 53 Front door belt line inner weather-strip—1990–94 vehicles

Liftgate Lock Cylinder

REMOVAL & INSTALLATION

▶ See Figure 12

1. Disconnect the negative battery cable.
2. Remove the rear liftgate trim.
3. If necessary, remove the rear combination light.
4. Unfasten the retainer, then remove the lock cylinder (vehicles without the theft deterrent system) r lock cylinder switch (vehicles with theft deterrent switch) from the liftgate.
5. Installation is the reverse of the removal procedure.

Door Glass and Regulator

REMOVAL & INSTALLATION

1990–94 Vehicles

▶ See Figures 53, 54 and 55

1. Disconnect the negative battery cable.
2. Remove the interior door trim panel and waterproof film.
3. Remove the door belt line inner weather-strip as follows:
   a. Remove the door mounted mirror.
   b. Pry upward and remove the front door inner belt weather-strip from the top of the door panel.
4. Remove the bolts holding the glass to the window regulator. Remove the door window glass.
5. Remove the door glass holder.
6. Remove the mounting bolts and the front door window regulator. Disconnect the electrical connector, if equipped with power windows.
   To install:
7. Install the window regulator into the door. Connect the electrical harness, if equipped with power windows.
8. Install the regulator retainer bolts and tighten to 3 ft. lbs. (4 Nm).
9. Install the window glass. Install the glass-to-regulator retaining bolts and tighten to 3 ft. lbs. (4 Nm).

➡Make sure the door glass holders are positioned between the glass and the heads of the retainer bolts. If the holders are not installed, the window glass may crack.

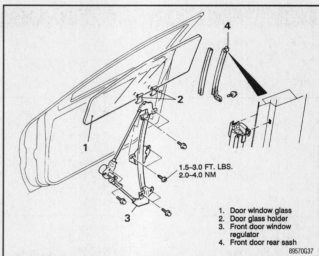

1.5–3.0 FT. LBS.
2.0–4.0 NM

1. Door window glass
2. Door glass holder
3. Front door window regulator
4. Front door rear sash

Fig. 54 Door glass and window regulator removal—1990–94 vehicles with manual windows

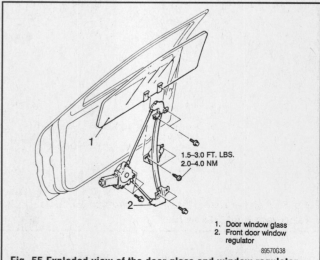

1.5–3.0 FT. LBS.
2.0–4.0 NM

1. Door window glass
2. Front door window regulator

Fig. 55 Exploded view of the door glass and window regulator—1990–94 vehicles with power windows

10. Install the front door inner belt weather-strip and related components.
11. Install the door trim panel and waterproof film.
12. Connect the negative battery cable.
13. Check for proper window regulator operation.

1995–98 Vehicles

▶ See Figure 56

1. Disconnect the negative battery cable.
2. Remove the door trim panel and waterproof film.
3. Remove the bolts, then remove the up-stops.
4. Remove the inner stabilizer.
5. Unfasten the retainers, then remove the delta sash.
6. Remove the retaining bolts, then remove the belt line molding.
7. Carefully remove the door window glass.
8. Unfasten the retainers, then remove the window regulator assembly.
9. If equipped, detach the connector, unfasten the retainers and remove the power window motor.
10. If necessary, remove the retainers, then remove the front and rear glass guide tracks.
11. Installation is the reverse of the removal procedure.

Electric Window Motor

For electric window motor replacement, please refer to the door glass and regulator procedures.

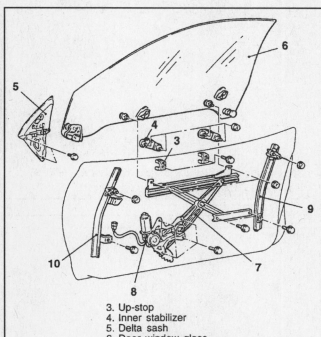

3. Up-stop
4. Inner stabilizer
5. Delta sash
6. Door window glass
7. Window regulator assembly
8. Power window motor (Vehicles with power window)
9. Glass guide rear track
10. Glass guide front track

89570G39

Fig. 56 Exploded view of the window, regulator and related components—1995–98 vehicles

Windshield & Fixed Glass

REMOVAL & INSTALLATION

If your windshield, or other fixed window, is cracked or chipped, you may decide to replace it with a new one yourself. However, there are two main reasons why replacement windshields and other window glass should be installed only by a professional automotive glass technician: safety and cost.

The most important reason a professional should install automotive glass is for safety. The glass in the vehicle, especially the windshield, is designed with safety in mind in case of a collision. The windshield is specially manufactured from two panes of specially-tempered glass with a thin layer of transparent plastic between them. This construction allows the glass to "give" in the event that a part of your body hits the windshield during the collision, and prevents the glass from shattering, which could cause lacerations, blinding and other harm to passengers of the vehicle. The other fixed windows are designed to be tempered so that if they break during a collision, they shatter in such a way that there are no large pointed glass pieces. The professional automotive glass technician knows how to install the glass in a vehicle so that it will function optimally during a collision. Without the proper experience, knowledge and tools, installing a piece of automotive glass yourself could lead to additional harm if an accident should ever occur.

Cost is also a factor when deciding to install automotive glass yourself. Performing this could cost you much more than a professional may charge for the same job. Since the windshield is designed to break under stress, an often life saving characteristic, windshields tend to break VERY easily when an inexperienced person attempts to install one. Do-it-yourselfers buying two, three or even four windshields from a salvage yard because they have broken them during installation are common stories. Also, since the automotive glass is designed to prevent the outside elements from entering your vehicle, improper installation can lead to water and air leaks. Annoying whining noises at highway speeds from air leaks or inside body panel rusting from water leaks can add to your stress level and subtract from your wallet. After buying two or three windshields, installing them and ending up with a leak that produces a noise while driving and water damage during rainstorms, the cost of having a professional do it correctly the first time may be much more alluring. We here at Chilton, therefore, advise that you have a professional automotive glass technician service any broken glass on your vehicle.

WINDSHIELD CHIP REPAIR

▶ See Figures 57 thru 71

➡Check with your state and local authorities on the laws for state safety inspection. Some states or municipalities may not allow chip repair as a viable option for correcting stone damage to your windshield.

Although severely cracked or damaged windshields must be replaced, there is something that you can do to prolong or even prevent the need for replacement of a chipped windshield. There are many companies which offer windshield chip repair products, such as Loctite's® Bullseye™ windshield repair kit. These kits usually consist of a syringe, pedestal and a sealing adhesive. The syringe is mounted on the pedestal and is used to create a vacuum which pulls the plastic layer against the glass. This helps make the chip transparent. The adhesive is then injected which seals the chip and helps to prevent further stress cracks from developing. Refer to the sequence of photos to get a general idea of what windshield chip repair involves.

➡Always follow the specific manufacturer's instructions.

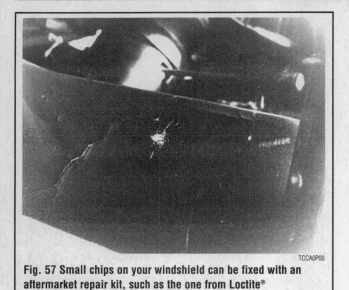

Fig. 57 Small chips on your windshield can be fixed with an aftermarket repair kit, such as the one from Loctite®

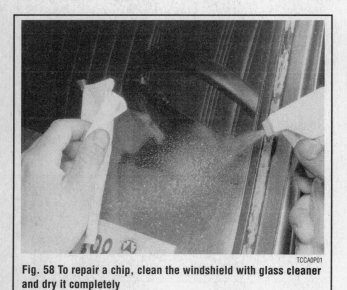

Fig. 58 To repair a chip, clean the windshield with glass cleaner and dry it completely

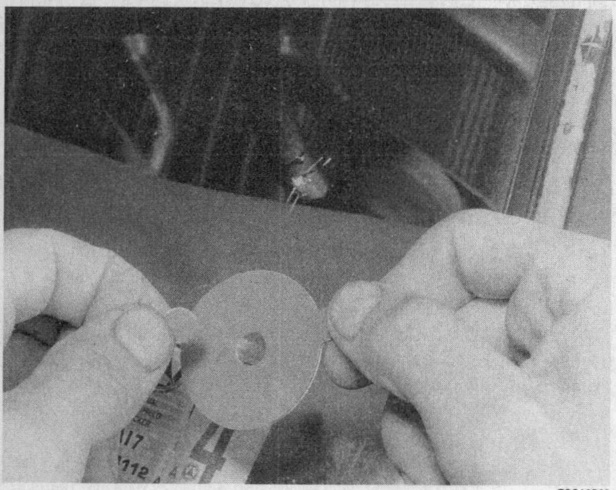

Fig. 59 Remove the center from the adhesive disc and peel off the backing from one side of the disc . . .

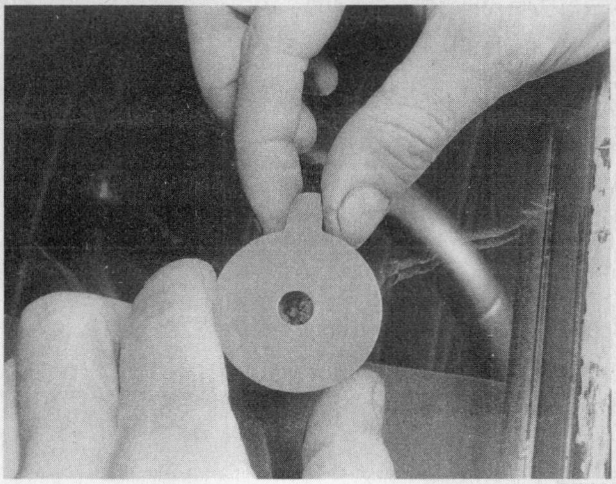

Fig. 60 . . . then press it on the windshield so that the chip is centered in the hole

Fig. 61 Be sure that the tab points upward on the windshield

Fig. 62 Peel the backing off the exposed side of the adhesive disc . . .

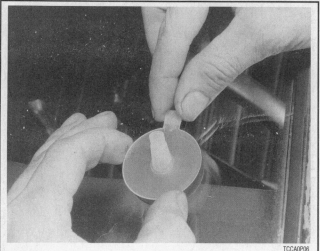

Fig. 63 . . . then position the plastic pedestal on the adhesive disc, ensuring that the tabs are aligned

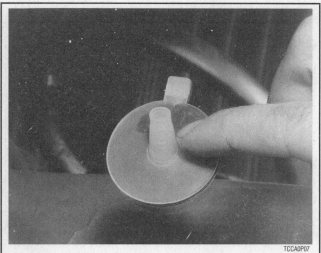

Fig. 64 Press the pedestal firmly on the adhesive disc to create an adequate seal . . .

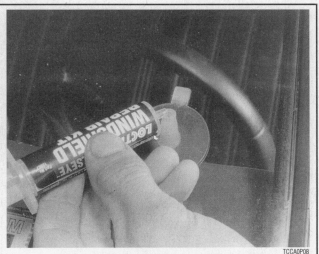

Fig. 65 . . . then install the applicator syringe nipple in the pedestal's hole

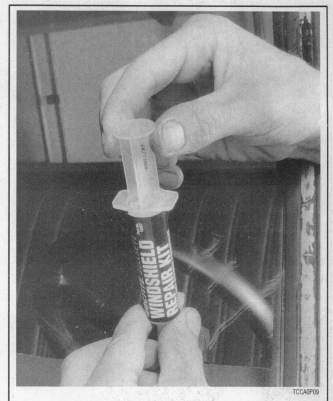

Fig. 66 Hold the syringe with one hand while pulling the plunger back with the other hand

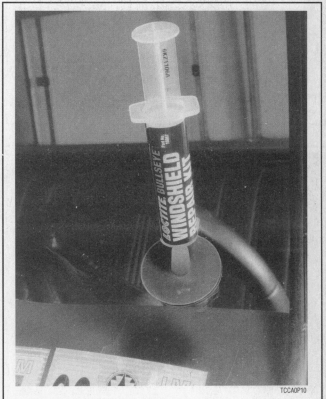

Fig. 67 After applying the solution, allow the entire assembly to sit until it has set completely

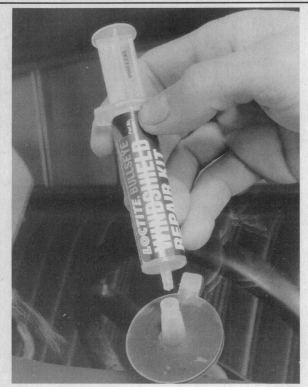

TCCA0P11

Fig. 68 After the solution has set, remove the syringe from the pedestal . . .

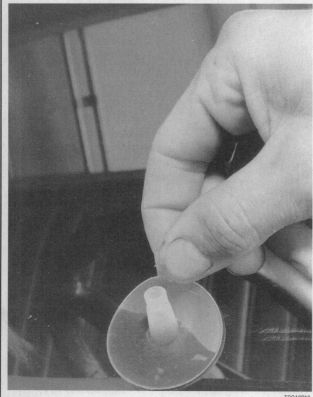

TCCA0P12

Fig. 69 . . . then peel the pedestal off of the adhesive disc . . .

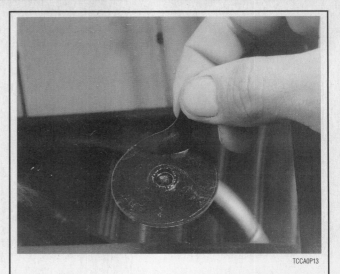

TCCA0P13

Fig. 70 . . . and peel the adhesive disc off of the windshield

TCCA0P14

Fig. 71 The chip will still be slightly visible, but it should be filled with the hardened solution

Inside Rear View Mirror

REPLACEMENT

▶ See Figure 72

Remove the inner rear view mirror by loosening the set screw on the mirror stem and lifting mirror off of the base, which is glued onto the windshield. On the Eclipse Spyder, you will also have to detach a connector. The installation is the reverse of the removal procedure. If the mirror base falls off of the windshield it can be installed as follows:

1. Scrape the base mounting area with a razor blade to remove the old adhesive.

2. Thoroughly clean the base mounting area with glass cleaner.

3. Obtain a mirror adhesive kit. Apply the cleaning compound to the windshield in the area that the base is to be mounted. Allow to dry.

4. Apply the adhesive to both the base plate and the windshield. Install the base to the glass. Hold in position until the adhesive has a chance to set. Make sure the correct side of the base is installed against the glass.

5. Allow around 24 hours for the adhesive to dry completely before installing the mirror to the base plate. This will assure proper adhesion.

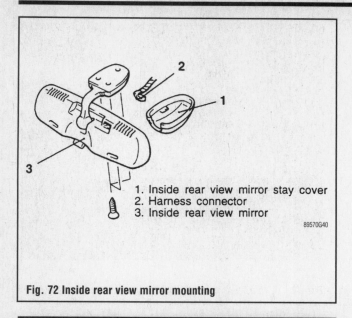

1. Inside rear view mirror stay cover
2. Harness connector
3. Inside rear view mirror

89570G40

Fig. 72 Inside rear view mirror mounting

Seats

REMOVAL & INSTALLATION

Front Seats

▶ **See Figures 73 thru 79**

1. Disconnect the negative battery cable.
2. If equipped with power seats and the motor doesn't work, perform the following to slide the seat in order to access the retainers:

a. Unfasten the bolts that secure the gear box to the left and right ends of the rails.

b. Remove the gear shaft from the left side. Pull the gear box at the right side toward you, to detach the gear from the side rail.

c. Use your hand to push the seat to a position where the mounting nuts and bolts can be removed.

3. For 1990–94 vehicles, remove the mounting screw and the side rail anchor cover.

4. Remove the seat anchor covers.

5. Disconnect the electrical connector from the seat, if equipped.

6. Unfasten the seat mounting nuts and bolts, then remove the seat from the vehicle.

To install:

7. Install the seat into the vehicle. Make sure the seat adjusters on both sides of the seat are locked in position.

8. Provisionally tighten the front mounting nuts first. After the front fasteners have been tightened, temporarily tighten the rear seat mounting bolts.

9. Tighten the front seat mounting nuts to 26 ft. lbs. (36 Nm) for 1990–94 vehicles or to 22 ft. lbs. (29 Nm) for 1995–98 vehicles. Tighten the rear mounting bolts to 40 ft. lbs. (55 Nm) for 1990–94 vehicles or to 33 ft. lbs. (44 Nm) for 1995–98 vehicles.

10. Install the seat anchor covers. On 1995–98 vehicles, insert the rear tab of the seat anchor cover in the front seat rear mounting bracket. Then rotate the cover in the direction of the arrow (shown in the accompanying figure) to install the side tabs in the side holes of the bracket.

11. For 1990–94 vehicles, install the seat side rail covers. Secure the rear pawl of the slider rail anchor cover to the mounting bracket on the rear of the slider rail and position over the rail.

12. If equipped with power seats, attach the electrical harness connector.

13. Connect the negative battery cable.

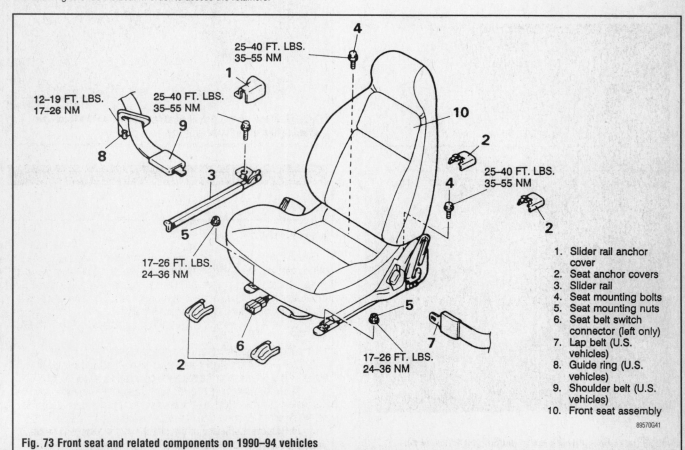

25–40 FT. LBS.
35–55 NM

12–19 FT. LBS.
17–26 NM

25–40 FT. LBS.
35–55 NM

25–40 FT. LBS.
35–55 NM

17–26 FT. LBS.
24–36 NM

17–26 FT. LBS.
24–36 NM

1. Slider rail anchor cover
2. Seat anchor covers
3. Slider rail
4. Seat mounting bolts
5. Seat mounting nuts
6. Seat belt switch connector (left only)
7. Lap belt (U.S. vehicles)
8. Guide ring (U.S. vehicles)
9. Shoulder belt (U.S. vehicles)
10. Front seat assembly

89570G41

Fig. 73 Front seat and related components on 1990–94 vehicles

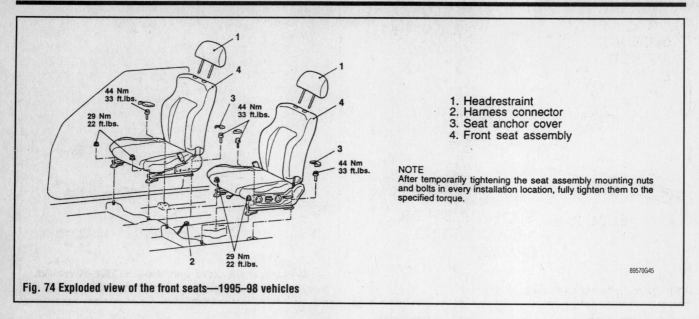

1. Headrestraint
2. Harness connector
3. Seat anchor cover
4. Front seat assembly

NOTE
After temporarily tightening the seat assembly mounting nuts and bolts in every installation location, fully tighten them to the specified torque.

Fig. 74 Exploded view of the front seats—1995–98 vehicles

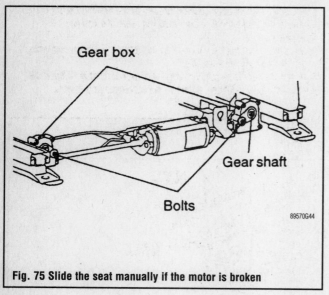

Fig. 75 Slide the seat manually if the motor is broken

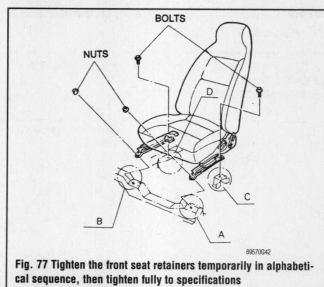

Fig. 77 Tighten the front seat retainers temporarily in alphabetical sequence, then tighten fully to specifications

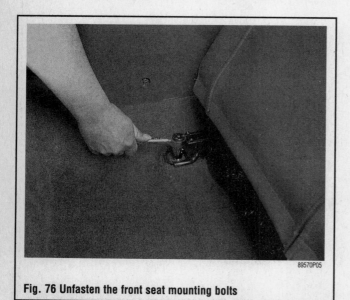

Fig. 76 Unfasten the front seat mounting bolts

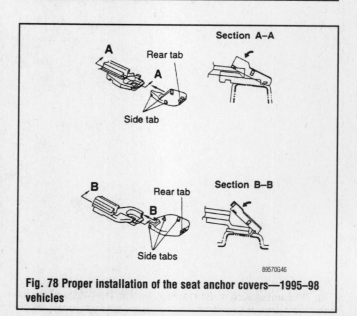

Fig. 78 Proper installation of the seat anchor covers—1995–98 vehicles

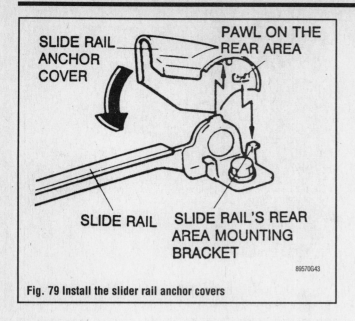

SLIDE RAIL ANCHOR COVER

PAWL ON THE REAR AREA

SLIDE RAIL

SLIDE RAIL'S REAR AREA MOUNTING BRACKET

89570G43

Fig. 79 Install the slider rail anchor covers

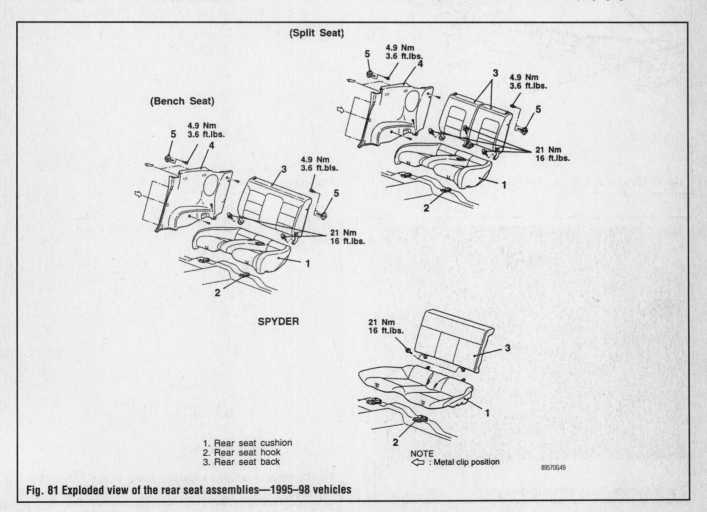

3-4 FT. LBS.
4-6 NM

12-19 FT. LBS.
17-26 NM

12-19 FT. LBS.
17-26 NM

1. Seat cushion
2. Clips
3. Seat back
4. Striker

89570G48

Fig. 80 Rear seat and related components on 1990–94 vehicles. Note that some models may have a bench style back cushion

Rear Seat

▶ **See Figures 80, 81, 82 and 83**

1. Disconnect the negative battery cable.
2. To remove the rear seat cushion, pull the levers under both side seat cushions and lift upward.
3. Remove the seat cushions from the vehicle.

4. Remove the seat back cushion retainer bolts. Release the lock from the striker and remove the seat back cushions from the vehicle.

To install:

5. Install the seat back cushions into the vehicle. Align the mounting bolt holes and install bolts loosely.
6. Press the seat back cushion into the striker assembly. Tighten the retainers to the specifications shown in the accompanying figures.

(Split Seat)

4.9 Nm
3.6 ft.lbs.

4.9 Nm
3.6 ft.lbs.

(Bench Seat)

4.9 Nm
3.6 ft.lbs.

4.9 Nm
3.6 ft.bls.

21 Nm
16 ft.lbs.

21 Nm
16 ft.lbs.

SPYDER

21 Nm
16 ft.lbs.

1. Rear seat cushion
2. Rear seat hook
3. Rear seat back

NOTE
◁ : Metal clip position

89570G49

Fig. 81 Exploded view of the rear seat assemblies—1995–98 vehicles

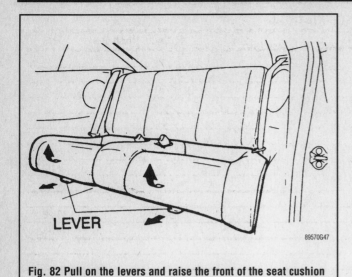

Fig. 82 Pull on the levers and raise the front of the seat cushion to remove it

Fig. 83 Remove the rear seat back cushion retainer bolts

7. Install the rear seat cushion as follows:

a. Securely insert the attachment wire of the rear seat cushion under the hinge bracket of the seat back.

b. Guide the seat belt buckles through the back seat cushions.

c. Securely insert the hook of the seat cushion into the seat support bracket in the floor of the vehicle. Make sure the hooks are locked in place.

8. Connect the negative battery cable.

Power Seat Motor

REMOVAL & INSTALLATION

1. Disconnect the negative battery cable.
2. Remove the front seat assembly from the vehicle.
3. Tag and detach the electrical connector(s).
4. Unfasten the retaining bolts, then remove the power seat motor from the vehicle.
5. Installation is the reverse of the removal procedure.

TORQUE SPECIFICATIONS

Component	ft. lbs.	inch lbs.	Nm
Doors			
Hinge-to-body bolts			
1990-94 vehicles	12-19		17-26
1995-98 vehicles			
Flange bolts	20		26
Washer-assembled bolts	16		22
Door striker bolts	18		25
1990-94 vehicles	7-10		9-14
1995-98 vehicles	16		22
Hood			
Hood hinge-to-body bolts	12-19		17-26
Hood hinge-to-hood bolts and nuts	7-10		9-14
Liftgate			
Hinge retainers			
1990-94 vehicles			
Nuts	8-12		11-16
Bolts	7-10		9-14
1995-98 vehicles			
Nuts	10		14
Bolts	8		12
Latch bolts			
1990-94 vehicles	5-8		7-11
1995-98 vehicles	7		9
Striker bolts			
1990-94 vehicles	7-10		9-14
1995-98 vehicles	8		12
Seats			
1988-94 vehicles			
Front seat-to-slider rail bolts	25-40		35-55
Front seat-to-floor pan nuts	17-26		24-36
Rear seat back mounting bolts	12-19		17-26
Reat seat back striker bolts	3-4		4-6
1995-98 vehicles			
Front seat-to-floor pan bolts	33		44
Front seat-to-floor pan nuts	22		29
Rear seat back mounting bolts	16		21
Rear seat back striker bolts	3.6		4.9
Trunk lid			
Hinge-to-lid bolts	9		13
Hinge-to-body bolts	8		12
Latch bolts	7		9

89570C01

GLOSSARY

AIR/FUEL RATIO: The ratio of air-to-gasoline by weight in the fuel mixture drawn into the engine.

AIR INJECTION: One method of reducing harmful exhaust emissions by injecting air into each of the exhaust ports of an engine. The fresh air entering the hot exhaust manifold causes any remaining fuel to be burned before it can exit the tailpipe.

ALTERNATOR: A device used for converting mechanical energy into electrical energy.

AMMETER: An instrument, calibrated in amperes, used to measure the flow of an electrical current in a circuit. Ammeters are always connected in series with the circuit being tested.

AMPERE: The rate of flow of electrical current present when one volt of electrical pressure is applied against one ohm of electrical resistance.

ANALOG COMPUTER: Any microprocessor that uses similar (analogous) electrical signals to make its calculations.

ARMATURE: A laminated, soft iron core wrapped by a wire that converts electrical energy to mechanical energy as in a motor or relay. When rotated in a magnetic field, it changes mechanical energy into electrical energy as in a generator.

ATMOSPHERIC PRESSURE: The pressure on the Earth's surface caused by the weight of the air in the atmosphere. At sea level, this pressure is 14.7 psi at 32°F (101 kPa at 0°C).

ATOMIZATION: The breaking down of a liquid into a fine mist that can be suspended in air.

AXIAL PLAY: Movement parallel to a shaft or bearing bore.

BACKFIRE: The sudden combustion of gases in the intake or exhaust system that results in a loud explosion.

BACKLASH: The clearance or play between two parts, such as meshed gears.

BACKPRESSURE: Restrictions in the exhaust system that slow the exit of exhaust gases from the combustion chamber.

BAKELITE: A heat resistant, plastic insulator material commonly used in printed circuit boards and transistorized components.

BALL BEARING: A bearing made up of hardened inner and outer races between which hardened steel balls roll.

BALLAST RESISTOR: A resistor in the primary ignition circuit that lowers voltage after the engine is started to reduce wear on ignition components.

BEARING: A friction reducing, supportive device usually located between a stationary part and a moving part.

BIMETAL TEMPERATURE SENSOR: Any sensor or switch made of two dissimilar types of metal that bend when heated or cooled due to the different expansion rates of the alloys. These types of sensors usually function as an on/off switch.

BLOWBY: Combustion gases, composed of water vapor and unburned fuel, that leak past the piston rings into the crankcase during normal engine operation. These gases are removed by the PCV system to prevent the buildup of harmful acids in the crankcase.

BRAKE PAD: A brake shoe and lining assembly used with disc brakes.

BRAKE SHOE: The backing for the brake lining. The term is, however, usually applied to the assembly of the brake backing and lining.

BUSHING: A liner, usually removable, for a bearing; an anti-friction liner used in place of a bearing.

CALIPER: A hydraulically activated device in a disc brake system, which is mounted straddling the brake rotor (disc). The caliper contains at least one piston and two brake pads. Hydraulic pressure on the piston(s) forces the pads against the rotor.

CAMSHAFT: A shaft in the engine on which are the lobes (cams) which operate the valves. The camshaft is driven by the crankshaft, via a belt, chain or gears, at one half the crankshaft speed.

CAPACITOR: A device which stores an electrical charge.

CARBON MONOXIDE (CO): A colorless, odorless gas given off as a normal byproduct of combustion. It is poisonous and extremely dangerous in confined areas, building up slowly to toxic levels without warning if adequate ventilation is not available.

CARBURETOR: A device, usually mounted on the intake manifold of an engine, which mixes the air and fuel in the proper proportion to allow even combustion.

CATALYTIC CONVERTER: A device installed in the exhaust system, like a muffler, that converts harmful byproducts of combustion into carbon dioxide and water vapor by means of a heat-producing chemical reaction.

CENTRIFUGAL ADVANCE: A mechanical method of advancing the spark timing by using flyweights in the distributor that react to centrifugal force generated by the distributor shaft rotation.

CHECK VALVE: Any one-way valve installed to permit the flow of air, fuel or vacuum in one direction only.

CHOKE: A device, usually a moveable valve, placed in the intake path of a carburetor to restrict the flow of air.

CIRCUIT: Any unbroken path through which an electrical current can flow. Also used to describe fuel flow in some instances.

CIRCUIT BREAKER: A switch which protects an electrical circuit from overload by opening the circuit when the current flow exceeds a predetermined level. Some circuit breakers must be reset manually, while most reset automatically.

COIL (IGNITION): A transformer in the ignition circuit which steps up the voltage provided to the spark plugs.

COMBINATION MANIFOLD: An assembly which includes both the intake and exhaust manifolds in one casting.

COMBINATION VALVE: A device used in some fuel systems that routes fuel vapors to a charcoal storage canister instead of venting them into the atmosphere. The valve relieves fuel tank pressure and allows fresh air into the tank as the fuel level drops to prevent a vapor lock situation.

COMPRESSION RATIO: The comparison of the total volume of the cylinder and combustion chamber with the piston at BDC and the piston at TDC.

CONDENSER: 1. An electrical device which acts to store an electrical charge, preventing voltage surges. 2. A radiator-like device in the air conditioning system in which refrigerant gas condenses into a liquid, giving off heat.

CONDUCTOR: Any material through which an electrical current can be transmitted easily.

CONTINUITY: Continuous or complete circuit. Can be checked with an ohmmeter.

COUNTERSHAFT: An intermediate shaft which is rotated by a mainshaft and transmits, in turn, that rotation to a working part.

CRANKCASE: The lower part of an engine in which the crankshaft and related parts operate.

CRANKSHAFT: The main driving shaft of an engine which receives reciprocating motion from the pistons and converts it to rotary motion.

CYLINDER: In an engine, the round hole in the engine block in which the piston(s) ride.

CYLINDER BLOCK: The main structural member of an engine in which is found the cylinders, crankshaft and other principal parts.

CYLINDER HEAD: The detachable portion of the engine, usually fastened to the top of the cylinder block and containing all or most of the combustion chambers. On overhead valve engines, it contains the valves and their operating parts. On overhead cam engines, it contains the camshaft as well.

DEAD CENTER: The extreme top or bottom of the piston stroke.

DETONATION: An unwanted explosion of the air/fuel mixture in the combustion chamber caused by excess heat and compression, advanced timing, or an overly lean mixture. Also referred to as "ping".

DIAPHRAGM: A thin, flexible wall separating two cavities, such as in a vacuum advance unit.

DIESELING: A condition in which hot spots in the combustion chamber cause the engine to run on after the key is turned off.

DIFFERENTIAL: A geared assembly which allows the transmission of motion between drive axles, giving one axle the ability to turn faster than the other.

DIODE: An electrical device that will allow current to flow in one direction only.

DISC BRAKE: A hydraulic braking assembly consisting of a brake disc, or rotor, mounted on an axle, and a caliper assembly containing, usually two brake pads which are activated by hydraulic pressure. The pads are forced against the sides of the disc, creating friction which slows the vehicle.

DISTRIBUTOR: A mechanically driven device on an engine which is responsible for electrically firing the spark plug at a predetermined point of the piston stroke.

DOWEL PIN: A pin, inserted in mating holes in two different parts allowing those parts to maintain a fixed relationship.

DRUM BRAKE: A braking system which consists of two brake shoes and one or two wheel cylinders, mounted on a fixed backing plate, and a brake drum, mounted on an axle, which revolves around the assembly.

DWELL: The rate, measured in degrees of shaft rotation, at which an electrical circuit cycles on and off.

ELECTRONIC CONTROL UNIT (ECU): Ignition module, module, amplifier or igniter. See Module for definition.

ELECTRONIC IGNITION: A system in which the timing and firing of the spark plugs is controlled by an electronic control unit, usually called a module. These systems have no points or condenser.

END-PLAY: The measured amount of axial movement in a shaft.

ENGINE: A device that converts heat into mechanical energy.

EXHAUST MANIFOLD: A set of cast passages or pipes which conduct exhaust gases from the engine.

FEELER GAUGE: A blade, usually metal, or precisely predetermined thickness, used to measure the clearance between two parts.

FIRING ORDER: The order in which combustion occurs in the cylinders of an engine. Also the order in which spark is distributed to the plugs by the distributor.

FLOODING: The presence of too much fuel in the intake manifold and combustion chamber which prevents the air/fuel mixture from firing, thereby causing a no-start situation.

FLYWHEEL: A disc shaped part bolted to the rear end of the crankshaft. Around the outer perimeter is affixed the ring gear. The starter drive engages the ring gear, turning the flywheel, which rotates the crankshaft, imparting the initial starting motion to the engine.

FOOT POUND (ft. lbs. or sometimes, ft.lb.): The amount of energy or work needed to raise an item weighing one pound, a distance of one foot.

FUSE: A protective device in a circuit which prevents circuit overload by breaking the circuit when a specific amperage is present. The device is constructed around a strip or wire of a lower amperage rating than the circuit it is designed to protect. When an amperage higher than that stamped on the fuse is present in the circuit, the strip or wire melts, opening the circuit.

GEAR RATIO: The ratio between the number of teeth on meshing gears.

GENERATOR: A device which converts mechanical energy into electrical energy.

HEAT RANGE: The measure of a spark plug's ability to dissipate heat from its firing end. The higher the heat range, the hotter the plug fires.

HUB: The center part of a wheel or gear.

HYDROCARBON (HC): Any chemical compound made up of hydrogen and carbon. A major pollutant formed by the engine as a byproduct of combustion.

HYDROMETER: An instrument used to measure the specific gravity of a solution.

INCH POUND (inch lbs.; sometimes in.lb. or in. lbs.): One twelfth of a foot pound.

INDUCTION: A means of transferring electrical energy in the form of a magnetic field. Principle used in the ignition coil to increase voltage.

INJECTOR: A device which receives metered fuel under relatively low pressure and is activated to inject the fuel into the engine under relatively high pressure at a predetermined time.

INPUT SHAFT: The shaft to which torque is applied, usually carrying the driving gear or gears.

INTAKE MANIFOLD: A casting of passages or pipes used to conduct air or a fuel/air mixture to the cylinders.

JOURNAL: The bearing surface within which a shaft operates.

KEY: A small block usually fitted in a notch between a shaft and a hub to prevent slippage of the two parts.

MANIFOLD: A casting of passages or set of pipes which connect the cylinders to an inlet or outlet source.

MANIFOLD VACUUM: Low pressure in an engine intake manifold formed just below the throttle plates. Manifold vacuum is highest at idle and drops under acceleration.

MASTER CYLINDER: The primary fluid pressurizing device in a hydraulic system. In automotive use, it is found in brake and hydraulic clutch systems and is pedal activated, either directly or, in a power brake system, through the power booster.

MODULE: Electronic control unit, amplifier or igniter of solid state or integrated design which controls the current flow in the ignition primary circuit based on input from the pick-up coil. When the module opens the primary circuit, high secondary voltage is induced in the coil.

NEEDLE BEARING: A bearing which consists of a number (usually a large number) of long, thin rollers.

OHM: (Ω) The unit used to measure the resistance of conductor-to-electrical flow. One ohm is the amount of resistance that limits current flow to one ampere in a circuit with one volt of pressure.

OHMMETER: An instrument used for measuring the resistance, in ohms, in an electrical circuit.

OUTPUT SHAFT: The shaft which transmits torque from a device, such as a transmission.

OVERDRIVE: A gear assembly which produces more shaft revolutions than that transmitted to it.

OVERHEAD CAMSHAFT (OHC): An engine configuration in which the camshaft is mounted on top of the cylinder head and operates the valve either directly or by means of rocker arms.

OVERHEAD VALVE (OHV): An engine configuration in which all of the valves are located in the cylinder head and the camshaft is located in the cylinder block. The camshaft operates the valves via lifters and pushrods.

OXIDES OF NITROGEN (NOx): Chemical compounds of nitrogen produced as a byproduct of combustion. They combine with hydrocarbons to produce smog.

OXYGEN SENSOR: Use with the feedback system to sense the presence of oxygen in the exhaust gas and signal the computer which can reference the voltage signal to an air/fuel ratio.

PINION: The smaller of two meshing gears.

PISTON RING: An open-ended ring with fits into a groove on the outer diameter of the piston. Its chief function is to form a seal between the piston and cylinder wall. Most automotive pistons have three rings: two for compression sealing; one for oil sealing.

PRELOAD: A predetermined load placed on a bearing during assembly or by adjustment.

PRIMARY CIRCUIT: the low voltage side of the ignition system which consists of the ignition switch, ballast resistor or resistance wire, bypass, coil, electronic control unit and pick-up coil as well as the connecting wires and harnesses.

PRESS FIT: The mating of two parts under pressure, due to the inner diameter of one being smaller than the outer diameter of the other, or vice versa; an interference fit.

RACE: The surface on the inner or outer ring of a bearing on which the balls, needles or rollers move.

REGULATOR: A device which maintains the amperage and/or voltage levels of a circuit at predetermined values.

RELAY: A switch which automatically opens and/or closes a circuit.

RESISTANCE: The opposition to the flow of current through a circuit or electrical device, and is measured in ohms. Resistance is equal to the voltage divided by the amperage.

RESISTOR: A device, usually made of wire, which offers a preset amount of resistance in an electrical circuit.

RING GEAR: The name given to a ring-shaped gear attached to a differential case, or affixed to a flywheel or as part of a planetary gear set.

ROLLER BEARING: A bearing made up of hardened inner and outer races between which hardened steel rollers move.

ROTOR: 1. The disc-shaped part of a disc brake assembly, upon which the brake pads bear; also called, brake disc. 2. The device mounted atop the distributor shaft, which passes current to the distributor cap tower contacts.

SECONDARY CIRCUIT: The high voltage side of the ignition system, usually above 20,000 volts. The secondary includes the ignition coil, coil wire, distributor cap and rotor, spark plug wires and spark plugs.

SENDING UNIT: A mechanical, electrical, hydraulic or electro-magnetic device which transmits information to a gauge.

SENSOR: Any device designed to measure engine operating conditions or ambient pressures and temperatures. Usually electronic in nature and designed to send a voltage signal to an on-board computer, some sensors may operate as a simple on/off switch or they may provide a variable voltage signal (like a potentiometer) as conditions or measured parameters change.

SHIM: Spacers of precise, predetermined thickness used between parts to establish a proper working relationship.

SLAVE CYLINDER: In automotive use, a device in the hydraulic clutch system which is activated by hydraulic force, disengaging the clutch.

SOLENOID: A coil used to produce a magnetic field, the effect of which is to produce work.

SPARK PLUG: A device screwed into the combustion chamber of a spark ignition engine. The basic construction is a conductive core inside of a ceramic insulator, mounted in an outer conductive base. An electrical charge from the spark plug wire travels along the conductive core and jumps a preset air gap to a grounding point or points at the end of the conductive base. The resultant spark ignites the fuel/air mixture in the combustion chamber.

SPLINES: Ridges machined or cast onto the outer diameter of a shaft or inner diameter of a bore to enable parts to mate without rotation.

TACHOMETER: A device used to measure the rotary speed of an engine, shaft, gear, etc., usually in rotations per minute.

THERMOSTAT: A valve, located in the cooling system of an engine, which is closed when cold and opens gradually in response to engine heating, controlling the temperature of the coolant and rate of coolant flow.

TOP DEAD CENTER (TDC): The point at which the piston reaches the top of its travel on the compression stroke.

TORQUE: The twisting force applied to an object.

TORQUE CONVERTER: A turbine used to transmit power from a driving member to a driven member via hydraulic action, providing changes in drive ratio and torque. In automotive use, it links the driveplate at the rear of the engine to the automatic transmission.

TRANSDUCER: A device used to change a force into an electrical signal.

TRANSISTOR: A semi-conductor component which can be actuated by a small voltage to perform an electrical switching function.

TUNE-UP: A regular maintenance function, usually associated with the replacement and adjustment of parts and components in the electrical and fuel systems of a vehicle for the purpose of attaining optimum performance.

TURBOCHARGER: An exhaust driven pump which compresses intake air and forces it into the combustion chambers at higher than atmospheric pressures. The increased air pressure allows more fuel to be burned and results in increased horsepower being produced.

VACUUM ADVANCE: A device which advances the ignition timing in response to increased engine vacuum.

VACUUM GAUGE: An instrument used to measure the presence of vacuum in a chamber.

VALVE: A device which control the pressure, direction of flow or rate of flow of a liquid or gas.

VALVE CLEARANCE: The measured gap between the end of the valve stem and the rocker arm, cam lobe or follower that activates the valve.

VISCOSITY: The rating of a liquid's internal resistance to flow.

VOLTMETER: An instrument used for measuring electrical force in units called volts. Voltmeters are always connected parallel with the circuit being tested.

WHEEL CYLINDER: Found in the automotive drum brake assembly, it is a device, actuated by hydraulic pressure, which, through internal pistons, pushes the brake shoes outward against the drums.

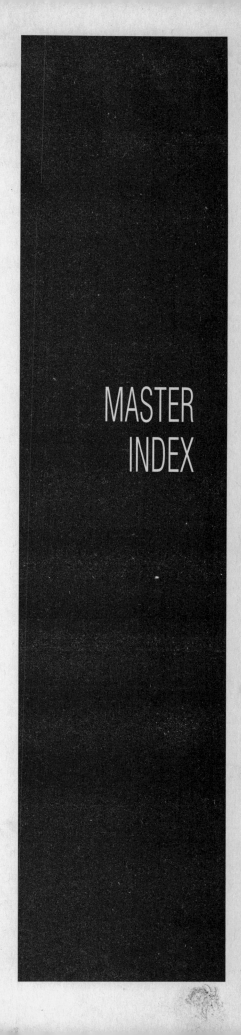

MASTER INDEX